W9-BET-587

A Gift from
GRACE
to You
www.gty.org

One Perfect Life

One Perfect Life:

The Complete Story of the Lord Jesus

John MacArthur

Thomas Nelson
Since 1798

NASHVILLE DALLAS MEXICO CITY RIO DE JANEIRO

ONE PERFECT LIFE: THE COMPLETE STORY OF THE LORD JESUS

Special thanks to Nathan Busenitz and also to the team at Thomas Nelson for their help in the completion of this project.

Published in Nashville, Tennessee, by Thomas Nelson. Thomas Nelson is a registered trademark of Thomas Nelson, Inc.

Unleashing God's Truth One Verse at a Time® is a trademark of Grace to You. all rights reserved.

Thomas Nelson, Inc., titles may be purchased in bulk for educational, business, fund-raising, or sales promotional use. For information, please e-mail SpecialMarkets@ThomasNelson.com.

Library of Congress Cataloging-in-Publication Data

Printed in the United States of America

13 14 15 16 [RRD] 6 5 4

CONTENTS

INTRODUCTION

Over the course of my ministry, I have spent decades studying, preaching, and writing commentaries on the four gospels. The Holy Spirit-inspired quartet is the pinnacle of Scripture because in it the Lord Jesus Christ is most perfectly revealed and God most clearly manifest. Nothing comes close to the rich reward of understanding the truth and glory of His matchless life.

The Holy Spirit gave us four gospels and, specifically, three of them are *synoptic* (from a Greek word meaning to share a common point of view) so that the truth concerning our Lord and Savior might be established on the basis of two or three witnesses (cf. Deut. 19:15; Matt. 18:16; 2 Cor. 13:1). Because each writer emphasized different themes from His life, the four historical testimonies provide a powerful and profound composite picture of the Son of God and Son of Man.

> *Matthew* wrote primarily to a Jewish audience, presenting Jesus of Nazareth as Israel's long-awaited Messiah and rightful King. His genealogy, unlike Luke's focuses on Jesus' royal descent from Israel's greatest King, David. Interspersed throughout Matthew are OT quotes presenting various aspects of Jesus' life and ministry as the fulfillment of OT messianic prophecy. Matthew alone uses the phrase "kingdom of heaven," avoiding the parallel phrase "kingdom of God" because of the unbiblical connotations it had in first-century Jewish thought. Matthew wrote his gospel, then, to strengthen the faith of Jewish Christians, and it provides a useful apologetic tool for Jewish evangelism.
>
> *Mark* targeted a Gentile audience, especially a Roman one. Mark is the gospel of action; the frequent use of "immediately" and "then" keeps his narrative moving rapidly along. Jesus appears in Mark as the Servant (cf. Mark 10:45) who came to suffer for the sins of many. Mark's fast-paced approach would especially appeal to the practical, action-oriented Romans.
>
> *Luke* addressed a broader Gentile audience. As an educated Greek, Luke wrote using the most sophisticated literary Greek of any NT writer. He was a careful researcher (Luke 1:1–4) and an accurate historian. Luke portrays Jesus as the Son of Man (a title appearing 26 times), the answer to the needs and hopes of the human race, who came to seek and save lost sinners (Luke 9:56; 19:10).

> *John*, the last gospel written, emphasizes the deity of Jesus Christ (e.g., 5:18; 8:58; 10:30–33; 14:9). John wrote to strengthen the faith of believers and to appeal to unbelievers to come to faith in Christ.
>
> Taken together, the 4 gospels weave a complete portrait of the God-Man, Jesus of Nazareth. In Him were blended perfect humanity and deity, making Him the only sacrifice for the sins of the world, and the worthy Lord of those who believe. *(The MacArthur Study Bible Introduction to the Gospels)*

These four are in perfect harmony with each other because the infallible Holy Spirit is the one divine author who inspired and guided the four writers into all truth (John 16:13). Each is an inerrant record that can be harmonized with the others down to the smallest details.

Through twenty-five years of preaching these four accounts, I have always started with the text being preached, paragraph by paragraph, and blended in parallel accounts from the other gospels. My aim was to pull together the full story known and show how each part of Matthew's gospel, for example, fit perfectly with the record in Mark or Luke; or, in the case of John, to demonstrate where his history fits and how it perfectly supplements the synoptic gospels. These four separate records can be reasonably harmonized, and any alleged discrepancies exist only in the minds of unbelieving critics, and not in the actual texts themselves. When all the details from all accounts are known, the full story is clear and divine authorship affirmed.

As I came to the end of preaching those gospel expositions and am still writing the final commentary volumes, I have felt a strong desire to provide a volume that would blend all four gospels into one story.

When *The MacArthur Study Bible* was first published in 1997, we included "A Harmony of the Gospels" in outline form set in separate columns, side by side, as harmonies have generally been arranged in the past. This volume, on the other hand, takes those separated accounts and blends them into one continuous narrative. All the details from the four gospels have been included without repeating exact parallel statements.

We used Matthew's gospel as the base text in keeping with our commitment to Matthean priority, and folded in the details from the others. This then becomes the blended harmony of the gospels. While the blending represents our effort, such that the order is not infallible, every word comes from Holy Spirit-inspired Scripture.

To explain portions of the text that may challenge the reader, we have incorporated notes from *The MacArthur Study Bible*, which are also harmonized, as a supplement.

Historically speaking, this work does not represent the first attempt to create a harmony of the gospels. The second-century church leader, Tatian, produced his *Diatesseron* that was used by churches in Syria for several centuries. Since that time, several harmonies have been produced—most of which keep the gospels separate (and present them in parallel columns) while others blend them together—as in this volume. For example, the separated approach done by Robert L. Thomas and Stanley N. Gundry (*A Harmony of the Gospels*) helped in this effort; as did the blended approach by Johnston M. Cheney, originally titled *The Life of Christ in Stereo*.

The end result is the best news the world has ever been given, about the most significant life in all history, Jesus Christ.

The objective is to bring into full view the One who is Immanuel, God with us, the Eternal Word made flesh, the preexistent, coexistent, self-existent Son of God who became the Son of Man to die and rise again for our salvation.

For believers, the full vision of the Lord Jesus is the supreme means by which we are sanctified—as we are enraptured by His glory and conformed into His image. As Paul explained to the Corinthians, "But we all, with unveiled face, beholding as in a mirror the glory of the Lord, are being transformed into the same image from glory to glory, just as by the Spirit of the Lord" (2 Cor. 3:18).

For unbelievers, the full vision of the Lord Jesus is the supreme means by which they are saved. John said this about His gospel and the three that came before: "These are written that you may believe that Jesus is the Christ, the Son of God, and that believing you may have life in His name." (John 20:31). May God use it to that end.

Part I | Anticipating the Lord Jesus Christ

1. Jesus Christ—the Preexistent Creator and Savior

Gen. 1:1; John 1:1–5a; 1 Cor. 8:6; Eph. 1:3–5; Col. 1:15–18; 2:9; 2 Tim. 1:9; Titus 1:2; Heb. 1:1b–3a

GEN In the beginning God created the heavens and the earth. JN In the beginning was [a]the Word, and the Word was with God, and the Word was God. He was in the beginning with God. All things were made through Him, and without Him nothing was made that was made.

1COR *There is* one God, the Father, of whom *are* all things, and we for Him; and one Lord Jesus Christ, through whom *are* all things, and through whom we *live,* HEB whom He has appointed heir of all things, through whom also He made the worlds; who being the brightness of *His* glory and the express image of His person, and upholding all things by the word of His power, COL is the image of the invisible God, [b]the firstborn over all creation.

---

[a] THE WORD. This title refers to Jesus Christ, the Second Person of the Trinity, who was in intimate fellowship with God the Father throughout all eternity. The phrase, "the Word was God" emphasizes the fact that the Son is equal in His essence, character, and being to the Father. The apostle John borrowed the use of the term *Word* not only from the vocabulary of the OT but also from Greek philosophy, in which the term was essentially impersonal, signifying the rational principle of "divine reason," "mind," or even "wisdom." John, however, imbued the term entirely with OT and Christian meaning (e.g., Gen. 1:3 where God's Word brought the world into being; Pss. 33:6; 107:20; Prov. 8:27 where God's Word is His omnipotent self-expression in creation, wisdom, revelation, and salvation) and made it refer to a person, i.e., Jesus Christ. Strategically, the term *Word* serves as a bridge-word to reach not only Jews but also the unsaved Greeks. John chose this concept because both Jews and Greeks were familiar with it.

[b] THE FIRSTBORN OVER ALL CREATION. The Greek word for firstborn can refer to one who was born first chronologically, but most often refers to preeminence in position, or rank (cf. Heb. 1:6; Rom. 8:29; Ps. 2:7). In both Greek and Jewish culture, the firstborn was the ranking son who had received the right of inheritance from his father, whether he was born first or not. It is used of Israel who, not being the first nation, was however the preeminent nation (cf. Ex. 4:22; Jer. 31:9). *Firstborn* in this context clearly means highest in rank, not first created (cf. Ps. 89:27; Rev. 1:5). Jesus is the firstborn in the sense that He has the preeminence (v. 18) and possesses the right of inheritance "over all creation" (cf. Heb. 1:2; Rev. 5:1–7, 13). He existed before the creation and is exalted in rank above it.

For by Him all things were created that are in heaven and that are on earth, visible and invisible, whether thrones or dominions or principalities or powers. All things were created through Him and for Him. And He is before all things, and in Him all things consist. JN In Him was life, and [c]the life was the light of men. COL For in Him dwells all the [d]fullness of the Godhead bodily.

EPH Blessed *be* the God and Father of our Lord Jesus Christ, 2TIM who has saved us and called *us* with a holy calling, not according to our works, but according to His own purpose and grace which was given to us in Christ Jesus [e]before time began. EPH He chose us in Him [f]before the foundation of the world, that we should be holy and without blame before Him in love, having predestined us to adoption as sons by Jesus Christ to Himself, according to the good pleasure of His will, to the praise of the glory of His grace, by which He made us accepted in the Beloved, TITUS in hope of eternal life which God, who cannot lie, promised before time began.

---

[c] THE LIFE. John uses the word *life* about thirty-six times in his gospel, far more than any other NT book. It refers not only in a broad sense to physical and temporal life that the Son imparted to the created world through His involvement as the agent of creation (John 1:3), but especially to spiritual and eternal life imparted as a gift through belief in Him (John 3:15; 17:3; Eph. 2:5).

[d] FULLNESS OF THE GODHEAD BODILY. Christ possesses the fullness of the divine nature and attributes (cf. Col. 1:19; John 1:14–16). In Greek philosophical thought, matter was evil; spirit was good. Thus, it was unthinkable that God would ever take on a human body. Paul refutes that false teaching by stressing the reality of Christ's incarnation. Jesus was not only fully God, but fully human as well.

[e] BEFORE TIME BEGAN. God's plan of salvation for sinful mankind was determined and decreed before man was even created. The promise was made by God the Father to God the Son (cf. John 6:37–44; 17:4–6; Eph. 1:4–5).

[f] BEFORE THE FOUNDATION OF THE WORLD. The doctrine of election is emphasized throughout Scripture (cf. Deut. 7:6; Isa. 45:4; John 6:44; Acts 13:48; Rom. 8:29; 9:11; 1 Thess. 1:3; 4 2; Thess. 2:13; 2 Tim. 2:10). The form of the Greek verb behind "chose" indicates that God not only chose by Himself but also for Himself to the praise of His own glory (cf. Eph. 1:6, 12, 14). Through God's sovereign will before the creation of the world and, therefore, obviously independent of human influence and apart from any human merit, those who are saved have become eternally united with Christ Jesus (cf. 1 Peter 1:20; Rev. 13:8; 17:8). However, God's election or predestination does not operate apart from or nullify man's responsibility to believe in Jesus as Lord and Savior (cf. Matt. 3:1, 2; 4:17; John 5:40).

2. The Fall of the Human Race into Sin

Gen. 3:1–12; John 8:44; 1 Cor. 11:3b; 1 Tim. 2:14b; James 1:13–15; Rev. 20:2b

GEN Now the serpent was more cunning than any beast of the field which the LORD God had made. REV That serpent of old, who is *the* Devil and Satan, JN was a murderer from the beginning, and does not stand in the truth, because there is no truth in him. When he speaks a lie, he speaks from his own *resources,* for he is a liar and the father of it. GEN And he said to the woman, "Has God indeed said, 'You shall not eat of every tree of the garden'?"

And the woman said to the serpent, "We may eat the fruit of the trees of the garden; but of the fruit of the tree which *is* in the midst of the garden, God has said, 'You shall not eat it, nor shall you touch it, lest you die.'" Then the serpent said to the woman, "[a]You will not surely die. For God knows that in the day you eat of it your eyes will be opened, and you will be like God, knowing good and evil."

1COR The serpent deceived Eve by his craftiness. GEN So when the woman saw that the tree *was* good for food, that it *was* pleasant to the eyes, and a tree desirable to make *one* wise, she took of its fruit and ate. 1TIM The woman being deceived, fell into transgression; GEN she also gave to her husband with her, and he ate.

Then [b]the eyes of both of them were opened, and they knew that they *were* naked; and they sewed fig leaves together and made themselves coverings. And they heard the sound of the LORD God walking in the garden in the cool of the day, and Adam and his wife hid themselves from the presence of the LORD God among the trees of the garden.

Then the LORD God called to Adam and said to him, [c]"Where *are* you?" So he

---

[a] YOU WILL NOT SURELY DIE. Satan, emboldened by her openness to him, spoke this direct lie. This lie actually led her and Adam to spiritual death (separation from God). So, Satan is called a liar and murderer from the beginning (John 8:44). His lies always promise great benefits (as in v. 5). Eve experienced this result—she and Adam did know good and evil; but by personal corruption they did not know as God knows in perfect holiness.

[b] THE EYES OF BOTH OF THEM WERE OPENED. The innocence noted in 2:25 had been replaced by guilt and shame (vv. 8–10), and from then on they had to rely on their conscience to distinguish between good and their newly acquired capacity to see and know evil.

[c] "WHERE ARE YOU?" The question was God's way of bringing man to explain why he was hiding, rather than expressing ignorance about man's location. Shame, remorse, confusion, guilt, and fear all led to their clandestine behavior. There was no place to hide; there never is (cf. Ps. 139:1–12). Adam's sin was evidenced by his new knowledge of the evil of nakedness, but God still waited for Adam to confess to what God knew they had done. The basic reluctance of sinful people to admit their iniquity is here established. Repentance is still the issue. When sinners refuse to repent, they suffer judgment; when they do repent, they receive forgiveness.

said, "I heard Your voice in the garden, and I was afraid because I was naked; and I hid myself." And He said, "Who told you that you *were* naked? Have you eaten from the tree of which I commanded you that you should not eat?" Then the man said, "[d]The woman whom You gave *to be* with me, she gave me of the tree, and I ate."

JAS Let no one say when he is tempted, "I am tempted by God"; for God cannot be tempted by evil, nor does He Himself tempt anyone. But each one is tempted when he is drawn away by his own desires and enticed. Then, when desire has conceived, it gives birth to sin; and sin, when it is full-grown, [e]brings forth death.

---

[d] THE WOMAN WHOM YOU GAVE. Adam pitifully put the responsibility on God for giving him Eve. That only magnified the tragedy in that Adam had knowingly transgressed God's prohibition, but still would not be open and confess his sin, taking full responsibility for his action, which was not made under deception (1 Tim. 2:14).

[e] BRINGS FORTH DEATH. Sin is not merely a spontaneous act, but the result of a process. The Greek words for "has conceived" and "brings forth" liken the process to physical conception and birth. Thus James personifies temptation and shows that it can follow a similar sequence and produce sin with all its deadly results. While sin does not result in spiritual death for the believer (because he or she has been forgiven), it can lead to physical death (1 Cor. 11:30; 1 John 5:16). In the fall of Gen. 3, the result of Adam's sin brought both physical and spiritual death to the entire human race (cf. Rom. 5:12–21).

3. The Curse upon Creation

Gen. 3:13; Ps. 90:10; 144:4; Eccl. 1:2b; 3:20; 12:7; Rom. 8:2b, 20a, 22; Gal. 4:4–5; 1 John 3:8b

GEN The LORD God said to the woman, "What *is* this you have done?" The woman said, "The serpent deceived me, and I ate." So the LORD God said to the serpent:

"Because you have done this,
You *are* cursed more than all cattle,
And more than every beast of the field;
On your belly you shall go,
And you shall eat dust
All the days of your life.
And I will put enmity
Between you and the woman,
And [a]between your seed and her Seed;
He shall bruise your head,
And you shall bruise His heel."

1JN For this purpose the Son of God, was manifested, that He might destroy the works of the devil. GAL When the fullness of the time had come, God sent forth His Son, born of a woman, born under the law, to redeem those who were under ROM the law of sin and death.

GEN To the woman He said:

"I will greatly multiply your sorrow and your conception;
In pain you shall bring forth children;
Your desire *shall be* for your husband,
And he shall rule over you."

---

[a] BETWEEN YOUR SEED AND HER SEED. After cursing the physical serpent, God turned to the spiritual serpent, the lying seducer, Satan, and cursed him. This "first gospel" is prophetic of the struggle and its outcome between "your seed" (Satan and unbelievers, who are called the Devil's children in John 8:44) and her Seed (Christ, a descendant of Eve, and those in Him), which began in the garden. In the midst of the curse passage, a message of hope shone forth—the woman's offspring called "He" is Christ, who will one day defeat the Serpent. Satan could only "bruise" Christ's heel (cause Him to suffer), while Christ will bruise Satan's head (destroy him with a fatal blow).

Then to Adam He said, "Because you have heeded the voice of your wife, and have eaten from the tree of which I commanded you, saying, 'You shall not eat of it':

"Cursed *is* the ground for your sake;
In toil you shall eat *of* it
All the days of your life.
Both thorns and thistles it shall bring forth for you,
And you shall eat the herb of the field.
In the sweat of your face you shall eat bread
Till you return to the ground,
For out of it you were taken;
For dust you *are,*
And to dust you shall return."

ROM For the creation was subjected to futility, not willingly, but because of Him who subjected *it.* ECCL Vanity of vanities, all *is* vanity. ROM For we know that the whole creation groans and labors with birth pangs together until now.

PS Man is like a breath; His days *are* like a passing shadow. ECCL All are from the dust, and all return to dust. PS The days of our lives *are* seventy years; and if by reason of strength *they are* eighty years, yet their boast *is* only labor and sorrow; for it is soon cut off, and we fly away. ECCL Then the dust will return to the earth as it was, and the spirit will return to God who gave it.

GEN And Adam called his wife's name Eve, because she was the mother of all living. Also for Adam and his wife the LORD God made [b]tunics of skin, and clothed them.

Then the LORD God said, "Behold, the man has become like one of Us, to know good and evil. And now, lest he put out his hand and take also of the tree of life, and eat, and live forever"—therefore the LORD God sent him out of the garden of Eden to till the ground from which he was taken. So He drove out the man; and He placed cherubim at the east of the garden of Eden, and a flaming sword which turned every way, to guard the way to the tree of life.

[b] TUNICS OF SKIN. The first physical deaths should have been the man and his wife, but it was an animal—a shadow of the reality that God would someday kill a substitute to redeem sinners.

4. Mankind's Need for a Savior

Ps. 7:11; Isa. 53:6a; 64:6; Ezek. 18:20a; Rom. 1:18–21; 3:10–18, 23; 5:12, 18–19; 6:23a; 1 Cor. 15:21; Eph. 2:1–3

ROM The wrath of God is revealed from heaven against all ungodliness and unrighteousness of men, who suppress the truth in unrighteousness, because what may be known of God is manifest in them, for God has shown *it* to them. For since the creation of the world His invisible *attributes* are clearly seen, being understood by the things that are made, *even* His eternal power and Godhead, so that [a]they are without excuse, because, although they knew God, they did not glorify *Him* as God, nor were thankful, but became futile in their thoughts, and their foolish hearts were darkened.

PS God *is* a just judge, and God is angry *with the wicked* every day. ROM As it is written:

"There is none righteous, no, not one;
There is none who understands;
There is none who seeks after God.
They have all turned aside;
They have together become unprofitable;
There is none who does good, no, not one.
Their throat *is* an open tomb;
With their tongues they have practiced deceit;
The poison of asps *is* under their lips;
Whose mouth *is* full of cursing and bitterness.
Their feet *are* swift to shed blood;
Destruction and misery *are* in their ways;
And the way of peace they have not known.
There is no fear of God before their eyes."

---

[a] THEY ARE WITHOUT EXCUSE. God holds all men responsible for their refusal to acknowledge what He has shown them of Himself in His creation. Even those who have never had an opportunity to hear the gospel have received a clear witness about the existence and character of God—and have suppressed it. If a person will respond to the revelation he has, even if it is solely natural revelation, God will provide some means for that person to hear the gospel (cf. Acts 8:26–39; 10:1–48; 17:27).

ISA All we like sheep have gone astray; ROM for all have sinned and fall short of the glory of God. ISA We are all like an unclean *thing,* and all our righteousnesses *are* like filthy rags; we all fade as a leaf, and our iniquities, like the wind, have taken us away.

ROM Through one man sin entered the world, and death through sin, and thus [b]death spread to all men, because all sinned. EZEK The soul who sins shall die, ROM for the wages of sin *is* death.

EPH And you were [c]dead in trespasses and sins, in which you once walked according to the course of this world, according to the prince of the power of the air, the spirit who now works in the sons of disobedience, among whom also we all once conducted ourselves in the lusts of our flesh, fulfilling the desires of the flesh and of the mind, and were by nature children of wrath, just as the others.

ROM Therefore, as through one man's offense *judgment came* to all men, resulting in condemnation, even so through one Man's righteous act *the free gift came* to all men, resulting in justification of life. For as by one man's disobedience many were made sinners, so also by one Man's obedience many will be [d]made righteous. 1COR For since by man *came* death, by Man also *came* the resurrection of the dead. For as in Adam all die, even so in Christ all shall be made alive.

---

[b] DEATH SPREAD TO ALL MEN. Adam was not originally subject to death, but through his sin it became a grim certainty for him and his posterity. Death has three distinct manifestations: (1) spiritual death or separation from God (cf. Eph. 1:1–2; 4:18); (2) physical death (Heb. 9:27); and (3) eternal death (also called the second death), which includes not only eternal separation from God, but eternal torment in the lake of fire (Rev. 20:11–15). Because all humanity existed in the loins of Adam and have through procreation inherited his fallenness and depravity, it can be said that all sinned in him.

[c] DEAD IN TRESPASSES AND SINS. A sobering reminder of the total sinfulness and lostness from which believers have been redeemed. "*In*" indicates the realm or sphere in which unregenerate sinners exist. They are not dead because of sinful acts that have been committed but because of their sinful nature (cf. Matt. 12:35; 15:18–19).

[d] MADE RIGHTEOUS. The believer is clothed in Christ's righteousness, which was manifest in His perfect obedience (cf. v. 19; Luke 2:49; John 4:34; 5:30; 6:38), culminating in the greatest demonstration of that obedience, His death on a cross (Phil. 2:8). The expression "made righteous" refers to one's legal status before God and not an actual change in character, since Paul is contrasting justification and condemnation throughout this passage, and he has not yet introduced the doctrine of sanctification (coming later in Rom. 6–8), which deals with the actual transformation of the sinner as a result of redemption.

5. The Promised Seed of Abraham

Gen. 12:1–3, 7, 22:1–18; Matt. 1:1; Acts 3:24–26; Rom. 4:3; Gal. 3:16, 19b; Heb. 11:8–9, 17–19

GEN Now the LORD had said to Abram:

"Get out of your country,
From your family
And from your father's house,
To a land that I will show you.
I will make you a great nation;
I will bless you
And make your name great;
And you shall be a blessing.
I will bless those who bless you,
And I will curse him who curses you;
And in you all the families of the earth shall be blessed."

ROM Abraham believed God, and it was [a]accounted to him for righteousness. HEB By faith Abraham obeyed when he was called to go out to the place which he would receive as an inheritance. And he went out, not knowing where he was going. By faith he dwelt in the land of promise as *in* a foreign country, dwelling in tents with Isaac and Jacob, the heirs with him of the same promise.

GEN Now it came to pass after these things that God tested Abraham, and said to him, "Abraham!" And he said, "Here I am." Then He said, "Take now your son, your only *son* Isaac, whom you love, and go to the land of Moriah, and offer him there as a burnt offering on one of the mountains of which I shall tell you." HEB By faith Abraham, when he was tested, offered up Isaac, and he who had received the promises offered up his only begotten *son,* of whom it was said, "In Isaac your seed

---

[a] ACCOUNTED TO HIM FOR RIGHTEOUSNESS. Abram's belief was in response to God's promise in Gen. 15:4–5, a reiteration of his promise in Gen. 12:2–3. Used in both financial and legal settings, the word *accounted* means to take something that belongs to someone and credit it to another's account. It is a one-sided transaction—Abraham did nothing to accumulate it; God simply credited it to him. God took His own righteousness and credited it to Abraham as if it were actually his. This God did because Abraham believed in Him. Abraham was a man of faith, but faith is not a meritorious work. It is never the ground of justification—it is simply the channel through which it is received, and it, too, is a gift (cf. Eph. 2:8).

shall be called," concluding that God *was* able to raise *him* up, even from the dead.

GEN And Abraham stretched out his hand and took the knife to slay his son. But the Angel of the Lord called to him from heaven and said, "Abraham, Abraham!" So he said, "Here I am." And He said, "Do not lay your hand on the lad, or do anything to him; for now I know that you fear God, since you have not withheld your son, your only *son,* from Me."

Then Abraham lifted his eyes and looked, and there behind *him was* a ram caught in a thicket by its horns. So Abraham went and took the ram, and offered it up for a burnt offering [b]instead of his son. And Abraham called the name of the place, The-Lord-Will-Provide; as it is said *to* this day, "In the Mount of the Lord it shall be provided."

Then the Angel of the Lord called to Abraham a second time out of heaven, and said: "By Myself I have sworn, says the Lord, because you have done this thing, and have not withheld your son, your only *son*—blessing I will bless you, and multiplying I will multiply your descendants as the stars of the heaven and as the sand which *is* on the seashore; and your descendants shall possess the gate of their enemies. In your seed all the nations of the earth shall be blessed, because you have obeyed My voice."

GAL Now to Abraham and his [c]Seed were the promises made. He does not say, "And to seeds," as of many, but as of one, "And to your Seed," who is Christ. ACTS And all the prophets, from Samuel and those who follow, as many as have spoken, have also foretold MT of Jesus Christ, the Son of David, the Son of Abraham— GAL till the Seed should come to whom the promise was made. ACTS You are sons of the prophets, and of the covenant which God made with our fathers, saying to Abraham, 'And in your seed all the families of the earth shall be blessed.' To you first, God, having raised up His Servant Jesus, sent Him to bless you, in turning away every one *of you* from your iniquities."

---

[b] Instead of his son. The ram was offered as a substitute for Isaac. In this way, the ram pictures Christ's substitutionary atonement. Though sinners deserved death, Christ took the punishment, as the perfect Substitute, for all who would believe in Him.

[c] Seed. The singular form of the Hebrew word, like its English and Greek counterparts, can be used in either an individual or a collective sense. Paul's point in Gal. 3:16 is that in some OT passages (e.g., Gen. 3:15; 22:18), "seed" refers to the greatest of Abraham's descendants, Jesus Christ.

6. The Coming Messiah as Prophet and King

Gen. 49:10; Num. 24:17b; Pss. 2:11–12; 72:2; 89:3–4; 110:1; Isa. 7:14; 9:6–7; 11:1–2; 42:1; 52:13; Jer. 23:5–6; Dan. 7:13–14; Mic. 5:2; Zech. 9:9; Acts 3:22–23; 10:42b–43; Rom. 1:2–3

ACTS For Moses truly said to the fathers, "The LORD your God will raise up for you a [a]Prophet like me from your brethren. Him you shall hear in all things, whatever He says to you. And it shall be *that* every soul who will not hear that Prophet shall be utterly destroyed from among the people."

ISA The Spirit of the LORD shall rest upon Him, the Spirit of wisdom and understanding, the Spirit of counsel and might, the Spirit of knowledge and of the fear of the LORD. PS He will judge Your people with righteousness, and Your poor with justice.

GEN The [b]scepter shall not depart from Judah, nor a lawgiver from between his feet, until Shiloh comes; and to Him *shall be* the obedience of the people. NUM A Star shall come out of Jacob; a Scepter shall rise out of Israel. ISA There shall come forth a Rod from the stem of Jesse, and a Branch shall grow out of his roots.

JER "Behold, *the* days are coming," says the LORD, "That I will raise to David a [c]Branch of righteousness; a King shall reign and prosper, and execute judgment and righteousness in the earth. In His days Judah will be saved, and Israel will dwell safely; Now this *is* His name by which He will be called: THE LORD OUR RIGHTEOUSNESS.

MIC "But you, Bethlehem Ephrathah, *though* you are little among the thousands of Judah, *yet* out of you shall come forth to Me the One to be Ruler in Israel, whose goings forth *are* from of old, from everlasting.

ISA "Behold! My Servant whom I uphold, My Elect One *in whom* My soul delights! I have put My Spirit upon Him; He will bring forth justice to the Gentiles."

---

[a] PROPHET. This prophecy comes from Deut. 18:15. Moses was revered by the Jews as their first and greatest prophet, and the Jews viewed the Prophet "like him" to refer to the Messiah.

[b] SCEPTER SHALL NOT DEPART FROM JUDAH. As strong as a young lion and entrenched as an old lion, to Judah's line belonged national prominence and kingship, including David, Solomon, and their dynasty (640 years after this), as well as "the one to whom the scepter belongs," i.e., Shiloh, the cryptogram for the Messiah, the One also called the "Lion of the Tribe of Judah" (Rev. 5:5).

[c] BRANCH. The Messiah is pictured as a branch (lit. "shoot") out of David's family tree (cf. Jer. 23:5; 33:15, 16; Isa. 4:2; 11:1–5; Zech. 3:8; 6:12–13), who will rule over God's people in the future.

PS "I have made a covenant with My chosen,
I have sworn to My servant David:
'Your seed I will establish forever,
And build up your throne to all generations.'"

ISA For unto us a Child is born, unto us a Son is given; and the government will be upon His shoulder. And His name will be called Wonderful, Counselor, Mighty God, Everlasting Father, Prince of Peace. Of the increase of *His* government and peace *there will be* no end, upon the throne of David and over His kingdom, to order it and establish it with judgment and justice from that time forward, even forever. The zeal of the LORD of hosts will perform this, ROM which He promised before through His prophets in the Holy Scriptures, concerning His Son Jesus Christ our Lord, who was born of the seed of David according to the flesh. ISA The Lord Himself will give you a sign: Behold, [d]the virgin shall conceive and bear a Son, and shall call His name [e]Immanuel.

ZECH Rejoice greatly, O daughter of Zion! Shout, O daughter of Jerusalem! Behold, your King is coming to you; He *is* just and having salvation, lowly and [f]riding on a donkey, a colt, the foal of a donkey.

ISA Behold, My Servant shall deal prudently; He shall be exalted and extolled and be very high. PS The LORD said to my Lord, "Sit at My right hand, till I make Your enemies Your footstool."

DAN Behold, *One* like the [g]Son of Man, coming with the clouds of heaven! He came to the Ancient of Days, and they brought Him near before Him. Then to Him was given dominion and glory and a kingdom, that all peoples, nations, and languages should serve Him. His dominion *is* an everlasting dominion, which shall not pass away, and His kingdom *the one* which shall not be destroyed.

---

[d] THE VIRGIN. This prophecy reached forward to the virgin birth of the Messiah, as the NT notes (Matt. 1:23). The Hebrew word refers to an unmarried woman and means "virgin" (Gen. 24:43; Prov 30:19; Song 1:3; 6:8), so the birth of Isaiah's own son (Isa. 8:3) could not have fully satisfied the prophecy.

[e] IMMANUEL. The title, applied to Jesus in Matt. 1:23, means "God with us."

[f] RIDING ON A DONKEY. Unlike Alexander the Great, this King comes riding on a donkey (cf. Jer. 17:25). This was fulfilled at Christ's triumphal entry (Matt. 21:1–5; John 12:12–16). The Jews should have been looking for someone from the line of David (cf. 2 Sam. 7; 1 Chron. 17). Four elements in this verse describe Messiah's character: (1) He is King; (2) He is just; (3) He brings salvation; and (4) He is humble.

[g] SON OF MAN. The Messiah (cf. Dan. 9:26), Christ is meant; He often designated Himself by this phrase (Matt. 16:26; 19:28; 26:64). "The clouds of heaven" are seen again in Rev. 1:7. Here He is distinct from the Ancient of Days, or Eternal One, the Father, who will coronate Him for the kingdom (Dan. 2:44). The picture of old age is not that of being feeble, rather it highlights eternality and divine wisdom to judge (as in Dan. 7:9–10).

PS Serve the Lord with fear, and rejoice with trembling. [h]Kiss the Son, lest He be angry, and you perish *in* the way, when His wrath is kindled but a little. Blessed *are* all those who put their trust in Him. ACTS It is He who was ordained by God *to be* Judge of the living and the dead. To Him all the prophets witness that, through His name, whoever believes in Him will receive remission of sins.

---

[h] Kiss the Son. This symbolic act would indicate allegiance and submission (cf. 1 Sam. 10:1; 1 Kings 19:18). The word for "Son" here is not the Hebrew word for "son" that was used in Ps. 2:7, but rather its Aramaic counterpart (cf. Dan. 7:13), which is a term that would especially be suitable for these commands being addressed to "nations" (Ps. 2:1). The imagery fluidly moves from the lesser David through the Davidic dynasty to the Greater David—Jesus Christ.

7. The Coming Messiah as the Suffering Servant

Pss. 16:10; 22:1, 13–14, 16b–18; 118:22–23; Isa. 11:10; 53:3–5, 6b–12; Dan. 9:25–27a; Zech 12:10b; Acts 26:22–23; Rom. 11:25b–27; 1 Peter 2:23

DAN "Know therefore and understand, *that* from the going forth of the command to restore and build Jerusalem until Messiah the Prince, *there shall be* [a]seven weeks and sixty-two weeks; the street shall be built again, and the wall, even in troublesome times. And after the sixty-two weeks Messiah shall be cut off, but not for Himself.

ISA He is [b]despised and rejected by men, a Man of sorrows and acquainted with grief. And we hid, as it were, *our* faces from Him; He was despised, and we did not esteem Him. Surely He has borne our griefs and carried our sorrows; yet we esteemed Him stricken, smitten by God, and afflicted. But He *was* [c]wounded for our transgressions, *He was* bruised for our iniquities; the chastisement for our peace *was* upon Him, and by His stripes we are healed.

PS They gape at Me *with* their mouths, *like* a raging and roaring lion. I am poured out like water, and all My bones are out of joint; My heart is like wax; it has melted within Me.

ISA The LORD has laid on Him the iniquity of us all. He was oppressed and He was afflicted, yet [d]He opened not His mouth; He was led as a lamb to the slaughter, and as a sheep before its shearers is silent, so He opened not His mouth. 1PET When He

---

[a] SEVEN WEEKS AND SIXTY-TWO WEEKS. These are weeks of years, whereas weeks of days are described in a different way (Dan. 10:2–3). The time spans from the Persian Artaxerxes' decree to rebuild Jerusalem, ca. 445 BC (Neh. 2:1–8), to the Messiah's kingdom. This panorama includes: (1) seven weeks or forty-nine years, possibly closing Nehemiah's career in the rebuilding of the "street and wall," as well as the end of the ministry of Malachi and the close of the OT; (2) sixty-two weeks or 434 more years for a total of 483 years to the first advent of Messiah. This was fulfilled at the triumphal entry in AD 30. The Messiah will be "cut off" (a common reference to death); and (3) the final seven years or seventieth week of the time of Antichrist (cf. v. 27). Roman people, from whom the Antichrist will come, will "destroy the city" of Jerusalem and its temple in AD 70.

[b] DESPISED AND REJECTED. The prophet foresees the hatred and rejection by mankind toward the Messiah/Servant, who suffered not only external abuse but also internal grief over the lack of response from those He came to save (e.g., Matt. 23:37; Luke 13:34).

[c] WOUNDED FOR OUR TRANSGRESSIONS. This verse is filled with the language of substitution. The Servant suffered not for His own sin, since He was sinless (cf. Heb. 4:15; 7:26), but as the substitute for sinners. The emphasis here is on Christ being the substitute recipient of God's wrath on sinners (cf. 2 Cor. 5:21; Gal. 1:3–4; Heb. 10:9–10).

[d] OPENED NOT HIS MOUTH. The Servant will utter no protest and will be utterly submissive to those who oppress Him. Jesus fulfilled this (Matt. 26:63; 27:12–14; Mark 14:61; 15:5; Luke 23:9; John 19:9).

was reviled, [He] did not revile in return; when He suffered, He did not threaten, but committed *Himself* to Him who judges righteously.

ISA He was taken from prison and from judgment, and who will declare His generation? For He was cut off from the land of the living; for the transgressions of My people He was stricken.

PS They pierced My hands and My feet; I can count all My bones. They look *and* stare at Me. They divide My garments among them, and for My clothing they cast lots.

ISA They made His grave with the wicked—but [e]with the rich at His death, because He had done no violence, nor *was any* deceit in His mouth. Yet it pleased the LORD to bruise Him; He has put *Him* to grief.

PS [f]My God, My God, why have You forsaken Me? *Why are You so* far from helping Me, *and from* the words of My groaning?

ISA When You make His soul an offering for sin, He shall see *His* seed, He shall prolong *His* days, and the pleasure of the LORD shall prosper in His hand. He shall see the labor of His soul, *and* be satisfied.

PS For You will not leave my soul in Sheol, nor will You [g]allow Your Holy One to see corruption.

ISA By His knowledge My righteous Servant shall justify many, for He shall bear their iniquities. Therefore I will divide Him a portion with the great, and He shall divide the spoil with the strong. PS The stone *which* the builders rejected has become the chief cornerstone. This was the LORD's doing; it *is* marvelous in our eyes. ISA He poured out His soul unto death, and He was numbered with the transgressors, and He bore the sin of many, and [h]made intercession for the transgressors.

ACTS Therefore, having obtained help from God, to this day I stand, witnessing both to small and great, saying no other things than those which the prophets and Moses said would come—that the Christ would suffer, that He would be the first

---

[e] WITH THE RICH AT HIS DEATH. Because of the nature of His disgraceful death, Roman law dictated that the Servant should have a disgraceful burial along with the thieves (but cf. Jewish law, Deut. 21:22–23; also cf. John 19:31). Instead He was buried with "the rich" in an honorable burial through the donated tomb of rich Joseph of Arimathea (Matt. 27:57–60; Mark 15:42–46; Luke 23:50–53; John 19:38–40).

[f] MY GOD, MY GOD, WHY HAVE YOU FORSAKEN ME? The repeated noun of direct address to God reflects a personal molecule of hope in a seemingly hopeless situation. *Forsaken* is a strong expression for personal abandonment, intensely felt by David and supremely experienced by Christ on the cross (Matt. 27:46).

[g] ALLOW YOUR HOLY ONE TO SEE CORRUPTION. These words expressed the confidence of the lesser David, but were applied messianically to the resurrection of the Greater David (the Lord Jesus Christ) both by Peter (Acts 2:25–28) and Paul (Acts 13:35).

[h] MADE INTERCESSION FOR THE TRANSGRESSORS. This speaks of the office of intercessory High-Priest, which began on the cross (Luke 23:34) and continues in heaven (cf. Heb. 7:25; 9:24).

to rise from the dead, and would proclaim light to the *Jewish* people and to the Gentiles.

ROM Blindness in part has happened to Israel until the fullness of the Gentiles has come in. And so all Israel will be saved, as it is written: "The Deliverer will come out of Zion, and He will turn away ungodliness from Jacob; for this *is* My covenant with them, when I take away their sins."

ZECH Then they will [i]look on Me whom they pierced. Yes, they will mourn for Him as one mourns for *his* only *son,* and grieve for Him as one grieves for a firstborn. ISA In that day there shall be a Root of Jesse, who shall stand as a banner to the people; for the Gentiles shall seek Him, and His resting place shall be glorious.

---

[i] look on Me whom they pierced. Israel's repentance will come because they look to Jesus, the One whom they rejected and crucified (cf. Isa. 53:5; John 19:37), in faith at the Second Advent (Rom. 11:25–27). When God says they pierced "Me," He is certainly affirming the incarnation of deity—Jesus was God (cf. John 10:30).

Part II | The Beginning of the Gospel of Jesus Christ

8. Introducing the History of Jesus Christ

Isa. 9:2; Mark 1:1; Luke 1:1–4; John 1:5, 9–13; 2 Tim. 1:10b

MK [a]The beginning of the gospel of [b]Jesus Christ, the [c]Son of God, 2TIM *who* has [d]abolished death and brought life and immortality to light through the gospel. JN And the [e]light shines in the darkness, and the darkness did not [f]comprehend it.

[a] The beginning . . . the Son of God. This is best viewed as Mark's title for his gospel. The historical record of the gospel message began with John the Baptist (cf. Matt. 11:12; Luke 16:16; Acts 1:22; 10:37; 13:24). The term *gospel* refers to the good news about the life, death, and resurrection of Jesus Christ, of which the four gospels are written records.

[b] Jesus Christ. *Jesus* is the Greek form of the Hebrew name Joshua (meaning, "the Lord is salvation"); *Christ* ("anointed one") is the Greek equivalent of the Hebrew word *Messiah*. *Jesus* is the Lord's human name (cf. Matt. 1:21; Luke 1:31); *Christ* signifies His office as ruler of God's coming kingdom (Dan. 9:25–26).

[c] Son of God. An affirmation of Jesus' deity, stressing His unique relationship to the Father (cf. Mark 3:11; 5:7; 9:7; 13:32; 15:39; John 1:34).

[d] abolished death . . . immortality to light. *Abolished* means "rendered inoperative." Physical death still exists, but it is no longer a threat or an enemy for Christians (1 Cor. 15:54–55; Heb. 2:14). It was not until the incarnation and the gospel that God chose to fully make known the truth of immortality and eternal life, a reality only partially understood by OT believers (cf. Job 19:26).

[e] light . . . darkness. John introduces the reader to contrastive themes that occur throughout this gospel. In Scripture *light* and *darkness* are very familiar symbols. Intellectually, light refers to biblical truth, while darkness refers to error or falsehood (cf. Ps. 119:105; Prov. 6:23). Morally, light refers to holiness or purity (1 John 1:5), while darkness refers to sin or wrongdoing (John 3:19; 12:35, 46; Rom. 13:11–14; 1 Thess. 5:4–7; 1 John 1:6; 2:8–11). Darkness has special significance in relationship to Satan (and his demonic cohorts) who rules the present spiritually-dark world (1 John 5:19) as the "prince of the power of the air," promoting spiritual darkness and rebellion against God (Eph. 2:2). John uses the term *darkness* fourteen times (eight in the gospel and six in 1 John) out of its seventeen occurrences in the NT, making it almost an exclusively Johannine word.

[f] comprehend. The better meaning of this term in context is "overcome." Darkness is not able to overcome or conquer the light. Just as a single candle can overcome a room filled with darkness, so also the powers of darkness are overcome by the person and work of the Son through His death on the cross (cf. 19:11a).

ISA The people who walked in darkness
Have seen a great light;
Those who dwelt in the land of the shadow of death,
Upon them a light has shined.

JN That was [g]the true Light [h]which gives light to every man coming into [i]the world. He was in the world, and the world was made through Him, and the world did not know Him. He came to [j]His own, and His own did not receive Him. But [k]as many as received Him, to them He [l]gave [m]the right to become children of God, to those who believe in [n]His name: who were born, not of blood, nor of the will of the flesh, nor of the will of man, but [o]of God.

---

[g] THE TRUE LIGHT . . . COMING INTO THE WORLD. The words "coming into the world" would be better grammatically if attached to "light" rather than "every man" and thus translated "the true Light coming into the world gives light to every man." This highlights the incarnation of Jesus Christ (John 1:14; 3:16).

[h] WHICH GIVES LIGHT TO EVERY MAN. Through God's sovereign power, every man has enough light to be responsible. God has planted His knowledge in man through general revelation in creation and conscience. The result of general revelation, however, does not produce salvation but either leads to the complete light of Jesus Christ or produces condemnation in those who reject such "light" (cf. Rom. 1:19, 20; 2:12–16). The coming of Jesus Christ was the fulfillment and embodiment of the light that God had placed inside the heart of man.

[i] THE WORLD. The basic sense of this Greek word meaning "an ornament" is illustrated by the word "*cosmetic*" (1 Peter 3:3). While the NT uses it a total of 185 times, John had a particular fondness for this term, using it seventy-eight times in his gospel, twenty-four times in 1-3 John and three times in Revelation. John gives it several shades of meaning: (1) the physical created universe (John 1:9; cf. v. 3; 21:24, 25); (2) humanity in general (John 3:16; 6:33, 51; 12:19); and (3) the invisible spiritual system of evil dominated by Satan and all that it offers in opposition to God, His Word, and His people (John 3:19; 4:42; 7:7; 14:17, 22, 27, 30; 15:18–19; 16:8, 20, 33; 17:6, 9, 14; cf. 1 Cor. 1:21; 2 Peter 1:4; 1 John 5:19). The latter concept is the significant new use that the term acquires in the NT and that predominates in John. Thus, in the majority of times that John uses the word, it has decidedly-negative overtones.

[j] HIS OWN. The first usage of "His own" most likely refers to the world of mankind in general, while the second refers to the Jewish nation. As Creator the world belongs to the Word as His property, but the world did not even recognize Him due to spiritual blindness (cf. also v. 10). John used the second occurrence of "His own" in a narrower sense to refer to Jesus' own physical lineage, the Jews. Although they possessed the Scriptures that testified of His person and coming, they still did not accept Him (Isa. 65:2–3; Jer. 7:25). This theme of Jewish rejection of their promised Messiah receives special attention in John's gospel (12:37–41).

[k] AS MANY AS RECEIVED HIM . . . TO THOSE WHO BELIEVE IN HIS NAME. The second phrase describes the first. To receive Him who is the Word of God means to acknowledge His claims, place one's faith in Him, and thereby yield allegiance to Him.

[l] GAVE. The term emphasizes the grace of God involved in the gift of salvation (cf. Eph. 2:8–10).

[m] THE RIGHT. Those who receive Jesus, the Word, receive full authority to claim the exalted title of "God's children."

[n] HIS NAME. Denotes the character of the person himself.

[o] OF GOD. The divine side of salvation: ultimately it is not a man's will that produces salvation, but God's will (cf. John 3:6–8; Titus 3:5; 1 John 2:29).

LK [p]Inasmuch as [q]many have taken in hand [r]to set in order a narrative of [s]those things which have been fulfilled [t]among us, just as those who from the beginning were [u]eyewitnesses and ministers of the word delivered them to us, it seemed good to me also, [v]having had perfect understanding of all things [w]from the very first, to

---

[p] Inasmuch. The opening four verses from Luke's gospel make a single sentence, written in the polished style of a Greek literary classic. It was common for Greek historical works to begin with such a prologue. After this formal prologue, however, Luke shifted into a simpler style of narrative, probably patterned after the familiar style of the Septuagint.

[q] many. Although Luke wrote direct, divine revelation inspired by the Holy Spirit, he acknowledged the works of others who had set down in writing events from Christ's life. All those sources have been long lost, except for the inspired gospels. Since Matthew and Mark were most likely written before Luke, it has been suggested that either one or both of those may have been among Luke's sources when he did his research. It is also known that he was personally acquainted with many firsthand witnesses to the events of Christ's life. And it is possible that some of his sources were word-of-mouth reports. About 60 percent of the material in Mark is repeated in Luke, and Luke seems to follow Mark's order of events closely.

[r] to set in order. Luke proposed to narrate the ministry of Christ in an authoritative, logical, and factual order (though not always strictly chronological).

[s] those things which have been fulfilled. i.e., the OT messianic promises fulfilled in Christ.

[t] among us. i.e., in our generation. This phrase does not mean Luke was personally an eyewitness to the life of Christ

[u] eyewitnesses and ministers of the word. Luke's primary sources were the apostles themselves, who delivered facts about Jesus' life and teaching—both orally and by means of recorded memoirs in written documents made available to Luke. In any case, Luke made no pretense of being an eyewitness himself but explained that these were facts supported by careful research

[v] having had perfect understanding. Lit. "having traced out carefully." Luke's gospel was the result of painstaking investigation. Luke, more than anyone else in the early church, had the abilities and the opportunity to consult with eyewitnesses of Jesus' ministry and consolidate their accounts. He spent more than two years during Paul's imprisonment at Caesarea (Acts 24:26–27), during which time he would have been able to meet and interview many of the apostles and other eyewitnesses of Jesus' ministry. We know, for example, that he met Philip (Acts 21:8), who was undoubtedly one of Luke's sources. In his travels he may also have encountered the apostle John. Joanna, wife of Herod's steward, is mentioned only in Luke's gospel (cf. Luke 8:3; 24:10), so she must have been a personal acquaintance of his. Luke also related details about Herod's dealings with Christ not found in the other gospels (Luke 13:31–33; 23:7–12). No doubt it was from Joanna (or someone in a similar position) that Luke learned those facts. However, his understanding was perfect because of the divine revelation he received from the Holy Spirit (2 Tim. 3:16, 17; 2 Peter 1:19–21).

[w] from the very first. This could mean from the beginning of Christ's earthly life. However, the word can mean "from above" (John 3:31; 19:11; James 3:15). "From the beginning" in Luke 1:2 uses a different Greek word, *arch*—so it is best to understand that Luke was saying he used earthly sources for his material but was given heavenly guidance as he did his research and writing. It is clear that he regarded his account as authoritative.

write to you [x]an orderly account, [y]most excellent Theophilus, that you may know the [z]certainty of those things in which you were[aa]instructed.

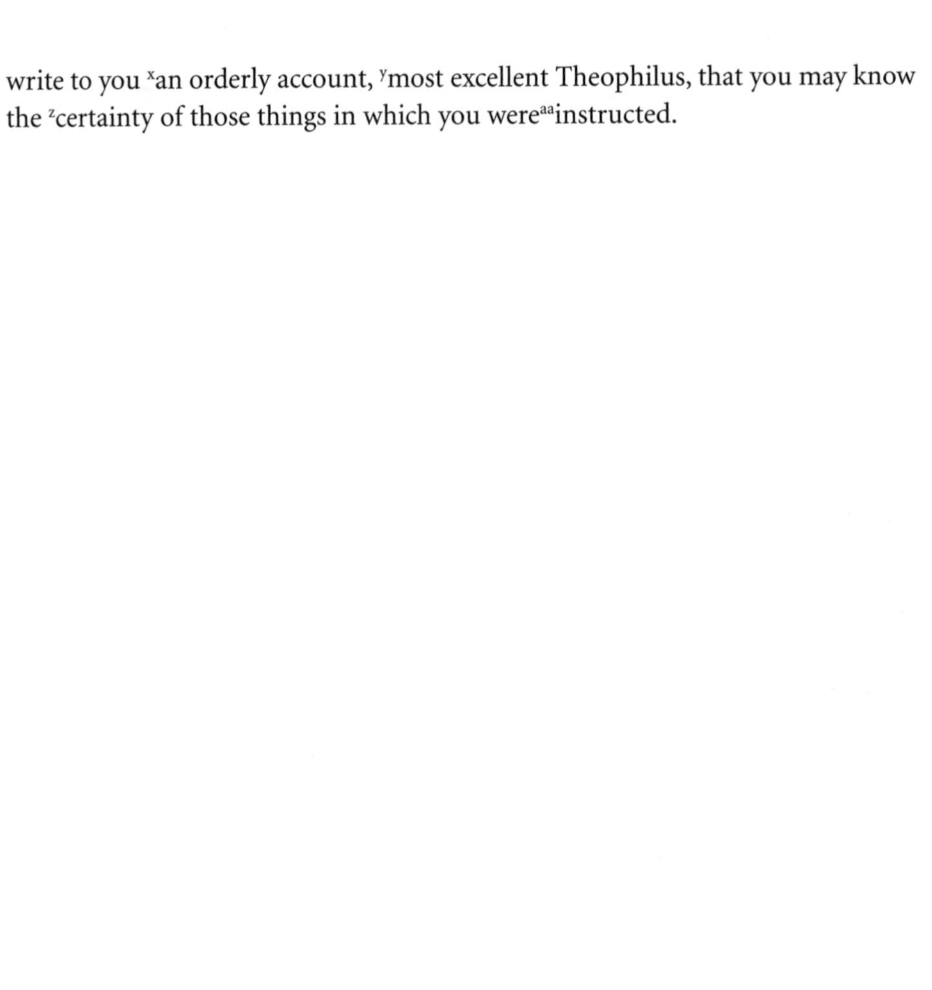

[x] AN ORDERLY ACCOUNT. Luke's account is predominantly ordered chronologically, but he does not follow such an arrangement slavishly.

[y] MOST EXCELLENT. This was a title used to address governors (Acts 23:26; 24:3; 26:25). This sort of language was reserved for the highest dignitaries, suggesting that "Theophilus" was a such a person.

[z] CERTAINTY. Note the implicit claim of authority. Though Luke drew from other sources, he regarded the reliability and authority of his gospel as superior to uninspired sources.

[aa] INSTRUCTED. Theophilus had been schooled in the apostolic tradition, possibly even by the apostle Paul himself. Yet the written Scripture by means of this gospel sealed the certainty of what he had heard.

9. The Royal Lineage of Jesus Christ Through Joseph

Matt. 1:1–17

MT The [a]book of the genealogy of [b]Jesus Christ, the [c]Son of David, the [d]Son of Abraham:

Abraham begot Isaac, Isaac begot Jacob, and Jacob begot Judah and his brothers. Judah begot Perez and Zerah by [e]Tamar, Perez begot Hezron, and Hezron begot Ram. Ram begot Amminadab, Amminadab begot Nahshon, and Nahshon begot Salmon. [f]Salmon begot Boaz by Rahab, Boaz begot Obed by Ruth, Obed begot Jesse, and Jesse begot David the king.

David the king begot Solomon by her *who had been the wife* of Uriah. Solomon begot Rehoboam, Rehoboam begot Abijah, and Abijah begot Asa. Asa begot Jehoshaphat, Jehoshaphat begot Joram, and [g]Joram begot Uzziah. Uzziah begot Jotham, Jotham begot Ahaz, and Ahaz begot Hezekiah. Hezekiah begot Manasseh,

[a] BOOK OF THE GENEALOGY OF JESUS CHRIST. This phrase is viewed by some as Matthew's title for the entire gospel. The Greek phrase translated "book of the genealogy" is exactly the same phrase used in Gen. 5:1 in the Septuagint.

[b] JESUS CHRIST. The Aramaic or Hebrew name *Jeshua* (*yeshua*) means "the Lord is Salvation." *Christos* means "anointed one" and is the exact equivalent of *mashiakh,* the Hebrew for "Messiah" (Dan. 9:25).

[c] SON OF DAVID. A messianic title used as such in only the synoptic gospels (cf. Matt. 22:42, 45).

[d] SON OF ABRAHAM. Takes His royal lineage all the way back to the nation's inception in the Abrahamic Covenant (Gen. 12:1–3).

[e] TAMAR. It is unusual for women to be named in genealogies. Matthew names 5: "Tamar" was a Canaanite woman who posed as a prostitute to seduce Judah (Gen. 38:13–30). "Rahab" (Matt. 1:5) was a Gentile and a prostitute (Josh. 2:1). "Ruth" (Matt. 1:5) was a Moabite woman (Ruth 1:3), and thus her offspring were forbidden to enter the assembly of the Lord for ten generations (Deut. 23:3). "Bathsheba" ("Uriah's wife" Matt. 1:6) committed adultery with David (2 Sam. 11). And "Mary" (Matt. 1:16) bore the stigma of pregnancy outside of wedlock. Each of these women is an object lesson about the workings of divine grace.

[f] SALMON BEGOT BOAZ BY RAHAB . . . AND JESSE BEGOT DAVID THE KING. This is not an exhaustive genealogy. Several additional generations must have elapsed between Rahab (in Joshua's time) and David (Matt. 1:6)—nearly four centuries later. Matthew's genealogy (like most of the biblical ones) sometimes skips over several generations between well-known characters in order to abbreviate the listing.

[g] JORAM BEGOT UZZIAH. Cf. 1 Chron. 3:10–12. Matthew skips over Ahaziah, Joash, and Amaziah, going directly from Joram to Uzziah (Azariah)—using a kind of genealogical shorthand. He seems to do this intentionally in order to make a symmetrical three-fold division in Matt. 1:17.

Manasseh begot Amon, and Amon begot Josiah. [h]Josiah begot Jeconiah and his brothers about the time they were carried away to Babylon.

And after they were brought to Babylon, Jeconiah begot Shealtiel, and [i]Shealtiel begot Zerubbabel. Zerubbabel begot Abiud, Abiud begot Eliakim, and Eliakim begot Azor. Azor begot Zadok, Zadok begot Achim, and Achim begot Eliud. Eliud begot Eleazar, Eleazar begot Matthan, and Matthan begot Jacob. And Jacob begot [j]Joseph the husband of Mary, of whom was born Jesus who is called Christ.

So all the generations from Abraham to David *are* [k]fourteen generations, from David until the captivity in Babylon *are* fourteen generations, and from the captivity in Babylon until the Christ *are* fourteen generations.

---

[h] Josiah begot Jeconiah. Again, Matthew skips a generation between Josiah and Jeconiah (cf. 1 Chron. 3:14–16). Jeconiah is also called Jehoiachin (2 Kings 24:6; 2 Chron. 36:8) and sometimes Coniah (Jer. 22:24). Jeconiah's presence in this genealogy presents an interesting dilemma. A curse on him forbade any of his descendants from the throne of David forever (Jer. 22:30). Since Jesus was heir through Joseph to the royal line of descent, but not an actual son of Joseph and thus not a physical descendant through this line, the curse bypassed him.

[i] Shealtiel begot Zerubbabel. See 1 Chron. 3:17–19, where Zerubbabel is said to be the offspring of Pedaiah, Shealtiel's brother. Elsewhere in the OT, Zerubbabel is always called the son of Shealtiel. (e.g., Hag. 1:1; Ezra 3:2; Neh. 12:1). Possibly Shealtiel adopted his nephew (cf. Hag. 2:23). Zerubbabel is the last character in Matthew's list who appears in any of the OT genealogies.

[j] Joseph the husband of Mary, of whom was born Jesus. This is the only entry in the entire genealogy where the word "*begot*" is not used—including those where whole generations were skipped. The pronoun *whom* is singular, referring to Mary alone. The unusual way in which this final entry is phrased underscores the fact that Jesus was not Joseph's literal offspring. The genealogy nonetheless establishes His claim to the throne of David as Joseph's legal heir.

[k] fourteen generations. The significance of the number fourteen is not clear, but Matthew's attention to numbers—a distinctly Hebrew characteristic—is evident throughout the gospel. The systematic ordering may be an aid for memorization. Note that Matthew counts Jeconiah in both the third and fourth groups, representing both the last generation before the Babylonian captivity and the first generation after.

10. The Physical Lineage of Jesus Christ Through Mary

Gal. 4:4; Luke 3:23b–38

GAL But when [a]the fullness of the time had come, [b]God sent forth His Son, [c]born of a woman, born [d]under the law, LK being (as was supposed) [e]*the* son of Joseph, *the son* of Heli, *the son* of Matthat, *the son* of Levi, *the son* of Melchi, *the son* of Janna, *the son* of Joseph, *the son* of Mattathiah, *the son* of Amos, *the son* of Nahum, *the son* of Esli, *the son* of Naggai, *the son* of Maath, *the son* of Mattathiah, *the son* of Semei, *the son* of Joseph, *the son* of Judah, *the son* of Joannas, *the son* of Rhesa, *the son* of Zerubbabel, *the son* of Shealtiel, *the son* of Neri, *the son* of Melchi, *the son* of Addi, *the son* of Cosam, *the son* of Elmodam, *the son* of Er, *the son* of Jose, *the son* of Eliezer, *the son* of Jorim, *the son* of Matthat, *the son* of Levi, *the son* of Simeon, *the son* of Judah, *the son* of Joseph, *the son* of Jonan, *the son* of Eliakim, *the son* of Melea, *the son* of Menan, *the son* of Mattathah, *the son* of Nathan, *the son* of David, *the son* of Jesse, *the son* of Obed, *the son* of Boaz, *the son* of Salmon, *the son* of Nahshon, *the son* of Amminadab, *the son* of Ram, *the son* of Hezron, *the son* of Perez, *the son* of Judah, *the son* of Jacob, *the son* of Isaac, *the son*

---

[a] THE FULLNESS OF THE TIME. In God's timetable, when the exact religious, cultural, and political conditions demanded by His perfect plan were in place, Jesus came into the world.

[b] GOD SENT FORTH HIS SON. As a father set the time for the ceremony of his son becoming of age and being released from the guardians, stewards, and tutors, so God sent His Son at the precise moment to bring all who believe out from under bondage to the law—a truth Jesus repeatedly affirmed (John 5:30, 36–37; 6:39, 44, 57; 8:16, 18, 42; 12:49; 17:21, 25; 20:21). That the Father sent Jesus into the world teaches His preexistence as the eternal second member of the Trinity (cf. Phil. 2:6, 7; Heb. 1:3–5).

[c] BORN OF A WOMAN. This emphasizes Jesus' full humanity, not merely His virgin birth (Isa. 7:14; Matt. 1:20–25). Jesus had to be fully God for His sacrifice to be of the infinite worth needed to atone for sin. But, He also had to be fully man so He could take upon Himself the penalty of sin as the substitute for man. See Luke 1:32, 35; John 1:1, 14, 18.

[d] UNDER THE LAW. Like all men, Jesus was obligated to obey God's law. Unlike anyone else, however, He perfectly obeyed that law (John 8:46; 2 Cor. 5:21; Heb. 4:15; 7:26; 1 Peter 2:22; 1 John 3:5). His sinlessness made Him the unblemished sacrifice for sins, who "fulfilled all righteousness," i.e., perfectly obeyed God in everything. That perfect righteousness is what is imputed to those who believe in Him.

[e] THE SON OF. Luke's genealogy moves backward, from Jesus to Adam; Matthew's moves forward, from Abraham to Joseph. Luke's entire section from Joseph to David differs starkly from that given by Matthew. The two genealogies are easily reconciled if Luke's is seen as Mary's genealogy, and Matthew's version represents Joseph's. Thus

of Abraham, *the son* of Terah, *the son* of Nahor, *the son* of Serug, *the son* of Reu, *the son* of Peleg, *the son* of Eber, *the son* of Shelah, *the son* of Cainan, *the son* of Arphaxad, *the son* of Shem, *the son* of Noah, *the son* of Lamech, *the son* of Methuselah, *the son* of Enoch, *the son* of Jared, *the son* of Mahalalel, *the son* of Cainan, *the son* of Enosh, *the son* of Seth, *the son* of Adam, *the son* of God.

---

the royal line is passed through Jesus' legal father, and His physical descent from David is established by Mary's lineage. Luke, unlike Matthew, includes no women in his genealogy—even Mary herself. Joseph was "the son of Heli" by marriage (Heli having no sons of his own) and thus is named here in Luke 3:23 as the representative of Mary's generation. Moses himself established precedent for this sort of substitution in Num. 27:1–11; 36:1–12. The men listed from Heli (Luke 3:23) to Rhesa (3:27) are found nowhere else in Scripture.

11. The Coming of Christ's Forerunner, John the Baptist

Mark 1:2–3; Luke 1:5–25; John 1:6–8

JN There was a man [a]sent from God, whose name *was* [b]John. This man came for a [c]witness, to bear witness of the Light, [d]that all through him might believe. [e]He was not that Light, but *was sent* to bear witness of that Light.

MK As [f]it is written [g]in the Prophets:

---

[a] SENT FROM GOD. As forerunner to Jesus, John was to bear witness to Him as the Messiah and Son of God. With John's ministry, the NT period began.

[b] JOHN. The name *John* always refers to John the Baptist in this gospel, never to the apostle John. The writer of the fourth gospel calls him merely *John* without using the phrase "the Baptist," unlike the other gospels, which use the additional description to identify him (Matt. 3:1; Mark 6:14; Luke 7:20). Moreover, John the apostle (or, son of Zebedee) never identified himself directly by name in his gospel even though he was one of the three most intimate associates of Jesus (Matt. 17:1). Such silence argues strongly that John the apostle authored the fourth gospel and that his readers knew full well that he composed the gospel that bears his name.

[c] WITNESS...BEAR WITNESS. The terms *witness* or *bear witness* receive special attention in John's gospel, reflecting the courtroom language of the OT where the truth of a matter was to be established on the basis of multiple witnesses (John 8:17–18; cf. Deut. 17:6; 19:15). Not only did John the Baptist witness regarding Jesus as Messiah and Son of God (John 1:19–34; 3:27–30; 5:35), but there were other witnesses: (1) the Samaritan woman (John 4:29); (2) the works of Jesus (10:25); (3) the Father (5:32–37); (4) the OT (5:39, 40); (5) the crowd (12:17); and (6) the Holy Spirit (15:26–27).

[d] THAT ALL THROUGH HIM MIGHT BELIEVE. The pronoun *him* refers not to Christ but to John the Baptist as the agent who witnessed to Christ. The purpose of his testimony was to produce faith in Jesus Christ as the Savior of the world.

[e] HE WAS NOT THAT LIGHT. While John the Baptist was the agent of belief, Jesus Christ is the object of belief. Although John's person and ministry were vitally important (Matt. 11:11), he was merely the forerunner who announced the coming of the Messiah. Many years after John's ministry and death, some still failed to understand John's subordinate role to Jesus (Acts 19:1–3).

[f] IT IS WRITTEN. A phrase commonly used in the NT to introduce OT quotes (cf. Matt. 2:5; 4:4, 6, 7; Mark 7:6; 9:13; 14:21, 27; Luke 2:23; 3:4; John 6:45; 12:14; Acts 1:20; 7:42; Rom. 3:4; 8:36; 1 Cor. 1:31; 9:9; 2 Cor. 8:14; 9:9; Gal. 3:10; 4:22; Heb. 10:7; 1 Peter 1:16).

[g] IN THE PROPHETS. The better Greek manuscripts read "Isaiah the prophet." Mark's quote is actually from two OT passages (Mal. 3:1; Isa. 40:3), which probably explains the reading "the Prophets" found in some manuscripts. The gospels all introduce John the Baptist's ministry by quoting Isa. 40:3 (cf. Matt. 3:3; Luke 3:4; John 1:23).

"Behold, I send [h]My messenger before Your face,
Who will prepare Your way before You.
The voice of one crying in the wilderness:
'Prepare the way of the LORD;
Make His paths straight.'"

LK There was in the days of Herod, the king of Judea, a certain priest named [i]Zacharias, of [j]the division of Abijah. His wife *was* of the [k]daughters of Aaron, and her name *was* Elizabeth. And they were both righteous before God, walking in all the commandments and ordinances of the Lord blameless. But they had no child, because Elizabeth was [l]barren, and they were both well advanced in years.

So it was, that while he was serving as priest before God in the order of his division, according to the custom of the priesthood, [m]his lot fell to burn incense when he went into the temple of the Lord. And the whole multitude of the people was praying outside at the hour of incense. Then an angel of the Lord appeared to him, standing on the right side of the altar of incense. And when Zacharias saw *him*, he was troubled, and [n]fear fell upon him.

But the angel said to him, "Do not be afraid, Zacharias, for [o]your prayer is heard; and your wife Elizabeth will bear you a son, and you shall call his name

---

[h] MY MESSENGER. John was the divinely-promised messenger, sent to prepare the way for the Messiah. In ancient times a king's envoys would travel ahead of him, making sure the roads were safe and fit for him to travel on, as well as announcing his arrival.

[i] ZACHARIAS. Lit. "Jehovah has remembered."

[j] THE DIVISION OF ABIJAH. The temple priesthood was organized into twenty-four divisions, with each division serving twice a year for one week (1 Chron. 24:4–19); Abijah's was the eighth division (1 Chron. 24:10). At this time, Zacharias's division was on duty for one of its two annual stints (Luke 1:8).

[k] DAUGHTERS OF AARON . . . RIGHTEOUS BEFORE GOD. Both husband and wife were from the priestly tribe, and both were believers, justified in God's sight.

[l] BARREN . . . WELL ADVANCED IN YEARS. This was seen by many as a sign of divine disfavor.

[m] HIS LOT FELL TO BURN INCENSE. A high honor (Ex. 30:7, 8; 2 Chron. 29:11). Because of the large number of priests, most would never be chosen for such a duty, and no one was permitted to serve in this capacity twice. Zacharias no doubt regarded this as the supreme moment in a lifetime of priestly service. The incense was kept burning perpetually, just in front of the veil that divided the holy place from the most holy place. The lone priest would offer the incense every morning and every evening, while the rest of the priests and worshipers stood outside the holy place in prayer (v. 10).

[n] FEAR. The normal response—and an appropriate one (12:5)—when someone is confronted by a divine visitation or a mighty work of God (Judg. 6:22; 13:22; Mark 16:5; Rev. 1:17). Luke seems especially to take note of this; he often reports fear in the presence of God and His works (cf. Luke 1:30, 65; 2:9–10; 5:10, 26; 7:16; 8:25, 37, 50; 9:34, 45; 23:40).

[o] YOUR PRAYER. Probably a prayer for children to be in his home (cf. Luke 1:7, 25).

[p]John. And you will have [q]joy and gladness, and many will rejoice at his birth. For he will be great in the sight of the Lord, and shall drink [r]neither wine nor strong drink. He will also be filled with the Holy Spirit, [s]even from his mother's womb. And he will turn many of the children of Israel to the Lord their God. He will also go before Him [t]in the spirit and power of Elijah, '[u]to turn the hearts of the fathers to the children,' and the disobedient to the wisdom of the just, to make ready a people prepared for the Lord."

And Zacharias said to the angel, [v]"How shall I know this? For I am an old man, and my wife is well advanced in years." And the angel answered and said to him, "I am [w]Gabriel, who stands in the presence of God, and was sent to speak to you and bring you these glad tidings. But behold, you will be mute and not able to speak until the day these things take place, because you did not believe my words which will be fulfilled in their own time."

And the people waited for Zacharias, and [x]marveled that he lingered so long in the temple. But when he came out, he could not speak to them; and they perceived that he had seen a vision in the temple, for he beckoned to them and remained speechless.

---

[p] John. Lit. "Jehovah has shown grace."

[q] joy and gladness. The hallmarks of the messianic kingdom (Isa. 25:9; Pss. 14:7; 48:11). The motif of joy runs through Luke's gospel (cf. Luke 1:44, 47, 58; 2:10; 6:23; 8:13; 10:17–21; 13:17; 15:5–10, 22–32; 19:6, 37; 24:52).

[r] neither wine nor strong drink. This was a key element of the Nazirite vow (Num. 6:1–21) and would probably have been understood as such by Zacharias. Usually such a vow was temporary, but Samson (Judg. 16:17) and Samuel (1 Sam. 1:11) were subject to it from birth. The language here is reminiscent of the angel's instructions to Samson's parents (Judg. 13:4–7). However, no mention is made here of any restriction on the cutting of John's hair. Luke may have simply omitted that detail to avoid weighing his Gentile audience down with the details of Jewish law.

[s] even from his mother's womb. Reminiscent of Jeremiah (Jer. 1:5). This illustrates God's sovereignty in salvation.

[t] in the spirit and power of Elijah. Elijah, like John the Baptist, was known for his bold, uncompromising stand for the Word of God—even in the face of a ruthless monarch (cf. 1 Kings 18:17–24; Mark 6:15). The final two verses of the OT (Mal. 4:5, 6) had promised the return of Elijah before the Day of the Lord (cf. Matt. 3:4; 11:14; Mark 9:11, 12).

[u] to turn the hearts. Quoted from Mal. 4:6, showing that John the Baptist fulfilled that prophecy.

[v] "How shall I know this?" Abraham also asked for a sign under similar circumstances (Gen. 15:8). The sign given Zacharias was also a mild rebuke for doubting (Luke 1:20).

[w] Gabriel. Lit. "strong man of God." Gabriel also appears in Dan. 8:16; 9:21. He is one of only two holy angels whose names are given in Scripture, the other being Michael (Dan. 10:13, 21; Jude 9; Rev. 12:7).

[x] marveled that he lingered so long. Zacharias was only supposed to offer incense, then come out to pronounce the familiar blessing of Num. 6:23–27 on the people who were waiting in the temple court. The conversation with the angel would have taken additional time.

So it was, as soon as the [y]days of his service were completed, that he departed to his own house. Now after those days his wife Elizabeth conceived; and she [z]hid herself five months, saying, "Thus the Lord has dealt with me, in the days when He looked on *me,* to take away my reproach among people."

---

[y] days of his service . . . to his own house. After his days of service were complete (which consisted of one week), Zacharias returned to his home in the hill country of Judea (v. 39).

[z] hid herself . . . my reproach. Elizabeth probably sought solitude as an act of devotion out of deep gratitude to the Lord. She no longer carried the social stigma of barrenness. Childlessness carried a reproach in a culture where blessings were tied to birthrights and family lines. Barrenness could occasionally be a sign of divine disfavor (Lev. 20:20, 21), but it was not always so (cf. Gen. 30:23; 1 Sam. 1:5–10).

12. Gabriel Announces the Coming of Jesus Christ

Luke 1:26–38

LK Now [a]in the sixth month the angel Gabriel was sent by God to a city of Galilee named Nazareth, to [b]a virgin betrothed to a man whose name was Joseph, of the house of David. The virgin's name *was* Mary. And having come in, the angel said to her, "Rejoice, [c]highly favored *one,* the Lord *is* with you; blessed *are* you among women!"

But when she saw *him,* she was troubled at his saying, and considered what manner of greeting this was. Then the angel said to her, " [d]Do not be afraid, Mary, for you have found favor with God. And behold, you will conceive in your womb and bring forth a Son, and shall call His name JESUS. He will be great, and will be called [e]the Son of the Highest; and the Lord God will give Him the throne of [f]His father David. And He will reign [g]over the house of Jacob forever, and of His kingdom there will be no end."

---

[a] IN THE SIXTH MONTH. i.e., Elizabeth's sixth month of pregnancy.

[b] A VIRGIN. The importance of the virgin birth cannot be overstated. A right view of the incarnation hinges on the truth that Jesus was virgin-born. Both Luke and Matthew expressly state that Mary was a virgin when Jesus was conceived (cf. Matt. 1:23). The Holy Spirit wrought the conception through supernatural means (cf. Matt. 1:18; Luke 1:35). The nature of Christ's conception testifies of both His deity and His sinlessness.

[c] HIGHLY FAVORED. Lit. "full of grace"—a term used of all believers in Eph. 1:6, where it is translated "accepted." This portrays Mary as a recipient, not a dispenser, of divine grace.

[d] DO NOT BE AFRAID. The same thing Gabriel had said to Zacharias (Luke 1:13).

[e] THE SON OF THE HIGHEST. Cf. Luke 1:76, where John the Baptist is called "the prophet of the Highest." The Greek term Luke uses for "Highest" is the one employed in the Septuagint to translate the Hebrew, "The Most High God." Since a son bears his father's qualities, calling a person someone else's "son" was a way of signifying equality. Here the angel was telling Mary that her Son would be equal to the Most High God.

[f] HIS FATHER DAVID. Cf. Matt. 9:27. Jesus was David's physical descendant through Mary's line. David's "throne" was emblematic of the messianic kingdom (cf. 2 Sam. 7:13–16; Ps. 89:26–29).

[g] OVER THE HOUSE OF JACOB FOREVER. This emphasizes both the Jewish character of the millennial kingdom and the eternal permanence of Christ's rule over all. Cf. Isa. 9:7; Dan. 2:44.

Then Mary said to the angel, "How can this be, since [h]I do not know a man?" And the angel answered and said to her, "*The* [i]Holy Spirit will come upon you, and the power of the Highest will overshadow you; therefore, also, that Holy One who is to be born will be called the Son of God. Now indeed, [j]Elizabeth your relative has also conceived a son in her old age; and this is now the sixth month for her who was called barren. For with God nothing will be impossible." Then Mary said, "Behold the maidservant of the Lord! [k]Let it be to me according to your word." And the angel departed from her.

---

[h] I DO NOT KNOW A MAN. i.e., conjugally. Mary understood that the angel was speaking of an immediate conception, and she and Joseph were still in the midst of the long betrothal, or engagement period (cf. Matt. 1:18), before the actual marriage and consummation. Her question was borne out of wonder, not doubt nor disbelief, so the angel did not rebuke her as he had Zacharias (v. 20).

[i] HOLY SPIRIT WILL COME UPON YOU. This was a creative act of the Holy Spirit, not the sort of divine-human cohabitation sometimes seen in ancient Near Eastern, Greek, and Roman mythology.

[j] ELIZABETH YOUR RELATIVE. It seems most reasonable to regard the genealogy of Luke 3:23–38 as Mary's. This would make her a direct descendant of David. Yet, Elizabeth was a descendant of Aaron. Therefore, Mary must have been related to Elizabeth through her mother, who would have been of Aaronic descent. Thus, Mary was a descendant of David through her father.

[k] LET IT BE TO ME ACCORDING TO YOUR WORD. Mary was in an extremely embarrassing and difficult position. Betrothed to Joseph, she faced the stigma of unwed motherhood. Joseph would obviously have known that the child was not his. She knew she would be accused of adultery—an offense punishable by stoning (Deut. 22:13–21; cf. John 8:3–5). Yet she willingly and graciously submitted to the will of God.

13. Mary Rejoices with Elizabeth

Luke 1:39–56

LK Now Mary arose in those days and went into the hill country with haste, to a city of Judah, and entered the house of Zacharias and greeted Elizabeth. And it happened, when Elizabeth heard the greeting of Mary, that the babe leaped in her womb; and Elizabeth was [a]filled with the Holy Spirit. Then she spoke out with a loud voice and said, "Blessed *are* you among women, and blessed *is* the fruit of your womb! But why *is* this *granted* to me, that [b]the mother of my Lord should come to me? For indeed, as soon as the voice of your greeting sounded in my ears, [c]the babe leaped in my womb for joy. Blessed *is* she who believed, for there will be a fulfillment of those things which were told her from the Lord."

And [d]Mary said:

"My soul magnifies the Lord,
And my spirit has rejoiced in God [e]my Savior.

---

[a] FILLED WITH THE HOLY SPIRIT. i.e., controlled by the Holy Spirit, who undoubtedly guided Elizabeth's remarkable expression of praise.

[b] THE MOTHER OF MY LORD. This expression is not in praise of Mary, but in praise of the Child whom she bore. It was a profound expression of Elizabeth's confidence that Mary's Child would be the long-hoped-for Messiah—the one whom even David called "Lord" (cf. Luke 20:44). Elizabeth's grasp of the situation was extraordinary, considering the aura of mystery that overshadowed all these events (cf. Luke 2:19). She greeted Mary not with skepticism but with joy. She understood the response of the child in her own womb. And she seemed to comprehend the immense importance of the Child whom Mary was carrying. All of this must be attributed to the illuminating work of the Spirit (Luke 1:41).

[c] THE BABE LEAPED IN MY WOMB FOR JOY. The infant, like his mother, was Spirit-filled (cf. Luke 1:15,41). His response, like that of Elizabeth, was supernaturally prompted by the Spirit of God.

[d] MARY SAID. Mary's *Magnificat* (the first word of her exaltation in the Latin translation of Luke 1:46–55) is filled with OT allusions and quotations. It reveals that Mary's heart and mind were saturated with the Word of God. It contains repeated echoes of Hannah's prayers, e.g., 1 Sam. 1:11; 2:1–10. These verses also contain numerous allusions to the law, the psalms, and the prophets. The entire passage is a point-by-point reciting of the covenant promises of God.

[e] MY SAVIOR. Mary referred to God as "Savior," indicating both that she recognized her own need of a Savior, and that she knew the true God as her Savior. Nothing here or anywhere else in Scripture indicates Mary thought of herself as "immaculate" (free from the taint of original sin). Quite the opposite is true; she employed language typical of someone whose only hope for salvation is divine grace. Nothing in this passage lends support to the notion that Mary herself ought to be an object of adoration.

For He has regarded the [f]lowly state of His [g]maidservant;
For behold, henceforth all generations will call me blessed.
For He who is mighty has done great things for me,
And holy *is* His name.
And His mercy *is* on those who fear Him
From generation to generation.
He has shown strength with His arm;
He has scattered *the* proud in the imagination of their hearts.
He has put down the mighty from *their* thrones,
And exalted *the* lowly.
He has filled *the* hungry with good things,
And *the* rich He has sent away empty.
He has helped His servant Israel,
In remembrance of *His* mercy,
As He spoke to our fathers,
To Abraham and to his seed forever."

And Mary remained with her [h]about three months, and returned to [i]her house.

---

[f] lowly state. The quality of Mary that shines most clearly through this passage is a deep sense of humility.

[g] maidservant. i.e., a female slave.

[h] about three months. Mary arrived in the sixth month of Elizabeth's pregnancy (Luke 1:26), so she evidently stayed until John the Baptist was born.

[i] her house. At this point Mary was still betrothed to Joseph, not yet living in his house (cf. Matt. 1:24).

14. John the Baptist Is Born

Luke 1:57–80

LK Now Elizabeth's full time came for her to be delivered, and she brought forth a son. When her neighbors and relatives heard how the Lord had shown great mercy to her, they rejoiced with her.

So it was, on [a]the eighth day, that they came to circumcise the child; and they would have called him by the name of his father, Zacharias. His mother answered and said, "[b]No; he shall be called John."

But they said to her, "There is no one among your relatives who is called by this name." So they [c]made signs to his father—what he would have him called.

And he asked for a writing tablet, and wrote, saying, "His name is John." So they all marveled. Immediately his mouth was opened and his tongue *loosed,* and he spoke, praising God. Then fear came on all who dwelt around them; and all these sayings were discussed throughout [d]all the hill country of Judea. And all those who heard *them* kept *them* in their hearts, saying, "What kind of child will this be?" And the hand of the Lord was with him.

Now his father Zacharias was [e]filled with the Holy Spirit, and prophesied, [f]saying:

---

[a] THE EIGHTH DAY. In accord with God's commandment (Gen. 17:12; Lev. 12:1–3; cf. Phil. 3:5), it had become customary to name a child at circumcision. The ritual brought together family and friends, who in this case pressured the parents to give the baby "the name of his father"—probably intending this as a gesture of respect to Zacharias.

[b] No. Elizabeth had learned from Zacharias in writing (Luke 1:63), everything Gabriel had said to him.

[c] MADE SIGNS TO HIS FATHER. The priests conducting the circumcision ceremony appear to have assumed that since he could not speak, he was also deaf.

[d] ALL THE HILL COUNTRY OF JUDEA. i.e., Jerusalem and the surrounding area. John the Baptist's reputation began to spread from the time of his birth (Luke 1:66).

[e] FILLED WITH THE HOLY SPIRIT. In every case where someone was Spirit-filled in Luke's nativity account, the result was Spirit-directed worship. Cf. Eph. 5:18–20.

[f] SAYING. The exaltation of Zacharias (in Luke 1:68–79) is known as the *Benedictus* (the first word of v. 68 in the Latin translation). Like Mary's *Magnificat,* it is liberally sprinkled with OT quotations and allusions. When Zacharias was struck mute in the temple (Luke 1:20), he was supposed to deliver a benediction. So it is fitting that when his speech was restored, the first words out of his mouth were this inspired benediction.

"Blessed *is* the Lord God of Israel,
For He has visited and redeemed His people,
And has raised up a [g]horn of salvation for us
In the house of His servant David,
As He spoke by the mouth of His holy prophets,
Who *have been* since the world began,
That we should be saved from our enemies
And from the hand of all who hate us,
To perform the mercy *promised* to our fathers
And to remember [h]His holy covenant,
The oath which He swore to our father Abraham:
To grant us that we,
Being delivered from the hand of our enemies,
Might serve Him without fear,
In holiness and righteousness before Him all the days of our life.
"And you, child, will be called the prophet of the Highest;
For you will go before the face of the Lord to prepare His ways,
To give knowledge of salvation to His people
By [i]the remission of their sins,
Through the tender mercy of our God,
With which the [j]Dayspring from on high has visited us;
To give light to those who sit in darkness and the shadow of death,
To guide our feet into the way of peace."

So the child grew and became strong in spirit, and [k]was in the deserts till the day of his manifestation to Israel.

---

[g] HORN OF SALVATION. A common expression in the OT (2 Sam. 22:3; Ps. 18:2; cf. 1 Sam. 2:1). The horn is a symbol of strength (Deut. 33:17). These words were clearly not meant to exalt John the Baptist. Since both Zacharias and Elizabeth were Levites (cf. Luke 1:5), the One raised up "In the house of . . . David" could not be John, but spoke of Someone greater than he (John 1:26, 27).

[h] HIS HOLY COVENANT. i.e., the Abrahamic Covenant (v. 73), with its promise of salvation by grace. Cf. Gen. 12:1–3.

[i] THE REMISSION OF THEIR SINS. Forgiveness of sins is the heart of salvation. God saves sinners from separation from Him and from eternal hell only by atoning for and forgiving their sins. Cf. Rom. 4:6–8; 2 Cor. 5:19; Eph. 1:7; Heb. 9:22.

[j] DAYSPRING. A messianic reference (cf. Isa. 9:2; 60:1–3; Mal. 4:2; 2 Peter 1:19; Rev. 22:16).

[k] WAS IN THE DESERTS. Several groups of ascetics inhabited the wilderness regions east of Jerusalem. One was the famous Qumran community, source of the Dead Sea Scrolls. John's parents, already old when he was born, might have given him over to the care of someone with ties to such a community. In a similar way, Hannah consecrated Samuel to the Lord by entrusting him to Eli (1 Sam. 1:22–28). However, there is nothing concrete in Scripture to suggest that John was part of any such group. On the contrary, he is painted as a solitary figure, in the spirit of Elijah.

15. Jesus' Miraculous Birth Explained to Joseph

Matt. 1:18–25

MT Now the birth of Jesus Christ was as follows: After His mother Mary was [a]betrothed to Joseph, before they came together, she was found with child of the Holy Spirit. Then [b]Joseph her husband, being a just *man*, and not wanting to make her a public example, was minded to put her away secretly. But while he thought about these things, behold, [c]an angel of the Lord appeared to him [d]in a dream, saying, "Joseph, son of David, do not be afraid to take to you Mary your wife, for that which is conceived in her is of the Holy Spirit. And she will bring forth a Son, and you shall call His name [e]JESUS, for He will save His people from their sins."

So all this was done [f]that it might be fulfilled which was spoken by the Lord through the prophet, saying: "Behold, the [g]virgin shall be with child, and bear a Son, and they shall call His name [h]Immanuel," which is translated, "God with us."

[a] BETROTHED. Jewish betrothal was as binding as modern marriage. A divorce was necessary to terminate the betrothal (Matt. 1:19), and the betrothed couple were regarded legally as husband and wife (v. 19)—although physical union had not yet taken place.

[b] JOSEPH . . . BEING A JUST MAN . . . WAS MINDED TO PUT HER AWAY SECRETLY. Stoning was the legal prescription for this sort of adultery (Deut. 22:23–24). Joseph's righteousness meant he was also merciful; thus he did not intend to make Mary "a public example." The phrase "a just man" is a Hebraism suggesting that he was a true believer in God who had thereby been declared righteous, and who carefully obeyed the law (see Gen. 6:9). To "put her away" would be to obtain a legal divorce (Matt. 19:8, 9; Deut. 24:1), which according to the Jewish custom was necessary in order to dissolve a betrothal.

[c] AN ANGEL OF THE LORD. This is one of only a few such angelic visitations in the NT, most of which are associated with Christ's birth. For others, see Matt. 28:2; Acts 5:19; 8:26; 10:3; 12:7–10; 27:23; Rev. 1:1.

[d] IN A DREAM. As if to underscore the supernatural character of Christ's advent, Matthew's narrative of the event describes five such revelatory dreams: Matt. 1:20; 2:12, 13, 19, 22. Here the angel told Joseph he was to take Mary into his own home.

[e] JESUS. Cf. Matt. 1:25; Luke 1:31. The name means "Savior."

[f] THAT IT MIGHT BE FULFILLED. Matthew points out fulfillments of OT prophecies no less than a dozen times (cf. Matt. 2:15, 17, 23; 4:14; 8:17; 12:17; 13:14, 35; 21:4; 26:54–56; 27:9, 35). He quotes from the OT more than sixty times, more frequently than any other NT writer, except Paul in Romans.

[g] VIRGIN. Scholars sometimes dispute whether the Hebrew term in Isa. 7:14 means "virgin" or "maiden." Matthew is quoting here from the Septuagint, which uses the unambiguous Greek term for "virgin" (Isa. 7:14). Thus Matthew, writing under the Spirit's inspiration, ends all doubt about the meaning of the word in Isa. 7:14.

[h] IMMANUEL. Cf. Isa. 8:8, 10.

Then Joseph, being aroused from sleep, did as the angel of the Lord commanded him and took to him his wife, and did not [i]know her till she had brought forth her firstborn Son. And he called His name Jesus.

[i] know her. A euphemism for sexual intercourse. See Gen. 4:1, 17, 25; 38:26; Judg. 11:39.

16. The Messiah Is Born in Bethlehem

Luke 2:1–7; John 1:14

LK And it came to pass in those days *that* a decree went out from [a]Caesar Augustus that all the world should be registered. This census first took place while [b]Quirinius was governing Syria. So all went to be registered, everyone to his [c]own city.

[a] CAESAR AUGUSTUS. Caius Octavius, grand-nephew, adopted son, and primary heir to Julius Caesar. Before and after Julius's death in 44 BC, the Roman government was constantly torn by power struggles. Octavius ascended to undisputed supremacy in 31 BC by defeating his last remaining rival, Antony, in a military battle at Actium. In 29 BC the Roman senate declared Octavius Rome's first emperor. Two years later they honored him with the title "Augustus" (*exalted one*—a term signifying religious veneration). Rome's republican government was effectively abolished, and Augustus was given supreme military power. He reigned until his death at age 76 (AD 14). Under his rule, the Roman Empire dominated the Mediterranean region, ushering in a period of great prosperity and relative peace (the *Pax Romana*). He ordered "all the world" (i.e., the world of the Roman Empire) to be "registered." This was not merely a one-time census; the decree actually established a cycle of enrollments that was to occur every fourteen years. Israel had previously been excluded from the Roman census, because Jews were exempt from serving in the Roman army, and the census was designed primarily to register young men for military service (as well as account for all Roman citizens). This new, universal census was ostensibly to number each nation by family and tribe (hence Joseph, a Judean, had to return to his ancestral home to register). Property and income values were not recorded in this registration. But soon the names and population statistics gathered in this census were used for the levying of poll taxes (see Matt. 22:17), and the Jews came to regard the census itself as a distasteful symbol of Roman oppression.

[b] QUIRINIUS WAS GOVERNING SYRIA. Fixing a precise date for this census is problematic. Publius Sulpicius Quirinius is known to have governed Syria during AD 6–9. A well known census was taken in Palestine in AD 6. Josephus records that it sparked a violent Jewish revolt (mentioned by Luke, quoting Gamaliel, in Acts 5:37). Quirinius was responsible for administering that census, and he also played a major role in quelling the subsequent rebellion. However, that cannot be the census Luke has in mind here, because it occurred about a decade after the death of Herod (cf. Matt. 2:1)—much too late to fit Luke's chronology (cf. Luke 1:5). In light of Luke's meticulous care as a historian, it would be unreasonable to charge him with such an obvious anachronism. Indeed, archaeology has vindicated Luke. A fragment of stone discovered at Tivoli (near Rome) in 1764 contains an inscription in honor of a Roman official who, it states, was twice governor of Syria and Phoenicia during the reign of Augustus. The name of the official is not on the fragment, but among his accomplishments are listed details that, as far as is known, can fit no one other than Quirinius. Thus, he must have served as governor in Syria twice. He was probably military governor at the same time that history records Varus was civil governor there. With regard to the dating of the census, some ancient records found in Egypt mention a worldwide census ordered in 8 BC. That date is not without problems, either. It is generally thought by scholars that 6 BC is the earliest possible date for Christ's birth. Evidently, the census was ordered by Caesar Augustus in 8 BC but was not actually carried out in Palestine until two to four years later, perhaps because of political difficulties between Rome and Herod. Therefore, the precise year of Christ's birth cannot be known with certainty, but it was probably no earlier than 6 BC and certainly no later than 4 BC. Luke's readers, familiar with the political history of that era, would no doubt have been able to discern a very precise date from the information he gave.

[c] OWN CITY. i.e., the place of tribal origin.

Joseph also went up from Galilee, out of the city of [d]Nazareth, into Judea, to the city of David, which is called Bethlehem, because he was of the house and lineage of David, to be registered with Mary, his [e]betrothed wife, who was with child. So it was, that while they were there, the days were completed for her to be delivered. And she brought forth her [f]firstborn Son, and wrapped Him in [g]swaddling cloths, and laid Him in a [h]manger, because there was [i]no room for them in the inn.

JN And [j]the Word became flesh and [k]dwelt among us, and [l]we beheld His glory, [m]the glory as of the [n]only begotten of the Father, [o]full of grace and truth.

---

[d] Nazareth . . . Bethlehem. Both Joseph and Mary were descendants of David and therefore went to their tribal home in Judea to be registered. This was a difficult trek of more than seventy miles through mountainous terrain—a particularly grueling journey for Mary, on the verge of delivery. Perhaps she and Joseph were conscious that a birth in Bethlehem would fulfill the prophecy in Mic. 5:2.

[e] betrothed. Matthew 1:24 indicates that when the angel told Joseph about Mary's pregnancy, he "took to him his wife"—i.e., he took her into his home. But they did not consummate their marriage until after the birth of Jesus (Matt. 1:25). Therefore, technically, they were still betrothed.

[f] firstborn. Mary had other children subsequent to this. Cf. 12:46.

[g] swaddling cloths. Strips of cloth used to bind a baby tightly. They kept the baby from injuring sensitive facial skin and eyes with its own (often sharp) fingernails and were believed to strengthen the limbs. This is still the custom in some Eastern cultures. The absence of swaddling cloths was a sign of poverty or lack of parental care (Ezek. 16:4).

[h] manger. A feeding trough for animals. This is the source of the notion that Christ was born in a stable, something nowhere stated in Scripture. Ancient tradition held that He was born in a cave (possibly one used as a shelter for animals). But no actual description of the location is given.

[i] no room for them in the inn. Possibly because many were returning to this ancient town to register in the census.

[j] the Word became flesh. While Christ as God was uncreated and eternal (cf. John 1:1), the term *became* emphasizes Christ's taking on humanity (cf. Heb. 1:1–3; 2:14–18). This reality is surely the most profound ever because it indicates that the Infinite became finite; the Eternal was conformed to time; the Invisible became visible; the supernatural One reduced Himself to the natural. In the incarnation, however, the Word did not cease to be God but became God in human flesh, i.e., undiminished deity in human form as a man (1 Tim. 3:16).

[k] dwelt. Meaning "to pitch a tabernacle," or "live in a tent." The term recalls to mind the OT tabernacle where God met with Israel before the temple was constructed (Ex. 25:8). It was called the "tabernacle of meeting" (Ex. 33:7; "tabernacle of witness"—Septuagint), where "the Lord spoke to Moses face to face, as a man speaks to his friend" (Ex. 33:11). In the NT, God chose to dwell among His people in a far more personal way through becoming a man. In the OT, when the tabernacle was completed, God's Shekinah glory filled the entire structure (Ex. 40:34; cf. 1 Kings 8:10). When the Word became flesh, the glorious presence of deity was embodied in Him (cf. Col. 2:9).

[l] we beheld His glory. Although His deity may have been veiled in human flesh, glimpses exist in the gospels of His divine majesty. The disciples saw glimpses of His glory on the Mount of Transfiguration (Matt. 17:1–8). The reference to Christ's glory, however, was not only visible but also spiritual. They saw Him display the attributes or characteristics of God (grace, goodness, mercy, wisdom, truth, etc.; cf. Ex. 33:18–23).

[m] THE GLORY AS OF . . . FATHER. Jesus as God displayed the same essential glory as the Father. They are one in essential nature (cf. John 5:17–30; 8:19; 10:30).

[n] ONLY BEGOTTEN. The term *only begotten* is a mistranslation of the Greek word. The word does not come from the term meaning "beget" but instead has the idea of "the only beloved one." It, therefore, has the idea of singular uniqueness, of being beloved like no other. By this word, John emphasized the exclusive character of the relationship between the Father and the Son in the Godhead (cf. 3:16, 18; 1 John 4:9). It does not connote origin but rather unique prominence; e.g., it was used of Isaac (Heb. 11:17), who was Abraham's second son (Ishmael being the first; cf. Gen. 16:15 with Gen. 21:2, 3).

[o] FULL OF GRACE AND TRUTH. John probably had Ex. 33, 34 in mind. On that occasion Moses requested that God display His glory to him. The Lord replied to Moses that He would make all His "goodness" pass before him, and then as He passed by, God declared "The Lord . . . merciful and gracious, longsuffering, and abounding in goodness and truth" (Ex. 33:18–19; 34:5–7). These attributes of God's glory emphasize the goodness of God's character, especially in relationship to salvation. Jesus as Yahweh of the OT (John 8:58; "I AM") displayed the same divine attributes when He tabernacled among men in the NT era (Col. 2:9).

17. Shepherds Pay Homage to the Lord Jesus

Luke 2:8–20

LK Now there were in the same country [a]shepherds living out in the fields, keeping watch over their flock by night. And behold, an angel of the Lord stood before them, and the glory of the Lord shone around them, and they were greatly afraid. Then the angel said to them, "Do not be afraid, for behold, I bring you good tidings of great joy which will be to all people. For there is born to you this day in the [b]city of David [c]a Savior, who is [d]Christ the [e]Lord. And this *will be* the sign to you: You will find a Babe wrapped in swaddling cloths, lying in a manger."

And suddenly there was with the angel a multitude of the heavenly [f]host praising God and saying: "Glory to God in [g]the highest, And on earth [h]peace, [i]goodwill toward men!"

---

[a] SHEPHERDS. Bethlehem was close to Jerusalem, and many of the sheep used in the temple sacrifices came from there. The surrounding hills were prime grazing land, and shepherds worked in the area day and night year-round. Therefore, it is not possible to draw any conclusion about the time of year by the fact that shepherds were living out in the fields.

[b] CITY OF DAVID. i.e., Bethlehem, the town where David was born—not the City of David, which was on the southern slope of Mount Zion (cf. 2 Sam. 5:7–9).

[c] A SAVIOR. This is one of only two places in the gospels where Christ is referred to as "Savior"—the other being John 4:42, where the men of Sychar confessed Him as "Savior of the world."

[d] CHRIST. "*Christ*" is the Greek equivalent of *Messiah*.

[e] LORD. The Greek word can mean "master"—but it is also the word used to translate the covenant name of God. Here (and in most of its NT occurrences), it is used in the latter sense, as a title of deity.

[f] HOST. A term used to describe an army encampment. Christ also used military imagery to describe the angels in Matt. 26:53. Rev. 5:11 suggests that the number of the angelic host may be too large for the human mind to fathom. Note that here the heavenly army brought a message of peace and goodwill.

[g] THE HIGHEST. i.e., heaven.

[h] PEACE. This is not to be taken as a universal declaration of peace toward all humanity. Rather, peace with God is a corollary of justification (cf. Rom. 5:1).

[i] GOODWILL TOWARD MEN. The Greek word for "goodwill" is also used in Luke 10:21. The verb form of the same word is used in Luke 3:22; 12:32. In each case, it refers to God's sovereign good pleasure. So a better rendering here might be "peace toward men on whom God's sovereign pleasure rests." God's peace is not a reward for those who have good will, but a gracious gift to those who are the objects of His good will.

\So it was, when the angels had gone away from them into heaven, that the shepherds said to one another, "Let us now go to Bethlehem and see this thing that has come to pass, which the Lord has made known to us." And they came with haste and found Mary and Joseph, and the Babe lying in a manger. Now when they had seen *Him,* they made widely known the saying which was told them concerning this Child. And [j]all those who heard *it* marveled at those things which were told them by the shepherds. But Mary kept all these things and pondered *them* in her heart. Then the shepherds returned, glorifying and [k]praising God for all the things that they had heard and seen, as it was told them.

[j] ALL THOSE WHO HEARD IT MARVELED. Wonderment at the mysteries of Christ's words and works is one of the threads that runs through Luke's gospel. Cf. Luke 1:21, 63; 2:19, 33, 47–48; 4:22, 36; 5:9; 8:25; 9:43–45; 11:14; 20:26; 24:12, 41.

[k] PRAISING GOD. Luke often reports this response. Cf. Luke 1:64; 2:28; 5:25–26; 7:16; 13:13; 17:15–18; 18:43; 19:37–40; 23:47; 24:52–53.

18. Jesus Is Presented in the Temple

Luke 2:21–39

LK And when eight days were completed for the circumcision of the Child, His name was called JESUS, the name given by the angel before He was conceived in the womb.

Now when the days of [a]her purification according to the law of Moses were completed, they brought Him [b]to Jerusalem [c]to present *Him* to the Lord (as it is written in the law of the Lord, "Every male who opens the womb shall be called holy to the LORD"), and to offer a sacrifice according to what is said in the law of the Lord, "A [d]pair of turtledoves or two young pigeons."

And behold, there was a man in Jerusalem whose name *was* [e]Simeon, and this man *was* just and devout, waiting for [f]the Consolation of Israel, and the Holy Spirit was upon him. And [g]it had been revealed to him by the Holy Spirit that he would not see death before he had seen the Lord's Christ. So he came by the Spirit into the temple. And when the parents brought in the Child Jesus, to do for Him according to the custom of the law, he took Him up in his arms and blessed God and [h]said:

---

[a] HER PURIFICATION. A woman who bore a son was ceremonially unclean for forty days (twice that if she bore a daughter—Lev. 12:2–5). After that she was to offer a yearling lamb and a dove or pigeon (Lev. 12:6). If poor, she could offer two doves or pigeons (Lev. 12:8). Mary's offering indicates that she and Joseph were poor (Luke 2:24).

[b] TO JERUSALEM. A journey of about six miles from Bethlehem.

[c] TO PRESENT HIM TO THE LORD. The dedication of the firstborn son was also required by Moses' law (Luke 2:23, cf. Ex. 13:2, 12–15).

[d] PAIR OF TURTLEDOVES. Quoted from Lev. 12:8.

[e] SIMEON. He is mentioned nowhere else in Scripture.

[f] THE CONSOLATION OF ISRAEL. A messianic title, evidently derived from verses like Isa. 25:9; 40:1, 2; 66:1–11.

[g] IT HAD BEEN REVEALED TO HIM. It is significant that with messianic expectation running so high (cf. Luke 3:15) and with the many OT prophecies that spoke of His coming, still only a handful of people realized the significance of Christ's birth. Most of them, including Simeon, received some angelic message or other special revelation to make the fulfillment of the OT prophecies clear.

[h] SAID. Simeon's psalm (in Luke 2:29–32) is known as the *Nunc Dimittis*, from the first two words of the Latin translation. It is the fourth of five psalms of praise Luke included in his birth narrative. It is a touching expression of Simeon's extraordinary faith.

"Lord, now You are letting Your servant depart in peace,
According to Your word;
For my eyes have seen [i]Your salvation
Which You have prepared before the face of [j]all peoples,
A light to *bring* revelation to the Gentiles,
And the glory of Your people Israel."

And Joseph and His mother marveled at those things which were spoken of Him. Then Simeon blessed them, and said to Mary His mother, "Behold, this *Child* is destined for the [k]fall and rising of many in Israel, and for a sign which will be [l]spoken against (yes, [m]a sword will pierce through your own soul also), [n]that the thoughts of many hearts may be revealed."

Now there was one, Anna, [o]a prophetess, the daughter of Phanuel, of the tribe of Asher. She was of a great age, and had lived with a husband seven years from her virginity; and this woman *was* [p]a widow of about eighty-four years, who did [q]not depart from the temple, but served *God* with fastings and prayers night and

---

[i] Your salvation. i.e., the One who would redeem His people from their sins.

[j] all peoples. i.e., all nations, tongues, and tribes (cf. Rev. 7:9)—both Israel and the Gentiles (v. 32).

[k] fall and rising of many in Israel. To those who reject Him, He is a stone of stumbling (1 Peter 2:8); those who receive Him are raised up (Eph. 2:6). Cf. Isa. 8:14–15; Hos. 14:9; 1 Cor. 1:23–24.

[l] spoken against. This was synecdoche. Simeon mentioned only the verbal insults hurled at Christ, but the expression actually embraced more than that—Israel's rejection and hatred and crucifixion of the Messiah.

[m] a sword. This was undoubtedly a reference to the personal grief Mary would endure when she watched her own Son die in agony (John 19:25).

[n] that the thoughts of many hearts may be revealed. The rejection of the Messiah (cf. Luke 2:34) would reveal the appalling truth about the apostate state of the Jews.

[o] a prophetess. This refers to a woman who spoke God's Word. She was a teacher of the OT, not a source of revelation. The OT mentions only three women who prophesied: Miriam (Ex. 15:20); Deborah (Judg. 4:4); Huldah (2 Kings 22:14; 2 Chron. 34:22). One other, the "prophetess" Noadiah, was evidently a false prophet, grouped by Nehemiah with his enemies. Isa. 8:3 refers to the prophet's wife as a "prophetess"—but there is no evidence Isaiah's wife prophesied. Perhaps she is so-called because the child she bore was given a name that was prophetic (Isa. 8:3–4). This use of the title for Isaiah's wife also shows that the title does not necessarily indicate an ongoing revelatory prophetic ministry. Rabbinical tradition also regarded Sarah, Hannah, Abigail, and Esther as prophetesses (apparently to make an even seven with Miriam, Deborah, and Huldah). In the NT, the daughters of Philip prophesied (Acts 21:9).

[p] a widow of about eighty-four years. This probably means she was an eighty-four-year-old widow, not that she had been widowed that long, since if she had been widowed eighty-four years after a seven-year marriage (Luke 2:35), she would have been at least 104 years old.

[q] not depart from the temple. She evidently had her living quarters on the temple grounds. There would have been several such dwelling places for priests in the outer court, and Anna must have been allowed to live there permanently because of her unusual status as a prophetess.

day. And coming in that instant she gave thanks to the Lord, and spoke of Him to all those who looked for redemption in Jerusalem.

So when they had performed all things according to the law of the Lord, [after a period of time] [r]they returned to Galilee, to their *own* city, Nazareth.

---

[r] THEY RETURNED TO GALILEE. Luke omitted the visit of the Magi and the flight into Egypt (Matt. 2:1–18), which occurred after these events at the temple but before the return to Nazareth. The theme of early rejection, so prominent in Matthew, was not where Luke focused his attention.

19. The Magi Pay Homage to Israel's True King

Matt. 2:1–12

MT Now after Jesus was born in [a]Bethlehem of Judea in the days of [b]Herod the king, behold, [c]wise men from the East came to Jerusalem, [d]saying, "Where is He who has been born King of the Jews? For we have seen His [e]star in the East and have come to worship Him."

When Herod the king heard *this,* he was troubled, and all Jerusalem with him. And when he had gathered all the [f]chief priests and [g]scribes of the people together, he inquired of them where the Christ was to be born.

So they said to him, "In Bethlehem of Judea, for thus it is written by [h]the prophet:

---

[a] BETHLEHEM. A small village on the southern outskirts of Jerusalem. Hebrew scholars in Jesus' day clearly expected Bethlehem to be the birthplace of the Messiah (cf. Mic. 5:2; John 7:42).

[b] HEROD THE KING. This refers to Herod the Great, the first of several important rulers from the Herodian dynasty who are named in Scripture. This Herod, founder of the famous line, ruled from 37–4 BC. He is thought to have been Idumean, a descendant of the Edomites, offspring of Esau. Herod was ruthless and cunning. He loved opulence and grand building projects, and many of the most magnificent ruins that can be seen in modern Israel date back to the days of Herod the Great. His most famous project was the rebuilding of the temple at Jerusalem (cf. Matt. 24:1). That project alone took several decades and was not completed until long after Herod's death (cf. John 2:20).

[c] WISE MEN FROM THE EAST. The number of wise men is not given. The traditional notion that there were three stems from the number of gifts they brought. These were not kings, but Magi, magicians or astrologers—possibly Persian priests whose knowledge of the Hebrew Scriptures could be traced back to the time of Daniel (cf. Dan. 5:11).

[d] SAYING. This present participle conveys the idea of continuous action. It suggests they went around the city questioning everyone they met.

[e] STAR. This could not have been a supernova or a conjunction of planets, as some modern theories suggest, because of the way the star moved and settled over one place (Matt. 2:9). It is more likely a supernatural reality similar to the Shekinah that guided the Israelites in the days of Moses (Ex. 13:21).

[f] CHIEF PRIESTS. These were the temple hierarchy. They were mostly Sadducees.

[g] SCRIBES. Primarily Pharisees, i.e., authorities on Jewish law. Sometimes they are referred to as "lawyers" (cf. Luke 10:25). They were professional scholars whose specialty was explaining the application of the law. They knew exactly where the Messiah was to be born, but lacked the faith to accompany the Magi to the place where He was.

[h] THE PROPHET. This ancient prophecy from Mic. 5:2 was written in the eighth century BC. The original prophecy, not quoted in full by Matthew, declared the deity of Israel's Messiah: "Out of you shall come forth to Me the One to be Ruler in Israel, whose goings forth are from of old, from everlasting."

'But you, Bethlehem, *in* the land of Judah,
Are not the least among the rulers of Judah;
For out of you shall come [i]a Ruler
Who will shepherd My people Israel.'"

Then Herod, when he had secretly called the wise men, determined from them what time the star appeared. And he sent them to Bethlehem and said, "Go and search carefully for the young Child, and when you have found *Him*, bring back word to me, [j]that I may come and worship Him also."

When they heard the king, they departed; and behold, the star which they had seen in the East went before them, till it came and stood over where the young Child was. When they saw the star, they rejoiced with exceedingly great joy. And when they had come [k]into the house, they saw [l]the young Child with Mary His mother, and fell down and worshiped Him. And when they had opened their treasures, they presented gifts to Him: [m]gold, frankincense, and myrrh.

Then, being divinely warned in a dream that they should not return to Herod, they departed for their own country another way.

---

[i] A RULER WHO WILL SHEPHERD MY PEOPLE ISRAEL. This portion of Matthew's quote actually seems to be a reference to God's words to David when Israel's kingdom was originally established (2 Sam. 5:2; 1 Chron. 11:2). The Greek word for "ruler" evokes the image of strong, even stern, leadership. "Shepherd" emphasizes tender care. Christ's rule involves both (cf. Rev. 12:5).

[j] THAT I MAY COME AND WORSHIP HIM. Herod actually wanted to kill the Child (Matt. 2:13–18), whom he saw as a potential threat to his throne.

[k] INTO THE HOUSE. By the time the wise men arrived, Mary and Joseph were situated in a house, not a stable (cf. Luke 2:7).

[l] THE YOUNG CHILD WITH MARY HIS MOTHER. Whenever Matthew mentions Mary in connection with her Child, Christ is always given first place (cf. Matt. 2:13–14, 20–21).

[m] GOLD, FRANKINCENSE, AND MYRRH. Gifts suitable for a king (cf. Isa. 60:6). The fact that Gentiles would offer such worship had prophetic significance as well (Ps. 72:10).

20. The Flight into Egypt and Return to Nazareth

Matt. 2:13–23; Luke 2:40

MT Now when they had departed, behold, an angel of the Lord appeared to Joseph in a dream, saying, "Arise, take the young Child and His mother, flee to Egypt, and stay there until I bring you word; for Herod will seek the young Child to destroy Him."

When he arose, he took the young Child and His mother by night and departed for Egypt, and was there until [a]the death of Herod, that it might be fulfilled which was spoken by the Lord through the prophet, saying, " [b]Out of Egypt I called My Son."

Then Herod, when he saw that he was deceived by the wise men, was exceedingly angry; and he sent forth and [c]put to death all the male children who were in Bethlehem and in all its districts, from two years old and under, according to the time which he had determined from the wise men. Then was [d]fulfilled what was spoken by Jeremiah the prophet, saying:

"A voice was heard in Ramah,
Lamentation, weeping, and great mourning,
Rachel weeping *for* her children,
Refusing to be comforted,
Because they are no more."

---

[a] THE DEATH OF HEROD. Recent scholarship sets this date at 4 BC. It is probable that the stay in Egypt was very brief—perhaps no more than a few weeks.

[b] OUT OF EGYPT. This quotation is from Hos. 11:1, which speaks of God's leading Israel out of Egypt in the Exodus. Matthew suggests that Israel's sojourn in Egypt was a pictorial prophecy, rather than a specific verbal one such as Matt. 1:23; 2:6. These are called *types* and all are always fulfilled in Christ, and identified clearly by the NT writers. Another example of a type is found in John 3:14.

[c] PUT TO DEATH ALL THE MALE CHILDREN. Herod's act is all the more heinous in light of his full knowledge that the Lord's Anointed One was the target of his murderous plot.

[d] FULFILLED. Again, this prophecy is in the form of a type. Matt. 2:18 quotes Jer. 31:15, which speaks of all Israel's mourning at the time of the Babylonian captivity (ca. 586 BC). That wailing prefigured the wailing over Herod's massacre.

Now when Herod was dead, behold, an angel of the Lord appeared in a dream to Joseph in Egypt, saying, "Arise, take the young Child and His mother, and go to the land of Israel, for those who sought the young Child's life are dead." Then he arose, took the young Child and His mother, and came into the land of Israel.

But when he heard that [e]Archelaus was reigning over Judea instead of his father Herod, he was afraid to go there. And being warned by God in a dream, he turned aside into the region of Galilee. And he came and dwelt in a city called Nazareth, that it might be fulfilled which was spoken by the prophets, "He shall be [f]called a Nazarene." [LK] And the Child grew and became strong in spirit, filled with wisdom; and the grace of God was upon Him.

---

[e] Archelaus. Herod's kingdom was divided three ways and given to his sons: Archelaus ruled Judea, Samaria, and Idumea; Herod Philip II ruled the regions north of Galilee (Luke 3:1); and Herod Antipas ruled Galilee and Perea (Luke 3:1). History records that Archelaus was so brutal and ineffective that he was deposed by Rome after a short reign and replaced with a governor appointed by Rome. Pontius Pilate was the fifth governor of Judea. Herod Antipas is the main Herod in the gospel accounts. He was the one who had John the Baptist put to death (Matt. 14:1–12) and examined Christ on the eve of the crucifixion (Luke 23:7–12).

[f] called a Nazarene. Nazareth, an obscure town seventy miles north of Jerusalem, was a place of lowly reputation and nowhere mentioned in the OT. Some have suggested that *Nazarene* is a reference to the Hebrew word for branch in Isa. 11:1. Others point out that Matthew's statement that "prophets" had made this prediction may be a reference to verbal prophecies nowhere recorded in the OT. A still more likely explanation is that Matthew is using *Nazarene* as a synonym for someone who is despised or detestable—for that was how people from the region were often characterized (cf. John 1:46). If that is the case, the prophecies Matthew has in mind would include Ps. 22:6–8; Isa. 49:7; 53:3.

21. Jesus Visits the Temple at Age Twelve

Luke 2:41–52

LK His parents went to Jerusalem every year at the [a]Feast of the Passover. And when He was twelve years old, they went up to Jerusalem according to the custom of the feast. When they had finished the days, as they returned, the Boy [b]Jesus lingered behind in Jerusalem. And Joseph and His mother did not know *it;* but supposing Him to have been [c]in the company, they went a day's journey, and sought Him among *their* relatives and acquaintances. So when they did not find Him, they returned to Jerusalem, seeking Him. Now so it was *that* after [d]three days they found Him in the temple, sitting in the midst of the teachers, both [e]listening to them and asking them questions. And all who heard Him were astonished at His understanding and answers. So when they saw Him, they were amazed; and His

[a] FEAST OF THE PASSOVER. Cf. Ex. 23:14–19. Passover was a one-day feast, followed immediately by the week-long Feast of Unleavened Bread (cf. Matt. 26:17).

[b] JESUS LINGERED. In stark contrast to the apocryphal gospels' spurious tales of youthful miracles and supernatural exploits, this lone biblical insight into the youth of Jesus portrays Him as a typical boy in a typical family. His lingering was neither mischievous nor disobedient; it was owing to a simple mistaken presumption on His parents' part that He was left behind.

[c] IN THE COMPANY. Obviously Joseph and Mary were traveling with a large caravan of friends and relatives from Nazareth. No doubt hundreds of people from their community went together to the feast. Men and women in such a group might have been separated by some distance, and it appears each parent thought He was with the other.

[d] THREE DAYS. This probably does not mean they searched Jerusalem for three days. They apparently realized He was missing at the end of a full day's travel. That required another full day's journey back to Jerusalem, and the better part of another day was spent seeking Him.

[e] LISTENING TO THEM AND ASKING THEM QUESTIONS. He was utterly respectful, taking the role of the student. But even at that young age, His questions showed a wisdom that put the teachers to shame.

mother said to Him, "Son, [f]why have You done this to us? Look, [g]Your father and I have sought You anxiously."

And He said to them, "Why did you seek Me? Did you not know that I must be about [h]My Father's business?" But they did not understand the statement which He spoke to them.

Then He went down with them and came to Nazareth, and [i]was subject to them, but His mother kept all these things in her heart. And Jesus increased in wisdom and stature, and in favor with God and men.

---

[f] Why have You done this to us? Mary's words convey a tone of exasperation and rebuke—normal for any mother under such circumstances, but misplaced in this case. He was not hiding from them or defying their authority. In fact, He had done precisely what any child should do under such circumstances (being left by His parents)—He went to a safe, public place, in the presence of trusted adults, where His parents could be expected to come looking for Him.

[g] Your father. i.e., Joseph, who was legally His father.

[h] My Father's business. Contrasting with Mary's "your father" in Luke 2:48. His reply was in no sense insolent, but reveals a genuine amazement that they did not know where to look for Him. This also reveals that even at so young an age, He had a clear consciousness of His identity and mission.

[i] Was subject. His relationship with His Heavenly Father did not override or nullify His duty to His earthly parents. His obedience to the fifth commandment was an essential part of the perfect legal obedience He rendered on our behalf (Heb. 4:4; 5:8–9). He had to fulfill all righteousness (cf. Matt. 3:15).

22. John the Baptist Begins His Ministry

Matt. 3:1–12; Mark 1:4–8; Luke 3:1–18

LK Now in the [a]fifteenth year of the reign of Tiberius Caesar, Pontius Pilate being governor of Judea, Herod being tetrarch of Galilee, his brother Philip tetrarch of Iturea and the region of Trachonitis, and [b]Lysanias tetrarch of Abilene, while [c]Annas and Caiaphas were high priests, the word of God came to [d]John the son of Zacharias in the wilderness.

[a] FIFTEENTH YEAR OF THE REIGN OF TIBERIUS. Because of the way Tiberius came to power, this date is hard to fix precisely. When the Roman senate declared Augustus emperor, they did so on condition that his power would end with his death, rather than passing to his heirs. The idea was that the senate, rather than the emperor himself, was to choose the heir to the throne. However, Augustus circumvented that difficulty by appointing a co-regent, on whom he planned gradually to confer the imperial powers. When he outlived his first choice for successor, Augustus next selected his son-in-law, Tiberius, whom he adopted and made his heir in AD 4. (Augustus disliked Tiberius but hoped to pass power to his grandsons through him.) Tiberius was made co-regent in AD 11, then automatically became sole ruler at the death of Augustus on Aug. 19, AD 14. If Luke's chronology is dated from Tiberius' appointment to the co-regency, the fifteenth year would be AD 25 or 26. If Luke was reckoning from the death of Augustus, this date would fall between Aug. 19, AD 28 and Aug. 18, AD 29. One other fact complicates the setting of a precise date: the Jews reckoned a ruler's term from the Jewish New Year following accession, so if Luke was using the Jewish system, the actual dates could be slightly later.

[b] LYSANIAS. Ruler of the area northwest of Damascus. History is virtually silent about him.

[c] ANNAS AND CAIAPHAS WERE HIGH PRIESTS. According to Josephus, Annas served as High-Priest AD 6–15, when he was deposed by Roman officials. He nonetheless retained de facto power, as seen in the fact that his successors included five of his sons and Caiaphas, a son-in-law. Caiaphas was the actual high priest during the time Luke describes, but Annas still controlled the office. This is seen clearly in the fact that Christ was taken to Annas first after His arrest, then to Caiaphas (cf. Matt. 26:57).

[d] JOHN. A common Jewish name in NT times, it is the Greek equivalent of the Hebrew name "Johanan" (cf. 2 Kings 25:23; 1 Chron. 3:15; Jer. 40:8), meaning "the Lord is gracious." John's name was given by the angel Gabriel to his father Zacharias, during his time of priestly service in the temple (Luke 1:13). His mother, Elizabeth, also a descendant of Aaron (Luke 1:5), was a relative of Mary the mother of Jesus (Luke 1:36). As the last OT prophet and the divinely ordained forerunner of the Messiah, John was the culmination of OT history and prophecy (Luke 16:16), as well as the beginning of the historical record of the gospel of Jesus Christ. Not surprisingly, Jesus designated John as the greatest man who had lived until his time (Matt. 11:11).

MT In those days John the Baptist MK came baptizing in [e]the wilderness MT of Judea. LK And he went into all the region around the Jordan, [f]preaching a [g]baptism of repentance [h]for the remission of sins, MT saying, "[i]Repent, for the [j]kingdom of heaven [k]is at hand!" For this is he who was [l]spoken of by the prophet Isaiah, LK saying: "The voice of one crying in the wilderness: 'Prepare the way of the Lord; [m]Make His paths straight. Every valley shall be filled And every mountain and hill brought low; The crooked places shall be made straight And the rough ways smooth; And [n]all flesh shall see the salvation of God.'"

---

[e] the wilderness of Judea. The region to the immediate west of the Dead Sea—an utterly barren desert. The Jewish sect of the Essenes had significant communities in this region. But there is no biblical evidence to suggest that John was in any way connected with that sect. John seems to have preached near the northern end of this region, close by where the Jordan flows into the Dead Sea (Matt. 3:6). This was a full day's journey from Jerusalem and seems an odd location to announce the arrival of a King. But it is perfectly in keeping with God's ways (1 Cor. 1:26–29).

[f] preaching. Better translated "proclaiming." John was Jesus' herald, sent to announce His coming.

[g] baptism of repentance. A baptism resulting from true repentance. John's ministry was to call Israel to repentance in preparation for the coming of Messiah. Baptism did not produce repentance, but was its result (cf. Matt. 3:7, 8). Far more than a mere change of mind or remorse, repentance involves a turning from sin to God (cf. 1 Thess. 1:9), which results in righteous living. Genuine repentance is a work of God in the human heart (Acts 11:18).

[h] for the remission of sins. John's rite of baptism did not produce forgiveness of sin (cf. Acts 2:38; 22:16); it was only the outward confession and illustration of the true repentance that results in forgiveness (cf. Luke 24:47; Acts 3:19; 5:31; 2 Cor. 7:10).

[i] Repent. This is no mere academic change of mind, nor mere regret or remorse. John the Baptist spoke of repentance as a radical turning from sin that inevitably became manifest in the fruit of righteousness (Matt. 3:8). Jesus' first sermon began with the same imperative (Matt. 4:17).

[j] kingdom of heaven. This is an expression unique to Matthew's gospel. Matthew uses the word *heaven* as a euphemism for God's name—to accommodate his Jewish readers' sensitivities (cf. Matt. 23:22). Throughout the rest of Scripture, the *kingdom* is called "the kingdom of God." Both expressions refer to the sphere of God's dominion over those who belong to Him. The kingdom is now manifest in heaven's spiritual rule over the hearts of believers (Luke 17:21) and one day will be established in a literal earthly kingdom (Rev. 20:4–6).

[k] is at hand. In one sense the kingdom is a present reality, but in its fullest sense it awaits a yet-future fulfillment.

[l] spoken of by the prophet Isaiah. John's mission had long ago been described in Isa. 40:3. All four of the gospels cite this passage as a prophecy pointing to John the Baptist (Matt. 3:3; Luke 3:4–6; Mark 1:3; John 1:23).

[m] Make His paths straight. Quoted from Isa. 40:3–5. A monarch traveling in wilderness regions would have a crew of workmen go ahead to make sure the road was clear of debris, obstructions, potholes, and other hazards that made the journey difficult. In a spiritual sense, John was calling the people of Israel to prepare their hearts for the coming of their Messiah.

[n] all flesh. i.e., Gentiles as well as Jews.

MT Now John himself was [o]clothed in camel's hair, with a leather belt around his waist; and his food was [p]locusts and wild honey. MK Then [q]all the land of [r]Judea, and those from Jerusalem, MT and all the region around the Jordan went out to him MK and were all baptized by him in the [s]Jordan River, [t]confessing their sins.

MT But when he saw many of the [u]Pharisees and Sadducees coming to his baptism, LK he said to the multitudes that came out to be [v]baptized by him, MT "Brood

---

[o] CLOTHED IN CAMEL'S HAIR, WITH A LEATHER BELT. The traditional clothes of a wilderness dweller, which were practical and sturdy, but neither fashionable nor comfortable. John's clothing would have reminded his audience of Elijah (cf. 2 Kings 1:8), whom they expected to come before Messiah (Mal. 4:5).

[p] LOCUSTS AND WILD HONEY. The OT dietary regulations permitted the eating of "locusts" (Lev. 11:21–22). "Wild honey" could often be found in the wilderness (Deut. 32:13; 1 Sam. 14:25–27). John's austere diet was in keeping with his status as a lifelong Nazirite (Luke 1:15; cf. Num. 6:2–13).

[q] ALL THE LAND OF JUDEA, AND THOSE FROM JERUSALEM. After centuries without a prophetic voice in Israel (Malachi had prophesied more than four hundred years earlier), John's ministry generated an intense amount of interest.

[r] JUDEA. The southernmost division of Israel (Samaria and Galilee being the others) in Jesus' day. It extended from about Bethel in the north to Beersheba in the south, and from the Mediterranean Sea in the west to the Dead Sea and Jordan River in the east. Included within Judea was the city of Jerusalem.

[s] JORDAN RIVER. Israel's major river, flowing through the Jordan Rift Valley from Lake Hula (drained in modern times), north of the Sea of Galilee, south to the Dead Sea. According to tradition, John began his baptizing ministry at the fords near Jericho.

[t] CONFESSING. To confess one's sins, as one is being baptized, is to agree with God about them. John baptized no one who did not confess and repent of his sins.

[u] PHARISEES AND SADDUCEES. The Pharisees were a small (about six thousand) sect within Judaism whose adherents were known for their interpretations of ceremonial fine points of the law and rigid adherence to those interpretations. Their name means "separated ones." Jesus' interaction with the Pharisees was usually adversarial. He rebuked them for using human tradition to nullify Scripture (Matt. 15:3–9) and especially for hypocrisy (Matt. 15:7, 8; 22:18; 23:13, 23, 25, 29; Luke 12:1). The Sadducees were known for their denial of things supernatural. They denied the resurrection of the dead (Matt. 22:23) and the existence of angels (Acts 23:8). Unlike the Pharisees, they rejected human traditions regarding interpretation of the law and accepted only the Pentateuch as authoritative. They tended to be wealthy, aristocratic members of the priestly tribe, and in the days of Herod their sect controlled the temple, though they were fewer in number than the Pharisees. Pharisees and Sadducees had little in common.. While Pharisees interpreted the law more strictly, resulting in separation from Roman society, Sadducees were known for compromise with Roman authorities and practices. Yet they united together in their opposition to Christ (Matt. 22:15–16, 23, 34–35). John publicly addressed them as deadly snakes.

[v] BAPTIZED. The symbolism of John's baptism likely had its roots in OT purification rituals (cf. Lev. 15:13). Baptism had also long been administered to Gentile proselytes coming into Judaism. The baptism of John thus powerfully and dramatically symbolized repentance. Jews accepting John's baptism were admitting they had been as Gentiles and needed to become the people of God genuinely, inwardly (an amazing admission, given many despised and distrusted Gentiles). The people were repenting in anticipation of the Messiah's arrival. The meaning of John's baptism differs somewhat from Christian baptism (cf. Acts 18:25). Actually, Christian baptism altered the significance of the ritual, symbolizing the believer's identification with Christ in His death, burial, and resurrection (Rom. 6:3–5; Col. 2:12).

of vipers! Who warned you to flee from [w]the wrath to come? Therefore bear [x]fruits worthy of repentance, and do not think to say to yourselves, 'We have Abraham as *our* father.' For I say to you that God is able to raise up [y]children to Abraham from these [z]stones. And even now [aa]the ax is laid to the root of the trees. Therefore every tree which does not bear good fruit is cut down and thrown into the fire."

LK So the people asked him, saying, "What shall we do then?" He answered and said to them, "He who has [bb]two tunics, let him give to him who has none; and he who has food, let him do likewise." Then tax collectors also came to be baptized, and said to him, "Teacher, what shall we do?" And he said to them, "Collect no more than what is appointed for you." Likewise the [cc]soldiers asked him, saying, "And what shall we do?" So he said to them, "[dd]Do not intimidate anyone or accuse falsely, and be content with your wages."

Now as the people were in expectation, and all reasoned in their hearts about John, whether he was the Christ *or* not, John answered, MK and he preached,

---

[w] THE WRATH TO COME. Possibly a reference to the coming destruction of Jerusalem. But this certainly also looks beyond any earthly calamity to the eschatological outpouring of divine wrath in the Day of the Lord (e.g., Ezek. 7:19; Zeph. 1:18), and especially the final judgment, where divine wrath will be the just fruit of all the unrepentant (cf. Rom. 1:18; 1 Thess. 1:10; Heb. 10:27). This must have been a particularly stinging rebuke to the Jewish leaders, who imagined that divine wrath was reserved only for non-Jews.

[x] FRUITS WORTHY OF REPENTANCE. Repentance itself is not a work, but works are its inevitable fruit. Repentance and faith are inextricably linked in Scripture. Repentance means turning from one's sin, and faith is turning to God (cf. 1 Thess. 1:9). They are like opposite sides of the same coin. That is why both are linked to conversion (Mark 1:15; Acts 3:19; 20:21). Note that the works John demanded to see were "fruits" of repentance. But repentance itself is no more a "work" than faith is (cf. 2 Tim. 2:25).

[y] CHILDREN TO ABRAHAM. Abraham's true children are not merely physical descendants, but those who follow his faith, believing God's Word the way he did (Rom. 4:11–16; 9:8; Gal. 3:7, 29). To trust one's physical ancestry is to shift the focus of faith away from God Himself—and that is spiritually fatal (cf. John 8:39–44).

[z] STONES. Cf. Luke 19:40. The imagery may echo OT verses such as Ezek. 11:19; 36:26; God can sovereignly turn a heart of stone into a believing heart. He can raise up children to Abraham from inanimate objects if He chooses—or even from stony-hearted Gentiles (cf. Gal. 3:29).

[aa] THE AX IS LAID TO THE ROOT. Irreversible judgment was imminent.

[bb] TWO TUNICS. Shirt-like garments. Only one could be worn at a time. John was still stressing the imminence of the coming judgment. This was not a time to hoard one's surplus goods.

[cc] SOLDIERS. These were most likely members of the forces of Herod Antipas, stationed at Perea, perhaps, along with Judean police.

LK saying to all, "I indeed [ee]baptize you with water MT unto repentance, but He who is coming after me is mightier than I, [ff]whose sandals I am not worthy to carry, [and] MK whose sandal strap I am not worthy to stoop down and loose. I indeed baptized you with water, but LK He will baptize you with the Holy Spirit and fire. His [gg]winnowing fan *is* in His hand, and He will thoroughly clean out His threshing floor, and gather the wheat into His barn; but the chaff He will burn with unquenchable fire." And with many other exhortations he preached to the people.

[dd] Do not intimidate anyone. John demanded integrity and high character in the practical matters of everyday life, not a monastic lifestyle or a mystical asceticism. Cf. James 1:27.

[ee] baptize. Three types of baptism are referred to here: (1) with water unto repentance. John's baptism symbolized cleansing; (2) with the Holy Spirit. All believers in Christ are Spirit-baptized (1 Cor. 12:13; cf. Acts 1:5; 8:16–17;); and (3) with fire. Because fire is used throughout this context as a means of judgment, this must speak of a baptism of judgment upon the unrepentant.

[ff] whose sandals. Unfastening the sandal strap was the lowliest slave's task, preliminary to washing the feet (cf. John 13:5).

[gg] winnowing fan. A tool for tossing grain into the wind so that the chaff is blown away.

23. John Baptizes Jesus

Matt. 3:13–17; Mark 1:9–11; Luke 3:21–23a; John 1:15–18

MK It came to pass [a]in those days *that* Jesus came from [b]Nazareth of Galilee MT to John at the Jordan to be [c]baptized by him. And [d]John *tried to* prevent Him, saying, "I need to be baptized by You, and are You coming to me?" But Jesus answered and said to him, "Permit *it to be so* now, for thus [e]it is fitting for us to fulfill all righteousness." Then he allowed Him.

LK When all the people were baptized, it came to pass that Jesus also was baptized. MT When He had been baptized, [f]Jesus came up immediately from the water; and behold, LK [g]while He prayed, MT the heavens were opened to Him, and He saw MK the heavens parting and the LK Holy Spirit MT of God descending LK in [h]bodily form

---

[a] IN THOSE DAYS. At some unspecified time during John's baptizing ministry at the Jordan.

[b] NAZARETH. An obscure village (not mentioned in the OT, or by Josephus, or in the Talmud) about seventy miles north of Jerusalem that did not enjoy a favorable reputation (cf. John 1:46). Jesus had apparently been living there before His public appearance to Israel.

[c] BAPTIZED BY HIM. The objections of John (cf. Matt. 3:14), who saw no need for the sinless Lamb of God (John 1:29) to participate in a baptism of repentance.

[d] JOHN TRIED TO PREVENT HIM. John's baptism symbolized repentance, and John saw this as inappropriate for the One he knew was the spotless Lamb of God (cf. John 1:29).

[e] IT IS FITTING FOR US TO FULFILL ALL RIGHTEOUSNESS. Christ was here identifying Himself with sinners. He will ultimately bear their sins; His perfect righteousness will be imputed to them (2 Cor. 5:21). This act of baptism was a necessary part of the righteousness He secured for sinners. This first public event of His ministry is also rich in meaning: (1) it pictured His death and resurrection (cf. Luke 12:50); (2) it therefore prefigured the significance of Christian baptism; (3) it marked His first public identification with those whose sins He would bear (Isa. 53:11; 1 Peter 3:18); and (4) it was a public affirmation of His messiahship by testimony directly from heaven.

[f] JESUS . . . THE SPIRIT OF GOD . . . A VOICE CAME FROM HEAVEN. Here all three Persons of the Trinity are clearly delineated—a strong proof against the heresy of modalism, which suggests that God is one Person who manifests Himself in three distinct modes, one at a time.

[g] WHILE HE PRAYED. Luke alone notes that Jesus was praying. Prayer is one of Luke's themes.

[h] BODILY FORM. i.e., physical and visible to all (cf. Matt. 3:16; John 1:32). The Father's command to hear His Son and the Spirit's vindication and empowerment officially inaugurated Christ's ministry.

[i]like a dove [MT] and alighting upon Him. And suddenly a voice *came* from heaven, saying, [LK] "You are [j]My beloved Son; in You I am well pleased."

[JN] John bore witness of Him and cried out, saying, "This was He of whom I said, 'He who comes after me is preferred before me, for He was before me.'" And of His fullness we have all received, and [k]grace for grace. For [l]the law was given through Moses, *but* grace and truth came through Jesus Christ. No one has seen God at any time. The only begotten Son, [m]who is in the bosom of the Father, He has [n]declared *Him.*

[LK] Now Jesus Himself began *His ministry at* [o]about thirty years of age.

---

[i] like a dove. A picture of gentleness (Matt. 10:16).

[j] My beloved Son, in You I am well pleased. This heavenly pronouncement combines language from Ps. 2:7 and Isa. 42:1—prophecies that would have been well known to those with messianic expectations. Cf. Matt. 17:5; Mark 1:11; 9:7; Luke 3:22; 9:35.

[k] grace for grace. This phrase emphasizes the superabundance of grace that has been displayed by God toward mankind, especially believers (Eph. 1:5–8; 2:7).

[l] the law. The law, given by Moses, was not a display of God's grace, but God's demand for holiness. God designed the law as a means to demonstrate the unrighteousness of man in order to show the need for a Savior, Jesus Christ (Rom. 3:19, 20; Gal. 3:10–14, 21–26). Furthermore, the law revealed only a part of truth and was preparatory in nature. The reality or full truth toward which the law pointed came through the person of Jesus Christ.

[m] who is in the bosom of the Father. This term denotes the mutual intimacy, love, and knowledge existing in the Godhead (cf. Luke 16:22–23; John 13:23).

[n] declared. Theologians derived the term *exegesis* "or 'to interpret'" from this word. John meant that all who Jesus is and all that He does interprets and explains who God is (John 14:8–10).

[o] about thirty years of age. Luke was probably not fixing an exact age. Rather, this was an approximation, thirty being a customary age for entering into the office of prophet (Ezek. 1:1), priest (Num. 4:3, 35, 39, 43, 47), or king (Gen. 41:46; 2 Sam. 5:4).

24. Jesus Is Tempted in the Wilderness

Matt. 4:1–11; Mark 1:12–13; Luke 4:1–13

LK Then Jesus, being filled with the Holy Spirit, returned from the Jordan and MK [a]immediately MT was [b]led up by the Spirit into the wilderness to be tempted by the devil. MK And He was there in [c]the wilderness [d]forty days, [e]tempted by [f]Satan, and was with the [g]wild beasts; LK and in those days He ate nothing. MT And when He had fasted forty days and forty nights, afterward, LK when they had ended, MT He was hungry.

Now when the tempter came to Him, LK the devil said to Him, " [h]If You are the Son of God, command this stone to become bread." LK But Jesus answered him,

---

[a] IMMEDIATELY. In keeping with his fast-paced narrative style, Mark used this adverb more than the other three gospel writers combined. Here it indicates that Jesus' temptation came right after His baptism.

[b] LED UP BY THE SPIRIT . . . TO BE TEMPTED BY THE DEVIL. God Himself is never the agent of temptation (James 1:13), but here—as in the book of Job—God uses even satanic tempting to serve His sovereign purposes. Jesus confronted Satan and took the first step toward overthrowing his evil kingdom (cf. 1 John 3:8). Christ was tempted in all points (Heb. 4:15; 1 John 2:16); Satan tempted Him with "the lust of the flesh" (Matt. 4:2–3); "the lust of the eyes" (Matt. 4:8–9); and "the pride of life" (Matt. 4:5–6).

[c] THE WILDERNESS. The exact location of Jesus' encounter with Satan is unknown. It most likely would have been the same wilderness where John lived and ministered, the desolate region farther south, or the arid Arabian desert across the Jordan.

[d] FORTY DAYS. Perhaps reminiscent of Israel's forty years of wandering in the wilderness (Num. 14:33; 32:13). Jesus went without food during this time. Moses (twice, Deut. 9:9, 18) and Elijah (1 Kings 19:8) also fasted for that length of time. Evidently the temptation of Christ encompassed the full forty days of His fast.

[e] TEMPTED. Both Matthew and Luke give a condensed recounting of only three specific temptations. Luke reverses the order of the last two temptations in Matthew's account. Luke occasionally ordered material logically, rather than chronologically. Luke may have had some purpose for doing so here—perhaps to end his account of Jesus' temptation at the temple in Jerusalem, a very important location in Luke's narrative.

[f] SATAN. From a Hebrew word meaning "adversary." Since He had no fallen nature, Jesus' temptation was not an internal emotional or psychological struggle, but an external attack by a personal being.

[g] WILD BEASTS. A detail unique to Mark's account, stressing Jesus' loneliness and complete isolation from other people.

[h] IF YOU ARE THE SON OF GOD. The conditional "if" carries the meaning of "since" in this context. There was no doubt in Satan's mind who Jesus was; but Satan's design was to get Him to violate the plan of God and employ the divine power that He had set aside in His humiliation (cf. Phil. 2:7).

saying, MT "[i]It is written, 'Man shall not live by bread alone, but by [j]every word that proceeds from the mouth of God.'"

Then the devil LK brought Him to Jerusalem, MT the holy city, set Him on the [k]pinnacle of the temple, and said to Him, "If You are the Son of God, throw Yourself down LK from here; [l]for it is written:

'He shall give His angels charge over you,
To keep you,'
and,
'In *their* hands they shall bear you up,
Lest you dash your foot against a stone.'"

And Jesus answered and said to him, MT "[m]It is written again, 'You shall not tempt the LORD your God.'"

Again, the devil took Him up on an exceedingly high mountain, and showed Him all the kingdoms of the world and their glory LK in a moment of time. MT And he said to Him, "All these things [and] LK all this authority [n]I will give You, and their glory; for *this* has been delivered to me, and I give it to whomever I wish.

---

[i] IT IS WRITTEN. All three of Jesus' replies to the Devil were taken from Deuteronomy. This one, from Deut. 8:3, states that God allowed Israel to hunger, so that He might feed them with manna and teach them to trust Him to provide for them. So the verse is directly applicable to Jesus' circumstances and a fitting reply to Satan's temptation.

[j] EVERY WORD THAT PROCEEDS FROM THE MOUTH OF GOD. A more important source of sustenance than food, it nurtures our spiritual needs in a way that benefits us eternally, rather than merely providing temporal relief from physical hunger.

[k] PINNACLE OF THE TEMPLE. This was probably a roof with a portico at the southeastern corner of the temple complex, where a massive retaining wall reached from a level well above the temple mount, deep into the Kidron Valley. According to the Jewish historian Josephus, this was a drop of nearly 450 feet.

[l] FOR IT IS WRITTEN . . . LEST YOU DASH YOUR FOOT AGAINST A STONE. Note that Satan also quoted Scripture (Ps. 91:11–12)—but utterly twisted its meaning, employing a passage about trusting God to justify testing Him.

[m] IT IS WRITTEN AGAIN. Christ replied with another verse from Israel's wilderness experience (Deut. 6:16)—recalling the experience at Massah, where the grumbling Israelites put the Lord to the test, angrily demanding that Moses produce water where there was none (Ex. 17:2–7).

[n] I WILL GIVE YOU. Satan is the "ruler of this world" (John 12:31; 14:30; 16:11) and the "god of this age" (2 Cor. 4:4). The whole world lies in his power (1 John 5:19). This is illustrated in Dan. 10:13, where demonic power controlled the kingdom of Persia, so that a demon is called the Prince of Persia.

Therefore, if You will [MT] fall down and [LK] worship before me, all will be Yours." [MT] Then Jesus said to him, "Away with you, Satan! [LK] Get behind Me! [MT] [o]For it is written, 'You shall worship the LORD your God, and Him only you shall serve.' "

[LK] Now when the devil had ended every temptation, he departed from Him until an opportune time, [MT] and behold, [p]angels came and ministered to Him.

---

[o] FOR IT IS WRITTEN. Here Christ was citing and paraphrasing Deut. 6:13–14. Again, these relate to the Israelites' wilderness experiences. Christ, like them, was led into the wilderness to be tested (cf. Deut. 8:2). Unlike them, He withstood every aspect of the test.

[p] ANGELS CAME AND MINISTERED TO HIM. Ps. 91:11–12—the verse Satan tried to twist—was thus fulfilled in God's way and in God's perfect timing. The tense of this Greek verb, "to minister" suggests the angels ministered to Jesus throughout His temptation.

25. John Further Testifies About Jesus

John 1:19–34

JN [a]Now this is the testimony of [b]John, when [c]the Jews sent priests and Levites from Jerusalem to ask him, "Who are you?"

He confessed, and did not deny, but confessed, [d]"I am not the Christ."

And they asked him, "What then? [e]Are you Elijah?" He said, "I am not." " [f]Are you the Prophet?" And he answered, "No."

Then they said to him, "Who are you, that we may give an answer to those who sent us? What do you say about yourself?"

---

[a] Now this is. In these verses the apostle John presented the first of many witnesses to prove that Jesus is the Messiah and Son of God, thus reinforcing his main theme (John 20:30–31). The testimony of John the Baptist was given on three different days to three different groups (cf. John 1:29, 35, 36). Each time, he spoke of Christ in a different way and emphasized distinct aspects regarding Him. The events in these verses took place in AD 26/27, just a few months after John's baptism of Jesus (cf. Matt. 3:13–17; Luke 3:21–22).

[b] John. John, born into a priestly family, was from the tribe of Levi (Luke 1:5). He began his ministry in the Jordan Valley when he was approximately twenty-nine or thirty years old and boldly proclaimed the need for spiritual repentance and preparation for the coming of the Messiah. He was the cousin of Jesus Christ and served as His prophetic forerunner (Matt. 3:3; Luke 1:5–25, 36).

[c] the Jews . . . from Jerusalem. This may refer to the Sanhedrin, the main governing body of the Jewish nation. The Sanhedrin was controlled by the family of the high priest, and thus the envoys would naturally be priests and Levites who would be interested in John's ministry, both his message and his baptism.

[d] "I am not the Christ." Some thought that John was the Messiah (Luke 3:15–17). The term *Christ* is the Greek equivalent of the Hebrew term for "Messiah."

[e] "Are you Elijah?" Mal. 4:5 promises that the prophet Elijah will return before Messiah establishes His earthly kingdom. If John was the forerunner of Messiah, was he Elijah, they asked? The angel announcing John's birth said that John would go before Jesus "in the spirit and power of Elijah" (Luke 1:17), thus indicating that someone other than literal Elijah could fulfill the prophecy. God sent John who was like Elijah, i.e., one who had the same type of ministry, the same power, and similar personality (2 Kings 1:8; cf. Matt. 3:4). If they had received Jesus as Messiah, John would have fulfilled that prophecy (cf. Matt. 11:14; Mark 9:13; Luke 1:17; Rev. 11:5, 6).

[f] "Are you the Prophet?" This is a reference to Deut. 18:15–18, which predicted God would raise up a great prophet like Moses who would function as His voice. While some in John's time interpreted this prophecy as referring to another forerunner of Messiah, the NT (Acts 3:22, 23; 7:37) applies the passage to Jesus.

He said: "I *am* 'The [g]voice of one crying in the wilderness: "Make straight the way of the Lord," ' as the prophet Isaiah said."

Now those who were sent were from the Pharisees. And they asked him, saying, "Why then do you [h]baptize if you are not the Christ, nor Elijah, nor the Prophet?"

John answered them, saying, "I baptize with water, but there stands [i]One among you whom you do not know. It is He who, coming after me, is preferred before me, whose sandal strap I am not worthy to loose."

These things were done in [j]Bethabara beyond the Jordan, where John was baptizing.

[k]The next day John saw Jesus coming toward him, and said, "Behold! [l]The

---

[g] voice. John quoted and applied Isa. 40:3 to himself (cf. Matt. 3:3; Mark 1:3; Luke 3:4). In the original context of Isa. 40:3, the prophet heard a voice calling for the leveling of a path. This call was a prophetic picture that foreshadowed the final and greatest return of Israel to their God from spiritual darkness and alienation through the spiritual redemption accomplished by the Messiah (cf. Rom. 11:25–27). In humility, John compared himself to a voice rather than a person, thus focusing the attention exclusively upon Christ (cf. Luke 17:10).

[h] baptize. Since John had identified himself as a mere voice, the question arose as to his authority for baptizing. The OT associated the coming of Messiah with repentance and spiritual cleansing (Ezek. 36–37; Zech. 13:1). John focused attention on his position as forerunner of Messiah, who used traditional proselyte baptism as a symbol of the need to recognize those Jews who were outside God's saving covenant like Gentiles. They, too, needed spiritual cleansing and preparation (repentance—Matt. 3:11; Mark 1:4; Luke 3:7, 8) for Messiah's advent.

[i] One among you. John the Baptist's words here continue a theme of the preeminence of Messiah in the prologue and demonstrate extraordinary humility. Each time John had opportunity to focus on himself in these encounters, he instead shifted the focus onto Messiah. John went so far as to state that he, unlike a slave that was required to remove his master's shoes, was not even worthy of performing this action in relationship to Messiah.

[j] Bethabara. This word has been substituted for "Bethany," which is in the original text because some feel that John incorrectly identified Bethany as the place of these events. The solution is that two Bethanys existed, i.e., one near Jerusalem where Mary, Martha, and Lazarus lived (John 11:1) and one "beyond the Jordan," near the region of Galilee. Since John made an effort to identify the other Bethany's close proximity to Jerusalem, he most likely was referring here to that other town with the same name.

[k] The next day. These events took place the day after John's response to those sent from the Pharisees. This portion deals with John's witness to a second group of Jews on the second day regarding Jesus. The verses also introduce a series of Messianic titles that refer to Jesus: Lamb of God (John 1:29, 36), Rabbi (vv. 38, 49), Messiah/ Christ (v. 41), Son of God (vv. 34, 49), King of Israel (v. 49), Son of Man (v. 51) and "Him of whom Moses in the law, and also the prophets, wrote" (v. 45).

[l] The Lamb of God. The use of a lamb for sacrifice was very familiar to Jews. A lamb was used as a sacrifice during Passover (Ex. 12:1–36); a lamb was led to the slaughter in the prophecies of Isaiah (Isa. 53:7); a lamb was offered in the daily sacrifices of Israel (Lev. 14:12–21; cf. Heb. 10:5–7). John the Baptist used this expression to point to the ultimate sacrifice of Jesus on the cross to atone for the sins of the world, a theme which John the apostle carries throughout his writings (John 19:36; cf. Rev. 5:1–6; 7:17; 17:14) and that appears in other NT writings (e.g., 1 Peter 1:19).

Lamb of God who takes away the [m]sin of the world! This is He of whom I said, 'After me comes a Man who is preferred before me, for He was before me.' I did not know Him; but that He should be revealed to Israel, therefore I came baptizing with water."

And [n]John bore witness, saying, "I saw the Spirit descending from heaven like a dove, and He remained upon Him. [o]I did not know Him, but He who sent me to baptize with water said to me, 'Upon whom you see [p]the Spirit descending, and remaining on Him, this is He who baptizes with the Holy Spirit.' And I have seen and testified that this is [q]the Son of God."

---

[m] sin of the world. In this context *world* has the connotation of humanity in general, not specifically every person. The use of the singular *sin* in conjunction with *of the world* indicates that Jesus' sacrifice for sin potentially reaches all people without distinction (cf. 1 John 2:2). John makes clear, however, that its efficacious effect is only for those who receive Christ (cf. John 1:11–12).

[n] Jesus bore witness. John is reflecting back on the events that occurred earlier at Jesus' baptism.

[o] I did not know Him. Although John was Jesus' cousin, he did not know Jesus as the "Coming One" or "Messiah" (v. 30).

[p] the Spirit descending. God had previously communicated to John that this sign was to indicate the promised Messiah, so when John witnessed this act, he was able to identify the Messiah as Jesus (cf. Matt. 3:16; Mark 1:10; Luke 3:22).

[q] the Son of God. Although, in a limited sense, believers can be called "sons of God" (e.g., Matt. 5:9; Rom. 8:14), John uses this phrase with the full force as a title that points to the unique oneness and intimacy that Jesus sustains to the Father as *Son*. The term carries the idea of the deity of Jesus as Messiah (John 1:49; 5:16–30; cf. 2 Sam. 7:14; Ps. 2:7; Heb. 1:1–9).

26. The Disciples of John Meet Jesus

John 1:35–51

JN Again, [a]the next day, John stood with two of his disciples. And looking at Jesus as He walked, he said, "Behold the Lamb of God!"

The two disciples heard him speak, and [b]they followed Jesus. Then Jesus turned, and seeing them following, said to them, "What do you seek?"

They said to Him, "Rabbi" (which is to say, when translated, Teacher), "where are You staying?"

He said to them, "Come and see." They came and saw where He was staying, and remained with Him that day (now it was about [c]the tenth hour).

One of the two who heard John *speak,* and followed Him, was Andrew, Simon Peter's brother. He first found his own brother Simon, and said to him, "We have found the [d]Messiah" (which is translated, the Christ). And he brought him to Jesus.

---

[a] THE NEXT DAY. This section deals with John the Baptist's witness to a third group, i.e., some of John's disciples, on the third day (see John 1:19–28; 29–34 for the first and second groups) regarding Jesus. Consistent with John's humility, he focuses the attention of his own disciples onto Jesus.

[b] THEY FOLLOWED JESUS. Although the verb *follow* usually means "to follow as a disciple" in the writing of the apostle (John 1:43; 8:12; 12:26; 21:19–20, 22), it may also have a neutral sense (11:31). The "following" here does not necessarily indicate that they became permanent disciples at this time. The implication may be that they went after Jesus to examine Him more closely because of John's testimony. This event constituted a preliminary exposure of John the Baptist's disciples to Jesus (e.g., Andrew). They eventually dedicated their lives to Him as true disciples and apostles when Jesus called them to permanent service after these events (Matt. 4:18–22; 9:9; Mark 1:16–20). At this point in the narrative, John the Baptist fades from the scene and the attention focuses upon the ministry of Christ.

[c] THE TENTH HOUR. The Jews divided the daytime, from sunrise to sunset, into twelve hours (starting at approximately 6:00 a.m.). This would make the time about 4:00 p.m. John mentions the precise time most likely to emphasize that he was the other disciple of John the Baptist who was with Andrew (John 1:40). As an eyewitness to these events occurring on three successive days, John's first meeting with Jesus was so life-changing that he remembered the exact hour when he first met the Lord. If John was reckoning time by the Roman method, beginning at midnight, the time would be about 10:00 a.m.

[d] MESSIAH. The term *Messiah* is transliterated from a Hebrew or Aramaic verbal adjective that means "Anointed One." It comes from a verb that means "to anoint" someone as an action involved in consecrating that person to a particular office or function. While the term at first applied to the king of Israel ("the Lord's anointed"—1 Sam. 16:6), the high priest ("the anointed priest," Lev. 4:3), and the patriarchs ("my anointed ones," Ps. 105:15), the term eventually came to point above all to the prophesied "Coming One" or "Messiah" in His role as prophet, priest, and king. The term *Christ,* a Greek word (verbal adjective) that comes from a verb meaning "to anoint," is used in translating the Hebrew term, so that the terms *Messiah* or *Christ* are titles and not personal names of Jesus.

Now [e]when Jesus looked at him, He said, "You are Simon the son of Jonah. [f]You shall be called Cephas" (which is translated, A Stone).

[g]The following day Jesus wanted to go to Galilee, and He found Philip and said to him, "Follow Me." Now Philip was from [h]Bethsaida, the city of Andrew and Peter. Philip found Nathanael and said to him, "We have found [i]Him of whom Moses in the law, and also the prophets, wrote—Jesus of Nazareth, the son of Joseph."

And Nathanael said to him, [j]"Can anything good come out of Nazareth?" Philip said to him, "Come and see."

Jesus saw Nathanael coming toward Him, and said of him, "Behold, an Israelite indeed, in whom is [k]no deceit!"

---

[e] WHEN JESUS LOOKED AT HIM. Jesus knows hearts thoroughly and not only sees into them but also transforms a person into what He wants him to become.

[f] YOU SHALL BE CALLED CEPHAS. Up to this time, Peter had been known as "Simon son of Jonah" (the name "Jonah" in Aramaic means "John"; cf. 21:15–17; Matt. 16:17). The term *cephas* means "rock" in Aramaic, which is translated "Peter" in Greek. Jesus' assignment of the name Cephas or Peter to Simon occurred at the outset of His ministry (cf. Matt. 16:18; Mark 3:16). The statement not only is predictive of what Peter would be called but also declarative of how Jesus would transform his character and use him in relationship to the foundation of the church (cf. John 21:18, 19; Matt. 16:16–18; Acts 2:14–4:32).

[g] THE FOLLOWING DAY. This section introduces the fourth day since the beginning of John the Baptist's witness (cf. John 1:19, 29, 35).

[h] BETHSAIDA, THE CITY OF ANDREW AND PETER. While Mark 1:21, 29 puts the location of Peter's house in Capernaum, John relates that he was from Bethsaida. Resolution centers in the fact that Peter (and Andrew) most likely grew up in Bethsaida and later relocated to Capernaum in the same way that Jesus was consistently identified with His hometown of Nazareth, though He lived elsewhere later (Matt. 2:23; 4:13; Mark 1:9; Luke 1:26).

[i] HIM OF WHOM MOSES IN THE LAW, AND ALSO THE PROPHETS, WROTE. This phrase encapsulates the stance of John's whole gospel: Jesus is the fulfillment of OT Scripture (cf. John 1:21; 5:39; Deut. 18:15–19; Luke 24:44, 47; Acts 10:43; 18:28; 26:22–23; Rom. 1:2; 1 Cor. 15:3; 1 Peter 1:10, 11; Rev. 19:10).

[j] "CAN ANYTHING GOOD COME OUT OF NAZARETH?" Nathanael was from Cana (21:2), another town in Galilee. Though Galileans were despised by Judeans, Galileans themselves looked down on people from Nazareth. In light of John 7:52, Nathanael's scorn may have centered in the fact that Nazareth was an insignificant village without seeming prophetic importance (cf., however, Matt. 2:23). Later, some would contemptuously refer to Christians as the "sect of the Nazarenes" (Acts 24:5).

[k] NO DECEIT. Jesus' point was that Nathanael's bluntness revealed him to be a man of sincerity and honesty who was open to the truth about Christ. The term reveals an honest, seeking heart. The reference here may be an allusion to Gen. 27:35, where Jacob, in contrast to the sincere Nathanael, was known for his trickery. The meaning may be that the employment of trickery characterized not only Jacob but also his descendants. In Jesus' mind, an honest and sincere Israelite had become an exception rather than the rule (cf. John 2:23–25).

Nathanael said to Him, "How do You know me?" Jesus answered and said to him, "Before Philip called you, when you were under the fig tree, [l]I saw you."

Nathanael answered and said to Him, "Rabbi, You are [m]the Son of God! You are the King of Israel!"

Jesus answered and said to him, "Because I said to you, 'I saw you under the fig tree,' do you believe? You will see greater things than these." And He said to him, " [n]Most assuredly, I say to you, hereafter you shall see [o]heaven open, and the angels of God ascending and descending upon the [p]Son of Man."

---

[l] I SAW YOU. A brief glimpse of Jesus' supernatural knowledge. Not only was Jesus' brief summary of Nathanael accurate, but also He revealed information that could only be known by Nathanael himself. Perhaps Nathanael had some significant or outstanding experience of communion with God at the location, and he was able to recognize Jesus' allusion to it. At any rate, Jesus had knowledge of this event not available to men.

[m] THE SON OF GOD! . . . THE KING OF ISRAEL! Christ's display of supernatural knowledge combined with Philip's witness removed Nathanael's doubts, so John added the witness of Nathanael to this section. The use of "the" with "Son of God" most likely indicates that the expression is to be understood as bearing its full significance (cf. John 1:34; 11:27). For Nathanael, here was One who could not be described merely in human terms.

[n] MOST ASSUREDLY. Cf. John 5:19, 24–25. A phrase used frequently for emphasizing the importance and truth of the coming statement.

[o] HEAVEN OPEN, AND THE ANGELS OF GOD ASCENDING AND DESCENDING. In light of the context of John 1:47, this verse most likely refers to Gen. 28:12, where Jacob dreamed about a ladder from heaven. Jesus' point to Nathanael was that just like Jacob experienced supernatural or heaven-sent revelation, Nathanael and the other disciples would experience supernatural communication confirming who Jesus was. Moreover, the term *Son of Man* replaced the ladder in Jacob's dream, signifying that Jesus was the means of access between God and man.

[p] SON OF MAN. This is Jesus' favorite self-designation, for it was mostly spoken by Jesus, who used it over eighty times. In the NT, it refers only to Jesus and appears mostly in the gospels (cf. Acts 7:56). While the term at times may refer merely to a human being or as a substitute for the personal pronoun (6:27; cf. 6:20), it especially takes on an eschatological significance referring to Dan. 7:13–14, where the "Son of Man" or Messiah comes in glory to receive the kingdom from the "Ancient of Days" (i.e., the Father).

27. Jesus' First Miracle: Water into Wine

John 2:1–12

JN [a]On the third day there was a [b]wedding in [c]Cana of Galilee, and the mother of Jesus was there. Now [d]both Jesus and His disciples were invited to the wedding. And when they ran out of [e]wine, the mother of Jesus said to Him, "They have no wine."

Jesus said to her, " [f]Woman, [g]what does your concern have to do with Me? [h]My hour has not yet come."

---

[a] ON THE THIRD DAY. This phrase has reference to the last narrated event, i.e., the calling of Philip and Nathanael (John 1:43). John relates the first great sign performed by Jesus to demonstrate His deity, the turning of water into wine. Only God can create from nothing. John identifies eight miracles in his gospel that constitute "signs" or confirmation of who Jesus is. Each of the eight miracles were different; no two were alike.

[b] WEDDING. A Jewish wedding celebration could last up to seven days. It was the groom's responsibility to pay for the festivities. To run out of wine for the guests would have been an embarrassment to the groom and may have even opened him to legal consequences from the extended family of the bride.

[c] CANA OF GALILEE. Cana was the home of Nathanael (John 21:2). Its exact location is unknown. A probable location is Khirbet Qana, a village now in ruins approximately nine miles north of Nazareth.

[d] BOTH JESUS AND HIS DISCIPLES WERE INVITED. The fact that Jesus, His mother, and His disciples were all present on this occasion probably indicates that the wedding was for a relative or friend of the family. The disciples that accompanied Him are the five mentioned in John 1: Andrew, Simon Peter, Philip, Nathanael, and the unnamed disciple (John 1:35) who was surely John, who also witnessed this miracle.

[e] WINE. The wine served was subject to fermentation. In the ancient world, however, to quench thirst without inducing drunkenness, wine was mixed with water to dilute its strength. Due to the climate and circumstances, even "new wine" fermented quickly and had an inebriating effect if not mixed (Acts 2:13). Because of a lack of water purification process, wine mixed with water was also safer to drink than water alone. While the Bible condemns drunkenness, it does not necessarily condemn the consumption of wine (Ps. 104:15; Prov. 20:1; Eph. 5:18).

[f] WOMAN. The term is not necessarily impolite, but it does have the effect of distancing Jesus from His mother and her request. Perhaps, it was the equivalent of "ma'am."

[g] WHAT DOES YOUR CONCERN HAVE TO DO WITH ME? Jesus' tone was not disrespectful, but abrupt. The phrase asks what is shared in common between the parties. The thrust of Jesus' comment was that He was fully focused on the purpose for His mission on earth, so that He subordinated all activities to the fulfillment of that mission. Mary had to recognize Him not so much as a son that she raised but as the promised Messiah and Son of God. Cf. Mark 3:31–35.

[h] MY HOUR HAS NOT YET COME. The phrase constantly refers to Jesus' death and exaltation (John 7:30; 8:20; 12:23, 27; 13:1; 17:1). He was on a divine schedule decreed by God before the foundation of the world. Since the prophets described the messianic kingdom as having an abundance of wine (Jer. 31:12; Hos. 14:7; Amos 9:13, 14), Jesus was likely referring to the fact that the necessity of the cross must come before the blessings of the millennial age.

His mother said to the servants, "Whatever He says to you, do *it.*"

Now there were set there six waterpots of stone, according to the manner of [i]purification of the Jews, containing twenty or thirty gallons apiece. Jesus said to them, "Fill the waterpots with water." And they filled them up to the brim. And He said to them, "Draw *some* out now, and take *it* to the master of the feast." And they took *it.* When the master of the feast had tasted the water that was made wine, and did not know where it came from (but the servants who had drawn the water knew), the master of the feast called the bridegroom. And he said to him, "Every man at the beginning sets out the good wine, and when the *guests* have well drunk, then the inferior. You have kept the good wine until now!"

This beginning of [j]signs Jesus did in Cana of Galilee, and manifested His glory; and His disciples believed in Him. [k]After this He went down to Capernaum, He, His mother, His brothers, and His disciples; and they did not stay there many days.

---

[i] PURIFICATION OF THE JEWS. Stone jars were used because stone was more durable than earthenware and less susceptible to uncleanness. As a result, stone was preferable for ceremonial washing (cf. Mark 7:3, 4).

[j] SIGNS. By this word, John emphasized that miracles were not merely supernatural displays of power but had a significance beyond the mere act themselves—authenticating the messianic claim of Christ.

[k] AFTER THIS. John often uses this phrase to connect two narratives in his gospel (e.g., John 3:22; 5:1, 14; 6:1; 7:1; 11:7, 11; 19:28, 38). John placed this verse here as a transition to explain Jesus' movement from Cana in Galilee to Capernaum and eventual arrival at Jerusalem for the Passover celebration. Capernaum was on the northwest shore of Galilee, about sixteen miles northeast of Cana.

Part IV | From Passover AD 27 to Passover AD 28

28. Jesus' First Cleansing of the Temple

John 2:13–25

JN [a]Now the [b]Passover of the Jews was at hand, and [c]Jesus went up to Jerusalem. And He found in the temple [d]those who sold oxen and sheep and doves, and the

---

[a] Now. John used this section where Jesus cleansed the temple in righteous indignation to reinforce his main theme that He was the promised Messiah and Son of God. In this section, he highlighted three attributes of Jesus that confirm His deity: (1) His passion for reverence (John 2:13–17); (2) His power of resurrection (vv. 18–22); and (3) His perception of reality (vv. 23–25). The first way John demonstrated Christ's deity in the narrative of the temple cleansing was to show His passion for reverence. God alone exercises the right to regulate His worship.

[b] Passover of the Jews. This is the first of three Passovers that John mentions (John 2:13; 6:4; 11:55). Jews selected the lamb on the tenth of the month and celebrated Passover on the fourteenth day of the lunar month of Nisan (in late March or early April). They slaughtered the lamb between 3:00 and 6:00 p.m. on the night of the feast. Passover commemorates the deliverance of the Jews from slavery in Egypt, when the angel of death "passed over" Jewish homes in Egypt whose "doorposts" were sprinkled with blood (Ex. 12:23–27).

[c] Jesus went up to Jerusalem. Jesus' journeying to Jerusalem for the Passover was a standard annual procedure for every devout Jewish male over twelve years old (Ex. 23:14–17). Jewish pilgrims crowded into Jerusalem for this greatest of Jewish feasts.

[d] those who sold . . . the money changers. During the celebration of Passover, worshipers came to Jerusalem from all over Israel and the Roman Empire. Because many traveled large distances, it was inconvenient to bring their sacrificial animals with them. Opportunistic merchants, seeing a chance to provide a service and probably eyeing considerable profit during this time, set up areas in the outer courts of the temple in order for travelers to buy animals. The money changers were needed because the temple tax, paid annually by all Jewish men (Ex. 30:13, 14; Matt. 17:24–27), had to be in Jewish or Tyrian coinage (because of its high purity of silver). Those coming from foreign lands would need to exchange their money into the proper coinage for the tax. The money changers charged a high fee for the exchange. With such a large group of travelers and because of the seasonal nature of the celebration, both the animal dealers and money exchangers exploited the situation for monetary gain ("den of thieves"; Matt. 21:13). Religion had become crass and materialistic.

money changers doing business. [e]When He had made a whip of cords, He [f]drove them all out of the temple, with the sheep and the oxen, and poured out the changers' money and overturned the tables. And He said to those who sold doves, "Take these things away! [g]Do not make [h]My Father's [i]house a house of merchandise!" Then His disciples remembered that it was written, "[j]Zeal for Your house has eaten Me up."

So [k]the Jews answered and said to Him, "What [l]sign do You show to us, since You do these things?"

---

[e] WHEN HE HAD MADE. As John recorded this cleansing of the temple at the outset of Jesus' ministry, the Synoptic Gospels record a temple cleansing at the end of Jesus' ministry during His passion week (Matt. 21:12–17; Mark 11:15–18; Luke 19:45, 46). The historical circumstances and literary contexts of the two temple cleansings differ so widely that attempts to equate the two are unsuccessful. Furthermore, that two cleansings occurred is entirely consistent with the overall context of Jesus' ministry, for the Jewish nation as a whole never recognized Jesus' authority as Messiah (Matt. 23:37–39). Instead, they rejected His message as well as His person, making such repeated cleansing of the temple highly probable (as well as necessary).

[f] DROVE THEM ALL OUT OF THE TEMPLE. When the holiness of God and His worship was at stake, Jesus took fast and furious action. The "all" indicates that He drove not only men out but also animals. Yet, although His actions required brute force, they were not cruel. The moderation of His actions is seen in the fact that no riotous uproar occurred; otherwise Roman troops would have swiftly intervened. Although the primary reference is to the actions of the Messiah in the millennial kingdom, Jesus' actions in cleansing the temple were an initial fulfillment of Mal. 3:1–3 (and Zech. 14:20–21) that speak of Messiah's purifying the religious worship of His people.

[g] DO NOT MAKE. The force of the Greek imperative should better be translated "stop making," indicating Jesus' demand that they stop their current practice. God's holiness demands holiness in worship.

[h] MY FATHER'S. John gave a subtle hint of Jesus' divine Sonship as well as His messiahship with the recording of this phrase (cf. John 5:17, 18).

[i] HOUSE A HOUSE OF MERCHANDISE. Jesus may have intended a play on words. The word *merchandise* pictures a trading house filled with wares.

[j] ZEAL FOR YOUR HOUSE. Quoted from Ps. 69:9 to indicate that Jesus would not tolerate irreverence toward God. When David wrote this psalm, he was being persecuted because of his zeal toward God's house and his defense of God's honor. The disciples were afraid that Jesus' actions would precipitate the same type of persecution. Paul quotes the latter half of Ps. 69:9 ("The reproaches of those who reproached You fell on Me") in Rom. 15:3, clearly indicating the messianic nature that the psalm had for the early church.

[k] THE JEWS. Most likely the temple authorities or members of the Sanhedrin (cf. John 1:19).

[l] SIGN. The Jews demanded that Jesus show some type of miraculous sign that would indicate His authority for the actions that He had just taken in regulating the activities of the temple. Their demand of a sign reveals that they had not grasped the significance of Jesus' rebuke that centered in their need for proper attitudes and holiness in worship. Such an action itself constituted a "sign" of Jesus' person and authority. Moreover, they were requesting from Jesus a crass display of miracles on demand, further displaying their unbelief.

Jesus answered and said to them, "Destroy this temple, and [m]in three days [n]I will raise it up."

Then the Jews said, "It has taken [o]forty-six years to build this temple, and will You raise it up in three days?"

But He was speaking of the temple of His body. Therefore, when He had risen from the dead, His disciples remembered that He had said this to them; and they believed the Scripture and the word which Jesus had said.

Now when He was in Jerusalem at the Passover, during the feast, [p]many believed in His name when they saw the signs which He did. But Jesus did not commit Himself to them, because [q]He knew all *men,* and had no need that anyone should testify of man, for He knew what was in man.

---

[m] In three days. At his trial the authorities charged Jesus (Mark 14:58; 15:29) with making a threatening statement against the temple, revealing that they did not understand Jesus' response here. Once again John's gospel supplements the other gospels at this point by indicating that Jesus enigmatically referred to His resurrection. As with His usage of parables, Jesus' cryptic statement most likely was designed to reveal the truth to His disciples but conceal its meaning from unbelievers who questioned Him (Matt. 13:10–11). Only after His resurrection, however, did the disciples understand the real significance of this statement (cf. Matt. 12:40). Through the death and resurrection of Christ, temple worship in Jerusalem was destroyed (cf. John 4:21) and reinstituted in the hearts of those who were built into a spiritual temple called the church (Eph. 2:19–22).

[n] I will raise it up. The second way John demonstrated Christ's deity in the account of the temple cleansing was to show His power over death through resurrection. Only God has this right.

[o] Forty-six years to build this temple. This was not a reference to the Solomonic temple, since it had been destroyed during the Babylonian conquest in 586 BC. When the captives returned from Babylon, Zerubbabel and Joshua began rebuilding the temple (Ezra 1–4). Encouraged by the prophets Haggai and Zechariah (Ezra 5:1–6:18), the Jews completed the work in 516 BC. In 20/19 BC Herod the Great began a reconstruction and expansion. Workers completed the main part of the project in ten years, but other parts were still being constructed even at the time Jesus cleansed the temple. Interestingly, the finishing touches on the whole enterprise were still being made at its destruction, along with Jerusalem, by the Romans in AD 70. The famous "Wailing Wall" is built on part of the Herodian temple foundation.

[p] Many believed in His name . . . But Jesus did not commit Himself. John based these two phrases on the same Greek verb for "believe." This verse subtly reveals the true nature of belief from a biblical standpoint. Because of what they knew of Jesus from His miraculous signs, many came to believe in Him. However, Jesus made it His habit not to wholeheartedly "entrust" or "commit" Himself to them, because He knew their hearts. John 2:24 indicates that Jesus looked for genuine conversion rather than enthusiasm for the spectacular. The latter verse also leaves a subtle doubt as to the genuineness of the conversion of some (cf. John 8:31–32). This emphatic contrast between John 2:23–24 in terms of type of trust, therefore, reveals that "belief into His name" involved much more than intellectual assent. It called for whole-hearted commitment of one's life as Jesus' disciple (cf. Matt. 10:37; 16:24–26).

[q] He knew all men. The third way John demonstrated Christ's deity in the account of the temple cleansing was to show His perception of reality. Only God truly knows the hearts of men.

29. Jesus Meets with Nicodemus

John 3:1–21

JN [a]There was a man of the [b]Pharisees named [c]Nicodemus, a [d]ruler of the Jews. This man [e]came to Jesus by night and said to Him, "Rabbi, we know that You are a teacher come from God; for no one can do these signs that You do unless God is with him."

---

[a] THERE WAS A MAN. The story of Jesus and Nicodemus reinforces John's themes that Jesus is the Messiah and Son of God (apologetic) and that He came to offer salvation to men (evangelistic). John 2:23–24 actually serves as the introduction to Nicodemus's story, since chapter 3 constitutes tangible evidence of Jesus' ability to know men's hearts and thereby also demonstrates Jesus' deity. Jesus also presented God's plan of salvation to Nicodemus, showing that He was God's messenger, whose redemptive work brings about the promised salvation to His people (John 3:14). John 3 may be divided into two sections: (1) Jesus' dialogue with Nicodemus (John 3:1–10) and (2) Jesus' discourse on God's plan of salvation (John 3:11–21).

[b] PHARISEES. The word *Pharisee* most likely comes from a Hebrew word meaning "to separate" and therefore probably means "separated ones." They were not separatists in the sense of isolationists but in the puritanical sense, i.e., they were highly zealous for ritual and religious purity according to the Mosaic law as well as their own traditions that they added to the OT legislation. Although their origin is unknown, they seem to have arisen as an offshoot from the "Hasidim" or "pious ones" during the Maccabean era. They were generally from the Jewish middle class and mostly consisted of laity (business men) rather than priests or Levites. They represented the orthodox core of Judaism and very strongly influenced the common people of Israel. According to Josephus, six thousand existed at the time of Herod the Great. Jesus condemned them for their hyperconcentration on externalizing religion (rules and regulations) rather than inward spiritual transformation.

[c] NICODEMUS. Although Nicodemus was a Pharisee, his name was Greek in origin and means "victor over the people." He was a prominent Pharisee and member of the Sanhedrin ("a ruler of the Jews"). Nothing is known about his family background. He eventually came to believe in Jesus (John 7:50–52), risking his own life and reputation by helping to give Jesus' body a decent burial (John 19:38–42).

[d] RULER OF THE JEWS. This is a reference to the Sanhedrin (cf. Matt. 26:59), the main ruling body of the Jews in Israel during the Greco-Roman period. It was the Jewish "supreme court" or ruling council of the time and arose most likely during the Persian period. In NT times, the Sanhedrin was composed of the high priest (president), chief priests, elders (family heads), and scribes for a total of seventy-one people. The method of appointment was both hereditary and political. It executed both civil and criminal jurisdiction according to Jewish law. However, capital punishment cases required the sanction of the Roman procurator (John 18:30–32). After AD 70 and the destruction of Jerusalem, the Sanhedrin was abolished and replaced by the Beth Din (court of judgment) that was composed of scribes whose decisions had only moral and religious authority.

[e] CAME TO JESUS BY NIGHT. While some have thought that Nicodemus's visit at night was somehow figurative of the spiritual darkness of his heart (cf. John 1:5; 9:4; 11:10; 13:30) or that he decided to come at this time because he could take more time with Jesus and be unhurried in conversation, perhaps the most logical explanation lies in the fact that, as a ruler of the Jews, Nicodemus was afraid of the implications of associating openly in conversation with Jesus. He chose night in order to have a clandestine meeting with Jesus rather than risk disfavor with his fellow Pharisees, among whom Jesus was generally unpopular.

Jesus answered and said to him, "Most assuredly, I say to you, unless one is [f]born again, he [g]cannot see the kingdom of God."

Nicodemus said to Him, " [h]How can a man be born when he is old? Can he enter a second time into his mother's womb and be born?"

Jesus answered, "Most assuredly, I say to you, unless one is [i]born of water and the Spirit, he cannot enter the kingdom of God. That which is born of the flesh is flesh, and that which is born of the Spirit is spirit. Do not marvel that I said to you, 'You must be born again.' [j]The wind blows where it wishes, and you hear the sound of it, but cannot tell where it comes from and where it goes. So is everyone who is born of the Spirit."

Nicodemus answered and said to Him, "How can these things be?"

Jesus answered and said to him, "Are you [k]the teacher of Israel, and do not

---

[f] BORN AGAIN. The phrase lit. means "born from above." Jesus answered a question that Nicodemus does not even ask. He read Nicodemus's heart and came to the very core of his problem, i.e., the need for spiritual transformation or regeneration produced by the Holy Spirit. New birth is an act of God whereby eternal life is imparted to the believer (2 Cor. 5:17; Titus 3:5; 1 Peter 1:3; 1 John 2:29; 3:9; 4:7; 5:1, 4, 18). John 1:12–13 indicates that "born again" also carries the idea "to become children of God" through trust in the name of the incarnate Word.

[g] CANNOT SEE THE KINGDOM OF GOD. In context, this is primarily a reference to participation in the millennial kingdom, fervently anticipated by the Pharisees and other Jews. Since the Pharisees were supernaturalists, they naturally and eagerly expected the coming of the prophesied resurrection of the saints and institution of the messianic kingdom (Isa. 11:1–16; Dan. 12:2). Their problem was that they thought that mere physical lineage and keeping of religious externals qualified them for entrance into the kingdom, rather than the needed spiritual transformation that Jesus emphasized (cf. John 8:33–39; Gal. 6:15).

[h] HOW CAN A MAN BE BORN. A teacher himself, Nicodemus understood the rabbinical method of using figurative language to teach spiritual truth, and he was merely picking up Jesus' symbolism.

[i] BORN OF WATER AND THE SPIRIT. Jesus referred not to literal water here but to the need for "cleansing" (e.g., Ezek. 36:24–27). The Old Testament sometimes uses water as a metaphor for spiritual cleansing or renewal (Num. 19:17–19; Ps. 51:9, 10; Isa. 32:15; 44:3–5; 55:1–3; Jer. 2:13; Joel 2:28, 29). Thus, Jesus made reference to the spiritual washing or purification of the soul, accomplished by the Holy Spirit through the Word of God at the moment of salvation (cf. Eph. 5:26; Titus 3:5), required for belonging to His kingdom.

[j] THE WIND BLOWS WHERE IT WISHES. Jesus' point was that just as the wind cannot be contained or controlled by human beings but its effects can be witnessed, so also it is with the Holy Spirit. He cannot be manipulated or understood, but the proof of His work is apparent. Where the Spirit works, there is undeniable and unmistakable evidence.

[k] THE TEACHER. The use of the definite article "the" indicates that Nicodemus was a renowned master-teacher in the nation of Israel, an established religious authority par excellence. He enjoyed a high standing among the rabbis or teachers of his day. Jesus' reply emphasized the spiritual bankruptcy of the nation at that time, since even one of the greatest of Jewish teachers did not recognize this teaching on spiritual cleansing and transformation based clearly in the OT. The net effect is to show that externals of religion may have a deadening effect on one's spiritual perception.

know these things? [l]Most assuredly, I say to you, We speak what We know and testify what We have seen, and [m]you do not receive Our witness. If I have told you earthly things and [n]you do not believe, how will you believe if I tell you heavenly things? No one has ascended to heaven but He who came down from heaven, *that is,* the Son of Man who is in heaven. And as Moses lifted up the serpent in the wilderness, even [o]so must the Son of Man be lifted up, that whoever believes in Him should not perish but have [p]eternal life. [q]For God so loved the world that He gave His only begotten Son, that whoever believes in Him should not perish but have everlasting life. For God did not send His Son into the world to condemn the world, but that the world through Him might be saved.

---

[l] MOST ASSUREDLY, I SAY TO YOU. The focus of these verses (John 3:11–21) turns away from Nicodemus and centers on Jesus' discourse regarding the true meaning of salvation. The key word in these verses is *believe,* used seven times. The new birth must be appropriated by an act of faith. While John 3:1–10 center on the divine initiative in salvation, vv. 11–21 emphasize the human reaction to the work of God in regeneration. In John 3:11–21 the section may be divided into three parts: (1) the problem of unbelief (vv. 11–12); (2) the answer to unbelief (vv. 13–17); and (3) the results of unbelief (vv. 18–21).

[m] YOU DO NOT RECEIVE OUR WITNESS. The plural "you" here refers back to the "we" of John 3:2, where Nicodemus was speaking as a representative of his nation Israel ("we know"). Jesus replied in John 3:11 with "you," indicating that Nicodemus's unbelief was typical of the nation as a collective whole.

[n] YOU DO NOT BELIEVE. Jesus focused on the idea that unbelief is the cause of ignorance. At heart, Nicodemus's failure to understand Jesus' words centered not so much in his mental capacity but in his unwillingness to embrace Jesus' testimony.

[o] SO MUST THE SON OF MAN BE LIFTED UP. Cf. John 8:28; 12:32, 34; 18:31–32. This is a veiled prediction of Jesus' death on the cross. Jesus referred to the story of Num. 21:5–9, where the Israelite people who looked at the serpent lifted up by Moses were healed. The point of this illustration or analogy is in the "lifted up." Just as Moses lifted up the snake on the pole so that all who looked upon it might live physically, those who look to Christ, who was "lifted up" on the cross, will live spiritually and eternally.

[p] ETERNAL LIFE. This is the first of ten references to "eternal life" in John's gospel. The same Greek word is translated eight times as "everlasting life." The two expressions appear in the NT nearly fifty times. Eternal life refers not only to eternal quantity but divine quality of life. It means lit. "life of the age to come" and refers therefore to resurrection and heavenly existence in perfect glory and holiness. This life for believers in the Lord Jesus is experienced before heaven is reached. This "eternal life" is in essence nothing less than participation in the eternal life of the Living Word, Jesus Christ. It is the life of God in every believer, yet not fully manifest until the resurrection (Rom. 8:19–23; Phil. 3:20–21).

[q] FOR GOD SO LOVED THE WORLD. The Son's mission is bound up in the supreme love of God for the evil, sinful "world" of humanity (cf. John 1:9; 6:32, 51; 12:47) that is in rebellion against Him. The word *so* emphasizes the intensity or greatness of His love. The Father gave His unique and beloved Son to die on behalf of sinful men (cf. 2 Cor. 5:21).

"He who believes in Him is not condemned; but he who does not believe is condemned already, because he has not [r]believed in the name of the only begotten Son of God. And this is the condemnation, that the light has come into the world, and men loved darkness rather than light, because their deeds were evil. For everyone practicing evil hates the light and does not come to the light, lest his deeds should be exposed. But he who does the truth comes to the light, that his deeds may be clearly seen, that they have been done in God."

---

[r] BELIEVED IN THE NAME. This phrase (lit. "to believe into the name") means more than mere intellectual assent to the claims of the gospel. It includes trust and commitment to Christ as Lord and Savior that results in receiving a new nature (v. 7) that produces a change in heart and obedience to the Lord (cf. John 2:23–25).

30. Jesus' Ministry Supersedes John's

John 3:22–36

JN [a]After these things Jesus and His disciples came [b]into the land of Judea, and there He remained with them and [c]baptized. Now John also was baptizing in [d]Aenon near Salim, because there was much water there. And they came and were baptized. For [e]John had not yet been thrown into prison.

Then [f]there arose a dispute between *some* of John's disciples and the Jews about purification. And [g]they came to John and said to him, "Rabbi, He who was

---

[a] AFTER THESE THINGS. This section constitutes John the Baptist's last testimony in this gospel regarding Christ. As his ministry faded away, Jesus' ministry moved to the forefront. In spite of the fact that John the Baptist received widespread fame in Israel and was generally accepted by the common people of the land as well as those who were social outcasts, his testimony regarding Jesus was rejected, especially by the leaders of Israel (cf. Matt. 3:5–10; Luke 7:29).

[b] INTO THE LAND OF JUDEA. While the conversation with Nicodemus took place in Jerusalem (John 2:23), which is located in Judea, the phrase here means that Jesus went out into the rural areas of that region.

[c] BAPTIZED. John 4:2 specifically says that Jesus did not personally baptize, but that His disciples carried on this work.

[d] AENON NEAR SALIM. The exact location of this reference is disputed. It could refer to either Salim near Shechem or Salim that is six miles south of Beth Shean. Both are in the region of Samaria. Aenon is a name that means "springs," and both of these possible sites have plenty of water ("much water there").

[e] JOHN HAD NOT YET BEEN THROWN INTO PRISON. This provides another indication that John supplemented the Synoptic Gospels by providing additional information that helps further understanding of the movements of John the Baptist and Jesus. In Matthew and Mark, Christ's temptation is followed by John's imprisonment. With this phrase John the apostle fills in the slot between Jesus' baptism and temptation and the Baptist's imprisonment.

[f] THERE AROSE A DISPUTE. The dispute probably concerned the relation of the baptismal ministries of John and Jesus to the Jews' purification practices alluded to in John 2:6. The real underlying impetus, however, centered on the concern of John's disciples that Jesus was in competition with him.

[g] THEY CAME TO JOHN. This section may be divided into three parts that highlight the significance of what was occurring in relationship to John's and Jesus' ministry: (1) John the Baptist constituted the end of the old age (John 3:25–29); (2) the transition to Jesus' ministry (v. 30); and (3) Jesus' ministry as constituting the beginning of the new age (vv. 31–36). Instead of jealousy, John exhibited humble faithfulness to the superiority of Jesus' person and ministry.

with you beyond the Jordan, to whom you have testified—behold, He is baptizing, and [h]all are coming to Him!"

John answered and said, "A man can receive nothing unless it has been [i]given to him from heaven. You yourselves bear me witness, that I said, 'I am not the Christ,' but, 'I have been sent before Him.' He who has the bride is the [j]bridegroom; but the friend of the bridegroom, who stands and hears him, rejoices greatly because of the bridegroom's voice. Therefore this joy of mine is fulfilled. [k]He must increase, but I *must* decrease. He who comes from above is above all; he who is of the earth is earthly and speaks of the earth. He who comes from heaven is above all. And what He has seen and heard, that He testifies; and no one receives His testimony. He who has received His testimony has certified that God is true. For He whom God has sent speaks the words of God, for God does not give [l]the Spirit by measure. The Father loves the Son, and has given all things into His hand. [m]He who believes in the Son has everlasting life; and he who does not believe the Son shall not see life, but the wrath of God abides on him."

---

[h] ALL ARE COMING TO HIM. The potential conflict between John and Jesus was heightened by the fact that both were engaged in ministry in close proximity to one another. Because baptism is mentioned in John 3:22, Jesus may have been close to Jericho near the fords of the Jordan, while John was a short distance north, baptizing at Aenon. John's followers were especially disturbed by the fact that so many were flocking to Jesus whereas formerly they had come to John.

[i] GIVEN TO HIM FROM HEAVEN. This verse emphasizes God's sovereign authority in granting ministry opportunity (cf. 1 Cor. 4:7; 15:10).

[j] BRIDEGROOM . . . FRIEND OF THE BRIDEGROOM. John used an illustration to clarify his role for his disciples. The "friend of the bridegroom" was essentially the best man. He helped organize the details of the ceremony and took great pleasure in seeing the wedding proceed without incident. Most likely, John was also alluding to OT passages where faithful Israel is depicted as the bride of the Lord (Isa. 62:4–5; Jer. 2:2; Hos. 2:16–20).

[k] HE MUST INCREASE. In these verses, John the Baptist gave five reasons for Christ's superiority to him: (1) Christ had a heavenly origin (John 3:31); (2) Christ knew what was true by firsthand experience (v. 32); (3) Christ's testimony always agreed with God (v. 33); (4) Christ experienced the Holy Spirit in an unlimited manner (v. 34); and (5) Christ was supreme because the Father sovereignly had granted that status to Him (v. 35).

[l] THE SPIRIT BY MEASURE. God gave the Spirit to the Son without limits (John 1:32, 33; Isa. 11:2; 42:1; 61:1).

[m] HE WHO BELIEVES . . . HE WHO DOES NOT BELIEVE. This constitutes an appropriate climax to the third chapter of John's gospel. John the Baptist laid out two divergent paths, sincere faith and stubborn disobedience. As John faded from the forefront, he offered an invitation to faith in the Son and clearly expressed the ultimate consequence of failure to believe, i.e., "the wrath of God."

31. Jesus Meets a Samaritan Woman at a Well

Matt. 4:12; Mark 1:14a; Luke 3:19–20; John 4:1–26

LK But Herod the tetrarch, being rebuked by [John] concerning Herodias, his brother Philip's wife, and for all the evils which Herod had done, also added this, above all, that he shut John up in prison.

JN Therefore, when the Lord knew that the Pharisees had heard that Jesus made and baptized more disciples than John (though Jesus Himself did not baptize, but His disciples), [and] MT when Jesus heard that [a]John had been put in prison, JN [b]He left Judea and departed again to Galilee. But [c]He needed to go through [d]Samaria.

---

[a] JOHN HAD BEEN PUT IN PRISON. He was incarcerated for rebuking Herod Antipas over his incestuous marriage to his niece, Herodias (cf. Mark 6:17–29).

[b] HE LEFT JUDEA. John the Baptist and Jesus had official scrutiny focused on them because of their distinctive message regarding repentance and the kingdom. Most likely, Jesus wanted to avoid any possible conflict with John's disciples, who were troubled by His growing popularity. The scrutiny on Jesus' ministry—along with the potential for conflict with John's disciples—only increased after John was imprisoned. Thus, Jesus decided to leave Judea and travel north to Galilee.

[c] HE NEEDED TO GO THROUGH. Several roads led from Judea to Galilee: one near the seacoast; another through the region of Perea; and one through the heart of Samaria. Although the verb "needed" may possibly refer to the fact that Jesus wanted to save time and needless steps, because of the gospel's emphasis on the Lord's consciousness of fulfilling His Father's plan (John 2:4; 7:30; 8:20; 12:23; 13:1; 14:31), the apostle may have been highlighting divine, spiritual necessity, i.e., Jesus had an appointment with divine destiny in meeting the Samaritan woman, to whom He would reveal His messiahship.

[d] SAMARIA. When the nation of Israel split politically after Solomon's rule, King Omri named the capital city of the northern kingdom "Samaria" (1 Kings 16:24). The name eventually referred to the entire region and sometimes to the whole of the northern kingdom, which had been taken captive by Assyria in 722 BC (2 Kings 17:1–6). While Assyria led most of the populace of the ten northern tribes away (into the region which today is northern Iraq), it left a sizable population of Israelites in the northern Samaritan region and transported many non-Israelites into Samaria. These groups intermarried to form a mixed race. Eventually tension developed between the Jews who returned from captivity and the Samaritans. The Samaritans withdrew from the worship of Yahweh at Jerusalem and established their worship at Mount Gerizim in Samaria. Samaritans regarded only the Pentateuch as authoritative. As a result of this history, Jews repudiated Samaritans and considered them heretical. Intense ethnic and cultural tensions raged historically between the two groups so that both avoided contact as much as possible (cf. Ezra 4:1–24; Neh. 4:1–6; Luke 10:25–37).

So [e]He came to a city of Samaria which is called [f]Sychar, near the plot of ground that Jacob gave to his son Joseph. Now [g]Jacob's well was there. Jesus therefore, being [h]wearied from *His* journey, sat thus by the well. It was about [i]the sixth hour.

[j]A woman of Samaria came to draw water. Jesus said to her, [k]"Give Me a drink." For His disciples had gone away into the city [l]to buy food.

Then the woman of Samaria said to Him, "How is it that You, being a Jew, ask a drink from me, a Samaritan woman?" For Jews have no dealings with Samaritans.

Jesus answered and said to her, "If you knew the gift of God, and who it is

---

[e] He came to a city of Samaria. The story of the Samaritan woman reinforces John's main theme that Jesus is the Messiah and Son of God. The thrust of these verses is not so much her conversion but that Jesus is Messiah. While her conversion is clearly implied, the apostle's focus centers on Jesus' declaration foretold in the Scriptures. Important also is the fact that this chapter demonstrates Jesus' love and understanding of people. His love for mankind involved no boundaries, for He lovingly and compassionately reached out to a woman who was a social outcast. In contrast to the limitations of human love, Christ exhibits the character of divine love that is indiscriminate and all-encompassing.

[f] Sychar. This town was probably located where the modern village of Askar is today, on the side of Mount Ebal, opposite Mount Gerizim. Very old tradition identifies Jacob's well as lying about a half-mile south of Askar.

[g] Jacob's well. These verses refer back to Genesis 48:22, where Jacob bequeathed a section of land to Joseph, which he had purchased from the "children of Hamor" (cf. Gen. 33:19). When the Jews returned from Egypt, they buried Joseph's bones in that land at Shechem. The precise location of "Jacob's well" has been set by a firm tradition among Jews, Samaritans, Muslims, and Christians. The term used here for "well" denotes a running spring, while in John 4:11–12 John used another term for "well" that means "cistern" or "dug-out-well," indicating that the well was both dug out and replenished by an underground spring. This spring is still active today.

[h] wearied from His journey. Since the Word became flesh (John 1:14), He also suffered from physical limitations in His humanity (Heb. 2:10–14).

[i] the sixth hour. If John used the Jewish reckoning of time, calculated from sunrise at about 6:00 a.m., the time was about noon. If John used Roman time, which started reckoning from 12:00 p.m., the time would be about 6:00 p.m.

[j] A woman of Samaria came to draw water. Women generally came in groups to collect water, either in the morning or the evening to avoid the sun's heat. If the Samaritan woman alone came at noon, this may indicate that her public shame caused her to be isolated from other women.

[k] "Give Me a drink." For a Jewish man to speak to a woman in public, let alone to ask from her, a Samaritan, a drink was a definite breach of rigid social custom as well as a marked departure from the social animosity that existed between the two groups. Further, a rabbi and religious leader did not hold conversations with women of ill-repute.

[l] to buy food. This verse indicates that since Jesus and His disciples were willing to buy food from Samaritans, they did not follow the beliefs of stricter Jews, who would never have ingested food from outcast Samaritans.

who says to you, 'Give Me a drink,' you would have asked Him, and He would have given you [m]living water."

The woman said to Him, "Sir, You have [n]nothing to draw with, and the well is deep. Where then do You get that living water? Are You greater than our father Jacob, who gave us the well, and drank from it himself, as well as his sons and his livestock?"

Jesus answered and said to her, "Whoever drinks of this water will thirst again, but whoever drinks of the water that I shall give him will never thirst. But the water that I shall give him will become in him a fountain of water springing up into everlasting life."

The woman said to Him, "Sir, give me this water, that I may not thirst, nor come here to draw."

Jesus said to her, "Go, [o]call your husband, and come here."

The woman answered and said, "I have no husband." Jesus said to her, "You have well said, 'I have no husband,' for you have had five husbands, and the one whom you now have is [p]not your husband; in that you spoke truly."

The woman said to Him, "Sir, I perceive that [q]You are a prophet. Our fathers worshiped [r]on this mountain, and you *Jews* say that in Jerusalem is the place where one ought to worship."

---

[m] LIVING WATER. The OT is the background for this term, which has important metaphorical significance. In Jer. 2:13, Yahweh decries the disobedient Jews for rejecting Him, the "fountain of living waters." The OT prophets eagerly anticipated a time when "living waters shall flow from Jerusalem" (Ezek. 47:9 ; Zech. 14:8). The OT metaphor spoke of the knowledge of God and His grace, which provides cleansing, spiritual life, and the regenerating work of the Holy Spirit (cf. Isa. 1:16–18; 12:3; 44:3; Ezek. 36:25–27). John applies these themes to Jesus Christ as the living water, which is symbolic of eternal life mediated by the Holy Spirit from Him (cf. John 4:14; 6:35; 7:37–39). Jesus used the woman's need for physical water to sustain life in this arid region in order to serve as an object lesson for her need for spiritual transformation.

[n] NOTHING TO DRAW WITH. The woman, like Nicodemus (in John 3:4), did not realize that Jesus was talking about her spiritual needs. Instead, in her mind, she wanted such water in order to avoid her frequent trips to Jacob's well.

[o] CALL YOUR HUSBAND. Since the woman failed to understand the nature of the living water He offered, Jesus abruptly turned the dialogue to focus sharply on her real spiritual need for conversion and cleansing from sin. His intimate knowledge of her morally depraved life not only indicated His supernatural ability, but also focused on her spiritual condition.

[p] NOT YOUR HUSBAND. She was living conjugally with a man who Jesus said was not her husband. By such an explicit statement, our Lord rejected the notion that when two people live together it constitutes marriage. Biblically, marriage is always restricted to a public, formal, official, and recognized covenant.

[q] YOU ARE A PROPHET. His knowledge of her life indicated He had supernatural inspiration.

[r] ON THIS MOUNTAIN. Both Jews and Samaritans understood that God had commanded their forefathers to identify a special place for worshiping Him (Deut. 12:5). The Jews, recognizing the entire Hebrew canon, chose Jerusalem (2 Sam. 7:5–13; 2 Chron. 6:6). The Samaritans, recognizing only the Pentateuch, noted that the first place Abraham built an altar to God was at Shechem (Gen. 12:6, 7), which was overlooked by Mount Gerizim, where the Israelites had shouted the blessings promised by God before they entered the promised land (Deut. 11:29–30). As a result, they chose Mount Gerizim for the place of their temple.

Jesus said to her, "Woman, believe Me, the hour is coming when you will [s]neither on this mountain, nor in Jerusalem, worship the Father. You worship what [t]you do not know; we know what we worship, for salvation is of the Jews. But the [u]hour is coming, and now is, when the [v]true worshipers will worship the Father in spirit and truth; for the Father is seeking such to worship Him. [w]God *is* Spirit, and those who worship Him [x]must worship [y]in spirit and truth."

The woman said to Him, "I know that [z]Messiah is coming" (who is called Christ). "When He comes, He will tell us all things."

Jesus said to her, "[aa]I who speak to you am *He*."

---

[s] NEITHER ON THIS MOUNTAIN, NOR IN JERUSALEM. There was no reason to debate locations, since both places would be obsolete soon and neither would have any role to play in the lives of those who genuinely worship God. Jerusalem would even be destroyed with its temple (AD 70).

[t] YOU DO NOT KNOW. The Samaritans did not know God. They did not have the full revelation of Him, and thus could not worship in truth. The Jews did have the full revelation of God in the OT; thus they knew the God they worshiped because salvation's truth came first to them (cf. Luke 19:9) and through them to the world (cf. Rom. 3:2; 9:4–5).

[u] HOUR. This refers to Jesus' death, resurrection, and ascension to God, having completed redemption.

[v] TRUE WORSHIPERS. Jesus' point is that in light of His coming as Messiah and Savior, worshipers will be identified, not by a particular shrine or location, but by their worship of the Father through the Son. With Christ's coming, previous distinctions between true and false worshipers based on locations disappeared. True worshipers are all those everywhere who worship God through the Son, from the heart (cf. Phil. 3:3).

[w] GOD IS SPIRIT. This verse represents the classical statement on the nature of God as Spirit. The phrase means that God is invisible (Col. 1:15; 1 Tim. 1:17; Heb. 11:27) as opposed to the physical or material nature of man (John 1:18; 3:6). The word order of this phrase puts an emphasis on "Spirit," and the statement is essentially emphatic. Man could never comprehend the invisible God unless He revealed Himself, as He did in Scripture and the incarnation.

[x] MUST WORSHIP. Jesus is not speaking of a desirable element in worship but that which is absolutely necessary.

[y] IN SPIRIT AND TRUTH. The word *spirit* does not refer to the Holy Spirit but to the human spirit. Jesus' point here is that a person must worship not simply by external conformity to religious rituals and places (outwardly) but inwardly ("in spirit") with the proper heart attitude. The reference to *truth* refers to worship of God consistent with the revealed Scripture and centered on the "Word made flesh" who ultimately revealed His Father (John 14:6).

[z] MESSIAH. The Samaritans also anticipated Messiah's coming.

[aa] I WHO SPEAK TO YOU AM HE. Jesus forthrightly declared Himself to be Messiah, though His habit was to avoid such declarations to His own Jewish people who had such crassly political and militaristic views regarding Messiah (cf. John 10:24; Mark 9:41). The "He" in this translation is not in the original Greek, for Jesus literally said, "I who speak to you am." The usage of "I am" is similar to John 8:58. This claim constitutes the main point of the story regarding the Samaritan woman.

32. Jesus Evangelizes the Village of Sychar

John 4:27–44

JN And [a]at this *point* His disciples came, and they marveled that He talked with a woman; yet no one said, "What do You seek?" or, "Why are You talking with her?"

The woman then left her waterpot, went her way into the city, and said [b]to the men, "Come, see a Man who told me all things that I ever did. Could this be the Christ?" Then they went out of the city and came to Him.

In the meantime His disciples urged Him, saying, "Rabbi, eat."

But He said to them, "[c]I have food to eat of which you do not know."

Therefore the disciples said to one another, "Has anyone brought Him *anything* to eat?"

Jesus said to them, "[d]My food is to do the will of Him who sent Me, and to finish His work. Do you not say, 'There are still [e]four months and *then* comes the

---

[a] AT THIS POINT. Had the disciples arrived earlier, they would have interrupted and destroyed the conversation, and if they had arrived any later, she would have gone, and they would not have heard His declaration of messiahship. This feature subtly reveals Jesus' divine control over the situation that was occurring.

[b] TO THE MEN. Jesus had such an impact on the woman that she was eager to share the news with those in her village whom she had previously avoided because of her reputation. Her witness and candor regarding her own life so impressed them that they came to see Jesus for themselves.

[c] I HAVE FOOD. Just like the Samaritan woman's misunderstanding of Jesus' words regarding literal water, Jesus' own disciples thought only of literal food. John commonly used such misunderstanding to advance the argument of his gospel (e.g., John 2:20; 3:3).

[d] MY FOOD IS TO DO THE WILL OF HIM WHO SENT ME. Most likely Jesus echoed Deut. 8:3, where Moses stated, "Man shall not live by bread alone; but man lives by every word that proceeds from the mouth of the Lord" (cf. Matt. 4:4; Luke 4:4). When He talked with the Samaritan woman, Jesus was doing the will of the Father and thereby received greater sustenance and satisfaction than any mere physical food could offer Him (cf. John 5:23–24; 8:29; 17:4). Obedience to and dependence upon God's will summed up Jesus' whole life (Eph. 5:17). God's will for Him to finish is explained in John 6:38–40.

[e] FOUR MONTHS AND THEN COMES THE HARVEST. The event probably happened in December or January, which was four months before the spring harvest (mid-April). Crops were planted in November, and by December or January, the grain would be sprouting up in vibrant green color. Jesus used the fact that they were surrounded by crops growing in the field and waiting to be harvested as an object lesson to illustrate His urgency about reaching the lost that the "harvest" symbolized. Jesus points out the Samaritan woman and people of Sychar ("lift up your eyes"), who were at that moment coming upon the scene looking like a ripened "harvest" that urgently need to be "gathered," i.e., evangelized.

harvest'? Behold, I say to you, lift up your eyes and look at the fields, for they are [f]already white for harvest! And [g]he who reaps receives wages, and gathers fruit for eternal life, that both he who sows and he who reaps may rejoice together. For in this the saying is true: 'One sows and another reaps.' I sent you to reap that for which you have not labored; others have labored, and you have entered into their labors."

And [h]many of the Samaritans of that city believed in Him because of the word of the woman who testified, "He told me all that I *ever* did." So when the Samaritans had come to Him, they urged Him to stay with them; and He stayed there two days. And many more believed because of His own word.

Then they said to the woman, "Now we believe, not because of what you said, for we ourselves have heard *Him* and we know that this is indeed the Christ, the [i]Savior of the world." Now after the two days He departed from there and [j]went to Galilee. For Jesus Himself testified that a [k]prophet has no honor in his own country.

---

[f] Already white for harvest. Their white clothing seen above the growing grain may have looked like white heads on the stalks, an indication of readiness for harvest. Jesus knew the hearts of all (John 2:24), so he was able to state their readiness for salvation.

[g] He who reaps. The Lord's call to His disciples to do the work of evangelism contains promises of reward ("wages"), fruit that brings eternal joy, and the mutual partnership of shared privilege.

[h] Many of the Samaritans . . . believed. This entire passage reinforces Jesus' acknowledgment that He was Messiah by offering proof for His claim. John gave five genuine, but subtle, proofs that Jesus was truly Messiah and Son of God, which reinforced his main theme of John 20:31: (1) proof from His immediate control of everything (John 4:27); (2) proof from His impact on the woman (vv. 28–30); (3) proof from His intimacy with the Father (vv. 31–34); (4) proof from His insight into men's souls (vv. 35–38); and (5) proof from His impression on the Samaritans (vv. 39–42).

[i] Savior of the world. This phrase occurs also in 1 John 4:14. The verse constitutes the climax to the story of the woman of Samaria. The Samaritans themselves became another in a series of witnesses in John's gospel that demonstrated the identity of Jesus as the Messiah and Son of God. This episode represents the first instance of crosscultural evangelism (Acts 1:8).

[j] Went to Galilee. After two days in Samaria, Jesus traveled to Galilee, resuming the trip that began in John 4:3.

[k] Prophet has no honor in his own country. This proverb (cf. Matt. 13:57; Mark 6:4) contrasts the believing response of the Samaritans with the characteristic unbelief of Jesus' own people in Galilee (and Judea), whose reticent faith depended so much on Jesus' performance of miracles. While in Samaria, Jesus had enjoyed His first unqualified and unopposed success. His own people's hearts were not open to Him, but exhibited reluctance and hardness.

33. Jesus Heals a Nobleman's Son

Mark 1:14b–15; Luke 4:14–15; John 4:43–54

LK Then Jesus returned in the power of the Spirit to [a]Galilee, MK preaching [b]the gospel of the kingdom of God, and saying, "[c]The time is fulfilled, and [d]the kingdom of God is [e]at hand. [f]Repent, and believe in the gospel." LK And news of Him went out through all the surrounding region.

JN [g]So when He came to Galilee, [h]the Galileans received Him, having seen all the things He did in Jerusalem at the feast; for they also had gone to the feast. LK And He taught in their synagogues, being glorified by all.

JN So Jesus came again to [i]Cana of Galilee where He had made the water wine.

---

[a] GALILEE. Galilee was the northernmost region of Israel and the most heavily populated.

[b] THE GOSPEL . . . OF GOD. The good news of salvation both about God and from Him (cf. Rom. 1:1; Rom. 15:16; 1 Thess. 2:2, 8, 9; 1 Tim. 1:11; 1 Peter 4:17).

[c] THE TIME IS FULFILLED. Not time in a chronological sense, but the time for decisive action on God's part. With the arrival of the King, a new era in God's dealings with men had come. Cf. Gal. 4:4.

[d] THE KINGDOM OF GOD. God's sovereign rule over the sphere of salvation; at present in the hearts of His people (Luke 17:21) and in the future, in a literal, earthly kingdom (Rev. 20:4–6).

[e] AT HAND. Because the King was present.

[f] REPENT, AND BELIEVE. Repentance and faith are man's required response to God's gracious offer of salvation (cf. Acts 20:21; Rom. 1:16).

[g] SO WHEN. The episode of Jesus' healing of the official's son constitutes the second major "sign" of eight that John used to reinforce Jesus' true identity for producing belief in his readers. In this episode, Jesus chided the official's unbelief in needing a miraculous sign in order to trust in Christ (John 4:48). While some believe that this story is the same as the healing of the centurion's servant (Matt. 8:5–13; Luke 7:2–10), sufficient differences exist to demonstrate that it is different from the Synoptic account; e.g., (1) no evidence exists that the official's son was a Gentile; (2) the official's son, not his servant, was healed; and (3) Jesus was far more negative regarding the official's faith than the centurion's (Matt. 8:10). One may divide this section into three parts: (1) Jesus contemplating unbelief (John 4:43–45); (2) Jesus confronting unbelief (John 4:46–49); and (3) Jesus conquering unbelief (John 4:50–54).

[h] THE GALILEANS RECEIVED HIM. The apostle may have meant these words as irony, especially in light of the surrounding context of John 4:44, 48. The reception was likely that of curiosity seekers whose appetite centered more on seeing miracles than believing in Jesus as Messiah—as it had been at "the feast" (cf. John 2:23–25).

[i] CANA OF GALILEE. The deep irony of the statement in John 4:45 increases with the fact that Jesus had only recently performed a miracle in Cana at the wedding. Instead of responding in belief, the people wanted more. The basis of their welcome was extremely crass.

And there was a certain [j]nobleman whose son was sick at [k]Capernaum. When he heard that Jesus had come out of Judea into Galilee, he went to Him and [l]implored Him to come down and heal his son, for he was at the point of death. Then Jesus said to him, "[m]Unless you *people* see signs and wonders, you will by no means believe."

The nobleman said to Him, "Sir, come down before my child dies!"

Jesus said to him, "Go your way; [n]your son lives." So the man believed the word that Jesus spoke to him, and he went his way. And as he was now going down, his servants met him and told *him,* saying, "Your son lives!"

Then he inquired of them the hour when he got better. And they said to him, "Yesterday at [o]the seventh hour the fever left him." So the father knew that *it was* [p]at the same hour in which Jesus said to him, "Your son lives." And he himself believed, and his whole household.

This again *is* the second sign Jesus did when He had come out of Judea into Galilee.

---

[j] Nobleman. The Greek term means "royal official" and most likely designated someone officially in the service of King Herod Antipas, Tetrarch of Galilee from 4 BC to AD 39.

[k] Capernaum. Capernaum was approximately sixteen miles northeast of Cana.

[l] Implored Him. The language here indicates that he repeatedly begged Jesus to heal his son. His approach to Jesus was out of desperation, but he had little appreciation of who Jesus was. In light of John 4:46, apparently the nobleman's motivation centered in Jesus' reputation as a miracle worker rather than as Messiah.

[m] Unless you people see signs and wonders. The "you" is plural. Jesus addresses these words to the Galileans as a whole and not just to the nobleman. The response of the Galileans was fundamentally flawed, because it disregarded the person of Christ and centered in the need for a constant display of miraculous signs. Such an attitude represents the deepest state of unbelief.

[n] Your son lives. Jesus met the demands of Galilean unbelief by healing the official's son, revealing not only His sympathy, but also His marvelous graciousness in spite of such a faithless demand for miracles.

[o] The seventh hour. About 1:00 p.m., reckoning from sunrise (6:00 a.m.). Or, if using the Roman reckoning, about 7:00 p.m. starting from noon.

[p] At the same hour. The time when the official's son improved corresponded precisely with the time when the official had spoken with Jesus. This served to strengthen the nobleman's faith and, as a result, the "whole household" believed.

34. Jesus Is Rejected at Nazareth

Luke 4:16–30

LK So [a]He came to Nazareth, where He had been brought up. And [b]as His custom was, He went into the synagogue on the Sabbath day, and stood up to read. And He was handed the book of the prophet Isaiah. And when He had opened the book, He found the place where it was written:

"The Spirit of the LORD *is* upon Me,
Because [c]He has anointed Me
To preach the gospel to *the* poor;
He has sent Me to heal the brokenhearted,
To proclaim liberty to *the* captives
And recovery of sight to *the* blind,
To set at liberty those who are oppressed;
To proclaim [d]the acceptable year of the LORD."

Then He closed the book, and gave *it* back to the attendant and [e]sat down. And the eyes of all who were in the synagogue were fixed on Him. And He began to say to them, "Today [f]this Scripture is fulfilled in your hearing." So all bore witness to Him, and marveled at the gracious words which proceeded out of His mouth. And they said, "Is this not Joseph's son?"

---

[a] HE CAME TO NAZARETH. Luke acknowledged in 4:23 that Christ had already ministered in Capernaum. Yet Luke purposely situated this episode at the beginning of his account of Christ's public ministry. Here is an example of Luke's ordering things logically rather than chronologically.

[b] AS HIS CUSTOM WAS. Nazareth was His hometown, so He would have been well known to all who regularly attended this synagogue.

[c] HE HAS ANOINTED ME. i.e., the Spirit Himself was the anointing.

[d] THE ACCEPTABLE YEAR OF THE LORD. Or, "the year of the Lord's favor." The passage Christ read was Isa. 61:1–2. He stopped in the middle of v. 2. The rest of the verse prophesies judgment in the day of God's vengeance. Since that part of the verse pertains to the second advent, He did not read it.

[e] SAT DOWN. It was customary for a teacher to stand respectfully during the reading of the Scriptures and sit humbly to teach.

[f] THIS SCRIPTURE IS FULFILLED. This was an unambiguous claim that He was the Messiah who fulfilled the prophecy. They correctly understood His meaning but could not accept such lofty claims from One whom they knew so well as the carpenter's son (cf. Matt. 13:55).

He said to them, "You will surely say this proverb to Me, 'Physician, heal yourself! Whatever we have heard done in [g]Capernaum, do also here in Your country.'" Then He said, "Assuredly, I say to you, no prophet is accepted in his own country. But I tell you truly, many widows were in Israel in the days of Elijah, when the heaven was shut up three years and six months, and there was a great famine throughout all the land; but to none of them was Elijah sent except to [h]Zarephath, *in the region* of Sidon, to a woman *who was* a widow. And many lepers were in Israel in the time of Elisha the prophet, and none of them was cleansed except Naaman the Syrian."

So all those in the synagogue, when they heard these things, were [i]filled with wrath, and rose up and thrust Him out of the city; and they led Him to the brow of the hill on which their city was built, that they might throw Him down over the cliff. Then [j]passing through the midst of them, He went His way.

[g] Capernaum. Obviously Christ had already gained a reputation for His miraculous works in Capernaum. Scripture gives few details about that first year of public ministry. Most of what we know about those months is found in John's gospel, and it suggests Christ ministered mostly in Judea. However, John 2:12 mentions a brief visit to Capernaum, with no other details. John 4:46–54 describes how, while Christ was at Cana, He healed a nobleman's son who lay sick in Capernaum. We also know that Christ had already gathered some of His disciples, who were men from the north shore of the Sea of Galilee (John 1:35–42; cf. Matt. 4:18). He might have visited there more than once during that first year of ministry. In any case He had been there long enough to do miracles, and His fame had spread throughout Galilee (cf. Luke 4:14).

[h] Zarephath . . . Naaman. Both the widow of Zarephath (1 Kings 17:8–24) and Naaman the Syrian (2 Kings 5) were Gentiles. Both lived during times in Israel of widespread unbelief. Jesus' point was that God bypassed all the widows and lepers in Israel, yet showed grace to two Gentiles. God's concern for Gentiles and outcasts is one of the thematic threads that runs through Luke's gospel.

[i] filled with wrath. This is Luke's first mention of hostile opposition to Christ's ministry. What seems to have sparked the Nazarenes' fury was Christ's suggestion that divine grace might be withheld from them yet extended to Gentiles.

[j] passing through the midst of them. The implication is that this was a miraculous escape—the first of several similar incidents in which He escaped a premature death at the hands of a mob (cf. John 7:30; 8:59; 10:39).

35. Jesus' First Call of the Four

Matt. 4:13–22; Mark 1:16–20; Luke 4:31a

MT And [a]leaving Nazareth LK He went down MT and dwelt in [b]Capernaum, which is by the sea, LK a city of Galilee, MT in the regions of Zebulun and Naphtali, that it might be fulfilled which was spoken by Isaiah the prophet, saying:

"The land of Zebulun and the land of Naphtali,
By the way of the sea, beyond the Jordan,
[c]Galilee of the Gentiles:
The people who sat in darkness have seen a great light,
And upon those who sat in the region and shadow of death
Light has dawned."

[d]From that time Jesus began to preach and to say, "[e]Repent, for the kingdom of heaven is at hand."

---

[a] LEAVING NAZARETH. Some time elapsed between Matt. 4:12 and 13. Jesus' stay in Nazareth ended abruptly when He was violently rejected by the people of Nazareth, who tried to murder Him (see Luke 4:16–30).

[b] CAPERNAUM. He settled in this important town on the trade route at the north end of the Sea of Galilee. Capernaum was the home of Peter and Andrew, James and John, and Matthew (cf. Matt. 9:9). A comparison of the gospels reveals that Christ had already ministered extensively in Capernaum.

[c] GALILEE OF THE GENTILES. This name was used even in Isaiah's time because Galilee lay on the route through which all Gentiles passed in and out of Israel. In Jesus' time, the region of Galilee had become an important center of Roman occupation. The prophecy cited by Matthew is from Isa. 9:1–2. See also Isa. 42:6–7.

[d] FROM THAT TIME JESUS BEGAN TO PREACH. This marks the beginning of His public ministry. Note that His message was an exact echo of what John the Baptist preached.

[e] REPENT, FOR THE KINGDOM OF HEAVEN IS AT HAND. The opening word of this first sermon sets the tone for Jesus' entire earthly ministry (cf. Luke 5:32). Repentance was a constant motif in all His public preaching. And in His closing charge to the apostles, He commanded them to preach repentance as well (Luke 24:47).

And Jesus, walking by the [f]Sea of Galilee, saw [g]two brothers, Simon called Peter, and Andrew his brother, casting a [h]net into the sea; for they were fishermen. MK Then Jesus said to them, "[i]Follow Me, and I will make you become [j]fishers of men." They immediately left their nets and [k]followed Him.

When He had gone a little farther from there, MT He saw two other brothers, [l]James *the son* of Zebedee, and John his brother, in the boat with Zebedee their father, mending their nets. MK And immediately He called them, and they left their father Zebedee in the boat with the [m]hired servants, and went after Him.

---

[f] Sea of Galilee. Also known as the Sea of Chinnereth (Num. 34:11), the Lake of Gennesaret (Luke 5:1), and the Sea of Tiberias (John 6:1). A large, freshwater lake about thirteen miles long and seven miles wide, and about 690 ft. below sea level (making it the lowest body of freshwater on earth), the Sea of Galilee was home to a thriving fishing industry.

[g] two brothers, Simon . . . and Andrew. Jesus had encountered Simon Peter and Andrew before, near Bethabara, in the Jordan region, where Andrew (and perhaps Peter as well) had become a disciple of John the Baptist (John 1:35–42). They left John to follow Jesus for a time before returning to fishing in Capernaum. (Possibly, they had returned to their fishing business after John's arrest (cf. Mark 1:14).) Perhaps they had returned to Capernaum during Jesus' earlier ministry here. In any case they had already met and spent time with Jesus (cf. Matt. 4:18) but were here called to follow Him permanently.

[h] net. A rope forming a circle about nine feet in diameter with a net attached. It could be thrown by hand into the water, then hauled in by means of the length of weighted rope attached to it.

[i] Follow Me. Used frequently in the gospels in reference to discipleship (Matt. 4:19; 8:22; 9:9; 10:38; 16:24; 19:21; Mark 2:14; 8:34; 10:21; Luke 9:23, 59, 61; 18:22; John 1:43; 10:27; 12:26).

[j] fishers of men. Evangelism was the primary purpose for which Jesus called the apostles, and it remains the central mission for His people (cf. Matt. 28:19, 20; Acts 1:8).

[k] followed Him. i.e., became His permanent disciples.

[l] James the son of Zebedee, and John his brother. The second set of fishermen brothers called by Jesus. Their mother and Jesus' mother may have been sisters (Mark 15:40; cf. Matt. 27:55, 56 with John 19:25). If so, they were Jesus' cousins. James the son of Zebedee is easy to distinguish from the other men named James in the NT, because he is never mentioned in Scripture apart from his brother John. His martyrdom by Herod Agrippa I marked the beginning of a time of severe persecution in the early church (Acts 12:2).

[m] hired servants. This indicates that Zebedee's fishing business was a prosperous one and that he was a man of importance (cf. John 18:15).

36. Jesus Heals in the Synagogue in Capernaum

Mark 1:21–28; Luke 4:31b–37

MK Then they went into [a]Capernaum, LK and [He] was teaching [the people] on the Sabbaths.

MK And immediately on the Sabbath He entered the [b]synagogue and [c]taught. And they were astonished at His teaching, for He taught them as one having [d]authority, and not as the scribes.

Now there was a man in their synagogue LK who had a spirit of an [e]unclean demon. And [f]he cried out with a loud voice, MK saying, "Let *us* alone! [g]What have we to do with You, Jesus of Nazareth? Did You come to destroy us? I know who You are—the [h]Holy One of God!"

---

[a] CAPERNAUM. A prosperous fishing village on the northwest shore of the Sea of Galilee, Capernaum was a more important city than Nazareth; it contained a Roman garrison and was located on a major road. Jesus made the city His headquarters (cf. Mark 2:1) after His rejection at Nazareth (Matt. 4:13; Luke 4:16–31).

[b] SYNAGOGUE. The place where Jewish people gathered for worship *(synagogue* is a transliteration of a Greek word meaning "to gather together"). Synagogues originated in the Babylonian captivity after the 586 BC destruction of the temple by Nebuchadnezzar. They served as places of worship and instruction. Jesus frequently taught in the synagogues (cf. Mark 1:39; 3:1; 6:2), as did Paul (cf. Acts 13:5; 14:1; 17:1).

[c] TAUGHT. Mark frequently mentions Jesus' teaching ministry (cf. Mark 2:13; 4:1–2; 6:2, 6, 34; 10:1; 11:17; 12:35; 14:49).

[d] AUTHORITY. Jesus' authoritative teaching, as the spoken Word of God, was in sharp contrast to that of the scribes (experts in the OT Scriptures), who based their authority largely on that of other rabbis. Jesus' direct, personal, and forceful teaching was so foreign to their experience that those who heard Him were "astonished" (cf. Titus 2:15).

[e] UNCLEAN. i.e., morally impure. The term *unclean spirit* is used interchangeably in the NT with *demon.*

[f] HE CRIED OUT. Satan and his demon hosts opposed Jesus' work throughout His ministry, culminating in the cross. Jesus always triumphed over their futile efforts (cf. Col. 2:15), convincingly demonstrating His ultimate victory by His resurrection.

[g] WHAT HAVE WE TO DO WITH YOU? Or, possibly, "Why do you interfere with us?" The demon was acutely aware that he and Jesus belonged to two radically different kingdoms and thus had nothing in common. That the demon used the plural pronoun "we" indicates he spoke for all the demons.

[h] HOLY ONE OF GOD. Cf. Ps. 16:10; Dan. 9:24; Luke 4:34; Acts 2:27; 3:14; 4:27; Rev. 3:7. Amazingly, the demon affirmed Jesus' sinlessness and deity—truths which many in Israel denied and still deny. In the gospel accounts, demons always recognized Christ immediately (cf. Matt. 8:29; Mark 1:24; 3:11; 5:7; Luke 4:41; 8:28).

But Jesus rebuked him, saying, "[i]Be quiet, and come out of him!" And when the unclean spirit had convulsed him LK in *their* midst MK and cried out with a loud voice, LK it came out of him and did not hurt him. MK Then they were all amazed, so that they questioned among themselves, saying, "What is this? What new doctrine *is* this? LK What a word this *is!* MK For [j]with authority LK and power He commands even the unclean spirits, and they obey Him MK and they come out."

And immediately His fame spread LK and the report about Him went out into every place MK throughout all the LK surrounding region MK around Galilee.

[i] Be quiet. Jesus wanted no testimony to the truth from the demonic realm to fuel charges that He was in league with Satan (cf. Mark 3:22; Acts 16:16–18).

[j] with authority. Jesus had absolute authority in His actions as well as His words (Matt. 28:18).

37. Jesus Heals Peter's Mother-in-Law

Matthew 8:14–17; Mark 1:29–34; Luke 4:38–41

LK Now He arose from the synagogue. MK As soon as they had come out of the synagogue, they entered the house of Simon and Andrew, with James and John.

MT Now when Jesus had come into Peter's house, He saw [a]his wife's mother lying sick with a LK high [b]fever, MK and they told Him about her at once. LK They made request of Him concerning her, MK so He came and LK stood over her and rebuked the fever. MT He touched her hand MK and took her by the hand and lifted her up, MK and immediately the fever left her. LK And immediately she arose and served them.

MT When evening had come, LK when [c]the sun was setting, MK they brought to Him all who were sick and those who were [d]demon-possessed. And [e]the whole city was gathered together at the door.

MT And He cast out the spirits with a word, LK and He laid hands on MT all who were sick MK with various diseases, LK and healed them, MT that it might be fulfilled which was [f]spoken by Isaiah the prophet, saying:

---

[a] HIS WIFE'S MOTHER. i.e., Peter's mother-in-law. Paul also affirmed that Peter was married (in 1 Cor. 9:5). That his mother-in-law was living with Peter and his wife may indicate that her husband was dead.

[b] FEVER. That she was too ill to get out of bed, coupled with Luke's description of her fever as a "high fever" (Luke 4:38), suggests her illness was serious, even life-threatening. Of the gospel writers, only Luke, the physician, remarks that the fever was "high" and makes note of the means Jesus used to heal her.

[c] THE SUN WAS SETTING. Marking the close of the Sabbath and the easing of the restrictions associated with it. Specifically, rabbinic law prohibited carrying any burdens (such as stretchers) on the Sabbath. As soon as they were free to travel, the multitudes came.

[d] DEMON-POSSESSED. This means "demonized," or under the internal control of a demon. All of the cases of demonization dealt with by Christ involved the actual indwelling of demons who utterly controlled the bodies of their victims, even to the point of speaking through them (Mark 5:5–9), causing derangement (John 10:20), violence (Luke 8:29), or rendering them mute (Mark 9:17–22).

[e] THE WHOLE CITY WAS GATHERED. The report of Jesus' healing of the demon-possessed man in the synagogue and Peter's mother-in-law created a sensation in Capernaum and aroused the hopes of other sufferers.

[f] SPOKEN BY ISAIAH THE PROPHET. In Isa. 53:4–5, the prophet predicted that the Messiah would bear the consequences of the sins of men, namely the griefs and sorrows of life, though incredibly the Jews who watched Him die thought He was being punished by God for His own sins. Matthew found an analogical fulfillment of these words in Jesus' healing ministry (in Matt. 8:16–17), because sickness results from sin for which the Servant paid with His life (cf. 1 Peter 2:24). In eternity, all sickness will be removed, so ultimately it is included in the benefits of the atonement. Both physical healing and ultimate victory over death are guaranteed by Christ's atoning work, but these will not be fully realized until the very end (1 Cor. 15:26).

"He Himself took our infirmities
And bore our sicknesses."

LK And demons also came out of many, crying out and saying, "[g]You are the Christ, the Son of God!" And He, rebuking *them,* did not allow them to speak, for they knew that He was the Christ.

[g] You are the Christ. The demons' theology is absolutely orthodox (James 2:19); but though they know the truth, they reject it and God, who is its source.

38. Jesus Ministers Throughout Galilee

Matt. 4:23–24; Mark 1:35–39; Luke 4:42–44

LK Now when it was MK morning, having risen a long while before daylight, He went out and departed to a solitary place; and there He prayed.

MK And [a]Simon and those *who were* with Him searched for Him. LK The crowd sought Him and MK when [b]they found Him, LK came to Him, and tried to keep Him from leaving them. MK They said to Him, "Everyone is looking for You." But He said to them, LK "I must preach the [c]kingdom of God to the other cities also. MK Let us go into the next towns, that I may preach there also, LK because for this purpose I have been sent."

MT And Jesus went about [d]all Galilee, [e]teaching in their synagogues, preaching the gospel of the kingdom, MK casting out demons, MT and healing all kinds of sickness and all kinds of disease among the people. Then His fame went throughout all [f]Syria; and they brought to Him all sick people who were afflicted with various diseases and torments, and those who were demon-possessed, epileptics, and paralytics; and He healed them.

---

[a] SIMON AND THOSE WHO WERE WITH HIM. The first instance in the Gospels of Peter's assuming of leadership. Those with Peter are not revealed, though Andrew, James, and John were likely among them.

[b] THEY FOUND HIM. Finding Jesus after a diligent search, Peter and the others excitedly implored Him to return to Capernaum and capitalize on the excitement generated by the previous night's healings.

[c] KINGDOM OF GOD. This term, so prominent throughout the remainder of Luke's gospel, is introduced here for the first time (in Luke 4:43). Cf. Matt. 3:2.

[d] ALL GALILEE. This terse statement summarizes a preaching tour that must have lasted for weeks or even months (cf. Matt. 4:23, 24).

[e] TEACHING . . . PREACHING . . . HEALING. The three main aspects of Christ's public ministry.

[f] SYRIA. The area immediately northeast of Galilee.

39. Jesus' Second Call of the Four

Luke 5:1–11

LK So it was, as the multitude pressed about Him to hear the word of God, that He stood by the [a]Lake of Gennesaret, and saw two boats standing by the lake; but the fishermen had gone from them and were [b]washing *their* nets. Then He got into one of the boats, which was Simon's, and asked him to put out a little from the land. And He sat down and taught the multitudes from the boat.

When He had stopped speaking, He said to Simon, "Launch out into the deep and [c]let down your nets for a catch."

But Simon answered and said to Him, "Master, we have toiled all night and caught nothing; nevertheless at Your word I will let down the net." And when they had done this, they caught a great number of fish, and their net was breaking. So they signaled to *their* partners in the other boat to come and help them. And they came and filled both the boats, so that they began to sink. When Simon Peter saw *it,* he fell down at Jesus' knees, saying, "[d]Depart from me, for I am a sinful man, O Lord!"

For he and all who were with him were astonished at the catch of fish which they had taken; and so also *were* James and John, the sons of Zebedee, who were partners with Simon. And Jesus said to Simon, "Do not be afraid. From now on you will catch men." So when they had brought their boats to land, they forsook all and followed Him.

---

[a] Lake of Gennesaret. i.e., the Sea of Galilee, sometimes also called the Sea of Tiberius (John 6:1; 21:1). It is actually a large freshwater lake, over 690 feet below sea level and serves as the main source of water and commerce for the Galilee region.

[b] washing their nets. Having fished all night with nothing to show for their labor, they were drying and mending their nets for another night's work.

[c] let down your nets. Normally, the fish that were netted in shallow water at night would migrate during the daylight hours to waters too deep to reach easily with nets, which is why Peter fished at night. Peter, no doubt, thought Jesus' directive made no sense, but he obeyed anyway and was rewarded for his obedience.

[d] Depart from me. The remarkable catch of fish was clearly a miracle, astonishing to all the fishermen in Capernaum. Peter immediately realized he was in the presence of the Holy One exercising His divine power, and he was stricken with shame over his own sin. Cf. Ex. 20:19; 33:20; Judg. 13:22; Job 42:5–6; Isa. 6:5.

40. Jesus Heals a Leperous Man

Matt. 8:2–4; Mark 1:40–45; Luke 5:12–16

LK And it happened when He was in a certain city, that behold, a man who was [a]full of leprosy saw Jesus; and he fell on *his* face MT and worshiped Him, MK imploring Him, kneeling down to Him and saying to Him, MT "Lord, [b]if You are willing, You can make me clean."

Then Jesus, MK moved with [c]compassion, MT put out *His* hand and [d]touched him, MK and said to him, "I am willing; be cleansed."

As soon as He had spoken, [e]immediately the leprosy left him, and he was cleansed. And He strictly warned him and sent him away at once; LK He charged him to [f]tell no one MK and said to him, "See that you [g]say nothing to anyone; but [h]go your way, show yourself to the priest, and offer for your cleansing those [i]things

---

[a] FULL OF LEPROSY. Luke's emphasis suggests this was an extremely serious case of leprosy. Lepers were considered ceremonially unclean and were outcasts from society (Lev. 13:11). While the OT term for leprosy included other skin diseases (cf. Lev. 13:2), this man may have actually had true leprosy (Hansen's Disease), or else his cure would not have created such a sensation.

[b] IF YOU ARE WILLING. He had no doubt about Christ's power, only His will (cf. Mark 1:40–45).

[c] COMPASSION. Only Mark records Jesus' emotional reaction to the leper's desperate plight. The Greek word appears only in the Synoptic Gospels and (apart from parables) is used only in reference to Jesus.

[d] TOUCHED HIM. Unlike rabbis, who avoided lepers lest they become ceremonially defiled, Jesus expressed His compassion with a physical gesture.

[e] IMMEDIATELY. One of the characteristics of Jesus' healings was immediate and total wholeness. Cf. Matt. 8:13; Mark 5:29; Luke 17:14; John 5:9.

[f] TELL NO ONE. Publicity over such miracles might hinder Christ's mission and divert public attention from His message. Mark records that this is precisely what happened. In this man's exuberance over the miracle, he disobeyed; as a result Christ had to move His ministry away from the city and into the desert regions (Mark 1:45).

[g] SAY NOTHING TO ANYONE. The ensuing publicity would hinder Jesus' ability to minister (as in fact happened) and divert attention away from His message. Cf. Mark 3:12; 5:43; 7:36.

[h] GO YOUR WAY, SHOW YOURSELF TO THE PRIEST. The "priest" was the one on duty at the temple. Jesus commanded the healed leper to observe the OT regulations concerning cleansed lepers (Lev. 14:1–32). Until the required offerings had been made, the man remained ceremonially unclean.

which Moses commanded, [j]as a testimony to them." However, he went out and began to [k]proclaim *it* freely, and to spread the matter.

LK The report went around concerning Him all the more MK so that Jesus could [l]no longer openly enter the city, but was outside in [m]deserted places; and they came to Him from every direction. LK Great multitudes came together to hear, and to be healed by Him of their infirmities. So He Himself *often* withdrew into the wilderness and prayed.

---

[i] THINGS WHICH MOSES COMMANDED. A sacrifice of two birds, one of which was killed and the other set free (Lev. 14:4–7).

[j] AS A TESTIMONY TO THEM. i.e., the priests. The priest's acceptance of the man's offering would be public affirmation of his cure and cleansing.

[k] PROCLAIM IT FREELY. Only Mark records the cleansed leper's disobedience, although Luke hints at it (Luke 5:15).

[l] NO LONGER OPENLY ENTER THE CITY. The result of the leper's disobedience was that Jesus could no longer enter a city without being mobbed by those seeking to be cured of diseases. Jesus' ministry of teaching in that area thus came to a halt.

[m] DESERTED PLACES. Jesus kept to the relatively uninhabited regions to allow the excitement over His cure of the leper to die down. Luke also notes that He used His time in the wilderness for prayer (Luke 5:16).

41. Jesus Heals and Forgives a Paralytic

Matt. 9:1–8; Mark 2:1–12; Luke 5:17–26

MT So MK after *some* days MT He got into a boat, crossed over, and came to [a]His own city. MK And again He entered Capernaum.

LK Now it happened on a certain day, as He was teaching, that there were Pharisees and [b]teachers of the law sitting by, who had come out of every town of Galilee, Judea, and Jerusalem. MK And it was heard that [c]He was in the house. Immediately many gathered together, so that there was no longer room to receive *them,* not even near the door. And He preached [d]the word to them. LK And the power of the Lord was *present* to heal them.

MT Then behold, MK four *men* LK brought on a bed a man [e]who was paralyzed, whom they sought to bring in and lay before Him. LK And when they could not find how they might bring him in, because of the crowd, they went up on the housetop and MK they [f]uncovered the roof where He was. So when they had broken through, they LK let him down with *his* bed [g]through the tiling into the midst before Jesus.

---

[a] HIS OWN CITY. Capernaum (cf. Matt. 4:13). Jesus had left there to get away from the crowds for a time (Matt. 8:18).

[b] TEACHERS OF THE LAW. i.e., scribes. These Jewish leaders came from as far away as Jerusalem. His reputation had spread, and already the scribes and Pharisees were watching Him critically.

[c] HE WAS IN THE HOUSE. This is better translated, "He was at home." This was likely Peter's home, where Jesus had taken up temporary residence (cf. Matt. 4:13).

[d] THE WORD. The good news of the gospel, that salvation is by grace alone, through faith alone, for the forgiveness of sins.

[e] WHO WAS PARALYZED. Since he was lying on a bed, the man's paralysis was severe—perhaps he was a quadriplegic.

[f] UNCOVERED THE ROOF. Most homes in Israel had flat roofs used for relaxation in the cool of the day and for sleeping on hot nights. And there was usually an external stairway that extended to the roof. Often, as here, the roof was made of slabs of burnt or dried clay that were placed on supporting beams, which stretched from wall to wall. The builder then spread a uniform coat of fresh, wet clay over those slabs. The hardened clay served as a seal against the rain. The paralytic's friends took him up to the top of such a house and dug out the top coat of clay, removing several of the slabs until they made enough room to lower him down into Jesus' presence.

[g] THROUGH THE TILING. This appears to have been a home with roof tiles that, when removed, gave access to lower the man between the roof beams. The extreme measures they took to lay this man before Jesus indicate that the crowds following Him were very large. With the press of people around Jesus, it would have been impossible for men carrying a paralytic to get close enough to Him, even if they waited until He left the house.

MT [h]When Jesus saw their faith, He said to the paralytic, "Son, be of good cheer; [i]your sins are forgiven you." And at once MK some of the scribes LK and the Pharisees MK were sitting there and reasoning in their hearts, "Why does this *Man* speak [j]blasphemies like this? Who can forgive sins but God alone?"

LK But when Jesus, MT [k]knowing their thoughts, MK perceived [l]in His spirit that they reasoned thus within themselves, LK He answered and said to them, MT "Why do you think evil, LK reasoning MK about these things MT in your hearts? For [m]which is easier, to say MK to the paralytic, MT '*Your* sins are forgiven you,' or to say, 'Arise, MK take up your bed MT and walk'? [n]But that you may know that the [o]Son of Man has power on earth to forgive sins"—then He said to the paralytic, LK "I say to you, arise, take up your bed, and go to your house." Immediately he rose up before them, MK took up the bed LK he had been lying on, and departed MK in the presence of them all LK to his own house, glorifying God.

---

[h] When Jesus saw their faith. The aggressive, persistent effort of the paralytic's friends was visible evidence of their faith in Christ to heal.

[i] your sins are forgiven. Many Jews in that day believed that all disease and affliction was a direct result of one's sins. This paralytic may have believed that as well; thus he would have welcomed forgiveness of his sins before healing. The Greek verb for "are forgiven" refers to sending or driving away (cf. Ps. 103:12; Jer. 31:34; Mic. 7:19). Thus Jesus dismissed the man's sin and freed him from the guilt of it (cf. Matt. 9:2). Christ ignored the paralysis and addressed the man's greater need first. In doing so He asserted a prerogative that was God's alone (cf. Luke 7:49). His subsequent healing of the man's paralysis was proof that He had the authority to forgive sins as well.

[j] blasphemies. This would be a true judgment about anyone but God incarnate, for only the One who has been sinned against has the prerogative to forgive. Jesus' words to the man were therefore an unequivocal claim of divine authority. The scribes were correct in saying that only God can forgive sins (cf. Isa. 43:25), but incorrect in saying Jesus blasphemed. They refused to recognize Jesus' power as coming from God, much less that He Himself was God.

[k] knowing their thoughts. Cf. Matt. 12:25; Mark 13:32; Luke 2:52; John 2:24. Though the Lord Jesus humbled Himself (Phil. 2:4–8) and set aside the independent use of His divine prerogatives in incarnation (John 5:30), He was still fully God and, therefore, omniscient.

[l] in His spirit. This can also be translated, "by His spirit." This is not the Holy Spirit, but the omniscient mind of the Savior.

[m] which is easier. It is certainly easier to claim the power to pronounce absolution from sin than to demonstrate the power to heal. Christ actually proved His power to forgive by instantly healing the man of his paralysis. If He could do the apparently-harder, He could also do what seemed easier. The actual forgiving of the sins was in reality the more difficult task because it ultimately required Him to sacrifice His life.

[n] But that you may know. Jesus' power to heal the paralytic's physical infirmities proved the veracity of His claim and power to forgive sins. His ability to heal anyone and everyone at will—totally and immediately—was incontrovertible proof of His deity. As God, He had all authority to forgive sins. This was a decisive moment and should have ended once and for all the Pharisees' opposition. Instead, they began to try to discredit Him by charging Him with violating their Sabbath rules.

[o] Son of Man. Jesus used this term for Himself to emphasize His humiliation (cf. Matt. 8:20; Mark 14:62). It appears fourteen times in Mark's gospel (Mark 2:10, 28; 8:31, 38; 9:9, 12, 31; 10:33, 45; 13:26; 14:21, 41, 62).

MT Now when the multitudes saw *it*, LK they were all amazed, and MT they marveled and glorified God, who had given such power to men. LK And [they] were filled with fear, MK saying, "We never saw *anything* like this! LK We have seen [p]strange things today!"

---

[p] STRANGE THINGS. The response is curiously noncommittal—not void of wonder and amazement, but utterly void of true faith.

42. Jesus Calls Matthew to Follow Him

Matt. 9:9–13; Mark 2:13–17; Luke 5:27–32

MK Then He went out again by the sea; and all the multitude came to Him, and He taught them. LK After these things He went out and, MT as Jesus passed on from there, He saw a LK tax collector named [a]Levi, MK the *son* of Alphaeus [b]sitting at the tax office. And He said to MT Matthew, LK "Follow Me." So he [c]left all, [d]rose up, and followed Him.

Then Levi gave Him a great feast in his own house. MK Now it happened, as He MT sat at the table MK [e]dining in *Levi's* house, MT *that* behold, LK a [f]great number of [g]tax collectors MK and [h]sinners also MT came and MK [i]sat together with Jesus and His disciples; for there were many, and they followed Him. And when the [j]scribes and Pharisees saw Him eating with the tax collectors and sinners, they LK complained

---

[a] LEVI, THE SON OF ALPHAEUS. One of the twelve, more commonly known as Matthew. Levi was Matthew's name prior to his conversion.

[b] SITTING AT THE TAX OFFICE. Whereas Mark 2:14 and Luke 5:27 employ his former name, Levi, Matthew himself used the name by which he was known after becoming a disciple (cf. Mark 3:18; Luke 6:15). By using the name *Matthew*, he demonstrated his humility. He did not disguise his past or make any excuse for it. Tax collectors (or publicans) were among the most despised persons in this society. They were Jews who had bought tax franchises from the Roman government. The money they collected was often partly extorted for personal gain (cf. Luke 19:8) and partly a tax for Rome, which made them not only thieves, but also traitors to the Jewish nation (cf. Matt. 5:46; Mark 2:15).

[c] LEFT ALL. This implies an irreversible action.

[d] ROSE UP AND FOLLOWED HIM. This simple action of Matthew signified his conversion. Because his response was so immediate, it is likely Matthew was already convicted of his sin and recognized his need of forgiveness.

[e] DINING. This can also be translated "reclining at table," a common posture for eating when guests were present. According to Luke 5:29, this was a feast that Matthew gave in Jesus' honor.

[f] GREAT NUMBER OF TAX COLLECTORS. Levi's immediate response was to introduce his former comrades to Christ.

[g] TAX COLLECTORS. There were two categories of tax collectors: (1) *gabbay* collected general taxes on land and property, and on income, referred to as poll or registration taxes; (2) *mokhes* collected a wide variety of use taxes, similar to our import duties, business license fees, and toll fees. There were two categories of *mokhes*: great *mokhes* hired others to collect taxes for them; small *mokhes* did their own assessing and collecting. Matthew was a small *mokhes*. It is likely representatives of both classes attended Matthew's feast. All of them were considered both religious and social outcasts.

[h] SINNERS. A term the Jews used to describe people who had no respect for the Mosaic law or rabbinic traditions and were, therefore, the most vile and worthless of people.

against [MK] His disciples, [LK] saying, [MT] "Why does your Teacher [LK] [k]eat and drink with tax collectors and sinners?" [MK] When Jesus heard *it,* He [LK] answered and [MK] said to them, "Those who are [l]well have no need of a physician, but those who are sick. [MT] But [m]go and learn what *this* means: 'I desire mercy and not sacrifice.' For [n]I did not come to call the righteous, but sinners, to repentance."

---

[i] SAT TOGETHER. Lit. "were reclining with." Jesus' willingness to associate with tax collectors and sinners by sharing in the feast with them deeply offended the scribes and Pharisees.

[j] SCRIBES AND PHARISEES. Lit. "the scribes of the Pharisees." This phrase indicates that not all scribes were Pharisees. The Pharisees were a legalistic sect of Jews known for their strict interpretations and adherence to the law (cf. Matt. 3:7).

[k] EAT AND DRINK. Consorting with outcasts on any level—even merely speaking to them—was bad enough. Eating and drinking with them implied a level of friendship that was abhorrent to the Pharisees (cf. Luke 7:34; 15:2; 19:7).

[l] WELL . . . SICK. The Pharisees thought they were well—religiously pure and whole. The outcasts knew they were not. Salvation can't come to the self-righteous (i.e., those who think they are whole and therefore fail to seek healing).

[m] GO AND LEARN WHAT THIS MEANS. This phrase was commonly used as a rebuke for those who did not know something they should have known. The verse Jesus cites is Hos. 6:6 (cf. 1 Sam. 15:22; Mic. 6:6–8), which emphasizes the absolute priority of the law's moral standards over the ceremonial requirements. The Pharisees tended to focus on the outward, ritual, and ceremonial aspects of God's law—to the neglect of its inward, eternal, and moral precepts. In doing so, they became harsh, judgmental, and self-righteously scornful of others. Jesus repeated this same criticism in Matt. 12:7.

[n] I DID NOT COME TO CALL THE RIGHTEOUS. The words "to repentance" do not appear in the better (earliest) manuscripts of Matthew. They do appear, however, in Luke 5:32, a parallel passage. The repentant person—the one who recognizes he is a sinner and who turns from his sin—is the object of Jesus' call. The person who is sinful but thinks he is righteous refuses to acknowledge his need to repent of his sin. Cf. Matt. 9:12–13; John 9:39–41.

43. Jesus Answers the Disciples of John

Matt. 9:14–17; Mark 2:18–22; Luke 5:33–39

MK The [a]disciples of John and [b]of the Pharisees were [c]fasting. Then they came MT to Him, saying, "Why do we, MK the disciples of John, LK and likewise those of the Pharisees MT [d]fast often LK and make prayers, MK but Your disciples LK eat and drink [and] MT do not fast?"

MK And Jesus said to them, "Can the [e]friends of the bridegroom MT mourn as long as the bridegroom is with them? MK As long as they have the bridegroom with them they cannot fast. But the days will come when the bridegroom will be [f]taken away from them, and [g]then they will fast in those days."

---

[a] DISCIPLES OF JOHN. Those followers of John the Baptist who did not transfer their allegiance to Jesus (cf. John 3:30; Acts 19:1–7). At this time John was in prison (Matt. 4:12). Their question indicates they were observing the Pharisaic traditions (cf. Matt. 9:14).

[b] OF THE PHARISEES. Evidently, some Pharisees were still present when John's disciples came. Both groups together may have asked this question. The association of John's disciples with the Pharisees indicates that both groups were disturbed about the problem raised by Jesus' association with tax collectors and sinners.

[c] FASTING. The twice-a-week fast was a major expression of orthodox Judaism during Jesus' day (cf. Luke 18:9–14). Yet the OT prescribed only one fast, and that on the Day of Atonement (Lev. 16:29, 31).

[d] FAST OFTEN. Jesus did fast on at least one occasion (Matt. 4:2)—but privately, in accordance with His own teaching (cf. Matt. 6:16–18). The law also prescribed a fast on the Day of Atonement (Lev. 16:29–31; 23:27), but all other fasts were supposed to be voluntary, for specific reasons such as penitence and earnest prayer. The fact that these Pharisees raised this question shows that they thought of fasting as a public exercise to display one's own spirituality. Yet, the OT also rebuked hypocritical fasting (Isa. 58:3–6). Cf. Matt. 6:17; 9:15.

[e] FRIENDS OF THE BRIDEGROOM. In Jesus' illustration, the "friends of the bridegroom" were the attendants the bridegroom selected to carry out the festivities. That certainly was not a time to fast, which was usually associated with mourning or times of great spiritual need. Jesus' point was that the ritual practiced by John's disciples and the Pharisees was out of touch with reality. There was no reason for Jesus' followers to mourn and fast while enjoying the unique reality that He was with them.

[f] TAKEN AWAY FROM THEM. This refers to a sudden removal or being snatched away violently—an obvious reference to Jesus' capture and crucifixion.

[g] THEN THEY WILL FAST. Using the analogy of a wedding party, Jesus answered that as long as Christ was present with them, there was too much joy for fasting, which was connected to seasons of sorrow and intense prayer. An appropriate time for mourning would come at the crucifixion of Jesus.

LK Then He spoke a [h]parable to them: MK "No one sews a piece of [i]unshrunk cloth LK from a new garment MK on an old garment; or else the new piece LK makes a tear—MT for the patch pulls away from the garment, and the tear is made worse. LK And also the piece that was *taken* out of the new does not match the old.

MK "And no one puts [j]new wine into old wineskins; or else the new wine bursts the wineskins, the wine is spilled, and the wineskins are ruined. MT But they put new wine into [k]new wineskins. LK New wine must be put into new wineskins, and both are preserved. And no one, having drunk old *wine,* immediately desires new; for he says, [l]'The old is better.'"

---

[h] PARABLE. Jesus offered two parables to illustrate that His new and internal gospel of repentance from and forgiveness of sin could not be connected to or contained in the old and external traditions of self-righteousness and ritual.

[i] UNSHRUNK CLOTH. That new cloth does not work on old material is analogous to trying to patch New Covenant truth onto old Mosaic ceremonial forms.

[j] NEW WINE INTO OLD WINESKINS. Animal skins were used for fermentation of wine because of their elasticity. As the wine fermented, pressure built up, stretching the wineskin. A previously stretched skin lacked elasticity and would rupture, ruining both wine and wineskin. Jesus used this as an illustration to teach that the forms of old rituals, such as the ceremonial fastings practiced by the Pharisees and John's disciples, were not fit for the new wine of the New Covenant era (cf. Col. 2:17). In both analogies (vv. 16–17) the Lord was saying that what the Pharisees did in fasting or any other ritual had no part with the gospel.

[k] NEW WINESKINS. Newly made and unused wineskins provided the necessary strength and elasticity to hold up as wine fermented.

[l] 'THE OLD IS BETTER.' Those who had acquired a taste for Old Covenant ceremonies and Pharisaic traditions were loath to give them up for the new wine of Jesus' teaching. Luke alone adds this saying.

Part V | From Passover AD 28 to Passover AD 29

44. Jesus Heals a Lame Man on the Sabbath

John 5:1–18

JN After this there was a [a]feast of the Jews, and Jesus went up to Jerusalem. [b]Now [c]there is in Jerusalem by the [d]Sheep *Gate* a pool, which is called in Hebrew, [e]Bethesda, having five porches. In these [f]lay a great multitude of sick people, blind, lame, paralyzed, [g]waiting for the moving of the water. For an angel went down at a certain time into the pool and stirred up the water; then whoever stepped in first, after the stirring of the water, was made well of whatever disease he had. Now a

---

[a] FEAST OF THE JEWS. Throughout his gospel, John highlighted various Jewish feasts: John 2:13—Passover (AD 27); 6:4—Passover (AD 29); 7:2—Tabernacles; 10:22—Hanukkah or Feast of Dedication; and 11:55—Passover (AD 30). This reference is the only instance when he did not identify the particular feast occurring at the time, but it may refer to Passover (AD 28).

[b] NOW THERE IS. Although opposition to Jesus smoldered beneath the surface (e.g., John 2:13–20), the story of Jesus' healing at the Pool of Bethesda highlights the beginning of open hostility toward Him. The passage may be divided into three parts: (1) the miracle performed (John 5:1–9); (2) the Master persecuted (vv. 10–16); and (3) the murder planned (vv. 16–18).

[c] THERE IS . . . A POOL. Some have suggested that John wrote his gospel prior to the destruction of Jerusalem in AD 70, because his usage of "is" here implies that the pool still existed. However, John frequently used what is known as a "historical present" when speaking of past events, so this argument carries little weight.

[d] SHEEP GATE. Most likely this is a reference to the gate identified in Neh. 3:1, 32; 12:39. It was a small opening in the north wall of the city, just west of the northeast corner.

[e] BETHESDA. "Bethesda" is the Greek transliteration of a Hebrew (or Aramic) name meaning "house of outpouring."

[f] LAY. It was a custom at that time for people with infirmities to gather at this pool. Intermittent springs may have fed the pool and caused the disturbance of the water. Some ancient witnesses indicate that the waters of the pool were red with minerals and thus thought to have medicinal value.

[g] WAITING FOR THE MOVING OF THE WATER. The statement in the latter half of John 5:3, "waiting for the moving of the water," along with v. 4 (regarding the angel), are not original to the gospel. The earliest and best Greek manuscripts, as well as the early versions, exclude the reading. The presence of words or expressions unfamiliar to John's writings also militate against its inclusion.

certain man was there who had an infirmity [h]thirty-eight years. When Jesus saw him lying there, and [i]knew that he already had been *in that condition* a long time, He said to him, "Do you want to be made well?"

The sick man answered Him, "Sir, I have no man to put me into the pool when the water is stirred up; but while I am coming, another steps down before me."

Jesus said to him, "[j]Rise, take up your [k]bed and walk." And immediately the man was made well, [l]took up his bed, and walked. And that day was the Sabbath.

The Jews therefore said to him who was cured, "It is [m]the Sabbath; [n]it is not lawful for you to carry your bed." He answered them, "He who made me well said to me, 'Take up your bed and walk.'"

Then they asked him, "Who is the Man who said to you, 'Take up your bed and walk'?" But the one who was healed did not know who it was, for Jesus had withdrawn, a multitude being in *that* place. Afterward Jesus found him in the temple, and said to him, "See, you have been made well. [o]Sin no more, lest a worse thing come upon you."

---

[h] THIRTY-EIGHT YEARS. John included this figure to emphasize the gravity of the debilitating disease that afflicted the individual. Since his sickness had been witnessed by many people for almost four decades, when Jesus cured him everyone knew the genuineness of the healing.

[i] KNEW. The word implies supernatural knowledge of the man's situation (John 1:47–48; 4:17). Jesus picked the man out from among many sick people. The sovereign initiative was His, and no reason is given as to His choice.

[j] RISE, TAKE . . . WALK. In the same way that He spoke the world into being at creation, (Gen. 1:3), Jesus' spoken words had the power to cure (cf. John 1:3; 8:58; Gen. 1:1; Col. 1:16; Heb. 1:2).

[k] BED. The straw mat was not heavy. It could easily be rolled up, lifted, and carried by an able-bodied individual (cf. Mark 2:3).

[l] TOOK UP HIS BED, AND WALKED. This phrase emphasizes the completeness of the cure.

[m] THE SABBATH. The OT prohibited working on the Sabbath but did not stipulate what kind of "work" was specifically indicated (Ex. 20:8–11). Scripture implies that "work" consisted of one's regular employment, but rabbinical opinion had developed oral tradition beyond the OT, which stipulated thirty-nine activities that were forbidden (*Mishnah Shabbath* 7:2; 10:5), including transporting an item from one area to another. Thus, the man had broken oral tradition, not OT law.

[n] IT IS NOT LAWFUL. The phrase reveals that the Judaism during Jesus' time had largely become characterized by pious hypocrisy. Such hypocrisy especially enraged the Lord Jesus (cf. Matt. 22–23), who used this incident to set up a confrontation with Jewish hyperlegalism and identified the need for national repentance.

[o] SIN NO MORE, LEST A WORSE THING COME UPON YOU. The basic thrust of Jesus' comments here indicates that sin has its inevitable consequences (cf. Gal 6:7, 8). Although Scripture makes clear that not all disease is a consequence of sin (cf. 9:1–3; Luke 13:1–5), illness at times may be directly tied into one's moral turpitude (cf. 1 Cor. 11:29, 30; James 5:15). Jesus may specifically have chosen this man in order to highlight this point.

The man departed and told the Jews that it was Jesus who had made him well.

For this reason the Jews [p]persecuted Jesus, and sought to kill Him, because He had done these things [q]on the Sabbath.

But [r]Jesus answered them, "[s]My Father has been working until now, and I have been working."

Therefore the Jews sought all the more to kill Him, because He not only broke the Sabbath, but also said that God was His Father, making Himself [t]equal with God.

---

[p] persecuted. The verb tense means that the Jewish leaders repeatedly persecuted Jesus, i.e., continued hostile activity. This was not an isolated incident of their hatred toward Him because of His healings on the Sabbath (cf. Mark 3:1–6).

[q] on the Sabbath. Jesus did not break God's law since in it there was no prohibition of doing good on that day (Mark 2:27). However, Jesus disregarded the oral law that the Pharisees had developed, i.e., "the traditions of men" (cf. also Matt. 15:1–9). Most likely, Jesus deliberately practiced such healing on the Sabbath to provoke a confrontation with their religious hypocrisy that blinded them to the true worship of God.

[r] Jesus answered. This begins one of the greatest Christological discourses in Scripture. In John 5:17–47, Jesus makes five claims to equality with God: (1) He is equal with God in His person (vv. 17–18); (2) He is equal with God in His works (vv. 19–20); (3) He is equal with God in His power and sovereignty (v. 21); (4) He is equal with God in His judgment (v. 22); and (5) He is equal with God in His honor (v. 23).

[s] My Father has been working. Jesus' point is that God is continuously at work, and since Jesus Himself worked continuously, He also must be God. Furthermore, God does not need a day of rest, for He never wearies (Isa. 40:28). For Jesus' assertion to be true, the same attributes that apply to God must also apply to Him. Jesus is Lord of the Sabbath (Matt. 12:8)! Interestingly, even the rabbis admitted that God's work had not ceased after the Sabbath, because He sustains the universe.

[t] equal with God. This verse confirms that the Jews instantly grasped the implications of His remarks that He was God.

45. Jesus Defends His Equality with the Father

John 5:19–47

JN Then Jesus answered and said to them, "[a]Most assuredly, I say to you, the Son can do nothing of Himself, but what He sees the Father do; for whatever He does, the Son also does in like manner. For the Father loves the Son, and shows Him all things that He Himself does; and He will show Him [b]greater works than these, that you may marvel. For as the Father raises the dead and gives life to *them,* even so the Son gives life to whom He will. For the Father judges no one, but has committed all judgment to the Son, that all should [c]honor the Son just as they [d]honor the Father. He who does not honor the Son does not honor the Father who sent Him.

"Most assuredly, I say to you, he who hears My word and believes in Him who sent Me has everlasting life, and shall not come into judgment, but has [e]passed from death into life. Most assuredly, I say to you, the [f]hour is coming, and now

---

[a] MOST ASSUREDLY. This is an emphatic way of saying, "I'm telling you the truth." In response to Jewish hostility at the implications of His assertions of equality with God, Jesus became even more fearless, forceful, and emphatic. Jesus essentially tied His activities of healing on the Sabbath directly to the Father. The Son never took independent action that opposed the Father's will because the Son only did those things that were in perfect agreement with the Father. Jesus thus implied His equality to the Father, since He alone could do what the Father does.

[b] GREATER WORKS. This refers to the powerful work of raising the dead. God has that power (cf. 1 Kings 17:17–24; 2 Kings 4:32–37; 5:7), and so does the Lord Jesus (John 5:21–29; 11:25–44; 14:19; 20:1–18).

[c] HONOR THE SON. This verse explains why God bestowed all judgment to the Son, i.e., so that "all men should honor the Son just as they honor the Father." Jesus is not a mere herald sent from the heavenly court. He is the King Himself, possessing full equality with the Father (cf. Phil. 2:9–11).

[d] HONOR THE FATHER. Jesus turned the tables on His opponents who accused Him of blasphemy. Instead, Jesus affirmed that the only way anyone can honor the Father is through receiving the Son. Therefore, the Jews were the ones who actually blasphemed the Father by rejection of His Son.

[e] PASSED FROM DEATH INTO LIFE. This develops the truth of John 5:21, that Jesus gives life to whomever He desires. The people who receive that life are here identified as those who hear the Word and believe in the Father and the Son. They are the people who have eternal life and never will be condemned (Rom. 8:1; Col. 1:13).

[f] HOUR IS COMING, AND NOW IS. Cf. John 4:23. This phrase reveals an already/not yet tension regarding the resurrection. Those who are born again are already "spiritually" resurrected ("now is"; Eph. 2:1; Col. 2:13), and yet a future physical resurrection still awaits them ("hour is coming"; 1 Cor. 15:35–54; Phil. 3:20–21).

is, when [g]the dead will hear the voice of the Son of God; and those who hear will live. For as the Father has life in Himself, so [h]He has granted the Son to have life in Himself, and has given Him authority to execute judgment also, because He is the Son of Man. Do not marvel at this; for the hour is coming in which all who are in the graves will hear His voice and come forth— [i]those who have done good, to the resurrection of life, and those who have done evil, to the resurrection of condemnation. I can of Myself do nothing. As I hear, I judge; and My judgment is righteous, because I do not seek My own will but [j]the will of the Father who sent Me.

"[k]If I bear witness of Myself, My witness is not true. There is another who bears witness of Me, and I know that the witness which He witnesses of Me is true. You have sent to John, and he has borne witness to the truth. Yet I do not receive testimony from man, but I say these things that you may be saved. He was the burning and shining lamp, and you were willing for a time to rejoice in his light. But I have a greater witness than John's; for the works which the Father has given Me to finish— [l]the very works that I do—bear witness of Me, that the Father has

---

[g] THE DEAD WILL HEAR. The theme of these verses is resurrection. Jesus related that all men, saved and unsaved, will be literally and physically resurrected from the dead. However, only the saved experience a spiritual ("born again"), as well as physical, resurrection unto eternal life. The unsaved will be resurrected unto judgment and eternal punishment through separation from God (i.e., the second death; cf. Rev. 20:6, 14; 21:8). These verses also constitute proof of the deity of Jesus Christ, since the Son has resurrection power (John 5:25–26), and the Father has granted Him the status of Judge of all mankind (v. 27). In the light of other Scripture, it is clear that Jesus speaks generally about resurrection, but not about one, general resurrection (cf. Dan. 12:2; 1 Cor. 15:23; 1 Thess. 4:16).

[h] HE HAS GRANTED THE SON. The Son from all eternity had the right to grant life (John 1:4). The distinction involves Jesus' deity versus His incarnation. In becoming a man Jesus voluntarily set aside the independent exercise of His divine attributes and prerogatives (Phil. 2:6–11). Jesus here affirmed that even in His humanity, the Father granted Him "life-giving" power, i.e., the power of resurrection.

[i] THOSE WHO HAVE DONE GOOD . . . EVIL. Jesus was not teaching justification by works (cf. John 6:29). In the context, the "good" is believing on the Son so as to receive a new nature that produces good works (John 3:21; James 2:14–20), while the "evil" done is to reject the Son (the unsaved) and hate the light, which has the result of evil deeds (John 3:1819). In essence, works merely evidence one's nature as saved or unsaved (cf. Rom. 2:5–10), but human works never determine one's salvation.

[j] THE WILL OF THE FATHER. In summarizing all He has said about His equality with God, Jesus claimed that the judgment He exercised was because everything He did was dependent upon the Father's word and will.

[k] IF I BEAR WITNESS. The background of these verses is Deut. 17:6; 19:15, where witnesses were to establish the truthfulness of a matter (cf. John 1:7). Jesus Himself emphasized the familiar theme of witnesses who testify to the identity of the Son: (1) John the Baptist (John 5:32–35); (2) Jesus' works (vv. 35–36); (3) the Father (vv. 37–38); and (4) the OT Scriptures (vv. 39–47).

[l] THE VERY WORKS THAT I DO. Cf. John 10:25. The miracles of Jesus were witness to His deity and messiahship. Such miracles are the major signs recorded by John in this gospel, so as to fulfill his purpose in John 20:30–31.

sent Me. And the [m]Father Himself, who sent Me, has testified of Me. You have neither heard His voice at any time, nor seen His form. But you do not have His word abiding in you, because whom He sent, Him you do not believe. [n]You search the Scriptures, for in them you think you have eternal life; and these are they which [o]testify of Me. But you are [p]not willing to come to Me that you may have life.

"I do not receive [q]honor from men. But I know you, that you do not have the love of God in you. I have come in My Father's name, and you do not receive Me; if another comes in his own name, [r]him you will receive. How can you believe, who receive honor from one another, and do not seek the honor that *comes* from the only God? Do not think that I shall accuse you to the Father; there is *one* who accuses you—Moses, in whom you trust. For if you believed [s]Moses, you would believe Me; for he wrote about Me. But if you do not believe his writings, how will you believe My words?"

---

[m] Father . . . has testified. Cf. Matt. 3:17; Mark 1:11; Luke 3:22.

[n] You search. Although the verb *search* could also be understood as a command (i.e., "Search the Scriptures!"), most prefer this translation as an indicative. The verb implies diligent scrutiny in investigating the Scriptures to find "eternal life." However, Jesus points out that with all their fastidious effort, they miserably failed in their understanding of the true way to eternal life through the Son of God (cf. Matt. 19:16–25; cf. 14:6; 2 Tim. 3:15).

[o] testify of Me. Christ is the main theme of Scripture.

[p] not willing. They searched for eternal life, but were not willing to trust its only source (John 1:11; 3:19; 5:24).

[q] honor from men. If Jesus agreed to be the kind of Messiah the Jews wanted, providing miracles and food along with political and military power, He would receive honor from them. But He sought only to please God.

[r] him you will receive. The Jewish historian, Josephus, records that a number of messianic pretenders arose in the years before AD 70. This verse contrasts the Jewish rejection of their true Messiah because they did not love or know God with their willing acceptance of charlatans.

[s] Moses . . . for he wrote about Me. Jesus does not mention any specific passage in the five books of Moses, although there are many (e.g., Deut. 18:15; cf. 1:21; 4:19; 6:14; 7:40, 52).

46. The Disciples Pick Grain on the Sabbath

Matt. 12:1–8; Mark 2:23–28; Luke 6:1–5

MK Now it happened MT at that time, LK on the second Sabbath after the first that MT Jesus went through the [a]grainfields [b]on the Sabbath. And His disciples were hungry.

MK And as they went His disciples began to [c]pluck the heads of grain MT and to eat LK *them,* rubbing *them* in *their* hands. MT And when LK some of MT the Pharisees saw *it,* they said to Him, "Look, LK why are MT Your disciples LK doing what is [d]not lawful to do on the Sabbath?"

MK But [e]He said to them, [f]"Have you never LK even read this, MK what [g]David did when he was in need and hungry, MT he and those who were with him: MK how he

[a] GRAINFIELDS. The roads in first-century Israel were primarily major arteries; so once travelers left those main roads, they walked along wide paths that bordered and traversed pastures and grainfields.

[b] ON THE SABBATH. "Sabbath" transliterates a Hebrew word that refers to a ceasing of activity or rest. In honor of the day when God rested from His creation of the world (Gen. 2:3), the Lord declared the seventh day of the week to be a special time of rest and remembrance for His people, which He incorporated into the Ten Commandments (Ex. 20:8). But hundreds of years of rabbinical teaching had added numerous unbearable and arbitrary restrictions to God's original requirement, one of which forbade any travel beyond three thousand feet of one's home (cf. Num. 35:5; Josh. 3:4).

[c] PLUCK THE HEADS OF GRAIN. Travelers who did not take enough food for their journey were permitted by Mosaic law to pick enough grain to satisfy their hunger (Deut. 23:24–25; cf. Matt. 12:2).

[d] NOT LAWFUL TO DO ON THE SABBATH. Actually, no OT law prohibited the plucking of grain in order to eat on the Sabbath. Gleaning handfuls of grain from a neighbor's field to satisfy one's immediate hunger was explicitly permitted (Deut. 23:25). What was prohibited was labor for the sake of profit (Ex. 34:21), but that was obviously not the situation here. Thus a farmer could not harvest for profit on the Sabbath, but an individual could glean enough grain to eat. Additionally, rabbinical tradition had interpreted the rubbing of grain in the hands (cf. Luke 6:1) as a form of threshing and forbidden it. In reality the Pharisees' charge was itself sinful, since they were holding their tradition on a par with God's Word (cf. Matt. 15:2–9).

[e] HE SAID. Jesus' answer points out that the Sabbath laws do not restrict deeds of necessity, service to God, or acts of mercy . He reaffirmed that the Sabbath was made for man's benefit and God's glory. It was never intended to be a yoke of bondage to the people of God.

[f] "HAVE YOU NEVER . . ."" Jesus' sarcasm pointed out the main fault of the Pharisees, who claimed to be experts and guardians of Scripture, yet were ignorant of what it actually taught (cf. Rom. 2:17–24). Christ's rebuke suggests that they were culpable for their ignorance of so basic a truth (cf. Matt. 12:5; 19:4; 21:16, 42; 22:31;).

[g] DAVID. David and his companions were fleeing for their lives from Saul when they arrived at Nob, where the tabernacle was located at that time. Because they were hungry, they asked for food (cf. 1 Sam. 21:1–6).

went into the house of God [h]*in the days* of Abiathar the high priest, and ate [i]the showbread, LK and also gave some to those MK who were with him, MT which was not lawful for him to eat, nor for those who were with him, [nor] LK for any but the priests?

MT "Or have you not read in the law that on the Sabbath the priests in the temple [j]profane the Sabbath, and are blameless? Yet I say to you that in this place there is *One* [k]greater than the temple. But if you had known what *this* means, 'I desire [l]mercy and not sacrifice,' you would not have condemned the guiltless." MK And He said to them, "The [m]Sabbath was made for man, and not man for the Sabbath. Therefore [n]the Son of Man is also Lord of the Sabbath."

---

[h] IN THE DAYS OF ABIATHAR THE HIGH PRIEST. The phrase "in the days" can mean "during the lifetime." According to 1 Sam. 21:1, Ahimelech was the priest who gave the bread to David. Abiathar was Ahimelech's son, who later was the high priest during David's reign. Since Ahimelech died shortly after this incident (cf. 1 Sam. 22:19–20), it is likely that Mark simply added this designation to identify the well-known companion of David who later became the high priest, along with Zadok (2 Sam. 15:35).

[i] THE SHOWBREAD. Twelve loaves of unleavened bread (representing the twelve tribes of Israel) were placed on the table in the sanctuary and at the end of the week replaced with fresh ones. The consecrated bread of the Presence was usually eaten by the priests only (Lev. 24:5–9). While it was not normally lawful for David and his companions to eat this showbread, neither did God want them to starve, so nowhere does Scripture condemn them for eating (1 Sam. 21:4–6).

[j] PROFANE THE SABBATH, AND ARE BLAMELESS. i.e., the priests have to do their work on the Sabbath, proving that some aspects of the Sabbath restrictions are not inviolable moral absolutes, but rather precepts pertaining to the ceremonial features of the law.

[k] GREATER THAN THE TEMPLE. This was a straightforward claim of deity. The Lord Jesus was God incarnate—God dwelling in human flesh—far superior to a building that God merely visited.

[l] MERCY AND NOT SACRIFICE. Quoted from Hos. 6:6.

[m] SABBATH WAS MADE FOR MAN. God instituted the Sabbath to benefit man by giving him a day to rest from his labors and to be a blessing to him. The Pharisees turned it into a burden and made man a slave to their myriad of man-made regulations.

[n] THE SON OF MAN IS ALSO LORD OF THE SABBATH. Again, this was an inescapable claim of deity—and as such it prompted the Pharisees' outrage. Based on His divine authority, Jesus could, in fact, reject the Pharisaic regulations concerning the Sabbath and restore God's original intention for Sabbath observance to be a blessing, not a burden.

47. Jesus Heals a Man's Hand on the Sabbath

Matt. 12:9–14; Mark 3:1–6; Luke 6:6–11

LK Now it happened MT when He had departed from there, LK on another Sabbath, MT He went into their [a]synagogue MK again LK and taught. MT [b]And behold, LK a man was there whose right hand was [c]withered. So the scribes and Pharisees watched Him closely, [d]whether He would heal on the Sabbath, that they might find [e]an accusation against Him. MT And they asked Him, saying, "[f]Is it lawful to heal on the Sabbath?"—that they might accuse Him.

LK But He [g]knew their thoughts, and said to the man who had the withered hand, "Arise, MK step forward, LK and [h]stand here." And he arose and stood. Then

---

[a] SYNAGOGUE. The Jews' local places of assembly and worship.

[b] AND BEHOLD. This is the last of the five conflict episodes (in this section of Mark's gospel), which began in Mark 2:1 (2:1–11; 13–17; 18–22; 23–28), and, as such, it gives a sense of climax to the growing antagonism between Jesus and the Jewish leaders. In this encounter, Jesus gave the Pharisees a living illustration of scriptural Sabbath observance and His sovereign authority over both man and the Sabbath.

[c] WITHERED. This describes a condition of paralysis or deformity from an accident, a disease, or a congenital defect.

[d] WHETHER HE WOULD HEAL ON THE SABBATH. The scribes and Pharisees spotted the man with the withered hand and, with Christ present, they immediately knew that this would be an occasion for the man's healing. In stark contrast to all other so-called healers, Christ was not selective. He healed all who came to Him (Matt. 8:16; Luke 4:40; 6:19).

[e] AN ACCUSATION. The Pharisees were not open to learning from Jesus, but only looked for an opportunity to charge Him with a violation of the Sabbath, an accusation they could bring before the Sanhedrin.

[f] IS IT LAWFUL TO HEAL ON THE SABBATH? Jewish tradition prohibited the practice of medicine on the Sabbath, except in life-threatening situations. But no actual law in the OT forbade the giving of medicine, healing, or any other acts of mercy on the Sabbath. It is always lawful to do good.

[g] KNEW THEIR THOUGHTS. Cf. Matt. 9:4; Luke 5:22.

[h] STAND HERE. Jesus purposely did this miracle openly, before all, as if to demonstrate His contempt for the Pharisees' man-made regulations.

Jesus said to them, "I will ask you one thing: MK "[i]Is it lawful on the Sabbath [j]to do [k]good or to do [l]evil, to save life or to kill?" [m]But they kept silent.

MT Then [n]He said to them, "What man is there among you who has one sheep, and if it falls into a pit on the Sabbath, will not lay hold of it and lift *it* out? Of how much more value then is a man than a sheep? Therefore it is lawful to do good on the Sabbath." MK And when He had [o]looked around at them LK all MK with [p]anger, being grieved by the [q]hardness of their hearts, He said to the man, "Stretch out your hand." MT And he stretched *it* out, and his hand was restored as whole as the other.

---

[i] IS IT LAWFUL. A reference to the Mosaic law. Jesus was forcing the Pharisees to examine their tradition regarding the Sabbath to see if it was consistent with God's OT law.

[j] TO DO GOOD . . . EVIL, TO SAVE . . . KILL. Christ used a device common in the Middle East—He framed the issue in terms of clear-cut extremes. The obvious implication is that failure to do good or save a life was wrong and not in keeping with God's original intention for the Sabbath (cf. Matt. 12:10; Mark 2:27).

[k] GOOD. The Sabbath laws forbade labor for profit, frivolous diversions, and things extraneous to worship. Activity, per se, was not unlawful. Good works were especially appropriate on the Sabbath—particularly deeds of charity, mercy, and worship. Works necessary for the preservation of life were also permitted. To corrupt the Sabbath to forbid such works was a perversion of God's design. Cf. Matt. 12:2, 3.

[l] EVIL. Refusal to do good is tantamount to doing evil (James 4:17).

[m] BUT THEY KEPT SILENT. The Pharisees refused to answer Jesus' question and by so doing implied that their Sabbath views and practices were false.

[n] HE SAID TO THEM. Jesus countered the Pharisees with a question that elevated the issue at hand from a legal to a moral problem.

[o] LOOKED AROUND AT THEM. i.e., giving them a chance to respond to His question. Evidently no one did.

[p] ANGER. Definite displeasure with human sin reveals a healthy, moral nature. Jesus' reaction was consistent with His divine nature and proved that He is the righteous Son of God. This kind of holy indignation with sinful attitudes and practices was to be more fully demonstrated when Jesus cleansed the temple (cf. Matt. 21:12, 13; Mark 11:15–18; Luke 19:45–48).

[q] HARDNESS OF THEIR HEARTS. This phrase refers to an inability to understand because of a rebellious attitude (Ps. 95:8; Heb. 3:8, 15). The Pharisees' hearts were becoming more and more obstinate and unresponsive to the truth (cf. Mark 16:14; Rom. 9:18).

MT Then [r]the Pharisees LK were [s]filled with rage. MK [They] went out and immediately plotted with the [t]Herodians against Him, LK and discussed with one another what they might do to Jesus—MK how they might destroy Him.

---

[r] THE PHARISEES . . . PLOTTED. They absolutely refused to be persuaded by anything Jesus said and did (cf. John 3:19), but were instead determined to kill Him. The Greek word for "plotted" (lit. "counseled together") includes the notion of carrying out a decision already made—the Pharisees were simply discussing how to implement theirs.

[s] FILLED WITH RAGE. A curious response in the face of so glorious a miracle. Such irrational hatred was their response to having been publicly humiliated—something they hated worse than anything (cf. Matt. 23:6–7). They were unable to answer His reasoning. And furthermore, by healing the man with only a command, He had performed no actual "work" that they could charge Him with. Desperately seeking a reason to accuse Him, they could find none. Their response was blind fury.

[t] HERODIANS. This secular political party, which took its name from Herod Antipas and was strong in its support for Rome, opposed the Pharisees on nearly every issue, but were willing to join forces with them because both desperately wanted to destroy Jesus. Cf. Matt. 22:16.

48. Jesus Withdraws to the Sea of Galilee

Matt. 4:25; 12:15–21; Mark 3:7–12

MT But when Jesus knew *it,* He withdrew from there MK with His disciples to the sea. MT And [a]great multitudes followed Him MK from Galilee and from Judea and Jerusalem and [b]Idumea MT and *from* [c]Decapolis MK and [d]beyond the Jordan; and those from [e]Tyre and Sidon, a great multitude, when they heard how many things He was doing, came to Him. MT And He [f]healed them all. Yet He warned them not to make Him known, that it might be fulfilled which was spoken by Isaiah the prophet, saying:

"[g]Behold! My Servant whom I have chosen,
My Beloved in whom My soul is well pleased!
I will put My Spirit upon Him,
And He will declare justice to the Gentiles.

---

[a] GREAT MULTITUDES. In spite of His conflicts with the Pharisees, Jesus remained very popular with the ordinary people.

[b] IDUMEA. An area southeast of Judea, mentioned only here in the NT and populated by many Edomites (originally descendants of Esau, cf. Gen. 36:43). By this time it had become mostly Jewish in population and was considered a part of Judea.

[c] DECAPOLIS. A confederation of ten Hellenized cities south of Galilee and mostly east of the Jordan. The league of cities was formed shortly after Pompey's invasion of Israel (ca. 64 BC) to preserve Greek culture in the Semitic region. These cities were naturally Gentile strongholds.

[d] BEYOND THE JORDAN. The region east of the Jordan River, also called Perea, and ruled by Herod Antipas. Its population contained a large number of Jews.

[e] TYRE AND SIDON. Two Phoenician cities on the Mediterranean coast, north of Galilee. Phoenicia as a whole was often designated by these cities (cf. Jer. 47:4; Joel 3:4; Matt. 11:21; Acts 12:20).

[f] HEALED THEM ALL. In all of OT history there was never a time or a person who exhibited such extensive healing power. Physical healings were very rare in the OT. Christ chose to display His deity by healing, raising the dead, and liberating people from demons. That not only showed the Messiah's power over the physical and spiritual realms, but also demonstrated the compassion of God toward those affected by sin. Cf. John 11:35.

[g] BEHOLD! MY SERVANT. Matthew 12:18–21 is quoted from Isa. 42:1–4, to demonstrate that (contrary to the typical first-century rabbinical expectations) the Messiah would not arrive with political agendas, military campaigns, and great fanfare, but with gentleness and meekness—declaring righteousness even "to the Gentiles."

He will [h]not quarrel nor cry out,
Nor will anyone hear His voice in the streets.
A [i]bruised reed He will not break,
And smoking flax He will not quench,
Till He sends forth justice to victory;
And in His name Gentiles will trust."

MK So He told His disciples that a small boat should be kept ready for Him because of the multitude, lest they should crush Him. For He healed many, so that as many as had [j]afflictions pressed about Him to touch Him. And the [k]unclean spirits, [l]whenever they saw Him, fell down before Him and cried out, saying, [m]"You are the Son of God." But He sternly [n]warned them that they should not make Him known.

---

[h] NOT QUARREL NOR CRY OUT. The Messiah would not try to stir up a revolution or force His way into power.

[i] BRUISED REED . . . SMOKING FLAX. The reed was used by shepherds to fashion a small musical instrument. Once cracked or worn, it was useless. A smoldering wick was also useless for giving light. These represent people who are deemed useless by the world. Christ's work was to restore and rekindle such people, not to "break" them or "quench" them. This speaks of His tender compassion toward the lowliest of the lost. He came not to gather the strong for a revolution, but to show mercy to the weak. Cf. 1 Cor. 1:26–29.

[j] AFFLICTIONS. Lit. "a whip, a lash," sometimes translated "plagues," or "scourges." This metaphorically describes various painful, agonizing, physical ailments and illnesses.

[k] UNCLEAN SPIRITS. This refers to demons (cf. Mark 1:23; Luke 4:41).

[l] WHENEVER THEY SAW HIM. The tense of the Greek verb means there were many times when demons looked at Jesus and contemplated the truth of His character and identity.

[m] "YOU ARE THE SON OF GOD." Cf. Mark 1:24. The demons unhesitatingly affirmed the uniqueness of Jesus' nature, which the gospel writers saw as clear proof of Jesus' deity.

[n] WARNED THEM THAT THEY SHOULD NOT MAKE HIM KNOWN. Jesus always rebuked demons for their testimonies about Him. He wanted His teaching and actions, not the impure words of demons, to proclaim who He was (cf. Mark 1:25; Acts 16:16–18). In Matthew's account, Jesus' warning was also directed toward the multitudes, not to publicize His miraculous deeds. Christ was likely concerned about the potential zealotry of those who would try to press Him into the conquering-hero mold that the rabbinical experts had interpreted from messianic prophecy.

49. Jesus Appoints the Twelve

Mark 3:13–19a; Luke 6:12–19

LK Now it came to pass in those days that MK He went up on the mountain LK to pray, and [a]continued all night in prayer to God. And when it was day, [b]He called His disciples to *Himself*—MK [c]those He Himself wanted. And they came to Him.

LK And from them He chose twelve whom He also named apostles. MK He [d]appointed twelve, that they might be with Him and that He might send them out to preach, and to [e]have power to heal sicknesses and to cast out demons: Simon, to whom He LK also MK gave the name [f]Peter, LK and Andrew his brother; MK James the *son* of Zebedee and John the brother of James, to whom He gave the name Boanerges, that is, [g]"Sons of Thunder"; LK Philip and Bartholomew; Matthew and

---

[a] CONTINUED ALL NIGHT IN PRAYER. Luke frequently shows Jesus praying—and particularly before major events in His ministry. Cf. Luke 3:21; 5:16; 9:18, 28–29; 11:1; 22:32, 40–46.

[b] HE CALLED HIS DISCIPLES. Cf. Matt. 10:1–4. Christ had many disciples. At one point He sent seventy out in pairs to proclaim the gospel (Luke 10:1). But on this occasion He chose twelve and specifically commissioned them as apostles, i.e., "sent ones," with a special authority to deliver His message on His behalf (cf. Acts 1:21–22).

[c] THOSE HE HIMSELF WANTED. The Greek verb "called" stresses that Jesus acted in His own sovereign interest when He chose the twelve disciples (cf. John 15:16).

[d] APPOINTED TWELVE. Christ, by an explicit act of His will, formed a distinct group of twelve men who were among His followers (cf. Matt. 10:1). This new group constituted the foundation of His church (cf. Eph. 2:20).

[e] HAVE POWER. This word is sometimes rendered "authority." Along with the main task of preaching, Jesus gave the twelve the right to expel demons (cf. Luke 9:1).

[f] PETER. From this point on (except in Mark 14:37), Mark uses this name for Simon, though this is not when the designation was first given (cf. John 1:42), nor does it signify the complete replacement of the name Simon (cf. Acts 15:14). The name means "stone" and describes Peter's character and activities, namely his position as a foundation rock in the building of the church (cf. Matt. 16:18; Eph. 2:20).

[g] "SONS OF THUNDER." Mark defines the Aramaic term "Boanerges" for his Gentile readers. This name for the two brothers probably referred to their intense, outspoken personalities (cf. Mark 9:38; Luke 9:54).

Thomas; James the *son* of Alphaeus, and Simon called [h]the Zealot; [i]Judas *the son* of James, and Judas [j]Iscariot who also [MK] betrayed Him.

[LK] And He came down with them and stood [k]on a level place with a crowd of His disciples and a great multitude of people from all Judea and Jerusalem, and from the seacoast of Tyre and Sidon, who came to hear Him and be healed of their diseases, as well as those who were tormented with [l]unclean spirits. And they were healed. And the whole multitude sought to touch Him, for [m]power went out from Him and healed *them* all.

[h] THE ZEALOT. In Mark's gospel, Mark refers to Simon as "Simon the Cananite." This does not indicate that this Simon was a native of Cana. Rather, the word is derived from the Aramaic which means "to be zealous" and was used for those who were zealous for the law. Luke uses the word transliterated from the Greek term that meant "the Zealot."

[i] JUDAS THE SON OF JAMES. In Mark's account he is listed as "Thaddaeus." His is the only name that is not the same in all the NT lists of the twelve (cf. Matt. 10:2–4; Luke 6:14–16; Acts 1:13). Matthew calls him Lebbaeus, with Thaddaeus as a surname (Matt. 10:3); Luke and Acts call him "Judas the son of James"; and John 14:22 refers to him as "Judas (not Iscariot)."

[j] ISCARIOT. This Hebrew term means "man of Kerioth," as in Kerioth-Hezron, south of Hebron (Josh. 15:25).

[k] ON A LEVEL PLACE. Some interpreters see this verse (Luke 6:17) as being parallel to Matthew 5:1, where Matthew writes that Jesus was "on a mountain." If this view is taken, these passages harmonize easily as long as Luke is referring to either a plateau or a level place on the mountainside. Indeed, there is such a place at the site near Capernaum where tradition says that the Sermon on the Mount (which begins in Luke 6:20) was delivered.

[l] UNCLEAN SPIRITS. Another name for demons, used ten times in the gospels.

[m] POWER WENT OUT FROM HIM. Cf. Mark 5:30; Luke 8:45–46.

50. The Sermon on the Mount: *True Righteousness and Divine Blessing*

Matt. 5:1–16; Luke 6:19–26

MT And seeing the multitudes, He went up on a mountain, and when He [a]was seated His disciples came to Him. LK Then [b]He lifted up His eyes toward His disciples, and MT He [c]opened His mouth and taught them, saying:

"[d]Blessed *are* the [e]poor in spirit,
For [f]theirs is the kingdom of heaven.

[a] WAS SEATED. This was the normal posture for rabbis while teaching (cf. Matt. 13:1–2; 26:55; Mark 4:1; 9:35; Luke 5:3; John 6:3; 8:2).

[b] HE LIFTED UP HIS EYES. Luke uses these words to introduce his account of Christ's sermon. The similarity to the Sermon on the Mount (Matt. 5:1–7:29) is remarkable. It is possible, of course, that Jesus simply preached the same sermon on more than one occasion. (It is evident that He often used the same material more than once—e.g., Luke 12:58–59; cf. Matt. 5:25–26.) It appears more likely, however, that these are variant accounts of the same event. Luke's version is abbreviated somewhat, because he omitted sections from the sermon that are uniquely Jewish (particularly Christ's exposition of the law). Aside from that the two sermons follow exactly the same flow of thought, beginning with the Beatitudes and ending with the parable about building on the rock. Differences in wording between the two accounts are undoubtedly owing to the fact that the sermon was originally delivered in Aramaic. Luke and Matthew translate into Greek with slight variances. Of course, both translations are equally inspired and authoritative.

[c] OPENED HIS MOUTH AND TAUGHT. The Sermon on the Mount (Matt. 5:1–7:29) introduces a series of five important discourses recorded in Matthew. This sermon is a masterful exposition of the law and a potent assault on Pharisaic legalism, closing with a call to true faith and salvation (Matt. 7:13–29). Christ expounded the full meaning of the law, showing that its demands were humanly impossible (cf. Matt. 5:48). This is the proper use of the law with respect to salvation: It closes off every possible avenue of human merit and leaves sinners dependent on nothing but divine grace for salvation (cf. Rom. 3:19–20; Gal. 3:23–24). Christ plumbed the depth of the law, showing that its true demands went far beyond the surface meaning of the words (Matt. 5:28, 39, 44) and set a standard that is higher than the most diligent students of the law had heretofore realized (Matt. 5:20).

[d] BLESSED. The word lit. means "happy, fortunate, blissful." Here it speaks of more than a surface emotion. Jesus was describing the divinely-bestowed well-being that belongs only to the faithful. The Beatitudes demonstrate that the way to heavenly blessedness is antithetical to the worldly path normally followed in pursuit of happiness. The worldly idea is that happiness is found in riches, merriment, abundance, leisure, and such things. The real truth is the very opposite. The Beatitudes give Jesus' description of the character of true faith.

[e] POOR IN SPIRIT. The opposite of self-sufficiency. This speaks of the deep humility of recognizing one's utter spiritual bankruptcy apart from God. It describes those who are acutely conscious of their own lostness and hopelessness apart from divine grace (cf. Matt. 9:12; Luke 18:13).

[f] THEIRS IS THE KINGDOM OF HEAVEN. Notice that the truth of salvation by grace is clearly presupposed in this opening verse of the Sermon on the Mount. Jesus was teaching that the kingdom is a gracious gift to those who sense their own poverty of spirit.

LK "Blessed *are* [g]*you* poor,
For yours is the kingdom of God.
MT "Blessed *are* [h]those who mourn,
For they shall be comforted.
LK "Blessed *are you* who weep now,
For you shall laugh.
MT "Blessed *are* [i]the meek,
For they shall inherit the earth.
LK "Blessed *are you* who [j]hunger now MT and thirst for righteousness,
LK For you shall be filled.
MT "Blessed *are* the merciful,
For [k]they shall obtain mercy.
"Blessed *are* the pure in heart,
For they shall [l]see God.
"Blessed *are* the [m]peacemakers,
For they shall be called sons of God.
"Blessed *are* those who are [n]persecuted for righteousness' sake,
For theirs is the kingdom of heaven.
LK "Blessed are you when men hate you MT and persecute you,
LK And when they exclude you,

---

[g] YOU POOR. Luke's account of the Beatitudes is abbreviated (cf. Matt. 5:3–12). He lists only four and balances them with four parallel woes. Here Luke used a personal pronoun ("you") where Matt. 5:3 employed a definite article ("the"); Luke was underscoring the tender, personal sense of Christ's words. A comparison of the two passages reveals that Christ was dealing with something more significant than mere material poverty and wealth, however. The poverty spoken of here refers primarily to a sense of one's own spiritual impoverishment.

[h] THOSE WHO MOURN. This speaks of mourning over sin, the godly sorrow that produces repentance leading to salvation without regret (2 Cor. 7:10). The "comfort" is the comfort of forgiveness and salvation (cf. Isa. 40:1, 2).

[i] THE MEEK. Meekness is the opposite of being out of control. It is not weakness, but supreme self-control empowered by the Spirit (cf. Gal. 5:23). The fact that "the meek shall inherit the earth" is quoted from Ps. 37:11.

[j] HUNGER NOW AND THIRST FOR RIGHTEOUSNESS. This is the opposite of the self-righteousness of the Pharisees. It speaks of those who seek God's righteousness rather than attempt to establish a righteousness of their own (Rom. 10:3; Phil. 3:9). What they seek will fill them, i.e., it will satisfy their hunger and thirst for a right relationship with God.

[k] THEY SHALL OBTAIN MERCY. The converse is also true. Cf. James 2:13.

[l] SEE GOD. Not only with the perception of faith, but in the glory of heaven. Cf. Heb. 12:14; Rev. 22:3–4.

[m] PEACEMAKERS. See Matt. 5:44–45 for more on this quality.

[n] PERSECUTED. Cf. James 5:10–11; 1 Peter 4:12–14.

And revile *you,* and cast out your name as evil,
MT And say all kinds of evil against you falsely,
LK [o]For the Son of Man's sake.

"Rejoice in that day MT and be exceedingly glad LK and leap for joy! For indeed your reward *is* great in heaven, for in like manner their fathers MT persecuted the prophets who were before you.

LK "But woe to you who are rich,
For you have received your consolation.
"Woe to you who are full,
For you shall hunger.
"Woe to you who laugh now,
For you shall mourn and weep.
"Woe to you when all men speak well of you,
For so did their fathers to the false prophets."

MT "You are the salt of the earth; but [p]if the salt loses its flavor, how shall it be seasoned? It is then good for nothing but to be thrown out and trampled underfoot by men.

"You are the light of the world. A city that is set on a hill cannot be hidden. Nor do they light a lamp and put it under a basket, but on a lampstand, and it gives light to all *who are* in the house. Let your [q]light so shine before men, that they may see your good works and glorify your Father in heaven."

---

[o] For the Son of Man's sake. Persecution, per se, is not something to be sought. But when evil is spoken against a Christian falsely and for Christ's sake (Matt. 5:11), such persecution carries with it the blessing of God.

[p] if the salt loses its flavor, how shall it be seasoned? Salt is both a preservative and a flavor enhancer. No doubt its use as a preservative is what Jesus had mostly in view here. Pure salt cannot lose its flavor or effectiveness, but the salt that is common in the Dead Sea area is contaminated with gypsum and other minerals and may have a flat taste or be ineffective as a preservative. Such mineral salts were useful for little more than keeping footpaths free of vegetation.

[q] light so shine. A godly life gives convincing testimony of the saving power of God. That brings Him glory. Cf. 1 Peter 2:12.

51. The Sermon on the Mount: *True Righteousness and External Morality*

Matt. 5:17–48; Luke 6:27–30, 32–36

MT "Do not think that I came [a]to destroy the Law or the Prophets. I did not come to destroy but [b]to fulfill. For assuredly, I say to you, [c]till heaven and earth pass away, [d]one jot or one tittle will by no means pass from the law till all is fulfilled. Whoever therefore breaks one of the least of these commandments, and teaches men so, [e]shall be called least in the kingdom of heaven; but whoever does and teaches *them*, he shall be called great in the kingdom of heaven. For I say to

---

[a] TO DESTROY. We are not to think that Jesus' teaching in this passage was meant to alter, abrogate, or replace the moral content of the OT law. He was neither giving a new law nor modifying the old, but rather explaining the true significance of the moral content of Moses' law and the rest of the OT. "The Law and the Prophets" speaks of the entirety of the OT Scriptures, not the rabbinical interpretations of them.

[b] TO FULFILL. This speaks of fulfillment in the same sense that prophecy is fulfilled. Christ was indicating that He is the fulfillment of the law in all its aspects. He fulfilled the moral law by keeping it perfectly. He fulfilled the ceremonial law by being the embodiment of everything the law's types and symbols pointed to. And he fulfilled the judicial law by personifying God's perfect justice (cf. Matt. 12:18, 20).

[c] TILL HEAVEN AND EARTH PASS AWAY . . . TILL ALL IS FULFILLED. Here Christ was emphasizing both the inspiration and the enduring authority of all Scripture. He was specifically affirming the utter inerrancy and absolute authority of the OT as the Word of God—down to the least jot and tittle. Again, this suggests that the NT should not be seen as supplanting and abrogating the OT, but as fulfilling and explicating it. For example, all the ceremonial requirements of the Mosaic law were fulfilled in Christ and are no longer to be observed by Christians (Col. 2:16, 17). Yet not one jot or tittle is thereby erased; the underlying truths of those Scriptures remain—and, in fact, the mysteries behind them are now revealed in the brighter light of the gospel. What Jesus is trying to convey here is that nothing has passed from the law, but rather every aspect of the law has been fulfilled in him.

[d] ONE JOT OR ONE TITTLE. A "jot" refers to the smallest Hebrew letter, the *yod*, which is a meager stroke of the pen, like an accent mark or an apostrophe. The "tittle" is a tiny extension on a Hebrew letter, like the serif in modern typefaces.

[e] SHALL BE CALLED LEAST . . . SHALL BE CALLED GREAT. The consequence of practicing or teaching disobedience of any of God's Word is to be called least in the kingdom of heaven (cf. James 2:10). Determining rank in the kingdom of heaven is entirely God's prerogative (cf. Matt. 20:23), and Jesus declares that He will hold those in lowest esteem who hold His Word in lowest esteem. There is no impunity for believers who disobey, discredit, or belittle God's law (cf. 2 Cor. 5:10). That Jesus does not refer to loss of salvation is clear from the fact that, though offenders will be called least, they will still be in the kingdom of heaven. The positive result is that whoever keeps and teaches God's Word, he shall be called great in the kingdom of heaven. Here again Jesus mentions the two aspects of doing and teaching. Kingdom citizens are to uphold every part of God's law both in their living and in their teaching.

you, that [f]unless your righteousness exceeds *the righteousness* of the scribes and Pharisees, you [g]will by no means enter the kingdom of heaven.

"[h]You have heard that it was said to those of old, 'You shall not murder, and whoever murders will be in danger of the judgment.' But I say to you that whoever is angry with his brother without a cause shall be in danger of the judgment. And whoever says to his brother, '[i]Raca!' shall be in danger of the council. But whoever says, 'You fool!' shall be in danger of [j]hell fire. Therefore if you bring your gift to the altar, and there remember that your brother has something against you, leave your gift there before the altar, and go your way. First be reconciled to your brother, and then come and offer your gift. [k]Agree with your [l]adversary quickly, while you are on the way with him, lest your adversary deliver you to the judge, the judge hand you over to the officer, and you be thrown into [m]prison. Assuredly, I say to you, you will by no means get out of there till you have paid the last penny.

"[n]You have heard that it was said to those of old, 'You shall not commit adultery.' But I say to you that whoever looks at a woman to lust for her has already

---

[f] UNLESS YOUR RIGHTEOUSNESS EXCEEDS THE RIGHTEOUSNESS OF THE SCRIBES AND PHARISEES. On the one hand Jesus was calling His disciples to a deeper, more radical holiness than that of the Pharisees. Pharisaism had a tendency to soften the law's demands by focusing only on external obedience. In the verses that follow, Jesus unpacks the full moral significance of the law and shows that the righteousness the law calls for actually involves an internal conformity to the spirit of the law, rather than mere external compliance to the letter.

[g] WILL BY NO MEANS ENTER THE KINGDOM OF HEAVEN. On the other hand this sets up an impossible barrier to works—salvation. Scripture teaches repeatedly that sinners are capable of nothing but a flawed and imperfect righteousness (e.g., Isa. 64:6). Therefore, the only righteousness by which sinners may be justified is the perfect righteousness of God that is imputed to those who believe (Gen. 15:6; Rom. 4:5).

[h] YOU HAVE HEARD . . . BUT I SAY TO YOU. Cf. Matt. 5:27, 31, 33, 38, 43. The quotes are from Ex. 20:13; Deut. 5:17. Jesus was not altering the terms of the law in any of these passages. Rather, He was correcting what they had "heard"—the rabbinical understanding of the law.

[i] RACA! Lit. "Empty-headed!" Jesus suggested here that the verbal abuse stems from the same sinful motives (anger and hatred) that ultimately lead to murder. The internal attitude is what the law actually prohibits, and therefore an abusive insult carries the same kind of moral guilt as an act of murder.

[j] HELL. A reference to the Hinnom Valley, southwest of Jerusalem. Ahaz and Manasseh permitted human sacrifices there during their reigns (2 Chron. 28:3; 33:6), so it was called "The Valley of Slaughter" (Jer. 19:6). In Jesus' day, it was a garbage dump where fires burned continually and was thus an apt symbol of eternal fire.

[k] AGREE . . . QUICKLY. Jesus calls for reconciliation to be sought eagerly, aggressively, quickly—even if it involves self-sacrifice. It is better to be wronged than to allow a dispute between brethren to be a cause for dishonoring Christ (1 Cor. 6:7).

[l] ADVERSARY. This speaks of one's opponent in a law case.

[m] PRISON. Debtor's prison, where the person could work to earn back what he had defrauded.

[n] "YOU SHALL NOT COMMIT ADULTERY." Quoted from Ex. 20:14; Deut. 5:18.

committed adultery with her in his heart. If your right eye causes you to sin, [o]pluck it out and cast *it* from you; for it is more profitable for you that one of your members perish, than for your whole body to be cast into hell. And if your right hand causes you to sin, cut it off and cast *it* from you; for it is more profitable for you that one of your members perish, than for your whole body to be cast into hell.

"Furthermore [p]it has been said, 'Whoever divorces his wife, let him give her a certificate of divorce.' But I say to you that whoever divorces his wife for any reason [q]except sexual immorality [r]causes her to commit adultery; and whoever marries a woman who is divorced commits adultery.

"Again you have heard that it was said to those of old, '[s]You shall not swear falsely, but shall perform your oaths to the Lord.' But I say to you, [t]do not swear at all: neither by heaven, for it is God's throne; nor by the earth, for it is His footstool; nor by Jerusalem, for it is the city of the great King. Nor shall you swear by your head, because you cannot make one hair white or black. But let your 'Yes' be 'Yes,' and your 'No,' 'No.' For whatever is more than these is from the evil one.

---

[o] pluck it out and cast it from you. Jesus was not advocating self-mutilation (for this would not cure lust, which is actually a problem of the heart). He was using this graphic hyperbole to demonstrate the seriousness of sins of lust and evil desire. The point is that it would be "more profitable" (Matt. 5:30) to lose a member of one's own body than to bear the eternal consequences of the guilt from such a sin. Sin must be dealt with drastically because of its deadly effects.

[p] it has been said. Cf. Deut. 24:1–4. The rabbis had taken liberty with what Scripture actually said. They referred to Deut. 24:1–4 as if it were given merely to regulate the paperwork when one sought divorce (cf. Matt. 19:7–9). Thus, they had wrongly concluded that men could divorce their wives for anything that displeased them, as long as they gave "a certificate of divorce." But Moses provided this as a concession to protect the woman who was divorced, not to justify or legalize divorce under all circumstances.

[q] except sexual immorality. Divorce was allowed in cases of adultery. Luke 16:18 must be understood in the light of this verse.

[r] causes her to commit adultery. The assumption is that divorced people will remarry. If the divorce was not for sexual immorality, any remarriage is adultery, because God does not acknowledge the divorce. Cf. 1 Cor. 7:15.

[s] You shall not swear falsely. This expresses teaching from Lev. 19:12; Num. 30:2; Deut. 23:21–23.

[t] do not swear at all. Cf. James 5:12. This should not be taken as a universal condemnation of oaths in all circumstances. God Himself confirmed a promise with an oath (Heb. 6:13–18; cf. Acts 2:30). Christ Himself spoke under oath (Matt. 26:63–64). And the law prescribed oaths in certain circumstances (e.g., Num. 5:19, 21; 30:2–3). What Christ is forbidding here is the flippant, profane, or careless use of oaths in everyday speech. In that culture such oaths were often employed for deceptive purposes. To make the person being victimized believe the truth was being told, the Jews would swear by "heaven," "earth," "Jerusalem," or their own "heads," not by God, hoping to avoid divine judgment for their lie. But it all was in God's creation, so it drew Him in and produced guilt before Him, exactly as if the oath were made in His name. Jesus suggested that all our speech should be as if we were under an oath to tell the truth.

"You have heard that it was said, '[u]An eye for an eye and a tooth for a tooth.' But I tell you [v]not to resist an evil person. But whoever slaps you on your right cheek, turn [and] LK offer the other also. MT If anyone wants to sue you and take away your tunic, let him have *your* cloak also. LK And from him who takes away your cloak, do not withhold *your* tunic either. MT And whoever [w]compels you to go one mile, go with him two. LK Give to everyone who asks of you. MT From him who wants to borrow from you do not turn away, LK and from him who takes away your goods do not ask *them* back.

MT "You have heard that it was said, 'You shall [x]love your neighbor and hate your enemy.' But I say to you LK who hear: [y]Love your enemies, MT bless those who curse you, do good to those who hate you, and pray for those who spitefully use you and persecute you, that you may be sons of your Father in heaven; for He makes His sun rise on the evil and on the good, and sends rain on the just and on the unjust. For if you love those who love you, what reward have you? LK What credit is that to you? MT Do not even the [z]tax collectors do the same? LK Even sinners

---

[u] AN EYE FOR AN EYE. The law did establish this standard as a principle for limiting retribution to that which was just (Ex. 21:24; Lev. 24:20; Deut. 19:21). Its design was to insure that the punishment in civil cases fit the crime. It was never meant to sanction acts of personal retaliation. So again Jesus made no alteration to the true meaning of the law. He was merely explaining and affirming the law's true meaning.

[v] NOT TO RESIST AN EVIL PERSON. Like Matt. 5:38, this deals only with matters of personal retaliation, not criminal offenses or acts of military aggression. Jesus applied this principle of nonretaliation to affronts against one's dignity (Matt. 5:39), lawsuits to gain one's personal assets (v. 40), infringements on one's liberty (v. 41), and violations of property rights (v. 42). He was calling for a full surrender of all personal rights.

[w] COMPELS. The word speaks of coercion or force. The NT picture of this is when Roman soldiers "compelled" Simon the Cyrene to carry Jesus' cross (Matt. 27:32).

[x] LOVE YOUR NEIGHBOR AND HATE YOUR ENEMY. The first half of this is found in Moses' law (Lev. 19:18). The second part was found in how the scribes and Pharisees explained and applied that OT command. Jesus' application was exactly the opposite, resulting in a much higher standard: Love for one's neighbors should extend even to those neighbors who are enemies (Matt. 5:44). Again, this was no innovation, since even the OT taught that God's people should do good to their enemies (Prov. 25:21).

[y] LOVE YOUR ENEMIES . . . THAT YOU MAY BE SONS OF YOUR FATHER. This plainly teaches that God's love extends even to His enemies. This universal love of God is manifest in blessings that God bestows on all, indiscriminately. Theologians refer to this as common grace. This must be distinguished from the everlasting love God has for the elect (Jer. 31:3), but it is a sincere goodwill nonetheless (cf. Ps. 145:9).

[z] TAX COLLECTORS. Disloyal Israelites hired by the Romans to tax other Jews for personal profit. They became symbols for the worst kind of people. Cf. Matt. 9:10–11; 11:19; 18:17; 21:31; Mark 2:14–16; Luke 5:30; 7:25, 29, 34; 18:11–13. Matthew had been one of them (cf. Matt. 9:9; Mark 2:15).

love those who love them. MT And if you greet your brethren only, what do you do more *than others?* Do not even the tax collectors do so? LK And if you do good to those who do good to you, what credit is that to you? For even sinners do the same.

"And if you lend *to those* from whom you hope to receive back, what credit is that to you? For even sinners lend to sinners to receive as much back. But love your enemies, do good, and lend, hoping for nothing in return; and your reward will be great, and you will be [aa]sons of the Most High. For He is kind to the unthankful and evil. Therefore be merciful, just as your Father also is merciful.

MT [bb]"You shall be perfect, just as your Father in heaven is perfect."

[aa] SONS OF THE MOST HIGH. i.e., God's children should bear the indelible stamp of His moral character. Since He is loving, gracious, and generous—even to those who are His enemies—we should be like Him. Cf. Eph. 5:1–2.

[bb] YOU SHALL BE PERFECT. Christ sets an unattainable standard. This sums up what the law itself demanded (James 2:10). Though this standard is impossible to meet, God could not lower it without compromising His own perfection. He who is perfect could not set an imperfect standard of righteousness. The marvelous truth of the gospel is that Christ has met this standard on our behalf (2 Cor. 5:21).

52. The Sermon on the Mount: *True Righteousness and Practical Religion*

Matt. 6:1–18

MT "[a] Take heed that you do not do your charitable deeds before men, to be seen by them. Otherwise you have no reward from your Father in heaven. Therefore, when you do a charitable deed, do not sound a trumpet before you as the [b]hypocrites do in the synagogues and in the streets, that they may have glory from men. Assuredly, I say to you, [c]they have their reward. But when you do a charitable deed, do not let your left hand know what your right hand is doing, that your charitable deed may be in secret; and your Father who [d]sees in secret will Himself reward you openly.

"And when you pray, you shall not be like the hypocrites. For they love to pray standing in the synagogues and on the corners of the streets, that they may be seen by men. Assuredly, I say to you, they have their reward. But you, when you pray, go into your room, and when you have shut your door, pray to your Father who *is* in the secret *place;* and your Father who sees in secret will reward you openly. And when you pray, do not use [e]vain repetitions as the heathen *do.* For they think that they will be heard for their many words.

"Therefore do not be like them. For your Father knows the things you have need of before you ask Him. [f]In this manner, therefore, pray:

---

[a] Take heed. In this section, Christ expands the thought of Matt. 5:20, showing how the Pharisees' righteousness was deficient by exposing their hypocrisy in the matters of "charitable deeds" (Matt. 6:1–4); "prayer" (vv. 5–15); and "fasting" (vv. 16–18). All of these acts are supposed to be worship rendered to God, never displays of self-righteousness to gain the admiration of others.

[b] hypocrites. This word had its origins in Greek theater, describing a character who wore a mask. The term, as used in the NT, normally described an unregenerate person who was self-deceived.

[c] they have their reward. Their reward is that they were seen by men, nothing more. God does not reward hypocrisy, but He does punish it (cf. Matt. 23:13–23).

[d] sees in secret. Cf. Prov. 15:3; Jer. 17:10; Heb. 4:13. God is omniscient.

[e] vain repetitions. Prayers are not to be merely recited, nor are our words to be repeated thoughtlessly or as if they were automatic formulas. But this is not a prohibition against importunity.

[f] In this manner. Cf. Luke 11:2–4 in which Christ gives similar instruction on a different occasion. The prayer is a model, not merely a liturgy. It is notable for its brevity, simplicity, and comprehensiveness. Of the six petitions, three are directed to God (Matt. 6:9, 10) and three toward human needs (vv. 11–13).

Our Father in heaven,
Hallowed be Your name.
Your kingdom come.
[g]Your will be done
On earth as *it is* in heaven.
Give us this day our daily bread.
And [h]forgive us our debts,
As we forgive our debtors.
And [i]do not lead us into temptation,
But deliver us from the evil one.
For Yours is the kingdom and the power and the glory forever.
Amen.

"For if you forgive men their trespasses, your heavenly Father will also forgive you. But if you do not forgive men their trespasses, [j]neither will your Father forgive your trespasses.

"Moreover, [k]when you fast, do not be like the hypocrites, with a sad countenance. For they disfigure their faces that they may appear to men to be fasting. Assuredly, I say to you, they have their reward. But you, when you fast, anoint your head and wash your face, so that you do not appear to men to be fasting, but to your Father who *is* in the secret *place;* and your Father who sees in secret will reward you openly."

---

[g] YOUR WILL BE DONE. All prayer, first of all, willingly submits to God's purposes, plans, and glory. Cf. Matt. 26:39.

[h] FORGIVE US OUR DEBTS. The parallel passage (Luke 11:4) uses a word that means "sins," so that in context spiritual debts are intended. Sinners are debtors to God for their violations of His laws (cf. Matt. 18:23–27). This request is the heart of the prayer; it is what Jesus stressed in the words that immediately follow the prayer (Matt. 6:14, 15; cf. Mark 11:25).

[i] DO NOT LEAD US INTO TEMPTATION. Cf. Luke 22:40. God does not tempt men (James 1:13), but He will subject them to trials that may expose them to Satan's assaults, as in the case of Job and Peter (Luke 22:31, 32). This petition reflects the believer's desire to avoid the dangers of sin altogether. God knows what one's need is before one asks (v. 8), and He promises that no one will be subjected to testing beyond what can be endured. He also promises a way of escape—often through endurance (1 Cor. 10:13). But still, the proper attitude for the believer is the one expressed in this petition.

[j] NEITHER WILL YOUR FATHER FORGIVE YOUR TRESPASSES. This is not to suggest that God will withdraw justification from those who have already received the free pardon He extends to all believers. Forgiveness in that sense—a permanent and complete acquittal from the guilt and ultimate penalty of sin—belongs to all who are in Christ (cf. John 5:24; Rom. 8:1; Eph. 1:7). Yet Scripture also teaches that God chastens His children who disobey (Heb. 12:5–7). Believers are to confess their sins in order to obtain a day-to-day cleansing (1 John 1:9). This sort of forgiveness is a simple washing from the worldly defilements of sin, not a repeat of the wholesale cleansing from sin's corruption that comes with justification. It is like a washing of the feet rather than a bath (cf. John 13:10). Forgiveness in this latter sense is what God threatens to withhold from Christians who refuse to forgive others (cf. Matt. 18:23–35).

[k] WHEN YOU FAST. This indicates that fasting is assumed to be a normal part of one's spiritual life (cf. 1 Cor. 7:5). Fasting is associated with sadness (Matt. 9:14–15), prayer (17:21), charity (Isa. 58:3–6), and seeking the Lord's will (Acts 13:2–3; 14:23).

53. The Sermon on the Mount: *True Righteousness and Mundane Things*

Matt. 6:19–34

MT "Do not lay up for yourselves [a]treasures on earth, where moth and rust destroy and where thieves break in and steal; but lay up for yourselves treasures in heaven, where neither moth nor rust destroys and where thieves do not break in and steal. For where your treasure is, there your heart will be also.

"[b]The lamp of the body is the eye. If therefore your eye is good, your whole body will be full of light. But if your eye is bad, your whole body will be full of darkness. If therefore the light that is in you is darkness, how great *is* that darkness!

"No one can serve two masters; for either he will hate the one and love the other, or else he will be loyal to the one and despise the other. You cannot serve God and [c]mammon.

"Therefore I say to you, do not worry about your life, what you will eat or what you will drink; nor about your body, what you will put on. Is not life more than food and the body more than clothing? Look at the birds of the air, for they neither sow nor reap nor gather into barns; yet [d]your heavenly Father feeds them. Are you not of more value than they? Which of you by worrying can [e]add one cubit to his stature?

"So why do you worry about clothing? Consider the lilies of the field, how they grow: they neither toil nor spin; and yet I say to you that even [f]Solomon in all his glory was not arrayed like one of these. Now if God so clothes the grass of

---

[a] TREASURES. Don't amass earthly wealth. He commends the use of financial assets for purposes which are heavenly and eternal. Cf. Luke 16:1–9.

[b] THE LAMP OF THE BODY. This is an argument from the lesser to the greater. The analogy is simple. If your eye is bad, no light can come in, and you are left with darkness because of that malady. How much worse when the problem is not merely related to external perception, but an internal corruption of one's whole nature, so that the darkness actually emanates from within and affects one's whole being. He was indicting them for their superficial earthly religion that left their hearts dark. Cf. Luke 11:34.

[c] MAMMON. Earthly, material treasures, especially money. Cf. Luke 16:13.

[d] YOUR HEAVENLY FATHER FEEDS THEM. Obviously this in no way advocates a sinful kind of idleness (Prov. 19:15). Birds are not idle, either. But it is God who provides them with food to eat.

[e] ADD ONE CUBIT TO HIS STATURE. The Greek phrase may also refer to adding time to one's lifespan.

[f] SOLOMON IN ALL HIS GLORY. The glory and pageantry of Solomon's kingdom was famous worldwide. Cf. 2 Chron. 9.

the field, which today is, and tomorrow is thrown into the oven, *will He* not much more *clothe* you, O [g]you of little faith?

"Therefore do not worry, saying, 'What shall we eat?' or 'What shall we drink?' or 'What shall we wear?' For after all these things the [h]Gentiles seek. For your heavenly Father knows that you need all these things. But seek first the [i]kingdom of God and His righteousness, and all these things shall be added to you. Therefore do not worry about tomorrow, for tomorrow will worry about its own things. Sufficient for the day *is* its own trouble."

---

[g] YOU OF LITTLE FAITH. Cf. Matt. 8:26; 14:31; 16:8; 17:20. This was the Lord's recurring rebuke of the weak disciples.

[h] GENTILES. i.e., those outside the people of promise and outside the blessing of God. Cf. Eph. 4:17–19.

[i] KINGDOM OF GOD. This is the same as kingdom of heaven. It refers to the sphere of salvation. He was urging them to seek salvation—and with it would come the full care and provision of God. Cf. Matt. 3:2; Rom. 8:32; Phil. 4:19; 1 Peter 5:7.

54. The Sermon on the Mount: *True Righteousness and Human Relationships*

Matt. 7:1–12; Luke 6:31, 37–42

LK "[a]Judge not, and you shall not be judged. Condemn not, and you shall not be condemned. Forgive, and you will be forgiven. MT For with what judgment you judge, you will be judged. LK Give, and it will be given to you: good measure, pressed down, shaken together, and running over will be [b]put into your bosom. For with the same measure that you use, it will be measured back to you."

And He spoke a parable to them: "Can the blind lead the blind? Will they not both fall into the ditch? A disciple is not above his teacher, but everyone who is perfectly trained will be like his teacher. And why do you look at the [c]speck in your brother's eye, but do not perceive the plank in your own eye? Or how can you say to your brother, 'Brother, let me remove the speck that *is* in your eye,' when you yourself do not see the plank that *is* in your own eye? Hypocrite! First remove the plank from your own eye, and then you will see clearly to remove the speck that is in your brother's eye.

MT "[d]Do not give what is holy to the dogs; nor cast your pearls before swine, lest they trample them under their feet, and turn and tear you in pieces.

---

[a] JUDGE NOT. As the context reveals, this does not prohibit all types of judging (Matt. 7:16). There is a righteous kind of judgment we are supposed to exercise with careful discernment (John 7:24). Censorious, hypocritical, self-righteous, or other kinds of unfair judgments are forbidden, but in order to fulfill the commandments that follow, it is necessary to discern dogs and swine (Matt. 7:6) from one's own brethren (Matt. 7:3–5).

[b] PUT INTO YOUR BOSOM. i.e., poured into your lap. A long robe was used to carry the overflow of grain. Cf. Ps. 79:12; Isa. 65:6; Jer. 32:18.

[c] SPECK . . . PLANK. The humor of the imagery was no doubt intentional. Christ often employed hyperbole to paint comical images (cf. Matt. 23:24; Luke 18:25).

[d] DO NOT GIVE WHAT IS HOLY TO THE DOGS. This principle is why Jesus Himself did not do miracles for unbelievers (Matt. 13:58). This is to be done in respect for what is holy, not merely out of contempt for the dogs and swine. Nothing here contradicts the principle of Matt. 5:44. That verse governs personal dealings with one's enemies; this principle governs how one handles the gospel in the face of those who hate the truth.

"Ask, and it will be given to you; seek, and you will find; knock, and it will be opened to you. For everyone who asks receives, and he who seeks finds, and to him who knocks it will be opened. Or what man is there among you who, if his son asks for bread, will give him a stone? Or if he asks for a fish, will he give him a serpent? If [e]you then, being evil, know how to give good gifts to your children, [f]how much more will your Father who is in heaven give good things to those who ask Him! Therefore, whatever you want men to do to you, LK you [g]also do to them likewise, MT for this is the Law and the Prophets."

[e] YOU . . . BEING EVIL. Jesus presupposes the doctrine of human depravity (cf. Romans 1:18–3:20).

[f] HOW MUCH MORE. If earthly fathers give what their sons need (Matt. 7:9–10), will not God give to His sons what they ask (vv. 7–8)? Cf. James 1:17.

[g] ALSO DO TO THEM. Versions of the "Golden Rule" existed before Christ in the rabbinic writings and even in Hinduism and Buddhism. All of them cast the rule as a negative command, such as Rabbi Hillel's version, "What is hateful to yourself do not to someone else." Jesus made it a positive command, enriching its meaning and underscoring that this one imperative aptly summarizes the whole gist of the ethical principles contained in the Law and the Prophets.

55. The Sermon on the Mount: *True Righteousness and Salvation*

Matt. 7:13–29; Luke 6:43–49

MT " [a]Enter by the narrow [b]gate; for wide *is* the gate and broad *is* the way that leads to destruction, and there are many who go in by it. Because narrow *is* the gate and [c]difficult *is* the way which leads to life, and there are few who find it.

"Beware of [d]false prophets, who come to you in [e]sheep's clothing, but inwardly they are ravenous wolves. [f]You will know them by their fruits. Do men gather grapes from thornbushes or figs from thistles? Even so, every good tree bears good fruit, but a bad tree bears bad fruit. A good tree cannot bear bad fruit, nor *can* a bad tree bear good fruit. LK For every tree is known by its own fruit. For *men* do not gather figs from thorns, nor do they gather grapes from a bramble bush. MT Every tree that does not bear good fruit is cut down and thrown into the fire. Therefore by their fruits you will know them. LK A good man out of the good treasure of his heart brings forth good; and an evil man out of the evil treasure of his heart brings forth evil. For out of the abundance of the heart his mouth speaks.

---

[a] ENTER. This closing section of the Sermon on the Mount is a gospel application. Here are two gates, two ways, two destinations, and two groups of people (Matt. 7:13, 14); two kinds of trees and two kinds of fruit (Matt. 7:17–20); two groups at the judgment (Matt. 7:21–23); and two kinds of builders, building on two kinds of foundations (Matt. 7:24–28). Christ is drawing the line as clearly as possible between the way that leads to destruction and the way that leads to life.

[b] GATE. Both the narrow gate and the wide gate are assumed to provide the entrance to God's kingdom. Two ways are offered to people. The narrow gate is by faith, only through Christ, constricted and precise. It represents true salvation in God's way that leads to life eternal. The wide gate includes all religions of works and self-righteousness, with no single way (cf. Acts 4:12), but leads to hell, not heaven.

[c] DIFFICULT IS THE WAY. Christ continually emphasized the difficulty of following Him (Matt. 10:38; 16:24–25; John 15:18–19; 16:1–3; cf. Acts 14:22). Salvation is by grace alone, but is not easy. It calls for knowledge of the truth, repentance, submission to Christ as Lord, and a willingness to obey His will and Word. Cf. Matt. 19:16–28.

[d] FALSE PROPHETS. These deceive not by disguising themselves as sheep, but by impersonating true shepherds. They promote the wide gate and the wide way.

[e] SHEEP'S CLOTHING. This may refer to the woolen attire that was the characteristic garb of a shepherd.

[f] YOU WILL KNOW THEM BY THEIR FRUITS. False doctrine cannot restrain the flesh, so false prophets manifest wickedness. Cf. 2 Peter 2:12–22.

"But why do [g]you call Me 'Lord, Lord,' and not do the things which I say? MT [h]Not everyone who says to Me, 'Lord, Lord,' shall enter the kingdom of heaven, but he who does the will of My Father in heaven. Many will say to Me in that day, 'Lord, Lord, [i]have we not prophesied in Your name, cast out demons in Your name, and done many wonders in Your name?' And then I will declare to them, 'I never knew you; depart from Me, you who practice [j]lawlessness!'

"Therefore LK whoever comes to Me, and hears My sayings and does them, I will show you whom he is like: He is like MT a wise man LK building a house, who dug deep and laid the foundation on the rock. MT And the rain descended, the floods came, and the winds blew and beat on that house; LK the stream beat vehemently against that house, and could not shake it, MT and it did not fall, for it was founded on the rock.

"But everyone who hears these sayings of Mine, and does not do them, will be like a foolish man who built his [k]house on the sand LK without a foundation: MT and the rain descended, the floods came, LK the stream beat vehemently, MT and the winds blew and beat on that house; LK and immediately it fell. And the ruin of that house was great— MT great was its fall."

And so it was, when Jesus had ended these sayings, that the people were astonished at His teaching, for He taught them as one having authority, and [l]not as the scribes.

---

[g] YOU CALL ME 'LORD, LORD.' It is not sufficient to give lip service to Christ's lordship. Genuine faith produces obedience. A tree is known by its fruits.

[h] NOT EVERYONE WHO SAYS . . . BUT HE WHO DOES. The barrenness of this sort of faith demonstrates its real character—the faith that says but does not do is really unbelief. Jesus was not suggesting that works are meritorious for salvation, but that true faith will not fail to produce the fruit of good works. This is precisely the point of James 1:22–25; 2:26.

[i] HAVE WE NOT PROPHESIED . . . CAST OUT DEMONS . . . AND DONE MANY WONDERS. Note that far from being totally devoid of works of any kind, these people were claiming to have done some remarkable signs and wonders. In fact their whole confidence was in these works—further proof that these works, spectacular as they might have appeared, could not have been authentic. No one so bereft of genuine faith could possibly produce true good works. A bad tree cannot bear good fruit.

[j] LAWLESSNESS. All sin is lawlessness (1 John 3:4), i.e., rebellion against the law of God (cf. Matt. 13:41).

[k] HOUSE. The house represents a religious life; the rain represents divine judgment. Only the one built on the foundation of obedience to God's Word stands, which calls for repentance, rejection of salvation by works, and trust in God's grace to save through His merciful provision.

[l] NOT AS THE SCRIBES. The scribes quoted others to establish the authority of their teachings; Jesus was His own authority (Matt. 28:18). This matter of authority was a major issue between Jesus and the Jewish religious leaders, who felt their authority challenged. Cf. Mark 1:22; 11:28–33; Luke 4:32; 20:2–8; John 12:49–50; 14:10.

56. Jesus Heals a Centurion's Servant

Matt. 8:1, 5–13; Luke 7:1–10

LK Now when He concluded all His sayings in the hearing of the people, [and] MT when He had come down from the mountain, great multitudes followed Him [and] LK He entered Capernaum.

And a certain [a]centurion's [b]servant, who was dear to him, was sick and ready to die. So when he heard about Jesus, MT when Jesus had entered Capernaum, LK he sent [c]elders of the Jews to Him, pleading with Him to come and heal his servant, MT saying, "Lord, my servant is lying at home paralyzed, dreadfully tormented." LK And when they came to Jesus, they begged Him earnestly, saying that the one for whom He should do this was deserving, "for he loves our nation, and has built us a synagogue." MT And Jesus said to [them], "I will come and heal him." LK Then Jesus went with them.

And when He was already not far from the house, the centurion sent friends to Him, saying to Him, "Lord, do not trouble Yourself, for [d]I am not worthy that You should enter under my roof. Therefore I did not even think myself worthy to come to You. But MT only LK say the word, and my servant will be healed. For I also am a man placed under authority, having soldiers under me. And I say to MT this LK one, 'Go,' and he goes; and to another, 'Come,' and he comes; and to my servant,

---

[a] CENTURION. A Roman military officer who commanded one hundred men. Luke indicates that the centurion appealed to Jesus through intermediaries (Luke 7:3–6) because of his own sense of unworthiness (cf. Luke 7:7). Matthew makes no mention of the intermediaries.

[b] SERVANT. The centurion's tender concern for a lowly slave was contrary to the reputation Roman army officers had acquired in Israel. Yet this is one of three centurions featured in the NT who gave evidence of genuine faith (cf. Matt. 27:54; Acts 10).

[c] ELDERS OF THE JEWS. Matthew 8:5–13 does not mention that the centurion appealed to Jesus through these intermediaries. It is a measure of the respect this man had in the community that Jewish elders would be willing to bring his cause to Jesus. He loved the Jewish nation and was somehow personally responsible for the building of the local synagogue. He obviously was being drawn to Christ by God Himself (cf. John 6:44, 65). Like all men under conviction, he deeply sensed his own unworthiness, and that is why he used intermediaries rather than speaking to Jesus personally.

[d] I AM NOT WORTHY THAT YOU SHOULD ENTER UNDER MY ROOF. Jewish tradition held that a person who entered a Gentile's house was ceremonially defiled (cf. John 18:28). The centurion, undoubtedly familiar with this law, felt unworthy of having Jesus suffer such an inconvenience for his sake. He also had faith enough to know that Christ could heal by merely speaking a word.

'Do this,' and he does *it*."

When Jesus heard these things, He marveled at him, and turned around and said to the crowd that followed Him, "[MT] Assuredly, [LK] I say to you, [e]I have not found such great faith, not even in Israel!" [MT] And I say to you that [f]many will come from east and west, and sit down with Abraham, Isaac, and Jacob in the kingdom of heaven. But the [g]sons of the kingdom [h]will be cast out into outer darkness. There will be [i]weeping and gnashing of teeth."

Then Jesus said to the centurion, "Go your way; and [j]as you have believed, *so* let it be done for you." And his servant was healed that same hour. [LK] And those who were sent, returning to the house, found the servant well who had been sick.

---

[e] I HAVE NOT FOUND SUCH GREAT FAITH, NOT EVEN IN ISRAEL! This centurion understood Jesus' absolute authority. Even some of Jesus' own disciples did not see things so clearly (cf. Matt. 8:26).

[f] MANY . . . FROM EAST AND WEST. Gentiles in the kingdom with Abraham will enjoy salvation and the blessing of God (cf. Isa. 49:8–12; 59:19; Mal. 1:11; Luke 13:28–29).

[g] SONS OF THE KINGDOM. The Hebrew nation, physical heirs of Abraham.

[h] WILL BE CAST OUT. This was exactly opposite to the rabbinical understanding, which suggested that the kingdom would feature a great feast in the company of Abraham and the Messiah—open to Jews only.

[i] WEEPING AND GNASHING. Cf. Matt. 22:13; 24:51; 25:30; Luke 13:28. This expression describes the eternal agonies of those in hell.

[j] AS YOU HAVE BELIEVED. Sometimes, faith was involved in the Lord's healings (in this case not by the one being healed, as in Matt. 9:2; 15:28); other times it was not a factor (Matt. 8:14–16; Luke 22:51).

57. Jesus Raises a Widow's Dead Son

Luke 7:11–17

LK Now it happened, the day after, *that* He went into a city called [a]Nain; and many of His disciples went with Him, and a large crowd. And when He came near the gate of the city, behold, a dead man was being carried out, the only son of his mother; and she was a widow. And a large crowd from the city was with her.

When the Lord saw her, He had compassion on her and said to her, "Do not weep." Then He came and [b]touched the open coffin, and those who carried *him* stood still. And He said, "Young man, I say to you, arise."

So he who was dead sat up and began to speak. And He presented him to his mother. Then fear came upon all, and they glorified God, saying, "A great prophet has risen up among us"; and, "God has visited His people." And this report about Him went throughout all Judea and all the surrounding region.

---

[a] NAIN. A small town southeast of Nazareth.

[b] TOUCHED THE OPEN COFFIN. A ceremonially-defiling-act normally. Jesus graphically illustrated how impervious He was to such defilements. When He touched the coffin, its defilement did not taint Him; rather, His power immediately dispelled the presence of all death and defilement (cf. Luke 7:39; 8:44). This was the first of three times Jesus raised people from the dead (cf. Luke 8:49–56; John 11). Luke 7:22 implies that Christ also raised others who are not specifically mentioned.

58. Jesus Replies to John the Baptist

Matt. 11:2–19; Luke 7:18–35

LK Then [a]the disciples of John reported to him concerning all these things. MT And when John had heard in prison about the works of Christ, he LK [called] two of his disciples to *him,* [and] sent *them* to Jesus, saying, "[b]Are You the Coming One, or do we look for another?"

When the men had come to Him, they said, "John the Baptist has sent us to You, saying, 'Are You the Coming One, or do we look for another?'" And that very hour He cured many of infirmities, afflictions, and evil spirits; and to many blind He gave sight.

MT Jesus answered and said to them, "[c]Go and tell John the things which you hear and see: *The* blind see and *the* lame walk; *the* lepers are cleansed and *the* deaf hear; *the* dead are raised up and *the* poor have the gospel preached to them. And blessed is [d]he who is not offended because of Me."

LK When the messengers of John had departed, MT Jesus began to say to the multitudes concerning John: "What did you go out into the wilderness to see? A reed shaken by the wind? But what did you go out to see? A man clothed in soft garments? Indeed, those who wear soft *clothing* are in kings' houses; LK those who are gorgeously appareled and live in luxury are in kings' courts. MT But what did

---

[a] THE DISCIPLES OF JOHN. John the Baptist evidently kept apprised of Christ's ministry—even after his imprisonment—through disciples who acted as messengers for him. Cf. Acts 19:1–7.

[b] ARE YOU THE COMING ONE. John the Baptist had introduced Christ as One who would bring a fierce judgment and "burn up the chaff with unquenchable fire" (Matt. 3:12). He was understandably confused by the turn of events: he was imprisoned, and Christ was carrying on a ministry of healing, not judgment, in Galilee, far from Jerusalem, the city of the King—and not finding a completely warm reception there (cf. Matt. 8:34). John wondered if he had misunderstood Jesus' agenda. John was not the sort of man who vacillated. We are not to think that his faith was failing or that he had lost confidence in Christ. But with so many unexpected turns of events, John wanted reassurance from Christ Himself. That is precisely what Jesus gave him.

[c] GO AND TELL JOHN. Luke 7:22–23 are quoted from Isa. 35:5–6; 61:1. These were messianic promises. (Isa. 61:1 is from the same passage Jesus read in the Nazareth synagogue—Luke 4:19.) John's disciples were to report that Jesus was doing precisely what Scripture foretold of the Messiah—even though the scheme of prophetic fulfillment was not unfolding quite the way John the Baptist had envisioned it. Jesus sent John's disciples back as eyewitnesses of many miracles. Evidently He performed these miracles in their presence just so that they could report back to John that they had personally seen proof that He was indeed the Messiah (cf. Isa. 29:18–19; 35:5–10). Note, however, that he offered no further explanation to John, knowing exactly how strong John's faith was (cf. 1 Cor. 10:13).

[d] HE WHO IS NOT OFFENDED. This was not meant as a rebuke for John the Baptist, but as encouragement for him.

you go out to see? A prophet? Yes, I say to you, and more than a prophet. For this is *he* of whom it is written: '[e]Behold, I send My messenger before Your face, Who will prepare Your way before You.'

"Assuredly, I say to you, among those born of women there has not risen [LK] a greater prophet [MT] than John the Baptist; but he who is [f]least in the kingdom of heaven is greater than he. And from the days of John the Baptist until now [g]the kingdom of heaven suffers violence, and the violent take it by force. For all the prophets and the law prophesied until John. And if you are willing to receive *it*, [h]he is Elijah who is to come. He who has ears to hear, let him hear!"

[LK] And when all the people heard *Him*, even the tax collectors [i]justified God, having been baptized with the baptism of John. But the Pharisees and lawyers [j]rejected the will of God for themselves, not having been baptized by him. And the Lord said, [MT] "But to what [LK] then shall I liken the men of this generation, and what are they like? They are [k]like children sitting in the marketplace and calling to [MT] their companions, and saying:

---

[e] BEHOLD, I SEND . . . Quoted from Mal. 3:1.

[f] LEAST . . . IS GREATER THAN HE. John was greater than the OT prophets because he actually saw with his eyes and personally participated in the fulfillment of what they only prophesied (cf. 1 Peter 1:10–11). But all believers after the cross are greater still because they participate in the full understanding and experience of something John merely foresaw in shadowy form—the actual atoning work of Christ.

[g] THE KINGDOM OF HEAVEN SUFFERS VIOLENCE. From the time he began his preaching ministry, John the Baptist evoked a strong reaction. Having been imprisoned already, John ultimately fell victim to Herod's savagery. But the kingdom can never be subdued or opposed by human violence. On a different occasion Jesus similarly said about the kingdom, "everyone is pressing into it" (Luke 16:16). So the sense of this verse may be rendered this way: "The kingdom presses ahead relentlessly, and only the relentless press their way into it." Thus again Christ is magnifying the difficulty of entering the kingdom (cf. Matt. 7:13–14).

[h] HE IS ELIJAH. i.e., he is the fulfillment of Mal. 4:5, 6 (see Matt. 17:12–13). The Jews were aware that Elijah had not died (cf. 2 Kings 2:11). This does not suggest that John was Elijah returned. In fact, John himself denied that he was Elijah (John 1:21), yet he came in the spirit and power of Elijah (Luke 1:17). If they had believed, John would have been the fulfillment of the Elijah prophecies. Cf. Mark 9:13; Rev. 11:5, 6.

[i] JUSTIFIED GOD. i.e. They testified to the righteousness of God. The common people and the outcast tax collectors who heard John the Baptist's preaching acknowledged that what he required by way of repentance was from God and was righteous.

[j] REJECTED THE WILL OF GOD. John's call to repentance was an expression of the will of God. By refusing repentance they rejected not just John the Baptist, but also God Himself.

[k] LIKE CHILDREN. Christ used strong derision to rebuke the Pharisees. He suggested they were behaving childishly, determined not to be pleased, whether invited to "dance" (a reference to Christ's joyous style of ministry, "eating and drinking" with sinners) or urged to "weep" (a reference to John the Baptist's call to repentance and John's more austere manner of ministry).

'We played the flute for you,
And you did not dance;
We mourned to you,
And you did not lament.'

[LK] For John the Baptist came neither eating bread nor drinking wine, and you say, 'He has a demon.' The Son of Man has come [l]eating and drinking, and you say, 'Look, a glutton and a winebibber, a friend of tax collectors and sinners!' But [m]wisdom is justified by all her children."

[l] EATING AND DRINKING. i.e., living an ordinary life. This passage explains why John's style of ministry differed so dramatically from Jesus' approach, although their message was the same (cf. Matt. 4:17). The different methods took away all the Pharisees' excuses. The very things they had professed to want to see in Jesus—rigid abstinence and a Spartan lifestyle—was what characterized the ministry of John the Baptist, yet they had already rejected him too. The real problem lay in the corruption of their own hearts, but they would not acknowledge that.

[m] WISDOM IS JUSTIFIED BY ALL HER CHILDREN. i.e., true wisdom is vindicated by its consequences—what it produces. Cf. James 2:14–17.

59. Woe upon Chorazin and Bethsaida

Matt. 11:20–30

MT Then He began to rebuke the cities in which most of His mighty works had been done, because they did not repent:

"[a]Woe to you, Chorazin! Woe to you, Bethsaida! For if the mighty works which were done in you had been done in [b]Tyre and Sidon, they would have repented long ago in sackcloth and ashes. But I say to you, it will be [c]more tolerable for Tyre and Sidon in the day of judgment than for you. And you, [d]Capernaum, who are exalted to heaven, will be brought down to Hades; for if the mighty works which were done in you had been done in Sodom, it would have remained until this day. But I say to you that it shall be more tolerable for the land of Sodom in the day of judgment than for you."

At that time Jesus answered and said, "I thank You, Father, Lord of heaven and earth, that You have hidden these things from *the* [e]wise and prudent and have revealed them to babes. Even so, Father, for so [f]it seemed good in Your sight. All things have been delivered to Me by My Father, and no one knows the Son

---

[a] Woe to you, Chorazin! . . . Bethsaida! Both were cities very close to Capernaum, near the northern shore of the Sea of Galilee.

[b] Tyre . . . Sidon. Phoenician cities on the shore of the Mediterranean. The prophecy about the destruction of Tyre and Sidon in Ezek. 26–28 was fulfilled in precise detail.

[c] more tolerable. This indicates that there will be degrees of punishment in hell for the ungodly (cf. Matt. 10:15; Mark 6:11; Luke 12:47, 48; Heb. 10:29).

[d] Capernaum . . . exalted . . . brought down. Capernaum, chosen by Jesus to be His headquarters, faced an even greater condemnation. Curiously, there is no record that the people of that city ever mocked or ridiculed Jesus, ran Him out of town, or threatened His life. Yet the sin of that city—indifference to Christ—was worse than Sodom's gross wickedness (cf. Matt. 10:15).

[e] wise and prudent . . . babes. There is sarcasm in these words, as the Jewish leaders are ironically identified as wise and prudent and the followers of Christ as the infants (cf. Matt. 18:3–10)—yet God has revealed to those followers the truth of the Messiah and His gospel. Cf. Matt. 13:10–17.

[f] it seemed good in Your sight. Cf. Luke 10:21–22. This is a powerful affirmation of the sovereignty of God over all the affairs of men, and in the verse that follows, Christ claimed that the task of executing the divine will had been committed to Him—a claim that would be utterly blasphemous if Jesus were anything less than sovereign God Himself.

except the Father. Nor does anyone know the Father except the Son, and *the one* to whom the Son wills to reveal *Him.* [g]Come to Me, all *you* who labor and are heavy laden, and I will give you rest. Take My yoke upon you and learn from Me, for I am gentle and lowly in heart, and [h]you will find rest for your souls. For My yoke *is* easy and My burden is light."

[g] Come to Me, all you who labor and are heavy laden. There is an echo of the first beatitude (Matt. 5:3) in this passage. Note that this is an open invitation to all who hear—but phrased in such a way that the only ones who will respond to the invitation are those who are burdened by their own spiritual bankruptcy and the weight of trying to save themselves by keeping the law. The stubbornness of humanity's sinful rebellion is such that without a sovereignly bestowed spiritual awakening, all sinners refuse to acknowledge the depth of their spiritual poverty. That is why, as Jesus says in Matt. 11:27, our salvation is the sovereign work of God. But the truth of divine election in v. 27 is not incompatible with the free offer to all in vv. 28–30.

[h] you will find rest. i.e., from the endless, fruitless effort to save oneself by the works of the law (cf. Heb. 4:1–3, 6, 9–11). This speaks of a permanent respite in the grace of God, which is apart from works (Matt. 11:30).

60. A Repentant Woman Anoints Jesus' Feet

Luke 7:36–8:3

LK Then [a]one of the Pharisees asked Him to eat with him. And He went to the Pharisee's house, and sat down to eat. And behold, a woman in the city who was a sinner, when she knew that *Jesus* sat at the table in the Pharisee's house, brought [b]an alabaster flask of fragrant oil, and [c]stood at His feet behind *Him* weeping; and she began to wash His feet with her tears, and wiped *them* with the hair of her head; and she kissed His feet and anointed *them* with the fragrant oil. Now when the Pharisee who had invited Him saw *this,* he spoke to himself, saying, "This Man, if He were a prophet, would know who and [d]what manner of woman *this is* who is touching Him, for she is a sinner."

And [e]Jesus answered and said to him, "Simon, I have something to say to you." So he said, "Teacher, say it."

"There was a certain creditor who had two debtors. One owed five hundred [f]denarii, and the other fifty. And when they had nothing with which to repay, he freely forgave them both. Tell Me, therefore, which of them will love him more?"

Simon answered and said, "I suppose the *one* whom he forgave more."

---

[a] ONE OF THE PHARISEES. His name was Simon (Luke 7:40). He does not appear to have been sympathetic to Jesus. Undoubtedly, his motive was either to entrap Jesus or to find some reason to accuse Him (cf. Luke 6:7).

[b] AN ALABASTER FLASK. This is similar in many ways to the events described in Matt. 26:6–13; Mark 14:3–9; and John 12:2–8, but it is clearly a different incident. That took place in Bethany, near Jerusalem, during the Passion Week. In the anointing at Bethany it was Mary, sister of Martha and Lazarus, who anointed Jesus. This incident takes place in Galilee and involves "a woman . . . who was a sinner"—i.e., a prostitute. There is no reason to identify this woman with Mary Magdalene, as some have done.

[c] STOOD AT HIS FEET BEHIND HIM. He was reclining at a low table, as was the custom. It would have been shocking to all for a woman of such low reputation to come to a Pharisee's house. Such dinners involving dignitaries were often open to spectators—but no one would have expected a prostitute to attend. Her coming took great courage and reveals the desperation with which she sought forgiveness. Her "weeping" was an expression of deep repentance.

[d] WHAT MANNER OF WOMAN. The Pharisees showed nothing but contempt for sinners. Simon was convinced that if Jesus knew her character, He would have sent her away, for her touching Him was presumed to convey ceremonial uncleanness.

[e] JESUS ANSWERED. Jesus knew Simon's thoughts (cf. Matt. 9:4; Luke 5:22)—demonstrating to Simon that He was indeed a Prophet.

[f] DENARII. Each denarius was worth a day's labor (cf. Matt. 22:19), so this was a large sum—about two years' full wages.

And He said to him, "You have rightly judged." Then He turned to the woman and said to Simon, "Do you see this woman? I entered your house; you gave Me [g]no water for My feet, but she has washed My feet with her tears and wiped *them* with the hair of her head. You gave Me no kiss, but this woman has not ceased to kiss My feet since the time I came in. You did not anoint My head with oil, but this woman has anointed My feet with fragrant oil. Therefore I say to you, her sins, which *are* many, are forgiven, [h]for she loved much. But to whom little is forgiven, *the same* loves little."

Then He said to her, "Your sins are forgiven."

And those who sat at the table with Him began to say to themselves, "Who is this who even [i]forgives sins?"

Then He said to the woman, "[j]Your faith has saved you. Go in peace."

Now it came to pass, afterward, that He went through every city and village, preaching and bringing the glad tidings of the kingdom of God. And the twelve *were* with Him, and [k]certain women who had been healed of evil spirits and infirmities— [l]Mary called Magdalene, out of whom had come seven demons, and [m]Joanna the wife of Chuza, Herod's steward, and [n]Susanna, and many others who provided for Him [o]from their substance.

---

[g] NO WATER FOR MY FEET. A glaring oversight. Washing a guest's feet was an essential formality (cf. John 13:4, 5). Not to offer a guest water for the washing of feet was tantamount to an insult—like it would be in modern Western culture if one did not offer to take a guest's coat.

[h] FOR SHE LOVED MUCH. This is not to suggest that she was forgiven because she loved much. The parable pictured a forgiveness that was unconditional, and love was the result. Therefore, to make the woman's love the reason for her forgiveness would be to distort the lesson Jesus is teaching here. "For" here has the sense of "wherefore." And her faith, not the act of anointing Jesus' feet, was the instrument by which she laid hold of His forgiveness.

[i] FORGIVES SINS. Cf. Matt. 9:13; Mark 2:7; Luke 5:20, 21.

[j] YOUR FAITH HAS SAVED YOU. Not all whom Jesus healed were saved, but those who exhibited true faith were (cf. Matt. 9:22; Mark 5:34; Luke 17:19; 18:42).

[k] CERTAIN WOMEN. Rabbis normally did not have women as disciples.

[l] MARY CALLED MAGDALENE. Her name probably derives from the Galilean town of Magdala. Some believe she is the woman described in Luke 7:37–50, but it seems highly unlikely that Luke would introduce her here by name for the first time if she were the main figure in the account he just completed. Also, while it is clear that she had suffered at the hands of "demons," there is no reason whatsoever to think that she had ever been a prostitute.

[m] JOANNA. This woman is also mentioned in Luke 24:10, but nowhere else in Scripture. It is possible that she was a source for some of the details Luke recounts about Herod (cf. Luke 23:8, 12).

[n] SUSANNA. Aside from this reference, she is nowhere mentioned in Scripture. She is probably someone Luke knew personally.

[o] FROM THEIR SUBSTANCE. It was a Jewish custom for disciples to support rabbis in this way. Cf. Luke 10:7; 1 Cor. 9:4–11; Gal 6:6; 1 Tim. 5:17–18.

61. The Pharisees Make Blasphemous Claims

Matt. 12:22–37; Mark 3:19b–30

MK And they [a]went into a house. Then the multitude came together again, so that they could not so much as eat bread. But when [b]His own people heard *about this,* they went out to [c]lay hold of Him, for they said, "He is [d]out of His mind."

MT Then one was brought to Him who was demon-possessed, blind and mute; and He healed him, so that the blind and mute man both spoke and saw. And all the multitudes were amazed and said, "Could this be the Son of David?" Now when the Pharisees MK and the [e]scribes who came down from Jerusalem MT heard *it* they said, MK "He has [f]Beelzebub," and MT "This *fellow* does not cast out demons except by Beelzebub, the ruler of the demons."

But Jesus knew their thoughts. MK So He called them to *Himself* and said to them in [g]parables: "How can Satan cast out Satan? MT Every kingdom divided against itself is brought to desolation, and every city or house divided against itself will not stand. If Satan casts out Satan, he MK has risen up against himself, and is divided, he cannot stand, but [h]has an end. MT How then will his kingdom

---

[a] WENT INTO A HOUSE. A clearer translation is "went home," which would refer to Jesus' return to Capernaum (cf. Mark 2:1). Verse divisions of the text are also misleading here; the phrase at the end of Mark 1:19 should be included with v. 20 and actually start the new paragraph.

[b] HIS OWN PEOPLE. In Greek this expression was used in various ways to describe someone's friends or close associates. In the strictest sense, it meant family, which is probably the best understanding here.

[c] LAY HOLD OF HIM. Mark used this same term elsewhere to mean the arrest of a person (Mark 6:17; 12:12; 14:1, 44, 46, 51). Jesus' relatives evidently heard the report of Mark 3:20 and came to Capernaum to restrain Him from His many activities and bring Him under their care and control, all supposedly for His own good.

[d] OUT OF HIS MIND. Jesus' family could only explain His unconventional lifestyle, with its willingness for others always to impose on Him, by saying He was irrational or had lost His mind.

[e] SCRIBES. Jewish scholars, also called lawyers (mostly Pharisees), who were experts on the law and its application (cf. Matt. 2:4).

[f] BEELZEBUB. i.e., Satan. Cf. Matt. 10:25. After all the displays of Jesus' deity, the Pharisees declared that He was from Satan—exactly opposite the truth, and they knew it (Matt. 9:34; Mark 3:22; Luke 11:15).

[g] PARABLES. Jesus answered the scribes by making an analogy between well-known facts and the truths He expounded (cf. Matt. 13:3).

[h] HAS AN END. An expression used only in Mark that refers to Satan's ultimate doom as head of the demonic world system. Cf. Rev. 20:1–10.

stand? And if I cast out demons by Beelzebub, by whom do your sons cast *them* out? Therefore they shall be your judges. But if I cast out demons by the Spirit of God, surely the [i]kingdom of God has come upon you. MK No one can [j]enter a strong man's house and plunder his goods, unless he first binds the strong man. And then he will plunder his house. MT He who is not with Me is against Me, and he who does not gather with Me scatters abroad.

"Therefore, MK [k]assuredly, MT I say to you, every sin MK will be forgiven the sons of men, and whatever blasphemies they may utter; but he who [l]blasphemes against the Holy Spirit [m]never has forgiveness, but is subject to eternal condemnation. MT Anyone who speaks a word against the Son of Man, [n]it will be forgiven him; but whoever speaks against the Holy Spirit, it will not be forgiven him, either in this age or in the *age* to come" — MK because they said, "He has an unclean spirit."

[Jesus said:] MT "Either make the tree good and its fruit good, or else make the tree bad and its fruit bad; for a tree is known by *its* fruit. Brood of vipers! How can you, being evil, speak good things? For out of the abundance of the heart the

---

[i] KINGDOM OF GOD HAS COME. That was precisely true. The King was in their midst, displaying His sovereign power. He showed it by demonstrating His ability to bind Satan and his demons (Matt. 12:29).

[j] ENTER A STRONG MAN'S HOUSE AND PLUNDER HIS GOODS. One must be stronger than Satan in order to enter his domain ("strong man's house"), bind him (restrain his action), and free ("plunder") people ("his goods") from his control. Only Jesus had such power over the devil. Cf. Rom. 16:20; Heb. 2:14, 15.

[k] ASSUREDLY, I SAY TO YOU. This is Mark's first use of this expression, which occurs throughout his gospel. It was employed as a formula that always introduced truthful and authoritative words from Jesus (cf. Mark 6:11; 8:12; 9:1, 41; 10:15, 29; 11:23; 12:43; 13:30; 14:9, 18, 25, 30).

[l] BLASPHEMES AGAINST THE HOLY SPIRIT. The sin He was confronting was the Pharisees' deliberate rejection of that which they knew to be of God (cf. John 11:48; Acts 4:16). They could not deny the reality of what the Holy Spirit had done through Him, so they attributed to Satan a work that they knew was of God (Matt. 12:24; Mark 3:22).

[m] NEVER HAS FORGIVENESS. Whenever someone deliberately and disrespectfully slanders the person and ministry of the Holy Spirit in pointing to the Lordship and redemption of Jesus Christ, he completely negates and forfeits any possibility of present or future forgiveness of sins, because he has wholly rejected the only basis of God's salvation.

[n] IT WILL BE FORGIVEN HIM. Someone never exposed to Christ's divine power and presence might reject Him in ignorance and be forgiven—assuming the unbelief gives way to genuine repentance. Even a Pharisee such as Saul of Tarsus could be forgiven for speaking "against the Son of Man" or persecuting His followers—because his unbelief stemmed from ignorance (1 Tim. 1:13). But those who know His claims are true and reject Him anyway sin "against the Holy Spirit"—because it is the Holy Spirit who testifies of Christ and makes His truth known to us (John 15:26; 16:14–15). No forgiveness was possible for these Pharisees who witnessed His miracles firsthand, knew the truth of His claims, and still blasphemed the Holy Spirit—because they had already rejected the fullest possible revelation. Cf. Heb. 6:4–6; 10:29.

mouth speaks. A good man out of the good treasure of his heart brings forth good things, and an evil man out of the evil treasure brings forth evil things. But I say to you that for °every idle word men may speak, they will give account of it in the day of judgment. For by your words you will be justified, and by your words you will be condemned."

° EVERY IDLE WORD. The most seemingly insignificant sin—even a slip of the tongue—carries the full potential of all hell's evil (cf. James 3:6). No infraction against God's holiness is therefore a trifling thing, and each person will ultimately give account of every such indiscretion. There is no truer indication of a bad tree than the bad fruit of speech (Matt. 12:33–35). The poisonous snakes were known by their poisonous mouths revealing evil hearts (cf. Luke 6:45). Every person is judged by his words, because they reveal the state of his heart.

62. Jesus Refuses to Perform a Sign

Matt. 12:38–45

MT Then some of the scribes and Pharisees answered, saying, "Teacher, [a]we want to see a sign from You."

But He answered and said to them, "An [b]evil and adulterous generation seeks after a sign, and no sign will be given to it except the sign of the prophet Jonah. For as Jonah was [c]three days and three nights in the belly of the great fish, so will the Son of Man be three days and three nights in the heart of the earth. The [d]men of Nineveh will rise up in the judgment with this generation and condemn it, because they repented at the preaching of Jonah; and indeed a greater than Jonah *is* here. The [e]queen of the South will rise up in the judgment with this generation and condemn it, for she came from the ends of the earth to hear the wisdom of Solomon; and indeed a greater than Solomon *is* here.

---

[a] WE WANT TO SEE A SIGN FROM YOU. They were hoping for a sign of astronomical proportions (Luke 11:16). Instead, he gives them a "sign" from Scripture. Cf. Matt. 16:1; 21:21.

[b] EVIL AND ADULTEROUS GENERATION. This speaks of spiritual adultery—unfaithfulness to God (cf. Jer. 5:7, 8).

[c] THREE DAYS AND THREE NIGHTS. Quoted from Jonah 1:17. This sort of expression was a common way of underscoring the prophetic significance of a period of time. An expression like "forty days and forty nights" may in some cases simply refer to a period of time longer than a month. "Three days and three nights" was an emphatic way of saying "three days," and by Jewish reckoning this would be an apt way of expressing a period of time that includes parts of three days. Thus, if Christ was crucified on a Friday, and His resurrection occurred on the first day of the week, by Hebrew reckoning this would qualify as three days and three nights. All sorts of elaborate schemes have been devised to suggest that Christ might have died on a Wednesday or Thursday, just to accommodate the extreme literal meaning of these words. But the original meaning would not have required that sort of wooden interpretation. Cf. Luke 13:32.

[d] MEN OF NINEVEH . . . REPENTED. See Jonah 3:5–10. The revival in Nineveh under Jonah's preaching was one of the most extraordinary spiritual revivals the world has ever seen. Some have suggested that the repentance of the Ninevites stopped short of saving faith, because the city reverted within one generation to its old pagan ways (cf. Nah. 3:7–8). From Jesus' words here, however, it is clear that the revival under Jonah represented authentic saving conversions. Only eternity will reveal how many souls from that one generation were swept into the kingdom as a result of the revival.

[e] QUEEN OF THE SOUTH. See 1 Kings 10:1–13. The queen of Sheba came to see Solomon's glory (cf. Matt. 6:29) and in the process encountered the glory of Solomon's God (1 Kings 10:9).

"When an unclean spirit goes out of a man, he goes through dry places, seeking rest, and finds none. Then he says, 'I will return to my house from which I came.' And when he comes, he finds *it* empty, swept, and put in order. Then he goes and takes with him seven other spirits more wicked than himself, and they enter and dwell there; and [f]the last *state* of that man is worse than the first. So shall it also be with this wicked generation."

[f] THE LAST STATE OF THAT MAN IS WORSE THAN THE FIRST. The problem is that the evil spirit found the house "empty." This is the description of someone who attempts moral reform without ever being indwelt by the Holy Spirit. Reform apart from regeneration is never effective and eventually reverts back to pre-reform behavior.

63. Jesus Describes His Spiritual Family

Matt. 12:46–50; Mark 3:31–35; Luke 8:19–21

MT While He was still talking to the multitudes, behold, [a]His mother and [b]brothers MK came LK to Him, and could not approach Him because of the crowd. MK And standing outside they sent to Him, calling Him, MT seeking to speak with Him. MK And a multitude was sitting around Him.

MT Then one said to Him, "Look, Your mother and Your brothers are standing outside, LK desiring to see You [and] MT speak with You."

But He answered and said to the one who told Him, "Who is My mother and [c]who are My brothers?"

MK And He looked around in a circle at those who sat about Him, MT and He stretched out His hand toward His disciples and said, "Here are My mother and My brothers—LK these who hear the word of God and do it! MT For whoever [d]does the will of My Father in heaven [e]is MK My brother and My sister and mother."

---

[a] His mother and brothers. Jesus' earthly family (cf. Matt. 12:46). The narrative that left off at Mark 3:21 resumes here (in Mark 3:31).

[b] brothers. These are actual siblings (half-brothers) of Jesus. Matthew explicitly connects them with Mary, indicating that they were not cousins or Joseph's sons from a previous marriage, as some of the church fathers imagined. They are mentioned in all the gospels (Matt. 12:46; Mark 3:31; Luke 8:19–21; John 7:3–5). Matthew and Mark give the names of four of Jesus' brothers and mention that He had sisters as well (Matt. 13:55; Mark 6:3).

[c] who are My brothers? Jesus was not repudiating His earthly family (cf. John 19:26–27). Rather, He was emphasizing the supremacy and eternality of spiritual relationships (cf. Matt. 10:37). After all, even His own family needed Him as Savior (cf. John 7:5).

[d] does the will of My Father. This is not salvation by works. Doing the will of God is the evidence of salvation by grace. Cf. Matt. 7:21–27.

[e] is My brother and My sister. Jesus made a decisive and comprehensive statement on true Christian discipleship. Such discipleship involves a spiritual relationship that transcends the physical family and is open to all who are empowered by the Spirit of God to come to Christ in repentance and faith and enabled to live a life of obedience to God's Word.

64. The Parable of the Soils

Matt. 13:1–9; Mark 4:1–9; Luke 8:4–8

MT On the same day Jesus went out of the house and [a]sat by the sea, MK and again He began to teach. MT And great multitudes were gathered together to Him, LK and they had come to Him from every city, MT so that He got into a boat and sat MK *in it* on the sea; and the whole multitude MT stood on the shore MK facing the sea.

Then He taught them many things by [b]parables, and said to them in His teaching: "Listen! MT Behold, [c]a sower went out [d]to sow LK his seed. MK And it happened, MT as he sowed, some *seed* fell by the [e]wayside; LK and it was trampled down, MK and the birds of the air came and devoured it. Some fell on [f]stony ground, where it did not have much earth; and immediately it sprang up because it had

---

[a] SAT. The typical rabbinical position for teaching; and more practically, Jesus may have sat because of the rocking of the boat in the water. Jesus' use of parables on this occasion marked a significant turning point in His ministry.

[b] PARABLES. Parables were a common form of teaching in Judaism. The Greek term for "parable" appears forty-five times in the Septuagint. A parable is a long analogy, often cast in the form of a story. Before this point in His ministry, Jesus had employed many graphic analogies (cf. Matt. 5:13–16), but their meaning was fairly clear in the context of His teaching. Parables required more explanation, and Jesus employed them to obscure the truth from unbelievers while making it clearer to His disciples. For the remainder of His Galilean ministry, He did not speak to the multitudes except in parable (Matt. 13:34). Jesus' veiling the truth from unbelievers this way was both an act of judgment and an act of mercy. It was "judgment" because it kept them in the darkness that they loved (cf. John 3:19), but it was "mercy" because they had already rejected the light, so any exposure to more truth would only increase their condemnation.

[c] A SOWER. This parable depicts the teaching of the gospel throughout the world and the various responses of people to it. Some will reject it; some will accept it for a brief time but then fall away; yet some will believe and will lead others to believe.

[d] TO SOW HIS SEED. Seed was sown by hand over plowed soil. In throwing seed toward the edges of a field, the sower would naturally throw some that landed or was blown onto the hard beaten path on the edges of the field, where it could not penetrate the soil and grow (cf. Matt. 13:4, 19). This could refer to the hard, obstinate Jewish leaders.

[e] WAYSIDE. Either a road near a field's edge or a path that traversed a field, both of which were hard surfaces due to constant foot traffic and the baking of the sun.

[f] STONY GROUND. Very shallow soil atop a layer of bedrock. From the top it looks fertile, but there is no depth to sustain a root system or reach water. This was caused by beds of solid rock, usually limestone, lying under the surface of good soil. They are a little too deep for the plow to reach and too shallow to allow a plant to reach water and develop a decent root system in the small amount of soil that covers them. This type of soil could refer to the fickle mob that followed Jesus only for His miracles.

no depth of earth. But when the sun was up it was scorched, and because it had no root it LK lacked moisture [and] MK withered away. And some *seed* fell among [g]thorns; and the thorns grew up LK with it MK and choked it, and it yielded no crop. But other *seed* fell on good ground and yielded a crop that sprang up, [h]increased and produced: some thirtyfold, some sixty, and some a hundred."
LK When He had said these things He cried, [i]"He who has ears to hear, let him hear!"

---

[g] THORNS. Tough, thistle-bearing weeds, which were still in the ground after plowing had been done. They would use up the available space, light, and water that good plants need. This could refer to the materialists to whom earthly wealth was more important than spiritual riches.

[h] INCREASED . . . A HUNDRED. An average ratio of harvested grain to what had been sown was 8 to 1, with a 10-to-1 ratio considered exceptional. The yields Jesus refers to constitute an unbelievable harvest.

[i] "HE WHO HAS EARS TO HEAR, LET HIM HEAR!" On the surface this is a call for the listener to be attentive and discern the meaning of His analogy. Yet more than human understanding is necessary to interpret the parable—only those who have been redeemed will have the true meaning explained to them by the divine Teacher. All three of the Synoptics include this admonition with the parable of the sower (cf. Matt. 13:9, Mark 4:9; Luke 8:8). Jesus often said this to stress particularly important statements cast in mysterious language (cf. Matt. 11:15; 13:43; Mark 4:23; Luke 14:35).

65. The Parable of the Soils Explained

Matt. 13:10–23; Mark 4:10–25; Luke 8:9–18

MK But when He was alone, those around Him with the twelve— LK His disciples— MT came to Him and MK asked Him about the parable, LK saying, "What does this parable mean?" [and] MT "Why do You speak to them in parables?"

He answered and said to them, "Because LK to you [a]it has been given to know the [b]mysteries of the kingdom of God, but to the rest MT it has not been given. MK To [c]those who are outside, all things come in parables. MT Therefore I speak to them in parables, [d]because seeing they do not see, and hearing they do not hear, nor do they understand. And in them the [e]prophecy of Isaiah is fulfilled, which says:

'Hearing you will hear and shall not understand,
And seeing you will see and not perceive;
For the hearts of this people have grown dull.
Their ears are hard of hearing,
And their eyes they have closed,
Lest they should see with *their* eyes and hear with *their* ears,

---

[a] IT HAS BEEN GIVEN TO KNOW. Here Jesus clearly affirms that the ability to comprehend spiritual truth is a gracious gift of God, sovereignly bestowed on the elect. The reprobate ones, on the other hand, are passed over. They reap the natural consequence of their own unbelief and rebellion—spiritual blindness.

[b] MYSTERIES OF THE KINGDOM. "Mysteries" are those truths which have been hidden from all ages in the past and revealed in the NT. Cf. 1 Cor. 2:7; 4:1; Eph. 3:4–5. Many specific doctrines of the NT are identified as "mysteries" (e.g., Rom. 11:25; 1 Cor. 15:51; Eph. 5:32; 6:19; Col. 1:26, 27; 2 Thess. 2:7; 1 Tim. 3:9, 16). In context the subject of the mystery is the kingdom of heaven (cf. Matt. 3:2), which Jesus communicates in the form of parables. Thus the mystery is revealed to those who believe, yet it remains concealed to those who reject Christ and His gospel (cf. Matt. 13:11).

[c] THOSE WHO ARE OUTSIDE. Those who are not followers of Christ.

[d] BECAUSE SEEING THEY DO NOT SEE. Matthew 13:13 seems to suggest that their own unbelief is the cause of their spiritual blindness. Luke 8:10, however, emphasizes God's initiative in obscuring the truth from these unbelievers. Both things are true, of course. Yet we are not to think that God blinds them because He somehow delights in their destruction (cf. Ezek. 33:11). This judicial blinding may be viewed as an act of mercy, lest their condemnation be increased.

[e] PROPHECY OF ISAIAH. Quoted from Isa. 6:9–10.

[f]Lest they should understand with *their* hearts and turn,
So that I should heal them.
MK And *their* sins be forgiven them.'

LK "But blessed *are* your eyes for they see, and your ears for they hear; for assuredly, I say to you that [g]many prophets and righteous *men* desired to see what you see, and did not see *it*, and to hear what you hear, and did not hear *it*."

MK And He said to them, "Do you not understand this parable? How then will you understand [h]all the parables? MT Therefore hear the parable of the sower. LK The parable is this: The seed is the word of God. MK [i]The sower sows the word. And these are the ones MT who received seed MK by the wayside where the word is sown. MT When anyone hears [j]the word of the kingdom, and does not understand *it*, LK the [k]devil MK comes immediately and MT snatches away MK the word that was sown in their hearts, LK lest they should believe and be saved.

MK "These likewise are the ones MT who received the seed MK on [l]stony ground who, when they hear the word, immediately [m]receive it with gladness; and they have [n]no root in themselves, LK who [o]believe for a while and in time of temptation

---

[f] Lest they should turn. The implication is that unbelievers do not want to turn from sin.

[g] many . . . desired to see. Cf. John 8:56; 1 Peter 1:9–12.

[h] all the parables. Understanding the parable of the sower was to be key in the disciples' ability to discern the meaning of Jesus' other parables of the kingdom (Matt. 13:21–34).

[i] The sower. Here Jesus begins His explanation of the parable of the sower, who is in fact Jesus Himself and anyone who proclaims the gospel of salvation.

[j] the word of the kingdom. The message of how to enter God's kingdom, the sphere of salvation, i.e., the gospel (cf. "word of reconciliation" in 2 Cor. 5:19).

[k] devil. The wicked one, Satan. Cf. 1 John 5:19. The gospel never penetrates these souls, so it disappears from the surface of their understanding—seen as the enemy snatching it away.

[l] stony ground. Some people make an emotional, superficial commitment to salvation in Christ, but it is not real. They remain interested only until there is a sacrificial price to pay and then abandon Christ. Cf. 1 John 2:19.

[m] receive it with gladness. An enthusiastic, emotional, yet superficial response to the gospel that does not take into account the cost involved.

[n] no root. Because the person's heart is hard, like the stony ground, the gospel never takes root in the individual's soul and never transforms his life—there is only a temporary, surface change.

[o] who believe for a while. i.e., with a nominal, nonsaving faith. Cf. Matt. 13:20.

fall away, [MK] and so endure only for a time. Afterward, when [p]tribulation or persecution arises for the word's sake, immediately they [q]stumble.

"Now these are the ones [MT] [r]who received seed [MK] sown among thorns; *they are* the ones who, [LK] when they have heard, go out and [MK] the [s]cares of this world, the [t]deceitfulness of riches, [LK] [the] pleasures of life, [MK] and the desires for other things entering in choke the word, and it becomes unfruitful. [LK] [They] bring no fruit to maturity.

[MK] "But these are the ones [MT] who received seed [MK] sown on [u]good ground, [LK] those who, having [v]heard the word with a noble and good heart, [MT] understand *it,* [MK] accept *it,* [LK] keep *it* and bear fruit with patience: [MK] some thirtyfold, some sixty, and some a hundred."

Also He said to them, [LK] "No one, when he has lit a [w]lamp, covers it with a [MK] basket [LK] or puts *it* [x]under a bed, but sets *it* on [y]a lampstand, that those who

---

[p] TRIBULATION OR PERSECUTION. Not the routine difficulties and troubles of life, but specifically the suffering, trials, and persecutions which result from one's association with God's Word.

[q] STUMBLE. The Greek word also means, "to fall" or "to cause offense," and from this comes the English word *scandalize.* All those meanings are appropriate since the superficial believer is offended, stumbles, and falls away when his faith is put to the test (cf. John 8:31; 1 John 2:19).

[r] WHO RECEIVED SEED SOWN AMONG THE THORNS. These make superficial commitments without a true repentance. They can't break with the love of money and the world (James 4:4; 1 John 2:15–17; cf. Matt. 19:16–22).

[s] CARES OF THIS WORLD. Lit. "the distractions of the age." A preoccupation with the temporal issues of this present age blinds a person to any serious consideration of the gospel (cf. James 4:4; 1 John 2:15–16).

[t] DECEITFULNESS OF RICHES. Not only can money and material possessions not satisfy the desires of the heart or bring the lasting happiness they deceptively promise, but they also blind those who pursue them to eternal, spiritual concerns (1 Tim. 6:9–10).

[u] GOOD GROUND. As there were three soils with no fruit, thus no salvation, there are three kinds of good soil with fruit. Not all believers are equally fruitful, but all are fruitful (cf. Matt. 7:16; John 15:8).

[v] HEARD . . . UNDERSTAND . . . ACCEPT . . . KEEP . . . BEAR FRUIT. Believers, in contrast to unbelievers, hear God's Word because God allows them to hear it. They "understand" and "accept" it—they genuinely believe because God opens their mind and heart and transforms their lives. "Keep" refers to ongoing obedience (cf. John 14:21–24). The result is that they produce spiritual fruit. "Fruit" is good works (Matt. 7:16–20; James 2:14–26).

[w] LAMP. This refers to a very small clay bowl made with a spout to hold a wick and containing a few ounces of oil that served as the fuel.

[x] UNDER A BED. The fact that Christ taught mysteries in parables was not to suggest that His message was meant for elite disciples or that it should be kept secret. A lamp is not lit to be hidden but must be put on a lampstand, where its light will reach furthest. Still, only those with eyes to see will see it.

[y] A LAMPSTAND. In common homes this was simply a shelf protruding from the wall. Wealthier homes might have separate, ornate stands (cf. Rev. 1:12).

enter may see the light. MK For [z]there is nothing hidden which will not be revealed, nor has anything been kept [aa]secret but that it should LK be known and come to light. MK If anyone has ears to hear, let him hear."

Then He said to them, LK [bb]"Take heed how you hear. MK [cc]With the same measure you use, it will be measured to you; and to you who hear, more will be given. For whoever has, to him [dd]more will be given, MT and he will have abundance; MK but whoever does not have, even what he has will be taken away from him."

---

[z] THERE IS NOTHING HIDDEN . . . REVEALED. The purpose in keeping something hidden is so that one day it can be revealed. Jesus' teaching was never intended to be just for an inner circle of followers. It would be the responsibility of the disciples to communicate the gospel of the kingdom to the world at large (cf. Matt. 28:19–20).

[aa] SECRET. All truth will be manifest in the judgment. Cf. Luke 12:2–3; 1 Cor. 4:5; 1 Tim. 5:24–25. God's ultimate purpose is not to hide the truth, but to make it known.

[bb] TAKE HEED HOW YOU HEAR. One's response to the light in this life is crucial, because at the throne of judgment there will be no opportunity to embrace truth that was formerly spurned (Rev. 20:11–15). Those who scorn the light of the gospel now will have all light removed from them in eternity. Cf. Matt. 25:29; Luke 19:26.

[cc] WITH THE SAME MEASURE. The spiritual results that the disciples realized were to be based on the amount of effort they put forth; they would reap as they had sown.

[dd] MORE WILL BE GIVEN. The one who has learned spiritual truth and applied it diligently will receive even more truth to faithfully apply.

66. Four Kingdom Parables

Matt. 13:24–35; Mark 4:26–34

MK And He said, "The kingdom of God is as if a man should [a]scatter seed on the ground, and should sleep by night and rise by day, and the seed should sprout and grow, he himself does not know how. For the earth yields crops by itself: first the blade, then the head, after that the full grain in the head. But when the grain ripens, immediately [b]he puts in the sickle, because the harvest has come."

MT Another parable He put forth to them, saying: "The kingdom of heaven is like a man who sowed good seed in his field; but while men slept, his enemy came and sowed [c]tares among the wheat and went his way. But when the grain had sprouted and produced a crop, then the tares also appeared. So the servants of the owner came and said to him, 'Sir, did you not sow good seed in your field? How then does it have tares?' He said to them, 'An enemy has done this.' The servants said to him, 'Do you want us then to go and gather them up?' But he said, 'No, lest while you gather up the tares you also uproot the wheat with them. Let both grow together until the harvest, and at the time of harvest I will say to the reapers, "First gather together the tares and bind them in bundles to burn them, but gather the wheat into my barn." ' "

[d]Another parable He put forth to them, saying: MK "To what shall we liken the kingdom of God? Or with what parable shall we picture it? MT The kingdom of

---

[a] SCATTER SEED. This parable is recorded only by Mark and complements the parable of the sower by explaining in more depth the results of spiritual growth accomplished in good soil.

[b] HE PUTS IN THE SICKLE, BECAUSE THE HARVEST HAS COME. When the grain is ripe, the sower of the seed must harvest the crop. There are two possible interpretations of this unexplained parable. It could be referring to the entire scope of the kingdom, from the time Jesus sowed the gospel message until the final harvest in the future. His disciples would continue the work of presenting the gospel that would eventually yield a harvest. The better interpretation pictures the gospel working in lives. After the gospel is presented, the Word of God works in the individual heart, sometimes slowly, until the time when God reaps the harvest in that individual and saves him.

[c] TARES. Probably darnel, a type of weed that can hardly be distinguished from wheat until the head matures. In an agricultural setting, sowing darnel in someone else's wheat field was a way for enemies to destroy someone's livelihood catastrophically. It pictures Satan's efforts to deceive the church by mingling his children with God's, in some cases making it impossible for believers to discern the true from the false. The parable is explained in Matt. 13:36–43.

[d] ANOTHER PARABLE. This parable of the mustard seed pictures the kingdom of God beginning with a small influence and then becoming worldwide in its scope.

heaven is like [e]a mustard seed, which a man took and sowed in his field, which indeed is [f]the least of all the seeds MK [g]on earth; but when it is sown, it grows up and becomes greater than all [h]herbs, and shoots out large branches MT and becomes [i]a tree, so that the birds of the air come and nest in its branches, MK under its shade."

MT Another parable He spoke to them: "[j]The kingdom of heaven is like leaven, which a woman took and hid in three measures of meal till it was all leavened."

MK With many such parables He spoke the word MT to the multitude, MK as they were able to hear *it.* But [k]without a parable He did not speak to them, MT that it might be fulfilled which was [l]spoken by the prophet, saying:

> "I will open My mouth in parables;
> I will utter things kept secret from the foundation of the world."

MK And when they were alone, He explained all things to His disciples.

---

[e] A MUSTARD SEED. A reference to the common black mustard plant. The leaves were used as a vegetable and the seed as a condiment. It also had medicinal benefits.

[f] THE LEAST OF ALL THE SEEDS. Smaller than all. The mustard seed is not the smallest of all seeds in existence, but it was in comparison to all the other seeds the Jews sowed in Israel.

[g] ON EARTH. Better translated as "on the soil."

[h] HERBS. Refers to garden vegetables grown specifically for eating.

[i] A TREE, SO THAT THE BIRDS OF THE AIR COME AND NEST IN ITS BRANCHES. Palestinian mustard plants are large shrubs, sometimes up to fifteen feet high—certainly large enough for birds to lodge in. This is undoubtedly a reference to several OT passages, including Ezek. 17:23; 31:6; Dan. 4:21—passages which prophesied the inclusion of Gentiles in the kingdom. The tree represents the sphere of salvation, which would grow so large that it would provide shelter, protection, and benefit to people (cf. Matt. 13:32). Even unbelievers have been blessed by association with the gospel and the power of God in salvation. Christians have been a benediction to the world. Cf. 1 Cor. 7:14.

[j] THE KINGDOM OF HEAVEN IS LIKE LEAVEN. Here the kingdom is pictured as yeast, multiplying quietly and permeating all that it contacts. The lesson is the same as the parable of the mustard seed. Some interpreters suggest that since leaven is nearly always a symbol of evil in Scripture (cf. Mark 8:15), it must carry that connotation here as well. They make the leaven some evil influence inside the kingdom. But that twists Jesus actual words and violates the context, in which Jesus is repeatedly describing that kingdom itself as the pervading influence.

[k] WITHOUT A PARABLE HE DID NOT SPEAK TO THEM. On that particular day, Jesus spoke to the larger crowd only in parables. This method of teaching left unbelievers with riddles and kept them from being forced to believe or disbelieve Him—they could make no decision to follow Him, since they did not understand what He taught. Moreover, for the remainder of His Galilean ministry, all Jesus' public teaching consisted only of parables.

[l] SPOKEN BY THE PROPHET. The "prophet" in this case was the psalmist. Cf. Ps. 78:2.

67. Jesus Explains the Parable of the Tares

Matt. 13:36–43

MT Then Jesus sent the multitude away and went into the house. And His disciples came to Him, saying, "Explain to us the parable of the tares of the field."

He answered and said to them: "[a] He who sows the good seed is the Son of Man. The field is the world, the good seeds are the sons of the kingdom, but the tares are the sons of the wicked *one.* The enemy who sowed them is the devil, the harvest is the end of the age, and the reapers are the angels. Therefore as the tares are gathered and burned in the fire, so it will be at the end of this age. The Son of Man will send out His angels, and they will gather out of His kingdom all things that offend, and those who practice lawlessness, and will cast them into the furnace of fire. There will be wailing and gnashing of teeth. Then the righteous will [b]shine forth as the sun in the kingdom of their Father. He who has ears to hear, let him hear!"

---

[a] HE WHO SOWS. The true sower of salvation seed is the Lord Himself. He alone can give the power in the heart to transform. He is the One who saves sinners, even through the preaching and witnessing of believers (Rom. 10:14).

[b] SHINE FORTH AS THE SUN. Cf. Dan. 12:3. Believers already shine in that they possess the Spirit of Christ and the glorious message of the gospel (Matt. 5:16; 2 Cor. 4:3–7). We will shine even more in the glory of Christ's kingdom and eternal heaven (Rom. 8:16–23; Phil. 3:20–21; Rev. 19:7–9).

68. Additional Kingdom Parables

Matt. 13:44–52

MT "Again, [a]the kingdom of heaven is like treasure hidden in a field, which a man found and hid; and for joy over it he goes and sells all that he has and buys that field.

"Again, the kingdom of heaven is like a merchant seeking beautiful pearls, who, when he had found one pearl of great price, went and sold all that he had and bought it.

"Again, the kingdom of heaven is like a [b]dragnet that was cast into the sea and gathered some of every kind, which, when it was full, they drew to shore; and they sat down and gathered the good into vessels, but threw the bad away. So it will be at the end of the age. The [c]angels will come forth, separate the wicked from among the just, and cast them into the furnace of fire. There will be wailing and gnashing of teeth."

Jesus said to them, "Have you understood all these things?" They said to Him, "Yes, Lord." Then He said to them, "Therefore every scribe instructed concerning the kingdom of heaven is like a householder who [d]brings out of his treasure *things* new and old."

---

[a] THE KINGDOM OF HEAVEN IS LIKE. These two parables have identical meanings. Both picture salvation as something hidden from most people, but so valuable that people who have it revealed to them are willing to give up all they have to possess it.

[b] DRAGNET. Some fishing was done with a large weighted net dragged along the bottom of the lake. When pulled in, it contained an assortment that had to be separated. In a similar way the visible kingdom, the sphere of those who claim to be believers, is full of both good and bad and will be sorted in the judgment.

[c] ANGELS. They serve God in judgment (cf. Matt. 13:41; 2 Thess. 1:7–10).

[d] BRINGS OUT OF HIS TREASURE THINGS NEW AND OLD. The disciples were not to spurn the old for the sake of the new. Rather, the new insights they gleaned from Jesus' parables were to be understood in light of the old truths and vice versa.

69. Jesus Calms the Storm

Matt. 8:18, 23–27; 13:53; Mark 4:35–41; Luke 8:22–25

MT Now [a]it came to pass, when Jesus had finished these parables, that He departed from there.

MK On the same day, when evening had come, MT and when Jesus saw great multitudes about Him, He gave a command to depart to [b]the other side. Now when He got into a boat, His disciples followed Him. LK And He said to them, "Let us cross over to the other side of the lake." And they launched out. MK Now when they had left the multitude, they took Him along in the boat as He was. And other little boats were also with Him. LK But as they sailed He fell asleep.

MT And [c]suddenly a [d]great tempest arose on the sea, so that the boat was covered with the waves. MK The waves beat into the boat, so that it was already filling, LK and [they] were in jeopardy. MK But [e]He was in the stern, asleep on a pillow. MT Then His disciples came to *Him* and awoke Him, saying, LK "Master, Master, MK do You not care that we are perishing? MT Lord, save us!"

MK Then He arose and rebuked the wind, and said to the LK raging MK sea, [f]"Peace, be still!" And the wind ceased and there was a great [g]calm. But He said to

---

[a] IT CAME TO PASS. This account demonstrates Jesus' unlimited power over the natural world.

[b] THE OTHER SIDE. Jesus and His disciples were on the western shore of the Sea of Galilee. To escape the crowds for a brief respite, Jesus wanted to go to the eastern shore, which had no large cities and therefore fewer people.

[c] SUDDENLY A GREAT TEMPEST AROSE. The Sea of Galilee is more than 690 feet below sea level. To the north Mount Hermon rises 9,200 feet, and from May to October strong winds often sweep through the narrow surrounding gorges into this valley, causing extremely sudden and violent storms.

[d] GREAT TEMPEST. Wind is a common occurrence on that lake, about 690 feet below sea level and surrounded by hills. The Greek word can also mean "whirlwind." In this case, it was a storm so severe that it took on the properties of a hurricane. The disciples, even though used to being on the lake in the wind, thought this storm would drown them.

[e] HE WAS . . . ASLEEP. Just before the disciples saw one of the most awesome displays of His deity, they were given a touching picture of His humanity. He was so weary that not even the violent tossing of the boat awakened Him—even though the disciples feared they would be killed. Jesus was so exhausted from a full day of healing and preaching, even that storm could not wake Him up.

[f] "PEACE, BE STILL!" Lit. "be silent, be muzzled." Storms normally subside gradually, but when the Creator gave the order, the natural elements of this storm ceased immediately.

them, "Why are you so fearful? How *is it* that you have no faith?" And [h]they feared exceedingly, [LK] and marveled, saying to one another, "[i]Who can this be? For He commands even [j]the winds and water, and they obey Him!"

---

[g] calm. Cf. Pss. 65:7; 89:9.

[h] they feared exceedingly. This was not fear of being harmed by the storm, but a reverence for the supernatural power Jesus had just displayed. The only thing more terrifying than having a storm outside the boat was having God in the boat!

[i] Who can this be? This statement betrayed the disciples' wonder at the true identity of Jesus.

[j] the winds and water . . . obey Him. This was convincing proof of His deity (cf. Pss. 29:3, 4; 89:9; 93:4; 107:25–29).

70. Jesus Casts Out Demons into Swine

Matt. 8:28–34; Mark 5:1–20; Luke 8:26–39

MK Then they LK sailed MK to [a]the other side of the sea, to the [b]country of the Gadarenes, LK which is opposite Galilee. MK And when He had LK stepped MK out of the boat LK on the land, MK immediately there met Him MT [c]two demon-possessed *men*, coming [d]out of the tombs, exceedingly fierce, so that no one could pass that way.

[One of these was] LK a certain man from the city who had demons for a long time. And he wore no clothes, nor did he live in a house but in the tombs. MK And [e]no one could bind him, not even with chains, because he had often been bound with [f]shackles and chains. And the chains had been pulled apart by him, and the shackles broken in pieces; neither could anyone tame him. And always, night and day, he was in the mountains and in the tombs, [g]crying out and cutting himself with stones. When he saw Jesus from afar, he ran and worshiped Him. And LK he cried out, fell down before Him, and with a loud voice said, MT" [h]What have we to

---

[a] THE OTHER SIDE OF THE SEA. The eastern shore of the Sea of Galilee (cf. Luke 8:26).

[b] COUNTRY OF THE GADARENES. Alternate readings are "Gergesenes" (cf. Matt. 8:28) or "Gerasenes" (cf. Mark 5:1). This refers to a small town on the lake opposite Tiberius, perhaps where the modern village of Khersa (Kursi) is located. Some ancient tombs are there, and the shoreline descends steeply into the water, exactly matching the description of the terrain in this account. "Country of" refers to the general region that included Gersa and was under the jurisdiction of the city of Gadara, which was located some six miles southeast of the Sea of Galilee; this was probably why Luke referred to the region as the country of the Gadarenes (Luke 8:26, 37).

[c] TWO DEMON-POSSESSED MEN. Mark 5:2 and Luke 8:27 mention only one of the men. Evidently one was more dominant than the other. Only one did the talking.

[d] OUT OF THE TOMBS. The "tombs"—common dwelling places for the demented of that day—were burial chambers carved out of rock hillsides on the outskirts of town.

[e] NO ONE COULD BIND HIM. Multiple negatives are used in the Greek text to emphasize the man's tremendous strength.

[f] SHACKLES AND CHAINS. "Shackles" (probably metal or perhaps, in part, cord or rope) were used to restrain the feet and "chains" were metal restraints for the rest of the body.

[g] CRYING OUT AND CUTTING HIMSELF WITH STONES. "Crying out" describes a continual unearthly scream uttered with intense emotion. The "stones" likely were rocks made of flint with sharp, jagged edges.

[h] WHAT HAVE WE TO DO WITH YOU? A common expression of protest (cf. Mark 1:24).

do with You, MK Jesus, [i]Son of the Most High God? MT Have You come here [j]to torment us before the time? MK I implore You by God that You do not torment me."

LK For He had commanded the [k]unclean spirit to come out of the man. For it had often seized him, and he was kept under guard, bound with chains and shackles; and he broke the bonds and was driven by the demon into the wilderness.

MK Then LK Jesus asked him, saying, [l]"What is your name?" MK And he answered, saying, "My name *is* [m]Legion; for we are many"— LK because many demons had entered him. And [n]they begged Him MK earnestly that He would [o]not send them out of the country [nor] LK command them to go out into the abyss.

MK Now a large [p]herd of swine was feeding there, MT a good way off from them, MK near the mountains. So all the demons begged Him, saying, MT "If You cast us out, permit us to go away into the herd of swine, MK that we may enter them." And at once [q]Jesus gave them permission [and] MT said to them, "Go." MK Then the

---

[i] Son of the Most High God? The demons knew that Jesus was deity, the God-Man. "Most High God" was an ancient title used by both Jews and Gentiles to identify the one, true, and living God of Israel and distinguish Him from all false idol gods (cf. Gen. 14:18–20; Num. 24:16; Deut. 32:8; Pss. 18:13; 21:7; Isa. 14:14; Dan. 3:26; Luke 1:32; Heb. 7:1).

[j] to torment us before the time? Evidently, even the demons not only recognized the deity of Jesus, but also knew there was a divinely appointed time for their judgment and He would be their judge. Their eschatology was factually correct, but it is one thing to know the truth and quite another thing to love it (cf. James 2:19). Mark adds "I implore you," which shows the demon tried to have Jesus soften the severity of his inevitable fate.

[k] unclean spirit. This refers to the demon who was controlling the man. Such spirits in themselves were morally filthy and caused much harm for those whom they possessed (cf. Mark 1:32–34; Luke 4:33, 36; 7:21; 8:2).

[l] "What is your name?" Most likely, Jesus asked this in view of the demon's appeal not to be tormented. However, He did not need to know the demon's name in order to expel him. Rather, Jesus posed the question to bring the reality and complexity of this case into the open.

[m] Legion. A Latin term, by then common to Jews and Greeks, that defined a Roman military unit of six thousand infantrymen. Such a name denotes that the man was controlled by an extremely large number of militant evil spirits, a truth reiterated by the expression "for we are many."

[n] they begged. The demons understood that Jesus had all power over them and addressed Him with an intense desire that their request be granted. Luke 8:31 relates they pleaded not to be sent into the abyss, meaning the pit, the underworld, the prison of bound demons who disobeyed (cf. 2 Peter 2:4; Jude 6). They knew Jesus had the power and authority to send them there if He desired.

[o] not send them out of the country. The demons wanted to remain in the same area where they had been exercising their evil powers.

[p] herd of swine. Such a large herd of unclean animals suggests that Gentiles dominated the region. It also suggests that the number of demons was large.

[q] Jesus gave them permission. According to His sovereign purposes Jesus allowed the demons to enter the pigs and destroy them—the text offers no other explanation (cf. Deut. 29:29; Rom. 9:20). By doing this, Jesus gave the man a graphic, visible, and powerful lesson on the immensity of the evil from which he had been delivered.

unclean spirits went out LK of the man MK and entered MT into the herd of [r]swine MK (there were about two thousand); and MT suddenly the whole herd of swine ran violently down the steep place into the sea, and perished in the water. LK When those who fed *them* saw what had happened, they fled MT and they went away into the city and told everything LK in the city and in the country MT including what *had happened* to the demon-possessed *men.* And behold, the whole city came out MK to see what it was that had happened.

Then they came to MT meet Jesus, LK and found the man MK *who had been* demon-possessed and had the legion, LK from whom the demons had departed, [s]sitting at the feet of Jesus, clothed and [t]in his right mind. And they were afraid.

MK And [u]those who saw it told them LK by what means he who had been demon-possessed was healed, MK and about the swine. Then LK the whole multitude of the surrounding region of the Gadarenes MT [v]begged *Him* to depart from their region, LK for they were seized with great fear. And He got into the boat and returned.

Now the man from whom the demons had departed begged Him that he might be with Him. MK However, Jesus did not permit him, but LK sent him away, saying, MK "Go home to your friends, and [w]tell them what great things the Lord has done for you, and how He has had compassion on you." And he departed and began to proclaim in [x]Decapolis, LK throughout the whole city what great things MK Jesus had done for him; and all marveled.

---

[r] swine. Pigs were unclean animals to the Jews, so the people tending this herd were most likely Gentiles.

[s] sitting. The man's restful condition was a strong contrast with his former restless, agitated state.

[t] in his right mind. He was no longer under the frenzied, screaming control of the demons.

[u] those who saw it told . . . about the swine. "Those" may refer to both the twelve disciples and the men who tended the pigs. They wanted people to know what had happened to the man and the pigs, and the relationship between the two events.

[v] begged Him to depart. The residents of the region became frightened and resentful toward Jesus because of what had happened. They may have been concerned about the disruption of their normal routine and the loss of property, and they wanted Jesus and His powers to leave the area so no more such financial losses would occur. More compelling, however, was the reality that they were ungodly people frightened by Christ's display of spiritual power.

[w] tell them . . . the Lord has done. Jesus was referring to Himself as God who controlled both the natural and the supernatural worlds (cf. Luke 8:39).

[x] Decapolis. A league of ten Greek-influenced (Hellenized) cities east of the Jordan River (cf. Matt. 4:25).

71. Jesus Heals a Woman and Raises a Girl

Matt. 9:18–26; Mark 5:21–43; Luke 8:40–56

MK Now when Jesus had crossed over again by boat to [a]the other side, a great multitude gathered to Him LK [and] welcomed Him, for they were all waiting for Him; MK and He was by the sea.

MT [b]While He spoke [certain] things to them, behold, MK one of the [c]rulers of the synagogue came, [d]Jairus by name. And when he saw Him, LK he fell down at Jesus' feet MT and worshiped Him, MK and begged Him earnestly LK to come to his house, MK saying, "My little daughter lies at the point of death. Come and lay Your hands on her, that she may be healed, and she will live." LK For he had an only daughter about twelve years of age, and she was dying. MT So Jesus arose and followed him, and so *did* His disciples. LK But as He went, MK a great multitude followed Him and [e]thronged Him.

MK Now a certain woman had [f]a flow of blood for twelve years, and had [g]suffered many things from many physicians LK and could not be healed by any. MK She had

---

[a] THE OTHER SIDE. Jesus and the disciples returned to the northwest shore of the Sea of Galilee.

[b] WHILE HE SPOKE. Though the phrase, "while He spoke these things" (in Matt. 9:18) might seem to suggest a chronological sequence between Matt. 9:14–17 and 9:18–26, it is more likely that Matthew did not intend such a sequence. This section of Matthew's gospel is not chronologically arranged. Thus, it is best to follow the sequence found in Mark and Luke.

[c] RULERS OF THE SYNAGOGUE. They presided over the elders of local synagogues. Those elder groups, made up of lay officials, were in charge of arranging the services and overseeing other synagogue affairs.

[d] JAIRUS. This man was a ruler of the synagogue. Jesus had once cast a demon out of a man in Jairus's synagogue (Luke 4:33–37).

[e] THRONGED. Lit. "choked," i.e., they almost crushed Him.

[f] A FLOW OF BLOOD FOR TWELVE YEARS. Denotes a chronic internal hemorrhage, perhaps from a tumor or other disease. This woman's affliction not only was serious physically but also left her permanently unclean for ceremonial reasons (cf. Lev. 15:25–27). This meant she would have been shunned by all, including her own family, and excluded from both synagogue and temple.

[g] SUFFERED MANY THINGS FROM MANY PHYSICIANS. In NT times, it was common practice in difficult medical cases for people to consult many different doctors and receive a variety of treatments. The supposed cures were often conflicting, abusive, and many times made the ailment worse, not better. (Luke, the physician, in Luke 8:43 suggested the woman was not helped because her condition was incurable.)

spent all that she had, LK all her livelihood, MK and was no better, but rather grew worse. When she heard about Jesus, she MT suddenly MK [h]came behind *Him* in the crowd and touched LK the [i]border of His garment. MT For she said to herself, "[j]If only I may touch His garment, I shall be made well." LK And immediately her [k]flow of blood stopped, MK and she felt in *her* body that she was healed of the affliction. And Jesus, immediately knowing in Himself that [l]power had gone out of Him, turned around in the crowd and said, [m]"Who touched My clothes?" LK When all denied it, Peter and those MK disciples LK with him said, "Master, the multitudes throng and press You, and You say, 'Who touched Me?'" But Jesus said, "Somebody touched Me, for I perceived power going out from Me."

MK And He looked around to see her who had done this thing. LK Now when the woman saw that she was not hidden, she came MK fearing and trembling, knowing what had happened to her, LK and falling down before Him, she declared to Him in the presence of all the people MK the whole truth— LK the reason she had touched Him and how she was healed immediately. MK And He said to her, MT "Be of good cheer, daughter; your faith has [n]made you well. MK Go in peace, and be healed of your affliction." MT And the woman was made well from that hour.

MK While He was still speaking, *some* came from the ruler of the synagogue's *house* who said, "Your daughter is dead. Why trouble the Teacher any further?" As soon as Jesus heard the word that was spoken, He said to the ruler of the syna-

---

[h] CAME BEHIND . . . AND TOUCHED. Because of her affliction, she would normally render anyone she touched unclean. The effect here was precisely the opposite. Cf. Luke 7:14, 39.

[i] BORDER OF HIS GARMENT. Cf. Matt. 14:36. Probably one of the tassels sewn to the corners of a garment, in order to remind the wearer to obey God's commandments (Num. 15:38–40; Deut. 22:12).

[j] IF ONLY I MAY TOUCH HIS GARMENT. The woman's faith in Jesus' healing powers was so great that she believed even indirect contact with Him through His garments (cf. Matt. 9:20) would be enough to produce a cure.

[k] FLOW OF BLOOD STOPPED. Mark refers to this as the "fountain of her blood" (Mark 5:29), the analogy being to the origin of a spring. Jesus' healing power cured her problem at its source.

[l] POWER HAD GONE OUT OF HIM. Christ's "power," His inherent ability to minister and work supernaturally, proceeded from Him under the conscious control of His sovereign will.

[m] "WHO TOUCHED MY CLOTHES?" Jesus asked this question not out of ignorance, but so He might draw the woman out of the crowd and allow her to praise God for what had happened.

[n] MADE YOU WELL. Jesus' public statement concerning the woman's faith and its results. The form of the Greek verb translated "has made you well," which can also be rendered "has made you whole," indicates that her healing was complete. It is the same Greek word often translated "to save" and is the normal NT word for saving from sin, which strongly suggests that the woman's faith also led to spiritual salvation.

gogue, "Do not be afraid; [o]only believe, LK and she will be made well." MK And He permitted no one to follow Him except [p]Peter, James, and John the brother of James, LK and the father and mother of the girl. MK Then He came to the house of the ruler of the synagogue, and saw a tumult and MT the [q]flute players and the noisy crowd MK who [r]wept and wailed LK and mourned for her MK loudly.

When He came in, He said to them, "Why make this commotion and weep? LK Do not weep. MT Make room, for the girl is [s]not dead, but sleeping." LK And they [t]ridiculed Him, knowing that she was dead. MT But when the crowd was [u]put outside, MK He took the father and the mother of the child, and those *who were* with Him, and entered where the child was lying. Then He took the child by the hand, and said to her, [v]"Talitha, cumi," which is translated, "Little girl, I say to you, arise."

---

[o] ONLY BELIEVE. Though not all Jesus' healings required faith (cf. Luke 22:51), at times He required it. The verb is a command for present, continuous action urging Jairus to maintain the faith he had initially demonstrated in coming to Jesus. Christ knew there was no other proper response to Jairus's helpless situation, and He was confident of faith's outcome (cf. Luke 8:50).

[p] PETER, JAMES, AND JOHN. In Mark's gospel, this is the first time he gives special status to these three disciples. Scripture never explains why these men were sometimes allowed to witness things that the other disciples were excluded from (cf. Mark 9:2; 14:33), but the trio did constitute an inner circle within the twelve. Even the Greek grammar implies this inner grouping by placing their three names under one definite article.

[q] FLUTE PLAYERS AND THE NOISY CROWD. Typical fixtures at a time of mourning in that culture (cf. 2 Chron. 35:25). The crowd at a funeral usually included professional mourners, women whose task it was to wail plaintively, while reciting the name of the departed one, as well as any other loved ones who had died recently. The result was a noisy, chaotic din.

[r] WEPT AND WAILED. In that culture a sure sign that a death had occurred. Because burial followed soon after death, it was the people's only opportunity to mourn publicly. The wailing was especially loud and mostly from paid mourners.

[s] NOT DEAD, BUT SLEEPING. With this figurative expression Jesus meant that the girl was not dead in the normal sense, because her condition was temporary and would be reversed (cf. Matt. 9:24; John 11:11–14; Acts 7:60; 13:36; 1 Cor. 11:30; 15:6, 18, 20, 51; 1 Thess. 4:13–14). Jesus was not saying that her death was a misdiagnosis. This was a prophecy that she would live again. He made a similar comment about Lazarus' death (John 11:11)—and then had to explain to the disciples that he was speaking metaphorically (John 11:14). Sleep is a designation for death in the NT (cf. 1 Cor. 11:30; 15:51; 1 Thess. 5:10).

[t] RIDICULED. This could more literally be translated, "laughed Him to scorn," or "were laughing in His face." They understood Jesus' words literally and thought they were absurd, so "ridiculed" most likely refers to repeated bursts of laughter aimed at humiliating the Lord. How quickly their paid act of mourning turned to derision! This reaction, although shallow and irreverent, indicates the people were convinced of the irreversible nature of the girl's death and underscores the reality of the miracle Jesus was about to do.

[u] PUT OUTSIDE. This was an emphatic, forceful expulsion that showed Christ's authority and was done because the disbelieving mourners had disqualified themselves from witnessing the girl's resurrection.

[v] "TALITHA, CUMI." Mark is the only gospel writer who recorded Jesus' original Aramaic words. "Talitha" is a feminine form of "lamb," or "youth." "Cumi" is an imperative meaning "arise." As in other such instances, Jesus addressed the person of the one being raised, not just the dead body (cf. Luke 7:14; John 11:43).

Immediately [LK] her spirit returned, and [MK] the girl arose and walked, for she was twelve years *of age.* [LK] And He commanded that she be given *something* to eat. And her parents were [MK] overcome with great amazement. [LK] But He charged them [MK] strictly [LK] to [w]tell no one what had happened.

[MT] And the report of this went out into all that land.

---

[w] TELL NO ONE. Knowledge of the miracle could not be completely withheld, but Christ did not want news of it to spread until after He had left the area, because He knew such news might cause His many Jewish opponents in Galilee to seek Him out and kill Him prematurely. He also wanted to be known for bringing the gospel, not as simply a miracle worker. Jesus was no doubt concerned that the girl and her parents not be made the center of undue curiosity and sensationalism.

72. Additional Miracles in Galilee

Matt. 9:27–34

MT When Jesus departed from there, two blind men followed Him, crying out and saying, "[a] Son of David, have mercy on us!"

And when He had come into the house, the blind men came to Him. And Jesus said to them, "Do you believe that I am able to do this?" They said to Him, "Yes, Lord."

Then He touched their eyes, saying, "According to your faith let it be to you." And their eyes were opened. And Jesus sternly warned them, saying, "See *that* no one knows *it*." But when they had departed, they spread the news about Him in all that country.

As they went out, behold, they brought to Him a man, mute and demon-possessed. And when the demon was cast out, the mute spoke. And the multitudes marveled, saying, "It was never seen like this in Israel!" But the Pharisees said, "He casts out demons by [b]the ruler of the demons."

---

[a] Son of David. Cf. Matt. 1:1; 12:23; 21:9, 15. A messianic title. See Matt. 20:29–34 for a remarkably similar, but separate, account.

[b] the ruler of the demons. The Pharisees had seen enough of Jesus' power to know it was God's power. But in their willful unbelief, they said His was the power of Satan. Cf. Matt. 12:24; 25:41; Mark 3:22; Luke 11:15.

73. Final Visit to Unbelieving Nazareth

Matt. 13:54–58; Mark 6:1–6a

MK Then He went out from there and came to [a]His own country, and [b]His disciples followed Him. And when the [c]Sabbath had come, He began to teach in the synagogue. And many hearing *Him* were [d]astonished, saying, MT "Where did this *Man* get this wisdom and *these* mighty works? MK What wisdom *is* this which is given to Him, that such mighty works are performed by His hands! MT Is this not the [e]carpenter's son? Is not [f]His mother called Mary? And [g]His brothers James, Joses, Simon, and Judas? MK And are not [h]His sisters here with us? MT Where then did this *Man* get all these things?"

---

[a] HIS OWN COUNTRY. i.e., Nazareth, Jesus' hometown.

[b] HIS DISCIPLES. This was not a private, family visit for Jesus, but a time for ministry.

[c] SABBATH. Cf. Mark 2:23. This implies that no public teaching was done until the Sabbath.

[d] ASTONISHED. The same word as used in Mark 1:22; however, here the people's initial reaction gave way to skepticism and a critical attitude toward Jesus.

[e] CARPENTER. The people of Nazareth still thought of Jesus as one who carried on his father's trade (cf. Matt. 13:55) as a craftsman who worked in wood and other hard materials (e.g., stones, bricks). The common earthly position of Jesus and His family caused the townspeople to stumble—they refused to see Him as higher than themselves and found it impossible to accept Him as the Son of God and Messiah.

[f] HIS MOTHER . . . MARY. In Mark's account Jesus is called, "the Son of Mary." Only there is Jesus called that. The normal Jewish practice was to identify a son by his father's (Joseph's) name. Perhaps that was not done here because Joseph was already dead, or because Christ's audience was recalling the rumors concerning Jesus' illegitimate birth (cf. John 8:41; 9:29)—a man was called the son of his mother if his father was unknown—and was purposely insulting Him with this title as a reference to illegitimacy.

[g] HIS BROTHERS JAMES, JOSES, SIMON, AND JUDAS. Cf. Matt. 12:46. These were actual half-brothers of Jesus. "James" was later the leader in the Jerusalem church (cf. Acts 12:17; 15:13; 21:18; 1 Cor. 15:7; Gal. 1:19; 2:9, 12) and wrote the epistle of James. "Judas" (Hebrew name "Judah") wrote the epistle of Jude. Nothing more is known of the other two. The fact that Joseph does not actually appear in any of these accounts suggests that he was no longer living.

[h] HIS SISTERS. Actual half-sisters whose names are never given in the NT. Nothing is known of them, not even if they became believers as the other family members did.

[MK] So [i]they were offended at Him. But Jesus said to them, "[j]A prophet is not without honor except in his own country, among his own relatives, and in his [k]own house." Now [l]He could do no mighty work there, [MT] because of their unbelief, [MK] except that He laid His hands on a few sick people and healed *them*. And [m]He marveled because of their unbelief.

---

[i] THEY WERE OFFENDED AT HIM. The English term *scandalize* comes from the Greek verb translated "were offended," which essentially means "to stumble," or "become ensnared," and fall into a sin. The residents of Nazareth were deeply offended at Jesus' posturing Himself as some great teacher because of His ordinary background, His limited formal education, and His lack of an officially sanctioned religious position.

[j] A PROPHET . . . IN HIS OWN COUNTRY. This is an ancient proverb paralleling the modern saying, "familiarity breeds contempt." They knew Jesus too well as a boy and a young man from their own town—and they concluded that He was nothing special. Jesus called Himself a prophet, in accord with one of His roles (cf. Matt. 21:11, 46; Mark 6:15; 8:28; Luke 7:16; 24:19; John 6:14; 7:40; 9:17).

[k] OWN HOUSE. His own family (cf. John 7:5; Acts 1:14)

[l] HE COULD DO NO MIGHTY WORK THERE. Cf. Matt. 13:58. This is not to suggest that His power was somehow diminished by their unbelief. It may suggest that people were not coming to Him for healing or miracles the way they did in Capernaum and Jerusalem. Or more importantly it may signify that Christ limited His ministry both as an act of mercy, so that the exposure to greater light would not result in a worse hardening that would only subject them to greater condemnation and a judgment on their unbelief. He had the power to do more miracles, but not the will, because they rejected Him. Miracles belonged among those who were ready to believe.

[m] HE MARVELED BECAUSE OF THEIR UNBELIEF. "Marveled" means Jesus was completely astonished and amazed at Nazareth's reaction to Him, His teaching, and His miracles. He was not surprised at the fact of the people's unbelief, but at how they could reject Him while claiming to know all about Him. Faith should have been the response in that town in Galilee, the region where Christ did so many miracles and so much teaching.

74. Jesus Commissions the Twelve: The Setting

Matt. 9:35–10:4; Mark 6:6b–9; Luke 9:1–2

MT Then Jesus went about all the cities and MK [a]villages in a circuit, MT teaching in their synagogues, preaching the gospel of the kingdom, and healing [b]every sickness and every disease among the people. But when He saw the multitudes, He was [c]moved with compassion for them, because [d]they were weary and scattered, like sheep having no shepherd. Then He said to His disciples, "The [e]harvest truly *is* plentiful, but the laborers *are* few. [f]Therefore pray the Lord of the harvest to send out laborers into His harvest."

LK Then He called His [g]twelve [h]disciples together, MK and began to [i]send them

---

[a] VILLAGES IN A CIRCUIT. The outcome of Jesus' visit to Nazareth was that He left there and made a teaching tour of other places in Galilee, concluding near where He started (cf. Matt. 9:35).

[b] EVERY SICKNESS AND EVERY DISEASE. Jesus banished illness in an unprecedented healing display, giving impressive evidence of His deity, and making the Jews' rejection all the more heinous. Cf. Matt. 12:15.

[c] MOVED WITH COMPASSION. Here the humanity of Christ allowed expression of His attitude toward sinners in terms of human passion. He was "moved" with compassion. Whereas God, who is immutable, is not subject to the rise and fall and change of emotions (Num. 23:19), Christ, who was fully human with all the faculties of humanity, was on occasion moved to literal tears over the plight of sinners (Luke 19:41; cf. Luke 13:34). God Himself expressed similar compassion through the prophets (Ex. 33:19; Ps. 86:15; Jer. 9:1; 13:17; 14:17).

[d] THEY WERE WEARY AND SCATTERED. The people's spiritual needs were even more desperate than the need for physical healing. Meeting that need would require more laborers.

[e] HARVEST. Cf. Luke 10:1–2. The Lord spoke of the spiritual harvest of souls for salvation.

[f] THEREFORE PRAY. Jesus affirmed the fact that believers' prayers participate in the fulfillment of God's plans.

[g] TWELVE. Cf. Matt. 10:2–4; Mark 3:16–19. The twelve disciples were by then a divinely-commissioned, recognized group.

[h] DISCIPLES . . . APOSTLES. "Disciple" means "student," one who is being taught by another. "Apostles" refers to qualified representatives who are sent on a mission. The two terms emphasize different aspects of their calling.

[i] SEND THEM OUT. The form of this Greek verb indicates that Jesus individually commissioned each pair to go out as His representatives.

out [j]two *by* two, LK and [k]gave them power and authority over all demons, MT to cast them out, and to heal all kinds of sickness and all kinds of disease. LK He sent them to preach the kingdom of God and to heal the sick. MK He commanded them to take nothing for the journey except [l]a staff— [m]no bag, no bread, no copper in *their* money belts—but [n]to wear sandals, and [o]not to put on two tunics.

MT Now [p]the names of the twelve apostles are these: first, Simon, who is called [q]Peter, and Andrew his brother; James the *son* of Zebedee, and John his brother; Philip and Bartholomew; Thomas and Matthew the tax collector; [r]James the *son* of Alphaeus, and [s]Lebbaeus, whose surname was Thaddaeus; [t]Simon the Cananite, and Judas Iscariot, who also betrayed Him.

---

[j] two by two. This was a prudent practice (cf. Eccl. 4:9–12) employed by Jewish alms collectors, by John the Baptist (Luke 7:19), by Jesus on other occasions (11:1; 14:13; Luke 10:1), and by the early church (Acts 13:2–3; 15:39–41; 19:22). The practice gave the disciples mutual help and encouragement and met the legal requirement for an authentic testimony (Deut. 19:15).

[k] gave them power. Cf. 2 Cor. 12:12. Jesus delegated His power to the apostles to show clearly that He and His kingdom were sovereign over the physical and spiritual realms, the effects of sin, and the efforts of Satan. This was an unheard-of display of power, never before seen in all redemptive history, to announce Messiah's arrival and authenticate Him plus His apostles who preached His gospel. This power was a preview of the power Christ will exhibit in His earthly kingdom, when Satan will be bound (Rev. 20) and the curse on physical life curtailed (Isa. 65:20–25).

[l] a staff. The walking stick, a universal companion of travelers in those days, which also provided potential protection from criminals and wild animals.

[m] no bag. They were not to carry the usual leather traveling bag or food sack.

[n] to wear sandals. Ordinary footwear consisting of leather or wood soles bound on by straps around the ankle and instep. "Sandals" were necessary protection for the feet in view of the hot, rough terrain of Israel.

[o] not to put on two tunics. "Tunics" were standard garments of clothing. Men of comparative wealth would wear two, but Jesus wanted the disciples to identify with common people and travel with just minimum clothing.

[p] the names of the twelve apostles. The twelve are always listed in a similar order (cf. Mark 3:16–19; Luke 6:13–16; Acts 1:13). Peter is always named first. The list contains three groups of four. The three subgroups are always listed in the same order, and the first name in each subgroup is always the same, though there is some variation in the order within the subgroups—but Judas Iscariot is always named last.

[q] Peter . . . Andrew . . . James . . . and John. The first subgroup of four are the most familiar to us. These two sets of brothers, all fishermen, represent an inner circle of disciples often seen closest to Jesus.

[r] James the son of Alphaeus. There are four men in the NT named James: (1) the apostle James, brother of John (cf. Matt. 4:21); (2) the disciple mentioned here, also called "James the Less" (Mark 15:40); (3) James, father of Judas (not Iscariot, Luke 6:16); and (4) James, the Lord's half-brother (Gal. 1:19; Mark 6:3), who wrote the epistle that bears the name. He also played a leading role in the early Jerusalem church (Acts 12:17; 15:13; Gal. 1:19).

[s] Lebbaeus, whose surname was Thaddaeus. Elsewhere he is called Judas, son of James (Luke 6:16; Acts 1:13).

[t] Simon the Cananite. The better manuscripts read "Cananaean"—a term for the party of the Zealots, a group determined to overthrow Roman domination in Israel. Acts 1:13 refers to him as "Simon the Zealot." Simon was probably a member of the Zealot party before coming to Christ. Cf. Mark 3:18.

75. Jesus Commissions the Twelve: The Send-Off

Matt. 10:5–11:1; Mark 6:10–13; Luke 9:3–6

MT [a]These twelve Jesus sent out and commanded them, saying:

MT "[b] Do not go into the way of the Gentiles, and do not enter a city of the Samaritans. But go rather to the [c]lost sheep of the house of Israel. And as you go, preach, saying, 'The kingdom of heaven is at hand.' Heal the sick, cleanse the lepers, raise the dead, cast out demons. [d]Freely you have received, freely give. LK [e]Take nothing for the journey. MT Provide neither gold nor silver nor copper in your money belts, nor bag for *your* journey, [f]nor two tunics LK apiece, MT nor sandals, nor staffs LK nor bread nor money; MT for a worker is worthy of his food.

"Now whatever city or town you enter, inquire who in it is worthy, and MK [when] you enter a house, [g]stay there till you depart from that place. MT And when

---

[a] These twelve Jesus sent. This passage presents the second of five major discourses recorded in Matthew.

[b] Do not go into the way of the Gentiles. Christ did not forbid the disciples to preach to Gentiles or Samaritans if they encountered them on the way, but they were to take the message first to the covenant people in the regions nearby (cf. Rom. 1:16).

[c] lost sheep of the house of Israel. Cf. Matt. 15:24; Jer. 50:6. Jesus narrowed this priority even more when He said the gospel was only for those who knew they were spiritually sick (Matt. 9:13) and needed a physician (Luke 5:31–32).

[d] Freely you have received, freely give. Jesus was giving them great power to heal the sick and raise the dead. If they sold these gifts for money, they could have made quite a fortune. But that would have obscured the message of grace Christ sent them to preach. So he forbade them to charge money for their ministry. Yet they were permitted to accept support to meet their basic needs, for a workman is worthy of such support.

[e] Take nothing. Slight differences between Matthew, Mark, and Luke have troubled some. Matthew 10:9–10 and Luke 9:3 say the disciples were not to take staffs; but Mark 6:8 prohibited everything "except a staff." Mark 6:9 also instructed them to "wear sandals," but in Matt. 10:10 sandals were included in the things they were not to carry. Actually, however, what Matt. 10:10 and Luke 9:3 prohibited was the packing of extra staffs and sandals. The disciples were not to be carrying baggage for the journey but merely to go with the clothes on their backs.

[f] nor two tunics. The restrictions on what they were to carry were unique for this mission. See Luke 22:36, where on a later mission Christ gave completely different instructions. The point here was to teach them to trust the Lord to supply their needs through the generosity of the people to whom they ministered and to teach those who received the blessing of their ministry to support the servants of Christ. Cf. 1 Tim. 5:18.

[g] stay there. The disciples were to carefully select where they stayed (cf. Matt. 10:11), but once there, the sole focus was to be on ministry. Contentment with their first host and his accommodations would be a testimony to others while the disciples ministered (cf. 1 Tim. 6:6).

you go into a household, greet it. If the household is worthy, let your [h]peace come upon it. But if it is not worthy, let your peace return to you. And whoever will not receive you nor [i]hear your words, when you depart from that house or city, [j]shake off the [LK] very [MT] dust from your feet. Assuredly, I say to you, it will be more tolerable for the land of [k]Sodom and Gomorrah in the day of judgment than for that city!

"Behold, I send you out as sheep in the midst of [l]wolves. Therefore be wise as serpents and harmless as doves. But beware of men, for they will [m]deliver you up to councils and scourge you in their synagogues. You will be brought before governors and kings for My sake, as a testimony to them and to the Gentiles. But when they deliver you up, do not worry about how or what you should speak. For it will be given to you in that hour what you should speak; for it is not you who speak, but the Spirit of your Father who speaks in you.

"Now [n]brother will deliver up brother to death, and a father *his* child; and children will rise up against parents and cause them to be put to death. And you will be hated by all for My name's sake. But he who endures to the end will be saved. When they persecute you in this city, flee to another. For assuredly, I say to you, you will not have gone through the cities of Israel before the Son of Man comes.

"A disciple is [o]not above *his* teacher, nor a servant above his master. It is

---

[h] PEACE. This is equivalent to the Hebrew *shalom* and refers to prosperity, well-being, or blessing.

[i] HEAR YOUR WORDS. The priority was to preach that the King had come and His kingdom was near. The message was the main thing. The signs and wonders were to authenticate it.

[j] SHAKE OFF THE VERY DUST FROM YOUR FEET. It was common for Jews to shake the dust off their feet—as an expression of disdain—when returning from Gentile regions. Paul and Barnabas also did this when expelled from Antioch (Acts 13:51). This was a visible protest, signifying that they regarded the place as no better than a pagan land. SHAKE OFF THE DUST. A symbolic act that signified complete renunciation of further fellowship with those who rejected them (cf. Matt. 10:14). When the disciples made this gesture, it would show that the people had rejected Jesus and the gospel and were hence rejected by the disciples and by the Lord.

[k] SODOM AND GOMORRAH. Those cities and the entire surrounding region were judged without warning and with the utmost severity. People who reject Christ's gracious, saving gospel will face a fate worse than those pagans killed by divine judgment on the two OT cities (cf. Gen. 19:24; Matt. 10:15).

[l] WOLVES. Used to describe false prophets who persecute the true ones and seek to destroy the church (cf. Matt. 7:15; Luke 10:3; Acts 20:29).

[m] DELIVER YOU UP. This is a technical word in this context, used for handing over a prisoner for punishment. Persecution of believers has often been the official policy of governments. Such persecutions give opportunity for testifying to the truth of the gospel. Cf. John 16:1–4; 2 Tim. 4:16.

[n] BROTHER WILL DELIVER UP BROTHER . . . These verses clearly have an eschatological significance that goes beyond the disciples' immediate mission. The persecutions he describes seem to belong to the tribulation period that precedes Christ's second coming, alluded to in Matt. 10:23.

[o] NOT ABOVE. If the Teacher (Christ) suffers, so will His pupils. If they attack the Master (Christ) with blasphemies, so will they curse the servants. This was the promise of persecution. Cf. John 15:20.

enough for a disciple that he be like his teacher, and a servant like his master. If they have called the master of the house [p]Beelzebub, how much more *will they call* those of his household! Therefore do not fear them. For there is nothing covered that will not be revealed, and hidden that will not be known.

"Whatever I tell you in the dark, speak in the light; and what you hear in the ear, preach on the housetops. And do not fear those who kill the body but cannot kill the soul. But rather [q]fear Him who is able to destroy both soul and body in hell. Are not two sparrows sold for a copper coin? And not one of them falls to the ground [r]apart from your Father's will. But the very hairs of your head are all numbered. Do not fear therefore; you are of more value than many sparrows.

"Therefore whoever [s]confesses Me before men, him I will also confess before My Father who is in heaven. But whoever denies Me before men, him I will also deny before My Father who is in heaven. Do not think that I came to bring peace on earth. I did [t]not come to bring peace but a sword. For I have come to [u]'set a man against his father, a daughter against her mother, and a daughter-in-law against her mother-in-law'; and 'a man's enemies *will be* those of his *own* household.' He who loves father or mother more than Me is not worthy of Me. And he who loves son or daughter more than Me is not worthy of Me. And he who does not [v]take his cross and follow after Me is not worthy of Me. He who finds his life will lose it, and he who loses his life for My sake will find it.

---

[p] BEELZEBUB. The Philistine deity associated with satanic idolatry. The name came to be used for Satan, the prince of demons (cf. 2 Kings 1:2; Luke 11:15).

[q] FEAR HIM. God is the one who destroys in hell. Cf. Luke 12:5. Persecutors can only harm the body.

[r] APART FROM YOUR FATHER'S WILL. Not merely "without His knowledge"; Jesus was teaching that God providentially controls the timing and circumstances of such insignificant events as the death of a sparrow. Even the number of hairs on our heads is controlled by His sovereign will. In other words divine providence governs even the smallest details and even the most mundane matters. These are very powerful affirmations of the sovereignty of God.

[s] CONFESSES ME. The person who acknowledges Christ as Lord in life or in death, if necessary, is the one whom the Lord will acknowledge before God as His own. Cf. 2 Tim. 2:10–13.

[t] NOT . . . PEACE BUT A SWORD. Though the ultimate end of the gospel is peace with God (John 14:27; Rom. 8:6), the immediate result of the gospel is frequently conflict. Conversion to Christ can result in strained family relationships, persecution, and even martyrdom. Following Christ presupposes a willingness to endure such hardships. Though He is called "Prince of Peace" (Isa. 9:6), Christ will have no one deluded into thinking that He calls believers to a life devoid of all conflict.

[u] SET A MAN AGAINST . . . Quoted from Mic. 7:6.

[v] TAKE HIS CROSS. Here is Jesus' first mention of the word *cross* to His disciples. To them it would have evoked a picture of a violent, degrading death (cf. Matt. 27:31). He was demanding total commitment from them—even unto physical death—and making this call to full surrender a part of the message they were to proclaim to others. This same call to life-or-death devotion to Christ is repeated in Matt. 16:24; Mark 8:34; Luke 9:23; 14:27. For those who come to Christ with self-renouncing faith, there will be true and eternal life.

"[w]He who receives you receives Me, and he who receives Me receives Him who sent Me. He who receives a prophet [x]in the name of a prophet shall receive a prophet's reward. And he who receives a righteous man in the name of a righteous man shall receive a righteous man's reward. And whoever gives one of these [y]little ones only a cup of cold *water* in the name of a disciple, assuredly, I say to you, he shall by no means lose his reward."

Now it came to pass, when Jesus finished commanding His twelve disciples, that He departed from there to teach and to preach [z]in their cities. [MK] So they went out [LK] and went through the towns, [aa]preaching the gospel—[MK] that *people* should repent. And they cast out many demons, and [bb]anointed with oil many who were sick, and healed *them* [LK] everywhere.

---

[w] He who receives you receives Me. Christ lives in His people. They also come in His name as His ambassadors (2 Cor. 5:20). Therefore, how they are treated is how He is treated (cf. Matt. 18:5; 25:45; Luke 9:48).

[x] in the name of a prophet . . . in the name of a righteous man. This expands on the principle of Matt. 10:40. To welcome Christ's emissaries is tantamount to welcoming Him (cf. Matt. 25:40).

[y] little ones. Believers. Cf. Matt. 18:3–10; 25:40.

[z] in their cities. i.e., in Galilee. Meanwhile, the disciples were also ministering in the Jewish towns in and around Galilee (Matt. 10:5, 6).

[aa] preaching . . . cast out many demons. They were heralds of the gospel and had repeated success in expelling evil spirits from people. This demonstrated Christ's power over the supernatural world and confirmed His claim to being God.

[bb] anointed with oil . . . sick. In Jesus' day olive oil was often used medicinally (cf. Luke 10:34). But here it represented the power and presence of the Holy Spirit and was used symbolically in relation to supernatural healing (cf. Isa. 11:2; Zech. 4:1–6; Matt. 25:2–4; Rev. 1:4, 12). As a well-known healing agent, the oil was an appropriate, tangible medium the people could identify with as the disciples ministered to the sick among them.

76. John the Baptist Is Killed

Matt. 14:1–12; Mark 6:14–29; Luke 9:7–9

MK Now MT at that time MK King [a]Herod MT the [b]tetrarch [c]heard the report LK of all that was done by MT Jesus, MK for His name had become well known. LK And he was perplexed, MK and he said, LK "John I have beheaded, but who is this of whom I hear such things?"

LK It was said by some that [d]John had risen from the dead, and MK others said, [e]"It is Elijah." And others said, "It is [f]the Prophet, or like one of the LK old MK prophets LK risen again." MK But when Herod heard, he MT said to his servants, "This is [g]John the Baptist, LK whom I beheaded; MT [h]he is risen from the dead, and therefore these powers are at work in him." LK So [i]he sought to see Him.

MK For Herod himself had sent and laid hold of [j]John, and bound him MT and

---

[a] HEROD. This was Herod Antipas, ruler of Galilee.

[b] TETRARCH. One of four rulers of a divided region. After the death of Herod the Great, Israel had been divided among his sons. Elsewhere, Matthew refers to Herod as "King" (Matt. 14:9), because that was the title by which he was known among the Galileans.

[c] HEARD. The context indicates Herod heard some exciting news centering on Jesus and resulting from the disciples' recent preaching and miracle working in Galilee. News of Christ reached to the highest levels of government.

[d] JOHN HAD RISEN FROM THE DEAD. Of course, this was not true, but Herod himself nonetheless seemed gripped by guilty fear (cf. Mark 6:16).

[e] "IT IS ELIJAH." This identification of Jesus, which probably had been discussed repeatedly among the Jews, was based on the Jewish expectation that the prophet Elijah would return prior to Messiah's coming (cf. Mal. 4:5; Matt. 11:14; Luke 1:17).

[f] THE PROPHET ... ONE OF THE OLD PROPHETS. Some saw Jesus as the fulfillment of Deut. 18:15, the messianic prophecy that looked to the One who, like Moses, would lead His people. Others were willing to identify Jesus only as a great prophet,or one who was resuming the suspended line of OT prophets. These and the other opinions, although misplaced, show that the people still thought Jesus was special or somehow supernatural.

[g] JOHN THE BAPTIST. The forerunner of Christ (cf. Matt. 3:1, 4, 6; Mark 1:4–7)

[h] JOHN ... RISEN FROM THE DEAD! By this excited, guilt-laden confession, Herod showed that he could not forget the evil he had done in beheading John the Baptist and that his conscience had led him to the eerie fear that John was back from the dead (cf. Matt. 14:1, 2; Luke 9:7–9).

[i] HE SOUGHT TO SEE HIM. Only Luke gives this detail (Luke 9:9; cf. 1:3; 8:3).

[j] JOHN ... BOUND HIM AND PUT HIM IN PRISON. Herod kept him fettered while imprisoned, probably at Machaerus, near the north eastern shore of the Dead Sea. Herod's intention was to protect John from the plots of Herodias.

put *him* MK in prison for the sake of [k]Herodias, his brother [l]Philip's wife; for he had married her. Because [m]John had said to Herod, "It is not lawful for you to have your brother's wife." Therefore Herodias held it against him and wanted to kill him, but she could not; for MT although he wanted to put him to death, MK Herod feared John, knowing that he *was* a just and holy man, and he protected him. And when he heard him, [n]he did many things, and heard him gladly. MT He [also] feared the multitude, because they counted him as a prophet.

MK Then an opportune day came when Herod on his birthday gave a feast for his [o]nobles, the [p]high officers, and the [q]chief *men* of Galilee. And when [r]Herodias' daughter herself came in and [s]danced MT before them, MK and pleased Herod and those who sat with him, the king said to the girl, "Ask me whatever you want, and I will give *it* to you." MT He promised with an oath to give her whatever she might ask [and] MK also swore to her, "Whatever you ask me, I will give you, [t]up to half my kingdom."

---

[k] Herodias, his brother Philip's wife. Herodias was the daughter of Aristobulus, another son of Herod the Great, so when she married Philip, she was marrying her own father's brother. What precipitated the arrest of John the Baptist was that Herod Antipas (another of Herodias' uncles) talked Herodias into leaving her husband (his brother) in order to marry him (Mark 6:17)—thus compounding the incest, as well as violating Lev. 18:16. John was outraged that a ruler in Israel would commit such a sin openly, so he rebuked Herod severely (v. 4). For this he was imprisoned and later killed (Mark 6:14–29).

[l] Philip's. Herod Philip II, another half-brother to Herod Antipas (the Herod in this passage). Therefore, Philip was also an uncle to Herodias.

[m] John had said . . . It is not lawful. The tense of the Greek verb and Mark's wording imply that John had repeatedly rebuked Herod Antipas in private confrontations that his marriage to Herodias was contrary to Mosaic law (cf. Matt. 3:7–10).

[n] he did many things. The preferred reading is "he was very perplexed," which indicates that Herod's interaction with John left him in great internal conflict—a moral struggle between his lust for Herodias and the prodding of his guilty conscience.

[o] nobles. This term may also be translated "lords," or "great ones." These were men who held high civil offices under Herod.

[p] high officers. High-ranking military officials who each commanded one thousand men.

[q] chief men of Galilee. The key social leaders of the region.

[r] Herodias' daughter. Salome, daughter of Herodias and Philip. According to Josephus, the Jewish historian, she married yet another son (her own father's brother and her mother's uncle) of Herod the Great, thus further tangling the web of incest in that family.

[s] danced. Refers to a solo dance with highly suggestive hand and body movements, comparable to a modern striptease. It was unusual and almost unprecedented that Salome would have performed in this way before Herod's guests (cf. Est. 1:11–12).

[t] up to half my kingdom. This was an exaggeration designed to enhance his previous statement of generosity. As a Roman tetrarch Herod actually had no "kingdom" to give.

So she went out and said to her mother, "What shall I ask?" And she said, "The head of John the Baptist!" Immediately she came in with haste to the king and asked, saying, "I want you to give me at once the head of John the Baptist on a platter."

And the king was exceedingly sorry; *yet*, [u]because of the oaths and because of those who sat with him, he did not want to refuse her. Immediately the king [MT] commanded *it* to be given to *her.* So he [MK] sent an [v]executioner and commanded his head to be brought. And he went and beheaded him in prison, brought his head on a platter, and gave it to the girl; and the girl gave it to her mother.

When his disciples heard *of it,* they came and took away his corpse and laid it in a tomb [MT] and went and told Jesus.

---

[u] BECAUSE OF THE OATHS. A promise made with a certain oath was considered sacred and inviolable (cf. Matt. 5:34)—especially when made by a ruling monarch. Herod was widely known for his duplicity, so it was not honesty that he was concerned about, but rather the appearance of things. He did not want to be embarrassed in front of his dinner guests.

[v] EXECUTIONER. Originally meant "spy" or "scout" but came to describe a staff member of a Roman tribune. They served as couriers and bodyguards as well as executioners. Herod had adopted the custom of surrounding himself with such men.

Part VI | From Passover AD 29 to Passover AD 30

77. Jesus Feeds the 5,000

Matt. 14:13–22; Mark 6:30–46; Luke 9:10–17; John 6:1–15

LK And the apostles, when they had returned, MK gathered to Jesus and LK told Him all that they had done MK and what they had taught.

JN [a]After these things Jesus MK said to them, "Come aside [b]by yourselves [c]to a deserted place and rest a while." For there were many coming and going, and they did not even have time to eat. LK Then He took them and went aside privately. MK So they [d]departed—JN over [e]the Sea of Galilee, which is *the Sea* of Tiberias—MK in the boat by themselves LK [to] a deserted place belonging to the city called [f]Bethsaida.

MK But the [g]multitudes saw them departing, and JN followed Him, because [h]they

---

[a] After these things. A large gap of time exists between chapters 5 and 6 of John's gospel. If the feast in John 5:1 is Tabernacles, then at least six months passed (October to April). If the feast of 5:1 is Passover, then a year passed between these chapters.

[b] by yourselves. Jesus' invitation for a retreat into the desert was restricted to the twelve. He knew they needed rest and privacy after their tiring ministry expedition and the continuing press of the people.

[c] to a deserted place. They were trying to get some rest and a break from the crowds.

[d] departed . . . in the boat by themselves. The disciples obeyed Jesus' proposal, departing from His headquarters in Capernaum using the same boat as in Mark 5:2.

[e] The Sea of Galilee. John 6 is very close to the same structure as John 5, since both occur around a Jewish feast and both lead to a discourse of Jesus' deity. While chapter 5 takes place in the south around Judea and Jerusalem, chapter 6 takes place in the north around Galilee. The result of both chapters is the same: He is rejected not only in the southern but also in the northern regions.

[f] Bethsaida. Bethsaida Julius is on the north shore of Galilee, where the Jordan River enters the lake.

[g] multitudes . . . followed Him on foot. They traveled great distances over land to reach the secluded spot where He had come by boat.

saw His signs which He performed on those who were diseased. [MK] Many knew Him and [i]ran there on foot from all the cities. They [j]arrived before them.

[MK] And Jesus, when He came out, [JN] went up on the mountain, and there He sat with His disciples. Now the Passover, a feast of the Jews, was near. Then Jesus lifted up *His* eyes, and [MT] saw a great multitude [JN] coming toward Him; [MT] and He was moved with compassion for them, [MK] because they were like [k]sheep not having a shepherd. [LK] And He received them and [MK] began to teach them many things [LK] about the kingdom of God, and healed those who had need of healing.

[MK] When the day was now far spent [and] [MT] it was evening, [LK] the twelve [MK] disciples came to Him and said, [MT] "This is a deserted place, and the hour is already late. Send the multitudes away, that they may go into [MK] the surrounding country and villages and buy themselves bread [LK] and lodge and get provisions; [MK] for they have nothing to eat."

[MT] But Jesus [MK] answered and [MT] said to them, "They do not need to go away. You [l]give them something to eat." And [JN] He said to Philip, "Where shall we buy bread, that these may eat?" But this He said to test him, for He Himself knew what He would do.

Philip answered Him, [MK] "Shall we go and buy two hundred denarii worth of bread and give them *something* to eat? [JN] [m]Two hundred denarii worth of bread is not sufficient for them, that every one of them may have a little." [MK] But He said to them, "How many [n]loaves do you have? Go and see."

---

[h] THEY SAW HIS SIGNS. The crowds followed not out of belief but out of curiosity concerning the miracles that He performed. However, in spite of the crowd's crass motivations, Jesus, having compassion on them, healed their sick and fed them.

[i] RAN THERE ON FOOT. The direction (toward the northeast shore of the lake) and speed of the boat, along with the immediate lack of other available boats, caused the crowd to follow by land.

[j] ARRIVED BEFORE THEM. Contained only in Mark's account, this does not necessarily mean everyone arrived before the boat, because the land distance was probably eight miles, twice as far as the four miles the boat had to travel. Rather, those young and eager in the crowd were able to outrun both the rest and the boat (probably because it encountered no wind or a contrary wind), and actually arrived at the shore before the boat.

[k] SHEEP NOT HAVING A SHEPHERD. An OT picture (cf. Num. 27:17; 1 Kings 22:17; 2 Chron. 18:16; Ezek. 34:5) used to describe the people as helpless and starving, lacking in spiritual guidance and protection, and exposed to the perils of sin and spiritual destruction.

[l] GIVE THEM SOMETHING TO EAT. Jesus knew they did not have enough food to feed the crowd. He wanted the disciples to state it plainly so the record would be clear that a miracle by His power occurred.

[m] TWO HUNDRED DENARII. A single denarius (cf. Matt. 22:19) was equivalent to a day's pay for the day laborer (cf. Matt. 20:2). "Two hundred" would therefore equal approximately eight months' wages and be quite beyond the disciples' (or any average person's) means. Moreover, the crowd was so large that such a significant amount was still inadequate to feed them.

[n] LOAVES. Lit. "bread-cakes," or "rolls."

JN One of His disciples, Andrew, Simon Peter's brother, said to Him, "There is a lad here who has five barley loaves and two small fish, but what are they among so many?" LK And they said, "We have no more than five loaves and two fish, unless we go and buy food for all these people." For there were about five thousand men. Then He said, MT "Bring them here to Me."

JN Then Jesus said LK to His disciples, JN "Make the people sit down LK in groups of fifty." And they did so, and made them all sit down MK in groups on the [o]green grass. So they sat down in ranks, [p]in hundreds and in fifties. JN Now there was much grass in the place.

LK Then He took the five loaves and the two fish, and MK [q]looked up to heaven; JN and when He had given thanks He MK broke the loaves, and gave *them* to His disciples; MT and the disciples gave JN to those sitting down; MK and the two fish He divided among *them* all. So they [r]all ate JN as much as they wanted MT and were filled.

JN So when they were filled, He said to His disciples, "Gather up the fragments that remain, so that nothing is lost." Therefore they gathered *them* up, and filled [s]twelve baskets MT full JN with the fragments of the five barley loaves which were left over by those who had eaten. MT Now those who had eaten were about [t]five thousand men, besides women and children. JN Then those men, when they had seen [u]the sign

---

[o] GREEN GRASS. This detail indicates it was the spring rainy season, before the hot summer would have turned the grass dry and brown.

[p] IN HUNDREDS AND IN FIFTIES. A symmetrical seating arrangement, possibly fifty semicircles of one hundred people each, with the semicircles one behind the other in ranks. Such an arrangement was familiar to the Jews during their festivals, and it made food distribution more convenient.

[q] LOOKED UP TO HEAVEN. A typical prayer posture for Jesus (cf. Mark 7:34; Luke 24:35; John 11:41; 17:1). Heaven was universally regarded as the Father's dwelling place (Matt. 6:9).

[r] ALL ATE . . . WERE FILLED. The hunger of everyone in the crowd was completely satisfied.

[s] TWELVE BASKETS FULL. The "baskets," apparently the same ones used to bring the food, were small wicker containers like the ones the Jews used to carry food.

[t] FIVE THOUSAND MEN. The Greek word for "men" means strictly males, so the numerical estimate did not include women and children (cf. Matt. 14:21). The women and children were traditionally seated separately from the men for meals. When everyone was added, there could have been at least twenty thousand.

[u] THE SIGN. Aside from the resurrection, the feeding of the five thousand is the only miracle of Jesus recorded in all four gospels. In John's gospel this account is the fourth sign John employed to demonstrate that Jesus is the Messiah and Son of God. Since John most likely wrote to supplement and provide additional information not recorded in the Synoptics, his recording of this miracle emphasized its strategic importance in two ways: (1) it demonstrated the creative power of Christ more clearly than any other miracle, and (2) it decisively supported John's purposes of demonstrating the deity of Jesus Christ, while also serving to set the stage for Jesus' discourse on the "bread of life" (John 6:22–40). Interestingly, both creative miracles of Jesus, the water into wine (John 2:1–10), and the multiplying of bread (John 6:1–14) speak of the main elements in the Lord's supper or communion (John 6:53).

that Jesus did, said, "This is truly [v]the Prophet who is to come into the world."

Therefore when Jesus perceived that they were about to come and [w]take Him by force to make Him king, [MK] immediately He made His disciples get into the boat and [x]go before Him to the other side, to [y]Bethsaida, while He sent the multitude away.

---

[v] THE PROPHET. The crowd referred to "the Prophet" of Deut. 18:15. Sadly, these comments, coming right after Jesus healed and fed them, indicate that the people desired a Messiah who met their physical rather than spiritual needs. Apparently, no recognition existed for the need of spiritual repentance and preparation for the kingdom (Matt. 4:17). They wanted an earthly, political Messiah to meet all their needs and to deliver them from Roman oppression. Their reaction typifies many who want a "Christ" that makes no demands of them (cf. Matt. 10:34–39; 16:24–26), but of whom they can make their selfish personal requests.

[w] TAKE HIM BY FORCE TO MAKE HIM KING. John supplemented the information in Matthew and Mark by indicating that the reason Jesus dismissed the disciples and withdrew from the crowd into a mountain alone was because of His supernatural knowledge of their intention to make Him king in light of His healing and feeding of them. The crowd, incited by mob enthusiasm, was ready to proceed with crassly political intentions that would have jeopardized God's will.

[x] GO BEFORE HIM. The implication is that Jesus was to rejoin the disciples later.

[y] BETHSAIDA. A different town by the same name, Bethsaida of Galilee, on the west side of the Sea of Galilee and south of Capernaum (cf. Matt. 11:21).

78. Jesus Walks on the Water

Matt. 14:23–36; Mark 6:47–56; John 6:15–21

MT And when He had sent the multitudes away, He went up on [a]the mountain by Himself to pray. Now when evening came, He was alone there. JN [Meanwhile,] His disciples went down to the sea, got into the boat, and went over the sea [b]toward Capernaum. And it was already dark, and Jesus had not come to them. [c]Then the sea arose because [d]a great wind was blowing.

MK The boat was MT now in the [e]middle of the sea, tossed by the waves, for the wind was contrary; MK and He *was* alone on the land. Then He saw them straining at rowing, for the wind was against them. MT Now in the [f]fourth watch of the night, JN when they had rowed about three or four miles, MT Jesus went to them, [g]walking on the sea, MK and [h]would have passed them by. And when they saw Him walking on

---

[a] THE MOUNTAIN. The entire east side of the Sea of Galilee is mountainous, with steep slopes leading up to a plateau. Up one of the slopes was a good place to pray, away from the crowd (cf. John 6:15).

[b] TOWARD CAPERNAUM. Matt. 14:22 and Mark 6:45 indicate that as soon as Jesus had fed the multitudes, He immediately dismissed His disciples to travel west toward Capernaum.

[c] THEN THE SEA AROSE. The story of Jesus walking on the water constituted the fifth sign in John's gospel designed to demonstrate the writer's purpose that Jesus is the Messiah and Son of God (John 20:30–31). The miracle demonstrates Jesus' deity by His sovereignty over the laws of nature.

[d] A GREAT WIND WAS BLOWING. The Sea of Galilee is almost seven hundred feet below sea level. Cooler air from the northern mountains and southeastern tablelands rushes down into the lake and displaces the warm moist air, causing violent churning of the water.

[e] MIDDLE OF THE SEA. Normally, in traveling across the northern end of the lake, they would have been within one or two miles of shore. But on that occasion, the wind had carried the boat several miles south, closer to the center of the lake.

[f] FOURTH WATCH. 3:00 a.m. to 6:00 a.m.

[g] WALKING ON THE SEA. The verb's tense depicts a steady progress, unhindered by the waves. The Synoptics reveal that in fear and the darkness, the disciples thought He was a ghost. The Son of God, who made the world, was in control of its forces and, in this case, He suspended the law of gravity. The act was not frivolous on Jesus' part, for it constituted a dramatic object lesson to the disciples of Jesus' true identity as the sovereign Lord of all creation (cf. John 1:3).

[h] WOULD HAVE PASSED THEM BY. The more literal rendering, "desired to come alongside of," indicates Jesus' intention here. He wanted to test the disciples' faith, so He deliberately changed course and came parallel to the boat to see if they would recognize Him and His supernatural powers and invite Him aboard.

the sea [JN] and drawing near the boat; [MK] they supposed it was [i]a ghost, and cried out [MT] for fear; [JN] and they were afraid [MK] for they all saw Him and were troubled.

[MT] But immediately Jesus spoke to them, saying, "[j]Be of good cheer! [k]It is I; do not be afraid." And Peter answered Him and said, "Lord, if it is You, command me to come to You on the water." So He said, "Come." And when Peter had come down out of the boat, he walked on the water to go to Jesus. But when he saw that the wind *was* boisterous, he was afraid; and beginning to sink he cried out, saying, "Lord, save me!" And immediately Jesus stretched out *His* hand and caught him, and said to him, "O you of little faith, why did you doubt?"

[MK] Then He went up into the boat to them, and [JN] they willingly received Him. [MT] And when they got into the boat, the wind ceased, [JN] and [l]immediately the boat was at the land where they were going. [MK] And they were greatly amazed in themselves beyond measure, and marveled. For [m]they had not understood about the loaves, because [n]their heart was hardened. [MT] Then those who were in the boat came and worshiped Him, saying, "Truly [o]You are the Son of God."

[MK] When they had crossed over, they came to the land of [p]Gennesaret and anchored there. And when they came out of the boat, immediately [MT] the men of that place [MK] recognized Him, [and] [MT] they sent out into all that surrounding region,

---

[i] A GHOST. An apparition or imaginary creature. The Greek term gives us the English *phantom.* Because of the impossibility of such an act and their fatigue and fear in the stormy conditions, the twelve, even though each one saw Him, did not at first believe the figure was actually Jesus.

[j] BE OF GOOD CHEER! This command, always linked in the gospels to a situation of fear and apprehension (cf. Matt. 9:2, 22; 14:27; Mark 10:49; Luke 8:48; John 16:33; Acts 23:11), urged the disciples to have a continuing attitude of courage.

[k] IT IS I. Lit. "I AM." This statement clearly identified the figure as the Lord Jesus, not some phantom. It also echoed the OT self-revelation of God (cf. Ex. 3:14).

[l] IMMEDIATELY THE BOAT WAS AT THE LAND. This wording indicates that another miracle occurred besides walking on the water, i.e., the boat miraculously and instantly arrived at its precise destination as soon as Jesus stepped into the boat.

[m] THEY HAD NOT UNDERSTOOD ABOUT THE LOAVES. An explanation of the disciples' overwhelming astonishment at what had just happened. Because they misunderstood the real significance of that afternoon's miracle, they could not grasp Jesus' supernatural character as displayed in His power over the lake.

[n] THEIR HEART WAS HARDENED. Cf. Mark 8:17. The disciples' minds were impenetrable, so that they could not perceive what Christ was saying (cf. Mark 4:11–12). This phrase conveys or alludes to rebellion, not just ignorance (cf. Mark 3:5).

[o] YOU ARE THE SON OF GOD. Cf. Matthew 27:43, 54.

[p] GENNESARET. A town on the northwest shore of the Sea of Galilee.

[MK] and began to carry about on beds [MT] all [MK] those who were sick to wherever they heard He was. [q]Wherever He entered, into villages, cities, or the country, they laid the sick in the [r]marketplaces, and begged Him that they might just touch [s]the hem of His garment. [MT] And as many as touched *it* were made perfectly well.

[q] WHEREVER HE ENTERED. This summary statement gives an overview of Christ's healing ministry during the days and weeks that followed His walking on water.

[r] MARKETPLACES. Open spaces, usually just inside city walls or near city centers, where people congregated for various business and social purposes. Here the term might indicate its original meaning of any place where people generally assembled. The people brought the sick to such locations because Jesus was more likely to pass by.

[s] THE HEM OF HIS GARMENT. Cf. Matt. 9:20; Mark 5:28.

79. Jesus Is the Bread of Life

John 6:22–40

JN [a]On the following day, when the people who were standing on the other side of the sea saw that there was no other boat there, except that one which His disciples had entered, and that Jesus had not entered the boat with His disciples, but His disciples had gone away alone—however, other boats came from Tiberias, near the place where they ate bread after the Lord had given thanks— [b]when the people therefore saw that Jesus was not there, nor His disciples, they also got into boats and came to Capernaum, seeking Jesus. And when they found Him on the other side of the sea, they said to Him, "Rabbi, when did You come here?"

Jesus answered them and said, "Most assuredly, I say to you, you seek Me, not because you saw the signs, but [c]because you ate of the loaves and were filled. Do not labor for the [d]food which perishes, but for the [e]food which endures to everlasting life, which the Son of Man will give you, because God the Father has set His seal on Him." Then they said to Him, "What shall we do, that we may work

---

[a] ON THE FOLLOWING DAY. This took place the day after Jesus walked on water. This section presents Jesus' famous discourse on the bread of life. The key theme is John 6:35, i.e., "I am the bread of Life," which is the first of seven emphatic "I AM" statements of Jesus in this gospel (John 8:12; 10:7, 9; 10:11, 14; 11:25; 14:6; 15:1, 5). This analogy of Jesus as "the bread" of life reinforces John's theme of Jesus as the Messiah and Son of God (John 20:30, 31). Although John records Jesus' miracles to establish His deity, he moves quickly to Jesus' discourse on the spiritual realities of His person in order to define correctly who Jesus Christ was, i.e., not merely a wonder worker but the Son of God who came to save mankind from sin (John 3:16).

[b] WHEN THE PEOPLE THEREFORE SAW . . . JESUS WAS NOT THERE. The crowds who witnessed Jesus' healings and His feeding of the multitudes were still at the original site of these miracles (east of the Lake) and, out of heightened curiosity, desired to find Jesus once again. Other boats loaded with people from Tiberias (on the northwest shore of the lake) also heard of the miracles and sought Him out.

[c] BECAUSE YOU ATE. This phrase emphasizes Jesus' point that the crowds that followed Him were motivated by superficial desires of food rather than any understanding of the true spiritual significance of Jesus' person and mission (Mark 6:52; John 8:14–21).

[d] FOOD WHICH PERISHES. Jesus rebuked the crowd for regarding the messianic kingdom in a wholly materialistic way (cf. John 4:15). Although Messiah's kingdom would be literal and physical someday, the people failed to see the overriding spiritual character and blessing of "everlasting life" given immediately to those who believe the witness of God to His Son.

[e] FOOD WHICH ENDURES TO EVERLASTING LIFE. The continuing discourse indicates that this was a reference to Jesus Himself.

the [f]works of God?" Jesus answered and said to them, "This is [g]the work of God, that you believe in Him whom He sent." Therefore they said to Him, "[h]What sign will You perform then, that we may see it and believe You? What work will You do? [i]Our fathers ate the manna in the desert; as it is written, 'He gave them bread from heaven to eat.'" Then Jesus said to them, "Most assuredly, I say to you, Moses did not give you the bread from heaven, but My Father gives you the [j]true bread from heaven. For the [k]bread of God is He who comes down from heaven and gives life to the world." Then they said to Him, [l]"Lord, give us this bread always."

And Jesus said to them, "[m]I am the bread of life. He who comes to Me shall never hunger, and he who believes in Me shall never thirst. But I said to you that you have seen Me and yet do not believe. [n]All that the Father gives Me will come

---

[f] WORKS OF GOD. They thought Jesus was saying that God required them to do some works to earn everlasting life, which they thought they would be able to do.

[g] THE WORK OF GOD, THAT YOU BELIEVE. The crowd misunderstood Jesus' prohibition in John 6:27 ("Do not labor"), which prompted Jesus to remind them that an exclusive focus on material blessings is wrong. The only work God desired was faith or trust in Jesus as Messiah and Son of God (cf. Mal. 3:1). The "work" that God requires is to believe in His Son (cf. John 5:24).

[h] WHAT SIGN WILL YOU PERFORM? The question demonstrated the obtuseness, the spiritual blindness of the crowd, and their shallow, selfish curiosity. The feeding of twenty thousand (John 6:10) was a sufficient enough sign to demonstrate Christ's deity (cf. Luke 16:31).

[i] OUR FATHERS ATE THE MANNA. The crowd's logic appeared to be that Jesus' miraculous feeding was a small miracle compared to what Moses did. In order for them to believe in Him, they would need to see Him feed the nation of Israel on the same scale that God did when He sent manna and fed the entire nation of Israel during their wilderness wanderings for forty years (Ex. 16:11–36). They were demanding that Jesus outdo Moses if they were to believe in Him. They quoted from Ps. 78:24.

[j] TRUE BREAD FROM HEAVEN. The manna God gave was temporary and perished and was only a meager shadow of what God offered them in the true bread, Jesus Christ, who gives spiritual and eternal life to mankind ("world").

[k] BREAD OF GOD. This phrase is synonymous with the phrase "bread of heaven" (v. 32).

[l] "LORD, GIVE US THIS BREAD ALWAYS." This statement once again demonstrated the blindness of the crowd, for they were thinking of some physical bread and failed to understand the spiritual implication that Jesus was that "bread" (cf. John 4:15).

[m] I AM THE BREAD OF LIFE. The obtuseness in John 6:34 prompted Jesus to speak very plainly that He was referring to Himself.

[n] ALL THAT THE FATHER GIVES ME WILL COME TO ME. This verse emphasizes the sovereign will of God in the selection of those who come to Him for salvation (cf. John 6:44, 65; 17:6, 12, 24). The Father has predestined those who would be saved (cf. Rom. 8:29, 30; Eph. 1:3–6; 1 Peter 1:2). The absolute sovereignty of God is the basis of Jesus' certainty that His mission will be successful (cf. Phil. 1:6). The security of salvation rests in the sovereignty of God, for God is the guarantee that "all" He has chosen will come to Him for salvation. The idea of "gives Me" is that every person chosen by God and drawn by God (John 6:44) must be seen as a gift of the Father's love to the Son. The Son receives each "love gift" (v. 37), holds on to each (v. 39), and will raise each to eternal glory (vv. 39, 40). No one chosen will be lost (cf. Rom. 8:31–39). This saving purpose is the Father's will that the Son will not fail to do perfectly (John 6:38; cf. 4:34; 10:28, 29; 17:6, 12, 24).

to Me, and the one who comes to Me I will by no means cast out. For I have come down from heaven, not to do My own will, but the will of Him who sent Me. This is the will of the Father who sent Me, that of all He has given Me I should lose nothing, but should raise it up at the last day. And this is the will of Him who sent Me, that °everyone who sees the Son and believes in Him may have everlasting life; and I will raise him up at the last day."

° everyone who sees the Son and believes in Him. This verse emphasizes human responsibility in salvation. Although God is sovereign, He works through faith, so that a man must believe in Jesus as the Messiah and Son of God who alone offers the only way of salvation (cf. John 14:6). However, even faith is a gift of God (Rom. 12:3; Eph. 2:8, 9). Intellectually harmonizing the sovereignty of God and the responsibility of man is impossible humanly, but perfectly resolved in the infinite mind of God.

80. Reaction to Jesus' Claim to Be the Bread of Life

John 6:41–71

JN [a]The [b]Jews then [c]complained about Him, [d]because He said, "I am the bread which came down from heaven." And they said, "Is not this Jesus, the son of Joseph, [e]whose father and mother we know? How is it then that He says, 'I have come down from heaven'?" Jesus therefore answered and said to them, "Do not murmur among yourselves. No one can come to Me unless the Father who sent Me [f]draws him; and I will raise him up at the last day. [g]It is written in the prophets, 'And they shall all be taught by God.' Therefore everyone who has heard

---

[a] THE JEWS THEN. This section constitutes the beginning of the crowd's reaction to Jesus' discourse on the bread of life and may be divided into three sections: (1) the murmuring reaction of the crowd (John 6:41, 42); 2) Jesus' rebuke of the crowd for their reaction (vv. 43–46); and (3) Jesus' reiteration of His message to the crowd (vv. 47–51).

[b] JEWS. In this gospel the term "Jews" is often associated with hostility toward Christ. It is used ironically to indicate the incongruity of their rising hostility toward their Messiah. Since they hardened their hearts, God judicially hardened their hearts also (cf. Isa. 6:10; 53:1; Matt. 13:10–15; John 12:37–40). In the tribulation Israel will turn to Jesus as their true Messiah and be saved (Rom. 11:25–27; Rev. 1:7; 7:1–8; cf. Zech. 12:10–14).

[c] COMPLAINED. The reaction of the synagogue crowds to Jesus' statements was the same as the Israelites in the wilderness who murmured against God both before and after the manna was given to them (Ex. 16:2, 8, 9; Num. 11:4–6).

[d] BECAUSE HE SAID, "I AM THE BREAD . . . FROM HEAVEN." The Jews' anger centered in two things: (1) that Jesus said He was the bread and (2) that He came down from heaven. Both the Jews in Jerusalem (John 5:18) and the Galileans reacted negatively when Jesus placed Himself equal with God.

[e] WHOSE FATHER AND MOTHER WE KNOW. On the human level they knew Jesus as a fellow Galilean. These words are reminiscent of Jesus' words in John 4:44, "a prophet has no honor in his own country." Their hostility sprang from the root of unbelief. Jesus' death was impending because hostility had resulted everywhere He went.

[f] DRAWS HIM. Cf. John 6:65. A comparison of John 6:37a and 44 demonstrates that the divine drawing of sinners to salvation cannot be relegated to what is referred to as "prevenient grace," i.e., that somehow the power to come to Christ is allegedly dispensed to all of mankind, thus enabling everyone to accept or reject the gospel according to their own will alone. Scripture indicates that no "free will" exists in man's nature, for man is enslaved to sin (total depravity) and unable to believe apart from God's empowerment (Rom. 3:1–19; Eph. 2:1–3; 2 Cor. 4:4; 2 Tim. 1:9). While "whosoever will" may come to the Father, only those whom the Father gives the ability to will toward Him will actually come to Him. The drawing here is selective and efficacious (producing the desired effect) upon those whom God has sovereignly chosen for salvation, i.e., those whom God has chosen will believe, because God has sovereignly determined that result from eternity past (Eph. 1:9–11).

[g] IT IS WRITTEN. Jesus paraphrased Isa. 54:13 to support the point that if someone comes to faith and repentance to God, it is because they have been "taught," and hence drawn, by God. The "drawing" and "learning" are just different aspects of God's sovereign direction in the person's life. Those taught by God to grasp the truth are also drawn by God the Father to embrace the Son.

and learned from the Father comes to Me. Not that anyone has seen the Father, except He who is from God; He has seen the Father. Most assuredly, I say to you, he who believes in Me has everlasting life. I am the bread of life. Your fathers ate the [h]manna in the wilderness, and are dead. This is the bread which comes down from heaven, that one may eat of it and not die. [i]I am the living bread which came down from heaven. If anyone eats of this bread, he will live forever; and the bread that I shall give is [j]My flesh, which I shall give for the life of the world."

The Jews therefore [k]quarreled among themselves, saying, "How can this Man give us *His* flesh to eat?" Then Jesus said to them, "Most assuredly, I say to you, unless you [l]eat the flesh of the Son of Man and drink His blood, you have no life in you. Whoever eats My flesh and drinks My blood has eternal life, and I will raise him up at the last day. For My flesh is food indeed, and My blood is drink indeed. He who eats My flesh and drinks My blood abides in Me, and I in him. As the living Father sent Me, and I live because of the Father, so he who feeds on Me will live because of Me. This is the bread which came down from heaven—not as your fathers ate the manna, and are dead. He who eats this bread will live forever." These things He said in the synagogue as He taught in Capernaum.

---

[h] MANNA. Jesus contrasted the earthly and heavenly bread. The manna that was given in the wilderness, although sent from heaven to help sustain the Israelites for their physical needs, could not impart eternal life nor meet their spiritual needs as could the "bread of life" that came down from heaven in the person of Jesus the Messiah. The proof of this contrast centers in the irrefutable fact that all the fathers died who ate the wilderness manna.

[i] I AM THE LIVING BREAD. This section (John 6:51–59) may be divided into three divisions: (1) Jesus' pronouncement (v. 51); (2) the crowd's perplexity (v. 52); and (3) Jesus' promises (vv. 53–59).

[j] MY FLESH, WHICH I SHALL GIVE FOR THE LIFE OF THE WORLD. Jesus refers here prophetically to His impending sacrifice upon the cross (cf. 2 Cor. 5:21; 1 Peter 2:24). Jesus voluntarily laid down His life for evil, sinful mankind (John 10:18; 1 John 2:2).

[k] QUARRELED. Once again the perplexity of the Jews indicates that they failed to understand the spiritual truth behind Jesus' illustration. Every time Jesus had given them a veiled saying or physical illustration, the Jews failed to see its spiritual significance (e.g., John 3:4; 4:15). The Mosaic law prohibited the drinking of blood or the eating of meat with blood still in it (Lev. 17:10–14; Deut. 12:16; Acts 15:29). The Jews, unable to go beyond the mere physical perspective, were perplexed and angered.

[l] EAT . . . DRINK. Jesus' point was an analogy that has spiritual, rather than literal, significance: just as eating and drinking are necessary for physical life, so also is belief in His sacrificial death on the cross necessary for eternal life. The eating of His flesh and drinking of His blood metaphorically symbolize the need for accepting Jesus' cross work. For the Jews, however, a crucified Messiah was unthinkable (cf. Acts 17:1–3). Once again, the Jews, in their willful and judicial blindness, could not see the real spiritual significance and truth behind Jesus' statements. Moreover, Jesus' reference here to eating and drinking was not referring to the ordinance of communion for two significant reasons: (1) communion had not been instituted yet, and (2) if Jesus was referring to communion, then the passage would teach that anyone partaking of communion would receive eternal life.

[m]Therefore many of His disciples, when they heard *this,* said, "This is a hard saying; who can understand it?" When Jesus knew in Himself that [n]His disciples complained about this, He said to them, "Does this offend you? *What* then if you should see the Son of Man ascend where He was before? It is the Spirit who gives life; the flesh profits nothing. The words that I speak to you are spirit, and *they* are life. But there are some of you who do not believe." For [o]Jesus knew from the beginning who they were who did not believe, and who would betray Him. And He said, "Therefore [p]I have said to you that no one can come to Me unless it has been granted to him by My Father." From that *time* many of His [q]disciples went back and walked with Him no more. Then Jesus said to the twelve, "Do you also want to go away?" But Simon Peter answered Him, "Lord, to whom shall we go? You have the words of eternal life. Also [r]we have come to believe and know that You are the Christ, the Son of the living God." Jesus answered them, "[s]Did I not choose

---

[m] THEREFORE. These verses (John 6:60–71) constitute the reaction of Jesus' disciples to His sermon on the "bread of life." As with the crowds' response in Jerusalem (chap. 5) and in Galilee (chap. 6), the response of many of His disciples was unbelief and rejection of Him. John lists two groups and their reactions: (1) the false disciples' reaction of unbelief (John 6:60–66), and (2) the true disciples' reaction of belief (vv. 67–71). After this sermon, only a small nucleus of disciples remained (v. 67).

[n] HIS DISCIPLES COMPLAINED. Many of Jesus' disciples had the same reaction as the Jews in John 6:41 and of the first generation of Israelites to manna, i.e., they murmured (Ex. 16:2).

[o] JESUS KNEW. Reminiscent of Jesus' words in John 2:23–25, Jesus knew the hearts of men, including those disciples who followed Him. He supernaturally knew that many did not believe in Him as Messiah and Son of God, so He did not entrust Himself to them. These false disciples were simply attracted to the physical phenomena (e.g., miracles and food) and failed to understand the true significance of Jesus' teaching.

[p] I HAVE SAID. Although sinners are commanded to believe and will be held responsible for rejecting the truth, genuine faith is a gift of God that He initiates. Once again, in the face of unbelief, Jesus reiterated God's sovereignty involved in selection for salvation.

[q] DISCIPLES . . . WALKED WITH HIM NO MORE. The language indicates that the abandonment was decisive and final (cf. 1 Peter 2:6–8; 1 John 2:19).

[r] WE HAVE COME TO BELIEVE. Peter's words were somewhat pretentious in that he implied that the true disciples somehow had superior insight and, as a result, came to belief through that insight.

[s] DID I NOT CHOOSE YOU, THE TWELVE? In response to Peter's words that the disciples had come to believe in Jesus, He reminds them that He sovereignly chose them (cf. John 6:37, 44, 65). They could take no credit for God's sovereign election of them.

you, the twelve, and one of you is [t]a devil?" He spoke of Judas [u]Iscariot, *the son* of Simon, for it was he who would betray Him, being one of the twelve.

[t] a devil. The word *devil* means "slanderer" or "false accuser." The idea perhaps is better translated, "one of you is the devil." This meaning is clear from Mark 8:33; Luke 22:3; John 13:2, 27. The foremost enemy of God so works behind the scenes through human agents that his malevolence becomes theirs (cf. Matt. 16:23). Jesus supernaturally knew the source and identified it precisely. This clearly fixes the character of Judas, not as a well-intentioned but misguided man trying to force Jesus to exert His power and set up His kingdom (as some suggest), but as a tool of Satan doing unmitigated wickedness (cf. John 13:21–30).

[u] Iscariot. The word most likely is from a Hebrew word meaning "man of Kerioth," the name of a village in Judah. As with the other three gospels, as soon as he was named, he became identified as the betrayer.

81. Jesus Confronts the Traditions of Men

Matt. 15:1–20; Mark 7:1–23; John 7:1

JN [a]After these things Jesus [b]walked in Galilee; for He did not want to walk in Judea, because the Jews sought to kill Him.

MK Then the [c]Pharisees and some of the scribes came together to Him, having come from Jerusalem. Now when they saw some of His disciples eat bread with [d]defiled, that is, with unwashed hands, they found fault. For the Pharisees and all the Jews do not eat unless they [e]wash *their* hands in a special way, holding the [f]tradition of the elders. *When they come* from the marketplace, they do not eat unless they wash. And there are many other things which they have received and hold, *like* the washing of cups, pitchers, copper vessels, and [g]couches. Then the Pharisees

---

[a] AFTER THESE THINGS. In John's gospel this phrase indicates a six-month gap between the events of John 6:1–71 (which occurred around Passover in April) and the events in chapter 7:2ff (which occurred around the Feast of Tabernacles in October). Although John skips this time period, the Synoptic Gospels fill in much of the gap. John's purpose in writing was not to present an exhaustive chronology of Christ's life, but to portray Him as the Messiah and Son of God and show how men reacted to Him.

[b] WALKED IN GALILEE. John 6 indicates Jesus spent two days with the multitude of twenty thousand people (John 6:22), but He spent the next seven months teaching His twelve disciples who believed in Him. This phrase subtly highlights the great importance of discipleship, for Jesus concentrated great lengths of time upon training His future spiritual leaders.

[c] PHARISEES . . . COME FROM JERUSALEM. This delegation of leading representatives of Judaism came from Jerusalem, probably at the request of the Galilean Pharisees.

[d] DEFILED. The disciples of Jesus were being accused of eating with hands that had not been ceremonially cleansed and thus had not been separated from the defilement associated with their having touched anything profane.

[e] WASH. This washing had nothing to do with cleaning dirty hands, but with a ceremonial rinsing. The ceremony involved someone pouring water out of a jar onto another's hands, whose fingers must be pointing up. As long as the water dripped off at the wrist, the person could proceed to the next step. He then had water poured over both hands with the fingers pointing down. Then each hand was to be rubbed with the fist of the other hand.

[f] TRADITION OF THE ELDERS. This was a body of extrabiblical law that had existed only in oral form and only since the time of the Babylonian captivity. Later it was committed to writing in the Mishnah near the end of the second century. The law of Moses contained no commandment about washing one's hands before eating—except for priests, who were required to wash before eating holy offerings (Lev. 22:6, 7). Such traditions had in actuality supplanted Scripture as the highest religious authority in Judaism

[g] COUCHES. This word does not appear in the better manuscripts.

and scribes asked Him, "[h]Why do Your disciples not walk according to the tradition of the elders? MT For they do not wash their hands when they eat bread."

He answered and said to them, "Why do you also [i]transgress the commandment of God MK that you may keep your tradition? MT For God [through] MK [j]Moses MT commanded, saying, 'Honor your father and your mother'; and, 'He who curses father or mother, let him be put to death.'

"But you say, 'Whoever says to his father or mother, "Whatever profit you might have received from me MK *is* [k]Corban"—' (that is, a gift *to God*),— MT then he need MK no longer do anything for his father or his mother.' MT Thus you have [l]made the commandment of God of no effect MK through your tradition which you have handed down. And many such things you do. MT [m]Hypocrites! Well [n]did Isaiah prophesy about you, MK as it is written:

> MT 'These people draw near to Me with their mouth,
> And honor Me with *their* lips,
> But their heart is far from Me.
> And in vain they worship Me,
> Teaching *as* doctrines the commandments of men.'

---

[h] WHY DO YOUR DISCIPLES NOT WALK? The Pharisees and scribes went to the disciples' Master for an explanation of the disciples' allegedly-disgraceful conduct. In reality they were accusing Jesus of teaching His disciples to disobey the traditions of the elders.

[i] TRANSGRESS. The nature of this sin is identified in Matt. 15:4–6 as dishonoring one's parents in a cleverly devised way. The commandments of God were clear (quoted from Ex. 20:12; 21:17; Deut. 5:16), but to circumvent them, some people claimed they could not financially assist their parents because they had dedicated a certain sum of money to God, who was greater than their parents. The rabbis had approved this exception to the commandments of Moses and thus, in effect, nullified God's law.

[j] MOSES COMMANDED. Quoted from Ex. 20:12 (the fifth commandment) and Ex. 21:17. Both refer specifically to the duty of honoring one's parents, which includes treating them with respect, love, reverence, and dignity, and assisting them financially. The second quotation indicates how seriously God regards this obligation.

[k] CORBAN. A Hebrew term meaning "given to God." It refers to any gift or sacrifice of money or goods an individual vowed to dedicate specifically to God. As a result of such dedication, the money or goods could be used only for sacred purposes.

[l] MADE THE COMMANDMENT OF GOD OF NO EFFECT THROUGH YOUR TRADITION. "Making . . . of no effect" means "to deprive of authority," or "to cancel." The "tradition" in question allowed any individual to call all his possessions "Corban." If a son became angry with his parents, he could declare his money and property "Corban." Since Scripture teaches that any vow made to God could not be violated (Num. 30:2), his possessions could not be used for anything but service to God and not as a resource of financial assistance for his parents. But Jesus condemned this practice by showing that the Pharisees and scribes were guilty of canceling out God's Word (and His command to honor one's parents) through their tradition.

[m] HYPOCRITES. Spiritual phonies (cf. Matt. 6:2). They followed the traditions of men because such teaching required only mechanical and thoughtless conformity without a pure heart.

[n] DID ISAIAH PROPHESY. Isa. 29:13 is quoted almost word for word from the Greek translation of the OT (Septuagint). Isaiah's prophecy perfectly fit the actions of the Pharisees and scribes (cf. Isa. 29:13).

MK "For laying aside the [o]commandment of God, you hold the tradition of men—the washing of pitchers and cups, and many other such things you do."

MT When He had called MK all the multitude to *Himself,* He said to them, "Hear Me, everyone, and understand: MK There is nothing that enters MT into the mouth MK from outside which can defile MT a man; MK but the things [p]which come out of MT the mouth, MK those are the things that defile a man. [q]If anyone has ears to hear, let him hear!"

MT Then His disciples came and said to Him, "Do You know that the Pharisees were offended when they heard this saying?" But He answered and said, "Every plant which My heavenly Father has not planted will be uprooted. [r]Let them alone. They are blind leaders of the blind. And if the blind leads the blind, both will fall into a ditch."

MK When He had entered a house away from the crowd, His disciples asked Him concerning the [s]parable. MT Then Peter answered and said to Him, "Explain this parable to us." So Jesus said, "Are you also still without understanding? Do you not yet understand that whatever enters the mouth [of] MK a man from outside [t]cannot defile him, because it does not enter his heart but MT goes into the stomach and is eliminated, MK *thus* [u]purifying all foods?"

---

[o] COMMANDMENT OF GOD . . . TRADITION OF MEN. Jesus first accused them of abandoning all the commandments contained in God's Word. Then He charged them with substituting God's standard with a humanly designed standard.

[p] WHICH COME OUT OF THE MOUTH . . . DEFILE A MAN. People might defile themselves ceremonially (under the Old Covenant) by eating something unclean, but they would defile themselves morally by saying something sinful (cf. James 3:6). Here Jesus clearly distinguished between the law's ceremonial requirements and its inviolable moral standard. Ceremonial defilement could be dealt with through ceremonial means. But moral defilement corrupts a person's soul.

[q] IF ANYONE HAS EARS TO HEAR, LET HIM HEAR! Mark 7:16 does not occur in the best manuscripts.

[r] LET THEM ALONE. This severe judgment is a form of God's wrath. It signifies abandonment by God and is described as "giving them over" in Rom. 1:18–32. Cf. Hos. 4:17.

[s] PARABLE. i.e., Matt. 15:11. The "parable" is not at all hard to understand, but it was hard for even the disciples to accept. Years later, Peter still found it hard to accept that all foods are clean (Acts 10:14).

[t] CANNOT DEFILE HIM. Since food is merely physical, no one who eats it will defile his heart or inner person, which is spiritual. Physical pollution, no matter how corrupt, cannot cause spiritual or moral pollution. Neither can external ceremonies and rituals cleanse a person spiritually.

[u] PURIFYING ALL FOODS. By overturning the tradition of hand washing, Jesus, in effect, removed the restrictions regarding dietary laws. This comment by Mark had the advantage of hindsight as he looked back on the event, and was no doubt influenced by Peter's own experience in Joppa (Acts 10:15).

And He said, MT "But those things which proceed out of the mouth MK of a man MT come from the heart, and they defile a man. MK For from within, out of the heart of men, proceed evil thoughts, adulteries, [v]fornications, murders, thefts, covetousness, wickedness, deceit, MT false witness, MK [w]lewdness, [x]an evil eye, blasphemy, pride, foolishness. All these [y]evil things come from within and defile a man, MT but to eat with unwashed hands does not defile a man."

---

[v] FORNICATIONS. Lit. illicit sexual activity.

[w] LEWDNESS. Lit. unrestrained, shameless behavior.

[x] AN EVIL EYE. A Hebrew expression referring to envy and jealousy (Deut. 28:54; Prov. 23:6; Matt. 20:15).

[y] EVIL THINGS COME FROM WITHIN. A person's defiled heart is expressed in both what he says and what he does (cf. Mark 12:34–37).

82. Jesus Ministers to a Syro-Phoenician Woman

Matthew 15:21–28; Mark 7:24–30

MT Then Jesus went out from there and departed to the region of Tyre and Sidon. MK And He entered a house and [a]wanted no one to know *it,* but He could not be hidden. For MT behold, a woman of Canaan MK whose young daughter had an [b]unclean spirit heard about Him. And she MT came from that region MK and fell at His feet MT and cried out to Him, saying, "Have mercy on me, O Lord, Son of David! My daughter is severely demon-possessed."

MK The woman was a [c]Greek, a [d]Syro-Phoenician by birth, and she kept asking Him to cast the demon out of her daughter. MT But He answered her not a word. And His disciples came and urged Him, saying, "Send her away, for she cries out after us." But He answered and said, "I was not sent except to the lost sheep of the house of Israel."

Then she came and worshiped Him, saying, "Lord, help me!" MK But Jesus said to her, "Let the children be filled [e]first, for it is not good to take [f]the children's bread and throw *it* to the [g]little dogs." And she answered and said to Him, "[h]Yes,

---

[a] WANTED NO ONE TO KNOW. Jesus did not seek a public ministry in the area. It is likely He wanted time to rest from the pressure of the Jewish leaders and an opportunity to further prepare the disciples for His coming crucifixion and their ministry.

[b] UNCLEAN SPIRIT. A demon (cf. Matt. 15:22; Mark 1:23).

[c] GREEK. A non-Jew in both her language and religion (cf. Rom. 1:14).

[d] SYRO-PHOENICIAN. The region of Phoenicia at that time was part of the province of Syria. Matthew 15:22 adds that she was a descendant of the Canaanites.

[e] FIRST. The illustration Jesus gave was, in essence, a test of the woman's faith. Jesus' "first" responsibility was to preach the gospel to the children of Israel (cf. Rom. 1:16; 15:8). But that also implied there would come a time when Gentiles would be the recipients of God's blessings.

[f] THE CHILDREN'S BREAD AND THROW IT TO THE LITTLE DOGS. "The children's bread" refers to God's blessings offered to the Jews. This picture indicates that the "little dogs" (Gentiles) had a place in the household of God, but not the prominent one (cf. Matt. 15:26).

[g] LITTLE DOGS. The diminutive form suggests that this reference is to dogs that were kept as pets. Jesus was referring to the Gentiles, but He did not use the derisive term the Jews usually employed for them that described mangy, vicious mongrels.

[h] YES, LORD. Indicative of the woman's humble faith and worshipful attitude. She knew she was sinful and undeserving of any of God's blessing. Her response was characterized by a complete absence of pride and self-reliance, which Jesus answered by granting her request (Mark 7:29–30).

Lord, yet even the little dogs under the table eat from [i]the children's crumbs
MT which fall from their masters' table."

Then Jesus answered and said to her, "O woman, great *is* your faith! Let it be to you as you desire. MK For this saying go your way; the demon has gone out of your daughter." MT And her daughter was healed from that very hour.

MK And when she had come to her house, she found the demon gone out, and her daughter lying on the bed.

---

[i] THE CHILDREN'S CRUMBS. The lost sheep of the house of Israel must be fed before the "little dogs" (cf. Matt. 10:5). Christ employed a word here that speaks of a family pet. His words with this woman are not to be understood as harsh or unfeeling. In fact, He was tenderly drawing from her an expression of her faith in Matt. 15:27.

83. Jesus Heals in Decapolis

Matthew 15:29–31; Mark 7:31–37

[MK] Again, [a]departing from the region of Tyre and Sidon, He [MT] skirted the Sea of Galilee, and [MK] came through the midst of the region of Decapolis to the Sea of Galilee. Then [He] [MT] went up on the mountain and sat down there. Then great multitudes came to Him, having with them *the* lame, blind, mute, maimed, and many others; and they laid them down at Jesus' feet, and He healed them.

[MK] They brought to Him one who was deaf and had an impediment in his speech, and they begged Him to put His hand on him. And He took him aside from the multitude, and [b]put His fingers in his ears, and [c]He spat and touched his tongue. Then, looking up to heaven, He sighed, and said to him, [d]"Ephphatha," that is, "Be opened." Immediately his ears were opened, and the impediment of his tongue was loosed, and he spoke plainly. Then He commanded them that they should [e]tell no one; but the more He commanded them, the more widely they proclaimed *it.*

[MT] So the multitude marveled when they saw *the* mute speaking, *the* maimed made whole, *the* lame walking, and *the* blind seeing; and they glorified the God of Israel. [MK] And they were astonished beyond measure, saying, "He has done all things well. He makes both the deaf to hear and the mute to speak."

---

[a] DEPARTING FROM THE REGION OF TYRE AND SIDON . . . SEA OF GALILEE. Jesus traveled twenty miles north from Tyre and passed through Sidon, which was deep into Gentile territory. From there He went east, crossed the Jordan, and traveled south along the eastern shore of the Sea of Galilee to the Decapolis (Mark 7:31), a primarily Gentile region. He may have taken this route to avoid the territory ruled by Herod Antipas (cf. Matt. 14:1, 2). The events that follow must have occurred in the Decapolis.

[b] PUT HIS FINGERS IN HIS EARS. Because the man could not hear, Jesus used His own form of sign language to tell him that He was about to heal the man's deafness.

[c] HE SPAT AND TOUCHED HIS TONGUE. Also a form of sign language in which Jesus offered the man hope for a restored speech.

[d] "EPHPHATHA." An Aramaic word that Mark immediately defines.

[e] TELL NO ONE. Although Jesus ministered to Gentiles as the need arose, His intention was not to have a public ministry among them.

84. Jesus Feeds Four Thousand in Decapolis

Matthew 15:32–38; Mark 8:1–9

MK In those days, [a]the multitude being very great and having nothing to eat, Jesus called His disciples *to Him* and said to them, "[b]I have compassion on the multitude, because they have now [c]continued with Me three days and have nothing to eat. And MT I do not want to MK send them away hungry to their own houses, MT lest they faint on the way; MK for some of them have come from afar."

MT Then His disciples said to Him, "[d]Where could we get enough bread [e]in the wilderness to fill such a great multitude?" Jesus MK asked them, "How many loaves do you have?" MT And they said, "[f]Seven, and a few little fish." So He commanded the multitude to sit down on the ground.

---

[a] THE MULTITUDE BEING VERY GREAT. Probably because of the widespread report of Jesus' healing of the deaf and mute man (Mark 7:36).

[b] I HAVE COMPASSION. Only here (Matt. 15:32; Mark 8:2) did Jesus use this word of Himself. When he fed the five thousand, Jesus expressed "compassion" for the people's lost spiritual condition (Mark 6:34); here, He expressed "compassion" for people's physical needs (cf. Matt. 6:8, 32). Jesus could empathize with their hunger, having experienced it Himself (Matt. 4:2).

[c] CONTINUED WITH ME THREE DAYS. This reflects the crowd's eagerness to hear Jesus' teaching and experience His healings (cf. Matt. 15:30). That they were with Him for that time before the miraculous feeding distinguishes this event from the earlier feeding of the five thousand, in which the crowd gathered, ate, and dispersed in one day (Matt. 14:14–15, 22–23).

[d] WHERE COULD WE GET ENOUGH BREAD? No wonder our Lord called them men of little faith (Matt. 8:26; 14:31; 16:8; 17:20), when they asked a question like that in the light of the recent feeding of the five thousand (Matt. 14:13–21). Some find the disciples' question incredible in light of the earlier feeding of the five thousand. But it was consistent with their spiritual dullness and lack of understanding (cf. Mark 8:14–21; 6:52).

[e] IN THE WILDERNESS. The Decapolis region was not as heavily populated as Galilee.

[f] SEVEN, AND A FEW LITTLE FISH. Again, the Lord had them confess for the record how little food they had in comparison to the size of the crowd. This made clear that the feeding was miraculous evidence of His deity.

And He took the seven [g]loaves and the fish and gave thanks, broke *them* and gave *them* to His disciples MK to set before *them;* MT and the disciples *gave* MK them MT to the multitude. So they all ate and were filled, and they took up [h]seven large baskets full of the fragments that were left. Now [i]those who ate were [j]four thousand men, besides women and children.

---

[g] LOAVES. Flat cakes of bread which could easily be broken into smaller pieces.

[h] SEVEN LARGE BASKETS. Not the same baskets mentioned in the feeding of the five thousand (Mark 6:43). Those were small baskets, commonly used by the Jewish people to hold one or two meals when traveling. The word here refers to large baskets (large enough to hold a man, Acts 9:25) used by Gentiles. What was done with the leftover food is not mentioned. It was likely given back to the people to sustain them on their trip home, since the disciples evidently did not take it with them (cf. Mark 6:14).

[i] THOSE WHO ATE. While all four gospels record the feeding of the five thousand, only Matthew and Mark record the feeding of the four thousand.

[j] FOUR THOUSAND. The number of the men only, not including the women and children (Matt. 15:38). This could indicate at least sixteen thousand people. Notably, Christ ended His ministry in Galilee with the feeding of the five thousand (Matt. 14:13–21). Here, He ended His ministry in the Gentile regions by feeding the four thousand. He later would end His Jerusalem ministry with a meal in the upper room with His disciples.

85. The Leaven of the Pharisees

Matthew 15:39–16:12; Mark 8:10–21

MT And He sent away the multitude, MK immediately got into the boat with His disciples, and came to the region of [a]Dalmanutha [near] MT Magdala. Then the Pharisees and Sadducees came MK out and began to dispute with Him, MT and testing Him asked that He would show them a [b]sign from heaven.

MK But He sighed deeply in His spirit, and MT answered and said to them, "When it is evening you say, '*It will be* [c]fair weather, for the sky is red'; and in the morning, '*It will be* foul weather today, for the sky is red and threatening.' Hypocrites! You know how to discern the face of the sky, but you cannot *discern* the signs of the times. A wicked and adulterous generation seeks after a sign, and MK assuredly, I say to you, MT no sign shall be given to MK this generation MT except the sign of the prophet Jonah." MK And He left them, and getting into the boat again, departed to [d]the other side.

---

[a] DALMANUTHA. This location is not mentioned in any secular literature and only mentioned here in the NT. The location is unknown, but clearly in the region near Magdala (cf. Matt. 15:39, where Magadan is the preferred reading). Recent archeological work in the area, when the water level of Galilee was at an all-time low, revealed several heretofore unknown anchorages. One small harbor has been found between Magadala and Capernaum, which may be Dalmanutha.

[b] SIGN FROM HEAVEN. The skeptical Pharisees demanded further miraculous proof of Jesus' messianic claims. Not content with the countless miracles He had performed on earth, they demanded some sort of astronomical miracle. Having already given them more than enough proof, Jesus refused to accommodate their spiritual blindness. This time, Jesus rebuked them for being so concerned with heavenly signs that they could not even interpret the signs of the times all around them. Then He referred them to the same sign He gave them before, the sign of the prophet Jonah (Mark 8:4; cf. 12:39). The supreme sign verifying His claim to be Son of God and Messiah was to be His resurrection (cf. Matt. 12:39, 40).

[c] FAIR WEATHER. As primitive as their method of predicting the weather was, their ability to discern spiritual matters was worse. They had the long-promised and long-awaited Messiah in their midst and refused to acknowledge Him.

[d] THE OTHER SIDE. To the northeast shore, where Bethsaida was located.

MT Now when His disciples had come to the other side, they had forgotten to take bread, MK and they did not have more than one loaf with them in the boat. MT Then Jesus said to them, "Take heed and beware of [e]the leaven of the Pharisees and the Sadducees MK and the leaven of Herod." MT And they reasoned among themselves, saying, "*It is* because we have taken no bread." But Jesus, being aware of *it,* said to them, "O you of little faith, [f]why do you reason among yourselves because you have brought no bread? Do you not yet MK perceive nor understand? Is your [g]heart still hardened? Having eyes, do you not see? And having ears, do you not hear? And [h]do you not remember? When I broke the five loaves for the five thousand, how many baskets full of fragments did you take up?" They said to Him, "Twelve."

"Also, when I broke the seven for the four thousand, how many large baskets full of fragments did you take up?" And they said, "Seven."

MT [i]"How is it you do not understand that I did not speak to you concerning bread?—*but* to beware of the leaven of the Pharisees and Sadducees." Then they understood that He did not tell *them* to beware of the leaven of bread, but of [j]the doctrine of the Pharisees and Sadducees.

---

[e] THE LEAVEN OF THE PHARISEES AND . . . OF HEROD. "Leaven" in the NT is an illustration of influence (cf. Matt. 13:33) and most often symbolizes the evil influence of sin. The "leaven" of the Pharisees included both their false teaching (Matt. 16:12) and their hypocritical behavior (Luke 12:1); the "leaven" of Herod Antipas was his immoral, corrupt conduct (cf. Mark 6:17–29). The Pharisees and the Herodians were allied against Christ (Mark 3:6). When Jesus warned of this dangerous influence, the disciples thought He was talking about bread. Again, He reminded them of the fact that the Lord provided plenty of bread, so they didn't need the bread the Pharisees were offering. How soon they forgot His miracles.

[f] WHY DO YOU REASON . . . NO BREAD? Jesus' question rebuked the disciples for completely missing His point. He was concerned with spiritual truth, not mundane physical matters.

[g] HEART STILL HARDENED. i.e., they were rebellious, spiritually insensitive, and unable to understand spiritual truth.

[h] DO YOU NOT REMEMBER? Jesus' rapid-fire questions further rebuked the disciples for their hardness of heart and also reminded them of His ability to provide anything they might lack.

[i] "HOW IS IT YOU DO NOT UNDERSTAND?" An appeal based on the questions He had just asked. As Matthew's account reveals, the disciples finally understood His point.

[j] THE DOCTRINE OF THE PHARISEES AND SADDUCEES. Here, the leaven of the Pharisees is their "doctrine." In Luke 12:1 it is their "hypocrisy." The two things are inextricably linked. The most sinister influence of the Jewish leaders was a pragmatic doctrine that made room for hypocrisy. They were too concerned with externals and ceremonies and the way things appeared and not concerned enough with matters of the heart. Jesus rebuked them for their hypocrisy again and again. Cf. Matt. 23:25.

86. Jesus Heals a Blind Man

Mark 8:22–26

MK [a]Then He came to Bethsaida; and they brought a blind man to Him, and begged Him to touch him. So He took the blind man by the hand and led him out of the town. And when He had [b]spit on his eyes and put His hands on him, He asked him if he saw anything. And he looked up and said, "I see men like trees, walking." Then He put *His* hands on his eyes again and made him look up. And he was restored and saw everyone clearly. Then He sent him away to his house, saying, "[c]Neither go into the town, nor tell anyone in the town."

---

[a] Then He came . . . This passage presents the second of Jesus' two miracles recorded only in Mark (cf. 7:31–37). It is also the first of two healings of blind men recorded in Mark (cf. 10:46–52).

[b] spit on his eyes. This action and Jesus' touching his eyes with His hands were apparently meant to reassure the blind man (who would naturally depend on his other senses, such as touch) that Jesus would heal his eyes (cf. Mark 7:33; John 9:6).

[c] Neither go into the town. Jesus led the blind man out of town before healing him, probably to avoid publicity and the mob scene that would otherwise result. Unlike others in the past (cf. Mark 1:45; 7:36), he apparently obeyed.

87. Peter Identifies Jesus as the Messiah

Matt. 16:13–20; Mark 8:27–30; Luke 9:18–21

MK Now Jesus and His disciples MT came into the region of MK the towns of [a]Caesarea Philippi. LK And it happened, as He was alone praying, *that* His disciples joined Him. MK And on the road He asked His disciples, saying to them, MT "Who do men say that I, the Son of Man, am?"

LK So they answered and said, MT "Some *say* [b]John the Baptist, MK but some *say,* [c]Elijah; MT and others LK say MT Jeremiah or LK that one of the old prophets has risen again."

MT He said to them, [d]"But who do you say that I am?" Simon Peter answered and said, [e]"You are [f]the Christ, the Son of [g]the living God."

Jesus answered and said to him, "Blessed are you, Simon Bar-Jonah, for [h]flesh and blood has not revealed *this* to you, but My Father who is in heaven. And I

[a] Caesarea Philippi. A district about twenty-five miles north of Galilee, at the base of Mount Hermon. This was different from the city of Caesarea built by Herod the Great on the Mediterranean coast, about sixty miles northwest of Jerusalem.

[b] John the Baptist . . . Elijah . . . one of the old prophets. Such rumors were apparently quite common. Cf. Matt. 11:14; Mark 9:13; Luke 1:17; Rev. 11:5–6.

[c] Elijah. Cf. Mal. 4:5; Matt. 11:14; Mark 6:15; Luke 1:17.

[d] "But who do you say that I am?" After they reported the prevailing erroneous views about Jesus, He asked the disciples to give their own evaluation of who He was. The answer every person gives to this question will determine his or her eternal destiny.

[e] "You are the Christ." Peter unhesitatingly replied on behalf of the twelve (cf. Matt. 14:28; 15:15; 17:4; 19:27; 26:33; John 6:68; 13:36), clearly and unequivocally affirming that they believed Jesus to be the Messiah.

[f] the Christ. i.e., the Messiah promised in the OT (Dan. 9:25–26). Cf. Matt. 16:16.

[g] the living God. An OT name for Yahweh (e.g., Deut. 5:26; Josh. 3:10; 1 Sam. 17:26, 36; 2 Kings 19:4, 16; Pss. 42:2; 84:2; Dan. 6:26; Hos. 1:10) as contrasted with the dead, dumb idols (Jer. 10:8; 18:15; 1 Cor. 12:2).

[h] flesh and blood has not revealed this to you. God the Father had opened Peter's eyes to the full significance of OT messianic truths and revealed to him who Jesus really was. In other words, God had opened Peter's heart to this deeper knowledge of Christ by faith. Peter was not merely expressing an academic opinion about the identity of Christ; this was a confession of Peter's personal faith, made possible by a divinely regenerated heart.

also say to you that you are Peter, and [i]on this rock I will build My [j]church, and [k]the gates of Hades shall not prevail against it. And I will give you [l]the keys of the kingdom of heaven, and whatever you bind on earth will be bound in heaven, and whatever you loose on earth will be loosed in heaven."

Then He [LK] strictly warned and [MT] commanded His disciples that they should [m]tell no one that He was Jesus the Christ.

---

[i] ON THIS ROCK. The word for "Peter," *Petros*, means a small stone (John 1:42). Jesus used a play on words here with *petra*, which means a foundation boulder (cf. Matt. 7:24, 25). Since the NT makes it abundantly clear that Christ is both the foundation (Acts 4:11, 12; 1 Cor. 3:11) and the head (Eph. 5:23) of the church, it is a mistake to think that here He is giving either of those roles to Peter. There is a sense in which the apostles played a foundational role in the building of the church (Eph. 2:20), but the role of primacy is reserved for Christ alone, not assigned to Peter. So Jesus' words here are best interpreted as a simple play on words in that a boulder-like truth came from the mouth of one who was called a small stone. Peter himself explains the imagery in his first epistle: the church is built of "living stones" (1 Peter 2:5) who, like Peter, confess that Jesus is the Christ, the Son of the living God. And Christ Himself is the "chief cornerstone" (1 Peter 2:6–7).

[j] CHURCH. Matthew is the only gospel where this term is found (cf. Matt. 18:17). Christ called it "My church," emphasizing that He alone is its Architect, Builder, Owner, and Lord. The Greek word for "church" means "called out ones." While God had since the beginning of redemptive history been gathering the redeemed by grace, the unique church He promised to build began at Pentecost with the coming of the Holy Spirit, by whom the Lord baptized believers into His body—which is the church (cf. Acts 2:1–4; 1 Cor. 12:12–13).

[k] THE GATES OF HADES. Hades is the place of punishment for the spirits of dead unbelievers. The point of entry for such is death. This, then, is a Jewish phrase referring to death. Even death, the ultimate weapon of Satan (cf. Heb. 2:14–15), has no power to stop the church. The blood of martyrs, in fact, has sped the growth of the church in size and spiritual power.

[l] THE KEYS OF THE KINGDOM OF HEAVEN. These represent authority, and here Christ gives Peter (and by extension all other believers) authority to declare what was bound or loosed in heaven. This echoed the promise of John 20:23, where Christ gave the disciples authority to forgive or retain the sins of people. All this must be understood in the context of Matt. 18:15–17, where Christ laid out specific instructions for dealing with sin in the church. The sum of it all means that any duly constituted body of believers, acting in accord with God's Word, has the authority to declare if someone is forgiven or unforgiven. The church's authority is not to determine these things, but to declare the judgment of heaven based on the principles of the Word. When they make such judgments on the basis of God's Word, they can be sure heaven is in accord. In other words, whatever they "bind" or "loose" on earth is already "bound" or "loosed" in heaven. When the church says the unrepentant person is bound in sin, the church is saying what God says about that person. When the church acknowledges that a repentant person has been loosed from that sin, God agrees.

[m] TELL NO ONE. Jesus' messianic mission cannot be understood apart from the cross, which the disciples did not yet understand (cf. Mark 8:31–33; 9:30–32). For them to have proclaimed Jesus as Messiah at this point would have only furthered the misunderstanding that the Messiah was to be a political-military deliverer. The fallout was that the Jewish people, desperate to be rid of the yoke of Rome, would seek to make Jesus king by force (John 6:15; cf. 12:12–19).

88. Jesus Foretells His Future Suffering and Glory

Matt. 16:21–28; Mark 8:27–9:1; Luke 9:22–27

MT [a]From that time Jesus began to MK teach MT His disciples that MK the Son of Man MT [b]must go to Jerusalem, and suffer many things MK and be rejected by MT the elders and [c]chief priests and [d]scribes, and be killed, and [e]be raised MK again MT the [f]third day. MK [g]He spoke this word openly.

MT Then [h]Peter took Him aside and began to rebuke Him, saying, "Far be it from You, Lord; this shall not happen to You!" MK But when He had turned around and looked at His disciples, He rebuked Peter, saying, MT [i]"Get behind Me, Satan! You are an offense to Me, for you are not mindful of the things of God, but the things of men."

---

[a] FROM THAT TIME. This section marks the beginning of a great turning point in Jesus' ministry. The disciples had confessed their faith in Him as Messiah. From then on He began to prepare them for His death.

[b] MUST . . . SUFFER MANY THINGS. Jesus' sufferings and death were inevitable because they were divinely ordained (Acts 2:22, 23; 4:13–15), though, humanly speaking, caused by His rejection from the Jewish leaders. Cf. Ps. 118:22–23; Isa. 53:3; cf. 12:10; Matt. 21:42.

[c] CHIEF PRIESTS. Members of the Sanhedrin and representatives of the twenty-four orders of ordinary priests (cf. Luke 1:8).

[d] SCRIBES. Experts in the OT law (cf. Matt. 2:4).

[e] BE RAISED AGAIN. Jesus always mentioned His resurrection in connection with His death (cf. Matt. 16:21; 17:23; 20:19; Mark 9:31; 10:34; Luke 9:22; 18:33), making it all the more incomprehensible that the disciples were so slow to understand.

[f] THE THIRD DAY. In keeping with the sign of Jonah (Matt. 12:40).

[g] HE SPOKE . . . OPENLY. i.e., not in parables or allusions (cf. John 16:29).

[h] PETER . . . BEGAN TO REBUKE HIM. The disciples still could not comprehend a dying Messiah (cf. Mark 8:30). Peter, as usual, expressed the thoughts of the rest of the twelve (cf. Mark 8:33). His brash outburst expressed not only presumption and misunderstanding, but also deep love for Jesus.

[i] "GET BEHIND ME, SATAN!" The harshness of this rebuke contrasts sharply with Christ's words of commendation in Matt. 16:17–19. Jesus suggested that Peter was being a mouthpiece for Satan. Jesus' death was part of God's sovereign plan (Acts 2:23; 4:27–28). "It pleased the Lord to bruise Him" (Isa. 53:10). Christ had come with the express purpose of dying as an atonement for sin (John 12:27). Whoever opposed His mission was, wittingly or not, advocating Satan's work.

Then Jesus MK called the people to *Himself* LK [and] said to *them* all, MK with His disciples also, MT "If anyone desires to come after Me, let him [j]deny himself, and [k]take up his [l]cross LK daily, MT and follow Me. For whoever desires to save his life will lose it, but whoever [m]loses his life for My sake MK and the gospel's MT will find it. MK For what will it profit a man if he gains the whole world, and loses his own [n]soul LK and is himself destroyed or lost? MT Or what will a man give in [o]exchange for his soul? MK For whoever is [p]ashamed of Me and My words in this adulterous and sinful generation, of him the Son of Man also will be ashamed [q]when He comes LK in His *own* glory, and MT in the glory of His Father with His angels, and then He [r]will reward each according to his works."

---

[j] DENY HIMSELF. No one who is unwilling to deny himself can legitimately claim to be a disciple of Jesus Christ.

[k] TAKE UP HIS CROSS. This reveals the extent of self-denial—to the point of death, if necessary. The extent of desperation on the part of the penitent sinner who is aware he can't save himself reaches the place where nothing is held back (cf. Matt. 19:21–22).

[l] CROSS. Self-denial was a common thread in Christ's teaching to his disciples (cf. Matt. 10:38; 16:24; Mark 8:34; Luke 14:26, 27; John 12:24–26). The kind of self-denial He sought was not a reclusive asceticism, but a willingness to obey His commandments, serve one another, and suffer—perhaps even die—for His sake.

[m] LOSES HIS LIFE . . . WILL FIND IT. This paradoxical saying reveals an important spiritual truth: those who pursue a life of ease, comfort, and acceptance by the world will not find eternal life. On the other hand, those who give up their lives for the sake of Christ and the gospel will find it. Cf. John 12:25. Aside from the command "follow Me," the saying "whoever loses his life for My sake" is repeated more times in the gospels than any other saying of Christ. Cf. Matt. 10:39; 16:25; Mark 8:35; Luke 17:33; John 12:25.

[n] SOUL. The real person, who will live forever in heaven or hell. To have all that the world has to offer yet not have Christ is to be eternally bankrupt; all the world's goods will not compensate for losing one's soul eternally.

[o] EXCHANGE. At the judgment when he faces the disastrous hell of remorse and suffering for his lost soul, with what will he buy it back from perdition? Nothing.

[p] ASHAMED OF ME AND MY WORDS. Those who reject the demands of discipleship prove themselves to be ashamed of Jesus Christ and the truth He taught, thus not redeemed from sin at all. They are unbelievers. Cf. Matt. 10:33; Rom. 9:33; 10:11; 2 Tim. 2:12.

[q] WHEN HE COMES. In Mark's gospel this is the first reference to Jesus' second coming, an event later described in detail in the Olivet Discourse (13:1–37).

[r] WILL REWARD. There is coming a time of rewards in the future for believers (1 Cor. 4:5; 2 Cor. 5:8–10; Rev. 22:12). Here, however, the Lord was concerned with the reward of the ungodly—final and eternal judgment (Rom. 2:5–11; 2 Thess. 1:6–10).

MK And He said to them, LK "But MT [s]assuredly, I say to you, there are [t]some standing here who shall [u]not taste death till they see the Son of Man coming in His kingdom MK [and] the kingdom of God present with power."

---

[s] ASSUREDLY, I SAY TO YOU. A solemn statement appearing only in the gospels and always spoken by Jesus. It introduces topics of utmost significance.

[t] SOME STANDING. In all three of the Synoptic Gospels, this promise is made immediately prior to the Transfiguration (Matt. 16:28; Mark 9:1–8; Luke 9:27–36). Furthermore, the word for "kingdom" can be translated "royal splendor." Therefore, it seems most natural to interpret this promise as a reference to the Transfiguration, which "some" of the disciples—Peter, James, and John, would witness only six days later.

[u] NOT TASTE DEATH TILL THEY SEE THE . . . KINGDOM. The event Jesus had in mind has been variously interpreted as His resurrection and ascension, the coming of the Spirit at Pentecost, the spread of Christianity, or the destruction of Jerusalem in AD 70. The most accurate interpretation, however, is to connect Christ's promise with the Transfiguration in the context, which provided a foretaste of His second-coming glory. That all three Synoptic Gospels place this promise immediately before the Transfiguration supports this view, as does the fact that "kingdom" can refer to royal splendor.

89. Jesus Is Gloriously Transfigured

Matt. 17:1–13; Mark 9:2–13; Luke 9:28–36

LK Now it came to pass, MT [a]after six days LK [b]after these sayings MT Jesus took [c]Peter, James, and John his brother, MK and led them up on [d]a high mountain MT by themselves LK to pray.

[e]As He prayed, MT He was [f]transfigured before them. LK The appearance of His face was altered [and] MT shone like the sun, and His clothes MK became [g]shining LK *and* [h]glistening, MK exceedingly white, like snow, MT as white as the light, MK such as no launderer on earth can whiten them. MT And behold, [i]Moses and Elijah appeared

---

[a] AFTER SIX DAYS. Matthew and Mark place the Transfiguration "six days" after Jesus' promise (Matt. 17:1; Mark 9:2); Luke, no doubt including the day the promise was made and the day of the Transfiguration itself, describes the interval as "about eight days" (Luke 9:28).

[b] AFTER THESE SAYINGS. This expression ties the promise of seeing the kingdom to the events that follow.

[c] PETER, JAMES, AND JOHN. These three are often seen alone together with Jesus (Matt. 26:37; Mark 5:37; 13:3). As the inner circle of Jesus' disciples, they were sometimes allowed to witness events that the other disciples were not, such as the raising of Jairus's daughter (Luke 8:51), the Transfiguration (Matt. 17:1), and Christ's agony in the garden (Mark 14:33).

[d] A HIGH MOUNTAIN. The traditional site, Mount Tabor, is unlikely. Jesus and the disciples had been in "the region of Caesarea Philippi" (Matt. 16:13), and Tabor is nowhere near there. Besides, Tabor had evidently been the site of pagan worship (Hos. 5:1), and in Jesus' day an army garrison had their fortress at the top. The actual location of the Transfiguration is nowhere identified, but Mount Hermon (at about 9,200 feet above sea level and closer to Caesarea Philippi) is most likely the place.

[e] AS HE PRAYED. As at His baptism, while He was praying, the Father's voice came from heaven.

[f] TRANSFIGURED. From a Greek word meaning "to change in form," or "to be transformed." In some inexplicable way Jesus manifested some of His divine glory to the three disciples (cf. 2 Peter 1:16). He underwent a dramatic change in appearance, so the disciples could behold Him in His glory.

[g] SHINING . . . EXCEEDINGLY WHITE. The divine glory emanating from Jesus made even his clothing radiate brilliant white light. Light is often associated with God's visible presence (cf. Ps. 104:2; Dan. 7:9; 1 Tim. 6:16; Rev. 1:14; 21:23).

[h] GLISTENING. Lit. "emitting light." This word is used only here in the NT. It suggests a brilliant flashing light, similar to lightning.

[i] MOSES AND ELIJAH. Representing the Law and the Prophets respectively, both of which had foretold Christ's death, and that is what Luke says the three of them were discussing (Luke 9:31).

to them, [MK] and they were talking with Jesus, [LK] who appeared in glory and spoke of [j]His decease which He was about to accomplish at Jerusalem.

But Peter and those with him were heavy with sleep; and when they were fully awake, they saw His glory and the two men who stood with Him. Then it happened, as they were parting from Him, *that* Peter said to Jesus, "Master, it is good for us to be here; [MT] if You wish, [k]let us make here three tabernacles: one for You, one for Moses, and one for Elijah"— [LK] not knowing what he said [MK] because he did not know what to say, for they were greatly afraid.

[MT] While he was still speaking, behold, a bright [l]cloud [MK] came and [MT] overshadowed them; [LK] and they were fearful as they entered the cloud. [MT] And suddenly [m]a voice came out of the cloud, saying, "[n]This is My beloved Son, in whom I am well pleased. [o]Hear Him!" And when the disciples heard *it,* they [p]fell on their faces and were greatly afraid.

[LK] When the voice had ceased, [MT] Jesus came and touched them and said, "Arise, and do not be afraid." When they had lifted up their eyes [MK] [and] had looked around, [MT] they saw no one but Jesus only [MK] with themselves.

---

[j] His decease. i.e., His death. Peter uses the same term to speak of his own death (2 Peter 1:15). Only Luke mentions the subject matter of their conversation and the fact that Peter, James, and John had fallen asleep.

[k] let us . . . make three tabernacles. This is undoubtedly a reference to the booths that were used to celebrate the Feast of Tabernacles, when the Israelites dwelt in booths for seven days (Lev. 23:34–42). Peter was expressing a wish that the three illustrious figures would stay permanently. It is also possible that Peter's suggestion reflected his belief that the millennial kingdom was about to be inaugurated (cf. Zech. 14:16).

[l] cloud . . . overshadowed them. This is the glory cloud, Shekinah, which throughout the OT was symbolic of God's presence (cf. Ex. 13:21; 33:18–23; 40:34–35; Num. 9:15; 14:14; Deut. 9:33; Rev. 1:7). Matt. 17:5 says "a bright cloud," i.e., enveloping the glory of God—similar to the pillar of cloud that led the Israelites in the OT (Ex. 14:19–20). The brightness of this cloud and the sleepiness of the disciples suggests that this event may have occurred at night.

[m] a voice came out of the cloud. The Father's voice from the cloud cut off Peter's fumbling words (Matt. 17:5; Luke 9:34).

[n] This is My beloved Son. The Father repeated the affirmation of His love for the Son, first given at Jesus' baptism (Mark 1:11). The apostle Peter also records these words in his second epistle (2 Peter 1:17).

[o] Hear Him! Peter erred in placing Moses and Elijah on the same level as Christ. Christ was the very one to whom Moses and Elijah (and the Law and Prophets) had pointed. He is the One whom the disciples are to listen to and obey (cf. Heb. 1:1, 2). The voice of the Father interrupted while Peter "was still speaking." The words were the same as those spoken from heaven at Christ's baptism (Matt. 3:17).

[p] fell on their faces. A common response to the realization that the Holy God of the universe is present. Cf. Isa. 6:5; Ezek. 1:28; Rev. 1:17.

[MT] Now as they came down from the mountain, Jesus commanded them, saying, "Tell the vision to no one [q]until the Son of Man is risen from the dead." [MK] So they kept this word to themselves, [LK] and told no one in those days any of the things they had seen, [MK] [while] [r]questioning what the rising from the dead meant.

[MT] And His disciples asked Him, saying, "[s]Why then do the scribes say that Elijah must come first?" Jesus answered and said to them, "Indeed, [t]Elijah is coming first and will restore all things. But I say to you that [u]Elijah has come already, and [v]they did not know him but did to him whatever they wished, [MK] [w]as it is written of him. [MT] Likewise, [MK] how is it written concerning the Son of Man, that He must [MT] also [MK] [x]suffer many things [MT] at their hands [MK] and be treated with contempt?"

[MT] Then the disciples understood that He spoke to them of John the Baptist.

---

[q] UNTIL THE SON OF MAN IS RISEN FROM THE DEAD. This looks to the time when the true nature of Jesus' messianic mission became evident to all, that He came to conquer sin and death, not the Romans.

[r] QUESTIONING WHAT THE RISING FROM THE DEAD MEANT. Like most of the Jewish people (the Sadducees being notable exceptions), the disciples believed in a future resurrection (cf. John 11:24). What confused them was Jesus' implication that His own resurrection was imminent, and thus so was His death. The disciples' confusion provides further evidence that they still did not understand Jesus' messianic mission.

[s] WHY . . . ELIJAH MUST COME FIRST? The scribes' teaching in this case was not based on rabbinical tradition, but on the OT (Mal. 3:1; 4:5–6). Malachi's prediction was well known among the Jews of Jesus' day, and the disciples were no doubt trying to figure out how to harmonize it with the appearance of Elijah they had just witnessed. The scribes and Pharisees also no doubt argued that Jesus could not be the Messiah based on the fact that Elijah had not yet appeared. Confused, the three disciples asked Jesus for His interpretation.

[t] ELIJAH IS COMING FIRST. Jesus affirmed the correctness of the scribal interpretation of Mal. 3:1; 4:5, which must have puzzled the disciples even more.

[u] ELIJAH HAS COME ALREADY. Jesus directly addressed the disciples' question: the prophecies of Elijah's coming had been fulfilled in John the Baptist. Though certainly not a reincarnation of Elijah (cf. John 1:21), John came in the "spirit and power of Elijah" and would have fulfilled prophecies if the Jewish leaders had believed (cf. Matt. 11:14; Luke 1:17). Because they rejected both John the Baptist and Jesus, there will be another who will come in the spirit and power of Elijah before the second coming of Christ (cf. Rev. 11:5–6). Though John came in the spirit and power of Elijah, he was put to death. The Messiah was "about to suffer" similarly.

[v] THEY . . . DID TO HIM. The Jewish leaders rejected John the Baptist (Matt. 21:25; Luke 7:33), and Herod killed him (6:17–29).

[w] AS IT IS WRITTEN OF HIM. No specific OT prophecies predicted that Messiah's forerunner would die. Therefore, this statement is best understood as having been fulfilled typically. The fate intended for Elijah (1 Kings 19:1, 2) had befallen John the Baptist. Cf. Matt. 11:11–14.

[x] SUFFER . . . BE TREATED WITH CONTEMPT. Jesus pointed out that the prophecies about Elijah in no way precluded the suffering and death of Messiah, for that, too, was predicted in the OT (e.g., Pss. 22; 69:20–21; Isa. 53; cf. Rom. 1:2).

90. Jesus Heals a Demon-Possessed Boy

Matt. 17:14–21; Mark 9:14–29; Luke 9:37–43a

LK Now it happened on the next day, when they had come down from the mountain, that MK He came to [a]the disciples. [And] He saw a great multitude around them, and scribes disputing with them. Immediately, when they saw Him, all the people were greatly amazed, and running to *Him,* greeted Him. And He asked the scribes, "What are you discussing with them?"

MK Then LK suddenly a man from the multitude cried out, saying, "Teacher, I implore You, MT have mercy on my son, MK who [b]has a mute spirit, LK for he is my only child. MT He is an epileptic and suffers severely. LK And behold, [c]a spirit seizes him, and he suddenly cries out; it MK throws him down LK [and] convulses him so that he foams *at the mouth,* MK gnashes his teeth, and becomes rigid. LK And it departs from him with great difficulty, bruising him. MT So I brought him to Your disciples, MK that they should cast it out, MT but [d]they could not cure him." Then Jesus answered and said, "[e]O faithless and perverse generation, how long shall I be with you? How long shall I bear with you? Bring LK your son MT here to Me."

MK Then they brought him to Him. And when he saw Him, LK as he was still coming, the demon MK immediately LK threw him down and MK convulsed him, and he fell on the ground and wallowed, foaming at the mouth. So He asked his father,

---

[a] THE DISCIPLES. The nine who had remained behind.

[b] HAS A MUTE SPIRIT. The boy had a demonically induced inability to speak, a detail found only in Mark's account.

[c] A SPIRIT SEIZES HIM. This was no mere case of epilepsy; it was plainly demon possession. There's no reason to think Luke, a physician, was merely accommodating the understanding of his readers. Besides, Jesus healed the boy by rebuking the demon (Mark 9:25; Luke 9:42).

[d] THEY COULD NOT. The disciples' failure is surprising, in light of the power granted them by Jesus (Mark 3:15; 6:13).

[e] O FAITHLESS AND PERVERSE GENERATION. Cf. Ps. 95:10. The word *generation* indicates that Jesus' exasperation was not merely with the father or the nine disciples, but also with the unbelieving scribes, who were no doubt gloating over the disciples' failure and with unbelieving Israel in general.

"How long has this been happening to him?" And he said, "From childhood. And often he has thrown him both into the fire and into the water [f]to destroy him. But if You can do anything, have compassion on us and help us." Jesus said to him, "If you can believe, [g]all things *are* possible to him who believes." Immediately the father of the child cried out and said with tears, "Lord, [h]I believe; help my unbelief!"

When Jesus saw that [i]the people came running together, He rebuked the unclean spirit, saying to it: "Deaf and dumb spirit, [j]I command you, come out of him and enter him no more!" Then *the spirit* cried out, convulsed him greatly, and came out of him. And he became as one dead, so that many said, "He is dead." But Jesus took him by the hand and lifted him up, and he arose; LK and [He] gave him back to his father. MT And the child was cured from that very hour. LK And they were all amazed at the majesty of God.

MK And when He had come into the house, His disciples MT came to Jesus privately and said, [k]"Why could we not cast it out?" So Jesus said to them, "Because of your unbelief; for assuredly, I say to you, if you have [l]faith as a mustard

---

[f] TO DESTROY HIM. This demon was an especially violent and dangerous one. Open fires and unfenced bodies of water were common in first-century Israel, providing ample opportunity for the demon's attempts to destroy the child. The father's statement added to the pathos of the situation. The boy himself was probably disfigured from burn scars and possibly further ostracized because of them. His situation also created a hardship for his family, who would have had to watch the boy constantly to protect him from harm.

[g] ALL THINGS ARE POSSIBLE. The issue was not His lack of power but the father's lack of faith. Though Jesus often healed apart from the faith of those involved, here He chose to emphasize the power of faith (cf. Matt. 17:20; Luke 17:6). Jesus healed multitudes, but many, if not most, did not believe in Him. Cf. Luke 17:15–19.

[h] I BELIEVE; HELP MY UNBELIEF! Admitting the imperfection of his faith, mixed as it was with doubt, the desperate father pleaded with Jesus to help him to have the greater faith the Lord demanded of him.

[i] THE PEOPLE CAME RUNNING. Noting the growing crowd, Jesus acted without further delay, perhaps to spare the boy and his anguished father any further embarrassment. Also, the Lord did not perform miracles to satisfy thrill seekers (cf. Mark 8:11; Luke 23:8, 9).

[j] I COMMAND YOU. Jesus' absolute authority over demons is well attested in the NT (e.g., Mark 1:32–34; 5:1–13; Luke 4:33–35). His healings demonstrated His deity by power over the natural world. His authority over demons demonstrated His deity by power over the supernatural world.

[k] "WHY COULD WE NOT CAST IT OUT?" When Christ sent the disciples out (Matt. 10:6–8), He explicitly commissioned them to do these kinds of miracles. Less than a year later, they failed where they had once succeeded. Christ's explanation for their failure was that their faith was deficient (Matt. 17:20). The deficiency did not consist in a lack of confidence; they were surprised that they could not cast out this demon. The problem probably lay in a failure to make God—rather than their own gifts—the object of their confidence.

seed, you will say to this mountain, 'Move from here to there,' and it will move; and [m]nothing will be impossible for you. However, MK [n]this kind can come out by [o]nothing but prayer and [p]fasting."

---

[l] FAITH AS A MUSTARD SEED. True faith, by Christ's definition, always involves surrender to the will of God. What He was teaching here is nothing like positive-thinking psychology. He was saying that both the source and the object of all genuine faith—even the weak, mustard-seed variety—is God. And "with God nothing will be impossible" (Luke 1:37).

[m] NOTHING WILL BE IMPOSSIBLE. Here, Christ assumes the qualifying thought that is explicitly added by 1 John 5:14: what we ask for must be "according to His will."

[n] THIS KIND. Some demons are more powerful and obstinate and thus more resistant to being cast out than others (cf. Matt. 12:45).

[o] NOTHING BUT PRAYER. Perhaps overconfident from their earlier successes (cf. Mark 6:13), the disciples became enamored with their own gifts and neglected to draw on divine power.

[p] FASTING. The earliest manuscripts of Mark omit this word. The earliest manuscripts of Matthew omit the entirety of Matt. 17:21.

91. Jesus Predicts His Resurrection a Second Time

Matt. 17:22–23; Mark 9:30–32; Luke 9:43b–45

MK Then they departed from there and [a]passed through Galilee, and He [b]did not want anyone to know *it.* MT Now while they were staying in Galilee, LK while everyone marveled at all the things which Jesus did, MK He taught His disciples and said to them, LK "[c]Let these words sink down into your ears, for the Son of Man is [d]about to be betrayed into the hands of men, MT and they will kill Him. MK And after He is killed, He will rise the third day." MT And they were exceedingly sorrowful, LK [even though] they did not understand this saying, and it was [e]hidden from them so that they did not perceive it; and they were afraid to ask Him about this saying.

---

[a] PASSED THROUGH GALILEE. Leaving the region around Caesarea Philippi, Jesus and the disciples began the journey to Jerusalem that would result in His crucifixion several months later. Their immediate destination was Capernaum (cf. Mark 9:33).

[b] DID NOT WANT ANYONE TO KNOW. Jesus continued to seek seclusion so He could prepare the disciples for His death (cf. Mark 7:24).

[c] LET THESE WORDS. Jesus continued His teaching about His upcoming death and resurrection—a subject the disciples still did not understand.

[d] ABOUT TO BE BETRAYED. By Judas Iscariot. Cf. Matt. 26:47, 50.

[e] HIDDEN FROM THEM. i.e., in accord with God's sovereign design. Cf. Luke 24:45.

92. Jesus Pays the Temple Tax

Matt. 17:24–27; Mark 9:33a

MT When they MK came to Capernaum, MT those who received the *temple* tax came to Peter and said, "Does your Teacher not pay [a]the *temple* tax?" He said, "Yes." And when he had come into the house, Jesus anticipated him, saying, "What do you think, Simon? From whom do the kings of the earth take customs or taxes, from their sons or from strangers?" Peter said to Him, "From strangers." Jesus said to him, "Then the sons are free. Nevertheless, lest we offend them, go to the sea, cast in a hook, and take the fish that comes up first. And when you have opened its mouth, you will find a piece of money; take that and give it to them for Me and you."

[a] THE TEMPLE TAX. A half-shekel tax (equivalent to about two-days' wages) collected annually from every male over twenty, for the upkeep of the temple (Ex. 30:13, 14; 2 Chron. 24:9). As kings did not tax their own sons, technically, Jesus, as God's son, was exempt from the tax. But to avoid offense, He paid on behalf of Himself and Peter. Cf. Rom. 13:1–7; Titus 3:1; 1 Peter 2:13–17.

93. Jesus Confronts the Disciples' Rivalry

Matt. 18:1–5; Mark 9:33b–37; Luke 9:46–48

MT At that time the disciples came to Jesus, MK when He was in [a]the house, MT saying, "Who then is greatest in the kingdom of heaven?"

Then Jesus MK asked them, "What was it you disputed among yourselves on the road?" But [b]they kept silent, for on the road they had disputed among themselves [c]who *would be the* greatest. And He [d]sat down, called the twelve, and said to them, " [e]If anyone desires to be first, he shall be [f]last of all and servant of all."

Then He, LK perceiving the thought of their heart, MK took [g]a little child and set him LK by Him MK in the midst of them. And when He had taken him in His arms, He said to them, MT "Assuredly, I say to you, unless you are converted and [h]become as little children, you will by no means enter the kingdom of heaven. Therefore whoever humbles himself as this little child is the greatest in the kingdom of

---

[a] THE HOUSE. The use of the definite article suggests this to be the house Jesus habitually stayed in when in Capernaum. Whether it was Peter's house (cf. Mark 1:29) or someone else's is not known.

[b] THEY KEPT SILENT. Convicted and embarrassed, the disciples were speechless.

[c] WHO WOULD BE THE GREATEST. A dispute possibly triggered by the privilege granted Peter, James, and John to witness the Transfiguration. The disciples' quarrel highlights their failure to apply Jesus' explicit teaching on humility (e.g., Matt. 5:3) and the example of His own suffering and death (Mark 8:30–33; 9:31–32). It also prompted them to ask Jesus to settle the issue, which He did—though not as they had expected.

[d] SAT DOWN. Rabbis usually sat down to teach (cf. Matt. 15:29; Luke 4:20; 5:3; John 8:2).

[e] IF ANYONE DESIRES TO BE FIRST. As the disciples undeniably did (cf. Mark 10:35–37).

[f] LAST OF ALL AND SERVANT OF ALL. The disciples' concept of greatness and leadership, drawn from their culture, needed to be completely reversed. Not those who lord their position over others are great in God's kingdom, but those who humbly serve others (cf. Matt. 19:30–20:16; 23:11–12; Mark 10:31, 43–45; Luke 13:30; 14:8–11; 18:14; 22:24–27).

[g] A LITTLE CHILD. The Greek word indicates an infant or toddler. If the house they were in was Peter's, this may have been one of his children. The child became in Jesus' masterful teaching an example of believers who have humbled themselves and become like trusting children.

[h] BECOME AS LITTLE CHILDREN. This is how Jesus characterized conversion. Like the Beatitudes, it pictures faith as the simple, helpless, trusting dependence of those who have no resources of their own. Like children, they have no achievements and no accomplishments to offer or commend themselves with.

heaven. [i]Whoever receives one little child like this in My name receives Me, [MK] and whoever receives Me, receives not Me but Him who sent Me. [LK] For [j]he who is least among you all will be great."

[i] Whoever receives one little child like this in My name. Not actual children, but true believers—those who have humbled themselves like little children.

[j] he who is least . . . will be great. The way to preeminence in Christ's kingdom is by sacrifice and self-denial.

94. Jesus Warns Against Stumbling Blocks

Matt. 18:6–14; Mark 9:38–50; Luke 9:49–50

MK Now [a]John answered Him, saying, "Teacher, we saw someone who does not follow us casting out demons in Your name, and we forbade him [b]because he does not follow LK with us."

MK But Jesus said, "[c]Do not forbid him, for no one who works a miracle in My name can soon afterward speak evil of Me. For [d]he who is not against us is on our side. For whoever gives you a cup of water to drink in My name, [e]because you belong to Christ, assuredly, I say to you, he will by no means lose [f]his reward. But MT [g]whoever causes one of these little ones who believe in Me to sin, it would be better for him if a [h]millstone were hung around his neck, and he were drowned

---

[a] JOHN ANSWERED. The only recorded instance in the Synoptic Gospels in which he alone speaks. In light of Jesus' rebuke (Mark 9:35–37), John's conscience troubled him about an earlier incident he had been involved in. It is clear that the unnamed exorcist was not a fraud, because he actually was casting out demons. He was apparently a true believer in Jesus; John and the others opposed him because he was not openly and officially allied with Jesus, as they were.

[b] BECAUSE HE DOES NOT FOLLOW WITH US. It is ironic that John, who came to be known as "the apostle of love," would be the one to raise this objection. John came to see that only legitimate tests of another person's ministry are the test of doctrine (1 John 4:1–3; 2 John 7–11) and the test of fruit (1 John 2:4–6, 29; 3:4–12; 4:5, 20; cf. Matt. 7:16). This man would have passed both tests, but John was inclined to reject him because of his group affiliation. That is the error of sectarianism.

[c] DO NOT FORBID HIM. Jesus ordered them not to hinder the exorcist, making the logical point that someone sincerely acting in His name would not soon turn against Him. There is no neutral ground regarding Jesus Christ; those "who [are] not against [Him are] on [His] side," but by the same token, "He who is not with Me is against Me, and he who does not gather with Me scatters abroad" (Matt. 12:30).

[d] HE WHO IS NOT AGAINST US IS ON OUR SIDE. Contrast this with Luke 11:23. There is no middle ground and no neutrality. Here Christ gave a test of outward conduct to use for measuring others. In Luke 11:23 He gave a test of the inward life that is to be applied to oneself.

[e] BECAUSE YOU BELONG TO CHRIST. Jesus considered acts of kindness done to His followers to have been done to Him (cf. Matt. 25:37–40).

[f] HIS REWARD. That is, his unique place and service in the eternal kingdom.

[g] WHOEVER CAUSES . . . TO SIN. To entice, trap, or cause a believer to fall into sin is a very serious matter.

[h] MILLSTONE. A stone used for grinding grain. It was so large, it took a donkey to turn it. Gentiles used this as a form of execution, and therefore it was particularly repulsive to the Jews. Even such a horrifying death is preferable to leading a Christian into sin.

in the depth of the sea. [i]Woe to the world because of offenses! For offenses must come, but woe to that man by whom the offense comes!

"If your hand or foot causes you to sin, [j]cut it off and cast *it* from you. It is better for you to enter into [k]life lame or maimed, rather than having two hands or two feet, MK to go to [l]hell, into the MT everlasting MK fire that shall [m]never be quenched where

'Their worm does not die
And the fire is not quenched.'

MT "And if your eye causes you to sin, pluck it out and cast *it* from you. It is better for you to enter into MK the kingdom of God MT with one eye, rather than having two eyes, to be cast into hell fire.

MK "For [n]everyone will be seasoned with fire, and every sacrifice will be seasoned with salt. [o]Salt *is* good, but if the salt loses its flavor, how will you season it? [p]Have salt in yourselves, and [q]have peace with one another.

MT "Take heed that you [r]do not despise one of these little ones, for I say to you

---

[i] Woe to the world. It is expected that those in the world will cause Christians to be offended, stumble, and sin, and they will be judged for it. But it should not be that fellow believers lead others into sin, directly or indirectly. One would be better off dead. Cf. Rom. 14:13, 19, 21; 15:2; 1 Cor. 8:13.

[j] cut it off. Cf. Matt. 5:29. Jesus' words are to be taken figuratively; no amount of self-mutilation can deal with sin, which is an issue of the heart. The Lord is emphasizing the seriousness of sin and the need to do whatever is necessary to deal with it.

[k] life. The contrast of "life" with "hell" indicates that Jesus was referring to eternal life.

[l] hell. The Greek word refers to the Valley of Hinnom near Jerusalem, a garbage dump where fires constantly burned, furnishing a graphic symbol of eternal torment (cf. Matt. 5:22).

[m] never be quenched. Cf. Matt. 25:46. That the punishment of hell lasts for eternity is the unmistakable teaching of Scripture (cf. Dan. 12:2; Matt. 25:41; 2 Thess. 1:9; Rev. 14:10–11; 20:10).

[n] everyone will be seasoned with fire. The meaning of this difficult verse seems to be that believers are purified through suffering and persecution. The link between salt and fire seems to lie in the OT sacrifices, which were accompanied by salt (Lev. 2:13).

[o] Salt is good. Salt was an essential item in first-century Palestine. In a hot climate without refrigeration, salt was the practical means of preserving food.

[p] Have salt in yourselves. The work of the Word (Col. 3:16) and the Spirit (Gal. 5:22–23) produces godly character, enabling a person to act as a preservative in society. Cf. Matt. 5:13.

[q] have peace with one another. Cf. Matt. 5:9; Rom. 12:18; 2 Cor. 13:11; 1 Thess. 5:13; James 3:18.

[r] do not despise. i.e., spurn or belittle another believer by treating him or her unkindly or indifferently.

that in heaven [s]their angels always see the face of My Father who is in heaven. For the Son of Man has come to save that which was lost.

"What do you think? If a man has a hundred sheep, and one of them goes astray, does he not leave the ninety-nine and go to the mountains to seek the one that is straying? And if he should find it, assuredly, I say to you, he rejoices more over that *sheep* than over the ninety-nine that did not go astray. Even so it is not the will of your Father who is in heaven that one of these little ones should [t]perish.

---

[s] THEIR ANGELS. This does not suggest that each believer has a personal guardian angel. Rather, the pronoun is collective and refers to the fact that believers are served by angels in general. These angels are pictured "always" watching the face of God so as to hear His command to them to help a believer when needed. It is extremely serious to treat any fellow believer with contempt, since God and the holy angels are so concerned for their well-being.

[t] PERISH. The word here can (and does in this context) refer to spiritual devastation rather than utter eternal destruction. This does not suggest that God's children ever could perish in the ultimate sense (cf. John 10:28).

95. Jesus Teaches about Forgiveness

Matt. 18:15–35

MT "Moreover [a]if your brother sins against you, go and tell him his fault between you and him alone. If he hears you, you have gained your brother. But [b]if he will not hear, take with you one or two more, that 'by the mouth of two or three witnesses every word may be established.' And if he refuses to hear them, [c]tell *it* to the church. But if he refuses even to hear the church, let him be to you like a heathen and a tax collector.

"Assuredly, I say to you, whatever you bind on earth will be bound in heaven, and whatever you loose on earth will be loosed in heaven.

"Again I say to you that [d]if two of you agree on earth concerning anything that they ask, it will be done for them by My Father in heaven. For where [e]two or three are gathered together in My name, I am there in the midst of them."

Then Peter came to Him and said, "Lord, how often shall my brother sin against me, and I forgive him? [f]Up to seven times?"

---

[a] IF YOUR BROTHER SINS. The prescription for church discipline in Matt. 18:15–17 must be read in light of the parable of the lost sheep in Matt. 18:12–14. The goal of this process is restoration. If successful, "you have gained your brother." Step 1 is to "tell him his fault" privately.

[b] IF HE WILL NOT HEAR. i.e., if he remains impenitent, follow step 2: "take with you one or two more," to fulfill the principle of Deut. 19:15.

[c] TELL IT TO THE CHURCH. If he still refuses to repent, step 3 requires that the matter be reported to the whole assembly (v. 17)—so that all may lovingly pursue the sinning brother's reconciliation. But failing that, step 4 means that the offender must be excommunicated, regarded by the church as "a heathen and a tax collector" (cf. 5:46). The idea is not merely to punish the offender, or to shun him completely, but to remove him as a detrimental influence from the fellowship of the church and henceforth to regard him as an evangelistic prospect rather than as a brother. Ultimately, the sin for which he is excommunicated is a hard-hearted impenitence.

[d] IF TWO OF YOU AGREE ON EARTH. This promise applies to the issue of discipline discussed in Matt. 18:15–17. The "two of you" spoken of here harks back to the two or three witnesses involved in step two of the discipline process.

[e] TWO OR THREE. Jewish tradition requires at least ten men (a *minyan*) to constitute a synagogue or even hold public prayer. Here, Christ promised to be present in the midst of an even smaller flock—"two or three witnesses" gathered in His name for the purpose of discipline (cf. Matt. 18:15).

[f] UP TO SEVEN TIMES. Peter thought he was being magnanimous. The rabbis, citing several verses from Amos (1:3, 6, 9, 11, 13), taught that since God forgave Israel's enemies only three times, it was presumptuous and unnecessary to forgive anyone more than three times.

Jesus said to him, "I do not say to you, up to seven times, but up to [g]seventy times seven. Therefore the kingdom of heaven is like a certain king who wanted to settle accounts with his [h]servants. And when he had begun to settle accounts, one was brought to him who owed him [i]ten thousand talents. But as he was not able to pay, his master commanded [j]that he be sold, with his wife and children and all that he had, and that payment be made. The servant therefore fell down before him, saying, 'Master, have patience with me, and I will pay you all.' Then the master of that servant was moved with compassion, released him, and [k]forgave him the debt.

"But that servant went out and found one of his fellow servants who owed him [l]a hundred denarii; and he laid hands on him and took *him* by the throat, saying, 'Pay me what you owe!' So his fellow servant fell down at his feet and begged him, saying, '[m]Have patience with me, and I will pay you all.' And he would not, but went and threw him into prison till he should pay the debt. So when his [n]fellow servants saw what had been done, they were very grieved, and came and told their master all that had been done. Then his master, after he had called him, said to him, 'You wicked servant! I forgave you all that debt because you begged me. Should you not also have had compassion on your fellow servant,

---

[g] SEVENTY TIMES SEVEN. Innumerable times. Cf. Luke 17:4.

[h] SERVANTS. Due to the large amounts of money involved, it is likely these "servants" would have been provincial governors who owed the king the money from taxation.

[i] TEN THOUSAND TALENTS. This represents an incomprehensible amount of money. The talent was the largest denomination of currency, and "ten thousand" in common parlance signified an infinite number.

[j] THAT HE BE SOLD. A way to recover some of this loss was for the king to sell the family members into slavery.

[k] FORGAVE HIM. Picturing the generous, compassionate forgiveness of God to a pleading sinner who owes him an unpayable debt. Cf. Col. 2:14.

[l] A HUNDRED DENARII. About three months' wages. This was not a negligible amount by normal standards, but it was a pittance in comparison to what the servant had been forgiven.

[m] HAVE PATIENCE . . . I WILL PAY YOU ALL. The forgiven man heard the same pleading he had given before his master, but was utterly without compassion.

[n] FELLOW SERVANTS . . . GRIEVED. A lack of forgiveness is offensive to fellow believers. Most of all it offends God, who chastens His unforgiving children severely. Cf. Matt. 6:15.

just as I had pity on you?' And [o]his master was angry, and delivered him to the [p]torturers until he should pay [q]all that was due to him.

"So My heavenly Father also will do to you if each of you, from his heart, does not forgive his brother his trespasses."

---

[o] HIS MASTER WAS ANGRY. Because He is holy and just, God is always angry at sin, including the sins of His children (cf. Heb. 12:5–11).

[p] TORTURERS. Not executioners. This pictures severe discipline, not final condemnation.

[q] ALL THAT WAS DUE TO HIM. The original debt was unpayable and the man was still without resources. So it seems unlikely that the slave was saddled once again with the same debt he had already been forgiven. Rather, what he now owed his master would be exacted in chastening by his master until he was willing to forgive others.

96. Jesus Is Ridiculed by His Half-Brothers

John 7:2–10

JN Now the Jews' [a]Feast of Tabernacles was at hand. [b]His brothers therefore said to Him, "Depart from here and go into Judea, that Your disciples also may see the works that You are doing. For no one does anything in secret while he himself seeks [c]to be known openly. If You do these things, show Yourself to the world." For even [d]His brothers did not believe in Him.

Then Jesus said to them, "[e]My time has not yet come, but [f]your time is always

---

[a] Feast of Tabernacles. The Feast of Tabernacles was connected in the OT with the harvest of grapes and olives (Ex. 23:16; Lev. 23:33–36, 39–43; Deut. 16:13–15). The feast lasted a full week from the fifteenth to the twenty-first of Tishri (September–October). The Jewish historian Josephus indicates that, of Israel's 3 major feasts (Passover, Pentecost, and Tabernacles), this one was the most popular. In order to commemorate the Israelites' trek through the wilderness, the people built makeshift shelters out of leaves and branches (hence, "booths," or "tabernacles"; cf. Lev. 23:42). Featured at the feast were both a water-drawing and a lamp-lighting ceremony.

[b] His brothers. Matthew 13:55 lists Jesus' brothers as "James, Joses, Simon, and Judas." James authored the NT epistle that bears his name and became the leader of the Jerusalem church, and Judas (or Jude) wrote the epistle that also bears his name. Because of Jesus' virgin birth, they were only the half-brothers of Jesus, since Mary, not Joseph, was Jesus' only human parent (cf. Matt. 1:16, 18, 23; Luke 1:35).

[c] to be known openly . . . show Yourself to the world. Jesus' brothers wanted Him to put on a display of His miracles. Although the text does not clearly state their motivation, perhaps they made the request for two reasons: (1) they wanted to see the miracles for themselves to determine their genuineness, and (2) they may have had similar crass political motives as did the people, namely that He would become their social and political Messiah. Jerusalem's acceptance of Him was to be the acid test for them as to whether His own family would believe in Him as Messiah.

[d] His brothers did not believe in Him. As with the crowds in Jerusalem and Galilee, even His own brothers did not believe in Him at first. They did not come to saving faith until after the resurrection (Acts 1:14; 1 Cor. 15:7).

[e] My time has not yet come. This recalls the response to Jesus' mother at the wedding in Cana (cf. John 2:4). It also reveals the first reason why Jesus would not go to the feast in the way His brothers wanted: it was not in God's perfect timing. The sentence reveals Jesus' complete dependence on and commitment to the Father's sovereign timetable for His life (cf. John 8:20; Acts 1:7; 17:26). Furthermore, Jesus never committed Himself to being motivated by unbelief, even that of His own half-brothers.

[f] your time is always ready. Because Jesus' brothers did not believe in Him, they were of the world and therefore knew nothing of God or His purposes. Because of unbelief, they did not listen to His word, did not recognize God's schedule, and could not perceive the incarnate Word before them. As a result, any time would do for them, preferably that moment.

ready. [g]The world cannot hate you, but it hates Me because [h]I testify of it that its works are evil. You go up to this feast. I am not yet going up to this feast, for [i]My time has not yet fully come."

When He had said these things to them, He remained in Galilee. But when His brothers had gone up, then He also went up to the feast, not openly, but as it were [j]in secret.

---

[g] The world cannot hate you. The world cannot hate Jesus' brothers, because they belonged to the world and the world loves its own (cf. John 15:18–19). The evil world system and all who reject the Word and Son of God lie in the control of the evil one himself (1 John 5:19).

[h] I testify of it that its works are evil. A true born-again believer who is living a life for God's glory can expect to experience the hatred and antagonism of the world (cf. John 15:18–25; 16:1–3; 2 Tim. 3:12).

[i] My time has not yet fully come. This reveals the second reason why Jesus would not go in the way His brothers wanted. The Jews could not kill Him before God's perfect timing and plan was ready (cf. Gal. 4:4). Jesus' commitment to God's timetable would not permit any deviance from what God had decreed.

[j] in secret. The assumption is that the Father had directed Jesus to permit Him to go to Jerusalem. In contrast to what his brothers demanded of Him, Jesus desired to maintain a low profile when He entered Jerusalem. Though He traveled toward Jerusalem with some of His disciples (cf. Matt. 8:19-22; Luke 9:51-62), He entered the city itself without the crowds knowing where He was (John 7:11).

97. Jesus Journeys to Jerusalem

Matt. 8:19–22; Luke 9:51–62

LK Now it came to pass, when the time had come for Him to be received up, that He [a]steadfastly set His face to go to Jerusalem, and [b]sent messengers before His face. And as they went, they entered a village of the [c]Samaritans, to prepare for Him.

But they did not receive Him, [d]because His face was *set* for the journey to Jerusalem. And when His disciples [e]James and John saw *this,* they said, "Lord, do You want us to command fire to come down from heaven and consume them,

---

[a] STEADFASTLY SET HIS FACE TO GO TO JERUSALEM. Though the specific events denoted here likely describe Jesus' journey to the Feast of Booths (John 7:11–36), Luke uses this phrase to begin a major section of his gospel, one which culminates in Christ's final journey to the cross. This was a dramatic turning point in Christ's ministry. After this, Galilee was no longer His base of operation. Although Luke 17:11–37 describes a return visit to Galilee, Luke included everything between this point and that short Galilean sojourn as part of the journey to Jerusalem. We know from a comparison of the gospels that, during this period of Christ's ministry, He made short visits to Jerusalem to celebrate feasts (cf. Luke 13:22; 17:11). Nonetheless, those brief visits were only interludes in this period of ministry that would culminate in a final journey to Jerusalem for the purpose of dying there.

[b] SENT MESSENGERS. These messengers were dispatched to secure accomodations in the Samaritan village. The Lord did not send messengers ahead of Him when He arrived in Jerusalem (cf. John 7:10).

[c] SAMARITANS. These people were descendants of mixed marriages between the Israelite and Judean remnants from the days of the captivity and the people who moved into the land after the Assyrian and Babylonian conquests. They were considered unclean by the Jews and were so hated that most Jewish travelers from Galilee to Judah took the longer route east of the Jordan to avoid traveling through Samaria. Perhaps Jesus chose the Samaritan route to maintain a lower profile as He traveled to Jerusalem (cf. John 7:10).

[d] BECAUSE HIS FACE WAS SET FOR . . . JERUSALEM. Traveling to Jerusalem for worship implied rejection of the temple on Mount Gerizim and a contempt for Samaritan worship. This was a strong point of contention between Jews and Samaritans (cf. John 4:20–22).

[e] JAMES AND JOHN. Jesus nicknamed these brothers "Boanerges"—Sons of Thunder (Mark 3:17)—a fitting title, apparently. This was John's second sin against charity in such a short time (cf. Luke 9:49). It is interesting to note that several years later, the apostle John journeyed through Samaria once again with Peter, this time preaching the gospel in Samaritan villages (Acts 8:25).

just as Elijah did?" But He turned and [f]rebuked them, and said, "You do not know what manner of spirit you are of. For the [g]Son of Man did not come to destroy men's lives but to save *them.*" And they went to another village.

Now it happened as they journeyed on the road, MT [h]a certain scribe came and said to Him, LK "Lord, I will follow You wherever You go." And Jesus said to him, "Foxes have holes and birds of the air *have* nests, but the Son of Man has nowhere to lay *His* head."

Then He said to another MT of His disciples, LK "Follow Me." But he said MT to Him, LK "Lord, [i]let me first go and bury my father." Jesus said to him, "[j]Let the dead bury their own dead, but you go and preach the kingdom of God."

And another also said, "Lord, I will follow You, but let me first go *and* bid them farewell who are at my house." But Jesus said to him, "No one, having put his hand to the plow, and [k]looking back, is fit for the kingdom of God."

---

[f] REBUKED THEM. Christ's response to the Samaritans exemplifies the attitude the church ought to have with regard to all forms of religious persecution. The Samaritans' worship was pagan at heart, plainly wrong (cf. John 4:22). Compounding that was their intolerance. Yet the Lord would not retaliate with force against them. Nor did He even revile them verbally. He had come to save, not to destroy, and so His response was grace rather than destructive fury. Nonetheless, Christ's words of disapproval here must not be taken as condemnation of Elijah's actions in 1 Kings 18:38–40 or 2 Kings 1:10–12. Elijah was commissioned to a special ministry as prophet in a theocracy, and it was his God-ordained task to confront an evil monarch (Ahab) who was attempting to usurp God's authority. Elijah was specifically authorized to measure out the reprisal of God's wrath. Elijah acted with an authority comparable to that of modern civil authorities (cf. Rom. 13:4)—not in a capacity that parallels that of ministers of the gospel.

[g] SON OF MAN. Cf. Mark 2:10; John 1:51. This is the name Jesus used for Himself more than any other. It is used eighty-three times in the Gospels, always by Jesus Himself. It was a messianic title (Dan. 7:13, 14), with an obvious reference to the humanity and the humility of Christ. Yet it also speaks of His everlasting glory, as Dan. 7:13–14 shows (cf. Matt. 24:27; Acts 7:56).

[h] A CERTAIN SCRIBE. As a scribe this man was breaking with his fellow scribes by publicly declaring his willingness to follow Jesus. Nonetheless, Jesus evidently knew that he had not counted the cost in terms of suffering and inconvenience.

[i] LET ME FIRST GO AND BURY MY FATHER. This does not mean that the man's father was already dead. The phrase "I must bury my father" was a common figure of speech meaning "Let me wait until I receive my inheritance."

[j] LET THE DEAD BURY THEIR OWN DEAD. Let the world (the spiritually dead) take care of mundane things.

[k] LOOKING BACK. A plowman looking back cuts a crooked furrow.

98. Jesus Teaches at the Feast of Tabernacles

John 7:11–36

JN Then [a]the Jews sought Him at the feast, and said, "Where is He?" And there was much [b]complaining among the people concerning Him. Some said, "He is good"; others said, "No, on the contrary, He deceives the people." However, no one spoke openly of Him for fear of the Jews.

Now about the [c]middle of the feast [d]Jesus went up into the temple and taught. And the Jews [e]marveled, saying, "How does this Man know letters, having never studied?"

Jesus answered them and said, "My doctrine is not Mine, but [f]His who sent

---

[a] THE JEWS SOUGHT HIM. The contrast between the phrase "the Jews" in this verse and "the people" in the next verse indicates that the term "Jews" designates the hostile Jewish authorities in Judea who were headquartered in Jerusalem. The search for Jesus was certainly hostile in intent.

[b] COMPLAINING AMONG THE PEOPLE. The crowds, made up of Judeans, Galileans, and Diaspora (scattered) Jews, expressed various opinions regarding Christ. The spectrum ranged from superficial acceptance ("He is good") to cynical rejection ("He deceives the people"). The Babylonian edition of the Jewish Talmud reveals that the latter view of deception became the predominant opinion of many Jews (*Sanhedrin* 43a).

[c] MIDDLE OF THE FEAST. Jesus may have waited until the middle of the feast in order to prevent a premature "triumphal entry" that some may have forced upon Him for political motivations.

[d] JESUS WENT . . . AND TAUGHT. The increasing hostility to Jesus did not prevent His teaching ministry. Instead, Jesus relentlessly set forth His claims regarding His identity and mission. In the midst of the Feast of Tabernacles, when Jews from all over Israel had migrated into Jerusalem, Jesus once again began to teach. Jesus taught according to the custom of the teachers or rabbis of His day. Prominent rabbis would enter the temple environs and expound on the OT to crowds who sat around them. In this section, Jesus set forth the justification of His ministry and taught with authority as God's Son. In this passage five reasons are set forth as to why Jesus' claims regarding Himself are true: (1) His supernatural knowledge originated from the Father Himself (John 7:15–16); (2) His teaching and knowledge could be confirmed by testing (v. 17); (3) His actions demonstrated His selflessness (v. 18); 4) His impact on the world was startling (vv. 19–20); and (5) His deeds demonstrated His identity as the Son of God (vv. 21–24).

[e] MARVELED. Jesus' knowledge of Scripture was supernatural. The people were amazed that someone who had never studied at any great rabbinical center or under any important rabbi could display such profound mastery of Scripture. Both the content and manner of Jesus' teachings were qualitatively different than any other teacher.

[f] HIS WHO SENT ME. The qualitative difference of Jesus' teaching was found in its source, i.e., the Father gave it to Him (John 8:26, 40, 46, 47; 12:49–50). It originated from God the Father Himself, in contrast to rabbis who received it from man (Gal. 1:12). While rabbis merely relied on the authority of others (the traditions of men), Jesus' authority centered in Himself (cf. Matt. 7:28–29; Acts 4:13).

Me. [g]If anyone wills to do His will, he shall know concerning the doctrine, whether it is from God or *whether* I speak on My own *authority.* He who speaks from himself seeks his own glory; but [h]He who seeks the glory of the One who sent Him is true, and no unrighteousness is in Him. Did not Moses give you the law, yet none of you keeps the law? Why do you seek to [i]kill Me?"

The people answered and said, "You have a demon. Who is seeking to kill You?"

Jesus answered and said to them, "I did [j]one work, and you all marvel. Moses therefore gave you circumcision (not that it is from Moses, [k]but from the fathers), and you circumcise a man on the Sabbath. If a man receives circumcision [l]on the Sabbath, so that the law of Moses should not be broken, are you angry with Me because [m]I made a man completely well on the Sabbath? Do not judge according to appearance, but judge [n]with righteous judgment."

---

[g] If anyone wills to do His will, he shall know. Those who genuinely seek to do God's will are guided by Him in the affirmation of His truth. God's truth is self-authenticating through the teaching ministry of the Holy Spirit (cf. John 16:13; 1 John 2:20, 27).

[h] He who seeks the glory of the One who sent Him. While other saviors and messiahs acted for their own selfish interests, thereby revealing their falseness, Jesus Christ as God's Son came solely to glorify the Father and accomplish the Father's will (2 Cor. 2:17; Phil. 2:5–11; Heb. 10:7).

[i] kill Me. If Jesus were another religious fake, the world never would have reacted in such hatred. Since the evil world system loves its own, its hatred toward Him demonstrates that He came from God (John 15:18, 19).

[j] one work. The context makes clear (John 7:22–23) that Jesus had reference to the healing of the paralytic that evoked the beginning of persecution against Him by the Jewish authorities, because it took place on the Sabbath (see John 5:1–16).

[k] but from the fathers. The patriarchal period during the time of Abraham when God instituted the sign of circumcision (Gen. 17:10–12), which was later included in the Mosaic covenant at Sinai (Ex. 4:26; 12:44–45). This observation demonstrated that this rite preceded the Mosaic law (Gal. 3:17). Furthermore, circumcision antedates the Sabbath law also.

[l] on the Sabbath. According to Mosaic Law, baby boys were to be circumcised on the eighth day (Lev. 12:1–3). If a son was born on the Sabbath, then the eighth day (including his birthday) would come on the following Sabbath, when the Jews would circumcise the child. Jesus' point was that the Jews who objected to His healings on the Sabbath broke their own Sabbath law with the circumcision of the child. Their hypocrisy is evident.

[m] I made a man completely well. Jesus used an argument of the lesser to the greater. If ceremonial cleansing of one part of the body is permitted on the Sabbath through the act of circumcision (the lesser), how much more so should the actual healing of the entire body be permitted on the Sabbath (the greater).

[n] with righteous judgment. While Jesus forbade harsh, censorious judgment that self-righteous legalism promotes (Matt. 7:1), He demanded the exercise of moral and theological discernment.

Now some of them from Jerusalem said, "[o]Is this not He whom they seek to kill? But look! [p]He speaks boldly, and they say nothing to Him. [q]Do the rulers know indeed that this is truly the Christ? However, we know where this Man is from; but when the Christ comes, [r]no one knows where He is from."

Then Jesus [s]cried out, as He taught in the temple, saying, "[t]You both know Me, and you know where I am from; and I have not come of Myself, but He who sent Me is true, [u]whom you do not know. But I know Him, for I am from Him, and He sent Me."

Therefore they sought to take Him; but no one laid a hand on Him, because [v]His hour had not yet come. And [w]many of the people believed in Him, and said, "When the Christ comes, will He do more signs than these which this *Man* has done?"

---

[o] Is this not He. In this section (John 7:25–36) John once again reiterated the claims of Jesus to His identity as the Messiah and Son of God. He focused on His divine origin and citizenship. While some believed in Him at this time (John 7:31), the religious leaders became even more angry at Him and nefariously planned to seize Him (v. 32). Jesus confronted the people with three dilemmas recorded in these verses: (1) the problem of dense confusion (John 7:25–29); (2) the problem of divided conviction (vv. 30–32); and (3) the problem of delayed conversion (vv. 33–36). These three problems left Jerusalem in a state of utter despair.

[p] He speaks boldly. What surprised the masses was that in spite of the ominous threat from the religious authorities (John 7:20, 32), Jesus boldly proclaimed His identity.

[q] Do the rulers know. The question indicates the crowds and the rulers were in great confusion and uncertainty as to who Jesus was and what to do about Him. They did not really have any firm convictions regarding Jesus' identity, for their question reveals their doubt and unbelief. They were also perplexed at the religious leaders' failure to arrest and silence Him if He really were a fraud. Such dense confusion caused the crowd to wonder if the religious authorities in private concluded that He was indeed the Christ. Mass confusion among all groups reigned regarding Jesus.

[r] no one knows where He is from. Only information regarding the Messiah's birthplace was revealed in Scripture (Mic. 5:2; Matt. 2:5, 6). Beyond that, a tradition had developed in Jewish circles that Messiah would appear suddenly to the people, based on a misinterpretation of Isa. 53:8 and Mal. 3:1. In light of this, the meaning of this phrase most likely is that the identity of the Messiah would remain unknown until He suddenly appeared in Israel and accomplished Israel's redemption. In contrast, Jesus had lived His life in Nazareth and was known (at least superficially) to the people.

[s] cried out. Jesus gave the greatest publicity to this important teaching by voicing it loudly (cf. John 1:15; 12:44).

[t] You both know Me, and you know where I am from. These words stand in antithesis with John 8:19, where Jesus told His enemies that they neither knew Him nor the Father, thus indicating a deep irony and sarcasm on Jesus' part here. Jesus' point is that contrary to what they thought, they really had no true understanding of who He was. They knew Him in the earthly sense, but not in the spiritual sense, because they didn't know God either.

[u] whom you do not know. Although they thought that they were acutely perceptive and spiritually oriented, their rejection of Jesus revealed their spiritual bankruptcy (Rom. 2:17–19).

[v] His hour had not yet come. This reveals the reason why they could not seize Him, i.e., God's sovereign timetable and plan for Jesus would not allow it.

The Pharisees heard the crowd murmuring these things concerning Him, and the [x]Pharisees and the chief priests sent [y]officers to take Him. Then Jesus said to them, "I shall be with you a little while longer, and *then* I go to Him who sent Me. You will seek Me and not find *Me*, and [z]where I am you cannot come."

Then the Jews said among themselves, "Where does He intend to go that we shall not find Him? Does He intend to go to the Dispersion among the Greeks and [aa]teach the Greeks? [bb]What is this thing that He said, 'You will seek Me and not find Me, and where I am you cannot come'?"

---

[w] MANY . . . BELIEVED. Divided conviction existed among the people regarding Jesus. While some wanted to seize Him, a small remnant of genuine believers existed among the crowds. The question here anticipates a negative answer, i.e., the Messiah could do no greater kinds of miracles than those Jesus had done.

[x] PHARISEES AND THE CHIEF PRIESTS. The Pharisees and chief priests historically did not have harmonious relationships with each other. Most of the chief priests were Sadducees, who were political and religious opponents to the Pharisees. John repeatedly links these two groups in his gospel (cf. John 11:47, 57; 18:3) in order to emphasize that their cooperation stemmed from their mutual hatred of Jesus. Both were alarmed at the faith of those indicated in John 7:31 and, in order to avoid any veneration of Jesus as Messiah, attempted unsuccessfully to arrest Him (John 7:30).

[y] OFFICERS. Temple guards who functioned as a kind of police force composed of Levites who were in charge of maintaining order in the temple environs. They could also be used by the Sanhedrin in areas outside the temple environs in religious disputes that did not affect Roman policy.

[z] WHERE I AM YOU CANNOT COME. Jesus referred here to His return to His heavenly origin with His Father after His crucifixion and resurrection (see John 17:15).

[aa] TEACH THE GREEKS. The phrase "teach the Greeks" probably had reference to Jewish proselytes, i.e., Gentiles. John may have been citing this phrase with ironic force, since the gospel eventually went to the Gentiles because of Jewish blindness and rejection of their Messiah. Cf. Rom. 11:7–11.

[bb] WHAT IS THIS THING. John again highlights the ignorance of the Jews regarding Jesus' words. The words were spoken to mock Jesus.

99. The Jewish Leaders Try to Arrest Jesus

John 7:37–52

JN [a]On the last day, that great *day* of the feast, [b]Jesus stood and cried out, saying, "[c]If anyone [d]thirsts, let him come to Me and drink. He who believes in Me, as the Scripture has said, out of his heart will flow rivers of [e]living water." But this [f]He spoke concerning the Spirit, whom those believing in Him would receive; for the Holy Spirit was not yet *given,* because Jesus was not yet glorified.

Therefore many from the crowd, when they heard this saying, said, "Truly this is the Prophet." Others said, "This is the Christ."

But some said, "Will the Christ come [g]out of Galilee? Has not the Scripture

[a] On the last day. This suggests that this occasion occurred on a different day than the controversy in John 7:11–36.

[b] Jesus stood and cried out. This section (John 7:37–52) catalogues the different reactions of people to Jesus' claims. These reactions have become universal patterns for reactions to Him through the ages. This section may be divided into the claim of Christ (John 7:37–39) and the reactions to Christ (vv. 40–52). The reactions may be subdivided into five sections: (1) the reaction of the convinced (vv. 40–41a); (2) the reaction of the contrary (vv. 41b–42); (3) the reaction of the hostile (vv. 43, 44); (4) the reaction of the confused (vv. 45, 46); and (5) the reaction of the religious authorities (vv. 47–52).

[c] If anyone thirsts. A tradition grew up in the few centuries before Jesus that on the seven days of the Feast of Tabernacles, a golden vessel containing water from the pool of Siloam was transported in a priestly procession back to the temple. As it came to the Water Gate three trumpet blasts sounded to mark the joy of the occasion and the people recited Isa. 12:3, "With joy you will draw water from the wells of salvation." At the temple, as the people watched, the priests would march around the altar carrying the water container while the temple choir sang the Hallel (Pss. 113–118). The water was then offered as a sacrifice to God. The use of the water symbolized the blessing of adequate rainfall for crops. Jesus used this event as an object lesson and opportunity to make a very public invitation on the last day of the feast for His people to accept Him as the living water. His words recall Isa. 55:1.

[d] thirsts . . . come . . . drink. These three words summarize the gospel invitation. A recognition of need leads to an approach to the source of provision, followed by receiving what is needed. The thirsty, needy soul feels the craving to come to the Savior and drink, i.e., receive the salvation that He offers.

[e] living water. The water-pouring rite also foreshadowed the millennial rivers of living water described in Ezek. 47:1–9 and Zech. 13:1. The significance of Jesus' invitation centers in the fact that He was the fulfillment of all the Feast of Tabernacles anticipated, i.e., He was the One who provided the living water that gives eternal life to man (cf. John 4:10, 11).

[f] He spoke concerning the Spirit. The impartation of the Holy Spirit is the source of spiritual and eternal life.

[g] out of Galilee? This betrays the people's great ignorance, because Jesus was born in Bethlehem of Judea not Galilee (Mic. 5:2; cf. Matt. 2:6; Luke 2:4). They did not even bother to investigate His true birthplace, showing their lack of interest in messianic credentials.

said that the Christ comes from the seed of David and from the town of Bethlehem, where David was?" So there was a [h]division among the people because of Him. Now some of them wanted to take Him, but no one laid hands on Him.

Then the officers came to the chief priests and Pharisees, who said to them, "Why have you not brought Him?"

[i]The officers answered, "No man ever spoke like this Man!"

Then the Pharisees answered them, "[j]Are you also deceived? Have any of the rulers or the Pharisees believed in Him? But this [k]crowd that does not know the law is [l]accursed."

[m]Nicodemus (he who came to Jesus by night, being one of them) said to them, "[n]Does our law judge a man before it hears him and knows what he is doing?"

They answered and said to him, "Are you also from Galilee? Search and look, for [o]no prophet has arisen out of Galilee."

---

[h] DIVISION. See Matt. 10:34–36; Luke 12:51–53.

[i] THE OFFICERS. The officers failed in their attempt to arrest Jesus when they were confronted with His person and powerful teaching. Since they were religiously trained, Jesus' words struck at their very heart.

[j] ARE YOU ALSO DECEIVED? The Pharisees mocked the officers, not on professional (as police officers), but religious grounds (as Levites). In essence, they accused them of being seduced by a deceiver (i.e., Jesus) in contrast to the Pharisees themselves who arrogantly and self-righteously felt that in their wisdom and knowledge no one could ever deceive them.

[k] CROWD. The Pharisees condescendingly labeled the people as a "crowd." The rabbis viewed the common people (or, people of the land) as ignorant and impious in contrast to themselves. This ignorance was not only because of their ignorance of Scripture, but especially the common people's failure to follow the Pharisees' oral traditions.

[l] ACCURSED. The people were considered damned because they did not belong to the elite group nor follow their beliefs regarding the law.

[m] NICODEMUS. Nicodemus's (see John 3:10) mind had not closed regarding Christ's claims, so that while not defending Jesus directly, he did raise a procedural point in Jesus' favor.

[n] DOES OUR LAW JUDGE. No explicit OT text can be cited that makes Nicodemus's point. Most likely he referred to rabbinical traditions contained in their oral law.

[o] NO PROPHET HAS ARISEN OUT OF GALILEE. The real ignorance lay with the arrogant Pharisees who did not carefully search out the facts as to where Jesus was actually born. While they accused the crowds of ignorance, they, too, were really as ignorant. Furthermore, the prophet Jonah did come from Galilee.

100. Jesus Forgives an Adulterous Woman

John 7:53–8:11

JN [a]Everyone went to his *own* house. But Jesus went to the Mount of Olives.

Now early in the morning He came again into the temple, and all the people came to Him; and He sat down and taught them. Then the scribes and Pharisees brought to Him a woman caught in adultery. And when they had set her in the midst, they said to Him, "Teacher, this woman was caught in adultery, in the very act. Now Moses, in the law, commanded us that such should be stoned. But what do You say?"

This they said, [b]testing Him, that they might have *something* of which to accuse Him. But Jesus stooped down and wrote on the ground with *His* finger, as though He did not hear. So when they continued asking Him, He raised Himself up and said to them, "[c]He who is without sin among you, let him throw a stone at her first."

And again [d]He stooped down and wrote on the ground. Then those who heard *it*, being convicted by *their* conscience, went out one by one, beginning with the oldest *even* to the last. And Jesus was left alone, and the woman standing in the midst. When Jesus had raised Himself up and saw no one but the woman, He

---

[a] EVERYONE WENT TO HIS OWN HOUSE. This section (John 7:53–8:11) dealing with the adulteress most likely was not a part of the original contents of John. It has been incorporated into various manuscripts at different places in the gospel (e.g., after John 7:36, 44, 52, or 21:25), while one manuscript places it after Luke 21:38. External manuscript evidence representing a great variety of textual traditions is decidedly against its inclusion, for the earliest and best manuscripts exclude it. Many manuscripts mark the passage to indicate doubt as to its inclusion. Significant early versions exclude it. No Greek church father comments on the passage until the twelfth century. The vocabulary and style of the section also are different from the rest of the gospel, and the section interrupts the sequence of John 7:52 with 8:12ff. Many, however, do think that it has all the earmarks of historical veracity, perhaps being a piece of oral tradition that circulated in parts of the western church, so that a few comments are in order. In spite of all these considerations of the likely unreliability of this section, it is possible to be wrong on the issue, and thus it is good to consider the meaning of this passage and leave it in the text.

[b] TESTING HIM . . . TO ACCUSE HIM. If Jesus rejected the law of Moses (Lev. 20:10; Deut. 22:22), His credibility would be gone. If He held to Mosaic law, His reputation for compassion and forgiveness would have been questioned.

[c] HE WHO IS WITHOUT SIN. This directly refers to Deut. 13:9; 17:7, where the witnesses of a crime are to start the execution. Only those who were not guilty of the same sin could participate.

[d] HE STOOPED DOWN AND WROTE ON THE GROUND. This seems to have been a delaying device, giving them time to think.

said to her, "Woman, where are those accusers of yours? Has no one condemned you?"

She said, "No one, Lord."

And Jesus said to her, "Neither do I condemn you; [e]go and sin no more."

[e] go and sin no more. Actually, "Leave your life of sin" (cf. Matt. 9:1–8; Mark 2:13–17; John 3:17; 12:47).

101. Jesus Is the Light of the World

John 8:12–30

JN [a]Then Jesus spoke to them again, saying, "[b]I am the light of the world. [c]He who follows Me shall not walk in darkness, but have the light of life."

The Pharisees therefore said to Him, "[d]You bear witness of Yourself; Your witness is not true." [e]Jesus answered and said to them, "Even if I bear witness of Myself, My witness is true, for I know where I came from and where I am going; but you do not know where I come from and where I am going. You judge according to the flesh; I judge no one. And yet if I do judge, My judgment is true; for I am not alone, but I *am* with the Father who sent Me. It is also [f]written in your law

[a] THEN JESUS SPOKE TO THEM AGAIN. Excluding the story of the adulterous woman in 7:53–8:11, the beginning of John 8:12 attaches itself well to John 7:52. The word "again" indicates that Jesus spoke once more to the people at this same Feast of Tabernacles (cf. John 7:2, 10). While Jesus first used the water-drawing rite (John 7:37–39) as a metaphor to portray the ultimate spiritual truth of Himself as Messiah who fulfills all that the feast anticipated, He then turned to another rite that traditionally occurred at the feast: the lighting ceremony. During Tabernacles four large lamps in the temple's court of women illuminated a joyous celebration that took place there, with people dancing, holding burning torches, and singing songs of praise. Levitical musicians also played. Jesus took this opportunity of the lighting celebration to portray another spiritual analogy for the people: "I am the light of the world."

[b] I AM THE LIGHT OF THE WORLD. This is the second "I AM" statement in John's gospel (see John 6:35). John has already used the "light" metaphor for Jesus (John 1:4; cf. 1 John 1:5). Jesus' metaphor here is steeped in OT allusions (Ex. 13:21, 22; 14:19–25; Pss. 27:1; 119:105; Prov. 6:23; Ezek. 1:4, 13, 26–28; Hab. 3:3, 4). The phrase highlights Jesus' role as Messiah and Son of God (Ps. 27:1; Mal. 4:2). The OT indicates that, in the coming age, the Lord will be the light for His people (Isa. 60:19–22; cf. Rev. 21:23–24) as well as for the whole earth (Isa. 42:6; 49:6). Zechariah 14:5b–8 has an emphasis on God as the light of the world who gives living waters to His people. This latter passage probably formed the liturgical readings for the Feast of Tabernacles.

[c] HE WHO FOLLOWS ME. The word *follows* conveys the idea of someone who gives himself completely to the person followed. No half-hearted followers exist in Jesus' mind (cf. Matt. 8:18–22; 10:38–39). A veiled reference exists here to the Jews, following the pillar of cloud and fire that led them during the exodus (Ex. 13:21).

[d] YOU BEAR WITNESS OF YOURSELF. The Jews mockingly brought up Jesus' own words from John 5:31. However, Jesus' words there and here are reconciled by the fact that OT law required not one but multiple witnesses to establish the truth of a matter (Deut. 17:6). Jesus was not alone in His witness that pointed to Him as Messiah, for many had already testified concerning this truth (cf. John 1:7).

[e] JESUS ANSWERED AND SAID TO THEM. These verses (John 8:14–18) give three reasons why Jesus' witness was true: (1) Jesus knew His origin and destiny, while the Jews were ignorant even of basic spiritual truths, making their judgment limited and superficial (vv. 14–15); (2) the intimate union of the Son with the Father guaranteed the truth of the Son's witness (v. 16); and (3) the Father and Son witnessed harmoniously together regarding the identity of the Son (vv. 17–18).

[f] WRITTEN IN YOUR LAW. See Deut. 17:6; 19:15.

that the testimony of two men is true. I am One who bears witness of Myself, and the Father who sent Me bears witness of Me."

Then they said to Him, "[g]Where is Your Father?" Jesus answered, "You know neither Me nor My Father. If you had known Me, you would have known My Father also."

These words Jesus spoke in the treasury, as He taught in the temple, and no one laid hands on Him, for His hour had not yet come.

Then Jesus said to them again, "[h]I am going away, and you will seek Me, and [i]will die in your sin. Where I go you cannot come."

So the Jews said, [j]"Will He kill Himself, because He says, 'Where I go you cannot come'?"

And He said to them, "[k]You are from beneath; I am from above. You are of this world; I am not of this world. Therefore I said to you that you will die in your sins; for [l]if you do not believe that [m]I am *He*, you will die in your sins."

---

[g] "Where is your Father?" The Jews, as was their habit (e.g., John 3:4; 4:11; 6:52), once again thought merely in human terms in asking about Jesus' paternity.

[h] I am going away. Jesus repeated His message of John 7:33–34, but with more ominous overtones regarding the consequences of rejecting Him. He would be going away by means of His impending death, resurrection, and ascension to the Father.

[i] will die in your sin. Jesus revealed the consequence of the rejection of Him as Messiah and Son of God, i.e., spiritual death (John 8:24; cf. Heb. 10:26–31). These verses (John 8:21–30) reveal four ways that ensure someone will die in their sins and, as a result, experience spiritual death: (1) being self-righteous (vv. 20–22); (2) being earthbound (vv. 23, 24); (3) being unbelieving (v. 24); and (4) being willfully ignorant (vv. 25–29). The Jews who rejected Jesus displayed all four of these characteristics.

[j] Will He kill Himself. The Jews spoke either in confusion (cf. John 7:34–35) or, perhaps more likely, in mockery of Christ. Jewish tradition condemned suicide as a particularly-heinous sin that resulted in permanent banishment to the worst part of Hades (Josephus, *Jewish Wars* 3.375). God did deliver Him to be killed (Acts 2:23); thus, as God, He gave up His own life (John 10:18).

[k] You are from beneath. The contrast here is between the realm of God and that of the fallen, sinful world (i.e., "from beneath"). The world in this context is the invisible spiritual system of evil dominated by Satan and all that it offers in opposition to God, His Word, and His people (cf. John 1:9; 1 John 5:19). Jesus declared that His opponents' true kinship was with Satan and his realm. By this domination they were spiritually blinded (see 2 Cor. 4:4; Eph. 2:1–3).

[l] if you do not believe. Jesus emphasized that the fatal, unforgivable, and eternal sin is failure to believe in Him as Messiah and Son of God. In truth all other sins can be forgiven if this one is repented of. Cf. John 16:8, 9.

[m] I am He. "He" is not part of the original statement. Jesus' words were not constructed normally but were influenced by OT Hebrew usage. It is an absolute usage meaning "I AM" and has immense theological significance. The reference may be to both Ex. 3:14, where the Lord declared His name as "I AM," and to Isa. 40–55, where the phrase "I am" occurs repeatedly (especially Isa. 43:10, 13, 25; 46:4; 48:12). In this Jesus referred to Himself as the God (Yahweh—the Lord) of the OT and directly claimed full deity for Himself, prompting the Jews' question of John 8:25.

Then they said to Him, "[n]Who are You?"

And Jesus said to them, "Just what I have been saying to you [o]from the beginning. I have many things to say and to judge concerning you, but He who sent Me is true; and I speak to the world those things which I heard from Him."

They did not understand that He spoke to them of the Father. Then Jesus said to them, "[p]When you lift up the Son of Man, then [q]you will know that I am *He,* and *that* I do nothing of Myself; but as My Father taught Me, I speak these things. And He who sent Me is with Me. The Father has not left Me alone, for I always do those things that please Him." As He spoke these words, many believed in Him.

---

[n] "WHO ARE YOU?" The Jews were willfully ignorant, because multiple witnesses testified to Jesus' identity, and Jesus Himself in words and actions persistently proved throughout His ministry on earth that He was the Son of God and Messiah.

[o] FROM THE BEGINNING. The start of Jesus' ministry among the Jews.

[p] WHEN YOU LIFT UP THE SON OF MAN. Jesus' impending crucifixion.

[q] YOU WILL KNOW THAT I AM HE. Having refused to accept Him by faith and having nailed Him to the cross, they would one day awaken to the terrifying realization that this One whom they despised was the One whom they should have worshiped (cf. Phil. 2:9–11; Rev. 1:7). Many Jews believed on Christ after His death and ascension, realizing that the One whom they rejected was truly the Messiah (Acts 2:36–37, 41).

102. Jesus' Relationship to Abraham

John 8:31–59

JN [a]Then Jesus said to those Jews [b]who believed Him, "[c]If you abide in My word, you are My disciples indeed. And you shall know [d]the truth, and the truth shall make you free."

They answered Him, "We are Abraham's descendants, and have [e]never been in bondage to anyone. How *can* You say, 'You will be made free'?"

Jesus answered them, "Most assuredly, I say to you, [f]whoever commits sin is [g]a slave of sin. And a slave does not abide in the house forever, *but* a son abides forever. Therefore if the Son makes you free, you shall be free indeed.

---

[a] THEN JESUS SAID. These verses (John 8:31–36) are a pivotal passage in understanding genuine salvation and true discipleship. John emphasized these realities by stressing truth and freedom. The focus in the passage is upon those who were exercising the beginnings of faith in Jesus as Messiah and Son of God. Jesus desired them to move on in their faith. Saving faith is not fickle but firm and settled. Such maturity expresses itself in full commitment to the truth in Jesus Christ resulting in genuine freedom. The passage has three features: (1) the progress of freedom (John 8:31–32); (2) the pretense of freedom (vv. 33, 34); and (3) the promise of freedom (vv. 35–36).

[b] WHO BELIEVED HIM. The first step in the progress toward true discipleship is belief in Jesus Christ as Messiah and Son of God.

[c] IF YOU ABIDE IN MY WORD, YOU ARE MY DISCIPLES INDEED. This reveals the second step in the progress toward true discipleship. Perseverance in obedience to Scripture (cf. Matt. 28:19–20) is the fruit or evidence of genuine faith (see Eph. 2:10). Here the word *abide* indicates habitual action, so a disciple habitually abides in Jesus' words. A genuine believer holds fast, obeys, and practices Jesus' teaching. The person who continues in His teaching has both the Father and the Son (2 John 9; cf. Heb. 3:14; Rev. 2:26). Real disciples are both learners (the basic meaning of the word) and faithful followers.

[d] THE TRUTH. "Truth" here has reference not only to the facts surrounding Jesus as the Messiah and Son of God but also to the teaching that He brought. A genuinely saved and obedient follower of the Lord Jesus will know divine truth and both freedom from sin and the search for reality. This divine truth comes not merely by intellectual assent (1 Cor. 2:14) but saving commitment to Christ (cf. Titus 1:1–2).

[e] NEVER BEEN IN BONDAGE TO ANYONE. Because Israel had experienced political subjection to many nations (Egypt, Assyria, Babylon, Greece, Syria, and Rome), these Jews must have been referring to their inward sense of freedom.

[f] WHOEVER COMMITS SIN. The kind of slavery that Jesus had in mind was not physical slavery but slavery to sin (cf. Rom. 6:17–18). The idea of "commits sin" means to practice sin habitually (1 John 3:4, 8–9). The ultimate bondage is not political or economic enslavement but spiritual bondage to sin and rebellion against God. Thus, this also explains why Christ did not allow Himself to be embraced as merely a political deliverer (John 6:14, 15).

[g] A SLAVE OF SIN. The notion of slavery in John 8:34 moves to the status of slaves. While the Jews thought of themselves only as free sons of Abraham, in reality, they were slaves of sin. The genuine son in the context is Christ Himself, who sets the slaves free from sin. Those whom Jesus Christ sets free from the bondage of sin and legalism are truly free (Rom. 8:2; Gal. 5:1).

"I know that you are Abraham's descendants, but you seek to kill Me, because My word has no place in you. I speak what I have seen with My Father, and you do what you have seen with your father."

They answered and said to Him, "Abraham is our father." Jesus said to them, "[h]If you were Abraham's children, you would do the [i]works of Abraham. But now you seek to kill Me, a Man who has told you the truth which I heard from God. Abraham did not do this. You do the deeds of your father."

Then they said to Him, "[j]We were not born of fornication; we have one Father—God."

Jesus said to them, "[k]If God were your Father, you would love Me, for I proceeded forth and came from God; nor have I come of Myself, but He sent Me. Why do you not understand My speech? Because you are not able to listen to My word. You are of [l]*your* father the devil, and the desires of your father you want to do. [m]He was a murderer from the beginning, and does not stand in the truth, because there is no truth in him. When he speaks a lie, he speaks from his own *resources,* for he is a liar and the father of it. But because I tell the truth, you do not

---

[h] If you were Abraham's children. The construction of this phrase indicates that Jesus was denying that mere physical lineage was sufficient for salvation (see Phil. 3:4–9). The sense would be, "if you were Abraham's children, but you are not, then you would act like Abraham did." Just as children inherit genetic characteristics from their parents, so also those who are truly Abraham's offspring will act like Abraham, i.e., imitate Abraham's faith and obedience (see Rom. 4:16; Gal. 3:6–9; Heb. 11:8–19; James 2:21–24).

[i] works of Abraham. Abraham's faith was demonstrated through his obedience to God (James 2:21–24). Jesus' point was that the conduct of the unbelieving Jews was diametrically opposed by the conduct of Abraham, who lived a life of obedience to all that God had commanded. Their conduct toward Jesus demonstrated that their real father was Satan (John 8:41, 44).

[j] We were not born of fornication. The Jews may well have been referring to the controversy surrounding Jesus' birth. The Jews knew the story about Mary's betrothal and that Joseph was not Jesus' real father; thus they implied that Jesus' birth was illegitimate (see Matt. 1:18–25; Luke 1:26–38).

[k] If God were your Father, you would love Me. The construction here denies that God is truly their Father. Although the OT calls Israel His "firstborn son" (Ex. 4:22) and affirms that God is Israel's father by creation and separation (Jer. 31:9), the unbelief of the Jews toward Jesus demonstrated that God was not their Father, spiritually. Jesus stressed that the explicit criterion verifying the claim to be a child of God is love for His Son, Jesus. Since God is love, those who love His Son also demonstrate His nature (1 John 4:7–11; 5:1).

[l] your father the devil. Sonship is predicated on conduct. A son will manifest his father's characteristics (cf. Eph. 5:1, 2). Since unbelieving Jews exhibited the patterns of Satan in their hostility toward Jesus and their failure to believe in Him as Messiah, their paternity was the exact opposite of their claims, i.e., they belonged to Satan.

[m] He was a murderer from the beginning. Jesus' words refer to the fall, when Satan tempted Adam and Eve and successfully killed their spiritual life (Gen. 2:17; 3:17–24; Rom. 5:12; Heb. 2:14). Some think that the reference may also refer to Cain's murder of Abel (Gen. 4:1–9; 1 John 3:12).

believe Me. Which of you [n]convicts Me of sin? And if I tell the truth, why do you not believe Me? He who is of God hears God's words; therefore you do not hear, because you are not of God."

Then the Jews answered and said to Him, "Do we not say rightly that [o]You are a Samaritan and have a demon?"

Jesus answered, "I do not have a demon; but I honor My Father, and you dishonor Me. And I do not seek My *own* glory; there is One who seeks and judges. Most assuredly, I say to you, if anyone keeps My word he shall [p]never see death."

Then the Jews said to Him, "Now we know that You have a demon! [q]Abraham is dead, and the prophets; and You say, 'If anyone keeps My word he shall never taste death.' Are You greater than our father Abraham, who is dead? And the prophets are dead. Who do You make Yourself out to be?"

Jesus answered, "If I honor Myself, My honor is nothing. It is My Father who honors Me, of whom you say that He is your God. Yet you have not known Him, but I know Him. And if I say, 'I do not know Him,' I shall be a liar like you; but I do know Him and keep His word. [r]Your father Abraham rejoiced to see My day, and he saw *it* and was glad."

Then the Jews said to Him, "You are not yet fifty years old, and have You seen Abraham?"

Jesus said to them, "Most assuredly, I say to you, before Abraham was, [s]I AM."

---

[n] convicts Me of sin. Only a perfectly-holy One who has the closest and most intimate communion with the Father could speak such words. The Jews arguing against Jesus could marshal no genuine evidence that He had ever sinned against God.

[o] You are a Samaritan. Since the Jews could not attack Jesus' personal life and conduct, they tried an ad hominem attack of personal abuse toward Him. The reference to Jesus as a "Samaritan" probably centers in the fact that the Samaritans, like Jesus, questioned the Jewish people's exclusive right to be called Abraham's children.

[p] never see death. Heeding Jesus' teaching and following Him results in eternal life (John 6:63, 68). Physical death cannot extinguish such life (see John 5:24; 6:40, 47; 11:25–26).

[q] Abraham is dead. Jesus' assertion that anyone who keeps His word will never die prompted the Jews to offer a retort that once again revealed their thinking on strictly a literal and earthly level (see John 3:4; 4:15).

[r] Your father Abraham rejoiced. Hebrews 11:13 indicates that Abraham saw Christ's day ("having seen them afar off"). Abraham particularly saw in the continuing seed of Isaac the beginning of God's fulfilling the covenant (Gen. 12:1–3; 15:1–21; 17:1–8; cf. 22:8) that would culminate in Christ.

[s] I AM. Cf. John 6:22–58. Here Jesus declared Himself to be Yahweh, i.e., the Lord of the OT. Basic to the expression are such passages as Ex. 3:14; Deut. 32:39; Isa. 41:4; 43:10 where God declared Himself to be the eternally preexistent God who revealed Himself in the OT to the Jews.

Then [t]they took up stones to throw at Him; but Jesus [u]hid Himself and went out of the temple, going through the midst of them, and so passed by.

[t] THEY TOOK UP STONES. The Jews understood Jesus' claim and followed Lev. 24:16, which indicates that any man who falsely claims to be God should be stoned.

[u] HID HIMSELF ... GOING THROUGH THE MIDST OF THEM. Jesus repeatedly escaped arrest and death because His hour had not yet come (cf. John 7:30, 44; 18:6). The verse most likely indicates escape by miraculous means.

103. Jesus Commissions the Seventy

Luke 10:1–16

LK After these things the Lord appointed [a]seventy others also, and sent them [b]two by two before His face into every city and place where He Himself was about to go. Then He said to them, "The harvest truly *is* great, but the laborers *are* few; therefore pray the Lord of the harvest to send out laborers into His harvest. Go your way; behold, I send you out as [c]lambs among wolves. Carry [d]neither money bag, knapsack, nor sandals; and [e]greet no one along the road. But whatever house you enter, first say, 'Peace to this house.' And if a son of peace is there, your peace will rest on it; if not, it will return to you. And remain in the same house, eating and drinking such things as they give, for the laborer is worthy of his wages. [f]Do not go from house to house. Whatever city you enter, and they receive you, eat such things as are set before you. And heal the sick there, and say to them, 'The kingdom of God has come near to you.' But whatever city you enter, and they do not receive you, go out into its streets and say, 'The very [g]dust of your city which clings to us we wipe off against you. Nevertheless know this, that the kingdom of God has come near you.' But I say to you that it will be more tolerable in that Day for Sodom than for that city.

[a] SEVENTY OTHERS. The commissioning of the seventy is recorded only in Luke. Moses also appointed seventy elders as his representatives (Num. 11:16, 24–25). The twelve disciples had been sent into Galilee (9:1–6); the seventy were sent into every city and place where He was about to go—i.e., into Judea, and possibly Perea (cf. Matt. 19:1).

[b] TWO BY TWO. As the twelve had been sent (Mark 6:7; cf. Eccl. 4:9, 11; Acts 13:2; 15:27, 39, 40; 19:22; Rev. 11:3).

[c] LAMBS AMONG WOLVES. i.e., they would face hostility (cf. Ezek. 2:3–6; John 15:20) and spiritual danger (cf. Matt. 7:15; John 10:12).

[d] NEITHER MONEY BAG, KNAPSACK, NOR SANDALS. i.e., travel without luggage. This does not mean they would be barefoot, but that they should not bring extra footwear.

[e] GREET NO ONE. A greeting in that culture was an elaborate ceremony involving many formalities, perhaps even a meal, and long delays (cf. 11:43). A person on an extremely urgent mission could be excused from such formalities without being thought rude. Everything in Jesus' instructions speaks of the shortness of time and the great urgency of the task.

[f] DO NOT GO FROM HOUSE TO HOUSE. i.e., for lodging. They were to establish headquarters in a village and not waste time moving around or seeking more comfortable housing.

[g] DUST . . . WIPE OFF AGAINST YOU. Jesus had given the twelve disciples similar instruction in Matt. 10:14–15.

"[h]Woe to you, Chorazin! Woe to you, Bethsaida! For if the mighty works which were done in you had been done in Tyre and Sidon, they would have repented long ago, sitting in sackcloth and ashes. But it will be more tolerable for Tyre and Sidon at the judgment than for you. And you, Capernaum, who are exalted to heaven, will be brought down to Hades. [i]He who hears you hears Me, he who rejects you rejects Me, and he who rejects Me rejects Him who sent Me."

---

[h] WOE TO YOU, CHORAZIN! Jesus gave a similar warning in Matt. 11:21, 23.

[i] HE WHO HEARS YOU HEARS ME. These words elevate the office of a faithful minister of Christ and magnify the guilt and the condemnation of those who reject the message.

104. The Seventy Return

Luke 10:17–24

LK Then the seventy [a]returned with joy, saying, "Lord, even the demons are subject to us in Your name."

And He said to them, "[b]I saw Satan fall like lightning from heaven. Behold, I give you the authority to trample on [c]serpents and scorpions, and over all the power of the enemy, and nothing shall by any means hurt you. Nevertheless [d]do not rejoice in this, that the spirits are subject to you, but rather rejoice [e]because your names are written in heaven."

In that hour Jesus rejoiced in the Spirit and said, "I thank You, Father, Lord of heaven and earth, that [f]You have hidden these things from *the* wise and prudent and revealed them to babes. Even so, Father, for so it seemed good in Your sight. All things have been delivered to Me by My Father, and no one knows who the Son is except the Father, and who the Father is except the Son, and *the one* to whom the Son wills to reveal *Him.*"

Then He turned to *His* disciples and said privately, "Blessed *are* the eyes which see the things you see; for I tell you that many prophets and kings have desired to see what you see, and have not seen *it,* and to hear what you hear, and have not heard *it.*"

---

[a] RETURNED WITH JOY. How long the mission lasted is not recorded. It may have been several weeks. The seventy probably did not return all at once, but this dialogue appears to have occurred after they had all reassembled.

[b] I SAW SATAN FALL. In this context it appears Jesus' meaning was, "Don't be so surprised that the demons are subject to you; I saw their commander cast out of heaven, so it is no wonder if his minions are cast out on earth. After all, I am the source of the authority that makes them subject to you" (Luke 10:19). He may also have intended a subtle reminder and warning against pride—the reason for Satan's fall (cf. 1 Tim. 3:6).

[c] SERPENTS AND SCORPIONS. Cf. Ps. 91:13; Ezek. 2:6. These appear to be figurative terms for demonic powers (cf. Rom. 16:20).

[d] DO NOT REJOICE IN THIS. Rather than being so enthralled with extraordinary manifestations such as power over demons and the ability to work miracles, they should have realized that the greatest wonder of all is the reality of salvation—the whole point of the gospel message and the central issue to which all the miracles pointed.

[e] BECAUSE YOUR NAMES ARE WRITTEN IN HEAVEN. Cf. Phil. 4:3; Heb. 12:23; Rev. 21:27. By contrast unbelievers are "written in the earth" (Jer. 17:13).

[f] YOU HAVE HIDDEN THESE THINGS. On another occasion Jesus made a similar statement in Matt. 11:25–26.

105. The Story About a Good Samaritan

Luke 10:25–37

LK And behold, a certain [a]lawyer stood up and tested Him, saying, "Teacher, [b]what shall I do to inherit eternal life?"

He said to him, "What is written in the law? What is your reading *of it?*"

So [c]he answered and said, "'You shall love the LORD your God with all your heart, with all your soul, with all your strength, and with all your mind,' and 'your neighbor as yourself.'"

And He said to him, "You have answered rightly; [d]do this and you will live."

But he, [e]wanting to justify himself, said to Jesus, "And [f]who is my neighbor?"

Then Jesus answered and said: "A certain *man* went [g]down from Jerusalem to Jericho, and fell among thieves, who stripped him of his clothing, wounded

---

[a] LAWYER. i.e., a scribe who was supposedly an expert in the law of God. Aside from one usage of this word in Matt. 22:35, Luke is the only one of the gospel writers who uses it (Luke 11:45–46).

[b] WHAT SHALL I DO TO INHERIT ETERNAL LIFE. The same question is raised by several inquirers (Matt. 19:16–22; Luke 18:18–23; John 3:1–15).

[c] HE ANSWERED. The lawyer summed up the requirements of the law (Lev. 19:18; Deut. 6:5) exactly as Christ did on another occasion (cf. Matt. 22:37–40).

[d] DO THIS AND YOU WILL LIVE. Cf. Lev. 18:5; Ezek. 20:11. "Do and live" is the promise of the law. But since no sinner can obey perfectly, the impossible demands of the law are meant to drive us to seek divine mercy (Gal. 3:10–13, 22–25). This man should have responded with a confession of his own guilt, rather than self-justification.

[e] WANTING TO JUSTIFY HIMSELF. This reveals the man's self-righteous character.

[f] WHO IS MY NEIGHBOR? The prevailing opinion among scribes and Pharisees was that one's neighbors were the righteous alone. According to them the wicked—including rank sinners (such as tax collectors and prostitutes), Gentiles, and especially Samaritans—were to be hated because they were the enemies of God. They cited Ps. 139:21–22 to justify their position. As that passage suggests, hatred of evil is the natural corollary of loving righteousness. But the truly righteous person's "hatred" for sinners is not a malevolent enmity. It is a righteous abhorrence of all that is base and corrupt—not a spiteful, personal loathing of individuals. Godly hatred is marked by a broken-hearted grieving over the condition of the sinner. And as Jesus taught here and elsewhere (Matt. 5:44–48; Luke 6:27–36;), it is also tempered by a genuine love. The Pharisees had elevated hostility toward the wicked to the status of a virtue, in effect nullifying the second Great Commandment. Jesus' answer to this lawyer demolished the pharisaical excuse for hating one's enemies.

[g] DOWN FROM JERUSALEM TO JERICHO. A rocky, winding, treacherous descent of about 3,300 feet in seventeen miles. That stretch of road was notorious for being beset with thieves and danger.

him, and departed, leaving *him* half dead. Now by chance a certain priest came down that road. And when he saw him, he passed by on the other side. Likewise a [h]Levite, when he arrived at the place, came and looked, and passed by on the other side. But a certain [i]Samaritan, as he journeyed, came where he was. And when he saw him, he had compassion. So he went to *him* and bandaged his wounds, pouring on [j]oil and wine; and he set him on his own animal, brought him to an inn, and took care of him. On the next day, when he departed, he took out [k]two denarii, gave *them* to the innkeeper, and said to him, 'Take care of him; and whatever more you spend, when I come again, I will repay you.' So which of these three do you think was [l]neighbor to him who fell among the thieves?"

And he said, "He who showed mercy on him."

Then Jesus said to him, "Go and do likewise."

---

[h] Levite. These were from the tribe of Levi, but not descendants of Aaron. They assisted the priests in the work of the temple.

[i] Samaritan. For a Samaritan to travel this road was unusual. The Samaritan himself was risking not only the thieves but also the hostility of other travelers.

[j] oil and wine. Probably carried by most travelers in small amounts as a kind of first-aid kit. The wine was antiseptic; the oil soothing and healing.

[k] two denarii. i.e., two-days' wages (cf. Matt. 20:2; 22:19). Probably more than enough to permit the man to stay until he recovered.

[l] neighbor to him. Jesus reversed the lawyer's original question (Luke 10:29). The lawyer assumed it was up to others to prove themselves neighbor to him. Jesus' reply makes it clear that each has a responsibility to be a neighbor—especially to those who are in need.

106. Jesus Visits Mary and Martha

Luke 10:38–42

LK Now it happened as they went that He entered [a]a certain village; and a certain woman named Martha welcomed Him into her house. And she had a sister called Mary, who also sat at Jesus' feet and heard His word.

But Martha was [b]distracted [c]with much serving, and she approached Him and said, "Lord, do You not care that my sister has left me to serve alone? Therefore tell her to help me."

And Jesus answered and said to her, "Martha, Martha, you are worried and troubled about many things. But [d]one thing is needed, and Mary has chosen that good part, which will not be taken away from her."

---

[a] A CERTAIN VILLAGE. Bethany, two miles east of the temple in Jerusalem, on the east slope of the Mount of Olives. This was the home of Mary, Martha, and Lazarus (cf. John 11:1).

[b] DISTRACTED. Lit. "dragging all around." The expression implies that Martha was in a tumult.

[c] WITH MUCH SERVING. Martha was evidently fussing about with details that were unnecessarily elaborate.

[d] ONE THING . . . GOOD PART. Jesus was not speaking of the number of dishes to be served. The one thing necessary was exemplified by Mary, i.e., an attitude of worship and meditation, listening with an open mind and heart to Jesus' words.

107. Jesus Teaches About Prayer

Luke 11:1–13

LK Now it came to pass, as He was praying in a certain place, when He ceased, *that* one of His disciples said to Him, "Lord, [a]teach us to pray, as John also taught his disciples."

So He said to them, "When you pray, say: [b]Our Father in heaven, Hallowed be [c]Your name. Your kingdom come. Your will be done On earth as *it is* in heaven. Give us day by day our daily bread. And forgive us our sins, For we also forgive everyone who is indebted to us. And do not lead us into temptation, But deliver us from the evil one."

And He said to them, "Which of you shall have a friend, and go to him at midnight and say to him, 'Friend, lend me three loaves; for a friend of mine has come to me on his journey, and I have nothing to set before him'; and he will answer from within and say, 'Do not trouble me; the door is now shut, and [d]my children are with me in bed; I cannot rise and give to you'? I say to you, though he will not rise and give to him because he is his friend, yet because of his [e]persistence he will rise and give him as many as he needs.

"So I say to you, ask, and it will be given to you; seek, and you will find; knock, and it will be opened to you. For everyone who asks receives, and he who seeks finds, and to him who knocks it will be opened. If a son asks for bread from any father among you, will he give him a stone? Or if *he asks* for a fish, will he give him a serpent instead of a fish? Or if he asks for an egg, will he offer him a scorpion? If you then, [f]being evil, know how to give good gifts to your children, how much more will *your* heavenly Father give the Holy Spirit to those who ask Him!"

---

[a] TEACH US TO PRAY. Rabbis often composed prayers for their disciples to recite. Having seen Jesus pray many times, they knew of His love for prayer, and they knew prayer was not just the reciting of words.

[b] OUR FATHER IN HEAVEN. Virtually the same prayer was given as a model on two separate occasions by Christ, first in the Sermon on the Mount (cf. Matt. 6:9–13), and then here, in response to a direct question. That accounts for minor variations between the two versions.

[c] YOUR NAME. God's name represents all His character and attributes. Cf. Pss. 8:1, 9; 9:10; 22:22; 52:9; 115:1.

[d] MY CHILDREN ARE WITH ME IN BED. The one-room houses that were common in Israel had a common sleeping area shared by the whole family. If one person arose and lit a lamp to get bread, all would be awakened.

[e] PERSISTENCE. The word can even mean "impudence." It conveys the ideas of urgency, audacity, earnestness, boldness, and relentlessness—like the persistent asking of a desperate beggar.

[f] BEING EVIL. i.e., by nature. Cf. Matt. 7:11.

108. The Pharisees Again Make Blasphemous Claims

Luke 11:14–36

LK And He was casting out a demon, and [a]it was mute. So it was, when the demon had gone out, that [b]the mute spoke; and the multitudes marveled. But [c]some of them said, "He casts out demons by [d]Beelzebub, the ruler of the demons." Others, testing *Him,* sought from Him [e]a sign from heaven.

But He, [f]knowing their thoughts, said to them: "Every [g]kingdom divided against itself is brought to desolation, and a house *divided* against a house falls. If Satan also is divided against himself, how will his kingdom stand? Because you say I cast out demons by Beelzebub. And if I cast out demons by Beelzebub, [h]by whom do your sons cast *them* out? Therefore they will be [i]your judges. But if I

---

[a] IT WAS MUTE. i.e., the demon.

[b] THE MUTE SPOKE. i.e., the man who had been delivered.

[c] SOME OF THEM SAID. Much like His earlier encounter with various Pharisees in Galilee (cf. Matt. 12:22–45; Mark 3:20–30), Jesus is similarly accused by Pharisees in Judea. The Lord answers their blasphemous charges in much the same way as before.

[d] BEELZEBUB. Originally this referred to Baal-Zebul ("Baal, the prince"), chief god of the Philistine city of Ekron; the Israelites disdainfully referred to him as Baal-Zebub ("Lord of Flies"). Cf. 2 Kings 1:2.

[e] A SIGN FROM HEAVEN. i.e., a miraculous work of cosmological proportions, like the rearranging of the constellations or something far greater than the casting out of a demon, which they had just witnessed. Cf. Matt. 12:38.

[f] KNOWING THEIR THOUGHTS. Jesus was God with full omniscience if He used it (cf. Mark 13:32; Luke 2:52; John 2:24–25).

[g] KINGDOM DIVIDED AGAINST ITSELF. This may have been a subtle jab at the Jewish nation, a kingdom divided in the time of Jeroboam and still marked by various kinds of bitter internal strife and factionalism, right up to the destruction of Jerusalem in AD 70.

[h] BY WHOM DO YOUR SONS CAST THEM OUT? There were Jewish exorcists who claimed power to cast out demons (Acts 19:13–15). Jesus' point was that if such exorcisms could be done via satanic power, the pharisaical exorcists must be suspect as well. And in fact the evidence in Acts 19 suggests that the sons of Sceva were charlatans who employed fraud and trickery to fabricate phony exorcisms.

[i] YOUR JUDGES. i.e., witnesses against you. This seems to suggest that the fraudulent exorcisms (which had their approval) stood as a testimony against the Pharisees themselves, who disapproved of Christ's genuine exorcisms.

cast out demons [j]with the finger of God, surely the kingdom of God has come upon you. When [k]a strong man, fully armed, guards his own palace, his goods are in peace. But when [l]a stronger than he comes upon him and overcomes him, he takes from him all his armor in which he trusted, and [m]divides his spoils. [n]He who is not with Me is against Me, and he who does not gather with Me scatters.

"When an [o]unclean spirit goes out of a man, he goes through dry places, seeking rest; and finding none, he says, 'I will return to my house from which I came.' And when he comes, he finds *it* swept and put in order. Then he goes and takes with *him* seven other spirits more wicked than himself, and they enter and dwell there; and the last *state* of that man is worse than the first."

And it happened, as He spoke these things, that a certain woman from the crowd raised her voice and said to Him, "Blessed *is* the womb that bore You, and *the* breasts which nursed You!" But He said, "[p]More than that, blessed *are* those who hear the word of God and keep it!" And while the crowds were thickly gathered together, He began to say, "This is an evil generation. [q]It seeks a sign, and no sign will be given to it except the sign of Jonah the prophet. For as [r]Jonah became a sign to the Ninevites, so also the Son of Man will be to this generation. The queen of the South will rise up in the judgment with the men of this generation

---

[j] WITH THE FINGER OF GOD. In Ex. 8:19 the phony magicians of Egypt were forced to confess that Moses' miracles were genuine works of God, not mere trickery such as they had performed. Here Jesus made a similar comparison between His exorcisms and the work of the Jewish exorcists.

[k] A STRONG MAN. i.e., Satan.

[l] A STRONGER THAN HE. i.e., Christ.

[m] DIVIDES HIS SPOILS. Probably a reference to Isa. 53:12. When a demon is defeated by the power of Christ, the soul vacated by the power of darkness is taken over by Christ.

[n] HE WHO IS NOT WITH ME IS AGAINST ME. Cf. Luke 9:50.

[o] UNCLEAN SPIRIT GOES OUT. Christ was characterizing the work of the phony exorcists (cf. Luke 11:19). What appears to be a true exorcism is merely a temporary respite, after which the demon returns with seven others (Luke 11:26).

[p] MORE THAN THAT. This has the sense of, "Yes, but rather . . ." While not denying the blessedness of Mary, Christ did not countenance any tendency to elevate Mary as an object of veneration. Mary's relationship to Him as His physical mother did not confer on her any greater honor than the blessedness of those who hear and obey the word of God. Cf. Luke 1:47.

[q] IT SEEKS A SIGN. Jesus always declined to give signs on demand. Evidences were not the primary means by which He appealed to unbelievers. Cf. Luke 16:31.

[r] JONAH BECAME A SIGN. i.e., a sign of judgment to come. Jonah's emergence from the fish's belly pictured Christ's resurrection. Jesus clearly regarded Jonah's account as historically accurate. Cf. Matt. 12:39–40.

and condemn them, for she came from the ends of the earth to hear the wisdom of Solomon; and indeed a greater than Solomon *is* here. The men of Nineveh will rise up in the judgment with this generation and condemn it, for they repented at the preaching of Jonah; and indeed a greater than Jonah *is* here.

"No one, when he has lit a lamp, puts *it* in a secret place or under a basket, but on a lampstand, that those who come in may see the light. [s]The lamp of the body is the eye. Therefore, when your eye is good, your whole body also is full of light. But [t]when *your eye* is bad, your body also *is* full of darkness. Therefore take heed that the light which is in you is not darkness. If then your whole body *is* full of light, having no part dark, *the* whole *body* will be full of light, as when the bright shining of a lamp gives you light."

---

[s] THE LAMP OF THE BODY. This is a different metaphor from the one in Luke 11:33. There the lamp speaks of the Word of God; here the eye is the "lamp"—i.e., the source of light—for the body. Cf. Matt. 6:22–23.

[t] WHEN YOUR EYE IS BAD. The problem was their perception, not a lack of light. They did not need a sign; they needed hearts to believe the great display of divine power they had already seen.

109. Jesus Warns the Scribes and Pharisees

Luke 11:37–54

LK And as He spoke, a certain Pharisee asked Him to dine with him. So He went in and sat down to eat. When the Pharisee saw *it,* he marveled that [a]He had not first washed before dinner. Then the Lord said to him, "Now you Pharisees make the outside of the cup and dish clean, but your inward part is [b]full of greed and wickedness. [c]Foolish ones! Did not He who made the outside make the inside also? But rather give [d]alms of such things as you have; then indeed all things are clean to you.

"But woe to you Pharisees! For you [e]tithe mint and rue and all manner of herbs, and pass by justice and the love of God. These you ought to have done, without leaving the others undone. Woe to you Pharisees! For you love the best seats in the synagogues and [f]greetings in the marketplaces. Woe to you, scribes and Pharisees, hypocrites! For you are like [g]graves which are not seen, and the men who walk over *them* are not aware *of them.*"

Then one of the [h]lawyers answered and said to Him, "Teacher, by saying these things You reproach us also."

---

[a] HE HAD NOT FIRST WASHED. The Pharisee was concerned with ceremony, not hygiene. The Greek word for "washed" refers to a ceremonial ablution. Nothing in the law commanded such washings, but the Pharisees practiced them, believing the ritual cleansed them of any accidental ceremonial defilement. Cf. Mark 7:2–3.

[b] FULL OF GREED AND WICKEDNESS. i.e., they were preoccupied with external ceremonies but overlooked the more important issue of internal morality. Cf. Matt. 23:25.

[c] FOOLISH ONES! i.e., persons who lack understanding. This was the truth and not the sort of coarse name-calling Christ forbade in Matt. 5:22.

[d] ALMS OF SUCH THINGS AS YOU HAVE. Lit. "Give that which is within as your alms." This contrasts inner virtues with external ceremonies. Alms are to be given not for show but as an expression of a faithful heart (cf. Matt. 6:1–4)—and the true almsgiving is not the external act, but one's attitude before God.

[e] TITHE. Cf. Matt. 23:23.

[f] GREETINGS. These were ostentatious ceremonies that were more or less elaborate, depending on the rank of the person being greeted.

[g] GRAVES WHICH ARE NOT SEEN. Hidden sources of defilement. They had carefully concealed their own inward corruption, but it still was a source of defilement. Cf. Matt. 23:27.

[h] LAWYERS. i.e., scribes. Cf. Luke 10:25.

And He said, "Woe to you also, lawyers! For you load men with burdens hard to bear, and you yourselves do not touch the burdens with one of your fingers. Woe to you! For [i]you build the tombs of the prophets, and your fathers killed them. In fact, you bear witness that you approve the deeds of your fathers; for they indeed killed them, and you build their tombs. Therefore [j]the wisdom of God also said, '[k]I will send them prophets and apostles, and *some* of them they will kill and persecute,' that the blood of all the prophets which was shed from the foundation of the world may be required of this generation, from the blood of Abel to the blood of Zechariah who perished between the altar and the temple. Yes, I say to you, it shall be required of this generation.

"Woe to you lawyers! For you have taken away [l]the key of knowledge. You did not enter in yourselves, and those who were entering in you hindered."

And as He said these things to them, the scribes and the Pharisees began to assail *Him* vehemently, and to cross-examine Him about many things, lying in wait for Him, and seeking [m]to catch Him in something He might say, that they might accuse Him.

---

[i] you build the tombs of the prophets. They thought they were honoring those prophets, but in reality they had more in common with those who killed the prophets (v. 48). Cf. Matt. 23:30.

[j] the wisdom of God also said. There is no OT source for this quotation. Christ is prophetically announcing the coming judgment of God, not quoting a previously written source, but giving them a direct warning from God.

[k] I will send them prophets. Cf. Matt. 23:34–36.

[l] the key of knowledge. They had locked up the truth of the Scriptures and thrown away the key by imposing their faulty interpretations and human traditions on God's Word. Cf. Matt. 23:13.

[m] to catch. The same word is used in Greek literature for the hunting of animals.

110. Jesus Warns Against Hypocrisy

Luke 12:1–12

LK In the meantime, when an [a]innumerable multitude of people had gathered together, so that they trampled one another, He began to say to His disciples first *of all,* "Beware of the [b]leaven of the Pharisees, which is hypocrisy. For there is [c]nothing covered that will not be revealed, nor hidden that will not be known. Therefore whatever you have spoken in the dark will be heard in the light, and what you have spoken in the ear in inner rooms will be proclaimed on the housetops.

"And I say to you, My friends, do not be afraid of those who kill the body, and after that have no more that they can do. But I will show you whom you should fear: [d]Fear Him who, after He has killed, has power to cast into hell; yes, I say to you, fear Him!

"Are not five sparrows sold for [e]two copper coins? And [f]not one of them is forgotten before God. But the very hairs of your head are all numbered. Do not fear therefore; you are of more value than many sparrows.

"Also I say to you, whoever confesses Me before men, him the Son of Man also will confess [g]before the angels of God. But [h]he who denies Me before men will be denied before the angels of God.

---

[a] INNUMERABLE. The Greek word is the same from which we get the word *myriads.*

[b] LEAVEN. Cf. Matt. 16:12; Mark 8:15.

[c] NOTHING COVERED THAT WILL NOT BE REVEALED. Cf. Mark 4:22; Luke 8:17.

[d] FEAR HIM. Cf. Matt. 10:28.

[e] TWO COPPER COINS. Greek, *assarion*, a Roman coin equal to a sixteenth of a denarius. One assarius would be less than an hour's wage.

[f] NOT ONE OF THEM IS FORGOTTEN BEFORE GOD. Divine providence governs even the most inconsequential details of God's creation. He cares for all that He created, regardless of how insignificant. Cf. Matt. 10:29.

[g] BEFORE THE ANGELS OF GOD. i.e., in the day of judgment. Cf. Matt. 10:32; 25:31–34; Jude 24.

[h] HE WHO DENIES ME BEFORE MEN. This describes a soul-damning denial of Christ, not the sort of temporary wavering Peter was guilty of (Luke 22:56–62), but the sin of those who through fear, shame, neglect, delay, or love of the world reject all evidence and revelation and decline to confess Christ as Savior and King until it is too late.

"And anyone who speaks a word against the Son of Man, it will be forgiven him; but to him who [i]blasphemes against the Holy Spirit, it will not be forgiven.

"Now when they bring you to the synagogues and magistrates and authorities, [j]do not worry about how or what you should answer, or what you should say. For the Holy Spirit will teach you in that very hour what you ought to say."

---

[i] blasphemes against the Holy Spirit. Cf. Matt. 12:31–32. This was not a sin of ignorance, but a deliberate, willful, settled hostility toward Christ—exemplified by the Pharisees in Matt. 12 (on a different occasion), who attributed to Satan the work of Christ (cf. Luke 11:15).

[j] do not worry. i.e., do not be anxious. This does not suggest that ministers and teachers should forego preparation in their normal spiritual duties. To cite this passage and others like it (Matt. 10:19; Luke 21:12–15) to justify the neglect of study and meditation is to twist the meaning of Scripture. This verse is meant as a comfort for those under life-threatening persecution, not an excuse for laziness in ministry. The exact same expression is used in Luke 11:22, speaking of concern for one's material necessities. In neither context was Jesus condemning legitimate toil and preparation. He was promising the Holy Spirit's aid for times of persecution when there can be no preparation. Cf. Mark 13:11.

111. Jesus Teaches About True Wealth

Luke 12:13–34

LK Then one from the crowd said to Him, "Teacher, [a]tell my brother to divide the inheritance with me." But He said to him, "Man, [b]who made Me a judge or an arbitrator over you?"

And He said to them, "Take heed and beware of covetousness, for one's life does not consist in the abundance of the things he possesses."

Then He spoke a parable to them, saying: "The ground of a certain rich man yielded plentifully. And he thought within himself, saying, 'What shall I do, since I have no room to store my crops?' So he said, 'I will do this: I will pull down my barns and build greater, and there I will store all my crops and my goods. And I will say to my soul, "Soul, you have many goods laid up for many years; take your ease; eat, drink, *and* be merry." ' But God said to him, 'Fool! This night your soul will be required of you; then whose will those things be which you have provided?'

"So *is* he who lays up treasure for himself, and is not rich toward God."

Then [c]He said to His disciples, "Therefore I say to you, do not worry about your life, what you will eat; nor about the body, what you will put on. Life is more than food, and the body *is more* than clothing. Consider the ravens, for they neither sow nor reap, which have neither storehouse nor barn; and God feeds them. Of how much more value are you than the birds? And which of you by worrying can add one cubit to his stature? If you then are not able to do *the* least, why are you anxious for the rest? Consider the lilies, how they grow: they neither toil nor spin; and yet I say to you, even Solomon in all his glory was not arrayed like one of these. If then God so clothes the grass, which today is in the field and tomorrow is thrown into the oven, how much more *will He clothe* you, O *you* of little faith?

"And do not seek what you should eat or what you should drink, nor have an anxious mind. For all these things the nations of the world seek after, and your

---

[a] TELL MY BROTHER TO DIVIDE THE INHERITANCE. "The right of the firstborn" was a double portion of the inheritance (Deut. 21:17). Perhaps this man wanted an equal share. In any case Jesus seemed unconcerned about the implied injustice and refused the man's request to arbitrate the family dispute.

[b] WHO MADE ME A JUDGE? One of Christ's roles is that of Judge of all the earth (John 5:22), but He did not come to be an arbiter of petty earthly disputes. Settling an inheritance dispute was a matter for civil authorities.

[c] HE SAID TO HIS DISCIPLES. The instruction in these verses (Luke 12:22–31) is similar to what Jesus said in the Sermon on the Mount (Matt. 6:26–33).

Father knows that you need these things. But seek the kingdom of God, and all these things shall be added to you.

"Do not fear, little flock, for it is your Father's [d]good pleasure to give you the kingdom. [e]Sell what you have and give alms; provide yourselves [f]money bags which do not grow old, a treasure in the heavens that does not fail, where no thief approaches nor moth destroys. For where your treasure is, there [g]your heart will be also."

---

[d] good pleasure. Cf. Luke 2:14. Christ stressed the Father's tender care over His little flock as an antidote to anxiety.

[e] Sell what you have and give alms. Those who amassed earthly possessions, falsely thinking their security lay in material resources (Luke 12:16–20), needed to lay up treasure in heaven instead. Cf. Matt. 6:20. Believers in the early church did sell their goods to meet the basic needs of poorer brethren (Acts 2:44–45; 4:32–37). But this commandment is not to be twisted into an absolute prohibition of all earthly possessions. In fact Peter's words to Ananias in Acts 5:4 make it clear that the selling of one's possessions was optional.

[f] money bags which do not grow old. These purses that do not wear out (so as to lose the money) are defined as "treasure in the heavens that does not fail." The surest place to put one's money is in such a purse—in heaven, where it is safe from thieves and decay as well.

[g] your heart will be also. Where one puts his money reveals the priorities of his heart. Cf. Matt 6:21; Luke 16:1–13.

112. Warning to Be Ready for the Master's Return

Luke 12:35–48

LK "Let your waist be [a]girded and *your* lamps burning; and you yourselves be like men who wait for their master, [b]when he will return from the wedding, that when he comes and knocks they may open to him immediately. Blessed *are* those servants whom the master, when he comes, will find [c]watching. Assuredly, I say to you that he will [d]gird himself and have them sit down *to eat*, and will come and serve them. And if he should come in the [e]second watch, or come in the [f]third watch, and find *them* so, blessed are those servants. But know this, that if the master of the house had known what hour the thief would come, he would have watched and not allowed his house to be broken into. Therefore you also be ready, for the Son of Man is coming at [g]an hour you do not expect."

Then Peter said to Him, "Lord, do You speak this parable *only* to us, or to all *people?*"

And the Lord said, "Who then is that faithful and wise steward, whom *his* master will make ruler over his household, to give *them their* portion of food in due season? [h]Blessed *is* that servant whom his master will find so doing when he comes. Truly, I say to you that he will make him ruler over all that he has. But if

---

[a] GIRDED. Speaks of preparedness. Long, flowing robes would be tucked into the belt to allow freedom in which to work. Cf. Ex. 12:11; 1 Peter 1:13.

[b] WHEN HE WILL RETURN. The servants were responsible to meet him with burning torches.

[c] WATCHING. The key here is readiness at all times for Christ's return. Cf. Matt. 25:1–13.

[d] GIRD HIMSELF. i.e., he will take the servant's role and wait on them. This remarkable statement pictures Christ at His return, ministering as a Servant to believers.

[e] SECOND WATCH. 9:00 p.m. to midnight.

[f] THIRD. Midnight to 3:00 a.m.

[g] AN HOUR YOU DO NOT EXPECT. Cf. Matt. 24:36, 42–44; Luke 21:34; 1 Thess. 5:2–4; 2 Peter 3:10; Rev. 3:3; 16:15.

[h] BLESSED IS THAT SERVANT. The faithful steward pictures the genuine believer, who manages well the spiritual riches God has put in his care for the benefit of others and the careful management of the master's estate. Faithful expression of the duty of such spiritual stewardship will result in honor and reward.

that servant says in his heart, 'My master is delaying his coming,' and begins [i]to beat the male and female servants, and to eat and drink and be drunk, the master of that servant will come on a day when he is not looking for *him,* and at an hour when he is not aware, and will [j]cut him in two and appoint *him* his portion with the unbelievers. And that servant who knew his master's will, and did not prepare *himself* or do according to his will, shall be beaten [k]many with *stripes.* But he who did not know, yet committed things deserving of stripes, shall be beaten with few. For everyone to whom much is given, from him much will be required; and to whom much has been committed, of him they will ask the more."

[i] TO BEAT THE . . . SERVANTS. This wicked steward's unfaithfulness and cruel behavior illustrates the evil of an unbelieving heart.

[j] CUT HIM IN TWO. i.e., utterly destroy him. This speaks of the severity of final judgment of unbelievers.

[k] WITH MANY STRIPES . . . WITH FEW. The degree of punishment is commensurate with the extent to which the unfaithful behavior was willful. Note that ignorance is nonetheless no excuse. That there will be varying degrees of punishment in hell is clearly taught in Matt. 10:15; 11:22, 24; and Heb. 10:29.

113. Coming Division and a Call to Readiness

Luke 12:49–59

LK "I came to send [a]fire on the earth, and how I wish it were already kindled! But I have [b]a baptism to be baptized with, and how distressed I am [c]till it is accomplished! Do *you* suppose that I came to give peace on earth? I tell you, [d]not at all, but rather division. For from now on five in one house will be divided: three against two, and two against three. Father will be divided against son and son against father, mother against daughter and daughter against mother, mother-in-law against her daughter-in-law and daughter-in-law against her mother-in-law."

Then He also said to the multitudes, "[e]Whenever you see a cloud rising out of the west, immediately you say, 'A shower is coming'; and so it is. And when *you see* the south wind blow, you say, 'There will be hot weather'; and there is. Hypocrites! You can discern the face of the sky and of the earth, but how *is it* you do not discern this time?

"Yes, and why, even of yourselves, do you not judge what is right? When you go with your adversary to the magistrate, [f]make every effort along the way to settle with him, lest he drag you to the judge, the judge deliver you to the officer, and the officer throw you into prison. I tell you, you shall not depart from there till you have paid the very last [g]mite."

---

[a] FIRE. i.e., judgment. Cf. Matt. 3:11. For the connection between fire and judgment, see Isa. 66:15; Joel 2:30; Amos 1:7, 10–14; 2:2, 5; Mal. 3:2, 5; 1 Cor. 3:13; 2 Thess. 1:7–8.

[b] A BAPTISM. A baptism of suffering. Christ was referring to His death. Christian baptism symbolizes identification with Him in death, burial, and resurrection.

[c] TILL IT IS ACCOMPLISHED. Though distressed about His coming passion, it was nonetheless the work He came to do, and He set His face steadfastly to accomplish it (cf. Luke 9:51; cf. John 12:23–27).

[d] NOT AT ALL. Cf. Matt. 10:34.

[e] WHENEVER YOU SEE A CLOUD. Cf. Matt. 16:2, 3.

[f] MAKE EVERY EFFORT ALONG THE WAY. Cf. Matt. 5:25.

[g] MITE. Cf. Mark 12:42; Luke 21:2.

114. Repent or Perish

Luke 13:1–9

LK There were present at that season some who told Him about the [a]Galileans whose blood Pilate had mingled with their sacrifices. And Jesus answered and said to them, "Do you suppose that these Galileans were [b]worse sinners than all *other* Galileans, because they suffered such things? I tell you, no; but [c]unless you repent [d]you will all likewise perish. Or those eighteen on whom the tower in [e]Siloam fell and killed them, do you think that they were worse sinners than all *other* men who dwelt in Jerusalem? I tell you, no; but unless you repent you will all likewise perish."

He also spoke this parable. "A certain *man* had a [f]fig tree planted in his vineyard, and he came seeking fruit on it and found none. Then he said to the keeper

---

[a] GALILEANS WHOSE BLOOD PILATE HAD MINGLED WITH THEIR SACRIFICES. This incident is in keeping with what was known about the character of Pilate. Evidently, some worshipers from Galilee were condemned by Rome—perhaps because they were seditious zealots (cf. Matt. 10:4)—and were sought out and killed in the temple by Roman authorities while in the process of offering a sacrifice. Such a killing would have been the grossest sort of blasphemy. Incidents like this inflamed the Jews' hatred of Rome and finally led to rebellion and the destruction of Jerusalem in AD 70.

[b] WORSE SINNERS. It was the belief of many that disaster and sudden death always signified divine displeasure over particular sins (cf. Job 4:7). Those who suffered in uncommon ways were therefore assumed to be guilty of some more severe immorality (cf. John 9:2).

[c] UNLESS YOU REPENT. Jesus did not deny the connection between catastrophe and human evil, for all such afflictions ultimately stem from the curse of humanity's fallenness (Gen. 3:17–19). Furthermore, specific calamities may indeed be the fruit of certain iniquities (Prov. 24:16). But Christ challenged the people's notion that they were morally superior to those who suffered in such catastrophes. He called all to repent, for all were in danger of sudden destruction. No one is guaranteed time to prepare for death, so now is the time for repentance for all (cf. 2 Cor. 6:2).

[d] YOU WILL ALL LIKEWISE PERISH. These words prophetically warned of the approaching judgment of Israel, which culminated in the catastrophic destruction of Jerusalem in AD 70. Thousands in Jerusalem were killed by the Romans. Cf. Matt. 23:36.

[e] SILOAM. An area at the south end of the lower city of Jerusalem, where there was a well-known pool (cf. John 9:7, 11). Evidently one of the towers guarding the aqueduct collapsed, perhaps while under construction, killing some people. Again, the question in the minds of people was regarding the connection between calamity and iniquity ("worse sinners"). Jesus responded by saying that such a calamity was not God's way to single out an especially-evil group for death, but as a means of warning to all sinners. Calamitous judgment was eventually coming to all if they did not repent.

[f] FIG TREE. Often used as a symbol for Israel (cf. Matt. 21:19; Mark 11:14). In this case, however, the parable's lesson about fruitlessness applies equally to the whole nation, and to each individual soul.

of his vineyard, 'Look, for three years I have come seeking fruit on this fig tree and find none. Cut it down; why does it use up the ground?' But he answered and said to him, 'Sir, [g]let it alone this year also, until I dig around it and fertilize *it.* And if it bears fruit, *well.* But if not, after that you can cut it down.'"

---

[g] LET IT ALONE THIS YEAR. This illustrates both the intercession of Christ and the extreme patience and graciousness of the Father.

115. Jesus Heals a Woman on the Sabbath

Luke 13:10–22

LK Now He was teaching in one of the [a]synagogues on [b]the Sabbath. And behold, there was a woman who [c]had a spirit of infirmity eighteen years, and was bent over and could in no way raise *herself* up. But when Jesus saw her, [d]He called *her* to *Him* and said to her, "Woman, you are loosed from your infirmity." And He laid *His* hands on her, and immediately she was made straight, and glorified God.

But the [e]ruler of the synagogue answered with indignation, because Jesus had healed on the Sabbath; and he said to the crowd, "There are six days on which men ought to work; therefore come and be healed on them, and not on the Sabbath day."

The Lord then answered him and said, "Hypocrite! Does not each one of you on the Sabbath [f]loose his ox or donkey from the stall, and lead *it* away to water it? So ought not this woman, being [g]a daughter of Abraham, [h]whom Satan has bound—think of it—for eighteen years, be loosed from this bond on the Sab-

---

[a] SYNAGOGUES. Cf. Mark 1:21.

[b] THE SABBATH. The Pharisees' Sabbath traditions were the issue that most frequently provoked controversy in Jesus' ministry. Cf. Matt. 12:2–10; Mark 2:23–3:4; Luke 6:5–11; 14:1–5.

[c] HAD A SPIRIT OF INFIRMITY. This suggests that her physical ailment, which left her unable to stand erect, was caused by an evil spirit. However, Christ did not have to confront and drive out a demon but simply declared her loosed, so her case appears somewhat different from other cases of demonic possession He often encountered (cf. Luke 11:14).

[d] HE CALLED HER TO HIM. The healing was unsolicited; He took the initiative (cf. Luke 7:12–14). Furthermore, no special faith was required on her part or anyone else's. Jesus sometimes called for faith, but not always (cf. Mark 5:34; Luke 8:48).

[e] RULER. An eminent layman whose responsibilities included conducting meetings, caring for the building, and supervising the teaching in the synagogue (cf. Matt. 9:18; Mark 5:38; Luke 8:41).

[f] LOOSE HIS OX. Nothing in Scripture forbade either the watering of an ox or the healing of the sick (cf. Matt. 12:2–3, 10; Luke 6:9). Their Sabbath traditions actually placed a higher value on animals than on people in distress—and therefore corrupted the whole purpose of the Sabbath (Mark 2:27).

[g] A DAUGHTER OF ABRAHAM. She was a Jew.

[h] WHOM SATAN HAS BOUND. Job's physical ailments and other disasters were also inflicted by Satan, with divine permission. This woman had apparently been permitted to suffer, not because of any evil she had done, but so that the glory of God might be manifest in her (cf. John 9:3).

bath?" And when He said these things, all His adversaries were put to shame; and all the multitude rejoiced for all the glorious things that were done by Him.

Then He said, "What is the kingdom of God like? And to what shall I compare it? It is [i]like a mustard seed, which a man took and put in his garden; and it grew and became a large tree, and the birds of the air nested in its branches."

And again He said, "To what shall I liken the kingdom of God? It is like leaven, which a woman took and hid in three measures of meal till it was all leavened."

And He went [j]through the cities and villages, teaching, and [k]journeying toward Jerusalem.

---

[i] like a mustard seed. Cf. Matt. 13:32–33.

[j] through the cities and villages. Luke's geographical points of reference are often vague; the readers he had in mind were probably largely unfamiliar with Palestinian geography anyway. Matthew 19:1; Mark 10:1; and John 10:40 all say that Christ moved His ministry to the region east of the Jordan, known as Perea. That move probably took place at about this point in Luke's narrative. Therefore the cities and villages He traveled through may have included places in both Judea and Perea.

[k] journeying toward Jerusalem. During His ministry in Judea to Perea, Christ actually went to Jerusalem on more than one occasion—at least once for the Feast of Tabernacles (John 7:11–8:59), another time for the Feast of Dedication (John 9:1–10:39), and another time when He raised Lazarus (John 11). Luke's focus was on Christ's constant progression toward His final trek to Jerusalem for the express purpose of dying there—and he therefore described all Christ's traveling as one long trek toward Jerusalem. Cf. Luke 9:51; 17:11.

116. Jesus Heals a Man Born Blind

John 9:1–12

JN Now as *Jesus* passed by, [a]He saw a man who was blind from birth. And His disciples asked Him, saying, "Rabbi, [b]who sinned, this man or his parents, that he was born blind?"

Jesus answered, "[c]Neither this man nor his parents sinned, but that the works of God should be revealed in him. I must work the works of Him who sent Me [d]while it is day; [e]*the* night is coming when no one can work. As long as I am in the world, [f]I am the light of the world."

When He had said these things, He spat on the ground and [g]made clay with the saliva; and He anointed the eyes of the blind man with the clay. And He said

---

[a] HE SAW A MAN WHO WAS BLIND. In this passage (John 9:1–12) Jesus performed a miracle by recreating the eyes of a man who was born with congenital blindness. Four features highlight this healing: (1) the problem that precipitated the healing (v. 1); (2) the purpose for the man's being born blind (vv. 2–5); (3) the power that healed him (vv. 6, 7); and (4) the perplexity of the people who saw the healing (vv. 8–12).

[b] WHO SINNED. While sin may be a cause of suffering, as clearly indicated in Scripture (cf. Num. 12; 1; John 5:14; Cor. 11:30; James 5:15), it is not always the case necessarily (see Job; 2 Cor. 12:7; Gal. 4:13). Like most first-century Jews, the disciples thought that sin was the primary, if not exclusive, cause of all suffering. In this instance, however, Jesus made it clear that personal sin was not the reason for the blindness.

[c] NEITHER THIS MAN NOR HIS PARENTS SINNED. Jesus did not deny the general connection between sin and suffering but refuted the idea that personal acts of sin were the direct cause. God's sovereignty and purposes play a part in such matters, as is clear from Job 1, 2.

[d] WHILE IT IS DAY. Jesus meant as long as He was still on earth with His disciples. The phrase does not imply that Christ somehow ceased to be the light of the world once He ascended but that the light shone most brightly among men when He was on the earth doing the Father's will (cf. John 8:12).

[e] THE NIGHT IS COMING. Cf. John 1:4–5; 1 John 1:5–7. The darkness has special reference to the period when Jesus was taken from His disciples during His crucifixion.

[f] I AM THE LIGHT OF THE WORLD. cf. John 1:5, 9; 3:19; 8:12; 12:35, 46. Not only was Jesus spiritually the light of the world, but He would also provide the means of physical light for this blind man.

[g] MADE CLAY WITH THE SALIVA. As He had done when He originally fashioned Adam out of the dust of the earth (Gen. 2:7), Jesus may have used the clay to fashion a new pair of eyes.

to him, "Go, [h]wash in the pool of Siloam" (which is translated, Sent). So he went and washed, and came back seeing.

Therefore the neighbors and those who previously had seen that he was blind said, "Is not this [i]he who sat and begged?" Some said, "This is he." Others *said,* "He is like him." He said, "I am *he.*"

Therefore they said to him, "How were your eyes opened?" He answered and said, "A Man called Jesus made clay and anointed my eyes and said to me, 'Go to the pool of Siloam and wash.' So I went and washed, and I received sight."

Then they said to him, "Where is He?" He said, "I do not know."

[h] wash in the pool of Siloam. The Greek term *Siloam* is from the Hebrew word for "sent." The pool of Siloam was southeast of the original City of David. Water flowed into it from the spring of Gihon in the Kidron Valley by way of Hezekiah's tunnel. It may be identified with the "lower pool" or "old pool" mentioned in Isa. 22:9, 11. Water for the water-pouring rites at the Feast of Tabernacles was drawn from this pool (cf. John 7:37–39).

[i] he who sat and begged. In ancient times such severe physical deformities as congenital blindness sentenced a person to begging as the only means of support (see Acts 3:1–7). The drastic change in the healed man caused many to faithlessly believe that he was not the person born blind.

117. The Pharisees Excommunicate the Formerly Blind Man

John 9:13–34

JN [a]They brought him who formerly was blind to [b]the Pharisees. Now it was a Sabbath when Jesus made the clay and opened his eyes. [c]Then the Pharisees also asked him again how he had received his sight. He said to them, "He put clay on my eyes, and I washed, and I see."

Therefore some of the Pharisees said, "This Man is [d]not from God, because He does not keep the Sabbath." Others said, "How can a man who is a sinner do such signs?" And there was [e]a division among them.

They said to the blind man again, "What do you say about Him because He opened your eyes?" He said, "[f]He is a prophet." But the Jews did not believe concerning him, that he had been blind and received his sight, until they [g]called the parents of him who had received his sight. And they asked them, saying, "Is this your son, who you say was born blind? How then does he now see?" His parents answered them and said, "We know that this is our son, and that he was born

[a] THEY. This was a reference to the blind man's "neighbors and those who previously had seen that he was blind" (John 8:8).

[b] TO THE PHARISEES. The people brought the blind man to the Pharisees most likely because the miracle had happened on the Sabbath, and they were aware that the Pharisees reacted negatively to those who violated the Sabbath (cf. John 5:1–15).

[c] THEN THE PHARISEES . . . This section in the story of the healing of the blind man (John 9:13–34) reveals some key characteristics of willful unbelief: (1) unbelief sets false standards; (2) unbelief always wants more evidence but never has enough; (3) unbelief does biased research on a purely subjective basis; (4) unbelief rejects the facts; and (5) unbelief is self-centered. John included this section on the dialogue of the Pharisees with the blind man most likely for two reasons: (1) the dialogue carefully demonstrates the character of willful and fixed unbelief, and (2) the story confirms the first great schism between the synagogue and Christ's new followers. The blind man was the first known person cast out of the synagogue because he chose to follow Christ (cf. John 16:1–3).

[d] NOT FROM GOD. The reasoning may have been that since Jesus violated their interpretation of the Sabbath law, He could not be the promised Prophet of God (Deut. 13:1–5).

[e] A DIVISION. Earlier the crowds were divided in opinion regarding Jesus (John 7:40–43); here the authorities also became divided.

[f] HE IS A PROPHET. While the blind man saw clearly that Jesus was more than a mere man, the sighted but obstinate Pharisees were spiritually blind to that truth. Blindness in the Bible is a metaphor for spiritual darkness, i.e., inability to discern God or His truth (2 Cor. 4:3–6; Col. 1:12–14).

[g] CALLED THE PARENTS. While neighbors may have been confused about the man's identity, the parents would know if this was their own son. The authorities completely disregarded the witness of the healed man himself.

blind; but by what means he now sees we do not know, or who opened his eyes we do not know. He is of age; ask him. He will speak for himself."

His parents said these *things* because they feared the Jews, for the Jews had agreed already that if anyone confessed *that* He *was* Christ, he would be put out of the synagogue. Therefore his parents said, "He is of age; ask him." So they again called the man who was blind, and said to him, "[h]Give God the glory! [i]We know that this Man is a sinner."

He answered and said, "Whether He is a sinner *or not* I do not know. One thing I know: that though I was blind, now I see." Then they said to him again, "What did He do to you? How did He open your eyes?"

He answered them, "I told you already, and you did not listen. Why do you want to hear *it* again? [j]Do you also want to become His disciples?" Then they reviled him and said, "[k]You are His disciple, but we are Moses' disciples. We know that God spoke to Moses; *as for* this *fellow,* we do not know where He is from."

[l]The man answered and said to them, "Why, this is a marvelous thing, that you do not know where He is from; yet He has opened my eyes! Now we know that God does not hear sinners; but if anyone is a worshiper of God and does His will, He hears him. Since the world began it has been unheard of that anyone opened the eyes of one who was born blind. If this Man were not from God, He could do nothing."

They answered and said to him, "You were completely born in sins, and [m]are you teaching us?" And they cast him out.

---

[h] GIVE GOD THE GLORY! The authorities invoked God in their attempt to coerce the man to say that Jesus was a sinner because He violated their traditions and threatened their influence (cf. Josh. 7:19).

[i] WE KNOW THAT THIS MAN IS A SINNER. Enough unanimity existed among the religious authorities to conclude that Jesus was a sinner (cf. John 8:46). Because of this already-predetermined opinion, they refused to accept any of the testimony that a miracle had actually taken place.

[j] DO YOU ALSO WANT TO BECOME HIS DISCIPLES? In order to forcefully emphasize their hypocrisy, the healed man resorted to biting sarcasm when he suggested they desired to be Jesus' disciples.

[k] YOU ARE HIS DISCIPLE, BUT WE ARE MOSES'. At this point the meeting degenerated into a shouting match of insults. The healed man's wit had exposed the bias of his inquisitors. As far as the authorities were concerned, the conflict between Jesus and Moses was irreconcilable. If the healed man defended Jesus, then such defense could only mean that he was Jesus' disciple.

[l] THE MAN ANSWERED AND SAID. The healed man demonstrated more spiritual insight and common sense than all of the religious authorities combined who sat in judgment of Jesus and him. His penetrating wit focused in on their intractable unbelief. His logic was that such an extraordinary miracle could only indicate that Jesus was from God, for the Jews believed that God responds in proportion to the righteous character of the one praying (see Job 27:9; 35:13; Pss. 66:18; 109:7; Prov. 15:29; Isa. 1:15; cf. 14:13, 14; 16:23–27; 1 John 3:21–22). The greatness of the miracle could only indicate that Jesus was actually from God.

[m] ARE YOU TEACHING US? The Pharisees were incensed with the man, and their anger prevented them from seeing the penetrating insight that the uneducated, healed man had demonstrated. The phrase also revealed their ignorance of Scripture, for the OT indicated that the coming messianic age would be evidenced by restoration of sight to the blind (Isa. 29:18; 35:5; 42:7; cf. Matt. 11:4, 5; Luke 4:18–19).

118. The Formerly Blind Man Receives Spiritual Sight

John 9:35–41

JN [a]Jesus heard that they had cast him out; and when He had found him, He said to him, "[b]Do you believe in the [c]Son of God?"

He answered and said, "Who is He, [d]Lord, that I may believe in Him?" And Jesus said to him, "You have both seen Him and it is He who is talking with you." Then he said, "Lord, I believe!" And he worshiped Him.

And Jesus said, "[e]For judgment I have come into this world, that [f]those who do not see may see, and that [g]those who see may be made blind."

Then *some* of the Pharisees who were with Him heard these words, and said to Him, [h]"Are we blind also?" Jesus said to them, "If you were blind, you would have no sin; but now you say, 'We see.' Therefore [i]your sin remains."

---

[a] JESUS HEARD. While John 9:1–34 dealt with Jesus' restoration of physical sight in the blind man, this section (John 9:35–41) featured Jesus bringing spiritual "sight" to him.

[b] DO YOU BELIEVE. Jesus invited the man to believe in Him. Jesus placed great emphasis on public acknowledgment of who He was and confession of faith in Him (Matt. 10:32; Luke 12:8).

[c] SON OF GOD. The correct reading, based on the best manuscripts, is Son of Man (cf. John 1:51; 3:13, 14; 5:27; 6:27, 53, 62; 8:28).

[d] LORD. The word here should be understood not as an indication that he understood Jesus' deity but as meaning "sir." Since the blind man had not yet seen Jesus, he did not recognize Jesus at first as the One who healed him.

[e] FOR JUDGMENT. Not that His purpose was to condemn, but rather to save (Luke 19:10; John 12:47). However, those who reject will be judged (cf. John 3:16–21). The last part of this verse is taken from Isa. 6:10; 42:19 (cf. Mark 4:12).

[f] THOSE WHO DO NOT SEE. Those people who know they are in spiritual darkness.

[g] THOSE WHO SEE. Refers in an ironic way to those who think they are in the light but are not (cf. Mark 2:17; Luke 5:31).

[h] "ARE WE BLIND ALSO?" Apparently Jesus found the man in a public place, where the Pharisees were present listening.

[i] YOUR SIN REMAINS. Jesus had particular reference to the sin of unbelief and rejection of Him as Messiah and Son of God. If they knew their lostness and darkness and cried out for spiritual light, they would no longer be guilty of the sin of unbelief in Christ. But satisfied that their darkness was light and continuing in rejection of Christ, their sin remained. Cf. Matt. 6:22–23.

119. Jesus Is the Good Shepherd

John 10:1–21

JN "[a]Most assuredly, I say to you, he who does not enter the [b]sheepfold by the door, but climbs up some other way, the same is a thief and a robber. But he who enters by the door is the shepherd of the sheep. To him [c]the doorkeeper opens, and [d]the sheep hear his voice; and [e]he calls his own sheep by name and leads them out. And when he brings out his own sheep, he goes before them; and [f]the sheep follow him, for they know his voice. Yet they will by no means follow a stranger, but will flee from him, for they do not know the voice of strangers."

Jesus used this [g]illustration, but they did not understand the things which He

---

[a] MOST ASSUREDLY, I SAY TO YOU. These words begin Jesus' discourse (in John 10:1–39) on Himself as the "Good Shepherd." This discourse flowed directly from John 9, as Jesus continued to talk to the very same people. The problem of John 9 was that Israel was led by false shepherds who drew them astray from the true knowledge and kingdom of Messiah (9:39–41). In John 10 Jesus declared Himself to be the "Good Shepherd" who was appointed by His Father as Savior and King, in contrast to the false shepherds of Israel who were self-appointed and self-righteous (Ps. 23:1; Isa. 40:11; Jer. 3:15; cf. Isa. 56:9–12; Jer. 23:1–4; 25:32–38; Ezek. 34:1–31; Zech. 11:16).

[b] SHEEPFOLD. Jesus spoke in John 10 using a lengthy illustration drawn from the tending of sheep. The sheep were kept in a pen, which had a gate through which the sheep entered and left. The shepherd engaged a "doorkeeper" (v. 3) or "hireling" (v. 12) as an undershepherd to guard the gate. The shepherd entered through that gate. But those who wanted to steal or harm the sheep would attempt entrance by another way. The words of Ezek. 34 most likely form the background to Jesus' teaching, since God decried the false shepherds of Israel (i.e., the spiritual leaders of the nation) for not caring properly for the flock of Israel (i.e., the nation). The gospels themselves contain extensive sheep/shepherd imagery (see Matt. 9:36; Mark 6:34; 14:27; Luke 15:1–7).

[c] THE DOORKEEPER. The doorkeeper was a hired undershepherd who recognized the true shepherd of the flock, opened the gate for Him, assisted the shepherd in caring for the flock, and especially guarded them at night.

[d] THE SHEEP HEAR HIS VOICE. Near Eastern shepherds stand at different locations outside the sheep pen, sounding out their own unique calls which their sheep recognize. As a result the sheep gather around the shepherd.

[e] HE CALLS HIS OWN SHEEP BY NAME. This shepherd goes even further by calling each sheep by its own special name. Jesus' point is that He comes to the fold of Israel and calls out those who belong to Him. In some way, they are already His sheep even before He calls them by name (see vv. John 6:37, 39, 44, 64, 65; 10:25–27; 17:6, 9, 24; 18:9).

[f] THE SHEEP FOLLOW HIM. In contrast to Western shepherds who drive their flocks from behind, Near Eastern shepherds lead their sheep, using their voice to prompt the sheep to follow. This draws a remarkable picture of the believer's relationship to Christ.

[g] ILLUSTRATION. The word here is best translated "illustration" or "figure of speech" and conveys the idea that something cryptic or enigmatic is intended in it. It is used again in John 16:25, 29, but not in the Synoptic Gospels. Having given the illustration (John 10:1–5), Jesus then began to draw salient spiritual truth from it.

spoke to them. Then Jesus said to them again, "Most assuredly, I say to you, I am the door of the sheep. All who *ever* came before Me are thieves and robbers, but the sheep did not hear them. [h]I am the door. [i]If anyone enters by Me, he will be saved, and will go in and out and find pasture. The thief does not come except to steal, and to kill, and to destroy. I have come that they may have life, and that they may have *it* more abundantly.

"[j]I am the good shepherd. The good shepherd [k]gives His life for the sheep. But a hireling, *he who is* not the shepherd, one who does not own the sheep, [l]sees the wolf coming and leaves the sheep and flees; and the wolf catches the sheep and scatters them. The hireling flees because he is a hireling and does not care about the sheep. I am the good shepherd; and I know My *sheep,* and am known by My own. As the Father knows Me, even so I know the Father; and I lay down My life for the sheep. And other sheep I have which are [m]not of this fold; them also I must bring, and they will hear My voice; and there will be one flock *and* one shepherd.

"Therefore My Father loves Me, because I lay down My life that I may take it again. No one takes it from Me, but I lay it down of Myself. I have power to lay it

---

[h] I AM THE DOOR. This is the third of seven "I AM" statements of Jesus (see John 6:35; 8:12). Here, He changes the metaphor slightly. In John 10:1–5 He was the shepherd; in these verses He is the gate. While in vv. 1–5 the shepherd led the sheep out of the pen, here He is the entrance to the pen (v. 9) that leads to proper pasture. This section echoes Jesus' words in John 14:6 that He is the only way to the Father. His point is that He serves as the sole means to approach the Father and partake of God's promised salvation. As some Near Eastern shepherds slept at night in the gateway to guard the sheep, Jesus here pictures Himself as the gate.

[i] IF ANYONE ENTERS BY ME. A proverbial way of indicating that belief in Jesus as the Messiah and Son of God is the only way of being "saved" from sin and hell and receiving eternal life. Only Jesus Christ is the one true source for the knowledge of God and the one basis for spiritual security.

[j] I AM THE GOOD SHEPHERD. Jesus picked up another expression from John 10:1–5, i.e., He is the "good shepherd" in contrast to the present evil leadership of Israel (John 9:40–41). This is the fourth of seven "I AM" statements of Jesus (see John 6:35; 8:12; 10:7, 9;). The term "good" has the idea of "noble" and stands in contrast to the "hireling" who cares only for self-interest.

[k] GIVES HIS LIFE FOR THE SHEEP. This is a reference to Jesus' substitutionary death for sinners on the cross. Cf. John 6:51; 10:15; 11:50–51; 17:19; 18:14.

[l] SEES THE WOLF COMING . . . FLEES. The hireling (or hired hand) likely represents religious leaders who pretend to care for the flock in good times but who abandon the sheep when danger comes. They stand in contrast to Jesus, who laid down His life for His flock (see John 15:13).

[m] NOT OF THIS FOLD. This refers to Gentiles who will obey His voice and become a part of the church (cf. Rom. 1:16). Jesus did not die only for Jews (cf. John 10:1–3), but also non-Jews whom He will make into one new body, the church (cf. John 11:51, 52; Eph. 2:11–22).

down, and I have power to [n]take it again. This command I have received from My Father."

Therefore there was [o]a division again among the Jews because of these sayings. And many of them said, "He has a demon and is mad. Why do you listen to Him?" Others said, "These are not the words of one who has a demon. Can a demon open the eyes of the blind?"

---

[n] TAKE IT AGAIN. Jesus repeated this phrase twice in these two verses, indicating that His sacrificial death was not the end. His resurrection followed in demonstration of His messiahship and deity (Rom. 1:4). His death and resurrection resulted in His ultimate glorification (John 12:23; 17:5) and the outpouring of the Holy Spirit (John 7:37–39; Acts 2:16–39).

[o] A DIVISION AMONG THE JEWS. The Jews once again had a mixed reaction to Jesus' words (see John 7:12–13). While some charged Him with demon possession (cf. Matt. 12:22–32; John 7:20; 8:48), others concluded His works and words were a demonstration of God's sanction upon Him.

120. The Jews Attempt to Stone Jesus

John 10:22–39

JN Now it was the [a]Feast of Dedication in Jerusalem, and it was winter. And Jesus walked in the temple, in Solomon's porch. Then the Jews surrounded Him and said to Him, "How long do You keep us in doubt? If You are the Christ, [b]tell us plainly."

Jesus answered them, "I told you, and you do not believe. The works that I do in My Father's name, they bear witness of Me. But you do not believe, because you are not of My sheep, as I said to you. My sheep hear My voice, and I know them, and they follow Me. And I give them eternal life, and they shall never perish; [c]neither shall anyone snatch them out of My hand. My Father, [d]who has given *them* to Me, is greater than all; and no one is able to snatch *them* out of My Father's hand. [e]I and *My* Father are one."

....

[a] Feast of Dedication. The Jewish celebration of Hanukkah, which celebrates the Israelite victory over the Syrian leader Antiochus Epiphanes, who persecuted Israel. In ca. 170 BC he conquered Jerusalem and desecrated the Jewish temple by displacing the altar of God with a pagan abomination. Under the leadership of an old priest named Mattathias (his family would become the Hasmonean dynasty), the Jews fought guerrilla warfare (known as the Maccabean Revolt-166–142 BC) against Syria and freed the temple and the land from Syrian dominance until 63 BC, when Rome (Pompey) took control of the region. It was in 164 BC on 25 Chislev (December approximately) that the Jews liberated the temple and rededicated it. The celebration is also known as the "Feast of Lights" on account of the lamps and candles lit in Jewish homes to commemorate the event. It was winter. John indicated by this phrase that the cold weather drove Jesus to walk on the eastern side of the temple in the sheltered area of Solomon's porch, which after the resurrection became the regular gathering place of Christians where they would proclaim the gospel (cf. Acts 3:11; 5:12).

[b] tell us plainly. In light of the context of John 10:31–39, the Jews were not seeking merely for clarity and understanding regarding who Jesus was, but rather wanted Him to declare openly that He was Messiah in order to justify attacking Him.

[c] neither shall anyone snatch them ... no one is able to snatch them. Jesus' sheep are secure because He is the Good Shepherd, possessing the power to keep them safe. Neither thieves and robbers (John 10:1, 8) nor the wolf (John 10:12) can harm them. John 10:29 makes clear that the Father ultimately stands behind the sheep's security, for no one is able to steal from God, who is in sovereign control of all things (Col. 3:3). No stronger passage in the OT or NT exists for the absolute, eternal security of every true Christian. Cf. Rom. 8:31–39.

[d] who has given them to Me. This clearly indicates that God has chosen His sheep, and it is they who believe and follow (cf. John 6:37–40, 44, 65; 10:3, 16).

[e] I and My Father are one. Both Father and Son are committed to the perfect protection and preservation of Jesus' sheep. The sentence, stressing the united purpose and action of both in the security and safety of the flock, presupposes unity of nature and essence (see John 5:17–23; 17:22).

Then the Jews [f]took up stones again to stone Him. Jesus answered them, "Many good works I have shown you from My Father. For which of those works do you stone Me?"

The Jews answered Him, saying, "For a good work we do not stone You, but for blasphemy, and because You, being a Man, [g]make Yourself God." Jesus answered them, "[h]Is it not written in your law, 'I said, "You are gods" '? If He called them gods, to whom the word of God came (and the [i]Scripture cannot be broken), do you say of Him whom the Father sanctified and sent into the world, 'You are blaspheming,' because I said, 'I am the Son of God'? If I do not do the works of My Father, do not believe Me; but if I do, though you do not believe Me, [j]believe the works, that you may know and believe that the Father *is* in Me, and I in Him."

Therefore they sought again to seize Him, but He escaped out of their hand.

---

[f] TOOK UP STONES TO STONE HIM. For the third time John records that the Jews attempted to stone Jesus (see John 5:18; 8:59). Jesus' assertion (John 10:30) that He was One with the Father affirmed His claim to deity and caused the people to seek His execution (v. 33). Although the OT permitted stoning in certain instances (e.g., Lev. 24:16), the Romans reserved the right of capital punishment for themselves (John 18:31). Nevertheless, incensed by Jesus' claims, some of the Jews attempted a mob action in lieu of legal proceedings (see Acts 7:54–60).

[g] MAKE YOURSELF GOD. There was no doubt in the minds of those Jews that Jesus was claiming to be God (cf. John 5:18).

[h] IS IT NOT WRITTEN. Quoted from Ps. 82:6, where God calls some unjust judges "gods" and pronounces calamity against them. This is an argument from the lesser to the greater. If mere men could, in some sense, be referred to as "gods," why would anyone object to the Son of God Himself being called by that title?

[i] SCRIPTURE CANNOT BE BROKEN. An affirmation of the absolute accuracy and authority of Scripture (cf. Matt. 5:17–19).

[j] BELIEVE THE WORKS. Jesus did not expect to be believed merely on His own assertions. Since He did the same things that the Father does (cf. John 5:19), His enemies should consider this in their evaluation of Him. The implication is, however, that they were so blind to the truth that they could not recognize the works of the Father or the One whom the Father sent (see also John 14:10–11).

121. Jesus Ministers in Judea and Perea

Luke 13:23–30; John 10:40–42

JN And [a]He went away again beyond the Jordan [b]to the place where John was baptizing at first, and there He stayed. Then many came to Him and said, "John performed no sign, but all the things that John spoke about this Man were true." And many believed in Him there.

LK Then one said to Him, "Lord, [c]are there few who are saved?" And He said to them, " [d]Strive to enter through the narrow gate, for [e]many, I say to you, will seek to enter and will not be able. When once the Master of the house has risen up and shut the door, and you begin to stand outside and knock at the door, saying, 'Lord, Lord, open for us,' and He will answer and say to you, ' [f]I do not know you, where you are from,' then you will begin to say, 'We ate and drank in Your presence, and

---

[a] HE WENT AWAY AGAIN BEYOND THE JORDAN. Because of the increasing hostility (John 10:39), Jesus went from the region of Judea into the unpopulated area across the Jordan.

[b] TO THE PLACE WHERE JOHN WAS BAPTIZING AT FIRST. Cf. Matt. 3:1–6; Mark 1:2–6; Luke 3:3–6. This is probably a reference to either Perea or Batanea, the general area in the tetrarchy of Philip in the east and northeast of the Sea of Galilee. The statement is ironic, since the area where John first began became the last area in which Jesus stayed before He left for Jerusalem and crucifixion. The people remembered John's testimony to Christ and affirmed their faith in Him.

[c] ARE THERE FEW WHO ARE SAVED? That question may have been prompted by a number of factors. The great multitudes that had once followed Christ were subsiding to a faithful few (cf. John 6:66). Great crowds still came to hear (Luke 14:25), but committed followers were increasingly scarce. Moreover, Christ's messages often seemed designed to discourage the half-hearted (cf. Luke 14:33). And He Himself had stated that the way is so narrow that few find it (Matt. 7:14). This contradicted the Jewish belief that all Jews, except for tax collectors and other notorious sinners, would be saved. Christ's reply once again underscored the difficulty of entering at the narrow gate. After the resurrection only 120 disciples gathered in the upper room in Jerusalem (Acts 1:15), and only about 500 in Galilee (1 Cor. 15:6; cf. Matt. 28:16; Luke 24:34).

[d] STRIVE. This signifies a great struggle against conflict. Christ was not suggesting that anyone could merit heaven by striving for it. No matter how rigorously they labored, sinners could never save themselves. Salvation is solely by grace, not by works (Eph. 2:8, 9). But entering the narrow gate is nonetheless difficult because of its cost in terms of human pride, because of the sinner's natural love for sin, and because of the world's and Satan's opposition to the truth. Cf. Matt. 11:12; Luke 16:16.

[e] MANY . . . WILL SEEK TO ENTER. i.e., at the judgment, when many will protest that they deserve entrance into heaven (cf. Matt. 7:21–23).

[f] I DO NOT KNOW YOU. Cf. Matt. 7:23; 25:12. Clearly, no relationship ever existed, though they had deluded themselves into thinking they knew the owner of the house. Despite their protests he repeated his denial emphatically.

You taught in our streets.' But He will say, 'I tell you I do not know you, where you are from. Depart from Me, all you workers of iniquity.' There will be [g]weeping and gnashing of teeth, when you see Abraham and Isaac and Jacob and all the prophets in the kingdom of God, and yourselves thrust out. [h]They will come from the east and the west, from the north and the south, and sit down in the kingdom of God. And indeed there are [i]last who will be first, and there are first who will be last."

[g] weeping and gnashing of teeth. Cf. Matt. 22:13.

[h] They will come. By including people from the four corners of the earth, Jesus made it clear that even Gentiles would be invited to the heavenly banquet table. This was contrary to prevailing rabbinical thought, but perfectly consistent with the OT Scriptures (Ps. 107:3; Isa. 66:18–19; Mal. 1:11). Cf. Mark 13:27; Luke 2:31.

[i] last . . . first . . . first . . . last. Cf. Matt. 20:16; Luke 14:11. In this context the saying seems to contrast Jews ("the first") and Gentiles ("the last").

122. Jesus Mourns over Jerusalem

Luke 13:31–35

LK On that very day some Pharisees came, saying to Him, "Get out and [a]depart from here, for Herod wants to kill You."

And He said to them, "Go, tell [b]that fox, 'Behold, I cast out demons and perform cures [c]today and tomorrow, and the third *day* I shall [d]be perfected.' Nevertheless I must journey today, tomorrow, and the *day* following; for [e]it cannot be that a prophet should perish outside of Jerusalem.

"[f]O Jerusalem, Jerusalem, the one who kills the prophets and stones those who are sent to her! How often [g]I wanted to gather your children together, as a

---

[a] DEPART FROM HERE. Herod Antipas ruled Galilee and Perea (cf. Matt. 2:22). Christ was probably either approaching Perea or ministering there already. The Pharisees—no friends of Herod themselves—may have warned Christ because they hoped the threat of violence from Herod would either silence Him—or drive Him back to Judea, where the Sanhedrin would have jurisdiction over Him.

[b] THAT FOX. Some have suggested that Jesus' use of this expression is hard to reconcile with Ex. 22:28; Eccl. 10:20; and Acts 23:5. However, those verses apply to everyday discourse. Prophets, speaking as mouthpieces of God and with divine authority, were often commissioned to rebuke leaders publicly (cf. Isa. 1:23; Ezek. 22:27; Hos. 7:3–7; Zeph. 3:3). Since Jesus spoke with perfect divine authority, He had every right to speak of Herod in such terms. Rabbinical writings often used "the fox" to signify someone who was both crafty and worthless. The Pharisees, who trembled at Herod's power, must have been astonished at Christ's boldness.

[c] TODAY AND TOMORROW, AND THE THIRD DAY. This expression signified only that Christ was on His own divine timetable; it was not meant to lay out a literal three-day schedule. Expressions like this were common in Semitic usage and seldom were employed in a literal sense to specify precise intervals of time. Cf. Matt. 12:40.

[d] BE PERFECTED. i.e., by death, in the finishing of His work. Cf. Heb. 2:10; John 17:4–5; 19:30. Herod was threatening to kill Him, but no one could kill Christ before His time (John 10:17–18).

[e] IT CANNOT BE. Not all prophets who were martyred died in Jerusalem, of course. John the Baptist, for example, was beheaded by Herod, probably at Herod's palace in Tiberias. This saying was probably a familiar proverb, like the adage in Matt. 13:57; Luke 4:24. The statement is full of irony, noting that most of the OT prophets were martyred at the hands of the Israelites, not by foreign enemies. Luke's inclusion of this saying underscores his theme in this section of his gospel—Jesus' relentless journey to Jerusalem for the purpose of dying (cf. Luke 9:51).

[f] O JERUSALEM, JERUSALEM. There is great tenderness in these words, as seen in the imagery of a hen with chickens. This outpouring of divine compassion foreshadows His weeping over the city as He approached it for the final time (Luke 19:41). Clearly, these are deep and sincere emotions (cf. Matt. 9:36).

[g] I WANTED . . . BUT YOU WERE NOT WILLING. Lit. "I willed, but you willed not." Christ's repeated expressions of grief over the plight of Jerusalem do not diminish the reality of His absolute sovereignty over all that happens. Nor should the truth of divine sovereignty be used to depreciate the sincerity of His compassion. Cf. Matt. 23:37.

hen *gathers* her brood under *her* wings, but you were not willing! See! [h]Your house is left to you desolate; and assuredly, I say to you, you shall not see Me until *the time* comes when you say, '[i]Blessed is He who comes in the name of the LORD!' "

[h] YOUR HOUSE IS LEFT TO YOU DESOLATE. This account of Luke's clearly falls at an earlier point in Christ's ministry than the parallel account in Matt. 23:37–39, which took place in the temple during Christ's final days in Jerusalem. The wording of the two laments is nonetheless virtually identical. Here Christ delivers prophetically the same message He would later pronounce as a final judgment.

[i] BLESSED . . . This quotation is from Ps. 118:26.

123. Jesus Heals a Man with Dropsy on the Sabbath

Luke 14:1–24

LK Now it happened, as He went into the house of one of the rulers of the Pharisees to eat bread on the [a]Sabbath, that they [b]watched Him closely. And behold, there was a certain man before Him who had [c]dropsy. And Jesus, answering, spoke to the [d]lawyers and Pharisees, saying, "[e]Is it lawful to heal on the Sabbath?" But they kept silent. And He took *him* and healed him, and let him go.

Then He answered them, saying, "Which of you, having [f]a donkey or an ox that has fallen into a pit, will not immediately pull him out on the Sabbath day?" And they could not answer Him regarding these things.

So He told a parable to those who were invited, when He noted how they chose the [g]best places, saying to them: "When you are invited by anyone to a wedding feast, do not sit down in the best place, lest one more honorable than you be invited by him; and he who invited you and him come and say to you, 'Give place to this man,' and then you begin with shame to take the lowest place. But when you are invited, go and sit down in the lowest place, so that when he who invited you comes he may say to you, 'Friend, go up higher.' Then you will have glory in

---

[a] SABBATH. Cf. Luke 13:10. Luke shows Christ healing on the Sabbath more frequently than any of the other gospels. Christ seems to have favored the Sabbath as a day for doing acts of mercy.

[b] WATCHED HIM CLOSELY. Evidently the Pharisee had less than honorable motives for inviting Him to a meal.

[c] DROPSY. A condition where fluid is retained in the tissues and cavities of the body—often caused by kidney or liver ailments, including cancer.

[d] LAWYERS. i.e., scribes. Cf. Luke 10:25.

[e] IS IT LAWFUL. He had repeatedly defended Sabbath healings, and His arguments consistently silenced the naysayers (cf. Luke 6:9–10; 13:14–17). Here and in Luke 6:9, He questioned the scribes about the legality of healing on the Sabbath beforehand—and still they could give no cogent reasons why they believed healing was a violation of Sabbath laws.

[f] A DONKEY OR AN OX. Cf. Matt. 12:11–12; Luke 13:15. Common humanitarianism (not to mention economic necessity) taught them that it was right to show mercy to animals on the Sabbath. Should not the same principles be applied in showing mercy to suffering people?

[g] BEST PLACES. i.e., the best seats at the table. Cf. Matt. 23:6; Luke 11:43.

the presence of those who sit at the table with you. For [h]whoever exalts himself will be humbled, and he who humbles himself will be exalted."

Then He also said to him who invited Him, "When you give a dinner or a supper, [i]do not ask your friends, your brothers, your relatives, nor rich neighbors, lest they also invite you back, and you be repaid. But when you give a feast, invite *the* poor, *the* maimed, *the* lame, *the* blind. And you will be blessed, because they cannot repay you; for you shall be [j]repaid at the resurrection of the just."

Now when one of those who sat at the table with Him heard these things, he said to Him, "Blessed *is* [k]he who shall eat bread in the kingdom of God!" Then He said to him, "A certain man gave [l]a great supper and [m]invited many, and sent his servant at supper time to say to [n]those who were invited, 'Come, for all things are now ready.' But they all with one *accord* began to make [o]excuses. The first said to him, 'I have bought a piece of ground, and I must go and see it. I ask you to have me excused.' And another said, 'I have bought five yoke of oxen, and I am going to test them. I ask you to have me excused.' Still another said, 'I have married a wife, and

[h] WHOEVER EXALTS HIMSELF WILL BE HUMBLED. Jesus favored this sort of paradoxical play on words (cf. Matt. 23:11–12; Luke 9:24; 13:30; 17:33; 18:14). This comment made the point of Luke 14:8–10 clear. The point of this whole lesson closely parallels Prov. 25:6–7.

[i] DO NOT ASK YOUR FRIENDS, YOUR BROTHERS. Clearly, this is not to be taken as an absolute prohibition against inviting friends or relatives to a meal. Christ employed similar hyperbole in Luke 14:26. Such language is common in Semitic discourse and is used for emphasis. His point here is that inviting one's friends and relatives cannot be classified as a spiritual act of true charity. It may also be a rebuke against those prone to reserve their hospitality for "rich neighbors," who they know will feel obligated to return the favor. Cf. Deut. 14:28–29.

[j] REPAID AT THE RESURRECTION. i.e., with treasure in heaven (cf. Luke 18:22).

[k] HE WHO SHALL EAT BREAD IN THE KINGDOM. The man probably held the common view that only Jews would be invited to the heavenly feast (cf. Matt. 8:12). Perhaps this was an idle or pious saying, made without much serious reflection. Christ replied with a parable that pictures the inclusion of Gentiles.

[l] A GREAT SUPPER. This parable, similar in many ways to the one in Matt. 22:2–14 and making the same point, is nonetheless distinct. That parable was told on a different occasion, and some key details differ.

[m] INVITED MANY. Apparently, no one declined the invitation. The man evidently had every reason to expect that all who were invited would attend.

[n] THOSE WHO WERE INVITED. Guests for a wedding, which could last a full week, were preinvited and given a general idea of the time. When all the many preparations were finally ready, the preinvited guests were notified that the event would commence. The preinvited guests refer to the people of Israel, who by the OT had been told to be ready for the arrival of the Messiah.

[o] EXCUSES. All the excuses smack of insincerity. One does not purchase property without seeing it first. And since the purchase was already complete, there was no urgency. The land would still be there after the banquet. Likewise, one does not purchase oxen without first testing them. The man who had recently married was excused from business travel or serving in the military (Deut. 24:5), but there was no legitimate reason for newlyweds to avoid such a social engagement.

therefore I cannot come.' So that servant came and reported these things to his master. Then the master of the house, being angry, said to his servant, 'Go out quickly into the streets and lanes of the city, and bring in here [p]*the* poor and *the* maimed and *the* lame and *the* blind.' And the servant said, 'Master, it is done as you commanded, and [q]still there is room.' Then the master said to the servant, 'Go out [r]into the highways and hedges, and [s]compel *them* to come in, that my house may be filled. For I say to you that [t]none of those men who were invited shall taste my supper.'"

---

[p] THE POOR AND THE MAIMED AND THE LAME AND THE BLIND. i.e., people the Pharisees tended to regard as unclean or unworthy. The religious leaders condemned Jesus for His associations with prostitutes and tax collectors (cf. Matt. 9:10–11; 11:19; 21:31–32; Mark 2:15–16; Luke 5:29–30; 15:1).

[q] STILL THERE IS ROOM. God is more willing to save sinners than sinners are to be saved.

[r] INTO THE HIGHWAYS AND HEDGES. This evidently represents the Gentile regions.

[s] COMPEL THEM TO COME IN. i.e., not by force or violence, but by earnest persuasion.

[t] NONE OF THOSE MEN WHO WERE INVITED. i.e., those who refused. Having spurned the invitation, Israel was shut out of the banquet. The master's judgment against them was to seal their own decision. Most of them were killed by divine judgment at the hands of the Romans in AD 70. Cf. Matt. 22:7; 23:36; 24:2.

124. The Cost of Following Christ

Luke 14:25–35

LK Now [a]great multitudes went with Him. And He turned and said to them, "If anyone comes to Me and does not [b]hate his father and mother, wife and children, brothers and sisters, yes, and his own life also, he cannot be My disciple. And whoever does not [c]bear his cross and come after Me cannot be My disciple. For which of you, intending to build a tower, does not sit down first and [d]count the cost, whether he has *enough* to finish *it*—lest, after he has laid the foundation, and is not able to finish, all who see *it* begin to mock him, saying, 'This man began to build and was not able to finish'? Or what king, going to make war against another king, does not sit down first and consider whether he is able with ten thousand to meet him who comes against him with twenty thousand? Or else, while the other is still a great way off, he sends a delegation and asks conditions of peace. So likewise, whoever of you does not [e]forsake all that he has cannot be My disciple.

"[f]Salt *is* good; but if the salt has lost its flavor, how shall it be seasoned? It is neither fit for the land nor for the dunghill, *but* men throw it out. He who has ears to hear, let him hear!"

---

[a] GREAT MULTITUDES. Christ's aim was not to gather appreciative crowds, but to make true disciples (cf. Luke 13:23). He never adapted His message to majority preferences, but always plainly declared the high cost of discipleship. Here He made several bold demands that would discourage the half-hearted.

[b] HATE. A similar statement in Matt. 10:37 is the key to understanding this difficult command. The "hatred" called for here is actually a lesser love. Jesus was calling His disciples to cultivate such a devotion to Him that their attachment to everything else—including their own lives—would seem like hatred by comparison. Cf. Gen. 29:30–31; Luke 16:13 for similar usages of the word "hate."

[c] BEAR HIS CROSS. i.e., willingly. This parallels the idea of hating one's own life. Cf. Matt. 10:38; Mark 8:34; Luke 9:23.

[d] COUNT THE COST. The multitudes were positive but uncommitted. Far from making it easy for them to respond positively, He set the cost of discipleship as high as possible—and encouraged them to do a careful inventory before declaring their willingness to follow. Cf. Luke 9:57–62.

[e] FORSAKE ALL. Only those willing to carefully assess the cost and invest all they had in His kingdom were worthy to enter. This speaks of something far more than mere abandonment of one's material possessions; it is an absolute, unconditional surrender. His disciples were permitted to retain no privileges and make no demands. They were to safeguard no cherished sins, treasure no earthly possessions, and cling to no secret self-indulgences. Their commitment to Him must be without reservation.

[f] SALT IS GOOD. Cf. Matt. 5:13; Mark 9:50. Christ employed this same imagery on at least three different occasions in His ministry.

125. The Lost Sheep and the Lost Coin

Luke 15:1–10

LK Then all [a]the tax collectors and the sinners drew near to Him to hear Him. And the Pharisees and scribes [b]complained, saying, "[c]This Man receives sinners and eats with them."

So He spoke this parable to them, saying: "What man of you, having a hundred sheep, if he loses one of them, does not leave the ninety-nine in the wilderness, and [d]go after the one which is lost until he finds it? And when he has found *it,* he [e]lays *it* on his shoulders, [f]rejoicing. And when he comes home, he calls together *his* friends and neighbors, saying to them, 'Rejoice with me, for I have found my sheep which was lost!' I say to you that likewise there will be more [g]joy in heaven over one sinner who repents than over ninety-nine just [h]persons who need no repentance.

"Or what woman, having ten [i]silver coins, if she loses one coin, does not [j]light

---

[a] THE TAX COLLECTORS AND THE SINNERS. Cf. Matt. 5:46; 21:32; Luke 14:21. Despite the difficulties of Christ's message (Luke 14:25–35), the outcasts of society were drawn to Him, while the religious leaders grew more and more determined to kill Him. Cf. 1 Cor. 1:26–29.

[b] COMPLAINED. Lit. "murmured greatly"—i.e., through the crowds. Their complaining prompted three parables designed to illustrate the joy of God over the repentance of sinners.

[c] THIS MAN RECEIVES SINNERS. This phrase is the key to the trilogy of parables that follow. Christ was not ashamed to be known as a "friend of tax collectors and sinners" (Luke 7:34).

[d] GO AFTER THE ONE WHICH IS LOST. The first two parables both picture God as taking the initiative in seeking sinners. The rabbis taught that God would receive sinners who sought His forgiveness earnestly enough, but here God is the One seeking the sinner (cf. Luke 19:10). The shepherd in the Middle East was responsible for every sheep. He was obligated to his master to see that none was lost, killed, or injured (cf. Matt. 18:11–14).

[e] LAYS IT ON HIS SHOULDERS. The picture of a loving shepherd. Cf. John 10:11; Ps. 24:1.

[f] REJOICING. Joy over the return of the lost is the most prominent feature in all three parable. (Luke 15:7, 10, 32).

[g] JOY IN HEAVEN. A reference to the joy of God Himself. There was complaining on earth, among the Pharisees, but there was great joy with God and among the angels.

[h] PERSONS WHO NEED NO REPENTANCE. i.e., those who think themselves righteous (cf. 5:32; 16:15; 18:9).

[i] SILVER COINS. The drachma was a Greek coin roughly equivalent in value to the Roman denarius (cf. Matt. 22:19).

[j] LIGHT A LAMP. The typical one-room house had no windows.

a lamp, [k]sweep the house, and search carefully until she finds *it?* And when she has found *it,* she calls *her* friends and neighbors together, saying, 'Rejoice with me, for I have found the piece which I lost!' Likewise, I say to you, there is joy in the presence of the angels of God over one sinner who repents."

[k] sweep the house. This illustrates the thoroughness of the search.

126. The Parable of the Prodigal Son

Luke 15:11–32

LK Then He said: "[a]A certain man had two sons. And the younger of them said to *his* father, 'Father, [b]give me the portion of goods that falls *to me.*' So he divided to them *his* livelihood. And not many days after, the younger son [c]gathered all together, journeyed to a far country, and there wasted his possessions with [d]prodigal living. But when he had spent all, there arose a severe famine in that land, and he began to be in want. Then he went and joined himself to a citizen of that country, and he sent him into his fields [e]to feed swine. And he [f]would gladly have filled his stomach with the pods that the swine ate, and [g]no one gave him *anything.*

"But when he [h]came to himself, he said, 'How many of my father's hired ser-

---

[a] A CERTAIN MAN HAD TWO SONS. The parable of the prodigal son is the most familiar and beloved of all Christ's parables. It is one of the longest and most-detailed parables. And unlike most parables, it has more than one lesson. The prodigal is an example of sound repentance. The elder brother illustrates the wickedness of the Pharisees' self-righteousness, prejudice, and indifference toward repenting sinners. And the father pictures God, eager to forgive and longing for the return of the sinner. The main feature, however, as in the other two parables in this chapter, is the joy of God, the celebrations that fill heaven when a sinner repents.

[b] GIVE ME THE PORTION OF GOODS THAT FALLS TO ME. A shocking request, tantamount to saying he wished his father were dead. He was not entitled to any inheritance while his father still lived. Yet the father graciously fulfilled the request, giving him his full portion, which would have been one-third of the entire estate—because the right of the firstborn (Deut. 21:17) gave the elder brother a double portion. This act pictures all sinners (related to God the Father by creation), who waste their potential privileges and refuse any relationship with Him, choosing instead a life of sinful self-indulgence.

[c] GATHERED ALL TOGETHER. The prodigal son evidently took his share in liquid assets and left, abandoning his father and heading into a life of iniquity.

[d] PRODIGAL LIVING. Not merely wasteful extravagance, but also wanton immorality. The Greek word for "prodigal" means "dissolute" and conveys the idea of an utterly debauched lifestyle.

[e] TO FEED SWINE. This was the worst sort of degradation imaginable for Jesus' Jewish audience; swine were the worst sort of unclean animals.

[f] WOULD GLADLY HAVE FILLED HIS STOMACH WITH THE PODS. i.e., carob pods, used to feed swine but virtually indigestible for humans. In other words the only reason he did not eat the same food as the swine is that he could not.

[g] NO ONE GAVE HIM ANYTHING. He could not even eke out a living by begging. His situation could hardly have been more desperate. Thus he symbolizes the estranged sinner who is helpless in despair.

[h] CAME TO HIMSELF. i.e., came to his senses. When his incessant sinning had left him utterly bankrupt and hungry, he was able to think more clearly. In that condition he was a candidate for salvation (cf. Matt. 5:3–6).

vants have bread enough and to spare, and I perish with hunger! I will arise and go to my father, and [i]will say to him, "Father, I have [j]sinned against heaven and before you, and I am no longer worthy to be called your son. Make me like one of your hired servants." '

"And he arose and came to his father. But when he was still a great way off, [k]his father saw him and had compassion, and [l]ran and fell on his neck and kissed him. And the son said to him, 'Father, I have sinned against heaven and in your sight, and am no longer worthy to be called your son.'

" [m]But [n]the father said to his servants, 'Bring out the best robe and put *it* on him, and put a ring on his hand and sandals on *his* feet. And bring [o]the fatted calf here and kill *it,* and let us eat and be merry; for this my son was dead and is alive again; he was lost and is found.' And they began to be merry.

"Now his [p]older son was in the field. And as he came and drew near to the house, he heard music and dancing. So he called one of the servants and asked what these things meant. And he said to him, 'Your brother has come, and because he has received him safe and sound, your father has killed the fatted calf.'

"But [q]he was angry and would not go in. Therefore his father came out and

---

[i] WILL SAY TO HIM. He carefully contemplated what he would say and counted the cost of his repentance.

[j] SINNED AGAINST HEAVEN. A euphemism meaning he had sinned against God. He not only realized the futility of his situation but also understood the gravity of his transgressions against the father.

[k] HIS FATHER SAW HIM. Clearly, the father had been waiting and looking for his son's return.

[l] RAN. The father's eagerness and joy at his son's return is unmistakable. This is the magnificent attribute of God that sets Him apart from all the false gods invented by men and demons. He is not indifferent or hostile, but a Savior by nature, longing to see sinners repent and rejoicing when they do. Cf. 1 Tim. 2:4; 4:10. From Gen. 3:8 to Rev. 22:17, from the fall to the consummation, God has been and will be seeking to save sinners and rejoicing each time one repents and is converted.

[m] BUT. Note that the son did not get to finish his rehearsed words of repentance before the father interrupted to grant forgiveness. This pictures God's eagerness to forgive.

[n] THE FATHER SAID. Without a single word of rebuke for the past, the father pours out his love for the son and expresses his joy that what was lost had been found. Each of the father's gifts said something unique about his acceptance of the son: the robe was reserved for the guest of honor; the ring was a symbol of authority; and the sandals (which were not usually worn by slaves) signified his full restoration to sonship.

[o] THE FATTED CALF. Reserved only for the most special of occasions—a sacrifice or a feast of great celebration. All this symbolizes the lavishness of salvation's blessings (cf. Eph. 1:3; 2:4–7).

[p] OLDER SON. He symbolizes the Pharisee, the hypocritical religious person who stays close to the place of the Father (the temple) but has no sense of sin, no real love for the Father (so as to share in His joy), and no interest in repenting sinners.

[q] HE WAS ANGRY. This parallels the complaining done by the scribes and Pharisees.

pleaded with him. So he answered and said to *his* father, 'Lo, these many years I have been serving you; [r]I never transgressed your commandment at any time; and yet [s]you never gave me a young goat, that I might make merry with my friends. But as soon as [t]this son of yours came, who has devoured your livelihood with harlots, you killed the fatted calf for him.'

"And he said to him, 'Son, you are always with me, and [u]all that I have is yours. [v]It was right that we should make merry and be glad, for your brother was dead and is alive again, and was lost and is found.'"

---

[r] I never transgressed your commandment at any time. Unlikely, given the boy's obvious contempt for his father, shown by his refusal to participate in the father's great joy. This statement reveals the telltale problem with all religious hypocrites. They will not recognize their sin and repent (cf. Matt. 9:12–13; 19:16–20). The elder son's comment reeks of the same spirit as the words of the Pharisee in 18:11.

[s] you never gave me a young goat. All those years of service to the father appear to have been motivated too much by concern what he could get for himself. This son's self-righteous behavior was more socially acceptable than the younger brother's debauchery, but it was equally dishonoring to the father—and called for repentance.

[t] this son of yours. An expression of deep contempt (cf. "this tax collector" in Luke 18:11). He could not bring himself to refer to him as "my brother."

[u] all that I have is yours. The inheritance had already been distributed. Everything the father had was literally in the elder son's possession. Yet the elder son was begrudging even the love the father showed to the prodigal son. The Pharisees and scribes had easy access to all the riches of God's truth. They spent their lives dealing with Scripture and public worship—but they never really possessed any of the treasures enjoyed by the repentant sinner.

[v] It was right that we should make merry. This summarizes the point of all three parables in Luke 15.

127. The Parable of the Unjust Steward

Luke 16:1–13

LK He also said to His disciples: "There was a certain rich man who had a [a]steward, and an accusation was brought to him that this man [b]was wasting his goods. So he called him and said to him, 'What is this I hear about you? Give an account of your stewardship, for [c]you can no longer be steward.'

"Then the steward said within himself, 'What shall I do? For my master is taking the stewardship away from me. [d]I cannot dig; I am ashamed to beg. I have [e]resolved what to do, that when I am put out of the stewardship, they may [f]receive me into their houses.'

"So he called every one of his master's debtors to *him,* and said to the first, 'How much do you owe my master?' And he said, 'A hundred measures of oil.' So he said to him, 'Take your bill, and sit down [g]quickly and write fifty.' Then he said to another, 'And how much do you owe?' So he said, 'A hundred measures of

---

[a] STEWARD. A steward was a trusted servant, usually someone born in the household, who was chief of the management and distribution of household provisions. He provided food for all the other servants, thus managing his master's resources for the well-being of others. He acted as an agent for his master, with full authority to transact business in the master's name.

[b] WAS WASTING HIS GOODS. His prodigality is a thread that ties this parable to the preceding one. Like the younger son in the earlier parable, this steward was guilty of wasting the resources available to him. Unlike the prodigal, however, he had enough sense to make sure that his wastefulness did not leave him friendless and destitute in the future.

[c] YOU CAN NO LONGER BE STEWARD. By announcing his intention to fire the man, the owner acted unwisely, and it cost him even more. Evidently, he thought the man guilty of incompetence, rather than fraud. That would explain his reaction in Luke 16:8.

[d] I CANNOT DIG. i.e., he did not consider himself fit for physical labor.

[e] RESOLVED WHAT TO DO. Cleverly, he arranged to give large discounts to his master's debtors, which they would eagerly agree to pay.

[f] RECEIVE ME INTO THEIR HOUSES. By reducing their debts to his master, he gained their indebtedness to him. They would thus be obligated to take him into their homes when he was put out of his master's home.

[g] QUICKLY. This was a secret transaction, unauthorized by the master. The borrower was guilty of deliberate complicity in the man's fraud.

wheat.' And he said to him, 'Take your bill, and write eighty.' So [h]the master commended the unjust steward because he had dealt shrewdly. For the sons of this world are [i]more shrewd in their generation than the sons of light.

"And I say to you, make friends for yourselves by unrighteous mammon, that when you fail, they may receive you into an everlasting home. [j]He who *is* faithful in *what is* least is faithful also in much; and he who is unjust in *what is* least is unjust also in much. Therefore if you have not been faithful in the [k]unrighteous mammon, who will commit to your trust the [l]true *riches?* And if you have not been faithful in [m]what is another man's, who will give you what is your own?

"No servant can serve two masters; for either he will hate the one and love the other, or else he will be loyal to the one and despise the other. [n]You cannot serve God and mammon."

---

[h] THE MASTER COMMENDED THE UNJUST STEWARD. Outwitted, he applauded the man's cunning. His admiration for the evil steward's criminal genius shows that he, too, was a wicked man. It is the natural tendency of fallen hearts to admire a villain's craftiness (Ps. 49:18). Note that all the characters in this parable are unjust, unscrupulous, and corrupt.

[i] MORE SHREWD. i.e., most unbelievers are wiser in the ways of the world than some believers ("sons of light," cf. John 12:36; Eph. 5:18) are toward the things of God.

[j] HE WHO IS FAITHFUL. Probably a common proverb. Cf. Matt. 25:21; Luke 19:17.

[k] UNRIGHTEOUS MAMMON. i.e., money. The unjust steward used his master's money to buy earthly friends; believers are to use their Master's money in a way that will accrue friends for eternity—by investing in the kingdom gospel that brings sinners to salvation, so that when they arrive in heaven ("an everlasting home"), those sinners will be there to welcome them. Christ did not commend the man's dishonesty; He pointedly called him "unjust." He only used him as an illustration to show that even the most wicked sons of this world are shrewd enough to provide for themselves against coming evil. Believers ought to be more shrewd, because they are concerned with eternal matters, not just earthly ones. Cf. Matt. 6:19–21; Luke 12:33.

[l] TRUE RICHES. Faithful use of one's earthly wealth is repeatedly tied to the accumulation of treasure in heaven (cf. Matt. 6:19–21; Luke 12:33; 18:22).

[m] WHAT IS ANOTHER MAN'S. Lit. "what is another's"—referring to God and the believer's stewardship of His money, which believers only manage as stewards.

[n] YOU CANNOT SERVE GOD AND MAMMON. Many of the Pharisees taught that devotion to money and devotion to God were perfectly compatible. This went hand-in-hand with the commonly held notion that earthly riches signified divine blessing. Rich people were, therefore, regarded as God's favorites (cf. Matt. 19:24). While not condemning wealth, per se, Christ denounced both love of wealth and devotion to mammon. On the love of money, see 1 Tim. 6:9–10, 17–19.

128. The Rich Man and Lazarus

Luke 16:14–31

LK Now the Pharisees, who were lovers of money, also heard all these things, and they derided Him. And He said to them, "You are those who [a]justify yourselves before men, but God knows your hearts. For what is highly esteemed among men is an abomination in the sight of God.

"The law and the prophets *were* [b]until John. Since that time the kingdom of God has been preached, and [c]everyone is pressing into it. And it is easier for heaven and earth to pass away [d]than for one tittle of the law to fail.

"Whoever divorces his wife and marries another [e]commits adultery; and whoever marries her who is divorced from *her* husband commits adultery.

"There was a certain rich man who was clothed in purple and fine linen and fared sumptuously every day. But there was a certain beggar named [f]Lazarus, full

---

[a] JUSTIFY YOURSELVES. The Pharisees' belief was that their own goodness was what justified them (cf. Rom. 10:3). This is the very definition of "self-righteousness." But as Jesus suggested, their righteousness was flawed, being an external veneer only. That might be enough to justify them before men, but not before God, because He knew their hearts. He repeatedly exposed their habit of seeking the approval of people (cf. Matt. 6:2, 5, 16; 23:28).

[b] UNTIL JOHN. John the Baptist's ministry marked the turning point of redemptive history. Prior to that, the great truths of Christ and His kingdom were veiled in the types and shadows of the law and promised in the writings of the prophets (cf. 1 Peter 1:10–12). But John the Baptist introduced the King Himself (see Matt. 11:11). The Pharisees, who thought of themselves as experts in the law and the prophets, missed the significance of the very One to whom the law and the prophets pointed.

[c] EVERYONE IS PRESSING INTO IT. Cf. Jer. 29:13. While the Pharisees were busy opposing Christ, sinners were entering His kingdom in droves. The language of this expression speaks of violent force—probably signifying the zeal with which sinners were seeking with all of their heart to enter the kingdom (cf. Isa. 55:6–7; Matt. 11:12; Luke 13:24).

[d] THAN FOR ONE TITTLE OF THE LAW TO FAIL. Lest anyone think the statement in Luke 16:16 meant He was declaring the law and the prophets annulled, He added this (cf. Matt. 5:18). The great moral principles of the law, the eternal truths contained in the law's types and symbols, and the promises recorded by the prophets all remain in force and are not abrogated by the kingdom message.

[e] COMMITS ADULTERY. i.e., if the divorce had no legitimate grounds. Luke gave an abbreviated record of Jesus' teaching on divorce, stressing only the main issue. Matthew's fuller account makes it clear that He permitted divorce in cases where one's spouse was guilty of adultery. Cf. Matt. 5:31–32; 19:3–9. This countered the rabbis' doctrine, which permitted men to divorce their wives easily and for almost any cause (Matt. 19:3).

[f] LAZARUS. Clearly not the Lazarus in John 11 (who died at a later time). This beggar was the only character in any of Jesus' parables ever given a name. Some therefore have speculated that this was no imaginary tale, but an actual incident that really took place. Either way, Christ employs it in the same fashion as all His parables, to teach a lesson, in this case for the benefit of the Pharisees. The rich man in the parable is sometimes called Dives, after the Latin word for "rich."

of sores, who was laid at his gate, desiring to be fed with the [g]crumbs which fell from the rich man's table. Moreover the dogs came and licked his sores. So it was that the beggar died, and was carried by the angels to [h]Abraham's bosom. The rich man also died and was buried. And being in torments [i]in Hades, he lifted up his eyes and saw Abraham afar off, and Lazarus in his bosom.

"Then he cried and said, 'Father Abraham, have mercy on me, and send Lazarus that he may dip the tip of his finger in water and cool my tongue; for [j]I am tormented in this flame.' But Abraham said, 'Son, remember that in your lifetime you received your good things, and likewise Lazarus evil things; but now he is comforted and you are tormented. And besides all this, between us and you there is a great gulf fixed, so that those who want to pass from here to you cannot, nor can those from there pass to us.'

"Then he said, 'I beg you therefore, father, that you would [k]send him to my father's house, for I have five brothers, that he may testify to them, lest they also come to this place of torment.' Abraham said to him, '[l]They have Moses and the

---

[g] crumbs . . . dogs. The mention of table scraps, sores, and dogs all made this poor man appear odious in the eyes of the Pharisees. They were inclined to see all such things as proof of divine disfavor. They would have viewed such a person as not only unclean but also despised by God.

[h] Abraham's bosom. This same expression (found only here in Scripture) was used in the Talmud as a figure for heaven. The idea was that Lazarus was given a place of high honor, reclining next to Abraham at the heavenly banquet.

[i] in Hades. The suggestion that a rich man would be excluded from heaven would have scandalized the Pharisees (cf. Matt. 19:24); especially galling was the idea that a beggar who ate scraps from his table was granted the place of honor next to Abraham. *Hades* was the Greek term for the abode of the dead. In the Septuagint it was used to translate the Hebrew *Sheol*, which referred to the realm of the dead in general, without necessarily distinguishing between righteous or unrighteous souls. However, in NT usage Hades always refers to the place of the wicked prior to final judgment in hell. The imagery Jesus used paralleled the common rabbinical idea that Sheol had two parts, one for the souls of the righteous and the other for the souls of the wicked—separated by an impassable gulf. But there is no reason to suppose, as some do, that "Abraham's bosom" spoke of a temporary prison for the souls of OT saints, who were brought to heaven only after He had actually atoned for their sins. Scripture consistently teaches that the spirits of the righteous dead go immediately into the presence of God (cf. Luke 23:43; 2 Cor. 5:8; Phil. 1:23). And the presence of Moses and Elijah on the Mount of Transfiguration (Luke 9:30) belies the notion that they were confined in a compartment of Sheol until Christ finished His work.

[j] I am tormented. Christ pictured Hades as a place where the unspeakable torment of hell had already begun. Among the miseries featured here are unquenchable flames (cf. Matt. 25:46); an accusing conscience fed by undying memories of lost opportunity (Luke 16:25); and permanent, irreversible separation from God and everything good (Luke 16:26).

[k] send him to my father's house. The rich man retained a condescending attitude toward Lazarus even in hell, repeatedly asking Abraham to "send" Lazarus to wait on him. The flames of hell do not atone for sin or purge hardened sinners from their depravity (cf. Rev. 22:11).

[l] They have Moses and the prophets. i.e., the OT Scriptures.

prophets; let them hear them.' And he said, 'No, father Abraham; but if one goes to them from the dead, they will repent.' But he said to him, 'If they do not hear Moses and the prophets, [m]neither will they be persuaded though one rise from the dead.'"

[m] NEITHER WILL THEY BE PERSUADED. This speaks powerfully of the singular sufficiency of Scripture to overcome unbelief. The gospel itself is the power of God unto salvation (Rom. 1:16). Since unbelief is at heart a moral, rather than an intellectual, problem, no amount of evidences will ever turn unbelief to faith. But the revealed Word of God has inherent power to do so (cf. John 6:63; Heb. 4:12; James 1:18; 1 Peter 1:23).

129. Forgiveness, Faith, and Faithfulness

Luke 17:1–10

LK Then He said to the disciples, "It is impossible that no [a]offenses should come, but woe *to him* through whom they do come! It would be better for him if [b]a millstone were hung around his neck, and he were thrown into the sea, than that he should offend one of these [c]little ones. Take heed to yourselves. If your brother sins against you, [d]rebuke him; and if he repents, forgive him. And if he sins against you [e]seven times in a day, and seven times in a day returns to you, saying, 'I repent,' you shall forgive him."

And the apostles said to the Lord, [f]"Increase our faith." So the Lord said, "If you have [g]faith as a mustard seed, you can say to this mulberry tree, 'Be pulled up by the roots and be planted in the sea,' and it would obey you. And which of you, having [h]a servant plowing or tending sheep, will say to him when he has come in from the field, 'Come at once and sit down to eat'? But will he not rather say to him, 'Prepare something for my supper, and gird yourself and serve me till I have eaten and drunk, and afterward you will eat and drink'? Does he thank that servant because he did the things that were commanded him? I think not. So likewise you, when you have done all those things which you are commanded, say, 'We are [i]unprofitable servants. We have done what was our duty to do.'"

---

[a] OFFENSES. Lit. "snares." Cf. Matt. 18:7.

[b] A MILLSTONE. Lit. "the millstone of a donkey." Cf. Matt. 18:6..

[c] LITTLE ONES. Believers; God's children who are under His care. Cf. Matt. 18:5.

[d] REBUKE HIM. It is the Christian's duty to deal straightforwardly with a brother or sister in sin. Cf. Matt. 18:15.

[e] SEVEN TIMES IN A DAY. i.e., no matter how many times he sins and repents. Cf. Matt 18:21–22. The number seven was not to set a limit on the number of times to forgive (cf. Ps. 119:164), but precisely the opposite. Christ meant that forgiveness should be granted unendingly (cf. Eph. 4:32; Col. 3:13).

[f] "INCREASE OUR FAITH." Lit. "Give us more faith." They felt inadequate in the face of the high standard He set for them.

[g] FAITH AS A MUSTARD SEED. Cf. Matt. 17:20.

[h] A SERVANT. The point of this parable was that a servant should expect no special reward for doing what was his duty in the first place. The demanding standards Christ set (Luke 17:1–4) may have seemed too high to the disciples, but they represented only the minimal duties for a servant of Christ. Those who obey are not to think their obedience is meritorious.

[i] UNPROFITABLE SERVANTS. i.e., not worthy of any special honor.

130. Lazarus Becomes Sick and Dies

John 11:1–16

JN [a]Now a certain *man* was sick, [b]Lazarus of [c]Bethany, the town of [d]Mary and her sister Martha. It was *that* Mary who anointed the Lord with fragrant oil and wiped His feet with her hair, whose brother Lazarus was sick. Therefore the sisters [e]sent to Him, saying, "Lord, behold, [f]he whom You love is sick."

When Jesus heard *that,* He said, "This sickness is not unto death, but for the glory of God, that [g]the Son of God may be glorified through it." Now Jesus loved

---

[a] Now a certain man was sick. As John 11 begins Jesus stands in the shadow of facing the cross. But all the rejection and hatred of the Jewish leaders could not dim His glory as displayed through the resurrection of Lazarus. That miracle evidences His glory in three ways: (1) it pointed to His deity; (2) it strengthened the faith of the disciples; and (3) it led directly to the cross (John 11:50). The chapter can be divided as follows: (1) the preparation for the miracle (John 11:1–16); (2) the arrival of Jesus (vv. 17–37); (3) the miracle itself (vv. 38–44); and (4) the results of the miracle (vv. 45–57).

[b] Lazarus. The resurrection of Lazarus is the climactic sign in John's gospel and the capstone of Jesus' public ministry. Six miracles have already been presented (water into wine [John 2:1–11], healing of the nobleman's son [John 4:46–54], restoring the impotent man [John 5:1–15], multiplying the loaves and fishes [John 6:1–14], walking on the water [John 6:15–21], and curing the man born blind [John 9:1–12]). Lazarus's resurrection is more potent than all those and even more monumental than the raising of the widow's son in Nain (Luke 7:11–16) or Jairus's daughter (Luke 8:40–56), because those two resurrections occurred immediately after death. Lazarus was raised after four days of being in the grave, with the process of decomposition already having started (John 11:39).

[c] Bethany. This Bethany is different from the other "Bethany beyond the Jordan" in John 1:28. It lies on the east side of the Mount of Olives, about two miles from Jerusalem along the road leading toward Jericho.

[d] Mary . . . Martha. This is the first mention of this family in John. John related the story of Mary's anointing of Jesus in John 12:1–8, but this reference may indicate that the original readers were already familiar with the event. Cf. Luke 10:38–42.

[e] sent to Him. Since Jesus was east of the Jordan and Lazarus was near Jerusalem, the message to Jesus would most likely have taken one whole day to reach Him. Surely by omniscience Jesus already knew of Lazarus's condition (cf. John 1:47; 11:6). He may have died before the messenger reached Jesus, since he was dead four days (John 11:17) when Jesus arrived, after a two-day delay (v. 6) and a one-day journey.

[f] he whom You love. This phrase is a touching hint at the close friendship that Jesus had with Lazarus. Cf. John 13:1.

[g] the Son of God may be glorified. This phrase reveals the real purpose behind Lazarus's sickness, i.e., not death, but that the Son of God might be glorified through his resurrection.

Martha and her sister and Lazarus. So, when He heard that he was sick, [h]He stayed two more days in the place where He was. Then after this He said to *the* disciples, "Let us go to Judea again."

The disciples said to Him, "Rabbi, lately [i]the Jews sought to stone You, and are You going there again?"

Jesus answered, "Are there not twelve hours in the day? [j]If anyone walks in the day, he does not stumble, because he sees the light of this world. But if one walks in the night, he stumbles, because the light is not in him." These things He said, and after that He said to them, "Our friend Lazarus [k]sleeps, but I go that I may wake him up."

Then His disciples said, "Lord, if he sleeps he will get well." However, Jesus spoke of his death, but they thought that He was speaking about taking rest in sleep. Then Jesus said to them plainly, "Lazarus is dead. And [l]I am glad for your sakes that I was not there, that you may believe. Nevertheless let us go to him."

Then [m]Thomas, who is called the Twin, said to his fellow disciples, "Let us also go, that we may die with Him."

---

[h] He stayed two more days. The decision to delay coming did not bring about Lazarus's death, since Jesus already supernaturally knew his plight. Most likely by the time the messenger arrived to inform Jesus, Lazarus was already dead. The delay was because He loved the family and that love would be clear as He greatly strengthened their faith by raising Lazarus from the dead. The delay also made certain that no one would wrongly think Lazarus's resurrection was merely a resuscitation, since he had been dead for so long.

[i] the Jews sought to stone You. The disciples realized that the animosity toward Jesus was so great that His return could result in His death because of the murderous intentions of the Jewish leaders (cf. John 8:59; 10:31).

[j] If anyone walks in the day. During the light of the sun, most people did their work safely. When darkness came, they stopped. The proverbial saying, however, had a deeper meaning. As long as the Son performed His Father's will (i.e., during the daylight period of His ministry when He is able to work), He was safe. The time would soon come (nighttime) when, by God's design, His earthly work would end and He would "stumble" in death. Jesus was stressing that as long as He was on earth, doing God's will, even at this late time in His ministry, He would safely complete God's purposes.

[k] sleeps. A euphemistic term used in the NT to refer to death, particularly with reference to believers who will be physically raised to eternal life (cf. 1 Cor. 11:30; 15:51; 1 Thess. 4:13).

[l] I am glad for your sakes. The resurrection of Lazarus was designed to strengthen His disciples' faith in Him as the Messiah and Son of God in the face of the strong Jewish rejection of Him.

[m] Thomas . . . said. Thomas's words reflect loyal devotion and, at the same time, pessimism over the fact that they would probably all die. His fears were not unrealistic in the face of bitter hostility toward Jesus, and had not the Lord protected them in the garden (John 18:1–11), they may also have been arrested and executed. Cf. John 20:24–29.

131. Jesus Raises Lazarus from the Dead

John 11:17–44

JN So when Jesus came, He found that he had already been [a]in the tomb four days. Now Bethany was near Jerusalem, about two miles away. And [b]many of the Jews had joined the women around Martha and Mary, to comfort them concerning their brother.

Now Martha, as soon as she heard that Jesus was coming, went and met Him, but Mary was sitting in the house. Now Martha said to Jesus, "Lord, [c]if You had been here, my brother would not have died. But even now I know that [d]whatever You ask of God, God will give You."

Jesus said to her, "Your brother will rise again." Martha said to Him, "I know that he will rise again in the resurrection at the last day."

Jesus said to her, "[e]I am the resurrection and the life. He who believes in Me, though he may die, he shall live. And whoever lives and believes in Me shall never die. Do you believe this?"

[f]She said to Him, "Yes, Lord, I believe that You are the Christ, the Son of God,

---

[a] IN THE TOMB. The term "tomb" means a stone sepulcher. In that region such a grave was common. Either a cave or rock area would be hewn out, the floor inside leveled and graded to make a shallow descent. Shelves were cut out or constructed inside the area in order to bury additional family members. A rock was rolled in front to prevent wild animals or grave robbers from entering. The evangelist made special mention of the fourth day in order to stress the magnitude of the miracle, for the Jews did not embalm and by then the body would have been in a state of rapid decomposition.

[b] MANY OF THE JEWS HAD JOINED THE WOMEN. The implication is that the family was well-known in that area. The mention of the Jews also reminds the reader of the great risk that Jesus faced by traveling so close to Jerusalem, which was seething with the leaders' hatred for Him.

[c] IF YOU HAD BEEN HERE. Not a rebuke of Jesus but a testimony of her trust in His healing power.

[d] WHATEVER YOU ASK OF GOD. Based on her later statement in John 11:39, she was not saying she believed Jesus could raise Lazarus from the dead, but that she knew He had a special relationship to God so that His prayers could bring some good from this sad event.

[e] I AM THE RESURRECTION AND THE LIFE. This is the fifth in a series of seven great "I AM" statements of Jesus recorded in John's gospel (see John 6:35; 8:12; 10:7, 9; 10:11, 14). With this statement, Jesus moved Martha from a general affirmation of the resurrection that will take place "at the last day" (cf. John 5:28, 29) to a personalized trust in Him who alone can raise the dead. No resurrection or eternal life exists outside of the Son of God. Time ("at the last day") is no barrier to the One who has the power of resurrection and life (John 1:4), for He can give life at any time.

[f] SHE SAID TO HIM. Her confession is representative of the very reason John wrote this inspired gospel (cf. John 20:30, 31). See Peter's confession in Matt. 16:16.

who is to come into the world." And when she had said these things, she went her way and secretly called Mary her sister, saying, "The Teacher has come and is calling for you." As soon as she heard *that,* she arose quickly and came to Him.

Now Jesus had not yet come into the town, but was in the place where Martha met Him. Then the Jews who were with her in the house, and comforting her, when they saw that Mary rose up quickly and went out, followed her, saying, "She is going to the tomb to weep there."

Then, when Mary came where Jesus was, and saw Him, she fell down at His feet, saying to Him, "Lord, if You had been here, my brother would not have died." Therefore, when Jesus saw her weeping, and [g]the Jews who came with her weeping, [h]He groaned in the spirit and was troubled.

And He said, "Where have you laid him?" They said to Him, "Lord, come and see." [i]Jesus wept. Then the Jews said, "See how He loved him!" And some of them said, "Could not this Man, who opened the eyes of the blind, also have kept this man from dying?"

Then Jesus, again groaning in Himself, came to the tomb. It was a cave, and a stone lay against it. Jesus said, "Take away the stone." Martha, the sister of him who was dead, said to Him, "Lord, by this time there is a [j]stench, for he has been *dead* four days."

Jesus said to her, "Did I not say to you that if you would believe you would see the glory of God?" Then they took away the stone *from the place* where the

---

[g] The Jews who came with her weeping. According to Jewish custom even a poor family must pay for at least a couple flute players and a professional mourner to weep for the dead. Because the family may have been well-to-do, a rather large group appears present.

[h] He groaned in the spirit and was troubled. The phrase here does not mean merely that Jesus was deeply touched or moved with sympathy at the sight. The Greek term "groaned" points to personal indignation (see John 11:38; cf. Matt. 9:30; Mark 1:43; 14:5). Most likely Jesus was angered at the emotional grief of the people because it implicitly revealed unbelief in the resurrection and the temporary nature of death. The group was acting like pagans who had no hope (1 Thess. 4:13). While grief is understandable, the group was acting in despair, thus indicating a tacit denial of the resurrection and the Scripture that promised it. Jesus may also have been angered because He was indignant at the pain and sorrow in death that sin brought into the human condition.

[i] Jesus wept. The Greek word here has the connotation of silently bursting into tears in contrast to the loud lament of the group. His tears here were not generated out of mourning, since He was to raise Lazarus, but out of grief for a fallen world entangled in sin-caused sorrow and death. He was "a Man of sorrows and acquainted with grief" (Isa. 53:3; John 3:16).

[j] stench. Although Jews used aromatic spices, their custom was not to embalm the body but to use the spices to counteract the repulsive odors from decomposition. They would wrap the body in linen cloth, adding spice in the layers and folds. The Jews did not wrap the body tightly like Egyptian mummies, but rather loosely with the head wrapped separately. This is indicated by the fact that Lazarus could move out of the tomb before he was unwrapped (John 11:44; cf. 20:7).

dead man was lying. And Jesus lifted up *His* eyes and said, "[k]Father, I thank You that You have heard Me. And I know that You always hear Me, but because of the people who are standing by I said *this,* that they may believe that You sent Me."

Now when He had said these things, He cried with a loud voice, "Lazarus, come forth!" And [l]he who had died came out bound hand and foot with grave-clothes, and his face was wrapped with a cloth. Jesus said to them, "Loose him, and let him go."

---

[k] Father, I thank You. Jesus' prayer was not really a petition, but thanksgiving to the Father. The reason for the miracle was to authenticate His claims to be the Messiah and Son of God.

[l] he who had died came out. This was a preview of the power to be fully displayed in the final resurrection, when all the dead hear the voice of the Son of God and live (John 5:25, 28–29).

132. The Jewish Leaders Plot to Kill Jesus

John 11:45–54

JN Then many of the Jews who had come to Mary, and had seen the things Jesus did, believed in Him. [a]But some of them went away to the Pharisees and told them the things Jesus did.

Then the chief priests and the Pharisees [b]gathered a council and said, "What shall we do? For this Man works many signs. If we let Him alone like this, everyone will believe in Him, and [c]the Romans will come and take away both our place and nation."

And one of them, [d]Caiaphas, being high priest that year, said to them, "You know nothing at all, nor do you consider that it is expedient for us that [e]one man should die for the people, and not that the whole nation should perish." Now this he did not say on his own *authority;* but being high priest that year [f]he prophesied

---

[a] BUT SOME OF THEM WENT AWAY. Jesus' teaching and actions often divided the Jews (e.g., John 6:14–15; 7:10–13, 45–52). While some believed, others, apparently with malicious intent, informed the Pharisees of Jesus' action.

[b] GATHERED A COUNCIL. Alerted by the Pharisees, a Sanhedrin committee consisting of chief priests (former high priests and members of high-priestly families) and Pharisees, called the Sanhedrin to session. The Pharisees could not by themselves take any judicial action against Jesus. Though subject to Roman control, the Sanhedrin was the most powerful judicial body in Israel and exercised judicial, legislative, and executive powers at that time. In Jesus' day the Sanhedrin was dominated by the Sadducees including the chief priests. The Pharisees made up a vocal minority. While the Pharisees and Sadducees were often in conflict, their mutual hatred of Jesus united them into action.

[c] THE ROMANS WILL COME. The Jews were not willing to believe in Jesus as the Son of God, even though Lazarus had been raised. They feared that escalating messianic expectations could start a movement against Roman oppression and occupation that would cause the Romans to come and take away all their rights and freedoms.

[d] CAIAPHAS. Caiaphas became high priest ca. AD 18, being appointed by the Roman prefect, Valerius Gratus. He was the son-in-law of Annas, who had previously functioned in that same position from ca. AD 7–14 and who exercised great influence over the office even after his tenure (see John 18:12–14). Caiaphas retained his position until AD 36, when, along with Pontius Pilate, he was removed by the Romans. He played a leading role in the trial and condemnation of Jesus. In his court or palace the chief priests (Sadducees) and Pharisees assembled "and plotted to take Jesus by trickery and kill Him" (see Matt. 26:3–4).

[e] ONE MAN SHOULD DIE FOR THE PEOPLE. He only meant that Jesus should be executed in order to spare their own positions and nation from Roman reprisals, but Caiaphas unwittingly used sacrificial, substitutionary language and prophesied the death of Christ for sinners. Cf. 2 Cor. 5:21; 1 Peter 2:24.

[f] HE PROPHESIED. Caiaphas did not realize the implications of what he spoke. While he uttered blasphemy against Christ, God parodied his statement into truth (cf. Ps. 76:10). The responsibility for the wicked meaning of his words belonged to Caiaphas, but God's providence directed the choice of words so as to express the heart of God's glorious plan of salvation (Acts 4:27–28). He actually was used by God as a prophet because he was the high priest, and originally the high priest was the means of God's will being revealed (2 Sam. 15:27).

that Jesus would die for the nation, and not for that nation only, but also that He would [g]gather together in one the children of God who were scattered abroad.

Then, [h]from that day on, they plotted to put Him to death. Therefore Jesus no longer walked openly among the Jews, but went from there into the country near the wilderness, to a city called [i]Ephraim, and there remained with His disciples.

---

[g] gather together in one the children of God. In context this had reference to believing Jews of the dispersion, who would be regathered in Israel to share in the Messianic kingdom (Isa. 43:5; Ezek. 34:12). In a wider sense this also anticipated the Gentile mission (see John 12:32). As a result of Christ's sacrificial death and resurrection, both Jew and Gentile have been made into one group, the church (Eph. 2:11–18).

[h] from that day on. The phrase indicates that their course of action toward Jesus was then fixed. It remained only to accomplish it. Notice that Jesus was not arrested to be tried. He had already been judged guilty of blasphemy. The trial was a mere formality for a sentence already passed (Mark 14:1–2).

[i] Ephraim. This probably refers to the OT city of Ephron (see 2 Chron 13:19). Its modern village name is Et-Taiyibeh, and it is located four miles northeast of Bethel and about twelve miles from Jerusalem. The location was far enough away for temporary safety from the Jewish leaders.

133. Jesus Heals Ten Lepers

Luke 17:11–21

LK Now it happened [a]as He went to Jerusalem that He passed through the midst of Samaria and Galilee. Then as He entered a certain village, there met Him ten men who were [b]lepers, who stood afar off. And they lifted up *their* voices and said, "Jesus, Master, [c]have mercy on us!"

So when He saw *them,* He said to them, "Go, [d]show yourselves to the priests." And so it was that as they went, they were cleansed. And [e]one of them, when he saw that he was healed, returned, and with a loud voice glorified God, and fell down on *his* face at His feet, giving Him thanks. And [f]he was a Samaritan.

So Jesus answered and said, "Were there not ten cleansed? But where *are* the nine? Were there not any found who returned to give glory to God except [g]this

[a] AS HE WENT TO JERUSALEM . . . THROUGH . . . SAMARIA AND GALILEE. Luke did not explain the reason for such a circuitous route, but a comparison of the gospels yields several clues. It appears that time elapsed between Luke 17:10 and 11. The raising of Lazarus at Bethany, near Jerusalem (John 11), appears to fit into this timeframe. John 11:54 states that after raising Lazarus, to avoid the authorities who were seeking to kill Him, Christ went to "a city called Ephraim"—north of Jerusalem, near the border of Samaria. From there He apparently traveled north through Samaria and Galilee one more time, possibly to join friends and family from Galilee who would be making a pilgrimage to Jerusalem for the Passover. From there He would have traveled south by the conventional route, which would have brought Him through Jericho (Luke 18:35) to Jerusalem.

[b] LEPERS. These men were ceremonially defiled and forced to live outside the village (Lev. 13:46; Num. 5:2–3). They were legally required to stand at a distance, and thus their communication with Christ was by shouting. Cf. Lev. 13:2.

[c] HAVE MERCY ON US. Cf. Matt. 9:27; 15:22; 17:15; 20:31; Mark 10:47–48; Luke 16:24; 18:38–39. This was a common plea from those desiring healing.

[d] SHOW YOURSELVES TO THE PRIESTS. i.e., to be declared clean (Lev. 13:2–3; 14:2–32). AS THEY WENT. The healing was sudden and immediately visible but occurred after they obeyed His command.

[e] ONE OF THEM . . . RETURNED. His response was reminiscent of the conduct of Naaman (2 Kings 5:15). The others, eager to be declared clean so that they could return to normal life in society, evidently continued on to the priest, forgetting to give thanks.

[f] HE WAS A SAMARITAN. Jesus' sending the lepers to show themselves to the priest suggests that they were Jewish. This Samaritan had been permitted to associate with them when all were ceremonially unclean, but in their healing they did not share his deep gratitude.

[g] THIS FOREIGNER. Evidently, Jesus did not view Samaritans as anything more or less than other Gentiles. Cf. John 4:4.

foreigner?" And He said to him, "Arise, go your way. Your faith has [h]made you well."

Now when He was asked by the Pharisees [i]when the kingdom of God would come, He answered them and said, "The kingdom of God [j]does not come with observation; nor will they say, 'See here!' or 'See there!' For indeed, the kingdom of God is [k]within you."

---

[h] made you well. Lit. "saved you" (cf. Matt. 9:22; Mark 5:34).

[i] when the kingdom of God would come. They may have asked the question mockingly, having already concluded that He was not the Messiah.

[j] does not come with observation. The Pharisees believed that the Messiah's triumph would be immediate. They were looking for Him to come, overthrow Rome, and set up the millennial kingdom. Christ's program was altogether different. He was inaugurating an era in which the kingdom would be manifest in the rule of God in men's hearts through faith in the Savior (Luke 17:21; cf. Rom. 14:17). That kingdom was neither confined to a particular geographical location nor visible to human eyes. It would come quietly, invisibly, and without the normal pomp and splendor associated with the arrival of a king. Jesus did not suggest that the OT promises of an earthly kingdom were hereby nullified. Rather that earthly, visible manifestation of the kingdom is yet to come (Rev. 20:1–6).

[k] within you. i.e., within people's hearts. The pronoun could hardly refer to the Pharisees in general.

134. Jesus Teaches About His Second Coming

Luke 17:22–37

LK Then He said to the disciples, "[a]The days will come when [b]you will desire to see one of the days of the Son of Man, and you will not see *it.* And [c]they will say to you, 'Look here!' or 'Look there!' Do not go after *them* or follow *them.* For as the lightning that flashes out of one *part* under heaven shines to the other *part* under heaven, so also the Son of Man will be in His day.

"But first He [d]must suffer many things and be rejected by this generation. And as it was [e]in the days of Noah, so it will be also in the days of the Son of Man: They ate, they drank, they married wives, they were given in marriage, until the day that Noah entered the ark, and the flood came and destroyed them all. Likewise as it was also [f]in the days of Lot: They ate, they drank, they bought, they sold, they planted, they built; but on the day that Lot went out of Sodom it rained fire and brimstone from heaven and destroyed *them* all. Even so will it be in the day when the Son of Man is revealed.

"In that day, he who is on the [g]housetop, and his goods *are* in the house, let him not come down to take them away. And likewise the one who is in the field,

---

[a] THE DAYS WILL COME. This introduces a brief discourse that has some similarities to the Olivet Discourse of Matt. 24, 25.

[b] YOU WILL DESIRE TO SEE ONE OF THE DAYS OF THE SON OF MAN. i.e., desire to have Him physically present. This suggests a longing for His return to set things right (cf. Rev. 6:9–11; 22:20).

[c] THEY WILL SAY TO YOU "LOOK HERE!" OR "LOOK THERE!" Cf. Matt. 24:26–27.

[d] MUST SUFFER. i.e., because it was the sovereign plan of God for Him to die as a substitute for sinners. Cf. Matt. 16:21; Mark 8:31; Luke 9:22; 18:31–33; 24:25–26.

[e] IN THE DAYS OF NOAH. Cf. Matt. 24:37–38.

[f] IN THE DAYS OF LOT. i.e., judgment came suddenly, destroying people in the midst of their everyday activities (Gen 19:24–25). None of the things Jesus cited with regard to Noah's day or Lot's day were inherently sinful. But people were so absorbed in the things of this life that they were utterly unprepared when the time of judgment came.

[g] HOUSETOP. The typical house had a flat roof with an external stairway. The danger would be so great that those on the roofs should flee, without going into the house to retrieve anything.

let him not turn back. [h]Remember Lot's wife. Whoever seeks to save his life will lose it, and [i]whoever loses his life will preserve it. I tell you, in that night there will be two *men* in one bed: the [j]one will be taken and the other will be left. Two *women* will be grinding together: the one will be taken and the other left. Two *men* will be in the field: the one will be taken and the other left."

And they answered and said to Him, "Where, Lord?" So He said to them, "Wherever the body is, there the [k]eagles will be gathered together."

[h] Remember Lot's wife. Lot's wife was destroyed on the very threshold of deliverance. Her attachment to Sodom was so powerful that she delayed and looked back; she was overwhelmed by oncoming judgment, just before reaching the place of safety (Gen. 19:26).

[i] whoever loses his life will preserve it. Cf. Luke 14:11.

[j] one will be taken and the other will be left. Matt 24:40–41.

[k] eagles. Better translated "vultures." Cf. Matt. 24:28.

135. The Unjust Judge and the Justified Tax Collector

Luke 18:1–14

LK Then He spoke a parable to them, that men [a]always ought to pray and [b]not lose heart, saying: "There was in a certain city a judge who [c]did not fear God nor regard man. Now there was a widow in that city; and she came to him, saying, 'Get justice for me from my adversary.' And he would not for a while; but afterward he said within himself, 'Though I do not fear God nor regard man, yet because this widow troubles me I will avenge her, lest by her continual coming she [d]weary me.'"

Then the Lord said, "[e]Hear what the unjust judge said. And shall God not avenge His own elect who cry out day and night to Him, though He bears long with them? I tell you that He will avenge them [f]speedily. Nevertheless, when the Son of Man comes, [g]will He really find faith on the earth?"

---

[a] ALWAYS . . . PRAY. A common theme in Paul's epistles. Cf. Rom. 1:9; 12:12; Eph. 6:18; 1 Thess. 5:17; 2 Thess. 1:11.

[b] NOT LOSE HEART. i.e., in light of the afflictions and hardships of life, and the evidence of approaching judgment (described in the preceding discourse—Luke 17:22–37).

[c] DID NOT FEAR GOD NOR REGARD MAN. This man was thoroughly wicked. Christ described him as "unjust"—like the steward in Luke 16:8. The judge is not given as a symbol of God, but rather in contrast to Him. If such an unjust man would respond to persistent pleas, would not God, who is not only just but also loving and merciful, do so more readily?

[d] WEARY ME. Lit. "hit under the eye." What the judge would not do out of compassion for the widow or reverence for God, he would do out of sheer frustration with her incessant pleading.

[e] HEAR WHAT THE UNJUST JUDGE SAID. i.e., listen to the point of the story, namely, that God, who always does right and is filled with compassion for believers who suffer, will certainly respond to His beloved ones who cry for His help.

[f] SPEEDILY. He may delay long, but He does so for good reason (cf. 2 Peter 3:8–9), and when He acts, His vengeance is swift.

[g] WILL HE REALLY FIND FAITH. This suggests that when He returns, the true faith will be comparatively rare—as in the days of Noah (Luke 17:26), when only eight souls were saved. The period before His return will be marked by persecution, apostasy, and unbelief (Matt. 24:9–13, 24).

Also He spoke this [h]parable to some who trusted in themselves that they were righteous, and despised others: "Two men went up to the temple to pray, one a Pharisee and the other a tax collector. The Pharisee stood and prayed thus with himself, 'God, I thank You that I am not like other men—extortioners, unjust, adulterers, or even as this tax collector. I [i]fast twice a week; I give tithes of all that I possess.' And the tax collector, [j]standing afar off, would not so much as raise *his* eyes to heaven, but beat his breast, saying, '[k]God, be merciful to me a sinner!' I tell you, this man went down to his house [l]justified *rather* than the other; for everyone who exalts himself will be humbled, and he who humbles himself will be exalted."

---

[h] PARABLE. This parable is rich with truth about the doctrine of justification by faith. It illustrates perfectly how a sinner who is utterly devoid of personal righteousness may be declared righteous before God instantaneously through an act of repentant faith. The parable is addressed to Pharisees who trusted their own righteousness. Such confidence in one's inherent righteousness is a damning hope (cf. Rom. 10:3; Phil 3:9), because human righteousness—even the righteousness of the most fastidious Pharisee—falls short of the divine standard (Matt. 5:48). Scripture consistently teaches that sinners are justified when God's perfect righteousness is imputed to their account (cf. Gen. 15:6; Rom. 4:4, 5; 2 Cor. 5:21; Phil. 3:4–9)—and it was only on that basis that this tax collector (or anyone else) could be saved.

[i] FAST TWICE A WEEK. i.e., more than is required by any biblical standard (cf. Luke 5:33). By exalting his own works the Pharisee revealed that his entire hope lay in his not being as bad as someone else. He utterly lacked any sense of his own unworthiness and sin. Cf. Matt. 19:17–20; Luke 17:7–10.

[j] STANDING AFAR OFF. The tax collector's humility is notable in everything about his posture and behavior. Here was a man who had been made to face the reality of his own sin, and his only response was abject humility and repentance. He contrasts with the Pharisee in virtually every detail.

[k] GOD, BE MERCIFUL. He had no hope but the mercy of God. This is the point to which the law aims to bring every sinner (cf. Rom. 3:19–20; 7:13; Gal 3:22–24).

[l] JUSTIFIED. i.e., reckoned righteous before God by means of an imputed righteousness.

Part VII | The Final Journey to Jerusalem for Passover AD 30

136. Jesus Teaches About Divorce

Matt. 19:1–12; Mark 10:1–12

MT Now it came to pass, when Jesus had finished these sayings, *that* MK He arose from there and MT departed from Galilee and came to [a]the region of Judea beyond the Jordan. And great multitudes followed Him, and He healed them there. MK And as He was accustomed, He taught them again.

MT The Pharisees also [b]came to Him, testing Him, and saying to Him, "[c]Is it lawful for a man to divorce his wife for *just* any reason?" MK And He answered and said to them, "[d]What did Moses command you?" They said, "[e]Moses [f]permitted *a man* to write a certificate of divorce, and to dismiss *her*." MT And He answered and

---

[a] THE REGION OF JUDEA BEYOND THE JORDAN. Perea was the name of the region just east of the Jordan River. It was not technically part of Judea, but the territory ruled by Herod the Great had included both regions, and it was commonly referred to this way. Christ's ministry in Perea lasted only a short time. It was from here that He would make His final journey to Jerusalem just prior to the Passion Week (cf. Matt. 20:17–19).

[b] CAME TO HIM, TESTING HIM. The Pharisees hoped to publicly discredit Jesus' ministry. The resulting loss of popularity, they hoped, would make it easier for them to destroy Him. Also, Perea was ruled by Herod Antipas—who had imprisoned John the Baptist for his views on divorce and remarriage (Mark 6:17–18). The Pharisees no doubt hoped a similar fate would befall Jesus.

[c] IS IT LAWFUL. A hotly debated difference of opinion existed between the Rabbis Shammai and Hillel (both near-contemporaries of Christ). The Shammaites interpreted the law rigidly and permitted a man to divorce his wife only if she was guilty of adultery. The Hillelites took a wholly pragmatic approach and permitted a man to divorce his wife indiscriminately. The Pharisees attempted to entrap Jesus with this volatile issue in first-century Judaism. The Pharisees undoubtedly expected Jesus to take one side, in which case He would lose the support of the other faction.

[d] "WHAT DID MOSES COMMAND YOU?" Jesus set the proper ground rules for the discussion. The issue was not rabbinical interpretations, but the teaching of Scripture.

[e] MOSES . . . PERMITTED YOU TO DIVORCE. The stress is certainly on the word "permitted." Thus Jesus clearly sides with the Shammai school of interpretation.

[f] PERMITTED. The Mosaic law, as the Pharisees were forced to concede, nowhere commanded divorce. The passage in question, Deut. 24:1–4, recognized the reality of divorce and sought to protect the wife's rights and reputation, and also regulated remarriage.

said to them, "Have you not read that He who made *them* at the beginning '[g]made them male and female,' and said, '[h]For this reason a man shall leave his father and mother and be joined to his wife, and the two shall become one flesh'? So then, they are no longer two but one flesh. [i]Therefore what God has joined together, let not man separate."

They said to Him, "[j]Why then did Moses command to give a [k]certificate of divorce, and to put her away?" He said to them, "Moses, because of [l]the hardness of your hearts, MK wrote you this precept, [and] MT permitted you to divorce your wives, but [m]from the beginning it was not so."

MK In the house His disciples also asked Him again about the same *matter.* So He said to them, MT "I say to you, whoever divorces his wife, except for [n]sexual immorality,

---

[g] MADE THEM MALE AND FEMALE. Quoted from Gen. 1:27; 5:2, in reference to Adam and Eve. Jesus' challenge to the Pharisees echoed the question raised by Mal. 2:15: "But did He not make them one . . . ?"

[h] FOR THIS REASON. Jesus took the issue beyond mere rabbinical quibbling over the technicalities of divorce to God's design for marriage. The passage Christ quotes (Gen. 2:24) presents three reasons for the inviolability of marriage: (1) God created only two humans, not a group of males and females who could configure as they pleased or switch partners as it suited them; (2) the word translated "be joined" lit. means "to glue," thus reflecting the strength of the marriage bond; (3) in God's eyes a married couple is "one flesh," forming an indivisible union, manifesting that oneness in a child.

[i] THEREFORE WHAT GOD HAS JOINED TOGETHER. Jesus added a fourth reason for the inviolability of marriage: God ordains marriages and thus they are not to be broken by man.

[j] WHY THEN DID MOSES COMMAND TO GIVE A CERTIFICATE OF DIVORCE? The Pharisees misrepresented Deut. 24:1–4. It was not a "command" for divorce, but a limitation on remarriage in the event of a divorce. While recognizing the legitimacy of divorce when a man "has found some uncleanness" (Deut. 24:1) in his wife (sexual sin, by Jesus' interpretation), Moses did not "command" divorce.

[k] CERTIFICATE OF DIVORCE. In this document, the husband was required to state the reason for the divorce, thus protecting the wife's reputation (if she were, in fact, innocent of wrongdoing). It also served as her formal release from the marriage and affirmed her right to remarry (assuming she was not guilty of immorality). The liberal wing of the Pharisees had misconstrued Deut. 24 to be teaching that divorce was "permitted" for any cause whatsoever (citing as legitimate grounds such trivial events as the wife's ruining dinner or the husband's simply finding a more desirable woman), providing the proper legal paperwork was done. They thus magnified a detail, mentioned merely in passing, into the main emphasis of the passage.

[l] THE HARDNESS OF YOUR HEARTS. This refers to the flagrant, unrepentant pursuit of sexual immorality—divorce was to be only used a last resort in dealing with such hard-heartedness. The Pharisees mistook God's gracious provision in permitting divorce (under certain circumstances) for His ordaining of it.

[m] FROM THE BEGINNING. Divorce formed no part of God's original plan for marriage, which was that one man be married to one woman for life (Gen. 2:24).

[n] SEXUAL IMMORALITY. This is a term that encompasses all sorts of sexual sins. Both here and in Matthew 5:32, Jesus includes this "exception clause," clearly permitting the innocent party in such a divorce to remarry without incurring the stigma of one who "commits adultery."

and [o]marries another, commits adultery [MK] against her. And if a woman divorces her husband and marries another, she commits adultery." [MT] His disciples said to Him, "If such is the case of the man with *his* wife, [p]it is better not to marry." But He said to them, "All cannot accept this saying, but only *those* to whom it has been given: For there are eunuchs who were born thus from *their* mother's womb, and there are eunuchs who were made eunuchs by men, and there are eunuchs who have made themselves eunuchs for the kingdom of heaven's sake. He who is able to accept *it*, [q]let him accept *it*."

---

[o] MARRIES ANOTHER, COMMITS ADULTERY. Remarriage after a divorce—except for legitimate biblical grounds—proliferates adultery. The innocent party—one whose spouse has committed prolonged, hard-hearted, unrepentant adultery—may remarry without being guilty of adultery, as may a believer whose unbelieving spouse has chosen to leave the marriage (cf. 1 Cor. 7:15).

[p] IT IS BETTER NOT TO MARRY. The disciples correctly understood the binding nature of marriage and that Jesus was setting a very high standard, permitting divorce only in the most extreme of circumstances.

[q] LET HIM ACCEPT IT. Since all cannot handle it, Christ is not enjoining celibacy here. Rather, He makes it entirely a matter of personal choice—except for those who are physically unable to marry, either through natural causes or because of the violence of other men. Still others may find there are pragmatic reasons not to marry for the good of the kingdom (cf. 1 Cor. 7:7–9). But in no way did Christ suggest that celibacy is superior to marriage (cf. Gen. 2:18; 1 Tim. 4:3).

137. Jesus Teaches About the Kingdom

Matt. 19:13–30; Mark 10:13–31; Luke 18:15–30

MT Then little children were brought to Him [a]that He might put *His* hands on them and pray, but the disciples rebuked MK those who brought *them.* But when Jesus saw *it,* He was greatly displeased and LK called them to *Him* and said MK to them, MT "Let the little children come to Me, and [b]do not forbid them; for [c]of such is the kingdom of heaven. MK Assuredly, I say to you, whoever does not receive the kingdom of God [d]as a little child will by no means enter it." And He took them up in His arms, laid *His* hands on them, and blessed them, MT and departed from there.

Now behold, MK as He was going out on the road, LK a certain ruler MK came running, knelt before Him, and asked Him, MT "[e]Good Teacher, [f]what good thing shall I do that I may have [g]eternal life?" LK So Jesus said to him, "[h]Why do you call Me

---

[a] THAT HE MIGHT PUT HIS HANDS ON THEM. i.e. lay His hands on them and pray for them. Jewish parents commonly sought the blessing of prominent rabbis for their children.

[b] DO NOT FORBID THEM. Jesus rebuked the disciples for their attempt to prevent the children from seeing Him. They were not the ones to decide who had access to Jesus (cf. Matt. 15:23).

[c] OF SUCH. These children were too young to have exercised personal faith. See Luke 18:15, where Luke refers to them as "infants." Therefore, it is all the more significant that Christ used them as an illustration of those who make up "the kingdom of heaven" (cf. 18:1–4). Mark 10:16 also says He "blessed them." God often shows a special mercy to those who because of age or mental deficiency are incapable of either faith or willful unbelief (cf. Jonah 4:11). They are called "innocents" in Jer. 19:4. This does not mean they are free from the inherited guilt and moral corruption of Adam's sin (cf. Rom. 5:12–19), but rather that they are not culpable in the same sense as those whose sins are premeditated and deliberate. Jesus' words here suggest that God's mercy is graciously extended to infants so that those who die are sovereignly regenerated and granted entrance into the kingdom—not because they are deserving of heaven, but because God in His grace chooses to redeem them. Cf. 2 Sam. 12:23. Most, if not all, of these children would have been too young to exercise personal faith. Jesus' words imply that God graciously extends salvation to those too young or too mentally impaired to exercise faith.

[d] AS A LITTLE CHILD. With humble, trusting dependence and the recognition of having achieved nothing of value or virtue.

[e] GOOD TEACHER. This is not necessarily a recognition of Christ's deity. The young man simply meant that Christ was righteous and a teacher from God who apparently had eternal life and might know how he could get it.

[f] WHAT . . . SHALL I DO. Steeped in the legalism of his day, the young man naturally thought in terms of some religious deed that would guarantee him eternal life. His lack of understanding about the true nature of salvation, however, does not mean he was insincere.

good? No one *is* good but One, *that is,* God. MT But [i]if you want to enter into life, keep the commandments." He said to Him, "Which ones?" Jesus said, "'[j]You shall not murder,' 'You shall not commit adultery,' 'You shall not steal,' 'You shall not bear false witness,' MK '[k]Do not defraud,' MT 'Honor your father and *your* mother,' and, 'You shall love your neighbor as yourself.'"

The young man MK answered and said to Him, MT "[l]All these things I have kept from my youth. What do I still lack?" LK So when [m]Jesus heard these things, He MK [looked] at him, loved him, and said to him, "One thing you LK still MK lack: Go your way, [n]sell whatever you have and give to the poor, and you will have [o]treasure

---

[g] ETERNAL LIFE. More than just eternal existence, it is a different quality of life. Eternal life is in Christ alone (cf. John 3:15–16; John 10:28; 17:2–3; Rom. 6:23; 1 John 5:11, 13, 20). Those who possess it have "passed from death to life" (John 5:24; 1 John 3:14; cf. Eph. 2:1–3); they have died to sin and are alive to God (Rom. 6:11); they have the very life of Christ in them (2 Cor. 4:11; Gal. 2:20); and enjoy a relationship with Jesus Christ that will never end (John 17:3).

[h] WHY DO YOU CALL ME GOOD? NO ONE IS GOOD BUT ONE. Jesus was not disclaiming His own deity, but rather teaching the young man that all but God are sinners. This young man's most serious spiritual defect was his reluctance to confess his own utter spiritual bankruptcy. Why do you call Me good? Jesus challenged the ruler to think through the implications of ascribing to Him the title "good." Since only God is intrinsically good, was he prepared to acknowledge Jesus' deity? By this query Jesus did not deny His deity; on the contrary, He affirmed it.

[i] IF YOU WANT TO ENTER INTO LIFE, KEEP THE COMMANDMENTS. This, of course, is law, not gospel. Before showing him the way to life, Jesus wanted to impress on the young man both the high standard required by God and the absolute futility of seeking salvation by his own merit. This should have elicited a response about the impossibility of keeping the law perfectly, but instead the young man confidently declared that he qualified for heaven under those terms.

[j] YOU SHALL NOT . . . These are five of the six commandments that make up the second table of the Ten Commandments—all dealing with human relationships (cf. Ex. 20:12–16; Deut. 5:16–20). In Matthew's account, the tenth commandment was omitted, which deals with covetousness, with Lev. 19:18 cited instead, as the summation of the second half of the Decalogue. Cf. Rom. 13:1–10.

[k] DO NOT DEFRAUD. This was not the wording of any of the Ten Commandments and is unique to Mark's account. It seems to be a paraphrase for the command against coveting.

[l] ALL THESE THINGS I HAVE KEPT. His answer was no doubt sincere, but superficial and untrue. He, like Paul (Phil. 3:6), may have been blameless in terms of external actions, but not in terms of internal attitudes and motives (cf. Matt. 5:21–48). The self-righteous young man would not admit to his own sin.

[m] JESUS . . . LOVED HIM. i.e., felt great compassion for this sincere truth-seeker who was so hopelessly lost. God does love the unsaved (cf. Matt. 5:43–48).

in heaven; and [p]come, take up the cross, and follow Me." MT But when the young man LK heard this, MK he was sad at this word, and [q]went away sorrowful, for LK he was very rich [and] MK had great possessions.

LK And when Jesus saw that he became very sorrowful, He MK looked around and said to His disciples, MT "Assuredly, I say to you that it is hard for a rich man to enter the kingdom of heaven." MK And the disciples were astonished at His words. But Jesus answered again and said to them, "Children, [r]how hard it is for those who trust in riches to enter the kingdom of God! MT And again I say to you, it is easier for a [s]camel to go through the eye of a needle than for a rich man to enter the kingdom of God." When His disciples heard *it,* they were greatly astonished

---

[n] SELL WHATEVER YOU HAVE. Again, Jesus was not setting forth terms for salvation, but rather exposing the young man's true heart. His refusal to obey here revealed two things: (1) he was not blameless as far as the law was concerned, because he was guilty of loving himself and his possessions more than his neighbors(cf. Lev. 19:18); and (2) he lacked true faith, which involves a willingness to surrender all at Christ's bidding (cf. Matt. 16:24). He refused to obey Christ's direct command, choosing to serve riches instead of God (Matt. 6:24). Jesus was not teaching salvation by philanthropy, but He was demanding that this young man give Him first place. The young man failed the test. The issue was to determine whether he would submit to the Lordship of Christ no matter what He asked of him. So as he would not acknowledge his sin and repent, neither would he submit to the Sovereign Savior. Such unwillingness on both counts kept him from the eternal life he sought.

[o] TREASURE IN HEAVEN. Salvation and all its benefits, given by the Father who dwells there, both in this life and the life to come (cf. Matt. 13:44–46).

[p] COME . . . FOLLOW ME. This was the answer to the young man's question. It was a call to faith. It is likely that the young man never even heard or contemplated it, though, because his own love of his possessions was such a stumbling block that he had already rejected Jesus' claim to lordship over his life. Thus he walked away in unbelief.

[q] WENT AWAY SORROWFUL. It was purely a worldly disappointment based on the fact that he didn't receive the eternal life he sought because the price of sacrifice was too high. He loved his wealth.

[r] HOW HARD IT IS. *Hard* in this context means impossible. "Riches" tend to breed self-sufficiency and a false sense of security, leading those who have them to imagine they do not need divine resources (see Luke 16:13; contrast Luke 19:2–10; cf. 1 Tim. 6:9, 17–18).

[s] CAMEL . . . EYE OF A NEEDLE. i.e., it is impossible. Jesus was underscoring the impossibility of anyone being saved by merit. The Persians expressed impossibility by saying it would be easier to put an elephant through the eye of a needle. This was a Jewish colloquial adaptation of that expression denoting impossibility (the largest animal in the region was a camel). Many improbable interpretations have arisen that attempt to soften this phrase, e.g., that "needle" referred to a tiny gate in the Jerusalem city wall that camels could enter only with difficulty (but there is no evidence that such a gate ever existed, and if it had, any sensible camel driver would have simply found a larger gate); or a copyist's error resulted in *kamelos* (camel) being substituted for *kamilos* (a large rope or cable) (but a large rope could no more go through the eye of a needle than a camel could, and it is extremely unlikely that the text of all three Synoptic Gospels would have been changed in exactly the same way). Jesus' use of this illustration was to explicitly say that salvation by human effort is impossible; it is wholly by God's grace. The Jews believed that with alms a man purchased salvation (as recorded in the Talmud), so the more wealth one had, the more alms he could give, the more sacrifices and offerings he could offer, thus purchasing redemption. Jesus destroyed that notion and along with it the notion that anyone can merit enough divine favor to gain entrance into heaven. The disciples' question makes it clear that they understood what Jesus meant—that not even the rich could buy salvation.

MK saying among themselves, "[t]Who then can be saved?" MT But Jesus looked at *them* and said to them, MK "[u]With men *it is* impossible, but not with God; for with God all things are possible."

MK Then Peter began to say to Him, "See, [v]we have left all and followed You. MT Therefore what shall we have?" MK So Jesus answered and said, MT "Assuredly I say to you, that in the [w]regeneration, when the Son of Man sits on the throne of His glory, you who have followed Me will also sit on twelve thrones, [x]judging the twelve tribes of Israel. And everyone who has left houses or brothers or sisters or father or mother or wife or children or lands, for My name's sake MK and the gospel's [and] LK for the sake of the kingdom of God, MT shall receive MK a hundredfold now [y]in this LK present MK time—houses and brothers and sisters and mothers and children and lands, with persecutions—and in the age to come, eternal life. But many *who are* [z]first will be last, and the last first."

---

[t] Who then can be saved? This was the right question to ask; it showed that they got Jesus' message. Salvation is possible only through divine grace. Jesus' teaching ran counter to the prevailing rabbinical teaching, which gave the wealthy a clear advantage for salvation. Jesus' emphatic teaching that even the rich could not be saved by their own efforts left the bewildered disciples wondering what chance the poor stood. Cf. Rom. 3:9–20; Gal. 3:10–13; Phil. 3:4–9.

[u] With men it is impossible, but not with God. It is impossible for anyone to be saved by his own efforts, since salvation is entirely a gracious, sovereign work of God. Cf. Rom. 3:21–28; 8:28–30; Gal. 3:6–9; 26–29.

[v] we have left all and followed You. Peter points out that they had already done what Christ demanded of the rich young ruler. They had embarked on the life of faith with Christ. Would that self-abandoning faith, Peter asked, qualify them for a place in the kingdom? Note that Jesus did not rebuke Peter for his expectation of reward (cf. Rev. 22:12).

[w] regeneration. Here the term does not carry its normal theological meaning of personal regeneration (cf. Titus 3:5). Instead, Jesus was speaking of "the times of restoration of all things, which God has spoken by the mouth of all His holy prophets since the world began" (Acts 3:21). This is a reference to the earthly kingdom described in Rev. 20:1–15, when believers will "sit on . . . thrones" with Christ (Rev. 3:21).

[x] judging. Governing. Cf. 1 Cor. 6:2, 3.

[y] in this present time . . . the age to come. Following Jesus brings rewards in this present age and when Messiah's glorious kingdom comes.

[z] first will be last, and the last first. This statement means that everyone ends up the same, a truth that is explained by the parable that follows (cf. Matt. 20:16). Believers will share equally in the blessings of heaven.

138. The Parable of the Equal Wages

Matt. 20:1–16

MT "For the kingdom of heaven is like a landowner who went out early in the morning to [a]hire laborers for his vineyard. Now when he had agreed with the laborers for [b]a denarius a day, he sent them into his vineyard. And he went out about the [c]third hour and saw others standing idle in the marketplace, and said to them, 'You also go into the vineyard, and whatever is right I will give you.' So they went.

"Again he went out about the sixth and the ninth hour, and did likewise. And about the eleventh hour he went out and found others standing idle, and said to them, 'Why have you been standing here idle all day?' They said to him, 'Because no one hired us.' He said to them, 'You also go into the vineyard, and [d]whatever is right you will receive.'

"So when evening had come, the owner of the vineyard said to his steward, 'Call the laborers and give them *their* wages, beginning with the last to the first.' And when those came who *were hired* about the [e]eleventh hour, they each received a denarius. But when the first came, they supposed that they would receive more; and they likewise received each a denarius. And when they had received *it,* they complained against the landowner, saying, 'These last *men* have worked *only* one hour, and you made them equal to us who have borne the burden and the heat of the day.' But he answered one of them and said, 'Friend, [f]I am doing you no

---

[a] HIRE LABORERS. This was typical during harvest. Day laborers stood in the market place from dawn, hoping to be hired for the day's work. The work day began at 6:00 a.m. and went to 6:00 p.m.

[b] A DENARIUS A DAY. A fair wage for a full day's labor (cf. Matt. 22:19).

[c] THIRD HOUR. 9:00 a.m. They were standing idle because no one had hired them.

[d] WHATEVER IS RIGHT. So eager to work, these men did not even negotiate a specific wage.

[e] ELEVENTH HOUR. i.e., 5:00 p.m. Desperate for work, they had waited nearly "all day." They would take whatever they could get.

[f] I AM DOING YOU NO WRONG. Everyone received a full day's wage, to their shock. The man was acting graciously to those whom he overpaid. This was no slight against those whom he paid a full wage for a full day's work. That was precisely what they agreed to in the beginning. But it was his privilege to extend the same generosity to all (cf. Rom. 9:15).

wrong. Did you not agree with me for a denarius? Take *what is* yours and go your way. I wish to give to this last man *the same* as to you. Is it not lawful for me to do what I wish with my own things? Or is your eye evil because I am good?' So [g]the last will be first, and the first last. For many are called, but few chosen."

---

[g] THE LAST WILL BE FIRST, AND THE FIRST LAST. In other words, everyone finishes in a dead heat. No matter how long each of the workers worked, they each received a full day's wage. Similarly, the thief on the cross will enjoy the full blessings of heaven alongside those who have labored their whole lives for Christ. Such is the grace of God (cf. Matt. 19:30).

139. Jesus Foretells His Death and Resurrection

Matt. 20:17–19; Mark 10:32–34; Luke 18:31–34

MK Now they were on the road, [a]going up to Jerusalem, and Jesus was going before them; and they were [b]amazed. And as [c]they followed they were afraid. Then He took the twelve MT disciples MK aside again and began to tell them the things that would happen to Him: "Behold, we are going up to Jerusalem, LK and [d]all things that are written by the prophets concerning the Son of Man will be accomplished. For MK the Son of Man will be betrayed to the chief priests and to the scribes; and they will [e]condemn Him to death and [f]deliver Him to the Gentiles; and they will mock Him, and scourge Him, and spit on Him, and kill Him. LK They will MT crucify LK Him. And the third day [g]He will rise again." But they understood none of these things; this saying was hidden from them, and [h]they did not know the things which were spoken.

---

[a] GOING UP TO JERUSALEM. From Perea, via Jericho (Mark 10:46). This is the first mention in Mark's gospel of Jerusalem as Jesus' destination. Because of the elevation of Jerusalem (about 2,550 feet above sea level), travelers always spoke of going up to the city, regardless of where in Israel they started.

[b] AMAZED. At Jesus' resolute determination to go to Jerusalem (cf. Luke 9:51) despite the cruel death that awaited Him there.

[c] THEY FOLLOWED. The Greek syntax makes it clear that this was a group distinct from the twelve, probably pilgrims en route to Jerusalem for Passover. They were afraid because they realized something significant was about to happen that they did not understand.

[d] ALL THINGS THAT ARE WRITTEN BY THE PROPHETS. e.g., Pss. 22; 69; Isa. 53; Dan. 9:26; Zech. 13:7.

[e] CONDEMN HIM TO DEATH. This was the third and last prediction of His death and resurrection that Jesus made to the twelve (cf. Matt. 16:21; 17:22–23; Mark 8:31; 9:31; Luke 9:22, 44). Plus three of the disciples had overheard Jesus discussing His death with Moses and Elijah at the Transfiguration (Luke 9:31). (Jesus also hinted at his future suffering in places like Luke 12:50; 13:32–33; 17:25). Of the three explicit predictions, this is the most detailed, specifically mentioning that He would be mocked (Mark 15:17–20; Luke 23:11, 35–39), scourged (Mark 15:15), and spat upon (Mark 14:65; 15:19).

[f] DELIVER HIM TO THE GENTILES. This is His first mention of being turned over to the Romans.

[g] HE WILL RISE AGAIN. Christ had predicted His resurrection on the third day before (Luke 9:22). But the disciples missed the import of these words, and when He actually did rise, they were surprised by it (Luke 24:6).

[h] THEY DID NOT KNOW. The whole matter of Christ's death and resurrection was not grasped by the twelve. The reason may have been that they were enamored with other ideas about the Messiah and how His earthly rule would operate (cf. Matt. 16:22; 17:10; Acts 1:6).

140. Jesus Warns Against Selfish Ambition

Matt. 20:20–28; Mark 10:35–45

MT Then the [a]mother of Zebedee's sons came to Him with her sons, kneeling down and asking something from Him. And He said to her, "What do you wish?" She said to Him, "[b]Grant that these two sons of mine may sit, one on Your right hand and the other on the left, [c]in Your kingdom."

MK [d]James and John, the sons of Zebedee, [were also] saying, "Teacher, we want You to do for us whatever we ask." MK And He said to them, "What do you want Me to do for you?" They said to Him, "Grant us that we may [e]sit, one on Your right hand and the other on Your left, [f]in Your glory."

MT But Jesus answered and said MK to them, MT "[g]You do not know what you ask. Are you able to drink [h]the cup that I am about to drink, and be baptized with [i]the baptism that I am baptized with?" They said to Him, "We are able." So He said to

---

[a] MOTHER OF ZEBEDEE'S SONS. Mark 10:35 says James and John themselves raised the question of Matt. 20:21. There is no contradiction. It is possible either that the three of them asked together, or perhaps even more likely that they had discussed it among themselves beforehand, and each posed the question to Jesus privately.

[b] GRANT . . . THESE TWO SONS OF MINE. Probably playing off the words of Jesus in Matt. 19:28, James and John had enlisted their mother to convey their proud, self-seeking request to Jesus. This was a recurring matter among the disciples (cf. Matt. 18:1, 4; 23:11; Mark 9:34, Luke 9:46; 22:24, 26), right up to the table at the Last Supper.

[c] IN YOUR KINGDOM. This incident reveals yet again the disciples' failure to grasp Jesus' teaching on humility (cf. Matt. 20:21; Mark 9:34). Ignoring the Lord's repeated instruction that He was going to Jerusalem to die, the disciples still thought the physical manifestation of the kingdom was about to appear and were busy maneuvering for the places of prominence in it (cf. Matt. 18:1).

[d] JAMES AND JOHN, THE SONS OF ZEBEDEE. Matthew reveals that their mother accompanied them and spoke first (Matt. 20:20–21), after which James and John reiterated her request. If she was Jesus' aunt, the three undoubtedly hoped to capitalize on the family ties.

[e] SIT . . . ON YOUR RIGHT . . . YOUR LEFT. In the places of highest prominence and honor beside the throne.

[f] IN YOUR GLORY. In the glorious majesty of His kingdom (cf. Matt. 20:21).

[g] YOU DO NOT KNOW WHAT YOU ASK. The greatest glory goes to those who suffer the most for Christ.

[h] THE CUP THAT I AM ABOUT TO DRINK. Endure suffering and the cup of God's wrath as Jesus would (cf. Matt. 26:39; Mark 14:36; Luke 22:42; John 18:11).

[i] THE BAPTISM THAT I AM BAPTIZED WITH. This refers to the immersion of the Lord into suffering (cf. Luke 12:50). However, the phrases referring to baptism here and in Matt. 20:23 do not appear in the best manuscripts.

them, "[j]You will indeed drink My cup, and be baptized with the baptism that I am baptized with; but to sit on My right hand and on My left is [k]not Mine to give, but *it is for those* [l]for whom it is prepared by My Father."

And when [m]the ten heard *it,* they were greatly displeased with the two brothers, [MK] James and John. [MT] But Jesus called them to *Himself* and said [MK] to them, [MT] "You know that [MK] those who are considered rulers over the Gentiles [n]lord it over them, [MT] and those who are great exercise authority over them. Yet it shall [o]not be so among you; but [p]whoever desires to become great among you, let him be your servant. And whoever desires to be first among you [MK] shall be slave of all. For even the Son of Man [q]did not come to be served, but to serve, and to [r]give His life a ransom for many."

---

[j] YOU WILL INDEED. James and John would suffer like their Master (cf. Acts 12:2; Rev. 1:9), but that in itself would not earn them the honors they desired. James was beheaded (Acts 12:2) and John tortured and exiled to Patmos (Rev. 1:9) for the sake of Christ.

[k] NOT MINE TO GIVE. Honors in the kingdom are bestowed not on the basis of selfish ambition, but of divine sovereign will.

[l] FOR WHOM IT IS PREPARED. God alone has chosen.

[m] THE TEN . . . WERE GREATLY DISPLEASED. Jealous displeasure, no doubt. Not righteous indignation, since they, too, had been guilty in the past of such self-serving conduct (Mark 9:33–34) and would be so in the future (Luke 22:24). The rest of the disciples resented James and John for their attempt to gain an advantage over the others in pursuing the honor they all wanted. They all would have petitioned Jesus for the exalted, favored positions, given the opportunity.

[n] LORD IT OVER THEM . . . EXERCISE AUTHORITY. These parallel phrases convey the sense of autocratic, domineering authority.

[o] NOT BE SO AMONG YOU. There is no place in the church for domineering leaders (cf. Matt. 23:8–12; Mark 9:35; 1 Peter 5:3–6; 3 John 9–10).

[p] WHOEVER DESIRES TO BECOME GREAT. In this rich text, the Lord was teaching the disciples that the style of greatness and leadership for believers is different. The Gentile leaders dominate in dictatorial fashion, using carnal power and authority. Believers are to do the opposite—they lead by being servants and giving themselves away for others, as Jesus did.

[q] DID NOT COME TO BE SERVED. Jesus was the supreme example of servant leadership (cf. John 13:13–15). The King of Kings, and Lord of Lords (Rev. 19:16) relinquished His privileges (Phil. 2:5–8) and gave His life as a selfless sacrifice in serving others.

[r] TO GIVE HIS LIFE A RANSOM FOR MANY. The word translated *for* means "in the place of," underscoring the substitutionary nature of Christ's sacrifice on behalf of those who would put their faith in Him (cf. Rom. 8:1–3; 1 Cor. 6:20; Gal. 3:13; 4:5; Eph. 1:7; Titus 2:14; 1 Peter 1:18–19). A "ransom" is a price paid to redeem a slave or a prisoner. Redemption does not involve a price paid to Satan, as some erroneous theories of the atonement teach. Satan is presented in Scripture as a foe to be defeated, not a ruler to be placated. Rather, the ransom was paid to God—to satisfy His justice and holy wrath against sin. The price paid was Christ's own life—as a blood atonement (cf. Lev. 17:11; Heb. 9:22). In paying the ransom, Christ "bore our sins in His own body on the [cross]" (1 Peter 2:24). This, then, is the meaning of the cross: Christ subjected Himself to the divine punishment against sin on our behalf (cf. Isa. 53:4–5; 2 Cor. 5:21). Suffering the brunt of divine wrath in the place of sinners was the "cup" He spoke of having to drink and the baptism He was preparing to undergo.

141. Jesus Heals Two Blind Men

Matt. 20:29–34; Mark 10:46–52; Luke 18:35–43

MK Now they came to [a]Jericho. LK Then it happened MK [b]as He went out of Jericho with His disciples, MT a great multitude followed Him. And behold, [c]two blind men [were] sitting by the road LK begging. And hearing a multitude passing by, MK blind Bartimaeus, the [d]son of Timaeus, LK asked what it meant. So they told him that Jesus of Nazareth was passing by.

MT When they heard that Jesus was passing by, [they] cried out, saying, "MK Jesus, MT have mercy on us, O Lord, [e]Son of David!" Then the multitude warned them that they should be quiet; but they cried out all the more, saying, "Have mercy on us, O Lord, Son of David!"

MK So [f]Jesus stood still and commanded MT them MK to be called [and] LK brought to Him. MK Then they called the blind man, saying to him, "Be of good cheer. Rise, He is calling you." And throwing aside his garment, [Bartimaeus] rose and came to Jesus. So Jesus answered and said to him [and his fellow beggar], "What do you

---

[a] JERICHO. A city located about fifteen miles northeast of Jerusalem and five miles from the Jordan River. The route from Perea to Jerusalem passed through it. This is the only recorded visit of Jesus to Jericho.

[b] AS HE WENT OUT. Mark and Matthew state that the healing took place as Jesus was leaving Jericho; Luke as He was entering the city. Mark and Matthew may be referring to the ancient walled city, just north of the NT city, while Luke refers to NT Jericho. It is a fact that there were two Jerichos—one the mound of the ancient city (the ruins of which may still be seen today) and the other, the inhabited city of Jericho, close by. Jesus may have been going "out of" old Jericho and entering new Jericho. Or it may also be that the events are telescoped for us, so that Christ first encountered the blind men on His way into the city, but the healing took place as he was departing. Or Luke's words may simply mean Jesus was in the vicinity of Jericho when the healing took place. In any case there is no contradiction here.

[c] TWO BLIND MEN. Mark 10:46 and Luke 18:35 mention only one blind man. This supposed difficulty is fairly simple to reconcile: there were two blind men, but Bartimaeus (Mark 10:46) was the spokesman of the two and was, therefore, the sole focus of both Luke's and Mark's accounts (cf. Matt. 8:28 with 5:2; Luke 8:27). If they were unable to work, blind people commonly made their living by begging (cf. John 9:8). These men had staked out a good site on the main road to Jerusalem.

[d] SON OF TIMAEUS. The translation of "Bartimaeus"; the Aramaic prefix "bar" means "son of."

[e] SON OF DAVID. A common messianic title, used as such only in the Synoptic Gospels.

[f] JESUS . . . COMMANDED . . . TO BE CALLED. Thus implicitly rebuking those trying to silence them.

want Me to do for you?" MT They said to Him, "Lord, MK [g]Rabboni, MT that [h]our eyes may be opened, LK that [we] may receive [our] sight."

So Jesus had compassion and touched their eyes. MK Then Jesus said, LK "Receive your sight. MK Go your way; [i]your faith has made you well." MT And immediately their eyes received sight, and they followed Him MK on the road, LK glorifying God. And all the people, when they saw *it,* gave praise to God.

---

[g] RABBONI. An intensified form of "rabbi."

[h] OUR EYES MAY BE OPENED. This is the second of two healings of blind men recorded in Mark (cf. Mark 8:22–26).

[i] YOUR FAITH HAS MADE YOU WELL. Lit. "saved you." Bartimaeus's physical and spiritual eyes were likely opened at the same time. The outward healing reflected the inner wellness of salvation.

142. Zacchaeus Encounters the Savior

Luke 19:1–10

LK Then *Jesus* entered and passed through Jericho. Now behold, *there was* a man named Zacchaeus who was a [a]chief tax collector, and he was rich. And he sought to see who Jesus was, but could not because of [b]the crowd, for he was of short stature. So he ran ahead and climbed up into a [c]sycamore tree to see Him, for He was going to pass that *way.* And when Jesus came to the place, He looked up and saw him, and said to him, "Zacchaeus, make haste and come down, for today [d]I must stay at your house."

So he made haste and came down, and received Him [e]joyfully. But when they saw *it,* [f]they all complained, saying, "He has gone to be a guest with a man who is a sinner." Then Zacchaeus stood and said to the Lord, "Look, Lord, I give half of

---

[a] CHIEF TAX COLLECTOR. Zacchaeus probably oversaw a large tax district and had other tax collectors working for him. Jericho alone was a prosperous trading center, so it is certain that Zacchaeus was a wealthy man. It is striking to note that only a chapter earlier, Luke recorded the account of the rich young ruler, and Jesus' statement about "how hard it is for those who have riches to enter the kingdom of God" (Luke 18:24). Here Jesus demonstrates that with God, nothing is impossible (cf. Luke 18:27).

[b] THE CROWD. Christ was probably traveling with a large entourage of pilgrims to the Passover in Jerusalem. But "the crowd" apparently refers to people in Jericho who lined the street to see Him pass through. They had undoubtedly heard about the recent raising of Lazarus in Bethany, less than fifteen miles away (John 11). That, combined with His fame as a healer and teacher, stirred the entire city when word arrived that He was coming.

[c] SYCAMORE TREE. A sturdy tree with low, spreading branches. A small person could get out on a limb and hang over the road. This was an undignified position for someone of Zacchaeus's rank, but he was desperate to see Christ.

[d] I MUST STAY AT YOUR HOUSE. This was worded as a mandate, not a request. It is the only place in all the gospels where Jesus invited Himself to be someone's guest (cf. Isa. 65:1).

[e] JOYFULLY. Such a despicable sinner as a typical tax collector (cf. Matt. 5:46) might have been distressed at the prospect of a visit from the perfect, sinless Son of God. But Zacchaeus's heart was prepared.

[f] THEY ALL COMPLAINED. Both the religious elite and the common people hated Zacchaeus. They did not understand, and in their blind pride refused to see what possible righteous purpose Jesus had in visiting such a notorious sinner. But He had come to seek and to save the lost. Cf. Luke 15:2.

my goods to the poor; and if I have taken anything from anyone by false accusation, [g]I restore fourfold."

And Jesus said to him, "Today salvation has come to this house, because he also is [h]a son of Abraham; for the Son of Man has come [i]to seek and to save that which was lost."

---

[g] I RESTORE FOURFOLD. Zacchaeus's willingness to make restitution was proof that his conversion was genuine. It was the fruit, not the condition, of his salvation. The law required a penalty of one-fifth as restitution for money acquired by fraud (Lev. 6:5; Num. 5:6, 7), so Zacchaeus was doing more than was required. The law required four-fold restitution only when an animal was stolen and killed (Ex. 22:1). If the animal was found alive, only two-fold restitution was required (Ex. 22:4). But Zacchaeus judged his own crime severely, acknowledging that he was as guilty as the lowest common robber. Since much of his wealth had probably been acquired fraudulently, this was a costly commitment. On top of that he gave half his goods to the poor. But Zacchaeus had just found incomprehensible spiritual riches and did not mind the loss of material wealth (cf. Matt. 13:44–46; Luke 14:28). He stands in stark contrast with the rich young ruler in Luke 18:18–24.

[h] A SON OF ABRAHAM. A Jew by race for whom Christ came as Savior (cf. Matt. 1:21; 10:6; 15:24; John 4:22).

[i] TO SEEK AND TO SAVE THAT WHICH WAS LOST. The main theme of Luke's gospel. See Luke 5:31, 32; 15:4–7, 32; cf. 1 Tim. 2:4; 4:10.

143. A Parable About the Kingdom's Delay

Luke 19:11–28

LK Now as they heard these things, He spoke another parable, because He was near Jerusalem and because [a]they thought the kingdom of God would appear immediately. Therefore He said: "A certain nobleman went into [b]a far country to receive for himself a kingdom and to return. So he called ten of his servants, delivered to them ten [c]minas, and said to them, 'Do business till I come.' But his citizens hated him, and [d]sent a delegation after him, saying, 'We will not have this *man* to reign over us.'

"And so it was that [e]when he returned, having received the kingdom, he then commanded these servants, to whom he had given the money, to be called to him, that he might know how much every man had gained by trading. Then came the first, saying, 'Master, your mina has earned ten minas.' And he said to him, 'Well *done,* good servant; because you were [f]faithful in a very little, have authority

---

[a] THEY THOUGHT. The disciples still mistakenly assumed that Christ would immediately establish His kingdom on earth at Jerusalem (cf. Luke 17:20).

[b] A FAR COUNTRY. Kings in Roman provinces like Galilee and Perea actually went to Rome to receive their kingdoms. The entire Herodian dynasty was dependent on Rome for ruling power, and Herod the Great himself had gone to Rome to be given his kingdom. This parable illustrates Christ, who would soon depart to receive His kingdom and will one day return to rule. It is similar to the parable of the talents (Matt. 25:14–30), but there are significant differences. That parable was told during the Olivet Discourse (cf. Matt. 24:1–25:46); this one was told on the road from Jericho up to Jerusalem (cf. Luke 19:28).

[c] MINAS. A Greek measure of money (cf. Luke 15:8), equal to slightly more than three-month's salary. The mina was one-sixtieth of a talent, meaning that the ten servants in this parable had been given a considerably smaller sum to account for than any of the three servants in the parable of the talents (Matt. 25:14–30).

[d] SENT A DELEGATION AFTER HIM. This was precisely what had happened to Archelaus (cf. Matt. 2:22), son of Herod the Great, when he went to Rome to be made tetrarch of Judea. A delegation of Jews traveled to Rome with a protest to Caesar Augustus. He refused their complaint and made Archelaus king anyway. Archelaus subsequently built his palace in Jericho, not far from where Jesus told this parable. Archelaus's rule was so inept and despotic that Rome quickly replaced him with a succession of procurators, of whom Pontius Pilate was the fifth. With this parable Jesus warned that the Jews were about to do the same thing, in a spiritual sense, to their true Messiah.

[e] WHEN HE RETURNED. This pictured Christ's return to earth. The full manifestation of His kingdom on earth awaits that time. Cf. Luke 17:20.

[f] FAITHFUL IN A VERY LITTLE. Those with relatively small gifts and opportunities are just as responsible to use them faithfully as those who are given much more.

[g]over ten cities.' And the second came, saying, 'Master, your mina has earned five minas.' Likewise he said to him, 'You also be over five cities.'

"Then another came, saying, 'Master, here is your mina, which I have kept put away in a handkerchief. For [h]I feared you, because you are an austere man. You collect what you did not deposit, and reap what you did not sow.' And he said to him, 'Out of your own mouth I will judge you, *you* wicked servant. [i]You knew that I was an austere man, collecting what I did not deposit and reaping what I did not sow. Why then did you not put my money in the bank, that at my coming I might have collected it with interest?'

"And he said to those who stood by, 'Take the mina from him, and give *it* to him who has ten minas.' (But they said to him, 'Master, he has ten minas.') 'For I say to you, that to everyone who has will be given; and from him who does not have, even what he has will be taken away from him. But bring here [j]those enemies of mine, who did not want me to reign over them, and [k]slay *them* before me.'" When He had said this, He went on ahead, going [l]up to Jerusalem.

---

[g] OVER TEN CITIES. The reward is incomparably greater than the ten minas warranted. Note also that the rewards were apportioned according to the servants' diligence: the one who gained ten minas was given ten cities, the one who gained five minas, five cities, and so on.

[h] I FEARED YOU. A craven fear, not borne out of love or reverence, but tainted with contempt for the master (cf. Matt. 25:24). Had he had any true regard for the master, a righteous "fear" would have provoked diligence rather than sloth.

[i] YOU KNEW. Cf. Matt. 25:26. This did not suggest that what the man "knew" about the master was true. However, even the knowledge he claimed to have was enough to condemn him. Thus will it be with the wicked in the day of judgment.

[j] THOSE ENEMIES OF MINE. These illustrated the Jews who actively opposed him.

[k] SLAY THEM BEFORE ME. This spoke of harsh, violent judgment and may be a reference to the destruction of Jerusalem (cf. Matt. 24:2).

[l] UP TO JERUSALEM. The road from Jericho to Jerusalem was a steep ascent, rising some four thousand feet in about twenty miles. This represented the last leg of the long journey that began in Luke 9:51.

Part VIII | The Passion Week of the Messiah AD 30

144. Jesus Arrives in Bethany

Matt. 21:1a; 26:6–13; Mark 11:1a; 14:3–9; Luke 19:29a; John 11:55–12:11

JN And the [a]Passover of the Jews was near, and many went from the country up to Jerusalem before the Passover, to purify themselves. Then [b]they sought Jesus, and spoke among themselves as they stood in the temple, "What do you think—that He will not come to the feast?" Now both the chief priests and the Pharisees had given a command, that [c]if anyone knew where He was, he should report *it*, that they might seize Him.

LK And it came to pass, JN [d]six days before the Passover, Jesus MK [e]drew near Jerusalem, to [f]Bethphage and JN came to [g]Bethany, MK at the [h]Mount of Olives,

---

[a] Passover. This is the third Passover explicitly mentioned in John (cf. John 2:13; 6:4) and the last in Jesus' earthly ministry at which His sacrificial death occurred.

[b] they sought Jesus. The Jews who filled Jerusalem for Passover were wondering if Jesus would show Himself at this time and were actively seeking to find Him. The plot of the chief priests and Pharisees (cf. John 7:12) was known widely enough to pique their curiosity as to whether Jesus would dare show Himself in Jerusalem.

[c] if anyone knew. The plotters ensured that the whole city was filled with potential informants.

[d] six days before the Passover. This may have been the previous Saturday, with Passover coming six days later on Thursday evening through sunset Friday. Or it may have been the previous Sunday, if Passover is included in the six days.

[e] drew near Jerusalem. A general transition statement marking the end of the narrative in Mark 10. It also indicates the beginning of the final phase of Christ's three-year ministry.

[f] Bethphage. A small town near Bethany, just east of Jerusalem, on the southeast slope of the Mount of Olives. It is mentioned nowhere else in Scripture except in connection with Christ's triumphal entry (Mark 11:1; Luke 19:29). Its name literally means "house of unripe figs."

[g] Bethany. The hometown of Mary, Martha, and Lazarus (John 11:1) on the eastern slope of the Mount of Olives, two miles east of Jerusalem. Jesus often stayed there during His visits to Jerusalem.

[h] Mount of Olives. This mountain stood between Bethany and Jerusalem (cf. Matt. 24:3). It was the main peak of a ridge running north to south, located east of the Kidron Valley adjacent to the temple. It derived its name from the dense olive groves that once covered it.

JN where Lazarus was who had been dead, whom He had raised from the dead. MT And when Jesus was in Bethany at the house of [i]Simon the leper, JN they made Him a supper; and Martha served, but Lazarus was one of those who sat at the table with Him. Then, MK as He sat at the table, JN Mary MT came to Him having [j]an alabaster flask [containing] JN a [k]pound of very costly oil of [l]spikenard. MK Then she [m]broke the flask and poured *it* on His head. MT And she JN [n]anointed the feet of Jesus, and wiped His feet with her hair MT as He sat *at the table.* JN And the house was filled with the fragrance of the oil.

MT But when His disciples saw *it,* MK there were some who [o]were indignant among themselves, and said, MT "Why this waste?" MK And they criticized her sharply. JN One of His disciples, Judas Iscariot, Simon's *son,* who would betray Him, said, "Why was this fragrant oil not sold for [p]three hundred denarii and [q]given to the

---

[i] Simon the leper. Simon was almost certainly someone whom Jesus had healed of leprosy, for lepers were deemed unclean and therefore not permitted to socialize or even live in cities. He may have planned this meal for Jesus in gratitude. Cf. Lev. 13:2; Matt. 26:6.

[j] an alabaster flask . . . costly oil. Mark sets the value at "more than three hundred denarii" (Mark 14:5), nearly a year's wages—very costly indeed. Even the expensive flask, a long-necked bottle, was broken (Mark 14:3), making the act that much more costly. "Alabaster" was a fine variety of marble, quarried in Egypt, which could be carved into delicate containers for storing and preserving costly perfumes and oils. John tells us this woman was Mary, sister of Martha and Lazarus (John 12:3), thus Martha and Mary were evidently serving the meal for Simon the leper. Matthew and Mark mention that she anointed his head. John adds that she anointed His feet and wiped them with her hair. A similar act of worship is related in Luke 7:36–38, but the differences in timing, location, and other details make it clear that the two occasions were different.

[k] pound. The term used for "pound" actually indicates a weight around three-fourths of a pound (approximately twelve ounces).

[l] spikenard. This actually represents two words in the Greek that could be translated "pure nard." The oil was derived from the root of the nard plant, which was native to India. That it was pure meant it was genuine and unadulterated, which is what made it so costly.

[m] broke the flask. She may have simply broken the neck of the bottle so that she could pour out the contents more quickly, an expression of her sincere and total devotion to the Lord.

[n] anointed the feet of Jesus. The dinner guests were reclined at the table with their feet extended away from it, making it possible for Mary to anoint the feet of Jesus. The act symbolized Mary's humble devotion and love for Him.

[o] were indignant. John says Judas was the spokesman who voiced the complaint and that he did it for hypocritical reasons (John 12:4–6). Evidently the other disciples, being undiscerning, were quick to voice sympathy with Judas's protest. Matt. 26:8 indicates that all the disciples, following Judas's lead, were angry with Mary's waste of a very valuable commodity.

[p] three hundred denarii. Since a denarius was a day's wage for a common laborer, it represented almost a year's work for such a person. Since one denarius was a day's wage given to common laborers, three hundred was equivalent to a year's wages (no money was earned on the Sabbath or other holy days).

poor?" This he said, not that he cared for the poor, but because he was [r]a thief, and had the money box; and he used to take what was put in it.

MT But when Jesus was aware of *it,* He said to them, MK "Let her alone. Why do you trouble her? She has done a good work for Me. [s]For you have the poor with you always, and whenever you wish you may do them good; but Me you do not have always. She has done what she could; JN she has kept this [t]for the day of My burial. MT For in pouring this fragrant oil on My body, she did *it* MK to anoint My body for burial. Assuredly, I say to you, wherever this gospel is preached in the whole world, what this woman has done will also be told as a [u]memorial to her."

JN Now a great many of the Jews knew that He was there; and they came, not for Jesus' sake only, but that they might also see Lazarus, whom He had raised from the dead. But the chief priests plotted to put Lazarus to death also, because on account of him many of the Jews [v]went away and believed in Jesus.

---

[q] GIVEN TO THE POOR. While eleven of the disciples would have agreed to this use of the money, the fact is the poor may never have seen it. Since Judas was in reality a thief masquerading as the treasurer of the twelve, he could have embezzled all of it (John 12:6).

[r] A THIEF. Judas's altruism was really a front for his own personal avarice. Because he was the apostolic band's treasurer, he was able to secretly pilfer the group treasury for his own desires.

[s] FOR YOU HAVE THE POOR WITH YOU ALWAYS. Jesus certainly was not disparaging ministry to the poor—especially so soon after the lesson of the sheep and goats judgment (cf. Matt. 25:35–36). However, He revealed here that there is a higher priority than any other earthly ministry, and that is worship rendered to Him. Opportunities to minister to the poor are "always" available, but Jesus would be in their presence for only a limited time. This was not a time for meeting the needs of the poor and the sick—it was a time for sacrificial worship of the One who would soon suffer and be crucified (cf. Matt. 26:11). This would be an utter blasphemy for anyone less than God, so yet again He was implicitly affirming His deity (cf. Matt. 8:27; 12:6, 8; 21:16; 22:42, 45).

[t] FOR . . . MY BURIAL. This does not necessarily mean that Mary was consciously aware of the significance of her act. It is doubtful that she knew of His approaching death, or at least how close it was. But her anointing of Jesus became a symbol that anticipated His death and burial (Matt. 26:12). Mary performed this act to signal her devotion, but, as in the case of Caiaphas (John 11:49–52), her act revealed more than she realized at the time. During the first century lavish sums were spent on funerals, which included costly perfumes to cover the smell of decay (cf. John 11:39).

[u] MEMORIAL TO HER. This promise was guaranteed by the inclusion of this story in the NT.

[v] WENT AWAY AND BELIEVED. This phrase signaled both a conscious, deliberate move away from the superficial religion of the Jewish leaders and a move toward true faith in Jesus as Messiah and Son of God.

145. The Presentation of the King

Matt. 21:1b–11, 14–17; Mark 11:1b–11; Luke 19:29b–44; John 12:12–19

JN [a]The next day, MT Jesus sent two disciples, saying to them, "Go into [b]the village opposite you, and MK as soon as you have entered it MT you will find [c]a donkey tied, and a colt with her, MK on which [d]no one has sat. MT Loose *them* and bring *them* to Me. MK And [e]if anyone says to you, 'Why are you doing this?' MT you shall say, 'The Lord has need of them,' and immediately he will send them MK here." So they went their way, and found the colt tied by the door outside on the street, and they loosed it. But some of those who stood there—LK the owners—MK said to them, "What are you doing, loosing the colt?" LK And they said, "The Lord has need of him," MK just as Jesus had commanded. So they let them go.

MT They brought the donkey and the colt MK to Jesus, MT laid their clothes on them, LK and they set Jesus on MK the colt. MT All this was done that it might be fulfilled which was spoken by the prophet, saying:

---

[a] THE NEXT DAY. This section marks Jesus' triumphal entry into Jerusalem. It is one of the few incidents in Jesus' life reported in all four gospels. By this action He presented Himself officially to the nation as the Messiah and Son of God. The Sanhedrin and other Jewish leaders wanted Him dead but did not want Him killed during the Passover time, because they feared stirring up the multitudes with whom He was popular (Matt. 26:5; Mark 14:2; Luke 22:2). Jesus entered the city, however, on His own time and forced the whole issue in order that it might happen exactly on the Passover day when the lambs were being sacrificed. As the Scripture says, "Christ, our Passover, was sacrificed for us" (1 Cor. 5:7; 1 Peter 1:19). In God's perfect timing (see 7:30; 8:20), at the precise time foreordained from eternity, He presented Himself to die (John 10:17, 18; 17:1; 19:10, 11; cf. Acts 2:23; 4:27–28; Gal. 4:4).

[b] THE VILLAGE OPPOSITE YOU. Most likely Bethphage. "Opposite" implies that it was somewhat off the main road.

[c] A DONKEY . . . AND A COLT. Matthew is the only gospel writer who mentions the mare donkey. But all mention the young age of the colt (John 12:14) or state that no man had ever sat on him (Mark 11:2; Luke 19:30). According to usage of this word in Greek papyri (ordinary written documents dating from NT times that were made of papyrus reed), this was most likely a young donkey—a definition also in harmony with other Scripture usage (cf. Gen. 49:11; Judg. 10:4; 12:14; Zech. 9:9). The mare was brought along, possibly to induce the colt to cooperate.

[d] NO ONE HAS SAT. The Jews regarded animals that had never been ridden as especially suited for holy purposes (cf. Num. 19:2; Deut. 21:3; 1 Sam. 6:7).

[e] IF ANYONE SAYS TO YOU. Because of its very nature, Jesus anticipated the disciples' action would be challenged. Mark recorded that this was in fact exactly what happened (Mark 11:5–6). Having just arrived in Bethphage, Jesus would have had no opportunity to make arrangements for the use of these animals. Yet He knew precisely the location of the animals and the disposition of the owners. Such detailed foreknowledge reveals His divine omniscience.

JN " [f]Fear not. MT Tell the daughter of Zion,
'Behold, your King is coming to you,
Lowly, and sitting on a donkey,
[g]A colt, the foal of a donkey.'"

JN His disciples did not understand these things at first; but when Jesus was glorified, then they remembered that these things were written about Him and *that* they had done these things to Him.

MT And a very great multitude JN that had come to the feast, when they heard that Jesus was coming to Jerusalem, [h]took branches of palm trees and went out to meet Him. LK And as He went, MK many [i]spread their clothes on the road, and others cut down leafy branches from the trees and spread *them* on the road. JN Therefore the people, who were with Him when He called Lazarus out of his tomb and raised him from the dead, bore witness. For this reason the people also met Him, because they heard that He had done this sign. The Pharisees therefore said among themselves, "You see that you are accomplishing nothing. Look, [j]the world has gone after Him!"

LK Then, as He was now drawing near the descent of the Mount of Olives, [k]the whole multitude of the disciples MT who went before and those who followed LK began to rejoice and praise God with a loud voice for all the [l]mighty works they

---

[f] Fear not. Jesus deliberately planned to present Himself to the nation in this manner as a conscious fulfillment of the messianic prophecy of Zech. 9:9. The words, "Fear not," do not come from the Zechariah passage but were added from Isa. 40:9. Only after His ascension did the disciples grasp the meaning of the triumphal entry (John 14:26).

[g] A colt, the foal of a donkey. An exact quotation from Zech. 9:9 (cf. Isa. 62:11). The precise fulfillment of this messianic prophecy would not have escaped the Jewish multitudes, who responded with titles and accolades fit only for the Messiah (cf. Rev. 7:9).

[h] took branches of palm trees. The supply of date palms was plentiful; they still grow in Jerusalem today. The waving of palm branches had become a symbol of the fervent hope of the Messiah's coming (John 6:14–15). The crowd was greatly excited and filled with praise for the Messiah who taught with such authority, healed the sick, and raised the dead (Lazarus; cf. John 12:12–18).

[i] spread their clothes on the road. Spreading one's garments on the street was an ancient act of homage reserved for high royalty (cf. 2 Kings 9:13), suggesting that they recognized His claim to be King of the Jews.

[j] the world has gone after Him. "The world" means the people in general, as opposed to everyone in particular. Clearly, most people in the world did not even know of Him at that time, and many in Israel did not believe in Him. Often, "world" is used in this general sense (cf. John 1:29; 3:17; 4:42; 14:22; 17:9, 21).

[k] the whole multitude of the disciples. Doubtless many in the crowd were not true disciples.

[l] mighty works. John 12:17–18 specifically mentions that news of the raising of Lazarus had provoked many in the crowd to come to see Him.

had seen, saying: MT "[m]Hosanna to the Son of David! LK '[n]Blessed *is* the King who comes in the name of the LORD!' [o]Peace in heaven and glory in the highest! MK Blessed *is* [p]the kingdom of our father David that comes in the name of the Lord! Hosanna in the highest!"

LK And some of the Pharisees called to Him from the crowd, "Teacher, [q]rebuke Your disciples." But He answered and said to them, "I tell you that if these should keep silent, [r]the stones would immediately cry out."

Now as He drew near, He saw the city and [s]wept over it, saying, "If you had known, even you, especially in this your day, the things *that make* for your peace! But now they are hidden from your eyes. For days will come upon you when your

---

[m] HOSANNA. The term *hosanna* is a transliteration of a Hebrew word that means "give salvation now." It was a term of adulation or praise occurring in Ps. 118:26, which was familiar to every Jew, since that psalm was part of the Hallel (Pss. 113–118) sung daily by the temple choir during the Feast of Tabernacles (7:37) and associated with the Feast of Dedication (10:22) and especially the Passover. After shouting out the "Hosanna," the crowds shouted Ps. 118:26; significantly, the original context of Ps. 118 may well have been the pronouncement of blessing upon a messianic leader. Jewish commentaries have understood the verse to bear messianic implications.

[n] BLESSED IS . . . This comes from Psalm 118:26. This phrase is part of the Hallel (the Hebrew word for "praise"), comprised of Pss. 113–118, which was sung at all the Jewish religious festivals, most notably at the Passover. This, along with the messianic title "Son of David," make it clear that the crowd was acknowledging Christ's messianic claim. "He who comes" was not an OT messianic title, but definitely had come to carry such implications for the Jews (cf. Matt. 11:3; Luke 7:19; John 3:31; 6:14; 11:27; Heb. 10:37).

[o] PEACE IN HEAVEN. Only Luke reported this phrase. It is reminiscent of the angels' message in Luke 2:14.

[p] THE KINGDOM OF OUR FATHER DAVID. This tribute, recorded only by Mark, acknowledges Jesus as bringing in the messianic kingdom promised to David's Son. The crowd paraphrased the quote from Ps. 118:26 in anticipation that Jesus was fulfilling prophecy by bringing in the kingdom.

[q] REBUKE YOUR DISCIPLES. The Pharisees were offended by people offering Him such worshipful praise. They wanted Him to stop them.

[r] THE STONES WOULD IMMEDIATELY CRY OUT. This was a strong claim of deity and perhaps a reference to the words of Hab. 2:11. Scripture often speaks of inanimate nature praising God. Cf. Pss. 96:11; 98:7–9; 114:7; Isa. 55:12. Cf. also the words of John the Baptist in Matt. 3:9; note the fulfillment of Jesus' words in Matt. 27:51.

[s] WEPT OVER IT. Only Luke recorded the weeping of Jesus over the city of Jerusalem. Christ grieved over Jerusalem on at least two other occasions (cf. Matt. 23:37; Luke 13:34). The timing of this lament may seem incongruous with the triumphal entry, but it reveals that Jesus knew the true superficiality of the peoples' hearts, and His mood was anything but giddy as He rode into the city. The same crowd would soon cry for His death (Luke 23:21).

enemies will build an embankment around you, [t]surround you [u]and close you in on every side, and level you, and your children within you, to the ground; and they will not leave in you one stone upon another, [v]because you did not know the time of your visitation."

MT And when He had come into Jerusalem, all the city was moved, saying, "Who is this?" So the multitudes said, "This is Jesus, the prophet from Nazareth of Galilee." MK And Jesus went into Jerusalem and into the [w]temple. MT Then *the* blind and *the* lame came to Him in the temple, and He healed them. But when the chief priests and scribes saw the wonderful things that He did, and the children crying out in the temple and saying, "Hosanna to the Son of David!" they were indignant and said to Him, "Do You hear what these are saying?" And Jesus said to them, "Yes. Have you never read, 'Out of the mouth of babes and nursing infants You have perfected praise'?"

MK So when He had [x]looked around at all things, MT He left them and [y]went out of the city to Bethany, MK as the hour was already late, MT and He lodged there MK with the twelve.

---

[t] SURROUND YOU AND CLOSE YOU IN. This is precisely the method used by Titus when he laid siege to Jerusalem in AD 70. He surrounded the city on April 9, cutting off all supplies and trapping thousands of people who had been in Jerusalem for the Passover and Feast of Unleavened Bread (just completed). The Romans systematically built embankments around the city, gradually starving the city's inhabitants. The Romans held the city in this manner through the summer, defeating various sections of the city one by one. The final overthrow of the city occurred in early September.

[u] AND LEVEL YOU. This was literally fulfilled. The Romans utterly demolished the city, temple, residences, and people. Men, women, and children were brutally slaughtered by the tens of thousands. The few survivors were carried off to become victims of the Roman circus games and gladiatorial bouts.

[v] BECAUSE YOU DID NOT KNOW THE TIME OF YOUR VISITATION. i.e., Jerusalem's utter destruction was divine judgment for their failure to recognize and embrace their Messiah when He visited them (cf. Luke 20:13–16; John 1:10, 11).

[w] TEMPLE. Not a reference limited to the inner, sacred sanctuary, but the entire area of courts and buildings.

[x] LOOKED AROUND AT ALL THINGS. A description distinctive to Mark, quite possibly based on one of Peter's eyewitness memories. Christ acted as one who had the authority to inspect temple conditions, and His observation missed nothing.

[y] WENT OUT OF THE CITY TO BETHANY. Nearby "Bethany" was a relatively safe place to avoid sudden, premature arrest by the Jewish leaders.

146. Jesus Cleanses the Temple a Second Time

Matt. 21:12–13; 18–19a; Mark 11:12–18; Luke 19:45–46

MK Now [a]the next day, MT in the morning, as He returned to the city MK from Bethany, He was hungry. And seeing from afar a [b]fig tree having leaves MT by the road, MK He went to see if perhaps He would find something on it. When He came to it, He found nothing but leaves, for it was [c]not the season for figs. In response Jesus said to it, MT "Let no fruit grow [and] MK [d]let no one eat fruit from you ever again." And His disciples heard *it.* MT [e]Immediately the fig tree withered away.

MK So they came to Jerusalem. Then Jesus went into the [f]temple MT of God MK

---

[a] THE NEXT DAY. Matthew 21:18 says this was "in the morning," probably before 6:00 a.m.

[b] FIG TREE HAVING LEAVES. Fig trees were common as a source of food. Three years were required from planting until fruit bearing. After that a tree could be harvested twice a year, usually yielding much fruit. The figs normally grew with the leaves. This tree had leaves but, strangely, no fruit. That this tree was along the side of the road (cf. Matt. 21:19) implies it was public property. It was also apparently in good soil, because its foliage was ahead of season and ahead of the surrounding fig trees. The abundance of leaves held out promise that the tree might also be ahead of schedule with its fruit.

[c] NOT THE SEASON FOR FIGS. The next normal fig season was in June, more than a month away. This phrase, unique to Mark, emphasizes the unusual nature of this fig tree.

[d] "LET NO ONE EAT FRUIT FROM YOU EVER AGAIN." Jesus' direct address to the tree personified it and condemned it for not providing what its appearance promised. This incident was not the acting out of the parable of the fig tree (Luke 13:6–9), which was a warning against spiritual fruitlessness. Here, Jesus cursed the tree for its misleading appearance that suggested great productivity without providing it. It should have been full of fruit but was barren. The fig tree was frequently an OT type of the Jewish nation (Hos. 9:10; Nah. 3:12; Zech. 3:10), and in this instance Jesus used the tree by the road as a divine object lesson concerning Israel's spiritual hypocrisy and fruitlessness (cf. Isa. 5:1–7).

[e] IMMEDIATELY. This is a relative term; the tree may have died at once, but Mark 11:14, 20 suggested that the withering was not visible until the following day. Jesus' cursing of the tree was a purposeful, divine object lesson, not an impetuous act of frustration. The fig tree is often employed in Scripture as a symbol of Israel (Hos. 9:10; Joel 1:7)—and the barren fig tree often symbolizes divine judgment on Israel because of her spiritual fruitlessness (cf. Matt. 3:8) despite an abundance of spiritual advantages (Jer. 8:13; Joel 1:12). Jesus' act therefore illustrates God's judgment against earthly Israel for shameful fruitlessness, exemplified in the rejection of their Messiah. One of Christ's parables taught a similar lesson (Luke 13:6–9).

[f] TEMPLE. The large Court of the Gentiles was the setting for the events that followed.

and [g]began to drive out [MT] all [h]those who [i]bought and sold in the temple, and overturned the tables of the [j]money changers and the seats of [k]those who sold doves. [MK] And He would [l]not allow anyone to carry wares through the temple. Then He taught, saying to them, "[m]Is it not written, 'My house shall be called [n]a house of prayer for all nations'? But you have made it [o]a 'den of thieves.' "

[g] BEGAN TO DRIVE OUT. This was the second time Jesus had cleansed the temple. John 2:14–16 describes a similar incident at the beginning of Christ's public ministry. There are distinct differences in the two incidents. In the first cleansing temple officials confronted Christ immediately afterward (cf. John 2:18); none of the accounts of this second cleansing mention any such confrontation. Instead, the Synoptics all describe how Jesus addressed all present and even made the incident an occasion for public teaching (Mark 11:17; Luke 19:46–47). Although Jesus had cleansed the temple three years earlier (John 2:14–16), it had become more corrupt and profane than ever and thus He was compelled to again offer clear testimony to God's holiness and to His judgment against spiritual desecration and false religion. Even as God sent His prophets repeatedly throughout the OT to warn His people of their sin and idolatry, Christ never stopped declaring God's will to a rebellious people, no matter how often they rejected it. With this temple cleansing Jesus showed vividly that He was on a divine mission as the Son of God.

[h] THOSE WHO BOUGHT AND SOLD. He regarded both merchants and customers guilty of desecrating the temple. Items being bought and sold included "doves" and other animals for sacrifice (cf. John 2:14).

[i] BOUGHT AND SOLD. Animals were needed by the Jews for their sacrificial temple offerings, and it was more convenient for the worshipers to buy them there rather than bring the animals from a distance and risk that they would not pass the high priest's inspection. The sellers either belonged to the high priestly hierarchy or paid a large fee to temple authorities for the privilege of selling. Whichever was the case, the high priest's family benefited monetarily.

[j] MONEY CHANGERS. This kind of commerce took place in the court of the Gentiles, a large area covering several acres on the temple mount. They were in the court to exchange Greek and Roman coins for Jewish or Tyrian coins, which pilgrims (every Jewish male twenty and older) had to use for the annual half-shekel payment for temple religious services. Roman coins and other forms of currency were deemed unacceptable for temple offerings. Evidently, both merchants and money changers were charging such excessive rates (as high as 10 or 12 percent) that the temple marketplace took on the atmosphere of a thieves' den.

[k] THOSE WHO SOLD DOVES. These birds were so often used for sacrifice that the gospel writers make a separate mention of their sellers. Doves were the normal offering of the poor (Lev. 5:7) and were also required for other purposes (Lev. 12:6; 14:22; 15:14, 29).

[l] NOT ALLOW ANYONE TO CARRY WARES. Jesus did not want people to continue the practice of using the court as a shortcut through which to carry utensils and containers with merchandise to other parts of Jerusalem, because such a practice revealed great irreverence for the temple—and ultimately for God Himself.

[m] IS IT NOT WRITTEN. Jesus defended Himself by appealing to Scripture (after His actions had caused a crowd to gather). He conflates two OT prophecies, Isa. 56:7 ("My house shall be called a house of prayer for all nations") and Jer. 7:11 ("Has this house, which is called by My name, become a den of thieves in your eyes?").

[n] A HOUSE OF PRAYER FOR ALL NATIONS. The true purpose for God's temple. Only Mark includes "for all nations" from Isaiah's text (56:7), probably because he was mainly addressing Gentiles. The Court of the Gentiles was the only part of the temple they were permitted to use for prayer and worship of God, and the Jews had frustrated that worship by turning it into a place of greedy business.

[o] A 'DEN OF THIEVES.' Using Jeremiah's phrase (Jer. 7:11), Jesus described the religious leaders as robbers who found refuge in the temple, comparable to how highwaymen took refuge in caves with other robbers. The temple had become a place where God's people, instead of being able to worship undisturbed, were extorted and their extortioners were protected.

And [p]the scribes and chief priests heard it and [q]sought how they might destroy Him; for they feared Him, because all the people were astonished at His teaching.

[p] THE SCRIBES AND CHIEF PRIESTS. These men were among those who comprised the principal leadership in the Sanhedrin (cf. Matt. 2:4; 26:59). The chief priests were the rulers of the temple. The scribes were mostly Pharisees, experts in the law and traditions. By bringing His ministry to the temple, Christ had walked into the very heart of the opposition against Him.

[q] SOUGHT HOW THEY MIGHT DESTROY HIM. The leaders had continuing discussions on how to kill Jesus (cf.; Matt. 26:3–4; Luke 22:2; John 5:16–18; 7:1, 19, 25).

147. The Son of Man Must Be Lifted Up

John 12:20–36

JN Now there were [a]certain Greeks among those who came up to worship at the feast. Then they came to Philip, who was from Bethsaida of Galilee, and asked him, saying, "Sir, we wish to see Jesus." Philip came and told Andrew, and in turn Andrew and Philip told Jesus. But Jesus answered them, saying, "The [b]hour has come that the Son of Man should be glorified. Most assuredly, I say to you, unless a grain of wheat falls into the ground and [c]dies, it remains alone; but if it dies, [d]it produces much grain. He who loves his life will lose it, and he who hates his life in this world will keep it for eternal life. If anyone serves Me, let him follow Me; and where I am, there My servant will be also. If anyone serves Me, him *My* Father will honor.

"Now [e]My soul is troubled, and what shall I say? 'Father, save Me from this hour'? But for this purpose I came to this hour. Father, [f]glorify Your name." Then a voice came from heaven, *saying,* "[g]I have both glorified *it* and will glorify *it* again." Therefore the people who stood by and heard *it* said that it had thundered. Others said, "An angel has spoken to Him." Jesus answered and said, "This

---

[a] CERTAIN GREEKS. Most likely Gentile proselytes to Judaism who had come up for the Passover and who, in their desire to see Jesus, stood in direct antithesis to the attitude of the national leaders who desired to kill Him. At the very time when the Jewish leaders plotted to kill Him, Gentiles began to desire His attention.

[b] HOUR. Refers to the time of Jesus' death, resurrection, and exaltation (John 13:1; 17:1). Until now, Jesus' hour had always been a future reality (John 2:4; 4:21, 23; 7:30; 8:20).

[c] DIES. Not only is the principle of death applicable to Jesus, but it is also applicable to His followers. They, too, as His disciples may have to lose their life in service and witness for Him (see Matt. 10:37–39; 16:24–25).

[d] IT PRODUCES MUCH GRAIN. As the sown kernel dies to produce a harvest, so also the death of Jesus will result in the salvation of many.

[e] MY SOUL IS TROUBLED. The term used here is strong and signifies horror, anxiety, and agitation. Jesus' contemplation of taking on the wrath of God for the sins of the world caused revulsion in the sinless Savior (cf. 2 Cor. 5:21).

[f] GLORIFY YOUR NAME. This request embodied the principle that Jesus lived by and would die by. See John 7:18; 8:29, 50.

[g] I HAVE . . . AND WILL GLORIFY. The Father answered the Son in an audible voice. This is only one of three instances during Jesus' ministry when this took place (cf. Matt. 3:17—His baptism; 17:5—His transfiguration).

voice did not come because of Me, but for your sake. Now is the judgment of this world; now [h]the ruler of this world will be cast out. And I, if I am [i]lifted up from the earth, will draw all *peoples* to Myself."

This He said, signifying by what death He would die. The people answered Him, "We have heard from the law that the Christ [j]remains forever; and how *can* You say, 'The Son of Man must be lifted up'? Who is this Son of Man?" Then [k]Jesus said to them, "A little while longer the light is with you. Walk while you have the light, lest darkness overtake you; he who walks in darkness does not know where he is going. While you have the light, believe in the light, that you may become sons of light."

---

[h] THE RULER OF THIS WORLD. A reference to Satan (cf. Matt. 4:8, 9; Luke 4:6, 7; John 14:30; 16:11; 2 Cor. 4:4; Eph. 2:2; 6:12). Although the cross might have appeared to signal Satan's victory over God, in reality it marked Satan's defeat (cf. Rom. 16:20; Heb. 2:14).

[i] LIFTED UP FROM THE EARTH. This refers to His crucifixion (John 18:32).

[j] REMAINS FOREVER. The term *law* was used broadly enough to include not only the five books of Moses but also the whole of the OT (see Rom. 10:4). Perhaps they had in mind Isa. 9:7, which promised that Messiah's kingdom would last forever, or Ezek. 37:25, where God promised that the final David would be Israel's prince forever (see also Ps. 89:35–37).

[k] JESUS SAID TO THEM. A final invitation from Jesus was recorded by John to focus on his theme of believing in the Messiah and Son of God (see John 20:30–31).

148. The Unbelief of the Jews

John 12:37–50

JN But although He had done so many signs before them, [a]they did not believe in Him, that the word of Isaiah the prophet might be fulfilled, which he spoke: "Lord, who has believed our report? And to whom has the arm of the LORD been revealed?"

Therefore they could not believe, because Isaiah said again: "He has blinded their eyes and hardened their hearts, Lest they should see with *their* eyes, Lest they should understand with *their* hearts and turn, So that I should heal them." These things [b]Isaiah said when he saw His glory and spoke of Him.

[c]Nevertheless even among the rulers many believed in Him, but because of the Pharisees they did not confess *Him,* lest they should be put out of the synagogue; for they loved the praise of men more than the praise of God.

Then Jesus cried out and said, "He who believes in Me, believes not in Me but in Him who sent Me. And he who sees Me sees Him who sent Me. I have come *as* a light into the world, that whoever believes in Me should not abide in darkness. And if anyone hears My words and does not believe, I do not judge him; for I did not come to judge the world but to save the world. He who rejects Me, and does not receive My words, has that which judges him—the word that I have spoken will judge him in the last day. For I have not spoken on My own *authority;* but the Father who sent Me gave Me a command, what I should say and what I should speak. And I know that His command is everlasting life. Therefore, whatever I speak, just as the Father has told Me, so I speak."

---

[a] THEY DID NOT BELIEVE IN HIM. In this section John gave the Scriptural explanation for such widespread unbelief on the part of the Jewish nation. The explanation was that the unbelief was not only anticipated in Scripture but necessitated by it. In John 12:38 the writer quotes Isa. 53:1 and in John 12:40 he quotes Isa. 6:10 (see Rom. 10:16), both of which stress the sovereign plan of God in His judicial hardening of Israel (cf. Paul's argument in Rom. 9–11). Although God predestined such judgment, it was not apart from human responsibility and culpability (see John 8:24).

[b] ISAIAH . . . SAW HIS GLORY AND SPOKE OF HIM. This is a reference to Isa. 6:1. John unambiguously ties Jesus to God or Yahweh of the OT (cf. John 8:58). Therefore, since John 12:41 refers to Jesus, it makes Him the author of the judicial hardening of Israel. That fits His role as Judge (see John 5:22–23, 27, 30; 9:39).

[c] NEVERTHELESS . . . MANY BELIEVED IN HIM. The indictment of John 12:37–41 is followed by the exceptions of vv. 42–43 (see John 1:10–11 vs. 1:12–13). While the people seemed to trust Jesus with much more candor and fervency, the leaders of Israel who believed in Him demonstrated inadequate, irresolute, even spurious faith (cf. John 2:23–25; 6:60; 8:30–31). The faith of the latter was so weak that they refused to take any position that would jeopardize their standing in the synagogue. This is one of the saddest statements about spiritual leadership, for they preferred the praises of men above the praises of God in their refusal to publicly acknowledge Jesus as Messiah and Son of God.

149. The Withered Fig Tree

Matt. 21:19b–22; Mark 11:19–26

MK When evening had come, He [a]went out of the city. Now in the morning, as they passed by, they saw the fig tree [b]dried up from the roots. And Peter, remembering, said to Him, "Rabbi, look! The fig tree which You cursed has withered away." MT And when the disciples saw *it,* they marveled, saying, "How did the fig tree wither away so soon?"

MK So Jesus answered and said to them, "[c]Have faith in God. For assuredly, I say to you, MT [d]if you have faith, MK whoever says to [e]this mountain, 'Be removed and be cast into the sea,' and does not doubt in his heart, but believes that those things he says will be done, he will have [f]whatever he says. Therefore I say to you, [g]whatever things you ask when you pray, believe that you receive *them,* and you will have *them.*

---

[a] WENT OUT OF THE CITY. Jesus' practice during the first three days of Passion Week was not to leave Jerusalem until sunset, when the crowds dispersed and the city gates were about to be closed.

[b] DRIED UP FROM THE ROOTS. The tree blight that prevented fruit had spread upward through the tree and killed it. Matthew described the event in a more compact fashion, but his account still allows the same time frame as Mark's.

[c] HAVE FAITH IN GOD. A gentle rebuke for the disciples' lack of faith in the power of His word. Such faith believes in God's revealed truth and His power and seeks to do His will (cf. 1 John 5:14).

[d] IF YOU HAVE FAITH . . . NOT DOUBT. This presupposes that the thing requested is actually God's will (cf. Matt. 17:20)—for only God-given faith is so doubt-free (cf. Mark 9:24).

[e] THIS MOUNTAIN . . . INTO THE SEA. This expression was related to a common metaphor of that day, "rooter up of mountains," which was used in Jewish literature of great rabbis and spiritual leaders who could solve difficult problems and seemingly do the impossible. Obviously, Jesus did not literally uproot mountains; in fact He refused to do such spectacular miracles for the unbelieving Jewish leaders (cf. Matt. 12:38). Jesus' point is that if believers sincerely trust in God and truly realize the unlimited power that is available through such faith in Him, they will see His mighty powers at work (cf. John 14:13–14).

[f] WHATEVER HE SAYS. A miracle on such a cosmic scale was precisely what the scribes and Pharisees wanted Christ to do, but He always declined (cf. Matt. 12:38). Here, He was speaking figuratively about the immeasurable power of God, unleashed in the lives of those with true faith.

[g] WHATEVER THINGS YOU ASK WHEN YOU PRAY. This places no limits on a believer's prayers, as long as they are according to God's will and purpose (cf. Matt. 17:20). This, therefore, means that man's faith and prayer are not inconsistent with God's sovereignty. And it is not the believer's responsibility to figure out how that can be true, but simply to be faithful and obedient to the clear teaching on prayer, as Jesus gives it in this passage. God's will is being unfolded through all of redemptive history, by means of the prayers of His people—as His saving purpose is coming to pass through the faith of those who hear the gospel and repent. Cf. James 5:16.

"And whenever you [h]stand praying, if you have [i]anything against anyone, [j]forgive him, that your Father in heaven may also forgive you your trespasses. But if you do not forgive, neither will your Father in heaven forgive your [k]trespasses."

---

[h] STAND PRAYING. The traditional Jewish prayer posture (cf. 1 Sam. 1:26; 1 Kings 8:14, 22; Neh. 9:4; Matt. 6:5; Luke 18:11, 13). Kneeling or lying with one's face on the ground were used during extraordinary circumstances or for extremely urgent requests (cf. 1 Kings 8:54; Ezra 9:5; Dan. 6:10; Matt. 26:39; Acts 7:60).

[i] ANYTHING AGAINST ANYONE. An all-inclusive statement that includes both sins and simple dislikes, which cause the believer to hold something against another person. "Anyone" incorporates believers and unbelievers.

[j] FORGIVE. Jesus states the believer's ongoing duty to have a forgiving attitude. Successful prayer requires forgiveness as well as faith. Cf. Matt. 5:22–24; Eph. 4:32.

[k] TRESPASSES. This is the only occurrence in Mark of "trespasses," a term that denotes a falling aside or departing from the path of truth and uprightness.

150. The Jewish Leaders Confront Jesus

Matt. 21:23–32; Mark 11:27–33; Luke 19:47–20:8

LK And He was teaching daily in the temple. But the chief priests, the scribes, and the leaders of the people sought to destroy Him, and were unable to do anything; for all the people were very attentive to hear Him.

Now it happened on one of those days, MK [that] they came again to Jerusalem [and] MT He came into the [a]temple. LK He taught the people in the temple and preached the gospel. MK [And] as He was walking in the temple, the [b]chief priests, the scribes, and the elders MT of the people confronted Him as He was teaching. MK And they said to Him, LK "Tell us, MK [c]by what authority are You doing [d]these things? And [e]who gave You this authority to do these things?"

But Jesus answered and said to them, "I also will ask you one question; MT which if you tell Me, I likewise will tell you by what authority I do these things: [f]The bap-

---

[a] TEMPLE. Again this was the Court of the Gentiles; this time, more specifically, Solomon's porch or the royal porch on the south side of the court (cf. Mark 11:11; John 10:23; Acts 5:12).

[b] CHIEF PRIESTS. The group that met Jesus might well have included Caiaphas and Annas, who served concurrently for several years (Luke 3:2). Because of the importance of this confrontation, the captain of the temple, the second highest official, may also have been present.

[c] BY WHAT AUTHORITY. This was the first in a series of questions designed to entrap Him. This question was raised by the chief priests, scribes, and elders—evidently representatives of the Sanhedrin. The leaders wanted to know what credentials Jesus—an untrained, unrecognized, seemingly self-appointed rabbi—claimed that would authorize Him to do what He was doing. They had recovered from the initial shock of the previous day's events and had become aggressive in demanding an explanation (cf. Matt. 21:23; John 2:18).

[d] THESE THINGS. Primarily a reference to His actions in cleansing the temple. But the undefined, vague nature of this expression leaves open the inclusion of everything Jesus had been doing and teaching during His public ministry, i.e., both His public teaching and miracles.

[e] WHO GAVE YOU THIS AUTHORITY? They were forced to acknowledge that He had some source of indisputable authority. His miracles were too obvious and too numerous to be fraudulent. Even His teaching was with such force and clarity that it was obvious to all that there was authority in His words (cf. Matt. 7:29).

[f] THE BAPTISM OF JOHN—WHERE WAS IT FROM? Jesus gave the Jewish leaders only those two alternatives in judging the source of John's authority and, by implication, His own authority. Christ was, in effect, forcing the men to carry out their roles as religious guides for the people and to go on record with an evaluation of both John's and His ministries. In so doing He caught them in their own trap. They had no doubt hoped that He would answer by asserting that His authority came directly from God (as He had many times before—cf. John 5:19–23; 10:18). They then accused Him of blasphemy and used the charge as an excuse to kill Him—as they had also attempted to do before (John 5:18; 10:31–33). Here, however, He asked a question that placed them in an impossible dilemma, because John was widely revered by the people. They could not affirm John's ministry without condemning themselves. And if they denied John's legitimacy, they feared the response of the people. In effect Jesus exposed their own lack of any authority to examine Him.

tism of John—where was it from? From heaven or from men? MK [g]Answer Me." MT And they reasoned among themselves, saying, "If we say, 'From heaven,' He will say to us, [h]'Why then did you not believe him?' But if we say, 'From men,' we fear the multitude, for LK all the people will stone us, for they are persuaded that John was a prophet MK indeed." So they answered and said to Jesus, "We do not know." And Jesus answered and said to them, "[i]Neither will I tell you by what authority I do these things."

MT "But what do you think? A man had two sons, and he came to the first and said, 'Son, go, work today in my vineyard.' He answered and said, 'I will not,' but afterward he regretted it and went. Then he came to the second and said likewise. And he answered and said, 'I *go,* sir,' but he did not go. [j]Which of the two did the will of *his* father?" They said to Him, "The first." Jesus said to them, "Assuredly, I say to you that [k]tax collectors and harlots enter the kingdom of God before you. For John came to you in [l]the way of righteousness, and you did not believe him; but tax collectors and harlots believed him; and when you saw *it,* you did not afterward relent and believe him."

---

[g] Answer Me. This challenge by Jesus is only in Mark's account. It implies that the Jews in the crowd did not have the courage to answer His question honestly.

[h] 'Why then did you not believe him?' John had clearly testified that Jesus was the Messiah. If John was a prophet whose words were true, they ought to believe his testimony about Christ. On the other hand, it would have been political folly for the Pharisees to attack the legitimacy of John the Baptist or deny his authority as a prophet of God. John was enormously popular with the people and a martyr at the hands of the despised Herod. For the Pharisees to question John's authority was to attack a national hero, and they knew better than that. So they pleaded ignorance.

[i] Neither will I tell you. Jesus exposed the hypocrisy of the question, unmasking their evil motives. He wasted no truth on them (cf. Matt. 7:6).

[j] Which of the two did the will of his father? Jesus forced them to testify against themselves. The point of the parable was that doing is more important than saying (cf. Matt. 7:21–27; James 1:22). They had to acknowledge this, yet in doing so they condemned themselves. The idea that repentant tax collectors and harlots would enter the kingdom before outwardly religious hypocrites was a recurring theme in His ministry (cf. Matt. 5:20), and this infuriated the Jewish leaders.

[k] tax collectors and harlots. See Matt. 5:46; 9:9; Mark 2:15. The pariahs of Jewish society, most publicly despised by the chief priests and elders, had found salvation, while the self-righteous leaders had not. Cf. Rom. 10:3.

[l] the way of righteousness. i.e., the repentance and faith that results in the imputation of God's righteousness (cf. Rom. 3:21).

151. The Parable of the Landowner

Matt. 21:33–46; Mark 12:1–12; Luke 20:9–19

LK Then He began to tell [a]the people this parable: MT "Hear another parable. There was a certain landowner who planted [b]a vineyard and set [c]a hedge around it, dug a winepress in it, MK [with] *a place for* the [d]wine vat, MT and built a [e]tower. And he [f]leased it to vinedressers and went into a far country LK for a long time.

MT "Now when [g]vintage-time drew near, MK he sent [h]a servant to the vinedressers, that he might receive some of the fruit of the vineyard from the vinedressers. And they took *him* and [i]beat him and sent *him* away empty-handed. LK Again he sent another servant; and they beat him also, treated *him* shamefully, and sent *him* away empty-handed. And again he sent a third; MK and at him they threw stones, wounded *him* in the head, LK cast him out MK and sent *him* away shamefully treated. And again he sent another, and him they killed. MT [Thus] he sent other servants, more than the first, and they did likewise to them, MK beating some and killing some.

---

[a] THE PEOPLE. Of the Synoptic writers Luke alone noted the parable was addressed to all the people, not just the Jewish leaders.

[b] A VINEYARD . . . A WINEPRESS. See Isa. 5:2. Jesus was clearly alluding to this OT passage, which would have been familiar to the Jewish leaders. Vineyards were a common sight in that region. The hillsides of Israel were covered with grape vineyards, the backbone of the economy. The "vineyard" is a common symbol for the Jewish nation in Scripture (cf. Ps. 80:8–16; Isa. 5:1–7; Jer. 2:21). Here the landowner, representing God, developed the vineyard with great care, then leased it to vinedressers, representing the Jewish leaders.

[c] A HEDGE. Lit. "a fence." It may have been a stone wall or a hedge of briars built for protection.

[d] WINE VAT. Located under the winepress. The grapes were squeezed in the press, and the juice ran through a trough into this lower basin, where it could be collected into wineskins or jars.

[e] TOWER. This structure had a three-fold purpose: (1) it served as a lookout post; (2) it provided shelter for the workers; and (3) it was used for storage of seed and tools.

[f] LEASED IT TO VINEDRESSERS. Jesus added to the picture from Isa. 5:1–2. The owner makes an agreement with men he believes are reliable caretakers, who are to pay a certain percentage of the proceeds to him as rent. The rest of the profit belonged to them for their work in cultivating the crop. The "vinedressers" represent the Jewish leaders.

[g] VINTAGE-TIME. Better translated, "harvest time." This usually occurred for the first time in the fifth year after the initial planting (cf. Lev. 19:23–25).

[h] A SERVANT. The servants in this parable represent the OT prophets.

[i] BEAT HIM AND SENT HIM AWAY. The terrible treatment toward the servants corresponds to the Jewish rulers' treatment of many of the OT prophets (1 Kings 22:24; 2 Chron. 24:20–21; 36:15–16; Neh. 9:26; Jer. 2:30).

LK "Then the owner of the vineyard said, 'What shall I do? I will send [j]my beloved son. Probably they will respect *him* when they see him.' MK Therefore still having one son, his beloved, he also sent him to them MT last of all.

LK "But when the vinedressers saw him, they reasoned among themselves, saying, MT 'This is the heir. Come, let us kill him and seize [k]his inheritance [which] MK will be ours.' MT So they took him and cast *him* out of the vineyard and killed *him.*

"Therefore, when the owner of the vineyard comes, what will he do to those vinedressers?" They said to Him, "He will [l]destroy those wicked men miserably, and [m]lease *his* vineyard to other vinedressers who will render to him the fruits in their seasons." Jesus said to them, LK "[Indeed,] he will come and destroy those vinedressers and give the vineyard to others." [But others,] when they heard *it* they said, "[n]Certainly not!" Then He looked at them and said, MT "Have you never read in the Scriptures LK this that is written:

MT [o]'The [p]stone which the builders rejected
Has become [q]the chief cornerstone.

---

[j] MY BELOVED SON. This person represents the Lord Jesus Christ, whom they killed and thereby incurred divine judgment.

[k] HIS INHERITANCE WILL BE OURS. The vinedressers were greedy; because they wanted the entire harvest and the vineyard for themselves and would stop at nothing to achieve that end, they plotted to kill the owner's son. Because Jesus had achieved such a following, the Jewish leaders believed the only way to maintain their position and power over the people was to kill Him (cf. John 11:48).

[l] DESTROY THE VINEDRESSERS. The owner of the vineyard will execute the vinedressers, thus serving as a prophecy of the destruction of Jerusalem (AD 70) and the nation of Israel. According to Matthew 21:41 this verdict was echoed by the chief priests, scribes, and elders.

[m] LEASE HIS VINEYARD TO OTHER VINEDRESSERS. Again the Jewish leaders pronounced their own judgment. Their verdict against the evil vinedressers was also Christ's judgment against them. The kingdom and all the spiritual advantages given to Israel would now be given to "other vinedressers," symbolizing the church, which consists primarily of Gentiles (cf. Rom. 11:11).

[n] CERTAINLY NOT! Only Luke recorded this hostile reaction from the crowd. The response suggests that they grasped the meaning of the parable.

[o] THE STONE . . . REJECTED. This messianic prophecy is a quotation of Ps. 118:22–23 from the Septuagint. This refers to His crucifixion, and the restoration of "the chief cornerstone" anticipates His resurrection. Jesus continued His teaching in the form of a parable, but here His kingdom is seen as a building instead of a vineyard. The point is that the rejected son and the rejected stone represent Christ .

[p] STONE WHICH THE BUILDERS REJECTED. Builders typically rejected stones until they found one perfectly straight in lines that could serve as the cornerstone, which was critical to the symmetry and stability of the building. In Jesus' metaphor, He Himself is the stone the builders (the Jewish religious leaders) rejected (crucified). But the resurrected Christ is the cornerstone (cf. Acts 4:10–12; 1 Peter 2:6–7).

[q] THE CHIEF CORNERSTONE. To the superficial eye this quotation from Ps. 118:22–23 is irrelevant to the parable that precedes it. But it is taken from a messianic psalm. Jesus cited it to suggest that the Son who was killed and thrown out of the vineyard was also "the chief cornerstone" in God's redemptive plan.

This was the Lord's doing,
And it is marvelous in our eyes'?

"Therefore I say to you, the kingdom of God will be taken from you and given to a [r]nation bearing the fruits of it. And [s]whoever falls on [t]this stone will be broken; but on whomever it falls, it will grind him to powder." Now when the chief priests and Pharisees heard His parables, [u]they perceived that He was speaking [LK] this parable [v]against them. [MT] They sought to lay hands on Him [LK] that very hour, but they feared the people, [MT] because they took Him for a prophet. [MK] So they left Him and went away.

---

[r] nation bearing the fruits of it. The church. Peter spoke of the church as "a holy nation" (1 Peter 2:9).

[s] whoever falls . . . on whomever it falls. The expression was a quotation from Isa. 8:13–15, which speaks of Jehovah. Like so many other OT passages applied to Christ, it proves that He was Jehovah incarnate.

[t] this stone. Christ is "a stone of stumbling and a rock of offense" to unbelievers (Isa. 8:14; 1 Peter 2:9). And the prophet Daniel pictured Him as a great stone "cut out of the mountain without hands," which falls on the kingdoms of the world and crushes them (Dan. 2:44–45). Whether a ceramic vessel "falls on" a rock or the rock "falls" on the vessel, the result is the same. The saying suggests that both enmity and apathy are wrong responses to Christ, and those guilty of either are in danger of judgment.

[u] they perceived that He was speaking this parable against them. By evoking so much familiar messianic imagery, Christ made His meaning inescapable to the chief priests and Pharisees.

[v] against them. The chief priests, scribes, and elders were completely aware that Christ was condemning their actions, but it only aroused their hatred, not their repentance.

152. The Parable of the Wedding Invitation

Matt. 22:1–14

MT And Jesus answered and spoke to them again by parables and said: "The kingdom of heaven is [a]like a certain king who arranged a marriage for his son, and sent out his servants to call those who were invited to the wedding; and they were not willing to come. [b]Again, he sent out other servants, saying, 'Tell those who are invited, "See, I have prepared my dinner; my oxen and fatted cattle *are* killed, and all things *are* ready. Come to the wedding." ' But they made light of it and went their ways, one to his own farm, another to his business. And the rest seized his servants, treated *them* spitefully, and killed *them.* But when the king heard *about it,* [c]he was furious. And he sent out his armies, destroyed those murderers, and [d]burned up their city.

"Then he said to his servants, 'The wedding is ready, but those who were invited were not worthy. Therefore go into the highways, and [e]as many as you find, invite to the wedding.' So those servants went out into the highways and gathered together all whom they found, both bad and good. And the wedding *hall* was filled with guests.

"But when the king came in to see the guests, he saw a man there who did not have on a wedding garment. So he said to him, 'Friend, how did you come in here

---

[a] LIKE A CERTAIN KING WHO ARRANGED A MARRIAGE. Jesus told a similar, but different, parable in Luke 14:16–23. Here, the banquet was a wedding feast for the king's own son, making the apathy and rejection of those invited much more of a personal slight against the king. Also, here they actually mistreated and killed the king's messengers—an unthinkable affront to the king's goodness.

[b] AGAIN, HE SENT OUT OTHER SERVANTS. This illustrates God's patience and forbearance with those who deliberately spurn Him. He continues to extend the invitation even after His goodness has been ignored or rebuffed.

[c] HE WAS FURIOUS. His vast patience finally exhausted, He judges them.

[d] BURNED UP THEIR CITY. The judgment Jesus described anticipated the destruction of Jerusalem in AD 70. Even the massive stone temple was destroyed by fire and reduced to rubble in that conflagration. Cf. Matt. 23:36; 24:2; Luke 19:43.

[e] AS MANY AS YOU FIND, INVITE TO THE WEDDING. This illustrates the free offer of the gospel, which is extended to all indiscriminately (cf. Rev. 22:17).

without a [f]wedding garment?' [g]And he was speechless. Then the king said to the servants, 'Bind him hand and foot, take him away, and cast *him* into [h]outer darkness; there will be [i]weeping and gnashing of teeth.'

"For [j]many are called, but few *are* chosen."

---

[f] WEDDING GARMENT. All without exception were invited to the banquet, so this man is not to be viewed as a common party-crasher. In fact, all the guests were rounded up hastily from "the highways," and, therefore, none could be expected to come with proper attire. That means the wedding garments were supplied by the king himself. So this man's lack of a proper garment indicates he had purposely rejected the king's own gracious provision. His affront to the king was actually a greater insult than those who refused to come at all, because he committed his impertinence in the very presence of the king. The imagery seems to represent those who identify with the kingdom externally, profess to be Christians, belong to the church in a visible sense—yet spurn the garment of righteousness Christ offers (cf. Isa. 61:10) by seeking to establish a righteousness of their own (cf. Rom. 10:3; Phil. 3:8, 9). Ashamed to admit their own spiritual poverty (cf. Matt. 5:3), they refuse the better garment the King graciously offers—and thus they are guilty of a horrible sin against His goodness.

[g] AND HE WAS SPEECHLESS. i.e., he had no excuse.

[h] OUTER DARKNESS. This would describe the darkness farthest from the light, i.e., outer darkness.

[i] WEEPING AND GNASHING OF TEETH. This speaks of inconsolable grief and unremitting torment. Jesus commonly used the phrases in this verse to describe hell (cf. Matt. 13:42, 50; 24:51).

[j] MANY ARE CALLED, BUT FEW ARE CHOSEN. The call spoken of here is sometimes referred to as the "general call" (or the "external" call)—a summons to repentance and faith that is inherent in the gospel message. This call extends to all who hear the gospel. "Many" hear it; "few" respond (see the many-few comparison in Matt. 7:13–14). Those who respond are the "chosen," the elect. In the Pauline writings the word *call* usually refers to God's irresistible calling extended to the elect alone (Rom. 8:30)—known as the "effectual call" (or the "internal" call). The effectual call is the supernatural drawing of God which Jesus speaks of in John 6:44. Here a general call is in view, and this call extends to all who hear the gospel—this call is the great "whosoever will" of the gospel (cf. Rev. 22:17). Here, then, is the proper balance between human responsibility and divine sovereignty: the "called" who reject the invitation do so willingly, and, therefore, their exclusion from the kingdom is perfectly just. The "chosen" enter the kingdom only because of the grace of God in choosing and drawing them.

153. The Pharisees and Herodians Test Jesus

Matt. 22:15–22; Mark 12:13–17; Luke 20:20–26

MT Then the Pharisees went and plotted how they might entangle Him in *His* talk. And LK they watched *Him,* and sent spies who pretended to be righteous; MK the Pharisees MT sent to Him their disciples with the [a]Herodians, MK to catch Him in *His* words, LK in order to deliver Him to the power and the authority of the governor.

MK When they had come, they said to Him, MT "Teacher, we know that You are true, and LK rightly MT teach the way of God in truth; nor do You LK [b]show personal favoritism, MT for You do not regard the person of men. [c]Tell us, therefore, what do You think? [d]Is it lawful to pay [e]taxes to Caesar, or not? MK Shall we pay, or shall we not pay?" MT But Jesus perceived LK their craftiness, and MK knowing their [f]hypocrisy, said to them, MT " [g]Why do you test Me, *you* hypocrites? Show Me the tax money. MK

---

[a] Herodians. A party of the Jews who supported the Roman-backed Herodian dynasty. The Herodians were not a religious party like the Pharisees, but a political party, probably consisting largely of Sadducees (including the rulers of the temple). By contrast the Pharisees hated Roman rule and the Herodian influence. The fact that these groups would conspire together to entrap Jesus reveals how seriously both groups viewed Him as a threat. Herod himself wanted Jesus dead (Luke 13:31), and the Pharisees were already plotting to kill Him as well (John 11:53). So they joined efforts to seek their common goal.

[b] show personal favoritism. In Mark this phrase is rendered, "regard the person of men." This speaks of impartiality or showing no favoritism. While this was flattery on the part of the Pharisees and Herodians, it was nonetheless true that Jesus would not be swayed by a person's power, prestige, or position.

[c] Tell us . . . what do you think? The second of a series of questions that the Jewish religious leaders hoped would trap Jesus into declaring Himself an insurrectionist (cf. Mark 11:28). This one concerns the controversial issue of paying taxes to Rome.

[d] Is it lawful to pay taxes to Caesar, or not? At issue was the poll tax, an annual fee of one denarius per person. Such "taxes" were part of the heavy taxation Rome assessed. Since these funds were used to finance the occupying armies, all Roman taxes were hated by the people. But the poll tax was the most hated of all because it suggested that Rome owned even the people, while they viewed themselves and their nation as possessions of God. It was therefore significant that they questioned Christ about the poll tax in particular. If He answered no to their question, the Herodians would charge Him with treason against Rome. If He said yes, the Pharisees would accuse Him of disloyalty to the Jewish nation, and He would lose the support of the multitudes.

[e] taxes. The Greek word for "taxes" was borrowed from the Latin word that gives us the English *census.* The Romans counted all the citizens and made each one pay an annual poll tax of one denarius.

[f] hypocrisy. The Pharisees and Herodians, using feigned interest in His teaching, attempted to hide their true intention to trap Jesus. But He perceived their true motives (cf. John 2:25).

[g] Why do you test Me? Jesus' response exposed the true motive of the Pharisees and Herodians and revealed their hypocrisy.

Bring Me a [h]denarius that I may see *it.*" MT So they brought Him a denarius. And He said to them, "Whose [i]image and [j]inscription *is* this?" LK They answered and said, "Caesar's." And He said to them, "[k]Render therefore to Caesar the things that are [l]Caesar's, and to God the things that are God's." But they could not catch Him in His words in the presence of the people.

MT When they had heard *these words,* LK they marveled at His answer and kept silent. MT And [they] left Him and went their way.

---

[h] DENARIUS. A small silver coin, the value of a day's wage for a Roman soldier. The coins were minted under the emperor's authority, since only he could issue gold or silver coins. The denarius of Jesus' day was minted by Tiberius. One side bore an image of his face; the other featured an engraving of him sitting on his throne in priestly robes. The Jews considered such images idolatry, forbidden by the second commandment (Ex. 20:4), which made this tax and these coins doubly offensive.

[i] IMAGE. On one side of the denarius was likely the image of the current emperor, Tiberius, though at that time it could have also been Augustus, since both coins were in circulation. Tiberius is most likely because the response was "Caesar's," indicating the current ruler rather than the past one.

[j] INSCRIPTION. If the coin was minted by Tiberius, it would have read, "Tiberius Caesar Augustus, the son of the Divine Augustus" on one side and "Chief Priest" on the other.

[k] RENDER . . . TO CAESAR. The Greek word for "render" means, "to pay or give back," which implies a debt. All who lived within the realm of Caesar were obligated to return to him the tax that was owed him. It was not optional. Thus Jesus declared that all citizens are under divine obligation to pay taxes to whatever government is over them (cf. Rom. 13:1–7; 1 Peter 2:13–17).

[l] CAESAR'S . . . GOD'S. Caesar's image is stamped on the coin; God's image is stamped on the person (Gen 1:26–27). The Christian must "render" obedience to Caesar in Caesar's realm (Rom. 13:1–7; 1 Peter 2:13–17), but "the things that are God's" are things that do not belong to Caesar and should be given only to God. Christ thus acknowledged Caesar's right to assess and collect taxes, and He made it the duty of Christians to pay them. But He did not suggest (as some suppose) that Caesar had sole or ultimate authority in the social or political realms. Ultimately, all things are God's (Rom. 11:36; 2 Cor. 5:18; Rev. 4:11)—including the realm in which Caesar or any other earthly ruler exercises authority.

154. The Sadducees Question Jesus

Matt. 22:23–33; Mark 12:18–27; Luke 20:27–39

MT The same day LK some of the [a]Sadducees, MT [b]who say there is no resurrection, came to Him and [c]asked Him, saying: MK "Teacher, [d]Moses wrote to us that MT if a man dies, MK and leaves *his* wife behind, and leaves no children, [e]his brother should take his wife and raise up offspring for his brother. MT Now there were with us seven brothers. MK The first took a wife MT [and] died after he had married, and having no offspring, left his wife to his brother. LK And the second took her as wife, and he died childless. Then the third took her, and in like manner the seven also; and they left no children, and died. Last of all the woman died also. MT Therefore, in the resurrection, MK when they rise, MT whose wife of the seven will she be? MK For all seven had her as wife."

Jesus answered and said to them, "Are you not therefore mistaken, because you do not know the Scriptures nor [f]the power of God? LK The sons of this age marry and are given in marriage. But those who are counted worthy to attain that age, and the resurrection from the dead, MK when they rise from the dead, they

---

[a] Sadducees. The most wealthy, influential, and aristocratic of all the Jewish sects. All the high priests, chief priests, and the majority of the Sanhedrin were Sadducees. They ignored the oral law, traditions, and scribal laws of the Pharisees, viewing only the Pentateuch as authoritative (cf. Matt. 3:7).

[b] who say there is no resurrection. This most distinctive aspect of the Sadducees' theology was adopted because they believed that only the Pentateuch was authoritative and that Moses did not teach a literal resurrection from the dead. With such a disregard for the future, the Sadducees lived for the moment and whatever profit they could make. Since they controlled the temple businesses, they were extremely upset when Jesus cleansed the temple of the money changers, because He cut into their profits (Mark 11:15–18)—the reason they also wanted to discredit Jesus in front of the people.

[c] asked Him. This was the third in a series of questions designed to entrap Him (cf. Luke 20:2, 22). This question was raised by the Sadducees. Matthew 22:34–40 and Mark 12:28–34 recorded one last question raised by a scribe. Luke omitted it from his record.

[d] Moses wrote. The Sadducees appealed to Moses because they were fully aware of Jesus' high regard for Scripture, and therefore, believed He would not contest the validity of the levirate marriage.

[e] his brother should take his wife. The Sadducees were summarizing Deut. 25:5–6, which refers to the custom of a levirate marriage (marriage to a dead husband's brother). God placed it in the law of Moses to preserve tribal names, families, and inheritances.

[f] the power of God. Their ignorance of the Scriptures extended to their lack of understanding regarding the miracles God performed throughout the OT. Such knowledge would have enabled them to believe in God's power to raise the dead.

[g]neither marry nor are given in marriage; [LK] nor can they die anymore, for they are [MT] [h]like angels of God in heaven [LK] and are sons of God, being sons of the resurrection.

[MK] "But concerning the dead, that they rise, have you not read [MT] what was spoken to you by God [MK] in the [i]book of Moses, in [j]the *burning* bush *passage,* [k]how God spoke to him, saying, 'I *am* the God of Abraham, the God of Isaac, and the God of Jacob'? [LK] Moses showed [therefore] that the dead are raised, when he called the Lord 'the God of Abraham, the God of Isaac, and the God of Jacob.' For He is [l]not the God of the dead but of the living, for [m]all live to Him. [MK] [n]You are therefore greatly mistaken." [MT] And when the multitudes heard *this,* they were astonished at His teaching. [LK] Then some of the scribes answered and said, [o]"Teacher, You have spoken well."

---

[g] NEITHER MARRY. Marriage was designed by God for companionship and the perpetuation of the human race on the earth. Jesus was emphasizing the fact that in heaven there will be no exclusive or sexual relationships. Believers will experience an entirely new existence in which they will have perfect spiritual relationships with everyone else.

[h] LIKE ANGELS OF GOD IN HEAVEN. The Sadducees did not believe in angels (cf. Matt. 3:7)—so here Jesus was exposing another of their false beliefs. Angels are deathless creatures who do not propagate and therefore have no need for marriage. "In the resurrection" the saints will have those same characteristics. They will be equal to angels in the sense that they do not procreate. Rather, they will be spiritual, eternal beings who will not die (cf. 1 Cor. 15:39–44, 48–49).

[i] BOOK OF MOSES. The Pentateuch—the first five books of the OT. Jesus appealed to the only Scriptures the Sadducees held as completely authoritative

[j] THE BURNING BUSH PASSAGE. A reference to Ex. 3:1–4:17, where God first appeared to Moses at the bush. In that passage God identified Himself to Moses as the God of Abraham, Isaac, and Jacob—using the present tense. He didn't say He *was* their God, but "I AM" their God, indicating that their existence had not ended with their deaths.

[k] HOW GOD SPOKE TO HIM, SAYING, 'I AM.' By keying on the emphatic present tense of Ex. 3:6, "I am the God of Abraham, the God of Isaac, and the God of Jacob," Jesus was underscoring the personal and perpetual covenantal relationship God established with the three patriarchs. Even though all three were dead when God spoke to Moses, God was still their God just as much as when they were alive on earth—and more so in that they were experiencing eternal fellowship with Him in heaven.

[l] NOT THE GOD OF THE DEAD. Jesus' argument (taken from the Pentateuch, because the Sadducees recognized only Moses' authority—cf. Matt. 3:7) was based on the emphatic present-tense "I AM" of Ex. 3:6. This subtle but effective argument utterly silenced the Sadducees.

[m] ALL LIVE TO HIM. Only Luke records this phrase. All people—whether departed from their earthly bodies or not—are still living and will live forever. No one is annihilated in death (cf. John 5:28–30).

[n] YOU ARE . . . GREATLY MISTAKEN. Jesus accused the Sadducees of making a complete error in teaching that there is no resurrection.

[o] "TEACHER, YOU HAVE SPOKEN WELL." Christ had given a powerful argument for the resurrection of the dead, and on that subject the Pharisees agreed with Him against the Sadducees. This scribe, in spite of his hatred for Christ, was pleased with the answer He had given.

155. A Scribe of the Pharisees Questions Jesus

Matt. 22:34–40; Mark 12:28–34; Luke 20:40

MT But when the Pharisees heard that He had silenced the Sadducees, they gathered together. MK Then one of the scribes, MT [a]a lawyer, MK came, and having heard them reasoning together, perceiving that He had answered them well, MT asked *Him a question,* testing Him, and saying, "Teacher, [b]which *is* the great commandment MK of all MT in the law?"

MK Jesus answered him, "The first of all the commandments *is:* '[c]Hear, O Israel, the LORD our God, the LORD is one. And you shall [d]love the LORD your God with all your [e]heart, with all your soul, with all your mind, and with all your strength.' MT This is *the* first and great commandment. And [f]*the* second *is* like it: MK 'You shall

---

[a] A LAWYER. A scribe whose specialty was interpreting the law. Cf. Matt. 2:4; Luke 10:25.

[b] WHICH IS THE GREAT COMMANDMENT. The rabbis had determined that there were 613 commandments contained in the Pentateuch, one for each letter of the Ten Commandments. Of the 613 commandments, 248 were seen as affirmative and 365 as negative. Those laws were also divided into heavy and light categories, with the heavy laws being more binding than the light ones. The scribes and rabbis, however, had been unable to agree on which were heavy and which were light. This orientation to the law led the Pharisees to think Jesus had devised His own theory. So the Pharisees asked this particular question to get Jesus to incriminate Himself by revealing His unorthodox and unilateral beliefs.

[c] HEAR, O ISRAEL. By quoting the first part of the Shema (Deut. 6:4–5), which is Hebrew for "hear," Jesus confirmed the practice of every pious Jew who recited the entire Shema (Num. 15:37–41; Deut. 6:4–9; 11:13–21) every morning and evening.

[d] LOVE THE LORD. Taken from Deut. 10:12; 30:6, Jesus used God's own word from the Pentateuch to answer the question, indicating the orthodox nature of His theology.

[e] HEART . . . SOUL . . . MIND. Mark 12:30 adds "strength." The quote is from Deut. 6:5, part of the *Shema,* (Hebrew for "hear"—Deut. 6:4). That verse says "heart . . . soul . . . strength." Some Septuagint manuscripts added "mind." The use of the various terms is not meant to delineate distinct human faculties but to underscore the completeness of the kind of love that is called for.

[f] THE SECOND. Jesus took the Pharisees' question one step further by identifying the second greatest commandment because it was critical to an understanding of the complete duty of love. This commandment, also from the books of Moses (Lev. 19:18), is of the same nature and character as the first. Genuine love for God is followed in importance by a genuine love for people.

love your [g]neighbor as yourself.' There is no other commandment greater than these. [MT] On these two commandments hang [h]all the Law and the Prophets."

[MK] So [i]the scribe said to Him, "Well *said,* Teacher. You have spoken the truth, for there is one God, and there is no other but He. And to love Him with all the heart, with all the understanding, with all the soul, and with all the strength, and to [j]love one's neighbor as oneself, is more than all the whole [k]burnt offerings and sacrifices." Now when Jesus saw that he answered wisely, He said to him, "You are [l]not far from the kingdom of God." But after that [m]no one dared question Him [LK] anymore.

---

[g] NEIGHBOR. Cf. Luke 10:29–37.

[h] ALL THE LAW AND THE PROPHETS. i.e., the whole OT. Thus Jesus subsumes man's whole moral duty under two categories: love for God and love for one's neighbors. These same two categories differentiate the first four commandments of the Decalogue from the final six.

[i] THE SCRIBE SAID. The scribe's response reveals he understood OT teaching that moral concerns took precedence over ceremonial practices (cf. 1 Sam. 15:22; Isa. 1:11–15; Hos. 6:6; Mic. 6:6–8).

[j] LOVE ONE'S NEIGHBOR AS ONESELF. This is a quotation from Lev. 19:18. Contrary to some contemporary interpretations, it is not a mandate for self-love. Rather, it contains in different words the very same idea as the Golden Rule (cf. Matt. 7:12). It prompts believers to measure their love for others by what they wish for themselves.

[k] BURNT OFFERINGS. Sacrifices that were completely consumed on the altar (cf. Lev. 1:1–17; 6:8–13).

[l] NOT FAR FROM THE KINGDOM. Jesus both complimented and challenged the scribe. Jesus acknowledged the scribe's insight regarding the importance of love. Yet by stating that the scribe was "not far" from the kingdom, He emphasized that he was not in the kingdom. He understood the requirements of love, he needed only to love and obey the One who alone could grant him entrance to the kingdom.

[m] NO ONE DARED QUESTION HIM. The more questions He answered, the clearer it became that His understanding and authority were vastly superior to that of the scribes and Pharisees.

156. Jesus Is Both David's Son and David's Lord

Matt. 22:41–46; Mark 12:35–37; Luke 20:41–44

MT While the Pharisees were gathered together, MK while He taught in the temple, MT [a]Jesus asked them, saying, "[b]What do you think about the [c]Christ? Whose Son is He?" They said to Him, "[d]*The Son* of David."

MK Then Jesus answered and said, "How *is it* that the scribes say that the Christ is the [e]Son of David? For [f]David himself said by the Holy Spirit LK in the Book of [g]Psalms:

'[h]The LORD said to my Lord,
"Sit at My right hand,
Till I make Your enemies Your footstool." '

---

[a] JESUS ASKED THEM. After the Jewish leaders gave up questioning Him, Christ turned the tables and posed a question to them.

[b] WHAT DO YOU THINK. A phrase often used by Christ to introduce a question designed to test someone (cf. Matt. 17:25; 18:12; 21:28; 26:66). Here, the Pharisees, Herodians, Sadducees, and scribes had all put Him to the test. He also had a test for them. Jesus' question exposed the Jewish religious leaders' ineptness as teachers and their ignorance of what the OT taught regarding the true nature of the Messiah.

[c] CHRIST. This is a translation of the OT Hebrew word *Messiah,* which means "anointed one" and refers to the King whom God had promised.

[d] THE SON OF DAVID. "Son of David" was the most common messianic title in the usage of Jesus' day. Their answer reflected their conviction that the Messiah would be no more than a man, and Jesus' reply was another assertion of His deity.

[e] SON OF DAVID. The common messianic title that was standard scribal teaching. The religious leaders were convinced that the Messiah would be no more than a man, thus they deemed such a title appropriate.

[f] DAVID HIMSELF SAID BY THE HOLY SPIRIT. David used his own words, yet he wrote under the inspiration of the Holy Spirit (cf. 2 Sam. 23:2).

[g] PSALMS. This quotation is from Ps. 110:1.

[h] THE LORD SAID TO MY LORD. In this quote from the Hebrew text (Ps. 110:1), the first word for "Lord" is *Yahweh,* which is God's covenant name. The second word for "Lord" is a different word that the Jews used as a title for God. Here David pictures God speaking to the Messiah, whom David calls his Lord. The religious leaders of Jesus' day recognized this psalm as messianic.

MK "Therefore David himself calls Him 'Lord.' MT If [i]David then calls Him 'Lord,' how is He his Son?"

MK And the [j]common people heard Him gladly.

---

[i] David then calls Him 'Lord.' Jesus interpreted Ps. 110:1 for the Pharisees. David would not have addressed a merely human descendant as "Lord." Here Jesus was not disputing whether "Son of David" was an appropriate title for the Messiah; after all the title is based on what is revealed about the Messiah in the OT (Isa. 11:1; Jer. 23:5), and it is used as a messianic title in Matt. 1:1. But Jesus was pointing out that the title "Son of David" did not begin to sum up all that is true about the Messiah, who is also "Son of God" (Luke 22:70). The Messiah is more than the "Son of David"—He is also the "Son of God." Jesus was proclaiming the Messiah's deity, and thus His own (cf. Rom. 1:3; 2 Tim. 2:8).

[j] common people. The multitude of people who observed this confrontation between Jesus and the religious leaders.

157. Woe to the Pharisees

Matt. 23:1–39; Mark 12:38–40; Luke 20:45–47

LK Then, MK in His teaching, LK in the hearing of all the people, He said to His disciples, "[a]Beware of the scribes, who desire to go around in [b]long robes, love [c]greetings in the marketplaces, the [d]best seats in the synagogues, and the best places at feasts, who [e]devour widows' houses, and for a pretense make [f]long prayers. These will receive greater condemnation."

MT Jesus spoke to the multitudes and to His disciples, saying: "The scribes and the Pharisees sit in [g]Moses' seat. Therefore whatever they tell you to observe, *that* [h]observe and do, but do not do according to their works; for they say, and do not do. For they bind heavy burdens, hard to bear, and lay *them* on men's shoulders; but they *themselves* will not move them with one of their fingers. But all their

---

[a] BEWARE. This means "to see" or "to watch." It carries the idea of guarding against the evil influence of the scribes.

[b] LONG ROBES. A long, flowing cloak that essentially trumpeted the wearer as a devout and noted scholar.

[c] GREETINGS. Accolades for those holding titles of honor.

[d] BEST SEATS IN THE SYNAGOGUES. The bench in the synagogue nearest the chest where the sacred scrolls were housed—an area reserved for leaders and people of renown (cf. James 2:3).

[e] DEVOUR WIDOWS' HOUSES. Jesus exposed the greedy, unscrupulous practice of the scribes. Scribes often served as estate planners for widows, which gave them the opportunity to convince distraught widows that they would be serving God by supporting the temple or the scribe's own holy work. In either case the scribe benefited monetarily and effectively robbed the widow of her husband's legacy to her.

[f] LONG PRAYERS. The Pharisees attempted to flaunt their piety by praying for long periods. Their motive was not devotion to God, but a desire to be revered by the people.

[g] MOSES' SEAT. The expression is equivalent to a university's "chair of philosophy." To "sit in Moses' seat" was to have the highest authority to instruct people in the law. The expression here may be translated, "[They] have seated themselves in Moses' seat"—stressing the fact that this was an imaginary authority they claimed for themselves. There was a legitimate sense in which the priests and Levites had authority to decide matters of the law (Deut. 17:9), but the scribes and Pharisees had gone beyond any legitimate authority and were adding human tradition to the Word of God (Matt. 15:3–9). For that Jesus condemned them.

[h] OBSERVE AND DO. i.e., insofar as it accords with the Word of God. The Pharisees were prone to bind "heavy burdens" of extrabiblical traditions and put them on others' shoulders. Jesus explicitly condemned that sort of legalism.

works they do to be seen by men. They make their [i]phylacteries broad and enlarge [j]the borders of their garments. They love the best places at feasts, the best seats in the synagogues, greetings in the marketplaces, and to be called by men, 'Rabbi, Rabbi.' But you, do not be called '[k]Rabbi'; for One is your Teacher, the Christ, and you are all brethren. Do not call anyone on earth your father; for One is your Father, He who is in heaven. And do not be called teachers; for One is your Teacher, the Christ. But he who is greatest among you shall be your servant. And whoever exalts himself will be humbled, and he who humbles himself will be exalted.

"But woe to you, scribes and Pharisees, hypocrites! For you shut up the kingdom of heaven against men; for you neither go in *yourselves,* [l]nor do you allow those who are entering to go in. Woe to you, scribes and Pharisees, hypocrites! For you devour widows' houses, and for a pretense make long prayers. Therefore you will receive greater condemnation.

"Woe to you, scribes and Pharisees, hypocrites! For you travel land and sea to win one [m]proselyte, and when he is won, you make him twice as much [n]a son of hell as yourselves.

"Woe to you, blind guides, who say, 'Whoever swears by the temple, [o]it is nothing; but whoever swears by the gold of the temple, he is obliged *to perform*

---

[i] phylacteries. Leather boxes containing a parchment on which is written in four columns Ex. 13:1–10, 11–16; Deut. 6:4–9; 11:13–21. These are worn by men during prayer—one on the middle of the forehead and one on the left arm just above the elbow. The use of phylacteries was based on an overly literal interpretation of passages like Ex. 13:9–10; Deut. 6:8. Evidently the Pharisees would broaden the leather straps by which the phylacteries were bound to their arms and foreheads, in order to make the phylacteries more prominent.

[j] the borders of their garments. i.e., the tassels. It's indicated that Jesus Himself wore them (cf. Matt. 9:20), so it was not the tassels themselves that He condemned, only the mentality that would lengthen the tassels to make it appear that one was especially spiritual.

[k] Rabbi . . . father . . . teachers. Here Jesus condemns pride and pretense, not titles, per se. Paul repeatedly speaks of "teachers" in the church and even refers to himself as the Corinthians' "father" (1 Cor. 4:15). Obviously, this does not forbid the showing of respect, either (cf. 1 Thess. 5:11–12; 1 Tim. 5:1). Christ is merely forbidding the use of such names as spiritual titles or in an ostentatious sense that accords undue spiritual authority to a human being, as if he were the source of truth rather than God.

[l] nor do you allow. The Pharisees, having shunned God's righteousness, were seeking to establish a righteousness of their own (Rom. 10:3)—and teaching others to do so as well. Their legalism and self-righteousness effectively obscured the narrow gate by which the kingdom must be entered (Matt. 7:13–14).

[m] proselyte. A Gentile convert to Judaism. See Acts 6:5.

[n] a son of hell. i.e., someone whose eternal destination is hell.

[o] it is nothing. This was an arbitrary distinction the Pharisees had made, which gave them a sanctimonious justification for lying with impunity. If someone swore "by the temple" (or the altar, Matt. 23:18; or heaven, v. 22), his oath was not considered binding, but if he swore "by the gold of the temple," he could not break his word without being subject to the penalties of Jewish law. Our Lord makes it clear that swearing by those things is tantamount to swearing by God Himself. Cf. Matt. 5:34.

it.' Fools and blind! For which is greater, the gold or the temple that sanctifies the gold? And, 'Whoever swears by the altar, it is nothing; but whoever swears by the gift that is on it, he is obliged *to perform it.'* Fools and blind! For which is greater, the gift or the altar that sanctifies the gift? Therefore he who swears by the altar, swears by it and by all things on it. He who swears by the temple, swears by it and by Him who dwells in it. And he who swears by heaven, swears by the throne of God and by Him who sits on it.

"Woe to you, scribes and Pharisees, hypocrites! For you pay [p]tithe of mint and anise and cummin, and have neglected the weightier *matters* of the law: justice and mercy and faith. These you ought to have done, without leaving the others undone. Blind guides, who [q]strain out a gnat and swallow a camel!

"Woe to you, scribes and Pharisees, hypocrites! For [r]you cleanse the outside of the cup and dish, but inside they are full of extortion and self-indulgence. Blind Pharisee, first cleanse the inside of the cup and dish, that the outside of them may be clean also.

"Woe to you, scribes and Pharisees, hypocrites! For you are like [s]whitewashed tombs which indeed appear beautiful outwardly, but inside are full of dead *men's* bones and all uncleanness. Even so you also outwardly appear righteous to men, but inside you are full of hypocrisy and lawlessness.

"Woe to you, scribes and Pharisees, hypocrites! Because you build the tombs of the prophets and adorn the monuments of the righteous, and say, 'If we had

---

[p] TITHE OF MINT AND ANISE AND CUMMIN. Garden herbs, not really the kind of farm produce that the tithe was designed to cover (Lev. 27:30). But the Pharisees fastidiously weighed out a tenth of every herb, perhaps even counting individual anise seeds. Jesus' point, however, was not to condemn their observance of the law's fine points. The problem was that they "neglected the weightier matters" of justice and mercy and faith—the moral principles underlying all the laws. They were satisfied with their focus on the incidentals and externals but willfully resisted the spiritual meaning of the law. He told them they should have concentrated on those larger issues "without leaving the others undone."

[q] STRAIN OUT A GNAT AND SWALLOW A CAMEL. Some Pharisees would strain their beverages through a fine cloth to make sure they did not inadvertently swallow a gnat—the smallest of unclean animals (Lev. 11:23). The camel was the largest of all the unclean animals (Lev. 11:4).

[r] YOU CLEANSE THE OUTSIDE. The Pharisees' focus on external issues lay at the heart of their error. Who would want to drink from a cup that had been washed on the outside but was still filthy inside? Yet the Pharisees lived their lives as if external appearance were more important than internal reality. That was the very essence of their hypocrisy, and Jesus rebuked them for it repeatedly (cf. Matt. 5:20; 16:12).

[s] WHITEWASHED TOMBS. Tombs were regularly whitewashed to make them stand out. Accidentally touching or stepping on a grave caused ceremonial uncleanness (Num. 19:16). A freshly whitewashed tomb would be brilliantly white and clean-looking—and sometimes spectacularly ornate. But the inside was full of defilement and decay. Contrast Jesus' words here and in Luke 11:44.

lived in the days of our fathers, [t]we would not have been partakers with them in the blood of the prophets.'

"Therefore you are witnesses against yourselves that you are sons of those who murdered the prophets. Fill up, then, the measure of your fathers' *guilt.* Serpents, brood of vipers! How can you escape the condemnation of hell? Therefore, indeed, I send you [u]prophets, wise men, and scribes: *some* of them you will kill and crucify, and *some* of them you will scourge in your synagogues and persecute from city to city, that on you may come all the righteous blood shed on the earth, from the blood of righteous [v]Abel to the blood of Zechariah, [w]son of Berechiah, whom you murdered between the temple and the altar. Assuredly, I say to you, all these things will come upon [x]this generation.

"O Jerusalem, Jerusalem, the one who kills the prophets and stones those who are sent to her! How often I wanted to gather your children together, as a hen gathers her chicks under *her* wings, but you were not willing! See! Your house is left to you desolate; for I say to you, you shall see Me no more till you say, 'Blessed *is* He who comes in the name of the Lord!' "

---

[t] we would not have been partakers. A ridiculous claim to self-righteousness when they were already plotting the murder of the Messiah (cf. John 11:47–53).

[u] prophets, wise men, and scribes. i.e., the disciples, as well as the prophets, evangelists, and pastors who followed them (cf. Eph. 4:11).

[v] Abel . . . Zechariah. The first and last OT martyrs, respectively.

[w] son of Berechiah. (Zech. 1:1). The OT does not record how he died. However, the death of another Zechariah, son of Jehoiada, is recorded in 2 Chron. 24:20–21. He was stoned in the court of the temple, exactly as Jesus describes here. All the best manuscripts of Matthew contain the phrase "Zechariah, son of Berechiah" (though it does not appear in Luke 11:51). Some have suggested that the Zechariah in 2 Chron. 24 was actually a grandson of Jehoiada, and that his father's name was also Berechiah. But there is no difficulty if we simply take Jesus' words at face value and accept His infallible testimony that Zechariah the prophet was martyred between the temple and the altar, in a way very similar to how the earlier Zechariah was killed.

[x] this generation. Historically, this was the generation that experienced the utter destruction of Jerusalem and the burning of the temple in AD 70. Jesus' lament over Jerusalem and His removal of the blessing of God from the temple strongly suggest that the sacking of Jerusalem in AD 70 was the judgment He was speaking about. Cf. Matt. 22:7; 24:2; Luke 19:43.

158. The Widow's Mite

Mark 12:41–44; Luke 21:1–4

MK Now Jesus sat opposite the [a]treasury and saw how the people put LK their gifts [of] MK money into the treasury. And many *who were* rich put in much. Then one [b]poor widow came and threw in [c]two mites, which make [d]a quadrans. So He called His disciples to *Himself* and said to them, "Assuredly, I say to you that this poor widow [e]has put in more than all those who have given to the treasury; LK for all these [f]out of their abundance have put in offerings for God, MK but she out of her poverty put in all that she had, [g]her whole livelihood."

---

[a] TREASURY. This refers to the thirteen trumpet-shaped receptacles on the walls in the court of the women where offerings and donations to the temple were placed. Each was labeled for a specific use, and donations were given accordingly.

[b] POOR WIDOW. The Greek expression signifies extreme poverty. This woman was desperately poor and more fit to be a recipient of charity than a donor.

[c] TWO MITES. A "mite" was a small copper coin, which was the smallest denomination in use. It was worth about an eighth of a cent.

[d] A QUADRANS. For the benefit of his Roman audience, Mark related the "mite" to this smallest denomination of Roman coinage. A "quadrans" was equal to 1/64 of a denarius, and a denarius was the equivalent of a day's wage.

[e] HAS PUT IN MORE. i.e., more in proportion to her means.

[f] OUT OF THEIR ABUNDANCE. There was nothing sacrificial about their giving.

[g] HER WHOLE LIVELIHOOD. This could be translated, "all she had to live on." That meant she would not be able to eat until she earned more. The religious system at the temple was thoroughly corrupt. It was literally devouring widows' houses (cf. Mark 12:40).

159. The Olivet Discourse: Beginning of Birth Pangs

Matt. 24:1–14; Mark 13:1–13; Luke 21:5–19

MT Then Jesus went out and departed from the temple, and His disciples came up to show Him [a]the buildings of the temple—LK how it was adorned with beautiful stones and [b]donations. MK One of His disciples said to Him, "Teacher, see what manner of stones and [c]what buildings *are here!*" MK And [d]Jesus answered and MT said to them, "Do you not see all MK these great buildings? MT Assuredly, I say to you, LK the days will come in which [e]not *one* stone shall be left upon another that shall not be thrown down."

[a] THE BUILDINGS OF THE TEMPLE. This temple was begun by Herod the Great in 20 BC and was still under construction when the Romans destroyed it in AD 70. At the time of Jesus' ministry, the temple was one of the most impressive structures in the world, made of massive blocks of stone bedecked with gold ornamentation. Some of the stones in the temple complex measured 40x12x12 feet and were expertly quarried to fit perfectly against one another. The temple buildings were made of gleaming white marble, and the whole eastern wall of the large main structure was covered with gold plates that reflected the morning sun, making a spectacle that was visible for miles. The entire temple mount had been enlarged by Herod's engineers, by means of large retaining walls and vaulted chambers on the south side and southeast corner. By this means the large courtyard area atop the temple mount was effectively doubled. The whole temple complex was magnificent by any standard. The disciples' conversation here may have been prompted by Jesus' words in Matthew 23:38. They were undoubtedly wondering how a site so spectacular could be left "desolate."

[b] DONATIONS. Wealthy people gave gifts of gold sculpture, golden plaques, and other treasures to the temple. Herod had donated a golden vine with clusters of golden grapes nearly six feet tall. The gifts were displayed on the walls and suspended in the portico. They constituted an unimaginable collection of wealth. All of these riches were looted by the Romans when the temple was destroyed.

[c] WHAT BUILDINGS. This unidentified disciple was admiring the magnificence and beauty of the temple and the surrounding buildings and was encouraging a like response from Jesus. It is likely that he could not comprehend how such an awesome structure could be left "desolate" (cf. Matt. 23:38).

[d] JESUS ANSWERED. In response to the disciple's admiration, Jesus again predicted that the temple would be destroyed. About forty years later, in AD 70, the Romans ransacked Jerusalem, killed a million Jews, and demolished the temple.

[e] NOT ONE STONE SHALL BE LEFT. These words were literally fulfilled in AD 70. Titus, the Roman general, built large wooden scaffolds around the walls of the temple buildings, piled them high with wood and other flammable items, and set them ablaze. The heat from the fires was so intense that the stones crumbled. The rubble was then sifted to retrieve the melted gold, and the remaining ruins were "thrown down" into the Kidron Valley. After the destruction was over, the only stones left undisturbed were huge foundation stones that were not actually a part of the temple edifice but formed footings for the retaining wall under the entire temple mount. These can be viewed today in the "Rabbi's Tunnel," which runs north-south along the Western Wall. It is a portion of the western side of the retaining wall that today is called the "Wailing Wall." More of that retaining wall, including the steps used to ascend and descend from the temple mount, has also been uncovered on the southern side.

[MT] Now [f]as He sat on the [g]Mount of Olives [MK] opposite the temple, [h]Peter, James, John, and Andrew [MT] came to Him privately, saying, [LK] "Teacher, [MT] tell us, [i]when will these things be? [MK] What *will be* the sign when all these things [LK] are about to take place? [MT] And [j]what *will be* [k]the sign of Your coming, and of the end of the age?"

And Jesus answered and said to them: "[l]Take heed that no one deceives you. For many will come in My name, saying, [m]'I am the Christ,' [LK] and, 'The time has drawn near,' [MT] and will deceive many. [LK] Therefore do not go after them. [MT] And you will hear of wars and rumors of wars. See that you are not troubled; for all

---

[f] As He sat. This is the last of the five discourses featured in Matthew's gospel. This great sermon by Jesus is commonly known as the Olivet Discourse, because Jesus delivered it on the Mount of Olives just east of the temple across the Kidron Valley. Jesus' prediction of the coming destruction of the temple prompted a question from the disciples about the character of the end times. The remainder of the passage is His response to their question, as He describes His second coming at the end of the present age.

[g] Mount of Olives. The hill directly opposite the temple, across the Kidron Valley to the east (cf. Luke 19:29). This spot affords the best panoramic view of Jerusalem. At the base of this mountain is Gethsemane (cf. Matt. 26:36).

[h] Peter, James, John, and Andrew came to Him privately. These four disciples were asking on behalf of all the twelve.

[i] when will these things be? The disciples were speculating that Jesus would imminently usher in the kingdom, so they asked a two-fold question: (1) When would the temple be destroyed and the kingdom begin? and (2) What event would herald the beginning of the kingdom? The first question, "when," implies immediacy. The disciples thought that Jesus was about to usher in the kingdom of God at any time (cf. Luke 19:11), at least by the end of the Passover season. "These things" refers to the desolation and destruction of the temple (cf. Matt. 23:38; 24:2).

[j] what will be the sign of Your coming. Luke 19:11 records that the disciples still "thought the kingdom of God would appear immediately." The destruction of the temple did not fit the eschatological scheme they envisioned, so they asked for clarification. Jesus addressed their questions in reverse order, describing the prophetic sign of His coming (actually a series of signs) in Matt. 24:4–35 and then addressing their question about the timing of these events beginning in v. 36. When they asked about His coming (Greek, parousia; lit. "presence"), they did not envision a second coming in the far-off future. They were speaking of His coming in triumph as Messiah, an event which they no doubt anticipated would occur presently. Even if they were conscious of His approaching death, which he had plainly prophesied to them on repeated occasions (cf. Matt. 20:19), they could not have anticipated His ascension to heaven and the long intervening church age. However, when Jesus used the term parousia in His discourse, He used it in the technical sense as a reference to His second coming.

[k] the sign. The disciples probably expected some miraculous occurrence—such as complete darkness, brilliant light, or an angel from heaven—to announce the coming millennial kingdom. All of those things will occur at that time.

[l] Take heed. This Greek word literally means, "to see," but was often used as it is here with the idea of "keep your eyes open" or "beware."

[m] 'I am the Christ.' Many false prophets will come forward claiming to be messiahs and deliverers, offering themselves as the solution to the world's problems. Some will even claim to be Christ Himself. The number of false christs will increase as the end nears.

these things must come to pass LK first, [n]but the end *will* not *come* immediately." Then He said to them, "Nation will rise against nation, and kingdom against kingdom. And there will be great earthquakes in various places, and famines and pestilences; and there will be fearful sights and great signs from heaven. MT All these *are* the beginning of [o]sorrows.

MK "But watch out for yourselves, for LK before all these things, they will lay their hands on you and persecute *you.* MK They will deliver you up to [p]councils LK and prisons MK and you will be [q]beaten [r]in the synagogues. MT They will deliver you up to tribulation and kill you, and you will be hated by all nations for My name's sake. MK You will be brought before rulers and kings for My sake. LK But it will turn out for you as [s]an occasion for testimony. MK When they arrest *you* and deliver you up, do not worry beforehand, or premeditate [t]what you will speak. LK Settle *it* in your hearts not to meditate beforehand on what you will answer. MK Whatever is given you in that hour, speak that; [u]for it is not you who speak, but the Holy Spirit; LK for I will

---

[n] BUT THE END WILL NOT COME IMMEDIATELY. False prophets, as well as wars and rumors of wars, characterize the whole of the present age, but will escalate toward the end (cf. 2 Tim. 3:13). "The end" refers to the consummation of the present age.

[o] SORROWS. The word means "birth pangs." Famines, earthquakes, and conflicts have always characterized life in a fallen world, but by calling these things "the beginning" of labor pains, He indicated that things will get notably and remarkably worse at the end of the era as these unique tribulations signal the soon arrival of Messiah to judge sinful humanity and set up His millennial kingdom. Birth pains signal the end of pregnancy—they are infrequent at first and gradually increase just before the child is born. Likewise, the signs described here (in Mark 13:6–8) will be infrequent, relatively speaking, in the beginning and will escalate to massive and tragic proportions just prior to Christ's second coming. Cf. 1 Thess. 5:3; Rev. 6:1–17; 8:1–9:21; 16:1–21.

[p] COUNCILS. The Greek word is lit. "sanhedrins." These were local, Jewish courts attached to the synagogues, which tried charges of heresy and normal infractions of the law. The historian Josephus says that each city's council was composed of seven judges (*Antiquities*, 4.214), and the Mishnah records that there were twenty-three judges in every city with more than one hundred Jewish men (*Mishnah Sanhedrin* 1:6). These "councils" were like smaller versions of the great Sanhedrin that convened in Jerusalem.

[q] BEATEN. These local councils usually administered thirty-nine stripes so as not to violate Deut. 25:2–3. The recipient of the punishment was stripped bare to the waist. He received thirteen lashings to his chest and twenty-six to his back (cf. 2 Cor. 11:24).

[r] IN THE SYNAGOGUES. The "synagogues" were the places for Jewish assembly and worship. When the "councils" convened, they typically met in the "synagogue."

[s] AN OCCASION FOR TESTIMONY. Trials are always opportunities (James 1:2–4), and persecution is often an opportunity to magnify one's testimony.

[t] WHAT YOU WILL SPEAK. Although the persecution will be terrifying, Christians are not to be anxious in anticipation of those events.

[u] FOR IT IS NOT YOU WHO SPEAK. Rather than being fearful, believers can remain calm and depend on the Holy Spirit, who will give them the appropriate and effective words to say in defense of their faith in Christ.

give you a mouth and wisdom which all your adversaries will not be able to contradict or resist.

[MT] "And then [v]many will be offended, will betray one another, and will hate one another. [MK] Brother will betray brother to death, and a father *his* child; and children will rise up against parents and cause them to be put to death. [LK] You will be betrayed even by parents and brothers, relatives and friends; [MK] and you will be hated by all for My name's sake. [LK] But [w]not a hair of your head shall be lost. [MT] Then many false prophets will rise up and deceive many. And because lawlessness will abound, the love of many will grow cold. But he who [x]endures to the end shall be saved. [LK] By your patience possess your souls. [MT] And this gospel of the kingdom [MK] must first be [y]preached [MT] in all the world as a witness to all the nations, [z]and then the end will come."

---

[v] MANY WILL BE OFFENDED. Lit. "caused to stumble"—suggesting professing believers who fall away—and even turn against "one another" in shocking acts of spiritual treachery. Those who fall away in such a manner give evidence that they never were true believers at all.

[w] NOT A HAIR. This was not a promise for the preservation of their physical lives, but a guarantee that they would suffer no eternal loss. God Himself sovereignly preserves His own. Cf. John 10:28–29.

[x] ENDURES TO THE END . . . BE SAVED. Cf. Matt. 10:22. The ones who persevere are the same ones who are saved—not the ones whose love grows cold. This does not suggest that our perseverance produces or secures our salvation. Scripture everywhere teaches precisely the opposite: God, as part of His saving work, secures our perseverance. True believers "are kept by the power of God through faith for salvation" (1 Peter 1:5). The guarantee of our perseverance is built into the New Covenant promise. God says: "I will put My fear in their hearts so that they will not depart from Me" (Jer. 32:40). Those who do fall away from Christ give conclusive proof that they were never truly believers to begin with (1 John 2:19). To say that God secures our perseverance is not to say that we are passive in the process, however. He keeps us "through faith" (1 Peter 1:5)—our faith. Scripture sometimes calls us to hold fast to our faith (Heb. 10:23; Rev. 3:11) or warns us against falling away (Heb. 10:26–29). Such admonitions do not negate the many promises that true believers will persevere (John 10:28–29; Rom. 8:38–39; 1 Cor. 1:8–9; Phil. 1:6). Rather, the warnings and pleas are among the means God uses to secure our perseverance in the faith. Notice that the warnings and the promises often appear side by side. For example, when Jude urges believers, "keep yourselves in the love of God" (Jude 21), he immediately points them to God, "who is able to keep you from stumbling" (Jude 24). Christ will eventually deliver all true believers out of the present evil system into God's eternal kingdom (cf. Matt. 10:22).

[y] PREACHED IN ALL THE WORLD. Before the end there will be a worldwide proclamation of the gospel. Despite all the tribulations that would come—the deception of false teachers, the wars, persecutions, natural disasters, defections from Christ, and all the obstacles to the spread of the gospel—the message ultimately penetrates every part of the globe. God is never without a witness, and He will proclaim the gospel from heaven itself if necessary (cf. Rev. 14:6).

[z] AND THEN THE END WILL COME. "The end" refers to the final, excruciating birth pangs (cf. Matt. 24:8). This is how Christ characterizes the time of Great Tribulation described in the verses that follow.

160. The Olivet Discourse: The Coming of the Son of Man

Matt. 24:15–31; Mark 13:14–27; Luke 21:20–28

LK "When you see Jerusalem surrounded by armies, then know that its desolation is near. MT Therefore when you see the '[a]abomination of desolation,' spoken of by Daniel the prophet, MK [b]standing where it ought not MT in the holy place" [c](whoever reads, let him understand), "then let those who are in Judea [d]flee to [e]the mountains, LK let those who are in the midst of her depart, and let not those who are in the country enter her. MT Let him who is on the housetop not go down MK [f]into the house, nor enter MT to take anything out of his house. And let him who is in the field not go back to get his [g]clothes. LK For these are the days of [h]vengeance, that

---

[a] ABOMINATION OF DESOLATION. See Dan. 9:27; 11:31. This phrase originally referred to the desecration of the temple by Antiochus Epiphanes, king of Syria in the second century BC. Antiochus invaded Jerusalem in 168 BC, made the altar into a shrine to Zeus, and even sacrificed pigs on it. However, Jesus clearly was looking toward a yet-future "abomination of desolation." Some suggest that this prophecy was fulfilled in AD 70, when Titus invaded Jerusalem and destroyed the temple. However, the apostle Paul saw a still-future fulfillment (2 Thess. 2:3–4), as did John (Rev. 13:14–15)—when the Antichrist sets up an image in the temple during the future tribulation. Christ's words here, therefore, look beyond the events of AD 70 to a time of even greater global cataclysm that will immediately precede His coming.

[b] STANDING WHERE IT OUGHT NOT. Matthew 24:15 indicates the location as the "holy place." On the only other occasion where this phrase from Matthew appears in the NT, it clearly refers to the temple (Acts 21:8). This specifically implies that the temple will be rebuilt in the future and that the daily sacrificial system will be reinstated. "Standing" indicates that the abomination of desolation will be continuous, actually lasting for three and one-half years (Dan. 12:11; cf. Rev. 12:6).

[c] (WHOEVER READS, LET HIM UNDERSTAND). This indicates that Jesus was not issuing these warnings to the disciples or to others of their generation who would not experience this event, but to believers in the end time. Those who will read these truths will be prepared and "understand" the trials they are enduring.

[d] FLEE. The Greek word for "flee" is related to the English word *fugitive*, a person who is on the run to escape danger. Jesus warns those who live in Judea to escape the holocaust by taking refuge in the mountains.

[e] THE MOUNTAINS. Probably a reference to the region southeast of Jerusalem, particularly the Dead Sea area, where there are many caves and places of refuge. David hid from Saul in this area (1 Sam. 23:29). This would also include the hills of Moab and Edom.

[f] INTO THE HOUSE. So urgent will be the need to flee that if a person happens to be on the roof of his house when he hears the news, he is to run down the outside stairway and leave town without going inside his house to retrieve any belongings.

[g] CLOTHES. The Greek word refers to the outer cloak. Jesus warns those working in the fields not to take the time to retrieve their cloaks that may be at home or some distance away at the entrance to the field.

[h] VENGEANCE. i.e., God's righteous retribution against sin.

all things which are written may be fulfilled. MT But woe to those who are [i]pregnant and to those who are nursing babies in those days! And pray that your flight may not be [j]in winter or on the Sabbath. LK For there will be great distress in the land and wrath upon this people. And they will fall by the edge of the sword, and be led away captive into all nations. And Jerusalem will be trampled by Gentiles until [k]the times of the Gentiles are fulfilled.

MK "*In* those days MT there will be [l]great tribulation, such as has not been since the beginning of the world MK which God created MT until this time, no, nor ever shall be. MK And unless the Lord had [m]shortened those days, no flesh would be saved; but for [n]the elect's sake, whom He chose, He shortened the days. Then if anyone says to you, [o]'Look, here *is* the Christ!' or, 'Look, *He is* there!' do not believe it. MT For false christs and false prophets will rise and show great [p]signs and wonders [q]to deceive, if possible, even the elect. MT Therefore if they say to you, 'Look, He is

---

[i] PREGNANT AND . . . NURSING BABIES. Jesus certainly felt compassion for those women who will be hindered from fleeing quickly because they carry children. But He may have been warning them about atrocities that could include unborn children being slashed in the wombs and tiny infants being crushed (cf. Hos. 13:16).

[j] IN WINTER. This refers to the rainy season in Israel, when streams could become impassable and it would be difficult to glean food from barren fields.

[k] THE TIMES OF THE GENTILES. This expression is unique to Luke's gospel. It identifies the era from Israel's captivity (ca. 586 BC to Babylon; cf. 2 Kings 25) to her restoration in the kingdom (Rev. 20:1–6). It has been a time during which, in accord with God's purpose, Gentiles have dominated or threatened Jerusalem. The era has also been marked by vast spiritual privileges for the Gentile nations (cf. Isa. 66:12; Mal. 1:11).

[l] GREAT TRIBULATION. The words "has not been" and "nor ever shall be"—along with the description that follows—identify this as the yet-future time in which God's wrath shall be poured out upon the earth. It will be of long duration and characterized by severe pressure and continual anguish. This is the Great Tribulation at the end of the age (cf. Rev. 7:14). Jesus' descriptions of the cataclysms that follow closely resemble the outpouring of divine wrath described in the bowl judgments of Rev. 16 and His subsequent appearing in Rev. 19.

[m] SHORTENED. Lit. "mutilated" or "amputated." If the afflictions of this time were to continue, "no flesh would be saved," i.e., no one would survive. But "for the elect's sake" (so that redeemed people do not suffer more than they can bear) the time is "shortened"—i.e., held short of total destruction. Both Dan. 7:25 and Rev. 12:14 suggest that the actual length of time the Beast will be permitted to terrorize the world is fixed at three and one-half years.

[n] THE ELECT'S SAKE. The "elect" could refer to the nation of Israel (cf. Isa. 45:4) or those who become Christians during the Tribulation (Rev. 17:14). In either case God cuts short the days for their benefit.

[o] 'LOOK, HERE IS THE CHRIST!' Satan will cause false christs to appear in an attempt to deceive the elect into leaving their places of refuge. False teachers will claim that Christ is in their midst or is back in Jerusalem or elsewhere in Judea.

[p] SIGNS AND WONDERS. Satanic inspired pseudo-miracles employed to support their claims to be the true Christ (cf. 2 Thess. 2:9).

[q] TO DECEIVE, IF POSSIBLE, EVEN THE ELECT. This clearly implies that such deception is not possible (John 10:4–5).

in the desert!' do not go out; *or* 'Look, *He is* in the inner rooms!' [r]do not believe *it.* [MK] But [s]take heed; see, I have told you all things beforehand. [MT] For as the lightning comes from the east and flashes to the west, so also will the coming of the Son of Man be. For wherever the carcass is, there [t]the eagles will be gathered together.

"Immediately [u]after the tribulation of those days [v]the sun will be darkened, and the moon will not give its light; the [w]stars will fall from heaven, and the [x]powers of the heavens will be shaken. [LK] And [y]there will be signs in the sun, in the moon, and in the stars; and on the earth distress of nations, with perplexity, the sea and the waves roaring; men's hearts failing them from fear and the expectation of those things which are coming on the earth, for the powers of the heavens will be shaken.

[MT] "Then [z]the sign of the Son of Man will appear in heaven, and then [aa]all

---

[r] DO NOT BELIEVE IT. No one should consider the claims of self-styled messiahs, because all of them are false. When Christ returns, no one will miss it.

[s] TAKE HEED. Jesus issues a prophetic warning to be on guard. He has told the elect refugees of the future all that they need to know to avoid being misled and deceived by Satan's emissaries.

[t] THE EAGLES WILL BE GATHERED TOGETHER. The location of a carcass is visible from great distances because of the circling carrion birds overhead (cf. Job 39:27–30). Similarly, Christ's return will be clearly evident to all near and far. The same point is made by the lightning in Matt. 24:27. The eagle-carcass imagery here also speaks of the judgment that will accompany His return (Rev. 19:21).

[u] AFTER THE TRIBULATION OF THOSE DAYS. "Those days" describes the events of the previous verses and, thus, "the tribulation" refers to the Great Tribulation Jesus just spoke of. This also means that what He was about to describe will occur immediately at the end of the future tribulation period.

[v] THE SUN WILL BE DARKENED. Such phenomena are a common feature of Day of the Lord prophecy (see Isa. 13:9, 10; Ezek. 32:7–8; Joel 2:10, 31; 3:15; Amos 8:9). The ultimate fulfillment of these prophecies takes place during the time of the Beast's reign. The sun will go black as the universe begins to disintegrate prior to the return of Christ (Rev. 6:12–13; 8:12; cf. Acts 2:20).

[w] STARS WILL FALL FROM HEAVEN. Heavenly bodies will careen at random through space (cf. Rev. 6:13–14; 8:10–13; 16:8, 17–20).

[x] POWERS OF THE HEAVENS. All the forces of energy that hold everything in space constant, and which Christ controls, He will allow to become random and chaotic (cf. Isa. 13:6–16; 34:1–5; 2 Peter 3:10–12).

[y] THERE WILL BE SIGNS. The celestial signs and wonders described here immediately precede the return of Christ.

[z] THE SIGN OF THE SON OF MAN. i.e., the Son of Man Himself is the sign. The events described here precisely parallel the description in Dan. 7:13; Rev. 19:11–21.

[aa] ALL THE TRIBES OF THE EARTH WILL MOURN. i.e., over their own rebellion. Israel in particular will mourn over their rejection of the Messiah (cf. Zech 12:10–12).

the tribes of the earth will mourn, and they will see the Son of Man [bb]coming on the clouds of heaven with [MK] great [MT] power and great glory. And He will send His [cc]angels with a great sound of a trumpet, and they will gather together His elect [dd]from the four winds, [MK] from [ee]the farthest part of earth to the farthest part of heaven. [LK] Now when these things begin to happen, look up and [ff]lift up your heads, because your [gg]redemption draws near."

[bb] COMING ON THE CLOUDS . . . WITH GREAT POWER AND GLORY. Jesus will return to earth in the same manner in which He left it (Acts 1:9–11; cf. Dan. 7:13–14; Rev. 1:7). The psalmist said that God uses "clouds" as His chariot (Ps. 104:3), and Isa. 19:1 pictures the Lord riding on a cloud. Although these "clouds" could be natural, they more likely describe the supernatural "glory cloud" that represented God's presence in OT Israel (cf. Rev. 1:7). While Christ possesses "great power and glory," His return will be accompanied with visible manifestations of that power and glory (cf. Rev. 6:15–17; 11:15–19; 16:17–21; 19:11–16)—He will redeem the elect, restore the devastated earth, and establish His rule on earth.

[cc] ANGELS . . . WILL GATHER. A number of angels return with Christ (cf. Matt. 16:27; Mark 8:38). Angels are God's gatherers—they gather unbelievers for judgment (Matt. 13:41, 49–50), and they gather the elect for glory. The "elect" will include the 144,000 Jewish witnesses (cf. Rev. 7:4), their converts (Rev. 7:9), and the converts of the angelic preachers (cf. Rev. 14:6). They will also include the OT saints, gathered out of their graves and united with their redeemed spirits (Dan. 12:1–3).

[dd] FROM THE FOUR WINDS. A colloquial expression meaning "from everywhere," and similar to the expression "from the four corners of the world." None of the elect on earth or in heaven will miss entering the kingdom.

[ee] THE FARTHEST PART . . . TO THE FARTHEST PART. All the "elect" from heaven and earth are gathered and assembled before Christ. This is the culmination of world history, ushering in the millennial reign of Christ (cf. Rev. 20:4).

[ff] LIFT UP YOUR HEADS. The dreadful tribulations and signs that mark the last days are a cause of great expectation, joy, and triumph for the true believer.

[gg] REDEMPTION. i.e., the final fullness of redemption, when the redeemed are reunited with Christ forever.

161. The Olivet Discourse: Watch and Pray

Matt. 24:32–51; Mark 13:28–37; Luke 21:29–36

LK Then He spoke to them a parable: "Look at the fig tree, and all the trees [which] are already budding. MT Now learn this [a]parable from the fig tree: When its branch has already become tender and puts forth leaves, LK you see and know for yourselves that summer is now near. MT So you also, when you see all these things MK happening, LK know that the kingdom of God is near—MT at the doors! Assuredly, I say to you, [b]this generation will by no means pass away till all these things take place. [c]Heaven and earth will pass away, but [d]My words will by no means pass away.

"But of that [e]day and hour [f]no one knows, not even the [g]angels of heaven, MK [h]nor

---

[a] PARABLE FROM THE FIG TREE. When the fig branch "puts forth leaves," only a short time remains until summer. Likewise, when the final labor pains begin (cf. Matt. 24:8, 14), Christ's return "is near; it is at the doors!"

[b] THIS GENERATION. This cannot refer to the generation living at that time of Christ, for "all these things"—the abomination of desolation (Matt. 24:15), the persecutions and judgments (vv. 17–22), the false prophets (vv. 23–26), the signs in the heavens (vv. 27–29), Christ's final return (v. 30), and the gathering of the elect (v. 31)—did not "take place" in their lifetime. It seems best to interpret Christ's words as a reference to the generation alive at the time when those final hard labor pains begin. This would fit with the lesson of the fig tree, which stresses the short span of time in which these things will occur.

[c] HEAVEN AND EARTH WILL PASS AWAY. The universe as we know it will be dramatically altered after the thousand-year reign of Christ. Cf. Isa. 24:18–20; 2 Peter 3:10–13.

[d] MY WORDS WILL BY NO MEANS PASS AWAY. It is impossible for God's Word to be negated, destroyed, or altered in any way (cf. Ps. 19:9; Matt. 5:18; Luke 16:17; John 10:35).

[e] DAY AND HOUR. The exact day and time of Christ's return. The disciples wanted to fix the precise time, but this was not for them to know (Acts 1:7). Christ's emphasis instead is on faithfulness, watchfulness, stewardship, expectancy, and preparedness. These are the lessons He taught in the parables that immediately follow.

[f] NO ONE KNOWS. The time of Christ's return will not be revealed in advance to any man. At this time it was known only to God the Father.

[g] ANGELS. While all the angelic beings enjoy intimacy with God, hover around His throne to do His bidding (Isa. 26:2–7), and continually behold Him (Matt. 18:10), they have no knowledge of the time of Christ's return.

[h] NOR THE SON. When Jesus spoke these words to the disciples, even He had no knowledge of the date and time of His return. Although Jesus was fully God (John 1:1, 14), when He became a man, He voluntarily restricted the use of certain divine attributes (Phil. 2:6–8). He did not manifest them unless directed by the Father (John 4:34; 5:30; 6:38). He demonstrated His omniscience on several occasions (cf. John 2:25; 3:13), but He voluntarily restricted that omniscience to only those things God wanted Him to know during the days of His humanity (John 15:15). Such was the case regarding the knowledge of the date and time of His return. After He was resurrected, Jesus resumed His full divine knowledge (cf. Matt. 28:18; Acts 1:7).

the Son, but only the Father. MT But [i]as the days of Noah *were,* so also will the coming of the Son of Man be. For as in the days before the flood, they were eating and drinking, marrying and giving in marriage, until the day that Noah entered the ark, and did not know until the flood came and took them all away, so also will the coming of the Son of Man be. Then two *men* will be in the field: [j]one will be taken and the other left. Two *women will be* grinding at the mill: one will be taken and the other left. Watch therefore, for you do not know what hour your Lord is coming. But know this, that if the master of the house had known what hour [k]the thief would come, he would have watched and not allowed his house to be broken into. Therefore you also be ready, for the Son of Man is coming [l]at an hour you do not expect.

MK "Take heed, [m]watch and pray; for you do not know when the time is. LK Take heed to yourselves, lest your hearts be weighed down with carousing, drunkenness, and cares of this life, and [n]that Day come on you unexpectedly. For it will come as a snare on all those who dwell on the face of the whole earth. Watch therefore, and pray always [o]that you may be counted worthy to escape all these things that will come to pass, and to stand before the Son of Man.

MK "*It is* like a man going to a far country, who left his house and gave au-

---

[i] AS THE DAYS OF NOAH WERE. Jesus' emphasis here is not so much on the extreme wickedness of Noah's day (Gen. 6:5), but on the people's preoccupation with mundane matters of everyday life ("eating and drinking, marrying and giving in marriage"), when judgment fell suddenly. They had received warnings, in the form of Noah's preaching (2 Peter 2:5)—and the ark itself, which was a testimony to the judgment that was to come. But they were unconcerned about such matters and therefore were swept away unexpectedly in the midst of their daily activities.

[j] ONE WILL BE TAKEN. i.e., taken in judgment just as in Noah's day. This is clearly not a reference to the catching away of believers described in 1 Thess. 4:16–17.

[k] THE THIEF. As no one knows what hour the thief will come, no one knows the hour of the Lord's return or the Day of the Lord that accompanies His coming (cf. 1 Thess. 5:2; 2 Peter 3:10). But the believer is to be ready at all times.

[l] AT AN HOUR YOU DO NOT EXPECT. The parables that follow teach Christ's followers to be ready in case He comes sooner than anticipated, and also to be prepared in case He delays longer than expected (Matt. 25:1–13).

[m] WATCH AND PRAY. Christ sounded a warning for believers to be on guard in two practical ways: (1) "watch" is a call to stay awake and be alert, looking for approaching danger; and (2) "pray" emphasizes the believer's constant need for divine assistance in this endeavor. Even believers do not have in themselves sufficient resources to be alert to spiritual dangers that can so easily surprise them.

[n] THAT DAY. i.e., the day of His return. When Christ mentions His return, he invariably enjoins watchfulness (cf. Luke 12:37–40).

[o] THAT YOU MAY BE COUNTED WORTHY. Older manuscripts say "that you may have strength."

thority to his servants, and to each his work, and commanded the [p]doorkeeper to watch. Watch therefore, for you do not know when the master of the house is coming— [q]in the evening, at midnight, at the crowing of the rooster, or in the morning—lest, coming suddenly, he find you sleeping. And what I say to you, I say to all: Watch!

MT "Who then is a faithful and wise servant, whom his master made ruler over his household, to give them food in due season? Blessed *is* that servant whom his master, when he comes, will find so doing. Assuredly, I say to you that he will make him ruler over all his goods. But if that [r]evil servant says in his heart, 'My master is delaying his coming,' and begins to beat *his* fellow servants, and to eat and drink with the drunkards, the master of that servant will come on a day when he is not looking for *him* and at an hour that he is not aware of, and will cut him in two and appoint *him* his portion with the hypocrites. There shall be weeping and gnashing of teeth."

---

[p] DOORKEEPER. In Jesus' day this individual guarded the outer gate of the house, so as to be ready to let the returning master in upon his arrival. All Christ's disciples are to be like doorkeepers, always remaining alert and vigilant for their Master's return.

[q] IN THE EVENING . . . OR IN THE MORNING. The normal expressions designating the four three-hour watches of the night from 6:00 p.m. to 6:00 a.m. Their names identify the ends of the three-hour periods rather than the periods' beginnings.

[r] EVIL SERVANT. The evil servant represents an unbeliever who refuses to take seriously the promise of Christ's return (cf. 2 Peter 3:4). Though he is an unbeliever, he is nonetheless accountable to Christ for the stewardship of his time. Jesus was teaching that every person in the world holds his life, natural abilities, wealth, and possessions in trust from God and must give account of how these things are used.

162. The Olivet Discourse: The Ten Virgins

Matt. 25:1–13

MT "Then [a]the kingdom of heaven shall be likened to [b]ten virgins who took their lamps and went out to meet the bridegroom. Now five of them were wise, and five *were* foolish. Those who *were* foolish took their lamps and took no oil with them, but the wise took oil in their vessels with their lamps. But while the bridegroom was delayed, they all slumbered and slept.

"And at midnight a cry was *heard:* 'Behold, the bridegroom is coming; go out to meet him!' Then all those virgins arose and trimmed their lamps. And the foolish said to the wise, 'Give us *some* of your oil, for our lamps are going out.' But the wise answered, saying, '*No,* lest there should not be enough for us and you; but go rather to those who sell, and buy for yourselves.' And while they went to buy, the bridegroom came, and those who were ready went in with him to the wedding; and the door was shut.

"Afterward the other virgins came also, saying, 'Lord, Lord, open to us!' But he answered and said, 'Assuredly, I say to you, I do not know you.'

"Watch therefore, for you know neither the day nor the hour in which the Son of Man is coming."

---

[a] THE KINGDOM OF HEAVEN SHALL BE LIKENED TO. The parable of the ten virgins is given to underscore the importance of being ready for Christ's return in any event—even if He delays longer than expected. For when He does return, there will be no second chances for the unprepared.

[b] TEN VIRGINS. i.e., bridesmaids. The wedding would begin at the bride's house when the bridegroom arrived to observe the wedding ritual. Then a procession would follow as the bridegroom took the bride to his house for the completion of festivities. For a night wedding, "lamps," which were actually torches, were needed for the procession.

163. The Olivet Discourse: The Parable of Talents

Matt. 25:14–30

MT "For [a]*the kingdom of heaven is* like a man traveling to a far country, *who* called his own servants and delivered his goods to them. And to one he gave five [b]talents, to another two, and to another one, to each according to his own ability; and immediately he went on a journey. Then he who had received the five talents went and traded with them, and made another five talents. And likewise he who *had received* two gained two more also. But he who had received one went and dug in the ground, and hid his lord's money. After a long time the lord of those servants came and settled accounts with them.

"So he who had received five talents came and brought five other talents, saying, 'Lord, you delivered to me five talents; look, I have gained five more talents besides them.' His lord said to him, 'Well *done,* good and faithful servant; you were faithful over a few things, I will make you ruler over many things. Enter into [c]the joy of your lord.' He also who had received two talents came and said, 'Lord, you delivered to me two talents; look, I have gained two more talents besides them.' His lord said to him, 'Well *done,* good and faithful servant; you have been faithful over a few things, I will make you ruler over many things. Enter into the joy of your lord.'

"Then he who had received the one talent came and said, 'Lord, I knew you to be [d]a hard man, reaping where you have not sown, and gathering where you have

---

[a] THE KINGDOM OF HEAVEN IS LIKE. The parable of the talents illustrates the tragedy of wasted opportunity. The man who goes on the journey represents Christ, and the servants represent professing believers given different levels of responsibility. Faithfulness is what he demands of them, but the parable suggests that all who are faithful will be fruitful to some degree. The fruitless person is unmasked as a hypocrite and utterly destroyed.

[b] TALENTS. A talent was a measure of weight, not a specific coin, so that a talent of gold was more valuable than a talent of silver. A talent of silver (the word translated "money" in Matt. 25:18 is lit. *silver*) was a considerable sum of money. The modern meaning of the word *talent,* denoting a natural ability, stems from the fact that this parable is erroneously applied to the stewardship of one's natural gifts.

[c] THE JOY OF YOUR LORD. Both the man with five talents and the man with two received exactly the same reward, indicating that the reward is based on faithfulness, not results.

[d] A HARD MAN. His characterization of the master maligns the man as a cruel and ruthless opportunist, "reaping and gathering" what he had no right to claim as his own. This slothful servant does not represent a genuine believer, for it is obvious that this man had no true knowledge of the master.

not scattered seed. And I was afraid, and went and hid your talent in the ground. Look, *there* you have *what is* yours.'

"But his lord answered and said to him, 'You wicked and lazy servant, [e]you knew that I reap where I have not sown, and gather where I have not scattered seed. So you ought to have deposited my money with the bankers, and at my coming I would have received back my own with interest. Therefore take the talent from him, and give *it* to him who has ten talents. 'For [f]to everyone who has, more will be given, and he will have abundance; but from him who does not have, even what he has will be taken away. And cast the unprofitable servant into the outer darkness. There will be weeping and gnashing of teeth.'"

---

[e] You knew that I reap where I have not sown. In repeating the servant's charge against him, the master was not acknowledging that it was true. He was allowing the man's own words to condemn him. If the servant really believed the master to be the kind of man he portrayed, that was all the more reason for him not to be slothful. His accusation against the master—even if it had been true—did not justify his own laziness.

[f] To everyone who has, more will be given. See Matt. 13:12. The recipients of divine grace inherit immeasurable blessings in addition to eternal life and the favor of God (cf. Rom. 8:32). But those who despise the riches of God's goodness, forbearance, and longsuffering (Rom. 2:4), burying them in the ground and clinging instead to the paltry and transient goods of this world, will ultimately lose everything they have (cf. Matt. 6:19; John 12:25).

164. The Olivet Discourse: The Son of Man's Judgment

Matt. 25:31–46

MT "When the Son of Man comes in His glory, and all the holy angels with Him, then [a]He will sit on the throne of His glory. All the nations will be gathered before Him, and He will separate them one from another, as a shepherd divides *his* [b]sheep from the [c]goats. And He will set the sheep on His right hand, but the goats on the left. Then the King will say to those on His right hand, 'Come, you blessed of My Father, inherit the kingdom [d]prepared for you from the foundation of the world: for I was hungry and you gave Me food; I was thirsty and you gave Me drink; I was a stranger and you took Me in; I *was* naked and you clothed Me; I was sick and you visited Me; I was in prison and you came to Me.'

"Then the righteous will answer Him, saying, 'Lord, when did we see You hungry and feed *You,* or thirsty and give *You* drink? When did we see You a stranger and take *You* in, or naked and clothe *You?* Or when did we see You sick, or in prison, and come to You?' And the King will answer and say to them, 'Assuredly, I say to you, inasmuch as you did *it* to one of [e]the least of these My brethren, you did *it* to Me.'

[a] HE WILL SIT ON THE THRONE OF HIS GLORY. This speaks of the earthly reign of Christ described in Rev. 20:4–6. The judgment described here is different from the Great White Throne judgment of Rev. 20:11–15. This judgment precedes Christ's millennial reign, and the subjects seem to be only those who are alive at His coming. This is sometimes referred to as the judgment of the nations, but His verdicts address individuals in the nations, not the nations as a whole.

[b] SHEEP. i.e., believers (Matt. 10:16; cf. Ps. 79:13; Ezek. 34). They are given the place at "His right hand"—the place of favor.

[c] GOATS. These represent unbelievers, consigned to the place of dishonor and rejection.

[d] PREPARED FOR YOU. This terminology underscores that their salvation is a gracious gift of God, not something merited by the deeds described in Matt. 25:35–36. Before "the foundation of the world," they were chosen by God and ordained to be holy (Eph. 1:4)—predestined to be conformed to Christ's image (Rom. 8:29). So the good deeds commended in Matt. 25:35–36 are the fruit, not the root of their salvation. The deeds are not the basis for their entrance into the kingdom, but merely manifestations of God's grace in their lives. They are the objective criteria for judgment, because they are the evidence of saving faith (cf. James 2:14–26).

[e] THE LEAST OF THESE MY BRETHREN. This refers in particular to other disciples. Some would apply this to national Israel; others to needy people in general. But here Christ is specifically commending "those on His right" (Matt. 25:34) for the way they received His emissaries.

"Then He will also say to those on the left hand, 'Depart from Me, you cursed, into the everlasting fire prepared for the devil and his angels: for I was hungry and you gave Me no food; I was thirsty and you gave Me no drink; I was a stranger and you did not take Me in, naked and you did not clothe Me, sick and in prison and you did not visit Me.'

"Then they also will answer Him, saying, 'Lord, when did we see You hungry or thirsty or a stranger or naked or sick or in prison, and did not minister to You?' Then He will answer them, saying, 'Assuredly, I say to you, inasmuch as you did not do *it* to one of the least of these, you did not do *it* to Me.' And these will go away into [f]everlasting punishment, but the righteous into eternal life."

[f] EVERLASTING PUNISHMENT . . . ETERNAL LIFE. The same Greek word is used in both instances. The punishment of the wicked is as never-ending as the bliss of the righteous. The wicked are not given a second chance, nor are they annihilated. The punishment of the wicked dead is described throughout Scripture as "everlasting fire" (Matt. 25:41); "unquenchable fire" (Matt. 3:12); "shame and everlasting contempt" (Dan. 12:2); a place where "their worm does not die, and the fire is not quenched" (Mark 9:44–49); a place of "torments" and "flame" (Luke 16:23–24); "everlasting destruction" (2 Thess. 1:9); a place of torment with "fire and brimstone" where "the smoke of their torment ascends forever and ever" (Rev. 14:10–11); and a "lake of fire and brimstone" where the wicked are "tormented day and night forever and ever" (Rev. 20:10). Here Jesus indicates that the punishment itself is everlasting—not merely the smoke and flames. The wicked are forever subject to the fury and the wrath of God. They consciously suffer shame and contempt and the assaults of an accusing conscience—along with the fiery wrath of an offended deity—for all of eternity. Even hell will acknowledge the perfect justice of God (Ps. 76:10); those who are there will know that their punishment is just and that they alone are to blame (cf. Deut. 32:3–5).

165. Judas Agrees to Betray Jesus

Matt. 26:1–5, 14–16; Mark 14:1–2, 10–11; Luke 21:37–22:6

LK And [a]in the daytime He was teaching in the temple, but at night He went out and stayed on the mountain called Olivet. Then early in the morning all the people came to Him in the temple to hear Him. Now the [b]Feast of Unleavened Bread drew near, [c]which is called Passover.

MT Now it came to pass, when Jesus had finished all these sayings, *that* He said to His disciples, "You know that [d]after two days is [e]the Passover, and the Son of Man will be delivered up to be crucified." Then the chief priests, the scribes, and the elders of the people assembled at the palace of the high priest, who was called [f]Caiaphas, and plotted MK how they might take Him by trickery and put *Him* to

---

[a] IN THE DAYTIME. i.e., during the days of that final week in Jerusalem.

[b] FEAST OF UNLEAVENED BREAD. This feast commemorated the departure of the Israelites from Egypt (Ex. 23:15). It began immediately after the Passover and lasted from Nisan 15–21. Unleavened bread refers to the type of bread the Israelites were to take with them in their escape, which represented the absence of the leaven of sin in their lives and household (cf. Ex. 12:14; Lev. 23:6–8).

[c] WHICH IS CALLED PASSOVER. Passover was a single day, followed immediately by the Feast of the Unleavened Bread (Lev. 23:5–6). The whole season could be referred to by either name.

[d] AFTER TWO DAYS. In the context Jesus predicted His crucifixion was to take place in "two days," which would be Friday since when He was speaking it was Wednesday evening.

[e] THE PASSOVER. Friday of Passover, which would have begun on Thursday at sunset. The Passover commemorated the "passing over" of the homes of the Israelites by the angel of death, who killed the firstborn of Egypt (Ex. 12:1–13:16). The Passover began on the fourteenth day of Nisan (the first month of the Jewish calendar) with the slaying of the Passover lamb and continued into the early hours of the fifteenth (cf. Ex. 12:6; Matt. 26:2). This was God's chosen time for Christ to die. He was the antitype to which the Passover Lamb had always referred. Christ had always avoided His enemies' plots to kill Him (Luke 4:29–30; John 5:18; 10:39), but now it was His time. The true Lamb of God would take away the sin of the world (John 1:29).

[f] CAIAPHAS. Caiaphas served as high priest from AD 18 to 36, an unusually long tenure for anyone in that role. His longevity suggests he had a close relationship with both Rome and the Herodian dynasty. He was son-in-law to his predecessor, Annas (John 18:13). He controlled the temple and no doubt personally profited from the corrupt merchandising that was taking place there (cf. Matt. 21:12). His enmity against Jesus seems intensely personal and especially malevolent; every time he appears in Scripture, he is seeking Jesus' destruction.

death. MT But they said, "[g]Not during the feast, lest there be an uproar among the people," LK [h]for they feared the people.

Then [i]Satan entered [j]Judas, surnamed Iscariot, who was numbered among the twelve. So he went his way and conferred with the chief priests and [k]captains, how he might betray Him to them. MT And [Judas] said, "What are you willing to give me if I deliver Him to you?" MK And when they heard *it*, they were glad, LK and agreed to give him money. MT And they counted out to him [l]thirty pieces of silver. So from that time [m]he sought opportunity [for] MK how he might conveniently LK betray Him to them in the absence of the multitude.

---

[g] NOT DURING THE FEAST. Because the Passover had to be celebrated in Jerusalem, the city would have been overflowing—perhaps as many as two million people were there. Since many would have been from Galilee—an area where Jesus had many followers—and the religious leaders did not want to start a riot, they determined to wait until after the Passover season, when the crowds would be diminished. They wanted to postpone their plot until a more politically opportune time. But they could not; God's chosen time had come.

[h] FOR THEY FEARED THE PEOPLE. They were therefore plotting secretly, hoping to eliminate Him after the Passover season, when Jerusalem would not be filled with so many people. But these events occurred according to God's timetable, not theirs.

[i] SATAN ENTERED. i.e., Judas was possessed by Satan himself. Satan evidently gained direct control over Judas on two occasions—once just before Judas arranged his betrayal with the chief priests, and again during the Last Supper (John 13:27), immediately before the betrayal was actually carried out.

[j] JUDAS, SURNAMED ISCARIOT. This disciple, who is understandably referred to last in the lists of the twelve, was the son of Simon, who was also called "Iscariot." The name "Iscariot" means "man of Kerioth," which was a small town in Judea about twenty-three miles south of Jerusalem (cf. Mark 3:19). Thus Judas was not a Galilean like the other disciples. It is clear that Judas never had any spiritual interest in Jesus—he was attracted to Him because he expected Jesus to become a powerful religious and political leader. He saw great potential for power, wealth, and prestige through his association with Him. But Jesus knew what Judas was like from the start, and that is why He chose him as one of the twelve. He was the one who would betray Him so that the Scripture and God's plan of salvation would be fulfilled (Pss. 41:9; 55:12–15, 20–21; Zech. 11:12–13; John 6:64, 70–71; 13:18; 17:12).

[k] CAPTAINS. i.e., the temple guard, a security force consisting of Levites.

[l] THIRTY PIECES OF SILVER. The price of a slave (Ex. 21:32).

[m] HE SOUGHT OPPORTUNITY. "Sought" is better translated "began to seek." "Conveniently" means that Judas was looking for a suitable occasion to carry out his evil plan, which would be when Jesus was away from the crowds (Luke 22:6).

Part IX | The Upper Room on the Night Before His Death

166. The Beginning of the Final Passover

Matt. 26:17–20; Mark 14:12–17; Luke 22:7–16

LK Then came MT the [a]first *day of the Feast* of [b]Unleavened Bread, MK when they [c]killed the Passover *lamb.* LK And He sent MK out [d]two of His disciples, LK Peter and John, saying, "[e]Go and prepare the Passover for us, that we may eat." So they said to Him, MK "Where do You want us to go and prepare, that You may eat the Passover?" LK And He said to them, "Behold, MK go into the city, and LK when you have

---

[a] FIRST DAY OF THE FEAST OF UNLEAVENED BREAD. The Passover lambs were killed (Mark 14:12) on 14 Nisan (March/April). That evening, the Passover meal was eaten. The Feast of Unleavened Bread followed immediately after Passover, from 15–21 Nisan. The entire time was often referred to either as Passover (Luke 22:1) or as the Feast of Unleavened Bread. Therefore the first day refers to 14 Nisan.

[b] UNLEAVENED BREAD. Passover and the Feast of Unleavened Bread were so closely associated that both terms were used interchangeably to refer to the eight-day celebration that began with the Passover. Although Unleavened Bread is used here by Mark, his clear intention is the preparation for Passover.

[c] KILLED THE PASSOVER LAMB. The lambs were killed on 14 Nisan at twilight (Ex. 12:6), a Hebrew term meaning "between the two evenings," or between 3:00 and 5:00 p.m. Because of differences in how a day was reckoned, the people from Galilee celebrated the Passover Thursday evening, so the lambs were killed in the afternoon of that day. The disciples and Jesus ate the Passover meal that evening, after sundown (when Passover officially began). Judeans would follow this same sequence one day later on Friday. After the lamb was slaughtered and some of its blood sprinkled on the altar, the lamb was taken home, roasted whole, and eaten in the evening meal with unleavened bread, bitter herbs, *charoseth* (a paste made of crushed apples, dates, pomegranates, and nuts, into which they dipped bread), and wine.

[d] TWO OF HIS DISCIPLES. Only two people were allowed to accompany a lamb to the sacrifice.

[e] GO AND PREPARE. This was no small task. They had to take the paschal lamb to be sacrificed and make preparations for a meal for thirteen (v. 14). But preliminary arrangements for the meal had apparently been made personally by Jesus Himself, and the owner of the upper room was taking care of many of those details for them.

entered the city, [MT] [f]a certain man [LK] will meet you carrying a pitcher of water; follow him into the house which he enters. [MK] Wherever he goes in, say to the master of the house, [LK] 'The Teacher says to you, [MT] "My time is at hand; [LK] where is the [g]guest room where I may eat the Passover with My disciples [MT] at your house?" ' [LK] Then he will show you a large, furnished [h]upper room; there [i]make ready [MK] for us."

[MT] So the disciples did as Jesus had directed them. [LK] They went [MK] out, and came into the city, and found it just as He had said to them; and they prepared the Passover.

[MK] [j]In the evening, [LK] when [k]the hour had come, [MK] He came [and] [LK] [l]sat down, and [m]the twelve apostles with Him. Then He said to them, "[n]With *fervent* desire I have desired to eat this Passover with you before I suffer; for I say to you, I will no longer eat of it until it is [o]fulfilled in the kingdom of God."

---

[f] A CERTAIN MAN. Mark 14:13 and Luke 22:10 say they would be able to identify the man because he would be "carrying a pitcher of water," a chore normally reserved for women. He was evidently someone they did not know, probably a servant of whoever owned the house with an "upper room," where the Passover meal was to be eaten (Mark 14:15; Luke 22:12). Jesus had evidently made these arrangements clandestinely, in order to prevent His premature betrayal. Had Judas known ahead of time where the meal was to be eaten, he would surely have alerted the chief priests and elders. But none of these things were to happen until the "time" was "at hand." All of this reveals how Jesus Himself was sovereignly in control of the details of His own crucifixion. Although Jesus made these arrangements, it is unlikely that the water pitcher was any sort of prearranged signal. Christ's knowledge of what the man would be doing at the precise moment the disciples arrived appears to be a manifestation of His divine omniscience.

[g] GUEST ROOM. The word is translated "inn" in Luke 2:7. It typically referred to a place where a traveler could spend the night—a place of lodging or a guest room in someone's home, as was the case here (cf. Matt. 26:18).

[h] UPPER ROOM. This indicates the room was located upstairs and may have been a roof chamber built on top of the house. It would have been just one of many such rooms for rent in Jerusalem that were maintained for the express purpose of providing pilgrims a place to celebrate feasts. The furnishings undoubtedly included a large banquet table and everything necessary to prepare and serve a meal.

[i] MAKE READY. Peter and John were to prepare the Passover meal for Jesus and the other disciples.

[j] IN THE EVENING. The Passover meal was to be eaten at night after sunset but had to be completed before midnight (Ex. 12:8–14).

[k] THE HOUR HAD COME. i.e., sundown, marking the official beginning of Passover.

[l] SAT DOWN. Lit. "reclined" (cf. Mark 14:18; John 13:25).

[m] THE TWELVE APOSTLES WITH HIM. Peter and John may have rejoined Jesus and the other disciples and led them to the upper room. This may also be a general reference to the twelve, meaning that Jesus came with the other ten disciples to meet Peter and John.

[n] WITH FERVENT DESIRE. Cf. John 13:1. He wanted to prepare them for what was coming.

[o] FULFILLED. Christ's death on the following day fulfilled the symbolism of the Passover meal. Passover was both a memorial of the deliverance from Egypt and a prophetic type of the sacrifice of Christ.

167. Jesus Washes the Disciples' Feet

John 13:1–20

JN Now before the Feast of the Passover, when Jesus knew that His hour had come that He should depart from this world to the Father, having loved His own who were in the world, He loved them [a]to the end. And [b]supper being ended, [c]the devil having already put it into the heart of Judas Iscariot, Simon's *son,* to betray Him, Jesus, knowing that the Father had given all things into His hands, and that He had come from God and was [d]going to God, rose from supper and laid aside His garments, took a towel and girded Himself.

After that, He poured water into a basin and began [e]to wash the disciples' feet, and to wipe *them* with the towel with which He was girded. Then He came to Simon Peter. And [f]*Peter* said to Him, "Lord, are You washing my feet?" Jesus answered and said to him, "What I am doing you do not understand now, but you will know after this." Peter said to Him, "You shall never wash my feet!" Jesus answered him, "If I do not wash you, you have no part with Me." Simon Peter said

---

[a] TO THE END. Meaning "to perfection" with perfect love. God loves the world (John 3:16) and sinners (Matt. 5:44–45; Titus 3:4) with compassion and common grace, but loves His own with perfect, saving, eternal love.

[b] SUPPER. Passover on Thursday night after sunset.

[c] THE DEVIL . . . THE HEART OF JUDAS. This does not exonerate Judas, because his wicked heart desired exactly what the devil desired, the death of Jesus. The devil and Judas were in accord.

[d] GOING TO GOD. He faced the betrayal, agony, and death because He knew He would be exalted to the Father afterward, where He would receive the glory and fellowship He had eternally enjoyed within the Trinity (see John 17:4–5). This was the "joy set before Him" that enabled Him to "endure the cross" (Heb. 12:2).

[e] TO WASH THE DISCIPLES' FEET. The dusty and dirty conditions of the region necessitated the need for footwashing. Although the disciples would have likely been willing to wash Jesus' feet, they would not consider washing each other's feet. In the society of the time, footwashing was a task assigned to the lowest-ranking household slaves. It was not an action performed by a peer, except possibly as a rare expression of profound love. Luke points out (Luke 22:24) that they were thinking about who was the greatest of them, so that none was willing to stoop to wash feet. When Jesus moved to wash their feet, they were shocked. His actions are symbolic of spiritual cleansing and a paradigm of Christian humility. Through this action Jesus taught the lesson of selfless service that was supremely exemplified by His death on the cross.

[f] PETER SAID TO HIM. These proceedings embarrassed all of the disciples. While others remained silent, Peter, perhaps on behalf of others (see Matt. 16:13–23), spoke up in indignation that Jesus would stoop so low as to wash his feet. He failed to see beyond the humble service itself to the symbolism of spiritual cleansing involved (cf. 1 John 1:7–9). Jesus' response made the real point of His actions clear: unless He cleanses a person from sin (i.e., as portrayed in the symbolism of washing), one can have no part with Him.

to Him, "Lord, not my feet only, but also *my* hands and *my* head!" Jesus said to him, "He who is bathed [g]needs only to wash *his* feet, but is completely clean; and you are clean, but not all of you." For He knew who would betray Him; therefore He said, "You are [h]not all clean."

So when He had washed their feet, taken His garments, and sat down again, He said to them, "Do you know what I have done to you? You call Me Teacher and Lord, and you say well, for *so* I am. If I then, *your* Lord and Teacher, have washed your feet, you also ought to wash one another's feet. For I have given you [i]an example, that you should do as I have done to you. Most assuredly, I say to you, a servant is not greater than his master; nor is he who is sent greater than he who sent him. If you know these things, [j]blessed are you if you do them.

"I do not speak concerning all of you. I know [k]whom I have chosen; but that the Scripture may be fulfilled, 'He who eats bread with Me has lifted up his heel against Me.' Now I tell you before it comes, that when it does come to pass, you may believe that I am *He.* Most assuredly, I say to you, he who receives whomever I send receives Me; and he who receives Me receives Him who sent Me."

---

[g] needs only to wash his feet. The cleansing that Christ does at salvation never needs to be repeated—atonement is complete at that point. But all who have been cleansed by God's gracious justification need constant washing in the experiential sense as they battle sin in the flesh. Believers are justified and granted imputed righteousness (Phil. 3:8–9) but still need sanctification and personal righteousness (Phil. 3:12–14).

[h] not all clean. This verse refers to Judas (John 6:70), who was soon to lead the mob to capture Jesus (John 18:3).

[i] an example. The word used here suggests both "example" and "pattern" (Heb. 4:11; 8:5; 9:25; James 5:10; 2 Peter 2:6). Jesus' purpose in this action was to establish the model of loving humility.

[j] blessed are you if you do them. Joy is always tied to obedience to God's revealed Word (see John 15:14).

[k] whom I have chosen. A reference to the twelve disciples whom the Lord had selected (see John 15:16), whom the Lord knew perfectly, including Judas, who was chosen that the prophecy of Ps. 41:9 would be fulfilled.

168. Jesus Identifies His Betrayer

Matt. 26:21–25; Mark 14:18–21; Luke 22:21–23; John 13:21–30

JN When Jesus had said these things, as they MK [a]sat and ate, JN He was troubled in spirit, and testified and said, "Most assuredly, I say to you, MK one of you who eats with Me will betray Me. LK Behold, the hand of My betrayer *is* with Me on the table."

JN Then the disciples looked at one another, perplexed about whom He spoke. LK They began to question among themselves, which of them it was who would do this thing. JN Now there was leaning on Jesus' bosom [b]one of His disciples, whom Jesus loved. Simon Peter therefore motioned to him to ask who it was of whom He spoke. Then, leaning back on Jesus' breast, he said to Him, "Lord, who is it?" MT And they were exceedingly sorrowful, and each of them began to say to Him, MK one by one, MT "Lord, is it I?" MK And another *said,* "*Is* it I?"

JN Jesus answered MK and said to them, "*It is* one of the twelve, who [c]dips with Me in the dish, JN to whom I shall give a piece of bread when I have dipped *it.* MK The Son of Man indeed goes just [d]as it is written of Him, [e]but woe to that man by whom the

---

[a] SAT AND ATE. The order of the Passover meal was: (1) drinking a cup of red wine mixed with water (cf. Luke 22:17); (2) the ceremonial washing of hands symbolizing the need for spiritual and moral cleansing; (3) eating the bitter herbs, symbolic of the bondage in Egypt; (4) drinking the second cup of wine, at which time the head of the household explained the meaning of Passover; (5) singing of the Hallel (Pss. 113–118)—at this point they sang the first two; (6) the lamb was brought out, and the head of the household distributed pieces of it with the unleavened bread; (7) drinking the third cup of wine (cf. 1 Cor. 10:16).

[b] ONE OF HIS DISCIPLES, WHOM JESUS LOVED. This is the first reference to John the apostle, the author of the gospel. He specifically mentioned himself at the cross (John 19:26–27), at the empty tomb (20:2–9), by the Sea of Tiberias (21:1, 20–23), and in the next to last verse, where he is referenced as the author of the gospel (21:24).

[c] DIPS WITH ME IN THE DISH. There were likely several dishes around the table—Judas was probably one of several sitting near Jesus and thus would have dipped in the same bowl with Him.

[d] AS IT IS WRITTEN. Jesus was no victim—His betrayal by Judas was prophesied in the OT (Ps. 22; Isa. 53) and was part of God's predetermined plan to provide salvation. Every detail of the crucifixion of Christ was under the sovereign control of God and in accord with His eternal purposes. Cf. Acts 2:23; 4:26–28.

[e] BUT WOE. The fact that Judas's betrayal was part of God's plan does not free him from the guilt of a crime he entered into willfully. God's sovereignty is never a legitimate excuse for human guilt.

Son of Man is betrayed! It would have been [f]good for that man if he had never been born." MT Then Judas, who was betraying Him, answered and said, "Rabbi, is it I?" He said to him, "You have said it."

JN And having dipped the bread, [g]He gave *it* to Judas Iscariot, *the son* of Simon. Now after the piece of bread, [h]Satan entered him. Then Jesus said to him, "What you do, do quickly." But no one at the table knew for what reason He said this to him. For some thought, because Judas had the money box, that Jesus had said to him, "Buy *those things* we need for the feast," or that he should give something to the poor. Having received the piece of bread, he then went out immediately. And [i]it was night.

---

[f] GOOD . . . IF HE HAD NEVER BEEN BORN. Cf. John 8:21–24; 16:8–11. This is because the terror Judas would experience in hell would be so great. The severest punishment is reserved for Judas and others like him (Heb. 10:29). This is one of the strongest statements in Scripture on human responsibility for believing in Jesus Christ, coupled with the consequences of such unbelief.

[g] HE GAVE IT TO JUDAS ISCARIOT. It was not uncommon for the host of a banquet to pass a choice morsel of food to a guest as a gesture marking honor and comradery. Here Jesus demonstrates a final gesture of friendship to Judas, even as Judas is about to betray Him.

[h] SATAN ENTERED HIM. Judas was personally possessed by Satan himself in his betrayal of Jesus.

[i] IT WAS NIGHT. Although this was a historical reminiscence of John, the phrase may also be imbued with profound theological implications. It was the hour for Judas to be handed over completely to the power of darkness (Satan; cf. Luke 22:53).

169. More Rivalry among the Disciples

Luke 22:24–30

LK [a]Now there was also [b]a dispute among them, as to which of them should be considered the greatest. And He said to them, "The kings of the Gentiles exercise lordship over them, and those who exercise authority over them are called [c]'benefactors.' But not so *among* you; on the contrary, he who is greatest among you, let him be as the younger, and he who governs as [d]he who serves. For who *is* greater, he who sits at the table, or he who serves? *Is* it not he who sits at the table? Yet I am among you as the One who serves.

"But you are those who have continued with Me in [e]My trials. And [f]I bestow upon you a kingdom, just as My Father bestowed *one* upon Me, that you may eat and drink at My table in My kingdom, and sit on thrones [g]judging the twelve tribes of Israel."

---

[a] Now there was also. At this point in the narrative, Judas had gone, and Jesus was alone with the remaining eleven disciples.

[b] a dispute. Cf. Matt. 20:20–24; Luke 9:46. This dispute is difficult to imagine following the Lord's washing of their feet (John 13:1–20). It reveals how large an issue this was in the minds of the disciples and how far they were from grasping all that He had taught them.

[c] 'benefactors.' Cf. Matt. 20:25. This title was used by the heathen rulers of both Egypt and Syria, though it was rarely a fitting description. The intent was to portray themselves as champions of their people, but it had a very condescending ring to it—especially when so many "benefactors" were actually ruthless tyrants.

[d] he who serves. Cf. Matt. 20:26–28. This is an apparent reference to the washing of their feet. Christ Himself had modeled such servitude throughout His ministry (cf. Phil. 2:5–8).

[e] My trials. Christ's entire life and ministry were filled with temptations (Luke 4:1–13); hardships (Luke 9:58); sorrows (Luke 19:41); and agonies (Luke 24:44)—not to mention the sufferings of the cross, which He knew were yet to come.

[f] I bestow upon you a kingdom. Christ confirmed the disciples' expectation of an earthly kingdom yet to come. It would not come in the timing or the manner that they hoped, but He affirmed the promise that such a kingdom would indeed be established and that they would have a principal role in it (cf. Matt. 19:28).

[g] judging the twelve tribes of Israel. The language identifies this as a millennial promise. Cf. Rev. 20:4.

170. Jesus Predicts That Peter Will Deny Him

Luke 22:31–38; John 13:31–38

JN So, when [Judas] had gone out, Jesus said, "Now the Son of Man is [a]glorified, and God is glorified in Him. If God is glorified in Him, God will also glorify Him in Himself, and glorify Him immediately. Little children, I shall be with you a little while longer. You will seek Me; and [b]as I said to the Jews, 'Where I am going, you cannot come,' so [c]now I say to you. [d]A new commandment I give to you, that you love one another; as I have loved you, that you also love one another. By this all will know that you are My disciples, if you have love for one another."

Simon Peter said to Him, "Lord, where are You going?" Jesus answered him, "Where I am going [e]you cannot follow Me now, but you shall follow Me afterward." Peter said to Him, "Lord, why can I not follow You now?" LK And the Lord said, "[f]Simon, Simon! Indeed, [g]Satan has asked for you, that he may [h]sift *you* as

---

[a] GLORIFIED. With Judas gone the final events were set in motion. Rather than looking at the agony of the cross, Jesus looked past the cross, anticipating the glory that He would have with the Father when it was over (John 17:4–5; Heb. 12:2).

[b] AS I SAID TO THE JEWS. That statement is recorded in John 8:21.

[c] NOW I SAY TO YOU. After indicating He was about to leave, Jesus specified what He expected of the disciples after His departure. Love is to serve as the distinguishing characteristic of discipleship (cf. 1 John 2:7–11; 3:10–12; 4:7–10, 20–21).

[d] A NEW COMMANDMENT . . . AS I HAVE LOVED YOU. The commandment to love was not new. Deut. 6:5 commanded love for God, and Lev. 19:18 commanded loving one's neighbor as oneself (cf. Matt. 22:34–40; Rom. 13:8–10; Gal. 5:14; James 2:8). However, Jesus' command regarding love presented a distinctly new standard for two reasons: (1) it was sacrificial love modeled after His love ("as I loved you"; cf. John 15:13), and (2) it is produced through the New Covenant by the transforming power of the Holy Spirit (cf. Jer. 31:29–34; Ezek. 36:24–26; Gal. 5:22).

[e] YOU CANNOT FOLLOW. His work was nearly finished; theirs was just beginning (Matt. 28:16–20; Mark 16:15; Luke 24:47). Particularly, Peter had a work to do (cf. John 21:15–19). Only Jesus, as the sinless sacrifice for the trespasses of the world, could go to the cross and die (1 Peter 2:22–24). Also, only He could be glorified in the presence of the Father with the glory that He possessed before His incarnation (see John 12:41; 17:1–5).

[f] SIMON, SIMON. The repetition of the name (cf. Luke 10:41; Acts 9:4) implied an earnest and somber tone of warning. Christ Himself had given Simon the name Peter (Luke 6:14), but here He reverted to his old name, perhaps to intensify His rebuke about Peter's fleshly overconfidence. The context also suggests that Peter may have been one of the more vocal participants in the dispute of Luke 22:24.

[g] SATAN HAS ASKED FOR YOU. Though addressed specifically to Peter, this warning embraced the other disciples as well. The pronoun *you* is plural in the Greek text.

[h] SIFT YOU AS WHEAT. The imagery is apt. It suggests that such trials, though unsettling and undesirable, have a necessary refining effect.

wheat. But [i]I have prayed for you, [j]that your faith should not fail; and when you have returned to *Me,* strengthen your brethren." But he said to Him, "Lord, I am ready to go with You, both to prison and to death. JN I will lay down my life for Your sake." Jesus answered him, "Will you lay down your life for My sake? Most assuredly, LK I tell you, Peter, the rooster shall not crow this day before [k]you will deny three times that you know Me."

And He said to them, "When I sent you without money bag, knapsack, and sandals, did you lack anything?" So they said, "Nothing." Then He said to them, "[l]But now, he who has a money bag, let him take *it,* and likewise a knapsack; and he who has no sword, let him sell his garment and buy one. For I say to you that [m]this which is written must still be accomplished in Me: 'And He was numbered with the transgressors.' For the things concerning Me have an end." So they said, "Lord, look, here *are* [n]two swords." And He said to them, [o]"It is enough."

---

[i] I have prayed for you. The pronoun *you* is singular. Although it is clear that He prayed for all of them (John 17:6–19), He personally assured Peter of His prayers and of Peter's ultimate victory, even encouraging Peter to be an encourager to the others.

[j] that your faith should not fail. Peter himself failed miserably, but his faith was never overthrown (cf. John 21:18–19).

[k] you will deny. This prediction of Peter's denial evidently took place in the upper room (cf. John 13:38). Matt. 26:34 and Mark 14:30 record a second, nearly identical incident, which took place on the Mount of Olives, on the way to Gethsemane (cf. Matt. 26:30; Mark 14:26).

[l] But now. When Christ sent them out before, He had sovereignly arranged for their needs to be met. Henceforth they were to use normal means to provide for their own support and protection. The money bag, knapsack, and sword were figurative expressions for such means (the sword being emblematic of protection, not aggression). But they mistakenly took His words literally.

[m] this which is written. Quoted from Isa. 53:12.

[n] two swords. These were short, dagger-like instruments—more like knives than swords. There was nothing unusual about the carrying of such weapons in that culture. They had many practical uses besides violence against other people.

[o] "It is enough." i.e., enough of such talk.

171. Jesus Institutes the Lord's Supper

Matt. 26:26–29; Mark 14:22–25; Luke 22:17–20; 1 Cor. 11:24–25

MT [a]And as [b]they were eating, LK [c]He took the cup, and gave thanks, and said, "Take this and divide *it* among yourselves; for I say to you, I will not drink of the fruit of the vine until the kingdom of God comes."

And He took bread, gave thanks and broke *it,* MT and gave *it* to the disciples and said, "Take, eat; [d]this is My body LK which is [e]given for you; [f]do this in [g]remembrance of Me."

Likewise He also [h]*took* the cup [i]after supper, MK and when He had given thanks

---

[a] AND AS . . . At this point in the narrative, it appears that Judas had gone (John 13:23–30), and Jesus was alone with the faithful eleven disciples (cf. Luke 22:21). Then it was that He transformed the Passover of the Old Covenant into the Lord's Supper of the New Covenant, creating a new memorial feast to remember God's deliverance from sin.

[b] THEY WERE EATING. There is no indication from any of the gospel accounts as to which part of the meal they were eating, but it is likely that this occurred just prior to eating the roasted lamb or concurrently with it. It is significant that Jesus established the truth of New Covenant while in the midst of eating the Passover.

[c] HE TOOK THE CUP. Luke mentions two cups. The Passover seder involved the sharing of four cups of diluted red wine. This cup was the first of the four (the cup of thanksgiving) and was preliminary to the institution of the Lord's Supper (cf. 1 Cor. 10:16). It represented the end of His time of eating and drinking with the disciples, particularly partaking of the Passover (cf. Matt. 9:15; 26:29; Mark 14:25; Luke 5:34–35).

[d] THIS IS MY BODY. i.e., it represented His body (cf. the words of Luke 8:11, "The seed is the word of God"—and also Luke 22:20). Such metaphorical language was a typical Hebraism. No eucharistic miracle of transubstantiation was implied, nor could the disciples have missed the symbolic intent of His statement, for His actual body—yet unbroken—was before their very eyes. Jesus gave new meaning to eating the bread. The unleavened bread symbolized the severing of the Israelites from the old life in Egypt. It represented a separation from worldliness, sin, and false religion and the beginning of a new life of holiness and godliness. From then on in the Lord's Supper, the bread would symbolize Christ's body, which He sacrificed for the salvation of men (cf. Matt. 26:26).

[e] GIVEN FOR YOU. Weak manuscript evidence in 1 Cor. 11:24 renders this phrase "broken for you." But see John 19:33, 36.

[f] DO THIS. Thus He established the observance as an ordinance for worship (cf. 1 Cor. 11:23–26).

[g] REMEMBRANCE OF ME. Passover had looked forward to the sacrifice of Christ; He transformed the seder into an altogether different ceremony, which looks back in remembrance at His atoning death.

[h] TOOK THE CUP. This is the third (the cup of blessing) of the four cups in the Passover celebration (cf. 1 Cor. 10:16).

[i] AFTER SUPPER. Cf. 1 Cor. 11:25. These two verses are virtually identical in form. Paul stated that he had received his information about this event from the Lord Himself (1 Cor. 11:23).

He gave *it* to them, [MT] saying, "Drink from it, all of you." [MK] And they all drank from it. And He said to them, " [LK] [j] This cup *is* the new covenant [k]in My blood, [MT] which is shed [l]for many for the remission of sins. [1COR] This do, as often as you drink *it,* [m]in remembrance of Me. [MK] Assuredly, [LK] I say to you, [n]I will not drink of the fruit of the vine [MT] from now on until that day when I [o]drink it new with you in [p]My Father's kingdom."

---

[j] This cup is the new covenant. Clearly, the cup only represented the New Covenant.

[k] in My blood. Covenants were ratified with the blood of a sacrifice (Gen. 8:20; 15:9–10; Ex. 24:5–8). Jesus' words here echo Moses' pronouncement in Ex. 24:8. The blood of the New Covenant is not an animal's blood, but Christ's own blood, shed for the remission of sins. The New Covenant has been ratified once and for all by the death of Christ. Cf. Jer. 31:31–34; Heb. 8:1–10:18; 8:6; 1 Peter 1:19.

[l] for many. This lit. means "for the benefit of many." The "many" are all who believe, both Jew and Gentile. Cf. Matt. 20:28; Luke 10:45.

[m] in remembrance of Me. Jesus transformed the third cup of the Passover into the cup of remembrance of His offering.

[n] I will not drink. Jesus declared that this would be the last Passover and that He would not even drink wine with them again, since this was His last meal. Until the inauguration of the millennial kingdom, believers are to share this memorial meal (cf. 1 Cor. 11:23–34).

[o] drink it new. This served as an assurance to them of Jesus' return and His establishment of His earthly, millennial kingdom. It possibly implies that the communion service will continue to be observed in the millennial kingdom, as a memorial to the cross. It more probably indicates that Jesus would not have another Passover with them until the kingdom (cf. Ezek. 45:18–25; 45:21–24). It is also true that in the kingdom, commemorative sacrifices from the Old Covenant will be restored (Ezek. 43–45), which will have meaning never understood before the cross of Christ to which they pointed.

[p] My Father's kingdom. i.e., the earthly millennial kingdom (cf. Luke 22:18, 29–30).

172. Jesus Comforts His Disciples

John 14:1–14

JN "[a]Let not your heart be [b]troubled; you believe in God, believe also in Me. In My Father's house are many [c]mansions; if *it were* not *so,* I would have told you. [d]I go to prepare a place for you. And if I go and prepare a place for you, I will come again and receive you to Myself; that where I am, *there* you may be also. And where I go you know, and the way you know."

Thomas said to Him, "Lord, we do not know where You are going, and how can we know the way?"

Jesus said to him, "[e]I am the way, the truth, and the life. No one comes to the

---

[a] LET NOT YOUR HEART. This whole chapter (John 14) centers in the promise that Christ is the One who gives the believer comfort, not only in His future return, but also in the present with the ministry of the Holy Spirit (John 14:26). The scene continues to be the upper room, where the disciples had gathered with Jesus before He was arrested. Judas had been dismissed (John 13:30), and Jesus had begun His valedictory address to the remaining eleven. The world of the disciples was about to be shattered; they would be bewildered, confused, and ridden with anxiety because of the events that would soon transpire. Anticipating their devastation, Jesus spoke to comfort their hearts. Instead of the disciples lending support to Jesus in the hours before His cross, He had to support them spiritually as well as emotionally. This reveals His heart of serving love (cf. Matt. 20:26–28).

[b] TROUBLED. Faith in Him can stop the heart from being agitated.

[c] MANSIONS. Lit. dwelling places, rooms, or even apartments (in modern terms). All are in the large "Father's house."

[d] I GO TO PREPARE. His departure would be for their advantage since He was going away to prepare a heavenly home for them and will return to take them so that they may be with Him. This is one of the passages that refers to the rapture of the saints at the end of the age when Christ returns. The features in this description do not describe Christ coming to earth with His saints to establish His kingdom (Rev. 19:11–15), but taking believers from earth to live in heaven. Since no judgment on the unsaved is described here, this is not the event of His return in glory and power to destroy the wicked (cf. Matt. 13:36–43, 47–50). Rather, this describes His coming to gather His own who are alive and raise the bodies of those who have died to take them all to heaven. This rapture event is also described in 1 Cor. 15:51–54; 1 Thess. 4:13–18. After being raptured the church will celebrate the marriage supper (Rev. 19:7–10), be rewarded (1 Cor. 3:10–15; 4:5; 2 Cor. 5:9–10), and later return to earth with Christ when He comes again to set up His kingdom (Rev. 19:11–20:6).

[e] I AM THE WAY, THE TRUTH, AND THE LIFE. This is the sixth "I AM" statement of Jesus in John (see 6:35; 8:12; 10:7, 9; 10:11, 14; 11:25; 15:1, 5). In response to Thomas's query, Jesus declared that He is the way to God because He is the truth of God (John 1:14) and the life of God (John 1:4; 3:15; 11:25). In this verse the exclusiveness of Jesus as the only approach to the Father is emphatic. Only one way, not many ways, exist to God, i.e., Jesus Christ (cf. Matt. 7:13–14; Luke 13:24; John 10:7–9; Acts 4:12).

Father except through Me. If you had known Me, you would have known My Father also; and [f]from now on you know Him and have seen Him."

Philip said to Him, "Lord, show us the Father, and it is sufficient for us."

Jesus said to him, "Have I been with you so long, and yet you have not known Me, Philip? He who has seen Me has seen the Father; so how can you say, 'Show us the Father'? Do you not believe that I am in the Father, and the Father in Me? The words that I speak to you I do not speak on My own *authority;* but the Father who dwells in Me does the works. Believe Me that I *am* in the Father and the Father in Me, or else believe Me for the sake of the works themselves.

"Most assuredly, I say to you, he who believes in Me, the works that I do he will do also; and [g]greater *works* than these he will do, [h]because I go to My Father. And [i]whatever you ask in My name, that I will do, that the Father may be glorified in the Son. If you ask anything in My name, I will do *it.*"

---

[f] FROM NOW ON YOU KNOW HIM. They know God because they had come to know Christ in His ministry and soon in His death and resurrection. To know Him is to know God. This constant emphasis on Jesus as God incarnate is unmistakably clear in this gospel (John 1:1–3, 14, 17–18; 5:10–23, 26; 8:58; 9:35; 10:30, 38; 12:41; 17:1–5; 20:28).

[g] GREATER WORKS THAN THESE HE WILL DO. Jesus did not mean greater works in power, but in extent. They would become witnesses to all the world through the power of the indwelling and infilling of the Holy Spirit (Acts 1:8) and would bring many to salvation because of the Comforter dwelling in them. The focus is on spiritual rather than physical miracles. The book of Acts constitutes the beginning historical record of the impact that the Spirit-empowered disciples had on the world (cf. Acts 17:6).

[h] BECAUSE I GO TO MY FATHER. The only way Jesus' disciples would be able to be used to do those greater works was through the power of the Holy Spirit, and He could not be sent as the Comforter until Jesus returned to the Father (John 7:39).

[i] WHATEVER YOU ASK. In their hour of loss at the departure of Jesus, He comforted them with the means that would provide them with the necessary resources to accomplish their task without His immediate presence, which they had come to depend upon. To ask in Jesus' "name" does not mean to tack such an expression on the end of a prayer as a mere formula. It means: (1) the believer's prayer should be for His purposes and kingdom and not selfish reasons; (2) the believer's prayer should be on the basis of His merits and not any personal merit or worthiness; and (3) the believer's prayer should be in pursuit of His glory alone.

173. The Promised Helper

John 14:15–31

JN "[a]If you love Me, keep My commandments. And I will [b]pray the Father, and He will give you [c]another [d]Helper, that He may abide with you forever— the [e]Spirit of truth, whom the world cannot receive, because it neither sees Him nor knows Him; but you know Him, for He [f]dwells with you and will be in you. I will not leave you [g]orphans; [h]I will come to you.

[a] IF YOU LOVE ME, KEEP MY COMMANDMENTS. In this section (John 14:15–31) Jesus promises believers comfort from five supernatural blessings that the world does not enjoy: (1) a supernatural Helper (vv. 15–17); (2) a supernatural life (vv. 18–19); (3) a supernatural union (vv. 20–25); (4) a supernatural Teacher (v. 26); and (5) a supernatural peace (vv. 27–31). The key to all of this is John 14:15, which relates that these supernatural promises are for those who love Jesus Christ, whose love is evidenced by obedience. Love for Christ is inseparable from obedience (see Luke 6:46; 1 John 5:2–3). "My commandments" are not only Jesus' ethical commandments in context (vv. 23–24), but the whole of God-given revelation (see 3:31–32; 12:47–49; 17:6).

[b] PRAY THE FATHER. The priestly and intercessory work of Christ began with the request that the Father send the Holy Spirit to indwell in the people of faith (John 7:39; 15:26; 16:7; 20:22; cf. Acts 1:8; 2:4, 33).

[c] ANOTHER. The Greek word specifically means another of the same kind, i.e., someone like Jesus Himself who will take His place and do His work. The Spirit of Christ is the Third Person of the Trinity, having the same essence of deity as Jesus and as perfectly one with Him as He is with the Father.

[d] HELPER. The Greek term here lit. means "one called alongside to help" and has the idea of someone who encourages and exhorts (cf. John 16:7). "Abiding" has to do with His permanent residence in believers (Rom. 8:9; 1 Cor. 6:19–20; 12:13).

[e] SPIRIT OF TRUTH. He is the Spirit of truth in that He is the source of truth and communicates the truth to His own (John 16:12–15). Apart from Him men cannot know God's truth (1 Cor. 2:12–16; 1 John 2:20, 27).

[f] DWELLS WITH YOU AND WILL BE IN YOU. This indicates some distinction between the ministry of the Holy Spirit to believers before and after Pentecost. While clearly the Holy Spirit has been with all who have ever believed throughout redemptive history as the source of truth, faith, and life, Jesus is saying something new is coming in His ministry. John 7:37–39 indicates this unique ministry would be like "rivers of living water." Acts 19:1–7 introduces some Old Covenant believers who had not received the Holy Spirit in this unique fullness and intimacy. Cf. Acts 1:8; 2:1–4; 1 Cor. 12:11–13.

[g] ORPHANS. In this veiled reference to His death, He promised not to leave them alone (Rom. 8:9).

[h] I WILL COME TO YOU . . . YOU WILL SEE ME. First, He was referring to His resurrection, after which they would see Him (John 20:19–29). There is no record that any unbelievers saw Him after He rose (see 1 Cor. 15:1–9). In another sense this has reference to the mystery of the Trinity. Through the coming and indwelling of the Holy Spirit at Pentecost, Jesus would be back with His children (cf. Matt. 28:20; John 16:16; Rom. 8:9; 1 John 4:13).

"A little while longer and the world will see Me no more, but you will see Me. Because I live, [i]you will live also. [j]At that day you will know that I *am* in My Father, and you in Me, and I in you. He who has My commandments and keeps them, it is he who loves Me. And he who loves Me will be loved by My Father, and I will love him and manifest Myself to him."

Judas (not Iscariot) said to Him, "Lord, how is it that You will manifest Yourself to us, and not to the world?"

Jesus answered and said to him, "If anyone loves Me, he will [k]keep My word; and My Father will love him, and We will come to him and make Our home with him. He who does not love Me does not keep My words; and the word which you hear is not Mine but the Father's who sent Me.

"These things I have spoken to you while being present with you. But the Helper, the Holy Spirit, whom the Father will send in My name, He [l]will teach you all things, and bring to your remembrance all things that I said to you. [m]Peace I leave with you, My peace I give to you; not as the world gives do I give to you. Let not your heart be troubled, neither let it be afraid. You have heard Me say to you,

---

[i] you will live also. Because of His resurrection and by the indwelling life of the Spirit of Christ, believers possess eternal life (see Rom. 6:1–11; Col. 3:1–4).

[j] At that day. This refers to His resurrection when He returns to them alive.

[k] keep My word. Once again, Jesus emphasized the need for the habitual practice of obedience to His commands as evidence of the believer's love for Him and the Father. This is consistent with the teaching of James 2:14–26 that true saving faith is manifest by works produced by God in the transforming, regenerating power of the Spirit. Those works are expressions of the love, which the Spirit pours into the believer's heart (Rom. 5:5; Gal. 5:22).

[l] will teach you all things. The Holy Spirit energized the hearts and minds of the apostles in their ministry, helping them to produce the NT Scripture. The disciples had failed to understand many things about Jesus and what He taught, but because of this supernatural work, they came to an inerrant and accurate understanding of the Lord and His work and recorded it in the gospels and the rest of the NT Scriptures (2 Tim. 3:16; 2 Peter 1:20–21).

[m] Peace I leave . . . not as the world gives. The word *peace* reflects the Hebrew *shalom*, which became a greeting to His disciples after the resurrection (John 20:19–26). On a personal level this peace, unknown to the unsaved, provides supernatural calm and comfort in the midst of trials (Phil. 4:7), and enables God's people to respond to others in harmony (Col. 3:15). The greatest reality of this peace will be in the messianic kingdom (Num. 6:26; Ps. 29:11; Isa. 9:6–7; 52:7; 54:13; 57:19; Ezek. 37:26; Hag. 2:9; cf. Acts 10:36; Rom. 1:7; 5:1; 14:17).

'I am going away and coming *back* to you.' If you loved Me, you would rejoice because I said, 'I am going to the Father,' for My Father is [n]greater than I.

"And now I have told you before it comes, that when it does come to pass, you may believe. I will no longer talk much with you, for [o]the ruler of this world is coming, and he has [p]nothing in Me. But that the world may know that I love the Father, and as the Father gave Me commandment, so I do. Arise, let us go from here."

---

[n] greater than I. He was not admitting inferiority to the Father (after claiming equality repeatedly, cf. John 14:7–11), but was saying that if the disciples loved Him, they would not be reluctant to let Him go to the Father, because He was returning to the realm where He belonged and to the full glory He gave up (John 17:5). He was going back to share equal glory with the Father, which would be greater than what He had experienced in His incarnation. He will in no way be inferior in that glory, because His humiliation was over.

[o] the ruler of this world. Judas was only a tool of the "prince" who rules the system of darkness—Satan (John 6:70; 13:21, 27).

[p] nothing in Me. The Hebrew idiom means that Satan had nothing on Jesus, could make no claim on Him, nor charge Him with any sin. Therefore, Satan could not hold Him in death. Christ would triumph and destroy Satan (Heb. 2:14). His death was no sign that Satan won, but that God's will was being done.

174. The Vine and the Branches

John 15:1–17

JN "[a]I am the true [b]vine, and My Father is the vinedresser. Every branch in Me that does not bear fruit [c]He takes away; and every *branch* that bears fruit [d]He prunes, that it may bear more fruit. You are already clean because of the word which I have spoken to you. [e]Abide in Me, and I in you. As the branch cannot bear fruit of itself, unless it abides in the vine, neither can you, unless you abide in Me.

"I am the vine, you *are* the branches. He who abides in Me, and I in him, bears much fruit; for without Me you can do nothing. If anyone does not abide in

---

[a] I AM THE TRUE VINE. This is the last of seven claims to deity in the form of "I AM" statements by Jesus in the gospel of John (see 6:35; 8:12; 10:7, 9; 10:11, 14; 11:25; 14:6).

[b] VINE . . . VINEDRESSER. Through this extended metaphor of the vine and branches, Jesus set forth the basis of Christian living. Jesus used the imagery of agricultural life at the time, i.e., vines and vine crops (see also Matt. 20:1–16; 21:23–41; Mark 12:1–9; Luke 13:6–9; 20:9–16). In the OT the vine is used commonly as a symbol for Israel (Ps. 80:9–16; Isa. 5:1–7; 27:2–6; Jer. 2:21; 12:10; Ezek. 15:1–8; 17:1–21; 19:10–14; Hos. 10:1–2). He specifically identified Himself as the "true vine" and the Father as the "vinedresser" or caretaker of the vine. The vine has two types of branches: (1) branches that bear fruit (John 15:2, 8), and (2) branches that do not (John 15:2, 6). The branches that bear fruit are genuine believers. Though in immediate context the focus is upon the eleven faithful disciples, the imagery also encompasses all believers down through the ages. The branches that do not bear fruit are those who profess to believe, but their lack of fruit indicates genuine salvation has never taken place, and they have no life from the vine. Especially in the immediate context, Judas was in view, but the imagery extends from him to all those who make a profession of faith in Christ but do not actually possess salvation. The image of non-fruit-bearing branches being burned pictures eschatological judgment and eternal rejection (cf. Ezek. 15:6–8).

[c] HE TAKES AWAY. The picture is of the vinedresser (i.e., the Father) getting rid of dead wood while preserving the living, fruit-bearing branches. The dead branches picture apostate Christians who never genuinely believed and will be taken away in judgment (Matt. 7:16; Eph. 2:10). They have never truly experienced the life of Christ within them (cf. Matt. 13:18–23; 24:12; John 8:31–32; Heb. 3:14–19; 6:4–8; 10:27–31; 1 John 2:19; 2 John 9).

[d] HE PRUNES. God removes all things in the believer's life that would hinder fruit-bearing, i.e., He chastises to cut away sin and hindrances that would drain spiritual life, just as the farmer removes anything on the branches that keep them from bearing maximum fruit (Heb. 12:3–11).

[e] ABIDE IN ME. The word *abide* means to remain or stay around. The "remaining" is evidence that salvation has already taken place (1 John 2:19) and not vice versa. The fruit or evidence of salvation is continuance in service to Him and in His teaching (John 8:31; 1 John 2:24; Col. 1:23). The abiding believer is the only legitimate believer. Abiding and believing actually are addressing the same issue of genuine salvation (Heb. 3:6–19). For a discussion of the perseverance of the saints, see Matt. 24:13.

Me, he is cast out as a branch and is withered; and they gather them and [f]throw *them* into the fire, and they are burned. [g]If you abide in Me, and My words abide in you, you will ask what you desire, and it shall be done for you. By this My Father is glorified, that you bear much fruit; so you will be My disciples.

"As the Father loved Me, I also have loved you; [h]abide in My love. If you keep My commandments, you will abide in My love, just as I have kept My Father's commandments and abide in His love.

"These things I have spoken to you, that My joy may remain in you, and *that* [i]your joy may be full. This is My commandment, that you love one another as I have loved you. Greater love has no one than this, than to [j]lay down one's life for his friends. You are My friends if you do whatever I command you. No longer do I call you servants, for a servant does not know what his master is doing; but I have called you [k]friends, for all things that I heard from My Father I have made known to you. You did not choose Me, but [l]I chose you and appointed you that you

---

[f] throw them into the fire. The imagery here is one of destruction (cf. Matt. 3:10–12; 5:22; 13:40–42, 50; 25:41; Mark 9:43–49; Luke 3:17; 2 Thess. 1:7–9; Rev. 20:10–15). It pictures the judgment awaiting all those who were never saved.

[g] If you abide in Me. True believers obey the Lord's commands, submitting to His Word (John 14:21, 23). Because of their commitment to God's Word, they are devoted to His will, thus their prayers are fruitful (John 14:13–14), which puts God's glory on display as He answers.

[h] abide in My love. Cf. Jude 21. This is not emotional or mystical, but defined in v. 10 as obedience. Jesus set the model by His perfect obedience to the Father, which we are to use as the pattern for our obedience to Him.

[i] your joy may be full. Just as Jesus maintained that His obedience to the Father was the basis of His joy, so also the believers who are obedient to His commandments will experience the same joy (John 17:13; cf. 16:24).

[j] lay down one's life for his friends. This is a reference to the supreme evidence and expression of Jesus' love, His sacrificial death upon the cross. Christians are called to exemplify the same kind of sacrificial giving toward one another, even if such sacrifice involves the laying down of one's own life in imitation of Christ's example (cf. 1 John 3:16).

[k] friends. Just as Abraham was called the "friend of God" (2 Chron. 20:7; James 2:23), so also those who follow Christ are privileged with extraordinary revelation through the Messiah and Son of God and, believing, become "friends" of God also. It was for His "friends" that the Lord laid down His life (John 10:11, 15, 17).

[l] I chose you. In case any pretense might exist among the disciples in terms of spiritual pride because of the extraordinary privileges they enjoyed, Jesus made it clear that such privilege rested not in their own merit but on His sovereign choice of them. God chose Israel (Isa. 45:4; Amos 3:2), but not for any merit (Deut. 7:7; 9:4–6). God elected angels to be forever holy (1 Tim. 5:21). He elected believers to salvation apart from any merit (Matt. 24:24, 31; Rom. 8:29–33; Eph. 1:3–6; Col. 3:12; Titus 1:1; 1 Peter 1:2).

should go and [m]bear fruit, and *that* your fruit should remain, that whatever you ask the Father in My name He may give you. These things I command you, that you love one another."

[m] BEAR FRUIT. One purpose of God's sovereign election is that believers should produce spiritual fruit. The NT describes fruit as godly attitudes (Gal. 5:22–23), righteous behavior (Phil. 1:11), praise (Heb. 13:15), and especially leading others to faith in Jesus as Messiah and Son of God (Rom. 1:13–16).

175. Hatred from the World

John 15:18–25

JN "[a]If the world hates you, you know that it hated Me before *it hated* you. If you were of the world, the world would love its own. Yet because you are not of the world, but I chose you out of the world, therefore the world hates you. Remember the word that I said to you, 'A [b]servant is not greater than his master.' If they persecuted Me, they will also persecute you. If they kept My word, they will keep yours also. But all these things they will do to you for My name's sake, because they do not know Him who sent Me. If I had not come and spoken to them, [c]they would have no sin, but now they have no excuse for their sin. He who hates Me hates My Father also. If I had not done among them the works which no one else did, they would have no sin; but now they have seen and also hated both Me and My Father. But *this happened* that the word might be fulfilled which is written in their law, [d]'They hated Me without a cause.'"

---

[a] IF THE WORLD HATES YOU. Since Satan is the one who dominates the evil world system in rebellion against God (John 14:30), the result is that the world hates not only Jesus but those who follow Him (2 Tim. 3:12). Hatred toward Jesus means also hatred toward the Father who sent Him.

[b] SERVANT ... MASTER. That axiom, spoken also in John 13:16, reflects the obvious truth that led Jesus to inform His disciples. They could expect to be treated like He was treated, because those who hated Him don't know God and would hate them also; conversely, those who listened with faith to Him, would hear them also.

[c] THEY WOULD HAVE NO SIN. He did not mean that if He had not come, they would have been sinless. But His coming incited the severest and most deadly sin, that of rejecting and rebelling against God and His truth. It was the decisive sin of rejection, the deliberate and fatal choice of darkness over light and death over life of which He spoke. He had done so many miracles and spoken innumerable words to prove He was Messiah and Son of God, but they—the world—were belligerent in their love of sin and rejection of the Savior. See Heb. 4:2–5; 6:4–6; 10:29–31.

[d] 'THEY HATED ME WITHOUT CAUSE.' Jesus quotes Pss. 35:19; 69:4. The logic here is that if David, a mere man, could have been hated in such a terrible manner by the enemies of God, how much more would the wicked hate David's perfect, divine Son who was the promised king that would confront sin and reign forever over His kingdom of righteousness (see 2 Sam 7:16).

176. Jesus Reiterates That the Helper Is Coming

John 15:26–16:15

JN "But [a]when the Helper comes, whom I shall send to you from the Father, the Spirit of truth who proceeds from the Father, He will testify of Me. And you also will bear witness, because you have been with Me from the beginning.

" [b]These things I have spoken to you, that you should not be made to [c]stumble. They will put you out of the synagogues; yes, the time is coming that whoever kills you will think that [d]he offers God service. And these things they will do to you because they have not known the Father nor Me. But these things I have told you, that when the time comes, you may remember that I told you of them.

"And these things I did not say to you at the beginning, because [e]I was with you.

"But now I go away to Him who sent Me, and [f]none of you asks Me, 'Where are You going?' But because I have said these things to you, sorrow has filled your

---

[a] WHEN THE HELPER COMES. Again, Jesus promised to send the Holy Spirit (John 7:39; 14:16–17, 26; 16:7, 13–14). This time He emphasized the Spirit's help for witnessing—proclaiming the gospel.

[b] THESE THINGS. In John 16:1–15, Jesus continued the thoughts of what He had just said in 15:18–25 regarding the world's hatred of His disciples and its opposition to the testimony of the Holy Spirit regarding Him as Messiah and Son of God. In this section He specified in greater detail how the Spirit confronts the world, i.e., not only does He testify about Jesus but He convicts men of sin. Through conviction of sin and testimony of the gospel, the Spirit turns the hostile hearts of men away from rebellion against God into belief regarding Jesus as Savior and Lord. This section may be divided into four parts: (1) the killing of the disciples by the world (John 16:1–4); (2) the comforting of the disciples by the Lord (vv. 5–7); (3) the conviction of men by the Holy Spirit (vv. 8–12); and (4) the guidance of the believer into all truth by the Holy Spirit (vv. 13–15).

[c] STUMBLE. The connotation of this word has the idea of setting a trap. The hatred of the world was such that it would seek to trap and destroy the disciples in an effort to prevent their witness to Jesus as Messiah and Son of God. Jesus did not want them to be caught unaware.

[d] HE OFFERS GOD SERVICE. Paul, before he was saved, personified this attitude as he persecuted the church thinking that he was doing service for God (Acts 22:4–5; 26:9–11; Gal. 1:13–17; Phil. 3:6; 1 Tim. 1:12–17). After Paul's conversion the persecutor became the persecuted because of the hatred of the world (2 Cor. 11:22–27; cf. Stephen in Acts 7:54–8:3).

[e] I WAS WITH YOU. He didn't need to warn them because He was there to protect them.

[f] NONE OF YOU ASKS. Earlier they had done so (John 13:36; 14:5), but they were then so absorbed in their own sorrow and confusion as to lose interest in where He was going. They were apparently consumed with what would happen to them.

heart. Nevertheless I tell you the truth. It is to your advantage that I go away; for if I do not go away, [g]the Helper will not come to you; but if I depart, I will send Him to you. And [h]when He has come, He will [i]convict the world of [j]sin, and of [k]righteousness, and of [l]judgment: of sin, because they do not believe in Me; of righteousness, because I go to My Father and you see Me no more; of judgment, because the ruler of this world is judged.

"I still have many things to say to you, but you cannot bear *them* now. However, when He, the Spirit of truth, has come, He will guide you into [m]all truth; for He will not speak on His own *authority*, but whatever He hears He will speak; and He

---

[g] THE HELPER WILL NOT COME. Again, the promise of the Holy Spirit being sent is given to comfort the disciples. The first emphasis was on His life-giving power (John 7:37–39). The next featured His indwelling presence (John 14:16–17). The next marked His teaching ministry (John 14:26). His ministry of empowering for witness is marked in John 15:26.

[h] WHEN HE HAS COME. The coming of the Holy Spirit at Pentecost was approximately forty or more days away at this point (see Acts 2:1–13).

[i] CONVICT. This word has two meanings: (1) the judicial act of conviction with a view toward sentencing (i.e., a courtroom term, conviction of sin) or (2) the act of convincing. Here the second idea is best, since the purpose of the Holy Spirit is not condemnation but conviction of the need for the Savior. The Son does the judgment with the Father (John 5:22, 27, 30). In John 16:14 it is said that He will reveal the glories of Christ to His people. He will also inspire the writing of the NT, guiding the apostles to write it (John 16:13), and He will reveal "things to come" through the NT prophecies.

[j] SIN. The singular indicates that a specific sin is in view, i.e., that of not believing in Jesus as Messiah and Son of God. This is the only sin, ultimately, that damns people to hell (cf. John 8:24). Though all men are depraved, cursed by their violation of God's law, and sinful by nature, what ultimately damns them to hell is their unwillingness to believe in the Lord Jesus Christ as Savior.

[k] RIGHTEOUSNESS. The Holy Spirit's purpose here is to shatter the pretensions of self-righteousness (hypocrisy), exposing the darkness of the heart (John 3:19–21; 7:7; 15:22, 24). While Jesus was on the earth, He performed this task especially toward the shallowness and emptiness of Judaism that had degenerated into legalistic modes without life-giving reality (e.g., John 2:13–22; 5:10–16; 7:24; Isa. 64:5–6). With Jesus gone to the Father, the Holy Spirit continues His convicting role.

[l] JUDGMENT. The judgment here in context is that of the world under Satan's control. Its judgments are blind, faulty, and evil, as evidenced in their verdict on Christ. The world can't make righteous judgments (John 7:24), but the Spirit of Christ does (John 8:16). All Satan's adjudications are lies (John 8:44–47), so the Spirit convicts men of their false judgment of Christ. Satan, the ruler of the world (John 14:30; Eph. 2:1–3) who, as the god of this world, has perverted the world's judgment and turned people from believing in Jesus as the Messiah and Son of God (2 Cor. 4:4), was defeated at the cross. While Christ's death looked like Satan's greatest victory, it actually was Satan's destruction (cf. Col. 2:15; Heb. 2:14–15; Rev. 20:10). The Spirit will lead sinners to true judgment.

[m] ALL TRUTH. This verse, like John 14:26, points to the supernatural revelation of all truth by which God has revealed Himself in Christ, particularly. This is the subject of the inspired NT writings.

will tell you things to come. [n]He will glorify Me, for He will take of what is Mine and declare *it* to you. All things that the Father has are Mine. Therefore I said that He will take of Mine and declare *it* to you."

[n] HE WILL GLORIFY ME. This is really the same as John 16:13, in that all NT truth revealed by God centers in Christ (Heb. 1:1–2). Christ was the theme of the OT, as the NT claims (Luke 24:27, 44; John 1:45; 5:37; Acts 10:43; 18:28; Rom. 1:1–2; 1 Cor. 15:3; 1 Peter 1:10–11; Rev. 19:10).

177. Jesus Speaks of His Death and Resurrection

John 16:16–33

JN "A little while, and [a]you will not see Me; and again a little while, and you will see Me, because I go to the Father." Then *some* of His disciples said among themselves, "What is this that He says to us, 'A little while, and you will not see Me; and again a little while, and you will see Me'; and, 'because I go to the Father'?" They said therefore, "What is this that He says, 'A little while'? We do not know what He is saying."

Now Jesus knew that they desired to ask Him, and He said to them, "Are you inquiring among yourselves about what I said, 'A little while, and you will not see Me; and again a little while, and you will see Me'? Most assuredly, I say to you that you will weep and lament, but the world will rejoice; and you will be sorrowful, but your [b]sorrow will be turned into joy. A woman, when she is in labor, has sorrow because her hour has come; but as soon as she has given birth to the child, she no longer remembers the anguish, for joy that a human being has been born into the world. Therefore you now have sorrow; but [c]I will see you again and your heart will rejoice, and your joy no one will take from you.

"And [d]in that day [e]you will ask Me nothing. Most assuredly, I say to you,

---

[a] YOU WILL NOT SEE ME. Jesus was referring to His ascension ("you will not see Me") and the coming of the Holy Spirit ("you will see Me"), emphatically claiming that the Spirit and He are one (Rom. 8:9; Phil. 1:19; 1 Peter 1:11; Rev. 19:10). Christ dwells in believers through the Holy Spirit—in that sense they see Him.

[b] SORROW WILL BE TURNED INTO JOY. The very event that made the hateful realm of mankind ("world") rejoice and cause grief to Jesus' disciples will be the same event that will lead to the world's sorrow and the believer's joy. The disciples would soon realize the marvelous nature of God's gift of salvation and the Spirit through what He accomplished and the blessing of answered prayer. Acts records the coming of the Holy Spirit and the power and joy (Acts 2:4–47; 13:52) of the early church.

[c] I WILL SEE YOU. After the resurrection Jesus did see His disciples (John 20:19–29; 21:1–23; cf. 1 Cor. 15:1–8). Beyond that brief time of personal fellowship (Acts 1:1–3), He would be with them permanently in His Spirit (John 14:16–19; 16:16–19).

[d] IN THAT DAY. This is a reference to Pentecost, when the Holy Spirit came (Acts 2:1–13) and sorrow turned to joy. This is a reference also to the "last days," which were inaugurated after His resurrection and the Spirit's coming (Acts 2:17; 2 Tim. 3:1; Heb. 1:2; James 5:3; 2 Peter 3:3; 1 John 2:18).

[e] YOU WILL ASK ME NOTHING. After His departure and sending of the Spirit, believers will no longer ask Him, since He is not present. Instead, they will ask the Father in His name (cf. John 14:13–14).

whatever you ask the Father in My name He will give you. Until now you have asked nothing in My name. Ask, and you will receive, that your [f]joy may be full.

"These things I have spoken to you [g]in figurative language; but the time is coming when I will no longer speak to you in figurative language, but I will tell you plainly about the Father. In that day you will ask in My name, and [h]I do not say to you that I shall pray the Father for you; for the Father Himself loves you, because you have loved Me, and have believed that I came forth from God. I came forth from the Father and have come into the world. Again, I leave the world and go to the Father."

His disciples said to Him, "See, now You are speaking plainly, and using no figure of speech! Now we are sure that You know all things, and have no need that anyone should question You. By this we believe that You came forth from God."

Jesus answered them, "Do you now believe? Indeed the hour is coming, yes, has now come, that you will be scattered, each to his own, and will leave Me alone. And yet I am not alone, because the Father is with Me. These things I have spoken to you, that in Me you may have peace. In the world you will have [i]tribulation; but be of good cheer, I have [j]overcome the world."

---

[f] joy may be full. In this case the believer's joy will be related to answered prayer and a full supply of heavenly blessing for everything consistent with the purpose of the Lord in one's life.

[g] in figurative language. The word means "veiled, pointed statement" that is pregnant with meaning, i.e., something that is obscure. What seemed hard to understand for the disciples during the life of Jesus would become clear after His death, resurrection, and the coming of the Holy Spirit (cf. 14:26; 15:26, 27; 16:13–14). They would actually understand the ministry of Christ better than they had while they were with Him, as the Spirit inspired them to write the gospels and epistles and ministered in and through them.

[h] I do not say. Christ was clarifying what He meant by praying in His name. He did not mean asking Him to ask the Father, as if the Father was indifferent to believers, but not to His Son. On the contrary, the Father loves Christ's own. In fact the Father sent the Son to redeem them and then return. Asking in Jesus' name means simply asking on the basis of His merit, His righteousness, and for whatever would honor and glorify Him so as to build His kingdom.

[i] tribulation. This word often refers to eschatological woes (Mark 13:9; Rom. 2:9) and to persecution of believers because of their testimony for Christ (cf. 15:18–16:4; Acts 11:19; Eph. 3:13).

[j] overcome. The fundamental ground for endurance in persecution is the victory of Jesus over the world (John 12:31; 1 Cor. 15:57). Through His impending death, He rendered the world's opposition null and void. While the world continues to attack His people, such attacks fall harmlessly, for Christ's victory has already accomplished a smashing defeat of the whole evil rebellious system. Cf. Rom. 8:35–39.

178. The High Priestly Prayer of Christ

John 17:1–26

JN [a]Jesus spoke these words, lifted up His eyes to heaven, and said: "Father, [b]the hour has come. Glorify Your Son, that Your Son also may glorify You, as You have given Him [c]authority over all flesh, that He should give eternal life to [d]as many as You have given Him. And this is [e]eternal life, that they may know You, the only true God, and Jesus Christ whom You have sent. I have glorified You on the earth. I have finished the work which You have given Me to do. And now, O Father, [f]glorify Me together with Yourself, with the glory which I had with You before the world was.

"I have manifested Your name to the men whom You have given Me out of

---

[a] JESUS SPOKE THESE WORDS. Although Matt. 6:9–13 and Luke 11:2–4 have become known popularly as the "Lord's Prayer," that prayer was actually a prayer taught to the disciples by Jesus as a pattern for their prayers. The prayer recorded here (in John 17) is truly the Lord's Prayer, exhibiting the face-to-face communion the Son had with the Father. Very little is recorded of the content of Jesus' frequent prayers to the Father (Matt. 14:23; Luke 5:16), so this prayer reveals some of the precious content of the Son's communion and intercession with Him. John 17 is a transitional chapter, marking the end of Jesus' earthly ministry and the beginning of His intercessory ministry for believers (Heb. 7:25). The prayer summarizes key themes from John's gospel. These include: (1) Jesus' faithful submission to the Father; (2) the Son's commitment to glorify the Father; (3) the election and protection of His disciples; (4) their witness to a hostile world; (5) their unity with Christ and with one another; and (6) the glorious future that awaits them. The chapter divides into three parts: (1) Jesus' prayer for Himself (John 17:1–5); (2) Jesus' prayer for the apostles (vv. 6–19); and (3) Jesus' prayer for all NT believers who will form the church (vv. 20–26).

[b] THE HOUR HAS COME. The time for His suffering and death.

[c] AUTHORITY OVER ALL FLESH. Cf. Matt. 28:18; John 5:27.

[d] AS MANY AS YOU HAVE GIVEN HIM. A reference to God's choosing of those who will come to Christ (see John 6:37, 44). The biblical doctrine of election or predestination is presented throughout the NT (15:16, 19; Acts 13:48; Rom. 8:29–33; Eph. 1:3–6; 2 Thess. 2:13; Titus 1:1; 1 Peter 1:2).

[e] ETERNAL LIFE. See John 3:15–16; 5:24; cf. 1 John 5:20.

[f] GLORIFY ME TOGETHER WITH YOURSELF. Having completed His work, Jesus looked past the cross and asked to be returned to the glory that He shared with the Father before the world began (cf. John 1:1; 8:58; 12:41). The actual completion of bearing judgment wrath for sinners was declared by Christ in the cry, "It is finished" (John 19:30).

the world. [g]They were Yours, You gave them to Me, and they have kept Your word. Now they have known that all things which You have given Me are from You. For I have given to them the words which You have given Me; and they have received *them,* and have known surely that I came forth from You; and [h]they have believed that You sent Me.

"I pray for them. I do not pray for the world but for those whom You have given Me, for they are Yours. And all Mine are Yours, and Yours are Mine, and I am glorified in them. Now [i]I am no longer in the world, but these are in the world, and I come to You. Holy Father, keep through Your name those whom You have given Me, that they may be one as We *are.* While I was with them in the world, [j]I kept them in Your name. Those whom You gave Me I have kept; and none of them is lost except the [k]son of perdition, that the Scripture might be fulfilled. But now I come to You, and these things I speak in the world, that they may have My joy fulfilled in themselves. I have given them Your word; and the world has hated them because they are not of the world, just as I am not of the world. I do not pray that You should take them out of the world, but that You should [l]keep them from the

---

[g] THEY WERE YOURS. Again, the Son emphasized that those who believed in Him were given by the Father. "They were Yours" (cf. John 17:9) is a potent assertion that before conversion, they belonged to God (cf. John 6:37). That is true because of God's election. They were chosen before the foundation of the world (Eph. 1:4), when their names were written in the Lamb's book of life (Rev. 17:8). Cf. Acts 18:10, where God says He has many people in Corinth who belong to Him but are not yet saved.

[h] THEY HAVE BELIEVED. The Son of God affirmed the genuine saving faith of His disciples.

[i] I AM NO LONGER IN THE WORLD. So sure was His death and departure back to the Father that Jesus treated His departure as an already accomplished fact. He prayed here for His disciples, because they would be exposed to the world's snares and hatred, but He would no longer be physically with them (John 15:18–16:4). Based on the eternal nature of immutable God ("name"), He prayed for the eternal security of those who believed. He prayed that as the Trinity experiences eternal unity, so may believers. See Rom. 8:31–39.

[j] I KEPT THEM IN YOUR NAME. Jesus protected them and kept them safe from the world as He said in John 6:37–40, 44. One illustration of that can be seen in John 18:1–11. Believers are secure forever, because they are held by Christ and by God. Cf. John 10:28–29.

[k] SON OF PERDITION. This identifies Judas by pointing to his destiny, i.e., eternal damnation (Matt. 7:13; Acts 8:20; Rom. 9:22; Phil. 1:28; 3:19; 1 Tim. 6:9; Heb. 10:39; 2 Peter 2:1; 3:7; Rev. 17:8, 11). The defection of Judas was not a failure on Jesus part, but was foreseen and foreordained in Scripture (Pss. 41:9; 109:8; cf. 13:18).

[l] KEEP THEM FROM THE EVIL ONE. The reference here refers to protection from Satan and all the wicked forces following him (Matt. 6:13; 1 John 2:13–14; 3:12; 5:18–19). Though Jesus' sacrifice on the cross was the defeat of Satan, he is still loose and orchestrating his evil system against believers. He seeks to destroy believers (1 Peter 5:8), as with Job and Peter (Luke 22:31–32) and in general (Eph. 6:12), but God is their strong protector (John 12:31; 16:11; cf. Ps. 27:1–3; 2 Cor. 4:4; Jude 24–25).

evil one. They are not of the world, just as I am not of the world. [m]Sanctify them by Your truth. Your word is truth. As You sent Me into the world, I also have sent them into the world. And for their sakes [n]I sanctify Myself, that they also may be sanctified by the truth.

"I do not pray for these alone, but also for those who will believe in Me through their word; that [o]they all may be one, as You, Father, *are* in Me, and I in You; that they also may be one in Us, that the world may believe that You sent Me. And [p]the glory which You gave Me I have given them, that they may be one just as We are one: I in them, and You in Me; that they may be [q]made perfect in one, and that the world may know that You have sent Me, and have loved them as You have loved Me.

"Father, I desire that they also whom You gave Me may [r]be with Me where I am, that they may behold My glory which You have given Me; for You loved Me before the foundation of the world. [s]O righteous Father! The world has not known You, but I have known You; and these have known that You sent Me. And I have declared to them Your name, and will declare *it,* that the love with which You loved Me may be in them, and I in them."

---

[m] SANCTIFY. This verb also occurs in John's gospel at 10:36 and 17:19. The idea of sanctification is the setting apart of something for a particular use. Accordingly, believers are set apart to serve the Lord exclusively so that the believer desires to obey God's commands and walk in holiness (Lev. 11:44–45; 1 Peter 1:16). Sanctification is accomplished by means of the truth, which is the revelation that the Son gave regarding all that the Father commanded Him to communicate and is now contained in the Scriptures left by the apostles. Cf. Eph. 5:26; 2 Thess. 2:13; James 1:21; 1 Peter 1:22–23.

[n] I SANCTIFY MYSELF. Meaning only that He was totally set apart for the Father's will (cf. 4:34; 5:19; 6:38; 7:16; 9:4). He did that in order that believers might be set apart to God by the truth He brought.

[o] THEY ALL MAY BE ONE. The basis of this unity is founded in obedience to the revelation of God given through the Son. Believers are also to be united in the common belief of the truth that was received in the Word of God (Phil. 2:2). This is not still a wish, but it became a reality when the Spirit came (cf. Acts 2:4; 1 Cor. 12:13). It is not experiential unity, but the unity of common eternal life shared by all who believe the truth, and it results in the one body of Christ all sharing His life. See Eph. 4:4–6.

[p] THE GLORY WHICH YOU GAVE ME. This refers to the believer's participation in all of the attributes and essence of God through the indwelling presence of the Holy Spirit (cf. Col. 1:27; 2 Peter 1:4), as John 17:23 makes clear ("I in them").

[q] MADE PERFECT IN ONE. The idea here is that they may be brought together in the same spiritual life around the truth that saves. That prayer was answered by the reality of 1 Cor. 12:12–13; Eph. 2:14–22.

[r] BE WITH ME. This will be in heaven, where one can see the full glory that is His. Someday believers will not only see His glory but share it (Phil. 3:20–21; 1 John 3:2). Until then we participate in it spiritually (2 Cor. 3:18).

[s] O RIGHTEOUS FATHER! These final verses summarize the prayer of John 17 and promise the continuing indwelling Christ and His love. Cf. Rom. 5:5.

179. Peter's Denial Predicted a Second Time

Matt. 26:30–35; Mark 14:26–31; Luke 22:39; John 18:1a

JN When Jesus had spoken these words, MT and when they had [a]sung a hymn, JN [b]He went out with His disciples over the [c]Brook Kidron MT to the Mount of Olives, LK as He was accustomed, and His disciples also followed Him.

MT Then Jesus said to them, "All of you will be made to stumble because of Me this night, for it is written: 'I will strike the Shepherd, And the sheep of the flock will be scattered.' But after I have been raised, I will go before you [d]to Galilee." Peter answered and said to Him, "Even if all are made to stumble because of You, I will never be made to [e]stumble." Jesus said to him, MK "Assuredly, I say to you that today, *even* this night, [f]before the rooster crows twice, you will deny Me three times." But he spoke more vehemently, "If I have to die with You, I will not deny You!" And MT the disciples MK all said likewise.

---

[a] SUNG A HYMN. Probably Ps. 118. The Talmud designated Pss. 113–118 as the Hallel (praise psalms) of Egypt. These psalms were sung at Passover (cf. Pss. 113–118).

[b] HE WENT OUT. Jesus' supreme courage is seen in His determination to go to the cross, where His purity and sinlessness would be violated as He bore the wrath of God for the sins of the world (John 3:16; 12:27). The time of "the power of darkness" had come (Luke 22:53; cf. John 1:5; 9:4; 13:30).

[c] BROOK KIDRON. "Brook" signifies that it was an intermittent stream that was dry much of the year but became a swift current during the rainy season. This stream ran through the Kidron Valley between the temple mount on the east of Jerusalem and the Mount of Olives further to the east.

[d] TO GALILEE. Jesus' promise to meet the disciples in His post-resurrection form (cf. 16:7; Matt. 28:16–17).

[e] STUMBLE. The Greek word is the same word Jesus used for "offended" in Matt. 24:10, describing the falling away and spiritual treachery that would occur in the last days. Here, however, Jesus spoke of something less than full and final apostasy. In a moment of fleshly fear they disowned Christ, but He prayed that their faith would not fail (Luke 22:32; John 17:9–11), and that prayer was answered. The verse Jesus quotes here is Zech. 13:7.

[f] BEFORE THE ROOSTER CROWS. In Jewish reckoning of time, "cock crow" was the third watch of the night, ending at 3:00 a.m., which was when roosters typically began to crow. Mark, alone of the gospels, indicates that the cock crowed two times (Mark 14:72). Though Peter and all the disciples insisted that they would never deny Christ, they were only a few hours away from fulfilling this prophecy (Matt. 26:74–75; Mark 14:66–72).

180. Jesus Prays in Gethsemane

Matt. 26:36–46; Mark 14:32–42; Luke 22:40–46; John 18:1b

MT Then Jesus came with them to a place called [a]Gethsemane, and JN there was a garden, which He and His disciples entered. MK And He said to His disciples, MT "Sit here while I go and pray over there." And He took with Him [b]Peter and the two sons of Zebedee—MK James and John— MT and He began to be sorrowful and [c]deeply distressed.

Then He said to them, "My soul is exceedingly [d]sorrowful, even to death. Stay here and watch with Me. LK [e]Pray that you may not enter into temptation." MT He went a little farther LK [being] withdrawn from them [f]about a stone's throw, and He knelt down MK on the ground MT and fell on His face, MK and prayed that [g]if it were possible, [h]the hour might pass from Him. And He said, "[i]Abba, Father, [j]all

---

[a] GETHSEMANE. The name means "oil press" and referred to a garden filled with olive trees on a slope of the Mount of Olives. This was a frequent meeting place for Christ and His disciples (John 18:2), just across the Kidron Valley from Jerusalem (John 18:1). A garden of ancient olive trees is there to this day. Jesus frequented this spot with the disciples when He wanted to get away from the crowds to pray (cf. John 18:12). Judas's familiarity with Jesus' patterns enabled him to find Jesus there—even though Christ had not previously announced His intentions.

[b] PETER . . . JAMES AND JOHN. Jesus left most of the disciples at the entrance to Gethsemane and took Peter, James, and John inside with Him to pray. He likely had them accompany Him into the garden because they were the leaders of the twelve and had to learn an important lesson to pass on to the others.

[c] DEEPLY DISTRESSED. Mark uses the synonym "troubled," a Greek word which refers to a feeling of terrified amazement. In the face of the dreadful prospect of bearing God's full fury against sin, Jesus was in the grip of terror.

[d] SORROWFUL, EVEN TO DEATH. Jesus' sorrow was so severe that it threatened to cause His death at that moment. His anguish had nothing to do with fear of men or the physical torments of the cross. He was sorrowful because within hours the full cup of divine fury against sin would be His to drink. It is possible for a person to die from sheer anguish.

[e] PRAY. He had already warned them—and Peter in particular—that an egregious trial was imminent (cf. Luke 22:31). Sadly, that warning, as well as His imploring them to pray, went unheeded.

[f] ABOUT A STONE'S THROW. i.e., within earshot. His prayer was partly for their benefit (cf. John 11:41–42).

[g] IF . . . POSSIBLE. Jesus was not asking God if He had the power to let the cup pass from Him, but if it were possible in God's plan. Christ was soon to partake of this cup in the cross as God's only sacrifice for sin (cf. Acts 4:12).

[h] THE HOUR. The time of His sacrificial death as decreed by God. It included everything from the betrayal to Jesus' trials, the mockery, and His crucifixion.

[i] ABBA. An endearing, intimate Aramaic term that is essentially equivalent to the English word "Daddy" (cf. Rom. 8:15; Gal. 4:6).

things *are* possible for You. LK If it is Your will, take [k]this cup away from Me; nevertheless [l]not My will, but Yours, be done."

Then an angel appeared to Him from heaven, strengthening Him. And being in agony, He prayed more earnestly. Then His sweat became [m]like great drops of blood falling down to the ground. When He rose up from prayer, and had come to His disciples, He found them [n]sleeping from sorrow.

Then He said MT to Peter, "What! MK [o]Simon, are you sleeping? MT Could you not watch with Me [p]one hour? LK Why do you sleep? [q]Rise, MK [r]watch and pray, lest you

---

[j] ALL THINGS ARE POSSIBLE. Jesus knew that it was in the scope of God's power and omniscience to provide an alternate plan of salvation, if He desired.

[k] THIS CUP. A cup is often the symbol of divine wrath against sin in the OT (Ps. 75:8; Isa. 51:17, 22; Jer. 25:15–17, 27–29; Lam. 4:21–22; Ezek. 23:31–34; Hab. 2:16). The next day Christ would "bear the sins of many" (Heb. 9:28)—and the fullness of divine wrath would fall on Him (Isa. 53:10–11; 2 Cor. 5:21). Christ was to endure the fury of God over sin, Satan, the power of death, and the guilt of iniquity (cf. Matt. 26:39; Luke 22:42; John 18:11). This was the price of the sin He bore, and He paid it in full. His cry of anguish in Matt. 27:46 reflects the extreme bitterness of the cup of wrath He was given.

[l] NOT MY WILL, BUT YOURS BE DONE. This implies no conflict between the Persons of the Godhead. It was a perfectly normal expression of His humanity that He shrank from the cup of divine wrath. But even though the cup was abhorrent to Him, He willingly took it, because it was the will of the Father. Christ's prayer graphically reveals how He in His humanity voluntarily surrendered His will to the will of the Father in all things—precisely so that there would be no conflict between the divine will and His desires. Thus there was neither conflict between Father and Son, nor between the deity of Christ and His human desires. Jesus came into the world to do God's will, and that remained His commitment while here. See John 4:34; 5:30; 6:38; 8:29; Phil. 2:8.

[m] LIKE GREAT DROPS OF BLOOD. Only Luke, the physician, provides this detail. This description suggests a dangerous condition known as *hematidrosis*, the effusion of blood in one's perspiration. It can be caused by extreme anguish or physical strain. Subcutaneous capillaries dilate and burst, mingling blood with sweat. Christ Himself stated that His distress had brought Him to the threshold of death.

[n] SLEEPING FROM SORROW. Cf. Luke 9:32. The emotional strain was wearing on the disciples as well as Christ. Their response, however, was to capitulate to fleshly cravings. Thus they gratified their immediate desire for sleep, rather than staying awake to pray for strength, as Christ had commanded them. All the reasons for their subsequent failure are found in their behavior in the garden.

[o] SIMON. Jesus' use of "Simon" may have implied that Peter was not living up to the significance and meaning of his new name, "Peter" (cf. Matt. 16:18).

[p] ONE HOUR. This suggests that Jesus had spent an hour praying, a duration in which Peter had been unable to stay awake.

[q] RISE AND PRAY. A tender appeal to the disciples, who in their weakness were disobeying Him at a critical moment. He may have been summoning them to a standing posture, to help overcome their drowsiness. Matthew 26:43 and Mark 14:40 reveal that He again found them sleeping at least one more time.

[r] WATCH. This Greek word means "to keep alert." Jesus was encouraging Peter, James, and John to discern when they were under spiritual attack. They were not to let their self-confidence lull them to sleep spiritually.

enter into temptation. The spirit indeed *is* willing, but [s]the flesh *is* weak."
MT Again, a second time, He went away and prayed, MK and spoke the same words, MT saying, "O My Father, if this cup cannot pass away from Me unless I drink it, Your will be done." MK And when He returned, He found them asleep again, for their eyes were heavy; and they did not know what to answer Him.

MT So He left them, went away again, and prayed the third time, saying the same words. Then He came to His disciples MK the third time MT and said to them, "[t]Are *you* still sleeping and resting? MK It is enough! MT Behold, the hour is at hand, and the Son of Man is being betrayed into the hands of sinners. Rise, let us be going. See, My betrayer is at hand."

---

[s] THE FLESH IS WEAK. The tenderness of this plea is touching. Because willing spirits are still attached to unredeemed flesh, believers are not always able to practice the righteousness they desire to do (cf. Rom. 7:15–23; also, Matt. 26:41). Christ Himself was well acquainted with the feeling of human infirmities (Heb. 4:15)—yet without sin. At that very moment He was locked in a struggle against human passions which, while not sinful in themselves, must be subjugated to the divine will if sin was to be avoided.

[t] ARE YOU STILL SLEEPING AND RESTING? The three disciples remained indifferent not only to the needs of Christ at that moment, but their need of strength and watchfulness for the impending temptation that all eleven would face. The disciples needed to learn that spiritual victory goes to those who are alert in prayer and depend on God, and that self-confidence and spiritual unpreparedness lead to spiritual disaster.

PART X | The Crucifixion, Resurrection, and Ascension

181. Jesus Is Arrested

Matt. 26:47–56; Mark 14:43–52; Luke 22:47–53; John 18:2–12

MK And immediately, while He was still speaking, LK behold, MT [a]a great multitude with swords and clubs, came LK and he who was called [b]Judas, one of the twelve, went before them and drew near to Jesus. JN [For] Judas, who betrayed Him, also knew the place; for Jesus often met there with His disciples. Then Judas, having received [c]a detachment *of troops,* and officers from the [d]chief priests MK and

---

[a] A GREAT MULTITUDE WITH SWORDS AND CLUBS. This "multitude" was a carefully selected group whose sole purpose was arresting Jesus so He could be put to death. These were heavily armed representatives of the Sanhedrin (Matt. 26:47; Mark 14:43), accompanied by a Roman cohort with lanterns, torches, and weapons (John 18:3). A cohort (six hundred men at full strength) of Roman soldiers (John 18:3, 12) was in this crowd because the Jewish leaders (cf. Luke 22:52) who organized the throng needed permission from Rome to carry out the death penalty and feared the crowds. The "swords" were the regular small hand weapons of the Romans, and the wood "clubs" were ordinary weapons carried by the Jewish temple police.

[b] JUDAS, ONE OF THE TWELVE. All four evangelists refer to Judas this way (Matt. 26:14, 47; Mark 14:10, 43; Luke 22:47; John 6:71). Only once (John 20:24) is another disciple so described. The gospel writers seem to use the expression to underscore the insidiousness of Judas' crime—especially here, in the midst of the betrayal. Clearly, they display remarkable restraint in describing and evaluating Judas. Especially in this context, such a simple description actually heightens the evil of his crime more than any series of derogatory epithets or negative criticisms could do. It also points out the precise fulfillment of Jesus' announcement in Mark 14:18–20.

[c] A DETACHMENT OF TROOPS, AND OFFICERS FROM THE CHIEF PRIESTS. The term "detachment of troops" refers to a cohort of Roman troops. A full cohort could have as many as one thousand men. Normally, however, a cohort consisted of six hundred men but could sometimes refer to as little as two hundred. Though they were regularly stationed at Caesarea, Roman auxiliary troops were brought into Jerusalem (to the Antonia Fortress near the temple) during feast days for added security. The second group designated as "officers" refers to temple police who were the main arresting officers since Jesus' destination after the arrest was to be brought before the High-Priest. They came ready for resistance from Jesus and His followers ("weapons").

[d] CHIEF PRIESTS . . . SCRIBES . . . ELDERS. Although three distinct sections of the Sanhedrin (as indicated by the Greek definite article with each), they were acting in unity. These Jewish leaders had evidently for some time (cf. Mark 3:6; 11:18) hoped to accuse Jesus of rebellion against Rome. Then, His execution could be blamed on the Romans, and the leaders could escape potential reprisals from those Jews who admired Jesus. The Sanhedrin likely had hurried to Pontius Pilate, the Roman governor, to ask immediate use of his soldiers, or perhaps acted on a prearranged agreement for troop use on short notice. Whatever the case, the leaders procured the assistance of the Roman military from Fort Antonia in Jerusalem.

the scribes JN and Pharisees MT and elders of the people, JN came there with lanterns, torches, and weapons.

MK Now His betrayer had given them a signal, saying, "Whomever I [e]kiss, He is the One; seize Him and lead *Him* away safely." As soon as he had come, MT immediately he went up to Jesus and said, "Greetings, [f]Rabbi!" and [g]kissed Him. But Jesus said to him, "[h]Friend, why have you come? LK Judas, are you betraying the Son of Man with a kiss?"

JN Jesus therefore, [i]knowing all things that would come upon Him, went forward and said to them, [j]"Whom are you seeking?" They answered Him, "Jesus of Nazareth." Jesus said to them, "I am *He.*" And Judas, who betrayed Him, also stood with them. Now when He said to them, "I am *He,*" they drew back and fell to the ground. Then He asked them again, "Whom are you seeking?" And they said, "Jesus of Nazareth." Jesus answered, "I have told you that I am *He.* Therefore, if you seek Me, let these go their way," that the saying might be fulfilled which He spoke, "Of those whom You gave Me [k]I have lost none." MT Then they came and laid MK their hands MT on Jesus and [seized] Him.

---

[e] kiss. In addition to being a special act of respect and affection, this kind of kiss was a sign of homage in Middle East culture. Out of the varieties of this kiss (on the feet, on the back of the hand, on the palm, on the hem of the garment), Judas chose the embrace and the kiss on the cheek—the one that showed the closest love and affection, normally reserved for one with whom a person had a close, intimate relationship (such as a pupil for his teacher). Judas could not have chosen a more despicable way to identify Jesus, because he perverted its usual meaning so treacherously and hypocritically.

[f] Rabbi. "My master."

[g] kissed Him. "Kissed" is an intensified form of the verb for "kiss" in Mark 14:44, and it denotes a fervent, continuous expression of affection (cf. Luke 7:38, 45; 15:20; Acts 20:37). It was with intensity that Judas pretended to love Christ. The act was likely prolonged enough so the crowd had time to identify Jesus.

[h] Friend. Not the usual Greek word for "friend," but another word meaning "comrade."

[i] knowing all things. John, in a matter-of-fact way, states that Jesus was omniscient, thus God.

[j] "Whom are you seeking?" By twice asking that question, to which they replied, "Jesus of Nazareth," Jesus was forcing them to acknowledge that they had no authority to take His disciples. In fact He demanded that they let the disciples go. The force of His demand was established by the power of His words. When He spoke, "I am He" (John 18:6), a designation He had used before to declare Himself God (John 8:28, 58; cf. 6:35; 8:12; 10:7, 9, 11, 14; 11:25; 14:6; 15:1, 5), they were jolted backward and to the ground. This power display and the authoritative demand not to take the disciples was of immense significance, as the next verse indicates.

[k] I have lost none. Jesus was saying that He protected the disciples from being arrested, so He would not lose any of them, thus fulfilling the promises He made earlier (John 6:39, 40, 44; 10:28; 17:12). He knew that being arrested and perhaps imprisoned or executed was more than they could bear, and it could shatter their faith. So He made sure it did not happen. All believers are weak and vulnerable if not protected by the Lord. But He will never let them be tempted beyond what they can bear (1 Cor. 10:13), as evidenced here. Believers are eternally secure, not in their own strength, but by the gracious and constant protection of the Savior (cf. Rom. 8:35–39).

LK When those around Him saw what was going to happen, they said to Him, "Lord, shall we strike with the sword?" JN Then [l]Simon Peter, having a sword, drew it and struck the [m]high priest's servant, and [n]cut off his right ear. The servant's name was Malchus. LK Jesus answered and said, [o]"Permit even this." And He [p]touched his ear and healed him.

JN Jesus said to Peter, "Put your sword into the sheath, MT for all who take the sword will [q]perish by the sword. Or do you think that I cannot now pray to My Father, and He will provide Me with [r]more than twelve legions of angels? How then could the Scriptures be fulfilled, that it must happen thus? JN Shall I not [s]drink the cup which My Father has given Me?"

MT In that hour Jesus said to the multitudes—LK the chief priests, captains of the temple, and the elders who had come to Him, MT "Have you come out, [t]as against a robber, with swords and clubs to take Me? I sat daily with you, teaching

---

[l] Simon Peter. He surely aimed for Malchus' head, ready to start the battle in defense of His Lord, but his was an ignorant love and courage.

[m] high priest's servant. Malchus. He was neither a soldier nor temple policeman, but rather was a high-ranking personal slave of Caiaphas, the High-Priest, probably sent along to observe Judas and report on the events of the evening.

[n] cut off his right ear. All four gospels record this incident. Only John reveals that the swordsman was Peter and the victim was named Malchus (John 18:10). And only Luke, the physician, records the subsequent healing.

[o] "Permit even this." i.e., the betrayal and arrest (cf. John 18:11). All was proceeding according to the divine timetable.

[p] touched his ear and healed him. This is the only instance in all of Scripture where Christ healed a fresh wound. The miracle is also unique in that Christ healed an enemy, unasked, and without any evidence of faith in the recipient. It is also remarkable that such a dramatic miracle had no effect whatsoever on the hearts of those men. Neither had the explosive power of Jesus' words, which knocked them to the ground (John 18:6). They carried on with the arrest as if nothing peculiar had happened.

[q] perish by the sword. Peter's action was vigilantism. No matter how unjust the arrest of Jesus, Peter had no right to take the law into his own hands in order to stop it. Jesus' reply was a restatement of the Gen. 9:6 principle: "Whoever sheds man's blood, by man his blood shall be shed," an affirmation that capital punishment is an appropriate penalty for murder.

[r] more than twelve legions. A Roman legion was composed of six thousand soldiers, so this would represent more than seventy-two thousand angels. In 2 Kings 19:35 a single angel killed more than 185,000 men in a single night, so this many angels would make a formidable army.

[s] drink the cup. Peter's impetuous bravery was not only misguided but exhibited failure to understand the centrality of the death that Jesus came to die. The "cup" in the OT is associated with suffering and especially judgment, i.e., the cup of God's wrath (Ps. 75:8; Isa. 51:17, 22; Jer. 25:15; Ezek. 23:31–34; Matt. 26:39; Mark 14:36; Luke 22:42; cf. Rev. 14:10; 16:19).

[t] as against a robber. Jesus expressed a righteous resentment toward the crowd's actions and attitudes. "Robber" was normally a highwayman or armed bandit who would resist arrest. The setting which the crowd orchestrated was completely inconsistent with His well-known ministry as a religious teacher.

in the [u]temple, and you did not LK try to seize Me. But [v]this is your hour, and the power of darkness. MT All this was done that the [w]Scriptures of the prophets might be fulfilled." JN Then the detachment *of troops* and the captain and the officers of the Jews arrested Jesus and bound Him. MT Then all the disciples [x]forsook Him and fled.

MK Now a [y]certain young man followed Him, having [z]a linen cloth thrown around *his* naked *body.* And the young men laid hold of him, and he left the linen cloth and [aa]fled from them naked.

---

[u] TEMPLE. Cf. Mark 11:11. This was the most public place in Jerusalem.

[v] THIS IS YOUR HOUR. i.e., nighttime, the hour of darkness. They had not the courage to confront Him in the presence of the crowds at the temple, where He had openly taught each day. Their skulking tactics betrayed the truth about their hearts. Nighttime was a fitting hour for the servants of the power of darkness (Satan) to be afoot (cf. John 3:20–21; Eph. 5:8, 12–15; 1 Thess. 5:5–7).

[w] SCRIPTURES . . . BE FULFILLED. God Himself had foreordained the very minutest details of how Jesus would die (Acts 2:23; 4:27–28). Dying was Christ's consummate act of submission to the Father's will. Jesus Himself was in absolute control (John 10:17–18). Yet it was not Jesus alone, but everyone around Him—His enemies included—who fulfilled precisely the details of the OT prophecies. Nonetheless, entirely apart from the crowd's sinful intentions against Jesus, God was sovereignly using it to fulfill prophecy (cf. Isa. 53:7–9, 12) and accomplish His gracious purposes. These events display His divine sovereignty. Cf. Matt. 1:22; 5:18; 27:50.

[x] FORSOOK HIM. The disciples found no comfort in Jesus' reference to Scripture, but instead their faith in Him collapsed as they realized He would not resist arrest and that they also might be captured.

[y] CERTAIN YOUNG MAN. Some commentators believe that this perhaps was Mark himself. However, ancient evidence from the church fathers (like Papias) suggests that Mark never personally saw the Lord—but rather that he received his eyewitness information from Peter. It is more likely, given the dramatic nature of this scene, that Mark included this detail to underscore the tumultuous nature of Christ's arrest. This man was probably an innocent bystander who lived nearby and was awakened in the night by the commotion. When he came to investigate, he was nearly arrested. Like the disciples, he fled the scene in terror.

[z] A LINEN CLOTH. Either a loose-fitting linen sleeping garment or a sheet that this man had hastily wrapped around himself after being roused from bed.

[aa] FLED . . . NAKED. The startled man escaped capture and ran, but in so doing his covering came off or was pulled off, and he left with nothing at all on, or nothing more than undergarments.

182. Jesus' Trial Before Annas; Peter's First Denial

Matt. 26:58, 69–70; Mark 14:54, 66–68; Luke 22:54–57; John 18:13–24

LK [a]Having arrested Him, JN they led Him away to [b]Annas first, for he was the father-in-law of Caiaphas who was high priest that year. Now it was Caiaphas who advised the Jews that it was expedient that one man should die for the people.

And [c]Simon Peter followed Jesus MT at a distance to the high priest's courtyard, JN and so *did* another disciple. Now that disciple was [d]known to the high priest, and went with Jesus into the courtyard of the high priest. But Peter stood at the door outside. Then the other disciple, who was known to the high priest, went out and spoke to her who kept the door, and brought Peter in. MT And he went in and sat with the servants to see the end.

LK When they had kindled a fire in the midst of the courtyard and sat down together, Peter sat among them. JN The servants and officers who had made a fire of coals stood there, for it was cold, and they warmed themselves. And [e]Peter stood with them and warmed himself.

---

[a] Having arrested Him. The gospel accounts of Jesus' trials make it clear that He was tried in two general phases: first, before the religious authorities (the Jewish Sanhedrin), and second, before the secular political authorities (Rome, represented by governor Pontius Pilate). Each of these phases had three parts: preliminary interrogation, formal arraignment, and formal sentencing. None of the gospel writers provide a comprehensive account of all the details and stages of these trials. A complete picture requires the material from all four gospels being combined.

[b] Annas first. Annas held the High-Priesthood from AD 6–15 until Valerius Gratus, Pilate's predecessor, removed him from office. In spite of this, Annas continued to wield influence over the office, most likely because he was still regarded as the true high priest and also because five of his sons, and his son-in-law Caiaphas, each held the position at different times. Two trials occurred: one Jewish and one Roman. The Jewish phase began with the informal examination by Annas (John 18:12–14, 19–23), probably giving time for the members of the Sanhedrin to hurriedly gather together. A session before the Sanhedrin was next (Matt. 26:57–68), at which consensus was reached to send Jesus to Pilate (Matt. 27:1–2). The Roman phase began when Jesus was examined before Pilate (Matt. 27:11–14; John 18:28–38a), and then Herod Antipas ("that fox"—Luke 13:32) interrogated Him (Luke 23:6–12). Last, Jesus appeared again before Pilate (Matt. 27:15–31; John 18:38b–19:16).

[c] Simon Peter followed . . . at a distance. All four gospels record this fact. John indicates that another disciple—presumably himself—also followed (John 18:15).

[d] known to the high priest. Apparently, John was more than just an acquaintance, because the term for "known" can mean a friend (Luke 2:44). The fact that he mentioned Nicodemus (John 3:1) and Joseph (John 19:38) may indicate his knowledge of other prominent Jews.

[e] Peter stood with them. Here is the record of the first of Peter's predicted three denials.

MK Now as Peter was [f]below in the courtyard, [g]one of the servant girls of the high priest JN who kept the door MK came. And when she saw Peter warming himself LK as he sat by the fire, MK she looked at him LK intently and said, MK "You also were with Jesus [h]of Nazareth. JN You are not also *one* of this Man's disciples, are you?" MT But he denied it before *them* all, saying, LK "Woman, JN I am not. LK I do not know Him. MK I neither know nor understand what you are saying." And he went out on [i]the porch, and [j]a rooster crowed.

JN The [k]high priest [Annas] then [l]asked Jesus about His disciples and His doctrine. Jesus answered him, "I spoke openly to the world. I always taught in synagogues and in the temple, where the Jews always meet, and in secret I have said nothing. Why do you ask Me? Ask those who have heard Me what I said to them. Indeed they know what I said." And when He had said these things, one of the officers who stood by struck Jesus with the palm of his hand, saying, "Do You answer the high priest like that?" Jesus answered him, "If I have spoken evil, bear

[f] BELOW. The apartments around it were higher than the courtyard itself.

[g] ONE OF THE SERVANT GIRLS. Female slave, or maid, in the household of the high priest. All four gospels mention her. She seems to have been the same gatekeeper (cf. John 18:15–16) who admitted Peter, and who being curious and suspicious of him, wanted a closer look.

[h] OF NAZARETH. Their reference to Jesus' hometown communicates a feeling of contempt, in keeping with the views of the Jewish leaders and the poor reputation Nazareth generally had (cf. John 1:46).

[i] THE PORCH. Used only here in the NT, this term denotes "the forecourt," or "entryway," a covered archway of the courtyard, opening onto the street.

[j] A ROOSTER CROWED. This phrase was probably not a part of Mark's original gospel, since it does not appear in the earliest manuscripts. It was likely inserted by a later scribe to account for the fact that, in Mark's gospel, the rooster is said to crow twice. Even if a rooster did crow at this point in the story, Peter apparently did not hear it or did not recognize the significance of it. When the rooster crowed the second time, Jesus looked at Peter (Luke 22:61), triggering Peter's memory and bringing conviction of his denials (cf. Mark 14:72).

[k] HIGH PRIEST. Here the gospel writer (John) referred to Annas as the high priest. This was appropriate and accurate, since Annas had formerly held that office, and he still continued to hold significant sway over it. A former high priest could still be addressed by that title.

[l] ASKED JESUS ABOUT. Their main objection was Jesus' claim that He was the Son of God (John 19:7). According to Jewish law, a case had to rest on the testimony of multiple witnesses. If this was an informal interrogation, Annas may have justified his actions on the premise that such rules did not apply in this case. Jesus, however, knew the law and demanded that witnesses be called (John 18:20–21). An official knew Jesus was rebuking Annas and retaliated (John 18:22).

witness of the evil; but if well, [m]why do you strike Me?" Then [n]Annas sent Him bound to Caiaphas the high priest. [LK] [And] they led *Him* and brought Him into the high priest's house.

---

[m] WHY DO YOU STRIKE ME? In essence Jesus had requested a fair trial, while His opponents, who had already decided on the sentence (see John 11:47–57), had no intention of providing one.

[n] ANNAS SENT HIM BOUND TO CAIAPHAS. Annas recognized that he was not getting anywhere with Jesus and sent Him to Caiaphas, because if Jesus was taken to Pilate for execution, an official charge had to be presented by the current high priest (i.e., Caiaphas) on behalf of the Sanhedrin.

183. Jesus' Trial Before Caiaphas

Matt. 26:57, 59–68; Mark 14:53, 55–65

MT Those who had laid hold of Jesus led *Him* away to [a]Caiaphas the high priest, where MK all the chief priests, the elders, and the scribes MT were assembled. MK Now the chief priests and all [b]the council sought MT false testimony against Jesus to put Him to death, but found none. Even though many false witnesses came forward, [c]they found none. MK For [d]many bore false witness against Him, but their testimonies [e]did not agree.

MT But at last two [f]false witnesses came forward MK and bore false witness

---

[a] CAIAPHAS THE HIGH PRIEST. From John 18:13 we learn that Christ was taken first to Annas (former high priest and father-in-law to Caiaphas). He then was sent bound to Caiaphas's house (John 18:24). Caiaphas was the leader of the Sanhedrin (cf. Matt. 26:3, 57; John 18:24) and the official high priest from AD 18–36. The conspiracy against Jesus was well planned, so that "the scribes and the elders" (the Sanhedrin) were already "assembled" at Caiaphas' house and ready to try Jesus. The time was sometime between midnight and the first rooster's crowing (Matt. 26:74). Such a hearing was illegal on two counts: criminal trials were not to be held at night, and trials in capital cases could only be held at the temple and only in public.

[b] THE COUNCIL. The great Sanhedrin was the Supreme Court of Israel, consisting of seventy-one members, presided over by the high priest. They met daily in the temple to hold court, except on the Sabbath and other holy days. Technically, they did not have the power to administer capital punishment (John 18:31), but in the case of Stephen, for example, this was no deterrent to his stoning (cf. Acts 6:12–14; 7:58–60). Roman governors evidently sometimes ignored such incidents as a matter of political expediency. In Jesus' case, the men who were trying Him were the same ones who had conspired against Him (cf. John 11:47–50).

[c] THEY FOUND NONE. Even though many were willing to perjure themselves, the Sanhedrin could not find a charge that had enough credibility to indict Jesus. Evidently the "false witnesses" could not agree between themselves. Because Jesus was innocent, the Jewish leaders could not convict Him except by relying on perjured testimony and perverted justice. The Jewish leaders were intent on doing whatever was necessary, even if they had to violate every biblical and rabbinical rule.

[d] MANY BORE FALSE WITNESS AGAINST HIM. There was no lack of people to come forward at the Sanhedrin's invitation to consciously present false, lying testimony.

[e] DID NOT AGREE. The testimonies were grossly inconsistent. The law, however, required exact agreement between two witnesses (Deut. 17:6; 19:15).

[f] FALSE WITNESS. The witnesses maliciously garbled and misrepresented Jesus' statements. Quite possibly they blended His figurative statement regarding His death and resurrection in John 2:19–22 with His prediction of a literal destruction of the temple in Mark 13:2. Their charge claimed He was disloyal to the present order of religion and worship (by replacing the current temple) and that He was blaspheming God (by saying He would so quickly rebuild the temple without hands).

against Him, saying, "We heard Him say, 'I will [g]destroy this temple MT of God MK made with hands, and within three days I will build another made without hands.'" But not even then did their testimony agree. And [h]the high priest stood up in the midst and asked Jesus, saying, "Do You answer nothing? What *is it* these men testify against You?" MT But Jesus [i]kept silent MK and answered nothing.

MT And the high priest answered and said to Him, "I put You [j]under oath by the living God: Tell us, MK are You the [k]Christ, the Son of the [l]Blessed?" MT Jesus said to him, "*It is as* you said. MK [m]I am. MT Nevertheless, I say to you, hereafter you will see [n]the Son of Man sitting at the [o]right hand of the Power, and coming on the [p]clouds of heaven."

---

[g] destroy this temple. See John 2:19–21. The witnesses' account was a distortion of Jesus' meaning. Jesus boldly made this assertion in front of the temple the Jews revered, but His words were not fully understood—since He was referring to the temple of His body, and to His death and resurrection.

[h] the high priest stood up. Caiaphas attempted to salvage the tense situation when the continued false charges were failing to establish a case or elicit a response from the Lord. The high priest could not understand how Jesus could remain silent and not offer any defense.

[i] kept silent. The silence of innocence, integrity, and faith in God. An answer by Jesus would have given all the false testimonies and illegal proceedings an appearance of legitimacy.

[j] under oath. Caiaphas was trying to break Jesus' silence. The oath was supposed to make Him legally obligated to reply. Jesus' answer implies acceptance of the oath.

[k] Christ. This term refers to Jesus' claim to be the promised Messiah.

[l] Blessed. Mark's account reads, "Son of the Blessed." This refers to Jesus claim to deity. This is the only NT use of the expression, and it is an example of Jewish wording that avoided using God's name (cf. John 8:58). Jesus' acceptance of messiahship and deity (cf. Luke 4:18–21; John 4:25–26; 5:17–18; 8:58) had always brought vigorous opposition from the Jewish leaders (John 5:19–47; 8:16–19; 10:29–39). Clearly, the high priest was asking this question in hopes that Jesus would affirm it and open Himself to the formal charge of blasphemy.

[m] I am. An explicit, unambiguous declaration that Jesus was and is both the Messiah and the Son of God.

[n] the Son of Man. Jesus used this commonly acknowledged messianic title of Himself more than eighty times in the gospels, here in a reference to Ps. 110:1 and Dan. 7:13 (cf. Rev. 1:13; 14:14).

[o] right hand of the Power. Cf. Mark 10:37; Acts 2:33; 7:55; Heb. 2:9; Rev. 12:5. Jesus' glorified position is next to the throne of God (the "Power" is another reference to God).

[p] clouds. See Matt. 13:26; cf. Matt. 24:30; 26:64; Luke 21:27; Acts 1:9–11; Rev. 1:7; 14:14.

Then [q]the high priest [r]tore his clothes, saying, MK "What [s]further need do we have of witnesses? You have heard the [t]blasphemy MT He has spoken! MK What do you think?" MT They MK all condemned Him MT and said, "He is deserving of death." MK Then some began to [u]spit MT in His face MK and to blindfold Him, and to beat Him; MT and MK the officers MT struck *Him* with the palms of their hands, saying, [v]"Prophesy to us, Christ! Who is the one who struck You?"

---

[q] THE HIGH PRIEST TORE HIS CLOTHES. Normally, this was an expression of deep grief (2 Kings 19:1; Job 1:20; Jer. 36:24). The high priest was forbidden to tear his clothes (Lev. 10:6; 21:10)—but the Talmud made an exception for high priests who witnessed a blasphemy. But Caiaphas's supposed grief was as phony as the charge of blasphemy against Jesus; he was gloating over having found something to base his charges on.

[r] TORE HIS CLOTHES. A ceremonial, and in this case contrived, display of grief and indignation over the presumed dishonoring of God's name by Jesus (cf. Gen 37:29; Lev. 10:6; Job 1:20; Acts 14:13, 19).

[s] FURTHER NEED . . . OF WITNESSES. A rhetorical question that expressed relief that the tense and embarrassing situation was finally over. Because Jesus had allegedly incriminated Himself in the eyes of the Sanhedrin, they would not need to summon any more lying witnesses.

[t] BLASPHEMY. Cf. Mark 2:7; 3:29. Strictly speaking, Jesus' words were not "blasphemy," or defiant irreverence of God (Lev. 24:10–23), but Caiaphas regarded them as such because Jesus claimed for Himself equal power and prerogative with God.

[u] SPIT IN HIS FACE . . . BEAT HIM. For the Jews, to "spit" in another's face was the grossest, most hateful form of personal insult (cf. Num. 12:14; Deut. 25:9). Their brutal cruelty reached a climax and revealed the great depravity of their hearts when they "beat Him," or hit Him with clenched fists.

[v] "PROPHESY!" They jeeringly and disrespectfully ordered Jesus to use the prophetic powers He claimed to have—even in the frivolous manner of telling them who struck Him (Matt. 26:68).

184. Peter's Second and Third Denials

Matt. 26:71–75; Mark 14:69–72; Luke 22:58–65; John 18:25–27

LK And after a little while, MT when [Peter] had gone out to [a]the gateway, MK the servant girl saw him again, and began to say to those who stood by, "This is *one* of them." MT Another *girl* saw him and said to those *who were* there, "This *fellow* also was with Jesus of Nazareth." LK [And] another saw him and said, "You also are of them." JN Now Simon Peter stood and warmed himself. Therefore they said to him, "You are not also *one* of His disciples, are you?" LK But Peter MK [b]denied it again MT with an oath, JN and said, LK "Man, I am not! MT I do not know the Man!"

MK A little later, LK [c]after about an hour had passed, MT those who stood by came up and said to Peter, "Surely you also are *one* of them, MK for you are a [d]Galilean, and your speech shows *it* [and] MT betrays you." LK Another confidently affirmed, saying, "Surely this *fellow* also was with Him, for he is a Galilean." JN One of the servants of the high priest, a relative *of him* whose ear Peter cut off, said, "Did I not see you in the garden with Him?" MK Then he JN denied again and MK [e]began to curse and

---

[a] THE GATEWAY. In Mark's parallel account (Mark 14:68) he uses the term "porch," denoting "the forecourt," or "entryway," a covered archway of the courtyard, opening onto the street.

[b] DENIED IT AGAIN. A comparison of the four gospel accounts indicates that all of these accusations were part of what occasioned Peter's second denial. Evidently, a small group of people, following the first servant girl's lead, were now accusing him all at once. Peter responded to their barrage of accusations by vehemently and repeatedly denying the Lord Jesus, probably in just a matter of a few moments. To the original maiden, "he denied it again" (Mark 14:70). To a second maiden, the girl mentioned by Matthew, "Again he denied with an oath, 'I do not know the Man!'" (Matthew 26:72). To one of the men who identified him as a disciple of Christ, he said, "Man, I am not" (Luke 22:58). And to the whole group who pressed him to admit that he was one of the Twelve, "He denied it and said, 'I am not!'" (John 18:25). Putting these four accounts together suggests that Peter emphatically denied all of these accusations in rapid-fire fashion, even using an oath to punctuate the seriousness of his rebuttal.

[c] AFTER ABOUT AN HOUR HAD PASSED. This span of time separates Peter's second denial from his third. As with the second denial, this third and final episode represented multiple accusers and a resolute and insistent denial on Peter's part.

[d] GALILEAN. They knew because of his accent (Matt. 26:73). The term *Galilean* was frequently used as a derisive label by people in Jerusalem toward their northern neighbors. It strongly suggested that natives of Galilee were deemed unsophisticated and uneducated (cf. Acts 4:13).

[e] HE . . . BEGAN TO CURSE AND SWEAR. i.e., calling on God as his witness, he declared, "I do not know the Man!" and pronounced a curse of death on himself at God's hand if his words were untrue. All four gospels record Peter's betrayal.

swear, LK "Man, I do not know what you are saying! MK I do not know this Man of whom you speak!" LK Immediately, while he was still speaking, the rooster crowed MK a second time.

LK And [f]the Lord turned and looked at Peter. Then [g]Peter remembered the word of the Lord, how He had said to him, MK "Before the rooster crows twice, you will deny Me three times." And when he thought about it, LK Peter went out and wept bitterly.

---

[f] The Lord turned and looked at Peter. Luke alone records that Jesus made eye contact with Peter. The verb used suggests an intent, fixed look. The fact that He could see Peter suggests that the men holding Jesus had already brought Him into the courtyard to beat Him.

[g] Peter remembered. Luke 22:61 records that Jesus made eye contact with Peter at this very moment, which must have magnified Peter's already unbearable sense of shame. "He went out"—evidently departing from Caiaphas's house—"and wept bitterly." The true Peter is seen not in his denial but in his repentance. This account reminds us of not only our own weakness but also the richness of divine grace (cf. John 21:15–19).

185. The Sanhedrin Confirms the Verdict

Matt. 27:1; Mark 15:1a; Luke 22:66–71

MK [a]Immediately, MT when morning came, LK [b]as soon as it was day, MK the chief priests held a consultation with the elders and scribes and the whole council. LK [They] came together and led Him into their council, saying, "[c]If You are the Christ, tell us."

But He said to them, "If I tell you, you will by no means believe. And if I also ask *you,* you will by no means answer Me or let *Me* go. Hereafter the Son of Man will sit on the right hand of the power of God."

Then they all said, "Are You then the Son of God?" So He said to them, "You *rightly* say that I am." And they said, "What further testimony do we need? For we have heard it ourselves from His own mouth." MT [And] all the chief priests and elders of the people plotted against Jesus to put Him to death.

---

[a] IMMEDIATELY . . . MORNING. At daybreak, probably between 5:00 and 6:00 a.m. Having illegally decided Jesus' guilt during the night (Mark 14:53–65; John 18:13–24), the Sanhedrin formally convened after daybreak to pronounce a sentence.

[b] AS SOON AS IT WAS DAY. Criminal trials were not deemed legal if held at night, so the Sanhedrin dutifully waited until daybreak to render the verdict they had already agreed on anyway.

[c] IF YOU ARE THE CHRIST. The Sanhedrin subjected Him to the same set of questions He had been asked in the nighttime trial, and the answers He gave were substantially the same.

186. Judas Regrets His Treachery

Matt. 27:3–10

MT Then Judas, His betrayer, seeing that He had been condemned, was [a]remorseful and brought back the thirty pieces of silver to the chief priests and elders, saying, "I have sinned by betraying innocent blood." And they said, "What *is that* to us? You see *to it!*" Then he threw down the pieces of silver in the temple and departed, and went and [b]hanged himself.

But the chief priests took the silver pieces and said, "It is not lawful to put them into the treasury, because they are the price of blood." And they consulted together and bought with them the potter's field, to bury strangers in. Therefore that field has been called the Field of Blood to this day. Then was fulfilled what was [c]spoken by Jeremiah the prophet, saying, "And they took the thirty pieces of silver, the value of Him who was priced, whom they of the children of Israel priced, and gave them for the potter's field, as the LORD directed me."

---

[a] REMORSEFUL. Judas felt the sting of his own guilt, but this was not genuine repentance. There is a godly sorrow that leads to repentance, but Judas's remorse was of a different kind, as demonstrated by his suicide. Cf. 2 Cor. 7:10.

[b] HANGED HIMSELF. See Acts 1:18.

[c] SPOKEN BY JEREMIAH. Actually, the statement paraphrases Zech. 11:12–13. But the Hebrew canon was divided into three sections: Law, Writings, and Prophets (cf. Luke 24:44). Jeremiah came first in the order of prophetic books, so the Prophets were sometimes collectively referred to by his name.

187. Jesus' Trial Before Pilate

Matt. 27:2, 11–14; Mark 15:1–5; Luke 23:1–5; John 18:28–38

MT And when they had MK bound Jesus, LK [a]the whole multitude of them arose and led Him MT away JN from Caiaphas to the [b]Praetorium MT and [c]delivered Him to Pontius Pilate the governor. JN And it was [d]early morning. But they themselves did not go into the Praetorium, [e]lest they should be defiled, but that they might eat the Passover.

Pilate then went out to them and said, "[f]What accusation do you bring against this Man?" They answered and said to him, "If He were not an evildoer, we would not have delivered Him up to you." Then Pilate said to them, "You take Him and judge Him according to your law." Therefore the Jews said to him, "[g]It

---

[a] THE WHOLE MULTITUDE OF THEM. i.e., the entire Sanhedrin, some seventy men. At least one member of the council, Joseph of Arimathea, dissented from the decision to condemn Christ (cf. Luke 23:50–52).

[b] PRAETORIUM. The headquarters of the Roman military commander or governor (i.e., Pilate). Pilate was normally in Caesarea, but he made sure to be in Jerusalem during the feasts in order to quell any riots. At such times, Jerusalem became his praetorium or headquarters.

[c] DELIVERED HIM . . . PILATE. Jesus had two trials, one Jewish and religious, the other Roman and secular. Rome reserved the right of execution in capital cases (cf. Matt. 26:59), so Jesus had to be handed over to the Roman authorities for execution of the death sentence. Pilate's headquarters were in Caesarea, on the Mediterranean coast, but he was in Jerusalem for the Passover celebrations, so he oversaw the trial (cf. Mark 15:1). Christ was brought before Pilate, then was sent to Herod for yet another hearing (Luke 23:6–12), then returned to Pilate for the final hearing and pronouncing of sentence.

[d] EARLY MORNING. The word is ambiguous. Most likely, it refers to around 6:00 a.m., since many Roman officials began their day very early and finished by 10:00 or 11:00 a.m.

[e] LEST THEY SHOULD BE DEFILED. Jewish oral law indicates that a Jew who went into a Gentile house or dwelling was considered ceremonially unclean. They stayed outside in the colonnade to avoid being tainted. John loads this statement with great irony by noting the chief priests' scrupulousness in the matter of ceremonial cleansing, when all the time they were incurring incomparably greater moral defilement by their proceedings against Jesus.

[f] WHAT ACCUSATION. This question formally opened the Roman civil phase of proceedings against Jesus (in contrast to the religious phase before the Jews in John 18:24).

[g] IT IS NOT LAWFUL. When Rome began to rule Judea through a governor, starting in AD 6, the Jews lost the right to administer capital punishment. Thus, the Jewish leaders were forced to ask Pilate to authorize the crucifixion of Jesus.

is not lawful for us to put anyone to death," that [h]the saying of Jesus might be fulfilled which He spoke, signifying by what death He would die. LK And they began to accuse Him, saying, "We found this *fellow* perverting the nation, and [i]forbidding to pay taxes to Caesar, [j]saying that He Himself is Christ, a King." JN Then [k]Pilate entered the Praetorium again, called Jesus, and said to Him, [l]"Are You the King of the Jews?"

MT Jesus stood before the governor JN [and] answered him, "Are you speaking for yourself about this, or did [m]others tell you this concerning Me?" Pilate answered, "Am I a Jew? Your own nation and the chief priests have delivered You to me. What have You done?"

Jesus answered, "[n]My kingdom is not of this world. If My kingdom were of this world, My servants would fight, so that I should not be delivered to the Jews; but now My kingdom is not from here." Pilate therefore said to Him, "Are You a king then?" Jesus answered, MT "[o]*It is* JN *rightly* MT *as* you say, JN that I am a king. For

---

[h] THE SAYING OF JESUS . . . FULFILLED. Jesus had said that He would die by being "lifted up" (John 3:14; 8:28; 12:32–33). If the Jews had executed Him, it would have been by throwing Him down and stoning Him. But God providentially controlled all the political procedures to assure that when sentence was finally passed, He would be crucified by the Romans and not stoned by the Jews, as was Stephen (Acts 7:59). The Jews may have preferred this form of execution based on Deut. 21:23.

[i] FORBIDDING TO PAY TAXES TO CAESAR. This was a deliberate lie. Members of the Sanhedrin had publicly questioned Jesus on this very issue (hoping to discredit Him before the Jews), and He expressly upheld Caesar's right to demand taxes (Luke 20:20–25).

[j] SAYING THAT HE . . . IS CHRIST, A KING. This was innuendo, implying that He was seditious against Rome—another untrue charge.

[k] PILATE . . . SAID TO HIM. John records (John 18:30) that the Jewish leaders demanded that Pilate simply agree to the death sentence they had already pronounced on Jesus (Mark 14:64). Pilate refused, and the Jewish leaders then presented their false charges against Jesus (Luke 23:2). Having heard those charges, Pilate then questioned Him.

[l] "ARE YOU THE KING OF THE JEWS?" The only charge Pilate took seriously was that Jesus claimed to be a king, thus making Him guilty of rebellion against Rome. Pilate's question reveals that he had already been informed of this charge (Luke 23:2).

[m] OTHERS. Again (cf. John 18:20–21), Jesus demanded witnesses.

[n] MY KINGDOM IS NOT OF THIS WORLD. By this phrase Jesus meant that His kingdom is not connected to earthly political and national entities, nor does it have its origin in the evil world system that is in rebellion against God. If His kingdom were of this world, He would have fought. The governments of this world protect their interests by fighting with force. Messiah's kingdom does not originate in the efforts of man but with the Son of Man forcefully and decisively conquering sin in the lives of His people and someday conquering the evil world system at His second coming when He establishes the earthly form of His kingdom. His kingdom was no threat to the national identity of Israel or the political and military identity of Rome. It exists in the spiritual dimension until the end of the age (Rev. 11:15).

[o] IT IS . . . AS YOU SAY. Jesus' answer acknowledged that He was the rightful king of Israel but implied that Pilate's concept of what that meant differed from His.

this cause I was born, and for this cause I have come into the world, that I should bear witness to the truth. Everyone who is of the truth hears My voice."

Pilate said to Him, [p]"What is truth?" And when he had said this, he went out again to the Jews, and said [LK] to the chief priests and the crowd, [JN] "I find [q]no fault in [LK] this Man [JN] at all." [LK] But they were the more fierce, saying, "He stirs up the people, teaching throughout all Judea, beginning from Galilee to this place." [MT] And while He was being accused [MK] of many things [MT] by the chief priests and elders, He answered nothing. [MK] Then Pilate asked Him again, saying, [r]"Do You answer nothing? [MT] Do You not hear how many things they testify against You?" But He answered him not one word, so that the governor marveled greatly.

---

[p] "WHAT IS TRUTH?" In response to Jesus' mention of "truth" in John 18:37, Pilate responded rhetorically with cynicism, convinced that no answer existed to the question. The retort proved that he was not among those whom the Father had given to the Son ("Everyone who is of the truth hears My voice"—John 18:37; cf. John 10:1–5).

[q] NO FAULT. Jesus was clearly not guilty of any sin or crime, thus exhibiting the severe injustice and guilt of both the Jews and Romans who executed Him. Despite the Jewish leaders' desperate attempts to accuse Him, Pilate was satisfied that Jesus was no insurrectionist, but the ferocity of the people made him afraid to exonerate Jesus. He was relieved to hear that Jesus was a Galilean, because that gave him an excuse to send Him to Herod. Cf. John 19:4.

[r] "DO YOU ANSWER NOTHING?" Pilate was amazed at Jesus' silence, since accused prisoners predictably and vehemently denied the charges against them. Jesus may have remained silent in fulfillment of prophecy (Isa. 42:1–2; 53:7), because Pilate had already pronounced him innocent (Luke 23:4; John 18:38), or both.

188. Jesus' Trial Before Herod Antipas

Luke 23:6–12

LK When Pilate heard of Galilee, he asked if the Man were a Galilean. And as soon as he knew that He belonged to Herod's jurisdiction, he [a]sent Him to Herod, who was also in Jerusalem at that time.

Now when Herod saw Jesus, he was exceedingly glad; for he had [b]desired for a long *time* to see Him, because he had heard many things about Him, and he hoped to see some miracle done by Him. Then he questioned Him with many words, but He [c]answered him nothing. And the chief priests and scribes stood and vehemently accused Him. Then Herod, with his [d]men of war, [e]treated Him with contempt and mocked *Him,* arrayed Him in [f]a gorgeous robe, and sent Him back to Pilate.

That very day Pilate and Herod became [g]friends with each other, for previously they had been at enmity with each other.

---

[a] SENT HIM TO HEROD. Herod had come to Jerusalem for the feasts, and Pilate seized the opportunity to free himself from a political dilemma by sending Jesus to his rival.

[b] DESIRED . . . TO SEE HIM. Herod's interest in Christ was fueled by the fact that Christ reminded him of his late nemesis, John the Baptist (cf. Luke 9:7–9). At one time Herod had apparently threatened to kill Jesus (Luke 13:31–33), but with Christ in Judea rather than Galilee and Perea (where Herod ruled), the king's concern seems to have been nothing more than an eager curiosity.

[c] ANSWERED HIM NOTHING. It is significant that in all Jesus' various interrogations, Herod was the only one to whom He refused to speak. Cf. Matt. 7:6. Herod had summarily rejected the truth when he heard it from John the Baptist, so it would have been pointless for Jesus to answer him. Cf. Isa. 53:7; Pss. 38:13–14; 39:1–2, 9; 1 Peter 2:23.

[d] MEN OF WAR. i.e., his security force.

[e] TREATED HIM WITH CONTEMPT. Herod made Christ and the charges against Him an occasion for a joke for Pilate's amusement.

[f] A GORGEOUS ROBE. Probably not the same robe mentioned in Matt. 27:28, which was a military cloak. This was an elegant king's garment, probably one that Herod was prepared to discard.

[g] FRIENDS. Based on their common unjust and cowardly treatment of Jesus.

189. Jesus Sentenced Before Pilate

Matt. 27:15–26a; Mark 15:6–15; Luke 23:13–25; John 18:39–19:15

MT Now [a]at the feast the governor was [b]accustomed to releasing to the multitude one prisoner, MK whomever they requested. MT And at that time they had a notorious prisoner, JN a [c]robber, MK named [d]Barabbas, *who was* chained with his fellow rebels; they had committed murder in LK a certain rebellion made in the city. MT Therefore, when they had gathered together, MK the multitude, crying aloud, began to ask *him to do* just as he had always done for them. But Pilate answered them, saying, JN "You have a custom that I should release someone to you at the Passover. MT Whom do you want me to release to you? Barabbas, or Jesus who is called Christ? MK Do you want me to release to you the King of the Jews?" For he knew that the chief priests had handed Him over [e]because of envy.

MT While he was sitting on the judgment seat, his wife sent to him, saying, "Have nothing to do with that just Man, for I have suffered many things today in a dream because of Him." LK Then Pilate, when he had [f]called together the chief priests, the rulers, and the people, said to them, "You have brought this Man to me, as one who misleads the people. And indeed, having examined *Him* in your presence, I have found no fault in this Man concerning those things of which you

---

[a] AT THE FEAST. The Passover.

[b] ACCUSTOMED TO. Ancient secular sources indicate that Roman governors occasionally granted amnesty at the request of their subjects. Assuming that the people would ask for their king (whom they had so acknowledged earlier in the week [Mark 11:1–10]) to be freed, Pilate undoubtedly saw this annual custom as the way out of his dilemma regarding Jesus.

[c] ROBBER. The word *robber* means "one who seizes plunder" and may depict not only a robber but a terrorist or guerrilla fighter who participated in bloody insurrection (see Mark 15:7)

[d] BARABBAS. A robber (John 18:40) and murderer (Luke 23:18–19) in some way involved as an anti-Roman insurrectionist. Whether his involvement was motivated by political conviction or personal greed is not known. It is impossible to identify the specific insurrection in question, but such uprisings were common in Jesus' day and were precursors of the wholesale revolt of AD 66–70.

[e] BECAUSE OF ENVY. Pilate realized that the Jewish authorities had not handed Jesus over to him out of loyalty to Rome. He saw through their deceit to the underlying reason—their jealousy over Jesus' popularity with the people.

[f] CALLED TOGETHER. Pilate intended to declare Christ not guilty, and it was his intention to make the verdict as public as possible. He undoubtedly expected that it would put an end to the whole matter.

accuse Him; no, [g]neither did Herod, for I sent you back to him; and indeed nothing deserving of death has been done by Him. I will therefore chastise Him and release *Him*" (for [h]it was necessary for him to release one to them at the feast).

[MT] But the chief priests and elders [MK] stirred up the crowd, so that [MT] they should ask for Barabbas and destroy Jesus. The governor answered and said to them, "Which of the two do you want me to release to you?" [LK] And they all cried out at once, saying, "Away with this *Man,* and release to us Barabbas. [JN] Not this Man, but Barabbas!" [LK] Pilate, therefore, wishing to release Jesus, [MK] answered and [LK] called out [MK] to them again, "What then do you want me to do with [MT] Jesus who is called Christ [MK] whom you call the King of the Jews?" [LK] But they [MT] all [LK] shouted [and] [MK] cried out again, [LK] saying [MT] to him, "Let Him be crucified! [LK] Crucify Him, crucify Him!" Then he said to them [j]the third time, "Why, what evil has He done? I have found no reason for death in Him. [k]I will therefore chastise Him and let *Him* go."

[JN] So then Pilate took Jesus and [l]scourged *Him.* And the soldiers twisted a [m]crown of thorns and put *it* on His head, and they put on Him a [n]purple robe.

---

[g] NEITHER DID HEROD. Pilate and Herod concurred in the verdict (cf. 1 Tim. 6:13).

[h] IT WAS NECESSARY. i.e., because it was a longstanding Jewish custom (John 18:39), traditionally honored by the Romans.

[i] CRUCIFIED. Crucifixion, the common Roman method of execution for slaves and foreigners, was described by the Roman writer Cicero as "the cruelest and most hideous punishment possible."

[j] THE THIRD TIME. Pilate repeatedly gave powerful testimony to the innocence of Christ (Luke 23:4, 14–15). In doing so, he not only condemned the Jews, who demanded Jesus' death, but also himself, because he handed the Savior over without cause.

[k] I WILL . . . CHASTISE HIM. Though Pilate found Him innocent of any wrongdoing, he was prepared to scourge Him merely to pacify the Jewish crowd. But even that punishment, severe as it was (cf. Matt. 27:26), could not quench their thirst for His blood.

[l] SCOURGED. Pilate appears to have flogged Jesus as a strategy to set Him free. This level of scourging, known as the *fustigatio,* was less severe than the later scourging Jesus received after He was sentenced. Pilate was hoping that the Jewish crowd would be appeased by this action and that sympathy for Jesus' suffering would result in their desire that He be released (see Luke 23:13–16).

[m] CROWN OF THORNS. This "crown" was made from the long spikes (up to twelve inches) of a date palm formed into an imitation of the radiating crowns which ancient Near Eastern kings wore. The long thorns would have cut deeply into Jesus' head, adding to the pain and bleeding.

[n] PURPLE ROBE. The color represented royalty. The robe (which was different than the one placed on Jesus by Herod in Luke 23:11) was likely a military cloak flung around Jesus' shoulders, intended to mock His claim to be King of the Jews.

Then they said, "Hail, King of the Jews!" And they struck Him with their hands. Pilate then went out again, and said to them, "Behold, I am bringing Him out to you, that you may know that I find no fault in Him."

Then Jesus came out, wearing the crown of thorns and the purple robe. And *Pilate* said to them, [o]"Behold the Man!" Therefore, when the chief priests and officers saw Him, [LK] they were insistent, [MT] [and] cried out all the more, [LK] demanding with loud voices, [JN] saying, "Crucify *Him,* crucify *Him!*" Pilate said to them, "[p]You take Him and crucify *Him,* for I find no fault in Him."

The Jews answered him, "[q]We have a law, and according to our law He ought to die, because He made Himself the Son of God." Therefore, when Pilate heard that saying, he was the [r]more afraid, and went again into the Praetorium, and said to Jesus, [s]"Where are You from?" But Jesus gave him no answer. Then Pilate said to Him, "Are You not speaking to me? Do You not know that I have power to crucify You, and power to release You?" Jesus answered, "[t]You could have no power at all against Me unless it had been given you from above. Therefore [u]the one who delivered Me to you has the greater sin."

---

[o] "Behold the Man!" Pilate dramatically presented Jesus after His torturous treatment by the soldiers. Jesus would have been swollen, bruised, and bleeding. By displaying Jesus as a beaten and pathetic figure, Pilate hoped to gain the people's choice of Jesus for release. Pilate's phrase is filled with sarcasm, since He was attempting to impress upon the Jewish authorities that Jesus was not the dangerous man that they had made Him out to be.

[p] You take Him and crucify Him. The pronouns "you" and "Him" have an emphatic force, indicating Pilate's disgust and indignation at the Jewish crowd for their callousness toward Jesus.

[q] We have a law. This probably refers to Lev. 24:16: "whoever blasphemes the name of the Lord shall surely be put to death." The charge of blasphemy (John 5:18; 8:58–59; 10:33, 36) was central in Jesus' trial before Caiaphas (see Matt. 26:57–68).

[r] more afraid. Many Roman officials were deeply superstitious. While Jews interpreted Jesus' claims as messianic, to the Greco-Roman person, the title "Son of God" would place Jesus in the category of "divine men" who were gifted with supernatural powers. Pilate was afraid because he had just whipped and tortured someone who, in his mind, could bring down a curse or vengeance upon him.

[s] "Where are You from?" He was concerned about Jesus' origins. His superstitious mind was wondering with just what kind of person was he dealing.

[t] You could have no power . . . unless. Jesus' statement here indicates that even the most heinous acts of wickedness cannot circumvent the sovereignty of God. Pilate had no real control, yet still stood as a responsible moral agent for his actions. When confronted with opposition and evil, Jesus often found solace in the sovereignty of His Father (e.g., John 6:43–44, 65; 10:18, 28–29).

[u] the one who delivered Me to you has the greater sin. This could refer either to Judas or Caiaphas. Since Caiaphas instigated the plot against Jesus (John 11:49–53) and presided over the Sanhedrin, the reference may center on him (John 18:30, 35). The critical point is not the identity of the person but the level of guilt. Both Judas and Caiaphas were involved in the deliberate, high-handed, and coldly calculated act of handing Jesus over to Pilate, after having seen and heard the overwhelming evidence that He was Messiah and Son of God. Pilate had not been exposed to that. Cf. John 9:41; 15:22–24; Heb. 10:26–31.

From then on Pilate sought to release Him, but the Jews cried out, saying, "If you let this Man go, you are [v]not Caesar's friend. Whoever makes himself a king speaks against Caesar." When Pilate therefore heard that saying, he brought Jesus out and sat down in [w]the judgment seat in a place that is called *The* Pavement, but in Hebrew, Gabbatha. Now it was the [x]Preparation Day of the Passover, and [y]about the sixth hour. And he said to the Jews, [z]"Behold your King!" But they cried out, "Away with *Him,* away with *Him!* Crucify Him!" Pilate said to them, "Shall I crucify your King?" The chief priests answered, "We have no king but Caesar!" LK And the voices of these men and of the chief priests prevailed.

MT When Pilate saw that he could not prevail at all, but rather *that* a tumult was rising, he took water and washed *his* hands before the multitude, saying, "I am innocent of the blood of this just Person. You see *to it.*" And all the people answered and said, "[aa]His blood *be* on us and on our children." MK So Pilate, wanting to gratify the crowd, LK [bb]gave sentence that it should be as they requested. And he released to them, MK Barabbas, LK the one they requested, who for rebellion and murder had been thrown into prison.

---

[v] NOT CAESAR'S FRIEND. This statement by the Jews was loaded with irony, for the Jews' hatred of Rome certainly indicated they too were no friends of Caesar. But they knew Pilate feared Tiberius Caesar (the Roman emperor at the time of Jesus' crucifixion) since he had a highly suspicious personality and exacted ruthless punishment. Pilate had already created upheaval in Jerusalem by several foolish acts that had infuriated the Jews, so he was under the scrutiny of Rome to see if his ineptness continued. The Jews were intimidating him by threatening another upheaval that could spell the end of his power in Jerusalem if he did not execute Jesus.

[w] THE JUDGMENT SEAT. Pilate broke under pressure and prepared to render judgment on the initial accusation of sedition against Rome. This "judgment seat" was the place Pilate sat to render the official verdict. The seat was placed on an area paved with stones known as the "Pavement." The irony is that Pilate rendered judgment on the One who would one day render a just condemnation of Pilate (John 5:22).

[x] PREPARATION DAY OF THE PASSOVER. This refers to the day of preparation for Passover Week (i.e., Friday of Passover Week).

[y] ABOUT THE SIXTH HOUR. John is here reckoning time by the Roman method of the day beginning at midnight.

[z] "BEHOLD YOUR KING!" That was Pilate's mockery—that such a brutalized and helpless man was a fitting king for them. This mockery continued in the placard on the cross (John 19:19–22).

[aa] HIS BLOOD BE ON US. The Jews in the crowd accepted the blame for the execution of Jesus and did not hold the Romans responsible. Cf. Matt. 21:38–39.

[bb] GAVE SENTENCE. Pilate's response reveals his lack of principle. His desire to please the Jews for political reasons (to save himself from Rome's displeasure) ultimately overcame his desire to set Jesus free (cf. Luke 23:20).

190. Further Mockery from the Roman Soldiers

Matt. 27:26b–30; Mark 15:16–19; John 19:16

MT When [Pilate] had [a]scourged Jesus, he delivered *Him* JN to them MT to be crucified. Then the soldiers of the governor JN took Jesus and led *Him* away MK into the hall called [b]Praetorium, and they called together the [c]whole garrison MT around Him. And they stripped Him and put a [d]scarlet robe on Him. MK And they [e]clothed Him with purple; and MT when they had twisted a crown of thorns, they put *it* on His head, and [f]a reed in His right hand MK and began to salute Him, [g]"Hail, King of the Jews!" MT And they bowed the knee before Him and mocked Him [and] MK worshiped Him. MT Then [h]they spat on Him, and took the reed and [i]struck Him on the head.

---

[a] SCOURGED. This was in addition to the earlier flogging (John 19:1–5). It followed sentencing and constituted the severest form of scourging, known as the *verberatio.* Scourging was a horribly cruel act in which the victim was stripped, tied to a post, and brutally beaten by multiple soldiers. For victims who were not Roman citizens, the preferred instrument was a short wooden handle to which several leather thongs were attached. This whip was known as a *flagellum.* Each leather thong had pieces of bones or metal on the end. The beatings were so vicious that they were sometimes fatal. The body could be torn or lacerated to such an extent that muscles, veins, or bones were exposed. Such flogging often preceded execution in order to weaken and dehumanize the victim (Isa. 53:5).

[b] PRAETORIUM. Pilate's residence in Jerusalem. It was probably located in the Antonia Fortress, adjacent to the northwest corner of the temple. "The soldiers of the governor" were part of a "garrison"—about six hundred soldiers—assigned to serve the governor (Pilate) during his stay in Jerusalem.

[c] WHOLE GARRISON. The Roman cohort, consisting of six hundred men, was stationed in Jerusalem. All the soldiers who were not on duty at that time gathered to heap additional mockery and torment on Jesus.

[d] SCARLET ROBE. Mark 15:17 says "purple," suggesting that the robe may have been something between royal purple and "scarlet," the closest thing they could find to the traditional garb of royalty. The word for "robe" refers to a military cloak undoubtedly belonging to one of the soldiers.

[e] CLOTHED HIM WITH PURPLE . . . CROWN OF THORNS. "Purple" was the color traditionally worn by royalty; the "crown of thorns" was in mockery of a royal crown. The callous soldiers decided to hold a mock coronation of Jesus as king of the Jews.

[f] A REED IN HIS RIGHT HAND. To imitate a royal scepter they purposely chose something flimsy-looking.

[g] "HAIL, KING OF THE JEWS!" The greeting was a parody of that given to Caesar.

[h] THEY SPAT ON HIM. See Isa. 50:6.

[i] STRUCK HIM ON THE HEAD. A reed long enough to make a mock scepter would be firm enough to be extremely painful, about like a broom handle. John 19:3 says they hit him with their fists as well.

191. Jesus' Journey to Golgotha

Matt. 27:31–34; Mark 15:20–23; Luke 23:26–33a; John 19:17

MT And when they had mocked Him, they took MK the purple MT robe off Him, put His *own* clothes on Him, and led Him away [a]to be crucified. JN And He, [b]bearing His cross, went out. MT Now as they came out, they found a man of Cyrene, Simon by name, MK the father of Alexander and Rufus LK who was coming from the country MK and passing by, LK and on him they laid the cross that he might bear *it* after Jesus. And a great multitude of the people followed Him, and women who also mourned and lamented Him. But Jesus, turning to them, said, "[c]Daughters of Jerusalem, do not weep for Me, but weep for yourselves and for your children. For indeed the days are coming in which they will say, '[d]Blessed *are* the barren,

---

[a] TO BE CRUCIFIED. Crucifixion was a form of punishment that had been passed down to the Romans from the Persians, Phoenicians, and Carthaginians. Roman crucifixion was a lingering doom—by design. Roman executioners had perfected the art of slow torture while keeping the victim alive. Some victims even lingered until they were eaten alive by birds of prey or wild beasts. Most hung on the cross for days before dying of exhaustion, dehydration, traumatic fever, or—most likely—suffocation. When the legs would no longer support the weight of the body, the diaphragm was constricted in a way that made breathing impossible. That is why breaking the legs would hasten death (John 19:31–33), but this was unnecessary in Jesus' case. The hands were usually nailed through the wrists, and the feet through the instep or the Achilles tendon (sometimes using one nail for both feet). None of these wounds would be fatal, but their pain would become unbearable as the hours dragged on. The most notable feature of crucifixion was the stigma of disgrace that was attached to it (Gal. 3:13; 5:11; Heb. 12:2). One indignity was the humiliation of carrying one's own cross, which might weigh as much as two hundred pounds. Normally a quaternion, four soldiers, would escort the prisoner through the crowds to the place of crucifixion. A placard bearing the indictment would be hung around the person's neck.

[b] BEARING HIS CROSS. This refers to horizontal bar of the cross. Condemned prisoners were required to carry the heavy crossbeam of their cross to the execution site. Jesus carried His cross as far as the city gate, but exhausted from a sleepless night and severely wounded and weakened by His scourging, Jesus was unable to continue. This is another touching picture of His humanity, beset with all human weaknesses except sin (Heb 4:15). As a result the Roman guards conscripted Simon, apparently at random, to carry Jesus' crossbeam the rest of the way. Simon, from the North African city of Cyrene, was on his way into Jerusalem. The identification of him by Mark as "the father of Alexander and Rufus" (cf. Rom. 16:13) is evidence of Mark's connection with the church at Rome.

[c] DAUGHTERS OF JERUSALEM. There is nothing to suggest that these women were Christ's disciples. They may have been professional mourners, obligatory at Jewish funerals (cf. Matt. 9:23), and probably present at high-profile executions as well.

[d] BLESSED ARE THE BARREN. Under normal circumstances motherhood is viewed as a blessing from God. But Christ warned of a time of judgment that was coming on national Israel, when those who had no children to mourn would be considered blessed.

wombs that never bore, and breasts which never nursed!' Then they will begin '[e]to say to the mountains, "Fall on us!" and to the hills, "Cover us!" ' For if they do these things in the [f]green wood, what will be done in the dry?" There were also two others, criminals, led with Him to be put to death. And when they had come to JN a place called *the* [g]*Place* of a Skull, which is called in Hebrew, Golgotha, MT they gave Him sour [h]wine mingled with gall to drink. But when He had tasted *it,* He would not drink. LK There they crucified Him.

---

[e] TO SAY. Quoted from Hos. 10:8. Cf. Rev. 6:16–17; 9:6.

[f] GREEN WOOD . . . DRY. This was probably a common proverb. Jesus' meaning seems to be this: if the Romans would perpetrate such atrocities on Jesus (the "green wood"—young, strong, and a source of life), what would they do to the Jewish nation (the "dry wood"—old, barren, and ripe for judgment)?

[g] PLACE OF A SKULL. *Golgotha* is an Aramaic word meaning "skull." The site may have been a skull-shaped hill, or it may have been so named because as a place of crucifixion, it accumulated skulls. None of the gospels mention a hill. In the Latin text, Luke 23:33 uses the name *Calvary,* from *calvaria*, "skull." Although the exact site is unknown, today two locations in Jerusalem are considered as possibilities: (1) Gordon's Calvary (named for the man who discovered it in modern times) to the north; and (2) the traditional site to the west at the Church of the Holy Sepulchre, a tradition dating to the fourth century.

[h] WINE MINGLED WITH GALL. "Gall" simply refers to something bitter. Mark 15:23 identifies it as myrrh, a narcotic. The Jews had a custom, based on Prov. 31:6, of administering a pain-deadening medication mixed with wine to victims of crucifixion, in order to deaden the pain. Tasting what it was, Christ, though thirsty, "would not drink," lest it dull His senses before He completed His work. The lessening of physical pain would probably not have diminished the efficacy of His atoning work. But He needed His full mental faculties for the hours yet to come. It was necessary for Him to be awake and fully conscious, for example, to minister to the dying thief (Luke 23:43).

192. The First Three Hours on the Cross

Matt. 27:35–44; Mark 15:24–32; Luke 23:33b–43; John 19:18–27

MT Then they [a]crucified Him, [and] LK Jesus said, "Father, [b]forgive them, for [c]they do not know what they do." MK Now it was the [d]third hour. LK And the people stood looking on.

JN Then the soldiers, when they had crucified Jesus, [e]took His garments and made four parts, to each soldier a part, and also the tunic. Now the tunic was without seam, woven from the top in one piece. They said therefore among themselves, "Let us not tear it, but cast lots for it, whose it shall be." LK And they divided His garments and cast lots MK for them *to determine* what every man should take, JN that the Scripture MT might be fulfilled which was spoken by the prophet:

---

[a] CRUCIFIED HIM. Jesus was forced to lie down while His arms were stretched out and nailed to the horizontal beam that He carried. The beam was raised up and affixed to the vertical post. His feet were then nailed to the vertical beam. Sometimes a small wooden board was added to create a makeshift seat that provided partial support for the victim's weight. The latter, however, was designed to prolong the agony, not alleviate it. Victims were stripped naked, beaten, and then hung outside where they would be exposed to both the mockery of the crowds and the elements of nature. Breathing was only possible by pushing up with the legs and straining the arms. It caused excruciating pain, but it was necessary to avoid asphyxiation.

[b] FORGIVE THEM. i.e., His tormentors, both Jews and Romans (cf. Acts 7:60). Some of the fruit of this prayer can be in the salvation of thousands of people in Jerusalem at Pentecost (Acts 2:41).

[c] THEY DO NOT KNOW WHAT THEY DO. i.e., they were not aware of the full scope of their wickedness. They did not recognize Him as the true Messiah (Acts 13:27–28). They were blind to the light of divine truth, "For if they had understood it, they would not have crucified the Lord of glory" (1 Cor. 2:8). Still, their ignorance certainly did not mean that they deserved forgiveness; rather, their spiritual blindness itself was a manifestation of their guilt (John 3:19). But Christ's prayer while they were in the very act of mocking Him is an expression of the boundless compassion of divine grace.

[d] THIRD HOUR. The crucifixion occurred at 9:00 a.m. based on the Jewish method of reckoning time. John notes that it was "about the sixth hour" when Pilate sentenced Jesus to be crucified (John 19:14). John apparently used the Roman method of reckoning time, which counted the hours from midnight. Thus John's "sixth hour" would have been about 6:00 a.m.

[e] TOOK HIS GARMENTS. This was in fulfillment of Ps. 22:18. Customarily, the clothes of the condemned person became the property of the executioners. The division of the garments suggests that the execution squad consisted of four soldiers (cf. Acts 12:4). The tunic was worn next to the skin. The plural "garments" probably refers to other clothes, including an outer garment, belt, sandals, and head covering.

"[f]They divided My garments among them,
And for My clothing they cast lots."

JN Therefore the soldiers did these things. MT Sitting down, they kept watch over Him there.

JN Now Pilate [g]wrote a title and put *it* on the cross. MT And they put up over His head MK the [h]inscription of MT [i]the accusation written against Him:

THIS IS JN JESUS OF NAZARETH,
[j]THE KING OF THE JEWS.

Then many of the Jews read this title, for the place where Jesus was crucified was near the city; and it was written in Hebrew, Greek, *and* Latin. Therefore the chief priests of the Jews said to Pilate, "Do not write, 'The King of the Jews,' but, 'He said, "I am the King of the Jews." '" Pilate answered, "What I have written, I have written."

MT Then two [k]robbers were crucified with Him, MK one on His right and the

---

[f] They divided My garments. John cites Ps. 22:18. In the psalm, David, beset by physical distress and mockery by his opponents, used the symbolism of the common practice in an execution scene in which the executioner divided the victim's clothes to portray the depth of his trouble. It is notable that David precisely described a form of execution that he had never seen. The passage was typologically prophetic of Jesus, David's heir to the messianic throne.

[g] wrote a title. A placard was often placed around the neck of the victim, listing his crimes, as he was taken to the execution site. The tablet would then be nailed to the victim's cross (cf. Matt. 27:37; Mark 15:26; Luke 23:38). Pilate used this opportunity for mocking revenge on the Jews who had so intimidated him into this execution.

[h] inscription of the accusation. The crime for which a condemned man was executed was written on a wooden board, which was fastened to the cross above his head. Jesus' inscription was written in Latin, Hebrew, and Greek (John 19:20).

[i] the accusation. The fact that the placard was placed "over His head" suggests that this cross was in the familiar shape with an upright protruding above the transom, and not the T-shaped cross that was also sometimes used.

[j] THE KING OF THE JEWS. Since Pilate had repeatedly declared Jesus to be innocent of any crime (Luke 23:4, 14–15, 22), he ordered this inscription written for Him. While Pilate's intent was probably neither to mock or honor Jesus, he certainly intended it as an affront to the Jewish authorities, who had given him so much trouble. When the outraged Jewish leaders demanded the wording be changed, Pilate bluntly refused (see John 19:22). All four gospel writers mentioned the inscription, but each reported a slightly different variation. Both Luke and John (19:20) said that the inscription was written in Greek, Latin, and Hebrew, so the varying reports in the gospels may simply reflect variant ways the inscription was translated on the placard itself. It is even more likely that all four evangelists simply reported the substance of the inscription elliptically, with each one omitting different parts of the full inscription. All four concurred with Mark that the inscription said THE KING OF THE JEWS (Matt. 27:37; Mark 15:26; Luke 23:38; John 19:19). Luke added "THIS IS" at the beginning, and Matthew started with "THIS IS JESUS." John's version began, "JESUS OF NAZARETH." Putting them all together, the full inscription would read "THIS IS JESUS OF NAZARETH, THE KING OF THE JEWS."

[k] robbers. This word denotes a rebel and brigand who plunders as he steals. Mere thieves were not usually crucified, since robbery was not a capital offense under Roman law. These were probably cohorts of Barabbas—e.g., rebels and guerilla fighters.

other on His left, JN and [l]Jesus in the center. MK So the Scripture was fulfilled which says, "And He was numbered with the transgressors." MT And those who passed by blasphemed Him, [m]wagging their heads and saying, MK "Aha! MT You who [n]destroy the temple and build *it* in three days, save Yourself! If You are the Son of God, [o]come down from the cross."

Likewise the chief priests also, mocking MK among themselves MT with the scribes and elders, LK [p]sneered, saying, MT "He saved others; Himself He cannot save; LK let Him save Himself if He is the Christ, the chosen of God. MT If He is the King of Israel, let Him now come down from the cross, MK that we may see [q]and believe MT Him. He trusted in God; let Him deliver Him now if He will have Him; for He said, 'I am the Son of God.'" LK The soldiers also mocked Him, coming and offering Him sour wine, and saying, "If You are the King of the Jews, save Yourself." MT Even [r]the robbers who were crucified with Him reviled Him with the same thing.

LK Then [s]one of the criminals who were hanged blasphemed Him, saying, "If You are the Christ, save Yourself and us." But the other, answering, rebuked him, saying, "Do you not even fear God, seeing you are under the same condemnation? And we indeed justly, for we receive the due reward of our deeds; but [t]this Man

---

[l] Jesus in the center. By placing Jesus' cross between the two robbers, Pilate may have intended to further insult the Jews, implying that their king was nothing but a common criminal. God intended it, however, as a fulfillment of prophecy (cf. Isa. 53:12).

[m] wagging their heads. A gesture of contempt and derision (cf. 2 Kings 19:21; Pss. 22:7; 44:14; 109:25; Jer. 18:16; Lam. 2:15).

[n] destroy the temple and build it in three days. See Matt. 26:61. The passersby repeated the false charge made during Jesus' trial before Caiaphas (Mark 14:58). The charge was a misunderstanding of Jesus' words in John 2:19–21. They had missed His point. "He was speaking of the temple of His body" (John 2:21). He would not "come down from the cross," but it was not because He was powerless to do so (John 10:18). The proof that He was the Son of God came "in three days" (see Matt. 12:40), when He returned with "the temple" (i.e., His body) rebuilt.

[o] come down from the cross. A final demand for a miracle by the unbelieving Jewish authorities (cf. Mark 8:11). Their claim that they would then see and believe was false, since they later refused to believe the even greater miracle of Christ's resurrection.

[p] sneered. Cf. Ps. 22:6–7, 16–18.

[q] and believe Him. Cf. Matt. 12:38; 16:1.

[r] the robbers who were crucified with Him. The two robbers joined in the reviling of Jesus, though one later repented (Luke 23:40–43).

[s] one of the criminals. Matthew 27:44 and Mark 15:32 report that both criminals were mocking Christ along with the crowd. As the hours wore on, however, this criminal's conscience was smitten, and he repented. When the impenitent thief resumed his mocking, this thief rebuked him and refused to participate again.

[t] this Man has done nothing wrong. Cf. Luke 23:4, 15, 22. Even the thief testified of His innocence.

has done nothing wrong." Then he said to Jesus, "[u]Lord, remember me when You come into Your kingdom." And Jesus said to him, "Assuredly, I say to you, today you will be with Me in [v]Paradise."

[JN] Now [w]there stood by the cross of Jesus His mother, and His mother's sister, Mary the *wife* of Clopas, and Mary Magdalene. When Jesus therefore saw His mother, and [x]the disciple whom He loved standing by, He said to His mother, "Woman, behold your son!" Then He said to the disciple, "Behold your mother!" And from that hour that disciple took her to his own *home.*

---

[u] Lord, remember me. The penitent thief's prayer reflected his belief that the soul lives on after death, that Christ had a right to rule over a kingdom of the souls of men, and that He would soon enter that kingdom despite His impending death. His request to be remembered was a plea for mercy, which also reveals that the thief understood he had no hope but divine grace and that the dispensing of that grace lay in Jesus' power. All of this demonstrates true faith on the part of the dying thief, and Christ graciously affirmed the man's salvation.

[v] Paradise. The only other places this word is used in the NT are 2 Cor. 12:4 and Rev. 2:7. The word suggests a garden (it is the word used of Eden in the Septuagint), but in all three NT uses, it speaks of heaven.

[w] there stood by the cross. Although the exact number of women mentioned here is questioned, John probably refers to four women rather than three, i.e., two by name and two without naming them: (1) "His mother" (Mary); (2) "His mother's sister" (probably Salome [Mark 15:40], the sister of Mary and mother of James and John, the sons of Zebedee [Matt. 27:56–57; Mark 15:40]); (3) "Mary the wife of Cleopas" (the mother of James the younger and Joses (Matt. 27:56); and (4) Mary Magdalene ("Magdalene" signifies "Magdala" a village along the west shore of Galilee, north of Tiberias). Mary Magdalene is a prominent figure in the resurrection account (see John 20:1–18; cf. Luke 8:2–3, where Jesus healed her from demon possession).

[x] the disciple whom He loved. This is a reference to John (cf. John 13:23). Jesus, as the first-born son of Mary, did not give the responsibility to His brothers, because they were not sympathetic to His ministry nor did they believe in Him (John 7:3–5) and they likely were not present at the time (i.e., their home was in Capernaum—see John 2:12).

193. The Final Three Hours on the Cross

Matt. 27:45–50; Mark 15:33–37; Luke 23:44–45a; John 19:28–30

MT Now [a]from the sixth hour until the ninth hour, LK the sun was darkened [and] MT there was [b]darkness over all the land. MT And about the ninth hour Jesus cried out with a loud voice, saying, "[c]Eli, Eli, lama sabachthani?" MK which is translated, "My God, My God, [d]why have You forsaken Me?" MT Some of those who stood there, when they heard *that,* said, MK "Look, MT this Man is calling for Elijah!"

JN After this, Jesus, knowing that all things were now accomplished, that the Scripture might be fulfilled, said, "I thirst!" Now a vessel full of sour wine was sitting there. MT Immediately one of them ran and took a sponge, filled *it* with [e]sour wine and put *it* on a reed [of] JN hyssop, and put *it* to His mouth MT and offered it to Him to drink. The rest said, "Let Him alone; let us see if [f]Elijah will come to save Him [and] MK take Him down." JN So when Jesus had received the sour wine, He said, [g]"It is finished!"

LK And when Jesus had [h]cried out with a loud voice, He said, "Father, '[i]into

---

[a] FROM THE SIXTH HOUR UNTIL THE NINTH HOUR. From noon until 3:00 p.m. The crucifixion began at 9:00 a.m. The sixth hour marked the halfway point of Jesus' six hours on the cross.

[b] DARKNESS. A mark of divine judgment (cf. Isa. 5:30; 13:10–11; Joel 2:1–2; Amos 5:20; Zeph. 1:14–15; Matt. 8:12; 22:13; 25:30). The geographical extent of the darkness is not known, although the writings of the church fathers hint that it extended beyond Israel. This could not have been caused by an eclipse, because the Jews used a lunar calendar, and Passover always fell on the full moon, making a solar eclipse out of the question. This was a supernatural darkness.

[c] ELI, ELI, LAMA SABACHTHANI. "Eli" is Hebrew; the rest Aramaic. (Mark 15:34 gives the entire wail in Aramaic.) This cry is a fulfillment of Psalm 22:1, one of many striking parallels between that psalm and the specific events of the crucifixion. Christ at that moment was experiencing the abandonment and despair that resulted from the outpouring of divine wrath on Him as sin-bearer (cf. Matt. 26:39).

[d] WHY HAVE YOU FORSAKEN ME? Jesus felt keenly His abandonment by the Father, resulting from God's wrath being poured out on Him as the substitute for sinners (cf. 2 Cor. 5:21).

[e] SOUR WINE. The drink here is not the same as the "wine mixed with myrrh" offered to Him as He marched to the cross (Matt. 27:34), which was intended to lessen the pain. The purpose of this cheap, sour wine (cf. Mark 15:36) was to prolong life and increase the torture. The term harkens back to Ps. 69:21 where the same word is found in the Septuagint. Hyssop is a little plant that is ideal for sprinkling (see Ex. 12:22).

[f] ELIJAH. Further mockery which in effect meant, "Let the forerunner come and save this so-called Messiah" (cf. Luke 1:17).

[g] "IT IS FINISHED!" The verb here carries the idea of fulfilling one's mission and religious obligations (see John 17:4). The entire work of redemption had been brought to completion. The single Greek word here (translated "it is finished") has been found in the papyri being placed on receipts for taxes meaning "paid in full" (see Col. 3:13, 14).

Your hands I commit My spirit.' " Having said this, JN and bowing His head, LK He breathed His last MT and [j]yielded up His spirit.

[h] CRIED OUT WITH A LOUD VOICE. Demonstrating amazing strength in light of the intense suffering He had endured, His shout reveals that His life did not slowly ebb away, but that He voluntarily gave it up (John 10:17–18).

[i] INTO YOUR HANDS. This quotes Ps. 31:5, and the manner of His death accords with John 10:18. Normally, victims of crucifixion died much slower deaths. He, being in control, simply yielded up His soul (John 10:18; 19:30), committing it to God. Thus He "offered Himself without spot to God" (Heb. 9:14).

[j] YIELDED UP HIS SPIRIT. A voluntary act. The sentence signaled that Jesus "handed over" His spirit as an act of His will. No one took His life from Him, for He voluntarily and willingly gave it up (see John 10:17–18).

194. Witnesses to Jesus' Death

Matt. 27:51–56; Mark 15:38–41; Luke 23:45b, 47–49

MT Then, behold, [a]the veil of the temple was torn in two from top to bottom; and the earth quaked, and the rocks were split, and the graves were opened; and many [b]bodies of the saints who had fallen asleep were raised; and coming out of the graves after His resurrection, they went into the holy city and appeared to many.

So when [c]the centurion, MK who stood opposite Him, MT and [d]those with him, who were guarding Jesus, MK [e]saw that He cried out like this and breathed His last, [and] MT saw the earthquake and the things that had happened, they feared greatly [and] LK glorified God, saying, MK "Truly this Man was the Son of God!" [and] LK "Certainly this was a righteous Man!" And the whole crowd who came together to that sight, seeing what had been done, [f]beat their breasts and returned.

---

[a] THE VEIL OF THE TEMPLE. i.e., the massive curtain separating the Holy of Holies from the rest of the sanctuary (Ex. 26:31–33; 40:20–21; Lev. 16:2; Heb. 9:3). The tearing of the veil signified that the way into God's presence was now open to all through a new and living way (Heb. 10:19–22). The fact that it tore "from top to bottom" showed that no man had split the veil. God did it.

[b] BODIES OF THE SAINTS . . . WERE RAISED. Matthew alone mentions this miracle. Nothing more is said about these people, which would be unlikely if they remained on earth for long. Evidently, these people were given glorified bodies; they appeared "to many," enough to establish the reality of the miracle; and then they no doubt ascended to glory—a kind of foretaste of 1 Thess. 4:16.

[c] THE CENTURION. The Roman officer in charge of the crucifixion. Centurions, considered the backbone of the Roman army, commanded one hundred soldiers.

[d] THOSE WITH HIM. These were probably men under his charge. Mark 15:39 says the centurion was the one who uttered the words of confession, but he evidently spoke for his men as well. Their "fear" speaks of an awareness of their sin, and the word "truly" suggests a certainty and conviction that bespeaks genuine faith. These men represent an answer to Jesus' prayer in Luke 23:34. Their response contrasts sharply with the mocking taunts of Matt. 27:39–44.

[e] SAW THAT HE CRIED OUT LIKE THIS. The centurion had seen many crucified victims die, but none like Jesus. The strength He possessed at His death, as evidenced by His loud cry, was unheard of for a victim of crucifixion. That, coupled with the earthquake that coincided with Christ's death (Matt. 27:51–54) convinced the centurion that Jesus "truly . . . was the Son of God." According to tradition this man actually became a believer.

[f] BEAT THEIR BREASTS. Only Luke records this expression of remorse and anguish (cf. Luke 18:13).

But all His acquaintances, MT and [g]many [h]women who followed Jesus from Galilee, ministering to Him, LK stood at a distance, watching these things. MT Among [them] were [i]Mary Magdalene, [j]Mary the mother of MK James the Less and of Joses, and [k]Salome, MT the mother of Zebedee's sons, MK who also followed Him and ministered to Him when He was in Galilee, and [l]many other women who came up with Him to Jerusalem.

---

[g] MANY WOMEN. Some of these women had earlier been at the foot of the cross (John 19:25–27). By then, unable to watch Jesus' suffering at such close range, they were "looking on from afar." Their sympathetic loyalty was in sharp contrast to the disciples who, except for John, were nowhere to be found.

[h] WOMEN . . . FROM GALILEE. Matthew 27:56 and Mark 15:40–41 report that this included Mary Magdalene; Mary, mother of James (the less) and Joses; Salome, mother of James and John, and many others. The same women were present at His burial (Matt. 27:61; Mark 15:47; Luke 23:55) and His resurrection (Matt. 28:1; Mark 16:1; Luke 24:1)—so they were eyewitnesses to all the crucial events of the gospel (cf. 1 Cor. 15:3–4).

[i] MARY MAGDALENE. She was from the village of Magdala, on the western shore of the Sea of Galilee, hence her name. Luke notes that Jesus had cast seven demons out of her (Luke 8:2). She is usually named first when the women who followed Jesus are listed, which may suggest that she was their leader.

[j] MARY THE MOTHER OF JAMES THE LESS AND OF JOSES. The other "Mary" ("wife of Clopas," John 19:25—a variant of Alphaeus) was distinguished from the other Marys by the name of her sons. "James the Less" (called "James the son of Alphaeus" in Matt. 10:2) was one of the twelve.

[k] SALOME, THE MOTHER OF ZEBEDEE'S SONS. Salome (Mark 15:40), mother of James and John. From John 19:26 we learn that Mary, the mother of Jesus, was also present at the cross—possibly standing apart from these three, who were "looking on from afar," as if they could not bear to watch His sufferings, but neither could they bear to leave Him.

[l] MANY OTHER WOMEN. They had been with Jesus since the days of His Galilean ministry, traveling with Him and the disciples, caring for their needs (cf. Luke 8:2–3).

195. Jesus' Body Removed from the Cross

Matt. 27:57–58; Mark 15:42–45; Luke 23:50–52; John 19:31–38

JN Therefore, MK when evening had come, because it was the [a]Preparation Day, that is, the day before the Sabbath, JN [in order] that the bodies [b]should not remain on the cross on the Sabbath (for that Sabbath was a high day), the Jews asked Pilate that [c]their legs might be broken, and *that* they might be taken away. Then the soldiers came and broke the legs of the first and of the other who was crucified with Him.

But when they came to Jesus and saw that He was already dead, they did not break His legs. But one of the soldiers [d]pierced His side with a spear, and immediately blood and water came out. And [e]he who has seen has testified, and his testimony is true; and he knows that he is telling the truth, so that you may believe. For these things were done that the Scripture should be fulfilled, "[f]Not *one* of His bones shall be broken." And again another Scripture says, "[g]They shall look on Him whom they pierced."

---

[a] PREPARATION DAY. Friday, the day before the Sabbath (Saturday).

[b] SHOULD NOT REMAIN ON THE CROSS ON THE SABBATH. Though the Romans had no problem leaving crucified victims hanging on crosses long after they died (allowing their corpses to rot or be eaten by birds), the Jewish leaders insisted that Jesus' body be taken down. The Mosaic Law stipulated that a person hanged on a tree should not remain there overnight (Deut. 21:22–23). They would have been especially wary of this in light of the Passover celebration.

[c] THEIR LEGS MIGHT BE BROKEN. In order to hasten death for certain reasons, soldiers would break the legs of the victim with an iron mallet. Doing so inhibited the dying man's ability to push up with his legs in order to breathe. Death by asphyxiation soon followed.

[d] PIERCED HIS SIDE WITH A SPEAR. The soldier's stabbing of Jesus' side caused significant penetration indicated by the sudden flow of blood and water. Either the spear pierced Jesus' heart, or the chest cavity was pierced at the bottom. In either event John mentioned the outflow of "blood and water" to emphasize that Jesus was unquestionably dead.

[e] HE WHO HAS SEEN. This has reference to John the apostle who was an eyewitness of these events (John 13:23; 19:26; 20:2; 21:7, 20; cf. 1 John 1:1–4).

[f] NOT ONE OF HIS BONES. John quoted from either Ex. 12:46 or Num. 9:12, since both stipulate that the bones of the Passover lamb must not be broken. Since the NT portrays Jesus as the Passover Lamb that takes away the sins of the world (John 1:29; cf. 1 Cor. 5:7; 1 Peter 1:19), these verses have special typologically prophetic significance for Him.

[g] THEY SHALL LOOK ON HIM. This quote comes from Zech. 12:10. The anguish and contrition of the Jews in the Zechariah passage, because of their wounding of God's Shepherd, is typologically prophetic of the time of the coming of the Son of God, Messiah, when at His return, Israel shall mourn for the rejection and killing of their King (cf. Rev. 1:7).

After this, LK behold, *there was* a man named [h]Joseph, MT a rich man from [i]Arimathea, LK a city of the Jews, [and] MK a prominent council member, who was himself [j]waiting for the kingdom of God; LK a good and just man [and] JN a disciple of Jesus, but secretly, for fear of the Jews. LK He had not consented to their decision and deed.

MK [k]Coming and taking courage, MT this man went to Pilate and [l]asked JN that he might take away the body of Jesus. MK [m]Pilate marveled that He was already dead; and summoning the centurion, he asked him if He had been dead for some time. So when he found out from the centurion, JN Pilate gave *him* permission [and] MT [n]commanded the body to be given to MK Joseph. JN So he came and took the body of Jesus.

---

[h] JOSEPH. This man appears in all four gospels, only in connection with Jesus' burial. The Synoptics relate that he was a member of the Sanhedrin (Mark. 15:43), he was rich (Matt. 27:57), and he was looking for the kingdom of God (Luke 23:51). Though part of the Sanhedrin, Luke says "he had not consented to their decision and deed" in condemning Christ. John treated the idea of secret disciples negatively (see 12:42–43), but since Joseph publicly risked his reputation and even his life in asking for the body of Jesus, John pictured him in a more positive light. Joseph and Nicodemus (John 19:39), both being prominent Jewish leaders, buried Christ in Joseph's own "new tomb," thus fulfilling exactly the prophecy of Isa. 53:9.

[i] ARIMATHEA. Known in the OT as Ramah, or Ramathaim-zophim (the birthplace of Samuel, 1 Sam. 1:1, 19; 2:11), this town was located about fifteen-to-twenty miles northwest of Jerusalem.

[j] WAITING FOR THE KINGDOM OF GOD. i.e., he believed Jesus' claims. John 19:38 refers to him as a secret disciple.

[k] COMING AND TAKING COURAGE. Pilate would not likely have been pleased to see a member of the Sanhedrin, after that group had forced him to crucify an innocent man. Further, Joseph's public identification with Jesus would enrage the other members of the Sanhedrin.

[l] ASKED THAT HE MIGHT TAKE AWAY THE BODY OF JESUS. Though prisoners sentenced to death forfeited the right to burial under Roman law, their bodies were usually granted to relatives who asked for them, but Jesus' mother was emotionally exhausted from the ordeal. There is no evidence that His brothers and sisters were in Jerusalem, and His closest friends, the disciples, had fled (except for John, who had Mary to take care of; John 19:26–27). In the absence of those closest to Jesus, Joseph courageously asked Pilate for Jesus' body.

[m] PILATE MARVELED. Victims of crucifixion often lingered for days, hence Pilate's surprise that Jesus was dead after only six hours. Before granting Jesus' body to Joseph, Pilate checked with the centurion in charge of the crucifixion to verify that Jesus was really dead.

[n] COMMANDED THE BODY TO BE GIVEN TO JOSEPH. Having received confirmation from the centurion that Jesus was dead, Pilate granted Jesus' body to Joseph. By that act the Romans officially pronounced Jesus dead.

196. Jesus' Body Is Placed in the Tomb

Matt. 27:59–66; Mark 15:46–47; Luke 23:53–56; John 19:39–42

MK Then MT Joseph MK bought fine linen [and] took Him down. JN And Nicodemus, who at first came to Jesus by night, also came, bringing a mixture of myrrh and aloes, [a]about a hundred pounds. Then they took the body of Jesus, and MT [b]wrapped JN it in [c]strips of MT clean linen cloth JN with the spices, as the custom of the Jews is to bury.

Now in the place where He was crucified there was a garden, and in the [d]garden a new tomb. MK And [Joseph] laid Him in MT his new [e]tomb which he had hewn out of the rock, JN in which no one had yet been laid LK before. MT And he rolled a large stone against the door of the tomb, and departed. JN There they laid Jesus, because of the Jews' [f]Preparation *Day,* for the tomb was nearby, LK and the Sabbath drew near.

---

[a] ABOUT A HUNDRED POUNDS. An inaccurate understanding of the term used in the original, this mixture of spices weighed closer to sixty-five pounds. Myrrh was a very fragrant gummy resin, which the Jews turned into a powdered form and mixed with aloes, a powder from the aromatic sandalwood. The Jews did not embalm but did this procedure to suppress the odor of decay (cf. John 11:39).

[b] WRAPPED IT IN . . . LINEN. The Jews did not embalm corpses, but wrapped them in perfumed burial cloths (cf. Mark 16:1). Nicodemus, another prominent member of the Sanhedrin (cf. John 7:50), assisted Joseph in caring for the body of Jesus (John 19:39–40). These men, who had kept their allegiance to Jesus secret during His lifetime, then came forward publicly to bury Him, while the disciples, who had openly followed Jesus, hid (John 20:19).

[c] STRIPS . . . SPICES. The spices most likely were spread along the full length of the cloth strips, which were then wrapped around Jesus' body. Additional spices were placed underneath the body and set around it. The sticky resin would help the cloth adhere.

[d] GARDEN . . . NEW TOMB. Only John relates that the tomb was near the place where Jesus was crucified. Since the Sabbath, when no more work was allowed, was nearly upon them (6:00 p.m., sunset), the close proximity of the tomb was helpful.

[e] TOMB . . . HEWN OUT OF THE ROCK. This "tomb" was located near Golgotha (John 19:42). Matthew adds that it was Joseph's own (Matt. 27:60), while Luke and John note that no one as yet had been buried in it (Luke 23:53; John 19:41). Joseph, a wealthy man, undoubtedly had the tomb built for his own family. It had remained unused. Christ's burial there was a wonderful fulfillment of Isa. 53:9.

[f] PREPARATION DAY. This was on Friday, the day before the Sabbath.

And the women who had come with Him from Galilee followed after, and they [g]observed the tomb and how His body was laid. MT Mary Magdalene was there, and the other Mary, sitting opposite the tomb. MK [So] Mary Magdalene and Mary *the mother* of Joses observed where He was laid. LK Then they returned and prepared spices and fragrant oils. And they rested on the Sabbath according to the commandment.

MT On [h]the next day, which followed the Day of Preparation, the chief priests and Pharisees gathered together to Pilate, saying, "Sir, we remember, while He was still alive, how that deceiver said, 'After three days I will rise.' Therefore command that the tomb be made secure until the third day, lest His disciples come by night and steal Him *away,* and say to the people, 'He has risen from the dead.' So the last deception will be worse than the first."

Pilate said to them, "You have a guard; go your way, make *it* as secure as you know how." So they went and made the tomb secure, sealing the stone and setting the guard.

---

[g] observed ... how His body was laid. According to John 19:39 Nicodemus brought a hundred pounds of spices and aloes (probably obtained while Joseph was negotiating with Pilate for Jesus' body), and he and Joseph wrapped the body with linen and the spices. These women, from Galilee, were probably unfamiliar with Joseph and Nicodemus, who were Judeans. After all, both men were associated with the Jewish leaders who orchestrated the conspiracy against Jesus (Luke 23:50; John 3:1). So the women were determined to prepare Jesus' body for burial themselves. So they returned (i.e., went to their homes) to prepare their own spices and perfumes (Luke 23:56). They had to have Jesus' body placed in the tomb before sunset, when the Sabbath began, so they were not able to finish preparing the body. Mark 16:1 says they purchased more spices "when the Sabbath was past," i.e., after sundown Saturday. Then they returned Sunday morning with the spices (Luke 24:1), expecting to finish the task that had been interrupted by the Sabbath.

[h] the next day. The Sabbath.

197. On Sunday Morning, the Tomb Is Empty

Matt. 28:1–8; Mark 16:1–8; Luke 24:1–8; John 20:1–2

MK Now when the [a]Sabbath was past, JN [on] the [b]first *day* of the week, MK [c]Mary Magdalene, Mary *the mother* of James, and Salome bought [d]spices, that they might come and [e]anoint Him.

MT And behold, there was [f]a great earthquake; for an angel of the Lord descended from heaven, and came and rolled back the stone from the door, and sat on it. His countenance was like lightning, and his clothing as white as snow. And the guards shook for fear of him, and [g]became like dead *men*.

JN [h]Mary Magdalene went to the tomb early, while it was still dark, and saw *that* the stone had been taken away from the tomb. Then she ran and came to Si-

---

[a] SABBATH WAS PAST. The Sabbath officially ended at sundown on Saturday, after which the women were able to purchase spices.

[b] FIRST DAY OF THE WEEK. A reference to Sunday. From then on, believers set aside Sunday to meet and remember the marvelous resurrection of the Lord (see Acts 20:7; 1 Cor. 16:2). It became known as the Lord's Day (Rev. 1:10).

[c] MARY MAGDALENE, MARY THE MOTHER OF JAMES, AND SALOME. Luke implies that Joanna and other women were also there (Luke 24:10; cf. 15:41).

[d] SPICES. The women bought more spices in addition to those prepared earlier (cf. Luke 23:56; John 19:39–40).

[e] ANOINT. Unlike the Egyptians, the Jewish people did not embalm their dead. Anointing was an act of love, to offset the stench of a decaying body. That the women came to anoint Jesus' body on the third day after His burial showed that they, like the disciples, were not expecting Him to rise from the dead (cf. Mark 8:31; 9:31; 10:34).

[f] A GREAT EARTHQUAKE. The second earthquake associated with Christ's death (Matt. 27:51). This one may have been confined to the immediate area around the grave, when "an angel" supernaturally "rolled back the stone from the door"—not to let Jesus out, for if He could rise from the dead, He would need no help escaping an earthly tomb, but to let the women and the apostles in.

[g] BECAME LIKE DEAD MEN. This suggests that they were not merely paralyzed with fear, but completely unconscious, totally traumatized by what they had seen. The word translated "shook" has the same root as the word for "earthquake" in Matt. 27:2. The sudden appearance of this angel was their first clue that anything extraordinary was happening.

[h] MARY MAGDALENE WENT TO THE TOMB EARLY, WHILE IT WAS STILL DARK. Mary went to the tomb first, before the other women. Perhaps the reason why Jesus first appeared to Mary Magdalene was to demonstrate grace by His personal, loving faithfulness to someone who formerly had a sordid past, but clearly also because she loved Him so dearly and deeply, that she appeared before anyone else at the tomb. Her purpose in coming was to finish the preparation of Jesus' body for burial by bringing more spices to anoint the corpse (Luke 24:1).

mon Peter, and to the [i]other disciple, whom Jesus loved, and said to them, [j]"They have taken away the Lord out of the tomb, and we do not know where they have laid Him."

MT [k]As [light] began to dawn, MK very early in the morning, MT the other Mary MK and Salome LK and certain *other women* with them, MT came to see the tomb, LK [l]bringing the spices which they had prepared. MK They came to the tomb [m]when the sun had risen. And they said among themselves, "[n]Who will roll away the stone from the door of the tomb for us?" But when they looked up, they saw that [o]the stone had been rolled away JN from the tomb—MK for it was very large.

LK Then they went in and, MK [p]entering the tomb, LK did not find the body of the Lord Jesus. And it happened, as they were greatly perplexed about this, that behold, [q]two men stood by them in shining garments. MK They were alarmed [and] LK afraid and bowed *their* faces to the earth.

MT But [one of] the angel[s]—MK a [r]young man clothed in a long white robe sitting on the right side—MT answered and said to the women, "Do not be afraid, for

---

[i] OTHER DISCIPLE, WHOM JESUS LOVED. This is the author of the fourth gospel, John.

[j] THEY HAVE TAKEN. Though Jesus had predicted His resurrection numerous times, it was more than she could believe at that point. It would take His showing Himself alive to them by many "infallible proofs" (Acts 1:3) for them to believe.

[k] AS LIGHT BEGAN TO DAWN. Sabbath officially ended with sundown on Saturday. At that time the women could purchase and prepare spices (Luke 24:1). The event described here occurred the next morning, at dawn on Sunday, the first day of the week.

[l] BRINGING THE SPICES. The women were not expecting to find Jesus risen from the dead; their only plan was to finish anointing His body for burial.

[m] WHEN THE SUN HAD RISEN. John 20:1 says that Mary Magdalene arrived at the tomb while it was still dark. Apparently, she had gone ahead of the other women, which explains why she alone left to find Peter and John.

[n] WHO WILL ROLL AWAY THE STONE. Only Mark records this discussion on the way to the tomb. The women realized they had no men with them to move the heavy stone away from the entrance to the tomb. Since they had last visited the tomb on Friday evening, they did not know it had been sealed and a guard posted, which took place on Saturday (Matt. 27:62–66). The Roman guards fainted with fear. Mark, Luke, and John make no mention of the guards, so it appears they fled when they awoke to find the empty tomb. The women must have arrived shortly after.

[o] THE STONE HAD BEEN ROLLED AWAY. This was not to let Jesus out, but to let the witnesses in. The earthquake when the angel rolled away the stone (Matt. 28:2) may have affected only the area around the tomb, since the women apparently did not feel it.

[p] ENTERING THE TOMB. The outer chamber, separated from the burial chamber by a small doorway.

[q] TWO MEN. These men were angels.

[r] YOUNG MAN CLOTHED IN A LONG WHITE ROBE. The angel, having rolled away the stone (Matt. 28:2), had then entered the burial chamber. Luke records that there were two angels in the tomb; Matthew and Mark focus on the one who spoke.

I know that you seek [s]Jesus MK of Nazareth MT who was crucified. LK Why do you seek the living among the dead? MT He is not here; for [t]He is risen, as He said. Come, see the place where MK they laid MT the Lord. MK But MT go quickly and MK tell His disciples—[u]and Peter—that MT He is risen from the dead, and indeed [v]He is going before you into Galilee; [w]there you will see Him, MK as He said to you. MT Behold, I have told you."

LK They said to them [further], "Remember how He spoke to you when He was still in Galilee, saying, 'The Son of Man must be delivered into the hands of sinful men, and be crucified, and the third day rise again.'" And they remembered His words.

MK So they went out quickly and fled from the tomb, for they trembled MT with fear and great joy, MK and were amazed. And they said nothing to anyone, for they were [x]afraid, MT [but] ran to bring His disciples word.

---

[s] Jesus of Nazareth who was crucified. Better, "the Nazarene" (cf. Matt. 2:23). The inspired account leaves no doubt about who had been in the tomb. The idea of some unbelievers that the women went to the wrong tomb is ludicrous.

[t] He is risen! Christ's resurrection is one of the central truths of the Christian faith (1 Cor. 15:4) and the only plausible explanation for the empty tomb. Even the Jewish leaders did not deny the reality of the empty tomb, but concocted the story that the disciples had stolen Jesus' body (Matt. 28:11–15). The idea that the fearful (John 19:19), doubting (Luke 24:10–11) disciples somehow overpowered the Roman guard detachment and stole Jesus' body is absurd. That they did it while the guards were asleep is even more preposterous. Surely, in moving the heavy stone from the mouth of the tomb, the disciples would have awakened at least one of the soldiers. And in any case, how could the guards have known what happened while they were asleep? Many other theories have been sinfully invented over the centuries to explain away the empty tomb, all of them equally futile.

[u] and Peter. Peter was not singled out as the leader of the disciples, but to be reassured that, despite his denials of Christ, he was still one of them.

[v] He is going before you into Galilee . . . as He said. The disciples' lack of faith made them slow to act on these words; they did not leave for Galilee (Matt. 28:7, 16) until after Jesus repeatedly appeared to them in Jerusalem (cf. Luke 24:13–32; John 20:19–31).

[w] there you will see Him. Cf. Matt. 26:32; John 21:1–14. This does not mean they would not see Him until then. He was seen by the apostles several times before they saw Him in Galilee (Luke 24:15, 34–36; John 20:19, 26). But His supreme post-resurrection appearance was in Galilee, where "He was seen by over five hundred brethren at once" (1 Cor. 15:6).

[x] afraid. They were overwhelmed by the frightening appearance of the angel and the awesome mystery of the resurrection.

198. Peter and John See the Empty Tomb

Luke 24:12; John 20:3–10

[After hearing from Mary Magdalene,] JN Peter therefore LK arose and JN went out, and the other disciple, and were going to the tomb.

So they both ran together, and the other disciple [a]outran Peter and came to the tomb first. And he, stooping down and looking in, saw the [b]linen cloths lying *there;* yet he did not go in. Then Simon Peter came, following him, and went into the tomb; and he saw the linen cloths lying *there* LK by themselves, JN and the handkerchief that had been around His head, not lying with the linen cloths, but [c]folded together in a place by itself.

Then [d]the other disciple, who came to the tomb first, went in also; and he saw and believed. For as yet they [e]did not know the Scripture, that He must rise again from the dead. Then the disciples LK departed [and] JN went away again to their own homes, LK marveling to [themselves] at what had happened.

---

[a] OUTRAN PETER. John ran with Peter, but reached the tomb first.

[b] LINEN CLOTHS. i.e., the empty shell of wrappings that had contained the body. A contrast existed between the resurrection of Lazarus (John 11:44) and that of Jesus. While Lazarus came forth from the grave wearing his grave clothes, Jesus' body, though physical and material, was glorified and was now able to pass through the grave clothes much in the same way that He later appeared in the locked room (cf. Phil. 3:21).

[c] FOLDED TOGETHER. The state of those items indicates no struggle, no hurried unwrapping of the body by grave robbers, who wouldn't unwrap the body anyway, since transporting it elsewhere would be easier and more pleasant if it was left in its wrapped and spiced condition. All appearances indicated that no one had taken the body, but that it had moved through the cloth and left it behind in the tomb.

[d] THE OTHER DISCIPLE. John saw the grave clothes and was convinced by them that He had risen.

[e] DID NOT KNOW THE SCRIPTURE. Neither Peter nor John understood that Scripture said Jesus would rise (Ps. 16:10). This is evident by the reports of Luke (24:25–27, 32, 44–47). Jesus had foretold His resurrection (Matt. 16:21; Mark 8:31; 9:31; Luke 9:22; John 2:17), but they would not accept it (Matt. 16:22; Luke 9:44–45). By the time John wrote this gospel, the church had developed an understanding of the OT prediction of Messiah's resurrection (cf. "as yet").

199. Jesus Appears to Mary Magdalene

John 20:11–18; [Mark 16:9–11]

JN Mary stood outside by the tomb [a]weeping, and as she wept she stooped down *and looked* into the tomb. And she saw [b]two angels in white sitting, one at the head and the other at the feet, where the body of Jesus had lain. Then they said to her, "Woman, why are you weeping?" She said to them, "Because they have taken away my Lord, and I do not know where they have laid Him."

Now when she had said this, she turned around and saw Jesus standing *there*, and [c]did not know that it was Jesus. Jesus said to her, "Woman, why are you weeping? Whom are you seeking?" She, supposing Him to be the gardener, said to Him, "Sir, if You have carried Him away, tell me where You have laid Him, and I will take Him away."

Jesus said to her, [d]"Mary!" She turned and said to Him, "Rabboni!" (which is to say, Teacher). Jesus said to her, [e]"Do not cling to Me, for I have not yet ascended to My Father; but go to [f]My brethren and say to them, 'I am ascending to My Father and

[a] WEEPING. Mary's grief may have driven her back to the tomb. She apparently had not crossed paths with Peter or John, after they visited the tomb, and thus did not know of Jesus' resurrection.

[b] TWO ANGELS. Luke (24:4) describes both. Matthew (28:2–3) and Mark (16:5) report only one. John's reason for the mention of angels is to demonstrate that no grave robbers took the body. This was an operation of the power of God.

[c] DID NOT KNOW THAT IT WAS JESUS. The reason for Mary's failure to recognize Jesus is uncertain. She may not have recognized Him because her tears blurred her eyes. Possibly also, the vivid memories of Jesus' bruised and broken body were still etched in her mind, and Jesus' resurrection appearance was so dramatically different that she failed to recognize Him. Perhaps, however, like the disciples on the road to Emmaus, she was supernaturally prevented from recognizing Him until He chose for her to do so (see Luke 24:16).

[d] "MARY!" Whatever the reason for her failure to recognize Jesus, the moment He spoke the single word, "Mary," she immediately recognized Him. This is reminiscent of Jesus' words "My sheep hear My voice, and I know them, and they follow Me" (John 10:27; cf. 10:3–4).

[e] DO NOT CLING TO ME, FOR I HAVE NOT YET ASCENDED. Mary was expressing a desire to hold on to His physical presence for fear that she would once again lose Him. Jesus' reference to His ascension signifies that He would only be temporarily with them and though she desperately wanted Him to stay, He could not. Jesus was with them only for forty more days and then He ascended (Acts 1:3–11). After He went to the Father, He sent the Holy Spirit ("The Helper") so that they would not feel abandoned (cf. John 14:18–19).

[f] MY BRETHREN. Disciples have been called "servants" or "friends" (John 15:15), but not "brothers," until here. Because of Jesus' work on the cross in place of the sinner, this new relationship to Christ was made possible (Rom. 8:14–17; Gal. 3:26–27; Eph. 1:5; Heb. 2:10–13).

your Father, and *to* My God and your God.'" Mary Magdalene came and told the disciples that she had seen the Lord, and *that* He had spoken these things to her.

[MK [g]Now when *He* rose early on the first *day* of the week, He appeared first to Mary Magdalene, out of whom He had cast seven demons. She went and told those who had been with Him, as they mourned and wept. And when they heard that He was alive and had been seen by her, they did not believe.]

[g] Now when He rose. The external evidence strongly suggests these verses (Mark 16:9–20) were not originally part of Mark's gospel. (Hence they are placed in brackets, at the end of the section.) While the majority of Greek manuscripts contain these verses, the earliest and most reliable do not. A shorter ending also existed, but it is not included in the text. Further, some that include the passage note that it was missing from older Greek manuscripts, while others have scribal marks indicating the passage was considered spurious. The fourth-century church fathers Eusebius and Jerome noted that almost all Greek manuscripts available to them lacked vv. 9–20. The internal evidence from this passage also weighs heavily against Mark's authorship. The transition between 16:8 and 16:9 is abrupt and awkward. The Greek particle translated "now" that begins v. 9 implies continuity with the preceding narrative. What follows, however, does not continue the story of the women referred to in v. 8, but describes Christ's appearance to Mary Magdalene (cf. John 20:11–18). The masculine participle in v. 9 expects "he" as its antecedent, yet the subject of v. 8 is the women. Although she had just been mentioned three times (v. 1; 15:40, 47), v. 9 introduces Mary Magdalene as if for the first time. Further, if Mark wrote v. 9, it is strange that he would only now note that Jesus had cast seven demons out of her. The angel spoke of Jesus' appearing to His followers in Galilee, yet the appearances described in vv. 9–20 are all in the Jerusalem area. Finally, the presence in these verses of a significant number of Greek words used nowhere else in Mark argues that Mark did not write them. Verses 9–20 represent an early (they were known to the second-century fathers Irenaeus, Tatian, and, possibly, Justin Martyr) attempt to complete Mark's gospel. While for the most part summarizing truths taught elsewhere in Scripture, vv. 9–20 should always be compared with the rest of Scripture, and no doctrines should be formulated based solely on them. Since, in spite of all these considerations of the likely unreliability of this section, it is possible to be wrong on the issue, it is good to consider the meaning of this passage and leave it in the text, just as with John 7:53–8:11.

200. Jesus Appears to the Other Women

Matt. 28:9–10; Luke 24:9–11

MT As [the other women] LK returned from the tomb and MT went to tell His disciples, behold, Jesus met them, saying, "Rejoice!" So they came and held Him by the feet and worshiped Him. Then Jesus said to them, "Do not be afraid. Go *and* tell [a]My brethren to go to Galilee, and there they will see Me."

LK Then they [went] and told all these things to [b]the eleven and to all the rest. It was [c]Mary Magdalene, [d]Joanna, [e]Mary *the mother* of James, and [f]the other *women* with them, who told these things to the apostles. And their words seemed to them like [g]idle tales, and they did not believe them.

---

[a] My brethren. i.e., the disciples.

[b] the eleven. This is a general reference to the apostles and would likely have excluded Peter and John who had already heard the news from Mary Magdalene earlier that morning.

[c] Mary Magdalene. Cf. Luke 8:2. She was the first to see Jesus alive (Mark 16:9; John 20:11–18). After her individual encounter with Jesus, Mary met up with the other women in order to tell the disciples what had happened.

[d] Joanna. Her husband was Herod's steward. Cf. Luke 8:3.

[e] Mary the mother of James. See Matt. 27:56.

[f] the other women. They are never explicitly identified (cf. Luke 23:49, 55).

[g] idle tales. i.e., nonsense. At this point the disciples found it impossible to believe what the women told them. Soon, however, the risen Christ would appear to them and dispel their doubts.

201. The Soldiers Report to the Jewish Authorities

Matt. 28:11–15

MT Now while they were going, behold, some of the guard came into the city and [a]reported to the chief priests all the things that had happened.

When they had assembled with the elders and consulted together, they gave [b]a large sum of money to the soldiers, saying, "Tell them, 'His disciples came at night and stole Him *away* [c]while we slept.' And if this comes to the governor's ears, we will appease him and make you secure."

So they took the money and did as they were instructed; and this saying is commonly reported among the Jews until this day.

---

[a] REPORTED TO THE CHIEF PRIESTS. The Jewish leaders' determination to cover up what had occurred reveals the obstinacy of unbelief in the face of evidence (Luke 16:31).

[b] A LARGE SUM OF MONEY. Lit. "silver" (cf. Matt. 26:15). The bribery was necessary because the soldiers' story, if true, could cost them their lives—since they were charged with guard duty under Pilate's personal orders (Matt. 27:65). The Jewish leaders also promised to cover for the soldiers if the false story they spread leaked back to Pilate.

[c] WHILE WE SLEPT. The story was obviously bogus and not a very good cover-up. They could not possibly know what had happened while they were asleep.

202. The Road to Emmaus

Luke 24:13–35; [Mark 16:12–13]

LK Now behold, [a]two of them were traveling that same day to a village called [b]Emmaus, which was seven miles from Jerusalem. And they talked together of all these things which had happened. So it was, while they conversed and reasoned, that Jesus Himself drew near and went with them. But [c]their eyes were restrained, so that they did not know Him.

And He said to them, "What kind of conversation *is* this that you have with one another as you walk and are sad?" Then the one whose name was Cleopas answered and said to Him, "[d]Are You the only stranger in Jerusalem, and have You not known the things which happened there in these days?"

And He said to them, "What things?" So they said to Him, "The things concerning Jesus of Nazareth, who was a Prophet mighty in deed and word before God and all the people, and how the chief priests and our rulers delivered Him to be condemned to death, and crucified Him. [e]But we were hoping that it was He who was going to redeem Israel. Indeed, besides all this, today is [f]the third day since these things happened. Yes, and certain women of our company, who arrived at the tomb early, astonished us. When they did not find His body, they came saying that they had also seen a vision of angels who said He was alive. And certain of

---

[a] TWO OF THEM. These evidently were not any of the eleven disciples. According to verse 18, one was named Cleopas.

[b] EMMAUS. Mentioned nowhere else in Scripture. Its exact location is not known, but tradition says it is a town known as Kubeibeh, seven miles northwest of Jerusalem.

[c] THEIR EYES WERE RESTRAINED. i.e., they were kept by God from recognizing Him.

[d] ARE YOU THE ONLY STRANGER IN JERUSALEM. The crucifixion of Jesus was already such a well known event around Jerusalem that they were shocked that He seemed not to know about it.

[e] BUT WE WERE HOPING. They had been looking for an immediate earthly kingdom. With Jesus crucified, they were probably struggling with doubt about whether He was the Messiah who would reign. But they still regarded Him as a true prophet.

[f] THE THIRD DAY. There may have been a glimmer of hope in these words. They had heard rumors of His resurrection already. Perhaps Cleopas recalled the Lord's promises of Luke 9:22; 18:33. More likely, however, it seems this was his way of expressing surprise that this Stranger did not yet know the news everyone else in Jerusalem had been discussing for the past three days.

those *who were* with us went to the tomb and found *it* just as the women had said; [g]but Him they did not see."

Then He said to them, "O foolish ones, and slow of heart to believe in all that the prophets have spoken! [h]Ought not the Christ to have suffered these things and to enter into His glory?" And beginning at [i]Moses and all the Prophets, He expounded to them in [j]all the Scriptures the things concerning Himself.

Then they drew near to the village where they were going, and He indicated that He would have gone farther. But they constrained Him, saying, "Abide with us, for it is toward evening, and the day is far spent." And He went in to stay with them. Now it came to pass, as He sat at the table with them, that He [k]took bread, blessed and broke *it,* and gave it to them. Then [l]their eyes were opened and they knew Him; and [m]He vanished from their sight.

And they said to one another, "Did not our heart burn within us while He talked with us on the road, and while He opened the Scriptures to us?" So they

[g] but Him they did not see. This was true. Evidently, Cleopas and his companion had not heard about the appearance to Mary Magdalene.

[h] Ought not. i.e., "Was it not necessary?" OT prophecies spoke often of a suffering servant of Jehovah.

[i] Moses and all the Prophets. Luke 24:44 gives the three-fold division; this expression is merely a shortened way to say the same thing.

[j] in all the Scriptures. In the inscrutable wisdom of divine providence, the substance of Christ's exposition of the OT messianic prophecies was not recorded. But the gist of what He expounded would have undoubtedly included an explanation of the OT sacrificial system, which was full of types and symbols that spoke of His sufferings and death. He also would have pointed them to the major prophetic passages which spoke of the crucifixion, such as Pss. 16:9–11; 22; 69; Isa. 52:14–53:12; Zech. 12:10; 13:7. And He would have pointed out the true meaning of passages like Gen. 3:15; Num. 21:6–9; Ps. 16:10; Jer. 23:5–6; Dan. 9:26—and a host of other key messianic prophecies, particularly those that spoke of His death and resurrection.

[k] took bread. A simple expression, meaning to share a meal.

[l] their eyes were opened. i.e., by God. They had been sovereignly kept from recognizing Him until this point. His resurrection body was glorified and altered from its previous appearance (see John's description in Rev. 1:13–16), and this surely explains why even Mary did not recognize Him at first (cf. John 20:14–16). But in this case, God actively intervened to keep them from recognizing Him until it was time for Him to depart.

[m] He vanished from their sight. His resurrection body, though real and tangible (John 20:27)—and even capable of ingesting earthly food (Luke 24:42, 43)—nonetheless possessed certain properties that indicate it was glorified, altered in a mysterious way (cf. 1 Cor. 15:35–54; Phil. 3:21). Christ could appear and disappear bodily, as seen in this text. His body could pass through solid objects—such as the grave clothes (Luke 24:12), or the walls and doors of a closed room (John 20:19, 26). He could apparently travel great distances in a moment, for by the time these disciples returned to Jerusalem, Christ had already appeared to Peter (Luke 24:34). The fact that He ascended into heaven bodily demonstrated that His resurrection body was already fit for heaven. Yet it was His body, the same one that was missing from the tomb, even retaining identifying features such as the nail wounds (John 20:25–27). He was no ghost or phantom.

rose up that very hour and returned to Jerusalem, and found the eleven and those *who were* with them gathered together, saying, "The Lord is risen indeed, and has [n]appeared to Simon!"

And they told about the things *that had happened* on the road, and how He was known to them in the breaking of bread.

[MK [o]After that, He appeared in another form to two of them as they walked and went into the country. And they went and told *it* to the rest, *but* they did not believe them either.]

---

[n] Appeared to Simon. Cf. 1 Cor. 15:5–8. Scripture describes at least ten distinct appearances of Christ between the resurrection and ascension. He appeared: (1) to Mary Magdalene at the tomb (Mark 16:9; John 20:11–18); (2) to the women on the road (Matt. 28:9, 10); (3) to the disciples on the road to Emmaus (Luke 24:13–32); (4) to Peter (Luke 24:34); (5) to ten of the eleven disciples, Thomas being absent (Luke 24:36–43; Mark 16:14; John 20:19–25); (6) to the eleven disciples (with Thomas present), eight days later (John 20:26–31); (7) to seven disciples by the shore of the Sea of Galilee (John 21:1–25); (8) to more than five hundred disciples, probably on a mountain in Galilee (1 Cor. 15:6; cf. Matt. 28:16); (9) to James (1 Cor. 15:7); and (10) to the apostles when He ascended into heaven (Acts 1:3–11). After His ascension, He appeared to Paul (1 Cor. 15:8). The next time He appears, it will be in glory (Matt. 24:30).

[o] After that. Both external and internal evidence strongly suggests these verses (Mark 16:9–20) were not originally part of Mark's gospel. (Hence they are placed in brackets, at the end of the section.)

203. The Upper Room with Thomas Absent

Luke 24:36–43; John 20:19–23; [Mark 16:14]

LK Now as they said these things, Jesus Himself JN came and LK stood in the midst of them. [It was] JN the same day at evening, being the first *day* of the week, [and] [a]the doors were shut where the disciples were assembled, for fear of the Jews.

Jesus LK said to them, "[b]Peace to you." But they were terrified and frightened, and supposed they had seen a spirit. And He said to them, "Why are you troubled? And why do doubts arise in your hearts? [c]Behold My hands and My feet, that it is I Myself. Handle Me and see, for a spirit does not have flesh and bones as you see I have." JN When He had said this, He showed them *His* hands LK and His feet JN and His side.

LK But while they still did not believe for joy, and marveled, He said to them, "Have you any food here?" So they gave Him a piece of a broiled fish and some honeycomb. And He took *it* and ate in their presence. JN Then the disciples were glad when they saw the Lord.

So Jesus said to them again, "Peace to you! As the Father has sent Me, I also send you." And when He had said this, He breathed on *them,* and said to them, "[d]Receive the Holy Spirit. [e]If you forgive the sins of any, they are forgiven them; if you retain the *sins* of any, they are retained."

[MK [f]Later He appeared to the eleven as they sat at the table; and He rebuked their unbelief and hardness of heart, because they did not believe those who had seen Him after He had risen.]

---

[a] THE DOORS WERE SHUT. The Greek word indicates the doors were locked for fear of the Jews. Since the authorities had executed their leader, they reasonably expected that Jesus' fate could be their own.

[b] PEACE TO YOU. Jesus' greeting complements His "It is finished," for His work on the cross accomplished peace between God and His people (Rom. 5:1; Eph. 2:14–17).

[c] BEHOLD MY HANDS AND MY FEET. He was showing them the nail wounds to prove it was really Him.

[d] RECEIVE THE HOLY SPIRIT. Since the disciples did not actually receive the Holy Spirit until the day of Pentecost, some forty days in the future (Acts 1:8; 2:1–3), this statement must be understood as a pledge on Christ's part that the Holy Spirit would be coming.

[e] IF YOU FORGIVE THE SINS OF ANY. This verse does not give authority to Christians to forgive sins. Jesus was saying that the believer can boldly declare the certainty of a sinner's forgiveness by the Father because of the work of His Son if that sinner has repented and believed the gospel. The believer with certainty can also tell those who do not respond to the message of God's forgiveness through faith in Christ that their sins, as a result, are not forgiven.

[f] LATER HE APPEARED. Both external and internal evidence strongly suggests these verses (Mark 16:9–20) were not originally part of Mark's gospel. (Hence they are placed in brackets, at the end of the section.)

204. The Upper Room with Thomas Present

John 20:24–31

JN Now Thomas, called the Twin, one of the twelve, was not with them when Jesus came. The other disciples therefore said to him, "We have seen the Lord."

So he said to them, "[a]Unless I see in His hands the print of the nails, and put my finger into the print of the nails, and put my hand into His side, I will not believe." And after eight days His disciples were again inside, and Thomas with them. Jesus came, the doors being shut, and stood in the midst, and said, "Peace to you!"

Then He said to Thomas, "Reach your finger here, and look at My hands; and reach your hand *here,* and put *it* into My side. Do not be unbelieving, but believing." And Thomas answered and said to Him, [b]"My Lord and my God!" Jesus said to him, "Thomas, because you have seen Me, you have believed. [c]Blessed *are* those who have not seen and *yet* have believed."

And truly Jesus did many other signs in the presence of His disciples, which are not written in this book; but [d]these are written that you may believe that Jesus is the Christ, the Son of God, and that believing you may have life in His name.

---

[a] UNLESS . . . I WILL NOT BELIEVE. Thomas has already been portrayed as loyal but pessimistic. Jesus did not rebuke Thomas for his failure, but instead compassionately offered him proof of His resurrection. Jesus lovingly met him at the point of his weakness. Thomas's actions indicated that Jesus had to convince the disciples rather forcefully of His resurrection, i.e., they were not gullible people predisposed to believing in resurrection. The point is they would not have fabricated it or hallucinated it, since they were so reluctant to believe even with the evidence they could see.

[b] "MY LORD AND MY GOD!" With these words, Thomas declared his firm belief in the resurrection and, therefore, the deity of Jesus the Messiah and Son of God (Titus 2:13). This is the greatest confession a person can make. Thomas's confession functions as the fitting capstone of John's purpose in writing.

[c] BLESSED ARE THOSE. Jesus looked ahead to a time when such physical evidence as Thomas received would not be available. When Jesus ascended permanently to the Father, believers would come to saving faith without the privilege of seeing the resurrected Lord. Jesus pronounced a special blessing on those who believe without having Thomas's privilege (1 Peter 1:8–9).

[d] THESE ARE WRITTEN. These verses constitute the goal and purpose for which John wrote the gospel.

205. Jesus Appears to the Disciples While Fishing

John 21:1–14

JN [a]After these things Jesus showed Himself again to the disciples at the [b]Sea of Tiberias, and in this way He showed *Himself:* Simon Peter, Thomas called the Twin, Nathanael of Cana in Galilee, the *sons* of Zebedee, and two others of His disciples were together.

[c]Simon Peter said to them, [d]"I am going fishing." They said to him, "We are going with you also." They went out and immediately got into the boat, and that night they caught nothing. But when the morning had now come, Jesus stood on the shore; yet [e]the disciples did not know that it was Jesus.

Then Jesus said to them, "Children, have you any food?" They answered Him, "No." And He said to them, "Cast the net on the right side of the boat, and you will find *some.*" So they cast, and now they were not able to draw it in because of the multitude of fish. Therefore [f]that disciple whom Jesus loved said to Peter, "It is the Lord!" Now when Simon Peter heard that it was the Lord, he put on *his* outer garment (for he had removed it), and plunged into the sea. But the other disciples

---

[a] AFTER THESE THINGS. John 21:1–25 constitutes the epilogue or appendix of John's gospel. While 20:30–31 constitute the conclusion of the main body of the work, the information here at the end provides a balance to his prologue in 1:1–18. The epilogue essentially answers five lingering questions. (1) Will Jesus no longer directly provide for His own (cf. 20:17)? This question is answered in vv. 1–14. (2) What happened to Peter? Peter had denied Christ three times and fled. The last time Peter was seen was in 20:6–8, where both he and John saw the empty tomb but only John believed (20:8). This question is answered in vv. 15–17. (3) What about the future of the disciples, now that they are without their Master? This question is answered in vv. 18–19. (4) Was John going to die? Jesus answers this question in vv. 20–23. (5) Why weren't other things that Jesus did recorded by John? John gives the answer to that in vv. 24–25.

[b] SEA OF TIBERIAS. An alternate name for the Sea of Galilee, found only in John (see 6:1).

[c] SIMON PETER. In all lists of the apostles, he is named first, indicating his general leadership of the group (e.g., Matt. 10:2).

[d] "I AM GOING FISHING." The most reasonable explanation for Peter and the others to be in Galilee was that they had gone there to obey the Lord's command to meet Him in Galilee (Matt. 28:16). Peter and the others occupied themselves with fishing, which was their former livelihood, while they awaited Jesus' appearance.

[e] THE DISCIPLES DID NOT KNOW THAT IT WAS JESUS. This could be another instance in which the Lord kept His disciples from recognizing Him (John 20:14–15; cf. Luke 24:16).

[f] THAT DISCIPLE WHOM JESUS LOVED. John immediately recognized that the Stranger was the risen Lord, for only He had such supernatural knowledge and power. Peter impulsively jumped in and headed to see the Lord.

came in the little boat (for they were not far from land, but about [g]two hundred cubits), dragging the net with fish.

Then, as soon as they had come to land, they saw a fire of coals there, and fish laid on it, and bread. Jesus said to them, "Bring some of the [h]fish which you have just caught." Simon Peter went up and dragged the net to land, full of large fish, [i]one hundred and fifty-three; and although there were so many, the net was not broken.

Jesus said to them, "Come *and* eat breakfast." Yet none of the disciples dared ask Him, "Who are You?"—knowing that it was the Lord. Jesus then came and took the bread and gave it to them, and likewise the fish. This *is* now [j]the third time Jesus showed Himself to His disciples after He was raised from the dead.

---

[g] TWO HUNDRED CUBITS. Approximately three hundred feet from the shore.

[h] FISH . . . AND BREAD. Apparently, the Lord created this breakfast as He had created food for the multitudes (John 6:1–13).

[i] ONE HUNDRED AND FIFTY-THREE. John's recording of the precise number reinforces the fact that he was an eyewitness author of the events he recorded (1 John 1:1–4). Jesus' action here in providing the fish also indicated that He would still provide for His disciples' needs (see Phil. 4:19; Matt. 6:25–33).

[j] THE THIRD TIME. The reference to the "third time" refers only to the appearances reported in John's gospel, i.e., the first being in John 20:19–23 and the second in John 20:26–29.

206. Jesus Restores Peter to Ministry

John 21:15–25

JN So when they had eaten breakfast, Jesus said to Simon Peter, "Simon, *son* of Jonah, [a]do you love Me [b]more than these?" He said to Him, "Yes, Lord; You know that I love You." He said to him, [c]"Feed My lambs."

He said to him again a second time, "Simon, *son* of Jonah, do you love Me?" He said to Him, "Yes, Lord; You know that I love You." He said to him, "Tend My sheep." He said to him the third time, "Simon, *son* of Jonah, do you love Me?"

[d]Peter was grieved because He said to him the third time, "Do you love Me?" And he said to Him, "Lord, You know all things; You know that I love You."

Jesus said to him, "Feed My sheep. Most assuredly, I say to you, when you were younger, you girded yourself and walked where you wished; but when you are old, you will stretch out your hands, and another will gird you and carry *you*

---

[a] DO YOU LOVE ME? The meaning of this section hinges upon the usage of two synonyms for love. In terms of interpretation, when two synonyms are placed in close proximity in context, a difference in meaning, however slight, is emphasized. When Jesus asked Peter if he loved Him, He used a word for love that signified total commitment. Peter responded with a word for love that signified his love for Jesus, but not necessarily his total commitment. This was not because he was reluctant to express that greater love, but because he had been disobedient and denied the Lord in the past. He was, perhaps, now reluctant to make a claim of supreme devotion when, in the past, his life did not support such a claim. Jesus pressed home to Peter the need for unswerving devotion by repeatedly asking Peter if he loved Him supremely. The essential message here is that Jesus demands total commitment from His followers. Their love for Him must place Him above their love for all else. Jesus confronted Peter with love because He wanted Peter to lead the apostles (Matt. 16:18), but in order for Peter to be an effective shepherd, his overwhelming drive must exemplify supreme love for his Lord.

[b] MORE THAN THESE. This probably refers to the fish (John 21:11), representing Peter's profession as a fisherman, for he had gone back to it while waiting for Jesus (see 21:3). Jesus wanted Peter to love Him so supremely as to forsake all that he was familiar with and be exclusively devoted to being a fisher of men (Matt. 4:19). The phrase may refer to the other disciples, since Peter had claimed he would be more devoted than all the others (Matt. 26:33).

[c] "FEED MY LAMBS." The word *feed* conveys the idea of being devoted to the Lord's service as an undershepherd who cares for His flock (see 1 Peter 5:1–4). The word has the idea of constantly feeding and nourishing the sheep. This served as a reminder that the primary duty of the messenger of Jesus Christ is to teach the Word of God (2 Tim. 4:2). Acts 1–12 records Peter's obedience to this commission.

[d] PETER WAS GRIEVED. The third time Jesus asked Peter, He used Peter's word for love that signified something less than total devotion, questioning even that level of love Peter thought he was safe in claiming. The lessons driven home to Peter grieved his heart, so that he sought for a proper understanding of his heart, not by what he said or had done, but based on the Lord's omniscience (cf. John 2:24–25).

where you do not wish." This He spoke, [e]signifying by what death he would glorify God. And when He had spoken this, He said to him, "Follow Me."

Then Peter, turning around, saw the disciple whom Jesus loved following, who also had leaned on His breast at the supper, and said, "Lord, who is the one who betrays You?" Peter, seeing him, said to Jesus, "But Lord, [f]what *about* this man?"

Jesus said to him, "If I will that he remain till I come, what *is that* to you? You follow Me." Then this saying went out among the brethren that this disciple would not die. Yet Jesus did not say to him that he would not die, but, "If I will that he remain [g]till I come, what *is that* to you?"

This is [h]the disciple who testifies of these things, and wrote these things; and we know that his testimony is true. And there are also [i]many other things that Jesus did, which if they were written one by one, I suppose that even the world itself could not contain the books that would be written. Amen.

---

[e] SIGNIFYING BY WHAT DEATH HE WOULD GLORIFY GOD. This was a prophecy of Peter's martyrdom. Jesus' call of devotion to Him would also mean that Peter's devotion would entail his own death (Matt. 10:37–39). Whenever any Christian follows Christ, he must be prepared to suffer and die (Matt. 16:24–26). Peter lived three decades serving the Lord and anticipating the death that was before him (2 Peter 1:12–15), but he wrote that such suffering and death for the Lord brings praise to God (1 Peter 4:14–16). Church tradition records that Peter suffered martyrdom under Nero (ca. AD 67–68), being crucified upside down, because he refused to be crucified like his Lord.

[f] WHAT ABOUT THIS MAN? Jesus' prophecy regarding Peter's martyrdom prompted Peter to ask what would happen to John ("the disciple whom Jesus loved"—John 13:23). He may have asked this because of his deep concern for John's future, since he was an intimate friend. Jesus' reply, "You follow Me," signified that his primary concern must not be John but his continued devotion to the Lord and His service, i.e., Christ's service must be his all-consuming passion, and nothing must detract from it.

[g] TILL I COME. Jesus' hypothetical statement for emphasis was that, if John lived until His second coming, it was none of Peter's concern. He needed to live his own life in faithfulness, not compare it with any other.

[h] THE DISCIPLE WHO TESTIFIES. John is a personal witness of the truth of the events that he recorded. The "we" most likely is an editorial device referring only to John (see John 1:14; 1 John 1:1–4; 3 John 12), or it may include the collective witness of his apostolic colleagues.

[i] MANY OTHER THINGS. John explained that he had been selective rather than exhaustive in his testimony. Although selective, the truth revealed in John's gospel is sufficient to bring anyone to faith in the Messiah and Son of God (John 14:26; 16:13).

207. Jesus Appears to Many Disciples in Galilee

Matt. 28:16–20; 1 Cor. 15:6–7; [Mark 16:15–18]

MT Then [a]the eleven disciples went away into Galilee, to the mountain which Jesus had appointed for them. 1COR [And there] He was seen by over [b]five hundred brethren at once, of whom the greater part remain to the present, but some have fallen asleep.

MT When they saw Him, they worshiped Him; [c]but some doubted. And Jesus came and spoke to them, saying, "[d]All authority has been given to Me in heaven and on earth. Go [e]therefore and make disciples of all the nations, baptizing them [f]in the name of the Father and of the Son and of the Holy Spirit, [g]teaching them to observe all things that I have commanded you; and lo, [h]I am with you always, *even* to the end of the age." Amen.

---

[a] THE ELEVEN DISCIPLES. This does not mean that only the eleven were present. The fact that some there "doubted" (Matt. 28:17) strongly suggests that more than the eleven were present. It is likely that Christ arranged this meeting in Galilee because that was where most of His followers were. This seems the most likely location for the massive gathering of disciples described in 1 Cor. 15:6.

[b] FIVE HUNDRED BRETHREN AT ONCE. The testimony of eyewitnesses, recorded in the NT, was added to support the reality of the resurrection. These included: (1) John and Peter together (John 20:19–20), but probably also separately before (Luke 24:34); (2) the twelve (John 20:19–20; Luke 24:36; Acts 1:22); (3) the five hundred, only referred to here, had all seen the risen Christ (cf. Matt. 28:9; Mark 16:9, 12, 14; Luke 24:31–39; John 21:1–23); (4) James, either one of the two so-named apostles (son of Zebedee or son of Alphaeus; cf. Mark 3:17–18) or even James the half-brother of the Lord, the author of the epistle by that name and the key leader in the Jerusalem church (Acts 15:13–21); and (5) the apostles (John 20:19–29). Such unspecified appearances occurred over a forty-day period (Acts 1:3) to all the apostles.

[c] BUT SOME DOUBTED. That simple phrase is one of countless testimonies to the integrity of Scripture. The transparent honesty of a statement like this shows that Matthew was not attempting to exclude or cover up facts that might lessen the perfection of such a glorious moment.

[d] ALL AUTHORITY. See Matt. 11:27; John 3:35. Absolute sovereign authority—lordship over all—is handed to Christ, "in heaven and on earth." This is clear proof of His deity. The time of His humiliation was at an end, and God had exalted Him above all (Phil. 2:9–11).

[e] THEREFORE. i.e., on the basis of His authority, the disciples were sent to "make disciples of all nations." The sweeping scope of their commission is consummate with His unlimited authority.

[f] IN THE NAME OF THE FATHER . . . SON AND . . . HOLY SPIRIT. Strong affirmation of the Trinity.

[g] TEACHING THEM TO OBSERVE ALL THINGS THAT I HAVE COMMANDED YOU. The kind of evangelism called for in this commission does not end with the conversion of the unbeliever.

[h] I AM WITH YOU. There's a touching echo of the beginning of Matthew's gospel here. Immanuel (Matt. 1:23) "which is translated, 'God with us'"—remains "with" us "even to the end of the age"—i.e., until He returns bodily to judge the world and establish His earthly kingdom.

1COR After that He was seen by James, then by all the apostles.

[MK [i]And He said to them, "Go into all the world and preach the gospel to every creature. He who believes and is baptized will be saved; but he who does not believe will be condemned. And these signs will follow those who believe: In My name they will cast out demons; they will speak with new tongues; they will take up serpents; and if they drink anything deadly, it will by no means hurt them; they will lay hands on the sick, and they will recover."]

---

[i] And He said to them. Both external and internal evidence strongly suggests these verses (Mark 16:9–20) were not originally part of Mark's gospel. (Hence they are placed in brackets, at the end of the section.)

208. Jesus Appears to the Disciples back in Jerusalem

Luke 24:44–49; Acts 1:3–8

ACTS He also [a]presented Himself alive [to His apostles] after His suffering by many infallible proofs, being seen by them during [b]forty days and speaking of the things pertaining to the kingdom of God. And [c]being assembled together with *them,* LK He said to them, "These *are* the words which I spoke to you while I was still with you, that all things must be fulfilled which were written in [d]the Law of Moses and *the* Prophets and *the* Psalms concerning Me."

And He [e]opened their understanding, that they might comprehend the Scriptures. Then He said to them, "Thus it is written, and thus it was necessary for the Christ to suffer and to rise from the dead the third day, and that repentance and remission of sins should be preached in His name to all nations, beginning at Jerusalem. And you are witnesses of these things. Behold, I send [f]the Promise of My Father upon you; but tarry in the city of Jerusalem until you are endued with power from on high."

[Thus,] ACTS He commanded them not to depart from Jerusalem, but to wait for the Promise of the Father, "which," *He said,* "you have heard from Me; for John

---

[a] PRESENTED HIMSELF . . . BY MANY INFALLIBLE PROOFS. Cf. John 20:30; 1 Cor. 15:5–8. To give the apostles confidence to present His message, Jesus entered a locked room (John 20:19), showed His crucifixion wounds (Luke 24:39), and ate and drank with the disciples (Luke 24:41–43).

[b] FORTY DAYS. The time period between Jesus' death and ascension, during which He appeared at intervals to the apostles and others (1 Cor. 15:5–8) and provided convincing evidence of His resurrection. KINGDOM OF GOD. Cf. 8:12; 14:22; 19:8; 20:25; 28:23, 31. Here this expression refers to the sphere of salvation, the gracious domain of divine rule over believers' hearts (see 1 Cor. 6:9; Eph. 5:5; cf. 17:7; Col. 1:13–14; Rev. 11:15; 12:10). This was the dominant theme during Christ's earthly ministry (cf. Matt. 4:23; 9:35; Mark 1:15; Luke 4:43; 9:2; John 3:3–21).

[c] BEING ASSEMBLED TOGETHER WITH THEM. An alternative reading, "eating with them," is preferred (cf. Luke 24:42–43; Acts 10:41). The fact that Jesus ate provides additional proof of His bodily resurrection.

[d] THE LAW OF MOSES AND THE PROPHETS AND THE PSALMS. i.e., the whole OT.

[e] OPENED THEIR UNDERSTANDING. He undoubtedly taught them from the OT, as He had on the road to Emmaus. But the gist of the expression also seems to convey a supernatural opening of their minds to receive the truths He unfolded. Whereas their understanding was once dull (Luke 9:45), they finally saw clearly (cf. Ps. 119:18; Isa. 29:18–19; 2 Cor. 3:14–16).

[f] THE PROMISE OF MY FATHER. Jesus repeatedly promised that God would send them His Spirit (Luke 11:13; 24:49; John 7:39; 14:16, 26; 15:26; 16:7; 20:22).

truly baptized with water, but you shall be baptized [g]with the Holy Spirit [h]not many days from now."

Therefore, when they had come together, they asked Him, saying, "Lord, will You at this time [i]restore the kingdom to Israel?" And [j]He said to them, "It is not for you to know [k]times or seasons which the Father has put in His own authority. But you shall [l]receive power when [m]the Holy Spirit has come upon you; and you shall be [n]witnesses to Me in Jerusalem, and in all [o]Judea and [p]Samaria, and to the end of the earth."

---

[g] with the Holy Spirit. The apostles had to wait until the Day of Pentecost, but since then all believers are baptized with the Holy Spirit at salvation (cf. 1 Cor. 12:13; cf. Rom. 8:9; 1 Cor. 6:19–20; Titus 3:5–6).

[h] not many days from now. God's promise was fulfilled just ten days later.

[i] restore the kingdom to Israel? The apostles still believed the earthly form of the kingdom of Messiah would soon be re-established (cf. Luke 19:11; 24:21). They also knew that Ezek. 36 and Joel 2 connected the coming of the kingdom with the outpouring of the Spirit whom Jesus had promised.

[j] He said to them. This verse shows that the apostles' expectation of a literal, earthly kingdom mirrored what Christ taught and what the OT predicted. Otherwise, He would have corrected them about such a crucial aspect of His teaching.

[k] times or seasons. These two words refer to features, eras, and events that will be part of His earthly kingdom reign, which will begin at the Second Coming (Matt. 25:21–34). The exact time of His return, however, remains unrevealed (Mark 13:32; cf. Deut. 29:29).

[l] receive power. The apostles had already experienced the Holy Spirit's saving, guiding, teaching, and miracle-working power. Soon they would receive His indwelling presence and a new dimension of power for witness (cf. 1 Cor. 6:19–20; Eph. 3:16, 20).

[m] the Holy Spirit has come upon you. The apostles' mission of spreading the gospel was the major reason the Holy Spirit empowered them. This event dramatically altered world history, and the gospel message eventually reached all parts of the earth (Matt. 28:19–20).

[n] witnesses. People who tell the truth about Jesus Christ (cf. John 14:26; 1 Peter 3:15). The Greek word means "one who dies for his faith," because that was commonly the price of witnessing.

[o] Judea. The region in which Jerusalem was located.

[p] Samaria. The region immediately to the north of Judea.

209. The Ascension of Christ

Luke 24:50–53; Acts 1:9–12; [Mark 16:19–20]

ACTS Now when He had spoken these things, LK He led them out as far as Bethany, and He lifted up His hands and blessed them. Now it came to pass, while He blessed them, that He was parted from them ACTS while they watched LK and [a]carried up into heaven. ACTS And [b]a cloud received Him out of their sight.

And while they looked steadfastly toward heaven as He went up, behold, [c]two men stood by them in white apparel, who also said, "[d]Men of Galilee, why do you stand gazing up into heaven? This *same* Jesus, who was taken up from you into heaven, will so come [e]in like manner as you saw Him go into heaven."

LK And [f]they worshiped Him, and returned to Jerusalem with great joy, ACTS from the [g]mount called Olivet, which is near Jerusalem, a [h]Sabbath day's journey. LK And [they] were continually [i]in the temple praising and blessing God. Amen.

---

[a] CARRIED UP INTO HEAVEN. i.e., visibly. Before when the resurrected Christ left them, He simply vanished (Luke 24:31). This time they saw Him ascend. God the Father took Jesus, in His resurrection body, from this world to His rightful place at the Father's right hand (cf. John 17:1–6).

[b] A CLOUD. A visible reminder that God's glory was present as the apostles watched the ascension. For some of them, this was not the first time they had witnessed divine glory (Mark 9:26); neither will it be the last time clouds accompany Jesus (Mark 13:26; 14:62; Rev. 1:7).

[c] TWO MEN . . . IN WHITE APPAREL. Two angels in the form of men (cf. Gen. 18:2; Josh. 5:13–15; Mark 16:5).

[d] MEN OF GALILEE. All the apostles were from Galilee except for Judas, who had killed himself by this time.

[e] IN LIKE MANNER. Christ one day will return to earth (to the Mount of Olives) in the same way He ascended (with clouds), to set up His kingdom (cf. Dan. 7:13; Zech. 14:4; Matt. 24:30; 26:64; Rev. 1:7; 14:14).

[f] THEY WORSHIPED HIM. i.e., a formal act of worship. Now that He had opened their understanding, they perceived the full truth of His deity, unclouded by the darkness of confusion or doubt. Cf. Matt. 28:9; John 20:28; contrast Matt. 28:17.

[g] MOUNT CALLED OLIVET. Located across the Kidron Valley, east of Jerusalem, this large hill rising about two hundred feet higher in elevation than the city, was the site from which Jesus ascended into heaven (Luke 24:50–51).

[h] SABBATH DAY'S JOURNEY. One-half of a mile (about two thousand cubits), the farthest distance a faithful Jew could travel on the Sabbath to accommodate the prohibition of Ex. 16:29. This measurement was derived from tradition based on Israel's encampments in the wilderness. The tents farthest out on the camp's perimeter were two thousand cubits from the center tabernacle—the longest distance anyone had to walk to reach the tabernacle on the Sabbath (Josh. 3:4; cf. Num. 35:5).

[i] IN THE TEMPLE. This became the first meeting-place of the church (Acts 2:46; 5:21, 42). There were rooms around the porticoes of the outer court available for such meetings.

[MK [j]So then, after the Lord had spoken to them, He was received up into heaven, and sat down at the right hand of God. And they went out and preached everywhere, the Lord working with *them* and confirming the word through the accompanying signs. Amen.]

---

[j] So then. Both external and internal evidence strongly suggests these verses (Mark 16:9–20) were not originally part of Mark's gospel. (Hence they are placed in brackets, at the end of the section.)

Part XI | New Testament Reflections on the Gospel of Jesus Christ

210. The Centrality of Christ's Death

Rom. 5:8–10; 1 Cor. 1:22–24; 2 Cor. 5:15, 21; Gal. 1:3–4; Eph. 2:13; Phil. 2:6–8; Col. 1:13–14; 2:13–14; Heb. 2:9, 17; 9:13–15, 27–28a; 12:2b; 1 Peter 1:18–19; 2:23–24; 3:18a

GAL Grace to you and peace from God the Father and our Lord Jesus Christ, who gave Himself for our sins, that He might deliver us from this present evil age, according to the will of our God and Father; [and] PHIL who, [a]being in the form of God, did [b]not consider it robbery to be [c]equal with God, but made Himself of no reputation, taking the form of a bondservant, *and* coming in [d]the likeness of men. HEB In all things He had to be made like *His* brethren, that He might be a merciful and

---

[a] BEING IN THE FORM OF GOD. Paul affirms that Jesus eternally has been God. The usual Greek word for "being" is not used here. Instead, Paul chose another term that stresses the essence of a person's nature—his continuous state or condition. Paul also could have chosen one of two Greek words for "form," but he chose the one that specifically denotes the essential, unchanging character of something—what it is in and of itself. The fundamental doctrine of Christ's deity has always encompassed these crucial characteristics (cf. John 1:1, 3–4, 14; 8:58; Col. 1:15–17; Heb. 1:3).

[b] NOT . . . ROBBERY. The Greek word is translated "robbery" here because it originally meant "a thing seized by robbery." It eventually came to mean anything clutched, embraced, or prized, and thus is sometimes translated "grasped" or "held onto." Though Christ had all the rights, privileges, and honors of deity—which He was worthy of and could never be disqualified from—His attitude was not to cling to those things or His position but to be willing to give them up for a season.

[c] EQUAL WITH GOD. The Greek word for "equal" defines things that are exactly the same in size, quantity, quality, character, and number. In every sense, Jesus is equal to God and constantly claimed to be so during His earthly ministry (cf. John 5:18; 10:33, 38; 14:9; 20:28; Heb. 1:1–3).

[d] THE LIKENESS OF MEN. Christ became more than God in a human body, but He took on all the essential attributes of humanity (Luke 2:52; Gal. 4:4; Col. 1:22), even to the extent that He identified with basic human needs and weaknesses (cf. Heb. 2:14, 17; 4:15). He became the God-Man: fully God and fully man.

faithful High Priest in things *pertaining* to God, to make [e]propitiation for the sins of the people. PHIL And being found [f]in appearance as a man, He humbled Himself and became obedient to *the point of* death, even the death of the cross.

HEB And as it is appointed for men to die once, but after this the judgment, so Christ was offered once to bear the sins of many. 1PET For Christ also suffered [g]once for sins, [h]the just for the unjust, that He might bring us to God, 2COR for He made Him who knew no sin *to be* sin for us, that we might become the righteousness of God in Him.

1PET When He was reviled, [He] did not revile in return; when He suffered, He did not threaten, but committed *Himself* to Him who judges righteously; who Himself [i]bore our sins in His own body on the tree, that we, having died to sins, might live for righteousness—by whose [j]stripes you were healed; [and] HEB who for the joy that was set before Him endured the cross, despising the shame, and has sat down at the right hand of the throne of God.

ROM But God demonstrates His own love toward us, in that while we were still

[e] PROPITIATION. The word means "to conciliate" or " to satisfy." Cf. Rom. 3:25. Christ's work of propitiation is related to His high-priestly ministry. By His partaking of a human nature, Christ demonstrated His mercy to mankind and His faithfulness to God by satisfying God's requirement for sin and thus obtaining for His people full forgiveness. Cf. 1 John 2:2; 4:10.

[f] IN APPEARANCE AS A MAN. This is not simply a repetition of the last phrase of Phil. 2:7, but a shift from the heavenly focus to an earthly one. Christ's humanity is described from the viewpoint of those who saw Him. Paul is implying that although He outwardly looked like a man, there was much more to Him (His deity) that many people recognized naturally (cf. John 6:42; 8:48).

[g] ONCE FOR SINS. Under the Old Covenant the Jewish people offered sacrifice after sacrifice and then repeated it all the next year, especially at the Passover. But Christ's one sacrifice for sins was of such perpetual validity that it was sufficient for all and would never need to be repeated (cf. Heb. 7:27; 9:26–28).

[h] THE JUST FOR THE UNJUST. This is another statement of the sinlessness of Jesus (cf. Heb. 7:26) and of His substitutionary and vicarious atonement. He, who personally never sinned and had no sin nature, took the place of sinners (cf. 2 Cor. 5:21). In so doing Christ satisfied God's just penalty for sin required by the law and opened the way to God for all who repentantly believe (cf. John 14:6; Acts 4:12).

[i] BORE OUR SINS. Christ suffered not simply as the Christian's pattern (1 Peter 2:21–23), but far more importantly as the Christian's substitute. To bear sins was to be punished for them (cf. Num. 14:33; Ezek. 18:20). Christ bore the punishment and the penalty for believers, thus satisfying a holy God (cf. 2 Cor. 5:21; Gal. 3:13). This great doctrine of the substitutionary atonement is the heart of the gospel. Actual atonement, sufficient for the sins of the whole world, was made for all who would ever believe, namely, the elect (cf. Lev. 16:17; 23:27–30; John 3:16; 2 Cor. 5:19; 1 Tim. 2:6; 2 Tim. 4:10; Titus 2:11; Heb. 2:9; 1 John 2:2; 4:9–10).

[j] STRIPES YOU WERE HEALED. From Isa. 53:5. Through the wounds of Christ at the cross, believers are healed spiritually from the deadly disease of sin. Physical healing comes at glorification only, when there is no more physical pain, illness, or death (Rev. 21:4). Cf. Isa. 53:4–6.

sinners, Christ died for us. Much more then, having now been [k]justified by His blood, we shall be saved from wrath through Him. For if when we were enemies we were reconciled to God through the death of His Son, much more, having been reconciled, we shall be [l]saved by His life. COL And you, being dead in your trespasses and the uncircumcision of your flesh, He has made alive together with Him, having [m]forgiven you all trespasses, having [n]wiped out the handwriting of requirements that was against us, which was contrary to us. And He has taken it out of the way, having [o]nailed it to the cross.

EPH But now in Christ Jesus you who once were far off have been brought near by the blood of Christ, 1PET knowing that you were not [p]redeemed with corruptible things, *like* silver or gold, from your aimless conduct *received* by tradition from your fathers, but with the precious blood of Christ, as of a lamb without blemish and without spot. HEB For if the blood of bulls and goats and the ashes of a heifer,

---

[k] JUSTIFIED. This verb, and related words from the same Greek root (e.g., justification), occur some thirty times in Romans and are concentrated in 2:13–5:1. This legal or forensic term comes from the Greek word for "righteous" and means "to declare righteous." This verdict includes: pardon from the guilt and penalty of sin, and the imputation of Christ's righteousness to the believer's account, which provides for the positive righteousness man needs to be accepted by God. God declares a sinner righteous solely on the basis of the merits of Christ's righteousness. God imputed a believer's sin to Christ's account in His sacrificial death (Isa. 53:4–5; 1 Peter 2:24), and He imputes Christ's perfect obedience to God's law to Christians (cf. Rom. 5:19; 1 Cor. 1:30; 2 Cor. 5:21; Phil. 3:9). The sinner receives this gift of God's grace by faith alone (Rom. 3:22, 25; 4:1–25). Sanctification, the work of God by which He makes righteous those whom He has already justified, is distinct from justification but without exception always follows it (Rom. 8:30).

[l] SAVED BY HIS LIFE. When we were God's enemies, Christ was able by His death to reconcile us to God. Certainly now that we are God's children, the Savior can keep us by His living power.

[m] FORGIVEN YOU ALL TRESPASSES. God's free (Rom. 3:24) and complete (Rom. 5:20; Eph. 1:7) forgiveness of guilty sinners who put their faith in Jesus Christ is the most important reality in Scripture (cf. Pss. 32:1; 130:3–4; Isa. 1:18; 55:7; Mic. 7:18; Matt. 26:28; Acts 10:43; 13:38, 39; Titus 3:4–7; Heb. 8:12).

[n] WIPED OUT THE HANDWRITING. The Greek work translated "handwriting" referred to the handwritten certificate of debt by which a debtor acknowledged his indebtedness. All people (Rom. 3:23) owe God an unpayable debt for violating His law (Gal. 3:10; James 2:10; cf. Matt. 18:23–27) and are thus under sentence of death (Rom. 6:23). Paul graphically compares God's forgiveness of believers' sins to wiping ink off a parchment. Through Christ's sacrificial death on the cross, God has totally erased our certificate of indebtedness and made our forgiveness complete.

[o] NAILED IT TO THE CROSS. This is another metaphor for forgiveness. The list of the crimes of a crucified criminal were nailed to the cross with that criminal, to declare the violations he was being punished for (as in the case of Jesus, as noted in Matt. 27:37). Believers' sins were all put to Christ's account, nailed to His cross as He paid the penalty in their place for them all, thus satisfying the just wrath of God against crimes requiring punishment in full.

[p] REDEEMED. That is, to buy back someone from bondage by the payment of a price; to set free by paying a ransom. *Redemption* was a technical term for money paid to buy back a prisoner of war. Here it is used of the price paid to buy the freedom of one in the bondage of sin and under the curse of the law (i.e., eternal death, cf. Gal. 3:13). The price paid to a holy God was the shed blood of His own Son (cf. Ex. 12:1–13; 15:13; Ps. 78:35; Acts 20:28; Rom. 3:24; Gal. 4:4–5; Eph. 1:7; Col. 1:14; Titus 2:14; Heb. 9:11–17).

sprinkling the unclean, sanctifies for the purifying of the flesh, [q]how much more shall [r]the blood of Christ, who through the eternal Spirit [s]offered Himself without spot to God, cleanse your conscience from dead works to serve the living God? And for this reason He is the Mediator of the new covenant, by means of death, for the redemption of the transgressions under the first covenant, that those who are called may receive the promise of the eternal inheritance.

1COR For Jews request a sign, and Greeks seek after wisdom; but we preach Christ [t]crucified, to the Jews a stumbling block and to the Greeks foolishness, but to those who are called, both Jews and Greeks, Christ the power of God and the wisdom of God. COL [God] has delivered us from the power of darkness and conveyed *us* into the kingdom of the Son of His love, in whom we have redemption through His blood, the forgiveness of sins.

HEB But we see Jesus, who was made a little lower than the angels, for the suffering of death crowned with glory and honor, that He, by the grace of God, might taste death for everyone. 2COR He died for all, that those who live should live no longer for themselves, but for Him who died for them and rose again.

---

[q] HOW MUCH MORE. Superior to the cleansing capability of the ashes of an animal is the cleansing power of the sacrifice of Christ.

[r] THE BLOOD OF CHRIST. This is an expression that refers not simply to the fluid, but the whole atoning sacrificial work of Christ in His death. Blood is used as a substitute word for death (cf. Matt. 23:30, 35; 26:28; 27:6, 8, 24, 25; John 6:54–56; Acts 18:6; 20:26; Rom. 3:25; 5:9; Col. 1:14).

[s] OFFERED HIMSELF. Cf. John 10:17–18. The animals in the Levitical system were brought involuntarily and without understanding to their deaths. Christ came of His own volition with a full understanding of the necessity and consequences of His sacrifice. His sacrifice was not just His blood, it was His entire human nature (cf. Heb. 10:10).

[t] CRUCIFIED. Though Paul expounded the whole counsel of God to the church (Acts 20:27) and taught the Corinthians the Word of God (Acts 18:11), the focus of his preaching and teaching to unbelievers was Jesus Christ, who paid the penalty for sin on the cross (Acts 20:20; 2 Cor. 4:2; 2 Tim. 4:1–2). Until someone understands and believes the gospel, there is nothing more to say to them. The preaching of the cross (1 Cor. 1:18) was so dominant in the early church that believers were accused of worshiping a dead man.

211. The Victory of Christ's Resurrection

Acts 2:32; 26:22–23; Rom. 6:5–9; 1 Cor. 15:1–8, 20–22, 51–55; 2 Cor. 13:4; 1 Thess. 4:13–18; 2 Tim. 2:8

1COR Moreover, brethren, I declare to you the gospel which I preached to you, which also you received and in which you stand, by which also you are saved, if you hold fast that word which I preached to you—unless you believed in vain. For I delivered to you first of all that which I also received: that Christ died for our sins according to the Scriptures, and that He was buried, and that He rose again the third day [a]according to the Scriptures.

ACTS This Jesus God has raised up, of which we are all witnesses. 1COR He was seen by Cephas, then by the twelve. After that He was seen by over five hundred brethren at once, of whom the greater part remain to the present, but some have fallen asleep. After that He was seen by James, then by all the apostles. Then last of all He was seen by me also, as by one born out of due time.

2TIM Jesus Christ, of the seed of David, was [b]raised from the dead according to my gospel, 2COR for though He was crucified in weakness, yet He lives by the power of God. For we also are weak in Him, but we shall live with Him by the power of God toward you. ROM For if we have been united together in the likeness of His death, certainly we also shall be *in the likeness* of *His* resurrection, knowing this, that our old man was crucified with *Him,* that the body of sin might be done away with, that we should no longer be slaves of sin. For he who has died has been freed from sin. Now if we died with Christ, we believe that we shall also live with Him, knowing that Christ, having been raised from the dead, dies no more. Death no longer has dominion over Him.

ACTS Therefore, having obtained help from God, to this day I stand, witnessing both to small and great, saying no other things than those which the prophets and Moses said would come—that the Christ would suffer, that He would be the first to rise from the dead, and would proclaim light to the *Jewish* people and to the Gentiles.

---

[a] ACCORDING TO THE SCRIPTURES. The OT spoke of the suffering and resurrection of Christ (see Luke 24:25–27; Acts 2:25–31; 26:22–23). Jesus, Peter, and Paul quoted or referred to such OT passages regarding the work of Christ as Pss. 16:8–11; 22; Isa. 53.

[b] RAISED FROM THE DEAD. The resurrection of Christ is the central truth of the Christian faith (1 Cor. 15:3–4, 17, 19). By it God affirmed the perfect redemptive work of Jesus Christ (cf. Rom. 1:4).

1COR But now Christ is risen from the dead, *and* has become the [c]firstfruits of those who have fallen asleep. For since by [d]man *came* death, by Man also *came* the resurrection of the dead. For as in Adam [e]all die, even so in Christ all shall be made alive.

1THS But I do not want you to be ignorant, brethren, concerning [f]those who have fallen asleep, lest you sorrow as others who have no hope. For if we believe that Jesus died and rose again, even so God will bring with Him those who sleep in Jesus. For this we say to you by the word of the Lord, that we who are alive *and* remain until the coming of the Lord will by no means precede those who are asleep. For the Lord Himself will descend from heaven with a shout, with the voice of an archangel, and with the trumpet of God. And the dead in Christ will rise first. Then we who are alive *and* remain shall be [g]caught up together with them in the clouds to meet the Lord in the air. And thus we shall always be with the Lord. Therefore [h]comfort one another with these words.

1COR Behold, I tell you a mystery: We shall not all sleep, but we shall all be changed—in a moment, in the twinkling of an eye, at the last trumpet. For the trumpet will sound, and the dead will be raised incorruptible, and we shall be

---

[c] FIRSTFRUITS. This speaks of the first installment of harvest to eternal life, in which Christ's resurrection will precipitate and guarantee that all of the saints who have died will be resurrected also. See John 14:19.

[d] MAN . . . MAN. Adam, who through his sin brought death on the whole human race, was human. So was Christ, who by His resurrection brought life to the race. Cf. Rom. 5:12–19.

[e] ALL . . . ALL. The two "alls" are alike only in the sense that they both apply to descendants. The second "all" applies only to believers (see Gal. 3:26, 29; 4:7; Eph. 3:6; cf. Acts 20:32; Titus 3:7) and does not imply universalism (the salvation of everyone without faith). Countless other passages clearly teach the eternal punishment of the unbelieving (e.g., Matt. 5:29; 10:28; 25:41, 46; Luke 16:23; 2 Thess. 1:9; Rev. 20:15).

[f] THOSE WHO HAVE FALLEN ASLEEP. Sleep is the familiar NT euphemism for death that describes the appearance of the deceased (cf. 1 Cor. 11:30). It describes the dead body, not the soul (cf. 2 Cor. 5:1–9; Phil. 1:23). Sleep is used of Jarius's daughter (Matt. 9:24), whom Jesus raised from the dead and Stephen, who was stoned to death (Acts 7:60; cf. John 11:11; 1 Cor. 7:39; 15:6, 18, 51; 2 Peter 3:4). Those who sleep are identified in 1 Thess. 4:16 as "the dead in Christ." The people, in ignorance, had come to the conclusion that those who die miss the Lord's return and they were grieved over their absence at such a glorious event. Thus the departure of a loved one brought great anguish to the soul. But there is no reason for Christians to sorrow when a brother dies as if some great loss to that person has come.

[g] CAUGHT UP. After the dead come forth, their spirits, already with the Lord (2 Cor. 5:8; Phil. 1:23), now being joined to resurrected new bodies (cf. 1 Cor. 15:35–50), the living Christians will be raptured, lit. snatched away (cf. John 10:28; Acts 8:39). This passage, along with John 14:1–3 and 1 Cor. 15:51–52, forms the biblical basis for "the Rapture" of the church.

[h] COMFORT ONE ANOTHER. The primary purpose of this passage is not to teach a scheme of prophecy, but rather to provide encouragement to those Christians whose loved ones have died. The comfort here is based on the following: (1) the dead will be resurrected and will participate in the Lord's coming for His own; (2) when Christ comes the living will be reunited forever with their loved ones; and (3) they all will be with the Lord eternally.

changed. For this corruptible must put on incorruption, and this mortal *must* put on immortality. So when this corruptible has put on incorruption, and this mortal has put on immortality, then shall be brought to pass the saying [i]that is written:

> "Death is swallowed up in victory."
> "O Death, where *is* your sting?
> O Hades, where *is* your victory?"

[i] THAT IS WRITTEN. Paul enhanced his joy at the reality of resurrection by quoting from Isa. 25:8 and Hos. 13:14. The latter quote taunts death as if it were a bee whose sting was removed. That sting was the sin that was exposed by the law of God (cf. Rom. 3:23; 4:15; 6:23; Gal. 3:10–13) but conquered by Christ in His death (cf. Rom. 5:17; 2 Cor. 5:21).

212. The Wonder of Christ's Ascended Glory

Acts 2:33–36; Eph. 1:20–23; Phil. 2:9–11; Col. 1:17–20; Heb. 10:10–12; 1 Peter 3:22; Rev. 1:10–18; 5:6–14

HEB We have been [a]sanctified through the offering of the body of Jesus Christ once *for all.* And every priest stands ministering daily and offering repeatedly the same sacrifices, which can never take away sins. But this Man, after He had offered one sacrifice for sins forever, sat down [b]at the right hand of God.

ACTS Therefore being exalted to the right hand of God, and having received from the Father the promise of the Holy Spirit, He poured out this which you now see and hear. For David did not ascend into the heavens, but [c]he says himself:

"The LORD said to my Lord,
'Sit at My right hand,
Till I make Your enemies Your footstool.'"

Therefore let all the house of Israel know assuredly that God has made this Jesus, whom you crucified, [d]both Lord and Christ. 1PET [He] has gone into heaven and is at the right hand of God, angels and authorities and powers having been made subject to Him.

---

[a] SANCTIFIED. "Sanctify" means to "make holy," to be set apart from sin for God (cf. 1 Thess. 4:3). When Christ fulfilled the will of God, He provided for the believer a continuing, permanent condition of holiness (Eph. 4:24; 1 Thess. 3:13). This is the believer's positional sanctification, as opposed to the progressive sanctification that results from daily walking by the will of God (cf. Rom. 6:19; 12:1–2; 2 Cor. 7:1).

[b] AT THE RIGHT HAND OF GOD. Jesus is frequently so depicted (cf. Matt. 22:44; 26:64; Luke 22:69; Acts 2:34; 7:55; Eph. 1:20; Col. 3:1; Heb. 1:3; 8:1; 10:11–12; 12:2). After Jesus accomplished His cross work and was raised from the dead, He was exalted to the place of prominence, honor, majesty, authority, and power (cf. Rom. 8:34; Phil. 2:9–11; Heb. 6:20).

[c] HE SAYS HIMSELF. Peter quoted another psalm (Ps. 110:1) concerning the exaltation of Messiah by ascension to the right hand of God, and reminds the reader that it was not fulfilled by David (as bodily resurrection had not yet been), but by Jesus Christ (Acts 2:36). Peter had been an eyewitness to that ascension (Acts 1:9–11).

[d] BOTH LORD AND CHRIST. Peter summarizes his sermon in Acts 2 with a powerful statement of certainty: The OT prophecies of resurrection and exaltation provide evidence that overwhelmingly points to the crucified Jesus as the Messiah. Jesus is God as well as anointed Messiah (cf. Rom. 1:4; 10:9; 1 Cor. 12:3; Phil. 2:9, 11).

PHIL God also has [e]highly exalted Him and given Him the [f]name which is above every name, that at the name of Jesus every knee should bow, of those in heaven, and of those on earth, and of those under the earth, and *that* every tongue should confess that Jesus Christ *is* Lord, to the glory of God the Father. COL And He is before all things, and in Him all things consist. And He is the [g]head of the body, the church, who is the beginning, the firstborn from the dead, that in all things He may have the preeminence. For it pleased *the Father that* in Him all the fullness should dwell, and by Him to reconcile all things to Himself, by Him, whether things on earth or things in heaven, having made peace through the blood of His cross.

EPH He raised Him from the dead and seated *Him* at His right hand in the heavenly *places,* far above all principality and power and might and dominion, and every name that is named, not only in this age but also in that which is to come. And He put all *things* under His [h]feet, and gave Him *to be* head over all *things* to the church, which is His body, the fullness of Him who fills all in all.

REV I was in the Spirit on the Lord's Day, and I heard behind me a loud voice, as of a trumpet, saying, "I am the Alpha and the Omega, the First and the Last," and, "What you see, write in a book and send *it* to the seven churches which are in Asia: to Ephesus, to Smyrna, to Pergamos, to Thyatira, to Sardis, to Philadelphia, and to Laodicea."

Then I turned to see the voice that spoke with me. And having turned I saw seven golden lampstands, and in the midst of the seven lampstands *One* like the

---

[e] HIGHLY EXALTED HIM. Christ's exaltation was four-fold. The early sermons of the apostles affirm His resurrection and coronation (His position at the right hand of God), and allude to His intercession for believers (Acts 2:32–33; 5:30–31; cf. Eph. 1:20–21; Heb. 4:15; 7:25–26). Hebrews 4:14 refers to the final element, His ascension. The exaltation did not concern Christ's nature or eternal place within the Trinity, but His new identity as the God-Man (cf. John 5:22; Rom. 1:4; 14:9; 1 Cor. 15:24–25). In addition to receiving back His glory (John 17:5), Christ's new status as the God-Man meant God gave Him privileges He did not have prior to the incarnation. If He had not lived among men, He could not have identified with them as the interceding High Priest. Had He not died on the cross, He could not have been elevated from that lowest degree back to heaven as the substitute for sin.

[f] NAME . . . ABOVE EVERY NAME. Christ's new name that further describes His essential nature and places Him above and beyond all comparison is *Lord.* This name is the NT synonym for OT descriptions of God as sovereign ruler. Both before (Isa. 45:21–23; Mark 15:2; Luke 2:11; John 13:13; 18:37; 20:28) and after (Acts 2:36; 10:36; Rom. 14:9–11; 1 Cor. 8:6; 15:57; Rev. 17:14; 19:16) the exaltation, Scripture affirms that this was Jesus' rightful title as the God-Man.

[g] HEAD OF THE BODY. Cf. Col. 2:19. Paul uses the human body as a metaphor for the church, of which Christ serves as the "head." Just as a body is controlled from the brain, so Christ controls every part of the church and gives it life and direction. Cf. Eph. 4:15; 5:23.

[h] FEET . . . HEAD. This is a quote from Ps. 8:6 indicating that God has exalted Christ over everything (cf. Heb. 2:8), including His church (cf. Col. 1:18). Christ is clearly the authoritative Head (not "source"), because all things have been placed under His feet.

[i]Son of Man, clothed with a [j]garment down to the feet and girded about the chest with a golden band. His head and hair *were* [k]white like wool, as white as snow, and His [l]eyes like a flame of fire; His [m]feet *were* like fine brass, as if refined in a furnace, and His [n]voice as the sound of many waters; He had in His right hand [o]seven stars, out of His mouth went a [p]sharp two-edged sword, and His countenance *was* like the sun shining in its strength. And when I saw Him, I [q]fell at His feet as dead. But He laid His right hand on me, saying to me, "Do not be afraid; I am the [r]First and the Last. I *am* He who lives, and was dead, and behold, I am alive forevermore. Amen. And I have the [s]keys of Hades and of Death."

REV And I looked, and behold, in the midst of the throne and of the four living

---

[i] Son of Man. According to the gospels this is the title Christ used most often for Himself during His earthly ministry (eighty-one times in the gospels). Taken from the heavenly vision in Dan. 7:13, it is an implied claim to deity.

[j] garment. Most occurrences of this word in the Septuagint, the Greek OT, refer to the garment of the high priest. The golden sash across His chest completes the picture of Christ serving in His priestly role (cf. Lev. 16:1–4; Heb. 2:17).

[k] white like wool. "White" does not refer to a flat white color but a blazing, glowing, white light (cf. Dan. 7:9). Like the glory cloud (or Shekinah), it is a picture of His holiness.

[l] eyes . . . flame of fire. Like two lasers, the eyes of the exalted Lord look with penetrating gaze into the depths of His church (Rev. 2:18; 19:12; cf. Heb. 4:13).

[m] feet . . . fine brass. The altar of burnt offering was covered with brass, and its utensils were made of the same material (cf. Ex. 38:1–7). Glowing hot, brass feet are a clear reference to divine judgment. Jesus Christ with feet of judgment is moving through His church to exercise His chastening authority upon sin.

[n] voice . . . sound of many waters. No longer was His voice like the crystal clear note of a trumpet (Rev. 1:10), but John likened it to the crashing of the surf against the rocks of the island (cf. Ezek. 43:2). It was the voice of authority.

[o] seven stars. These are the messengers who represent the seven churches (cf. Rev. 1:20). Christ holds them in His hand, which means that He controls the church and its leaders.

[p] sharp two-edged sword. A large, two-edged broad sword. It signifies judgment (cf. Rev. 2:16; 19:15) on those who attack His people and destroy His church.

[q] fell at His feet. A common response to seeing the awesome glory of the Lord (Gen. 17:3; Num. 16:22; Ezek. 1:28; Isa. 6:1–8; Acts 9:4).

[r] First and the Last. Jesus Christ applies this OT name for Yahweh (Rev. 22:13; cf. Isa. 41:4; 44:6; 48:12) to Himself, clearly claiming to be God. Idols will come and go. He was before them, and He will remain after them.

[s] keys of Hades and of Death. Cf. Luke 16:23. Death and Hades are essentially synonyms, but death is the condition and Hades, equivalent to the OT Sheol, the place of the dead (cf. Rev. 20:13). Christ decides who lives, who dies, and when.

creatures, and in the midst of the elders, stood a [t]Lamb [u]as though it had been slain, having [v]seven horns and seven eyes, which are the seven Spirits of God sent out into all the earth. Then He came and took the scroll out of the right hand of Him who sat on the throne.

Now when He had taken the scroll, the four living creatures and the twenty-four elders fell down before the Lamb, each having a harp, and golden bowls full of incense, which are the prayers of the saints. And they sang a new song, saying:

"You are worthy to take the scroll,
And to open its seals;
For You were slain,
And have [w]redeemed us to God by Your blood
Out of every tribe and tongue and people and nation,
And have made us kings and priests to our God;
And we shall reign on the earth."

Then I looked, and I heard the voice of many angels around the throne, the living creatures, and the elders; and the number of them was ten thousand times ten thousand, and thousands of thousands, saying with a loud voice:

"Worthy is the Lamb who was slain
To receive power and riches and wisdom,
And strength and honor and glory and blessing!"

And every creature which is in heaven and on the earth and under the earth and such as are in the sea, and all that are in them, I heard saying:

"Blessing and honor and glory and power
Be to Him who sits on the throne,
And to the Lamb, forever and ever!"

Then the four living creatures said, "Amen!" And the twenty-four elders fell down and worshiped Him who lives forever and ever.

---

[t] LAMB. Having just heard of a lion (Rev. 5:5), John turns to see a lamb (lit. "a little, pet lamb"). God required the Jews to bring the Passover lamb into their houses for four days, essentially making it a pet, before it was to be violently slain (Ex. 12:3, 6). This is the true Passover Lamb, God's Son (cf. Isa. 53:7; Jer. 11:19; John 1:29).

[u] AS THOUGH IT HAD BEEN SLAIN. The scars from its slaughter are still clearly visible, but it is standing—it is alive.

[v] SEVEN HORNS. In Scripture horns always symbolize power, because in the animal kingdom they are used to exert power and inflict wounds in combat. Seven horns signify complete or perfect power. Unlike other defenseless lambs, this One has complete, sovereign power.

[w] REDEEMED US TO GOD BY YOUR BLOOD. The sacrificial death of Christ on behalf of sinners made Him worthy to take the scroll (cf. 1 Cor. 6:20; 7:23; 2 Cor. 5:21; Gal. 3:3; 1 Peter 1:18–19; 2 Peter 2:1).

213. The Certainty of Christ's Return

Phil. 3:20–21; 1 Thess. 1:9b–10; 2 Thess. 1:6–10; 1 Tim. 6:13–16; Titus 2:11–14; Heb. 9:28b; 2 Peter 3:8–10; Rev. 19:11–16; 22:12–13, 20

TITUS For the grace of God that brings salvation has appeared to [a]all men, teaching us that, denying ungodliness and worldly lusts, we should live soberly, righteously, and godly in the present age, looking for the [b]blessed hope and [c]glorious appearing of our great [d]God and Savior Jesus Christ, who gave Himself for us, that He might redeem us from every lawless deed and purify for Himself *His* own special people, zealous for good works. 1THS [For] you turned to God from idols to serve the living and true God, and [e]to wait for His Son from heaven, whom He raised from the dead, *even* Jesus who delivers us from the wrath to come.

PHIL For our citizenship is in heaven, from which we also [f]eagerly wait for the Savior, the Lord Jesus Christ, who will [g]transform our lowly body that it may be

---

[a] ALL MEN. This does not teach universal salvation. "All men" is used as "man" in Titus 3:4, to refer to humanity in general, as a category, not to every individual. Cf. 2 Cor. 5:19; 2 Peter 3:9. Jesus Christ made a sufficient sacrifice to cover every sin of every one who believes (John 3:16–18; 1 Tim. 2:5–6; 4:10; 1 John 2:2). Paul makes clear in the opening words of this letter to Titus that salvation becomes effective only through "the faith of God's elect" (Titus 1:1). Out of all humanity only those who believe will be saved (John 1:12; 3:16; 5:24, 38, 40; 6:40; 10:9; Rom. 10:9–17).

[b] BLESSED HOPE. A general reference to the second coming of Jesus Christ, including the resurrection (cf. Rom. 8:22–23; 1 Cor. 15:51–58; Phil. 3:20–21; 1 Thess. 4:13–18; 1 John 3:2–3) and the reign of the saints with Christ in glory (2 Tim. 2:10).

[c] GLORIOUS APPEARING. Cf. 2 Tim. 1:10. Lit. "the appearing of the glory." This will be our salvation from the presence of sin.

[d] GOD AND SAVIOR. A clear reference to the deity of Jesus. Cf. 2 Peter 1:1.

[e] TO WAIT. This is a recurring theme in the Thessalonian letters (1 Thess. 3:13; 4:15–17; 5:8, 23; 2 Thess. 3:6–13; cf. Acts 1:11; 2 Tim. 4:8; Titus 2:11–13). These passages indicate the imminency of the deliverance; it was something Paul felt could happen in their lifetime.

[f] EAGERLY WAIT. The Greek verb is found in most passages dealing with the second coming and expresses the idea of waiting patiently, but with great expectation (Rom. 8:23; 2 Peter 3:11–12).

[g] TRANSFORM OUR LOWLY BODY. The Greek word for "transform" gives us the word "schematic," which is an internal design of something. Those who are already dead in Christ, but alive with Him in spirit in heaven (2 Cor. 5:8; Phil. 1:23; Heb. 12:23), will receive new bodies at the resurrection and rapture of the church, when those alive on earth will have their bodies transformed (cf. Rom. 8:18–23; 1 Cor. 15:51–54; 1 Thess. 4:16).

[h]conformed to His glorious body, according to the working by which He is able even to subdue all things to Himself. HEB To those who eagerly wait for Him He will appear a [i]second time, apart from sin, for salvation.

> REV "And behold, [j]I am coming quickly, and My reward *is* with Me, to give to every one according to his work. I am the Alpha and the Omega, *the* Beginning and *the* End, the First and the Last."

2PET But, beloved, do not forget this one thing, that with the Lord [k]one day *is* as a thousand years, and a thousand years as one day. The Lord is [l]not slack concerning *His* promise, as some count slackness, but is longsuffering toward us, [m]not

---

[h] CONFORMED TO HIS GLORIOUS BODY. The believer's new body will be like Christ's after His resurrection and will be redesigned and adapted for heaven (1 Cor. 15:42–43; 1 John 3:2).

[i] SECOND TIME. On the Day of Atonement the people eagerly waited for the high priest to come back out of the Holy of Holies. When he appeared they knew that the sacrifice on their behalf had been accepted by God. In the same way when Christ appears at His second coming, it will be confirmation that the Father has been fully satisfied with the Son's sacrifice on behalf of believers. At that point salvation will be consummated (cf. 1 Peter 1:3–5).

[j] I AM COMING QUICKLY! This isn't the threatening temporal judgment described in Rev. 1:3; 2:5, 16, nor the final judgment of Rev. 19; it is a hopeful event. Christ will return to take His church out of the hour of trial.

[k] ONE DAY IS AS A THOUSAND YEARS. God understands time much differently than man. From man's viewpoint Christ's coming seems like a long time away (cf. Ps. 90:4). From God's viewpoint it will not be long. Beyond that general reference, this may be a specific indication of the fact that there are actually one thousand years between the first phase of the Day of the Lord at the end of the Tribulation (Rev. 6:17), and the last phase one thousand years later at the end of the millennial kingdom when the Lord creates the new heaven and new earth (cf. 1 Peter 3:10, 13; Rev. 20:1–21:1).

[l] NOT SLACK. That is, not loitering or late (cf. Gal. 4:4; Titus 1:6; Heb. 6:18; 10:23, 37; Rev. 19:11). LONGSUFFERING TOWARD US. "Us" is the saved, the people of God. He waits for them to be saved. God has an immense capacity for patience before He breaks forth in judgment (Joel 2:13; Luke 15:20; Rom. 9:22; 1 Peter 3:15). God endures endless blasphemies against His name, along with rebellion, murders, and the ongoing breaking of His law, waiting patiently while He is calling and redeeming His own. It is not impotence or slackness that delays final judgment; it is patience.

[m] NOT WILLING THAT ANY SHOULD PERISH. The "any" must refer to those whom the Lord has chosen and will call to complete the redeemed, i.e., the "us." Since the whole passage is about God's destroying the wicked, his patience is not so He can save all of them, but so that He can receive all His own. He can't be waiting for everyone to be saved, since the emphasis is that He will destroy the world and the ungodly. Those who do perish and go to hell, go because they are depraved and worthy only of hell and have rejected the only remedy, Jesus Christ, not because they were created for hell and predetermined to go there. The path to damnation is the path of a nonrepentant heart; it is the path of one who rejects the person and provision of Jesus Christ and holds on to sin (cf. Isa. 55:1; Jer. 13:17; Ezek. 18:32; Matt. 11:28; 13:37; Luke 13:3; John 3:16; 8:21, 24; 1 Tim. 2:3–4; Rev. 22:17).

willing that any should perish but that [n]all should come to repentance. But [o]the day of the Lord will come [p]as a thief in the night, in which the heavens will pass away with a great noise, and the elements will melt with fervent heat; both the earth and the works that are in it will be burned up.

REV Now I saw [q]heaven opened, and behold, a [r]white horse. And He who sat on him *was* called Faithful and True, and in righteousness He judges and makes war. His eyes *were* like a flame of fire, and on His head *were* many crowns. He had a name written that no one knew except Himself. He *was* clothed with a robe dipped in blood, and His name is called The Word of God.

And the [s]armies in heaven, clothed in fine linen, white and clean, followed Him on white horses. Now out of His mouth goes a [t]sharp sword, that with it He

---

[n] ALL SHOULD COME TO REPENTANCE. "All" (cf. "us," "any") must refer to all who are God's people who will come to Christ to make up the full number of the people of God. The reason for the delay in Christ's coming and the attendant judgments is not because He is slow to keep His promise, or because He wants to judge more of the wicked, or because He is impotent in the face of wickedness. He delays His coming because He is patient and desires the time for His people to repent.

[o] THE DAY OF THE LORD. "The Day of the Lord" is a technical term pointing to the special interventions of God in human history for judgment. It ultimately refers to the future time of judgment whereby God judges the wicked on earth and ends this world system in its present form. The OT prophets saw the final Day of the Lord as unequaled darkness and damnation, a day when the Lord would act in a climactic way to vindicate His name, destroy His enemies, reveal His glory, establish His kingdom, and destroy the world (cf. Isa. 2:10–21; 13:6–22; Ezek. 13:30; Joel 1–2; Amos 5; Obad. 15; Zech. 14; Mal. 4; 2 Thess. 1:7; 2:2). It occurs at the time of the tribulation on earth (Rev. 6:17) and again one thousand years later at the end of the millennial kingdom before the creation of the new heavens and new earth (Rev. 20:1–21:1).

[p] AS A THIEF IN THE NIGHT. The Day of the Lord will have a surprise arrival—sudden, unexpected, and disastrous to the unprepared.

[q] HEAVEN OPENED. The One who ascended to heaven (Acts 1:9–11) and had been seated at the Father's right hand (Heb. 8:1; 10:12; 1 Peter 3:22) will return to take back the earth from the usurper and establish His kingdom (Rev. 5:1–10). The nature of this event shows how it differs from the Rapture. At the Rapture Christ meets His own in the air—in this event He comes with them to earth. At the Rapture there is no judgment; in this event it is all judgment. This event is preceded by blackness—the darkened sun, moon gone out, stars fallen, smoke—then lightning and blinding glory as Jesus comes. Such details are not included in Rapture passages (John 14:1–3; 1 Thess. 4:13–18).

[r] WHITE HORSE. In the Roman triumphal processions the victorious general rode his white war horse up the Via Sacra to the temple of Jupiter on the Capitoline Hill. Jesus' first coming was in humiliation on a colt (Zech. 9:9). John's vision portrays Him as the conqueror on His war horse, coming to destroy the wicked, to overthrow the Antichrist, to defeat Satan, and to take control of the earth (cf. 2 Cor. 2:14).

[s] ARMIES IN HEAVEN. Composed of the church (Rev. 19:8), tribulation saints (Rev. 7:13), OT believers (Jude 14; cf. Dan. 12:1–2), and even angels (Matt. 25:31). They return not to help Jesus in the battle (they are unarmed), but to reign with Him after He defeats His enemies (1 Cor. 6:2; 2 Tim. 2:12; Rev. 20:4). Cf. Ps. 149:5–9.

[t] SHARP SWORD. This symbolizes Christ's power to kill His enemies (Rev. 1:16; cf. Isa. 11:4; Heb. 4:12–13). That the sword comes out of His mouth indicates that He wins the battle with the power of His word. Though the saints return with Christ to reign and rule, they are not the executioners. That is His task and that of His angels (Matt. 13:37–50).

should strike the nations. And He Himself will rule them with a [u]rod of iron. He Himself treads the winepress of the fierceness and wrath of Almighty God. And He has on *His* robe and on His thigh a name written:

KING OF KINGS AND LORD OF LORDS.

2THS *It is* a righteous thing with [v]God to repay with tribulation those who trouble you, and to *give* you who are troubled rest with us [w]when the Lord Jesus is revealed from heaven with His mighty angels, in flaming fire taking vengeance on those who do not know God, and on those who do not obey the gospel of our Lord Jesus Christ. These shall be punished with everlasting destruction from the presence of the Lord and from the glory of His power, [x]when He comes, in that Day, to be glorified in His saints and to be admired among all those who believe, because our testimony among you was believed.

1TIM I urge you in the sight of God who gives life to all things, and *before* Christ Jesus who witnessed the good confession before Pontius Pilate, that you keep *this* commandment without spot, blameless until our Lord Jesus Christ's [y]appearing, which [God] will manifest in His own time, *He who is* the blessed and only Potentate, the King of kings and Lord of lords, who alone has immortality, dwelling in unapproachable light, whom no man has seen or can see, to whom *be* honor and everlasting power. Amen.

REV He who testifies to these things says, "Surely I am coming quickly." Amen. Even so, come, Lord Jesus!

---

[u] ROD OF IRON. Swift, righteous judgment will mark Christ's rule in the kingdom. Believers will share His authority (Rev. 2:26–27; 1 Cor. 6:2; cf. Ps. 2:8–9; Rev. 12:5).

[v] GOD TO REPAY. Just as the righteous judgment of God works to perfect believers (v. 5), so it works to "repay" the wicked. Vindication and retribution are to be exercised by God, not man, in matters of spiritual persecution (cf. Deut. 32:35; Prov. 25:21–22; Rom. 12:19–21; 1 Thess. 5:15; Rev. 19:2). When God repays and how God repays are to be determined by Him.

[w] WHEN THE LORD JESUS IS REVEALED. This undoubtedly refers to Christ being unveiled in His coming as Judge. The first aspect of this revealing occurs at the end of the seven-year tribulation period (cf. Matt. 13:24–30, 36–43; 24:29–51; 25:31–46; Rev. 19:11–15). The final and universal revelation of Christ as Judge occurs at the Great White Throne judgment following Christ's millennial reign on the earth (Rev. 20:11–15). Angels always accompany Christ in His coming for judgment (cf. Matt 13:41, 49; 24:30–31; 25:31; Rev. 14:14–15).

[x] WHEN HE COMES. When the Day of the Lord arrives, bringing retribution and ruin for unbelievers. As Christ's great glory is displayed, the result will be rest and relief for believers and the privilege of sharing His glory (cf. Phil. 3:21; 1 John 3:2). This is the "glorious manifestation" of believers of which Paul spoke (Rom. 8:18–19). At the time, all believers will adore and worship Him, including those in the Thessalonian church who believed Paul's testimony of the gospel.

[y] APPEARING. When the Lord returns to earth in glory (cf. 2 Tim. 4:1, 8; Titus 2:13) to judge and to establish His kingdom (Matt. 24:27, 29–30; 25:31). Because Christ's return is imminent, that ought to be motivation enough for the man of God to remain faithful to his calling until he dies or the Lord returns (cf. Acts 1:8–11; 1 Cor. 4:5; Rev. 22:12).

214. Salvation Is by Grace Alone Through Faith Alone in Christ Alone

Acts 4:12; 15:11a; Rom. 3:23–26; 4:2–5, 24–25; 5:1–2; 8:1, 29–39; 11:6; Gal. 2:16; 3:11–14; Eph. 1:13–14; 2:8–9; Phil. 3:8–10a; 1 Tim. 2:5–6a; 2 Tim. 1:8b–11; Titus 3:4–7; Heb. 7:25; 1 John 2:1b–2

GAL A man is not [a]justified by the [b]works of the law but by faith in Jesus Christ, [and] we have believed in Christ Jesus, that we might be justified by faith in Christ and not by the [c]works of the law; for by the works of the law no flesh shall be justified. ROM For all have sinned and fall short of the glory of God, being justified [d]freely by His grace through the [e]redemption that is in Christ Jesus, whom God set forth *as* a [f]propitiation by His blood, [g]through faith, to demonstrate His

---

[a] JUSTIFIED. This basic forensic Greek word describes a judge declaring an accused person not guilty and therefore innocent before the law. Throughout Scripture it refers to God's declaring a sinner not guilty and fully righteous before Him by imputing to him the divine righteousness of Christ and imputing the man's sin to his sinless Savior for punishment, (cf. Rom. 3:24; Phil. 3:8–9).

[b] WORKS . . . FAITH. Three times in this verse (Gal. 2:16), Paul declares that salvation is only through faith in Christ and not by law. The first is general, "a man is not justified"; the second is personal, "we might be justified"; and the third is universal, "no flesh shall be justified."

[c] WORKS OF THE LAW. Keeping the law is a totally unacceptable means of salvation, because the root of sinfulness is in the fallenness of man's heart, not his actions. The law served as a mirror to reveal sin, not a cure for it (cf. Rom. 7:7–13; Gal. 3:22–24; 1 Tim. 1:8–11).

[d] FREELY BY HIS GRACE. Justification is a gracious gift that God extends to the repentant, believing sinner, wholly apart from human merit or work.

[e] REDEMPTION. The imagery behind this Greek word comes from the ancient slave market. It meant paying the necessary ransom to obtain the prisoner or slave's release. The only adequate payment to redeem sinners from sin's slavery and its deserved punishment was "in Christ Jesus" (1 Tim. 2:6; 1 Peter 1:18–19), and was paid to God to satisfy His justice.

[f] PROPITIATION. Crucial to the significance of Christ's sacrifice, this word carries the idea of appeasement or satisfaction—in this case Christ's violent death satisfied the offended holiness and wrath of God against those for whom Christ died (Isa. 53:11; Col. 2:11–14). The Heb. equivalent of this word was used to describe the mercy seat—the cover to the ark of the covenant—where the high priest sprinkled the blood of the slaughtered animal on the Day of Atonement to make atonement for the sins of the people. In pagan religions it is the worshiper—not the god—who is responsible to appease the wrath of the offended deity. But in reality, man is incapable of satisfying God's justice apart from Christ, except by spending eternity in hell. Cf. 1 John 2:2.

[g] THROUGH FAITH. To believe, trust in, rely on, or have faith in. True saving faith is supernatural, a gracious gift of God that He produces in the heart (cf. Eph. 2:8) and is the only means by which a person can appropriate true righteousness (cf. Rom. 3:22, 25; 4:5, 13, 20; 5:1). Saving faith consists of three elements: (1) mental: the mind understands the gospel and the truth about Christ (Rom. 10:14–17); (2) emotional: one embraces the truthfulness of those facts with sorrow over sin and joy over God's mercy and grace (Rom. 6:17; 15:13); and (3) volitional: the sinner submits his will to Christ and trusts in Him alone as the only hope of salvation (Rom. 10:9). Genuine faith will always produce authentic obedience (Rom. 4:3; cf. John 8:31; 14:23–24).

righteousness, because in His forbearance God had [h]passed over the sins that were previously committed, to demonstrate at the present time His righteousness, that He might be [i]just and the justifier of the one who has faith in Jesus.

EPH In Him you also [j]*trusted,* after you heard the word of truth, the gospel of your salvation; in whom also, having believed, you were [k]sealed with the Holy Spirit of promise, who is the guarantee of our inheritance until the redemption of the purchased possession, to the praise of His glory. ROM Therefore, [l]having been justified by faith, we have [m]peace with God through our Lord Jesus Christ, through whom also we have access by faith into this grace in which we stand, and rejoice in hope of the glory of God.

HEB Therefore He is also able to save to the [n]uttermost those who come to God through Him, since He always lives to make [o]intercession for them. 1JN And if anyone sins, we have an Advocate with the Father, Jesus Christ the righteous. And

---

[h] PASSED OVER THE SINS. This means neither indifference nor remission. God's justice demands that every sin and sinner be punished. God would have been just when Adam and Eve sinned to destroy them, and with them, the entire human race. But in His goodness and forbearance (see Rom. 2:4), He withheld His judgment for a certain period of time (cf. Ps. 78:38–39; Acts 17:30, 31; 2 Peter 3:9).

[i] JUST AND THE JUSTIFIER. The wisdom of God's plan allowed Him to punish Jesus in the place of sinners and thereby justify those who are guilty without compromising His justice.

[j] TRUSTED, AFTER YOU HEARD THE WORD. The God-revealed gospel of Jesus Christ must be heard (Rom. 10:17) and believed (John 1:12) to bring salvation.

[k] SEALED WITH THE HOLY SPIRIT. God's own Spirit comes to indwell the believer and secures and preserves his eternal salvation. The sealing of which Paul speaks refers to an official mark of identification placed on a letter, contract, or other document. That document was thereby officially under the authority of the person whose stamp was on the seal. Four primary truths are signified by the seal: (1) security (cf. Dan. 6:17; Matt. 27:62–66); (2) authenticity (cf. 1 Kings 21:6–16); (3) ownership (cf. Jer. 32:10); and (4) authority (cf. Est. 8:8–12). The Holy Spirit is given by God as His pledge of the believer's future inheritance in glory (cf. 2 Cor. 1:21).

[l] HAVING BEEN JUSTIFIED. The Greek construction—and its English translation—underscores that justification is a one-time legal declaration with continuing results, not an ongoing process.

[m] PEACE WITH GOD. Not a subjective, internal sense of calm and serenity, but an external, objective reality. God has declared Himself to be at war with every human being because of man's sinful rebellion against Him and His laws (cf. Ex. 22:24; Deut. 32:21–22; Ps. 7:11; John 3:36; Rom. 1:18; 8:7; Eph. 5:6). But the first great result of justification is that the sinner's war with God is ended forever (Col. 1:21–22). Scripture refers to the end of this conflict as a person's being reconciled to God (Rom. 5:10–11; 2 Cor. 5:18–20).

[n] UTTERMOST. Virtually the same concept as was expressed in "perfection" (Heb. 7:11) and "make perfect" (Heb. 7:19). The Greek term is used only here and in Luke 13:11 (the woman's body could not be straightened completely).

[o] INTERCESSION. The word means "to intercede on behalf of another." It was used to refer to bringing a petition to a king on behalf of someone. See Rom. 8:34. Cf. the high-priestly intercessory prayer of Christ in John 17. Since rabbis assigned intercessory powers to angels, perhaps the people were treating angels as intercessors. The writer makes it clear that only Christ is the intercessor (cf. 1 Tim. 2:5).

He Himself is the propitiation for our sins, and not for ours only but also [p]for the whole world. 1TIM For *there is* one God and [q]one Mediator between God and men, *the* Man Christ Jesus, who gave Himself [r]a ransom for all. ACTS Nor is there salvation in any other, for there is no other name under heaven given among men by which we must be saved.

TITUS But when the kindness and the love of God our Savior toward man appeared, not by works of righteousness which we have done, but according to His mercy He saved us, through the [s]washing of regeneration and renewing of the Holy Spirit, whom He poured out on us abundantly through Jesus Christ our Savior, that having been justified by His grace we should become heirs according to the hope of eternal life. EPH For by grace you have been saved through [t]faith, and that not of yourselves; *it is* the gift of God, not of works, lest anyone should boast. ROM And if by grace, then *it is* no longer of works; otherwise grace is no longer grace. ACTS [For] we believe that through the grace of the Lord Jesus Christ we shall be saved.

---

[p] FOR THE WHOLE WORLD. This is a generic term, referring not to every single individual, but to mankind in general. Christ actually paid the penalty only for those who would repent and believe. A number of Scriptures indicate that Christ died for the world (John 1:29; 3:16; 6:51; 1 Tim. 2:6; Heb. 2:9). Most of the world will be eternally condemned to hell to pay for their own sins, so they could not have been paid for by Christ. The passages that speak of Christ's dying for the whole world must be understood to refer to mankind in general (as in Titus 2:3–4). "World" indicates the sphere, the beings toward whom God seeks reconciliation and has provided propitiation. God has mitigated His wrath on sinners temporarily, by letting them live and enjoy earthly life (cf. 1 Tim. 4:10). In that sense Christ has provided a brief, temporal propitiation for the whole world. But He actually satisfied fully the wrath of God eternally only for the elect who believe. Christ's death in itself had unlimited and infinite value because He is Holy God. Thus His sacrifice was sufficient to pay the penalty for all the sins of all whom God brings to faith. But the actual satisfaction and atonement was made only for those who believe (cf. John 10:11, 15; 17:9, 20; Acts 20:28; Rom. 8:32, 37; Eph. 5:25). The pardon for sin is offered to the whole world but received only by those who believe (cf. John 5:24; 1 John 4:9, 14). There is no other way to be reconciled to God.

[q] ONE MEDIATOR. This refers to someone who intervenes between two parties to resolve a conflict or ratify a covenant. Jesus Christ is the only "Mediator" who can restore peace between God and sinners (Heb. 8:6; 9:15; 12:24).

[r] A RANSOM. This describes the result of Christ's substitutionary death for believers, which He did voluntarily (John 10:17–18) and reminds one of Christ's own statement in Matt. 20:28, "a ransom for many." The "all" is qualified by the "many." Not all will be ransomed (though His death would be sufficient), but only the many who believe by the work of the Holy Spirit and for whom the actual atonement was made. Christ did not pay a ransom only; He became the object of God's just wrath in the believer's place—He died his death and bore his sin (cf. 2 Cor. 5:21; 1 Peter 2:24).

[s] WASHING OF REGENERATION. Cf. Ezek. 36:25–29; Eph. 5:26; James 1:18; 1 Peter 1:23. Salvation brings divine cleansing from sin and the gift of a new, Spirit-generated, Spirit-empowered, and Spirit-protected life as God's own children and heirs (Titus 3:7). This is the new birth (cf. John 3:5; 1 John 2:29; 3:9; 4:7; 5:1)

[t] FAITH, AND THAT NOT OF YOURSELVES. "That" refers to the entire previous statement of salvation, not only the grace but the faith. Although men are required to believe for salvation, even that faith is part of the gift of God that saves and cannot be exercised by one's own power. God's grace is preeminent in every aspect of salvation (cf. Rom. 3:20; Gal. 2:16).

ROM *There is* therefore now no condemnation to those who are in Christ Jesus, who do not walk according to the flesh, but according to the Spirit. GAL But that no one is justified by the law in the sight of God *is* evident, for "the just shall live by faith." Yet the law is not of faith, but "the man who does them shall live by them." Christ has redeemed us from the curse of the law, [u]having become a curse for us (for it is written, "Cursed *is* everyone who hangs on a tree"), that the blessing of Abraham might come upon the Gentiles in Christ Jesus, that we might receive the promise of the Spirit through faith.

ROM For if Abraham was justified by works, he has *something* to [v]boast about, but not before God. For what does the Scripture say? "[w]Abraham believed God, and it was accounted to him for righteousness." Now to him who works, the wages are not counted as grace but as debt. But to him who does not work but believes on Him who justifies the ungodly, his faith is [x]accounted for righteousness. [And righteousness] shall be imputed to us who believe in Him who raised up Jesus our Lord from the dead, who was delivered up because of our offenses, and was raised [y]because of our justification.

PHIL Indeed I also count [z]all things loss for the excellence of the knowledge of Christ Jesus my Lord, for whom I have suffered the loss of all things, and count them as rubbish, that I may gain Christ and be found in Him, not having my own

---

[u] HAVING BECOME A CURSE FOR US. By bearing God's wrath for believers' sins on the cross (cf. 2 Cor. 5:21; cf. Heb. 9:28; 1 Peter 2:24; 3:18), Christ took upon Himself the curse pronounced on those who violated the law (cf. Gal. 3:10).

[v] BOAST. If Abraham's own works had been the basis of his justification, he would have had every right to boast in God's presence. That makes the hypothetical premise of v. 2 unthinkable (Eph. 2:8–9; 1 Cor. 1:29).

[w] ABRAHAM BELIEVED GOD. A quotation of Gen. 15:6, one of the clearest statements in all Scripture about justification. Abraham was a man of faith (cf. Rom. 1:16; 4:18–21; Gal. 3:6–7, 9; Heb. 11:8–10). But faith is not a meritorious work. It is never the ground of justification—it is simply the channel through which it is received, and it, too, is a gift. Cf. Eph. 2:8.

[x] ACCOUNTED. Cf. Rom. 4:5, 9–10, 22. Also translated "imputed" (Rom. 4:6, 8, 11, 23–24). Used in both financial and legal settings, this Greek word, which occurs nine times in Romans 4 alone, means to take something that belongs to someone and credit to another's account. It is a one-sided transaction—Abraham did nothing to accumulate it; God simply credited it to him. God took His own righteousness and credited it to Abraham as if it were actually his. This God did because Abraham believed in Him.

[y] BECAUSE OF OUR JUSTIFICATION. The resurrection provided proof that God had accepted the sacrifice of His Son and would be able to be just and yet justify the ungodly.

[z] ALL THINGS LOSS. The Greek word for "loss" also is an accounting term, used to describe a business loss. Paul used the language of business to describe the spiritual transaction that occurred when Christ redeemed him. All his Jewish religious credentials that he thought were in his profit column, were actually worthless and damning (cf. Luke 18:9–14). Thus, he put them in his loss column when he saw the glories of Christ (cf. Matt. 13:44–45; 16:25–26).

righteousness, which *is* from the law, but that which *is* through faith in Christ, the righteousness which is from God by faith; that I may know Him and the power of His resurrection.

2TIM [This is] the gospel according to the power of God, who has saved us and called *us* with a holy calling, [aa]not according to our works, but according to His own purpose and grace which was given to us in Christ Jesus before time began, but has now been revealed by the appearing of our Savior Jesus Christ, *who* has abolished death and brought life and immortality to light through the gospel, to which I was appointed a preacher, an apostle, and a teacher of the Gentiles.

ROM For whom He foreknew, He also predestined *to be* conformed to the image of His Son, that He might be the firstborn among many brethren. Moreover whom He predestined, these He also called; whom He called, these He also justified; and whom He justified, these He also glorified.

[bb]What then shall we say to these things? If God *is* for us, who *can be* against us? He who did not spare His own Son, but delivered Him up for us all, how shall He not with Him also freely give us all things? Who shall bring a charge against God's elect? *It is* God who justifies. Who *is* he who condemns? *It is* Christ who died, and furthermore is also risen, who is even at the right hand of God, who also makes intercession for us. Who shall separate us from the love of Christ? *Shall* tribulation, or distress, or persecution, or famine, or nakedness, or peril, or sword? As it is written:

"For Your sake we are killed all day long;
We are accounted as sheep for the slaughter."

Yet in all these things we are more than conquerors through Him who loved us. For I am persuaded that neither death nor life, nor angels nor principalities nor powers, nor things present nor things to come, nor height nor depth, nor any other created thing, shall be able to separate us from the love of God which is in Christ Jesus our Lord.

[aa] NOT . . . WORKS, BUT . . . GRACE. This truth is the foundation of the gospel. Salvation is by grace through faith, apart from works (cf. Rom. 3:20–25; Gal. 3:10–11; Eph. 2:8–9; Phil. 3:8–9). Grace is also the basis for God's sustaining work in believers (cf. Phil. 1:6; Jude 24–25)

[bb] WHAT THEN SHALL WE SAY. In Romans 8:31–39 Paul closes his teaching about the believer's security in Christ with a crescendo of questions and answers for the concerns his readers might still have. The result is an almost-poetic expression of praise for God's grace in bringing salvation to completion for all who are chosen and believe—a hymn of security.

215. Today Is the Day of Salvation

Acts 10:43; 13:38–39; 16:31a; 17:30b–31; Rom. 10:9–13; 2 Cor. 5:17, 20–6:2; 1 Thess. 5:9–10; 1 Tim. 1:15a; 2:3–4; 1 John 4:9–10; 5:1a, 11–13, 20; Jude 24–25

2COR Now then, we are [a]ambassadors for Christ, [b]as though God were pleading through us: we implore *you* on Christ's behalf, be reconciled to God. For He made Him [c]who knew no sin *to be* [d]sin for us, that we might become [e]the righteousness of God in Him. We then, *as* workers together *with Him* also plead with *you* not to receive the grace of God in vain. For He says:

"In an acceptable time I have heard you,
And in the day of salvation I have helped you."

---

[a] AMBASSADORS. A term that is related to the more familiar Greek word often translated "elder." It described an older, more experienced man who served as a representative of a king from one country to another. Paul thus described his role—and the role of all believers—as a messenger representing the King of heaven with the gospel, who pleads with the people of the world to be reconciled to God, who is their rightful King (cf. Rom. 10:13–18).

[b] AS THOUGH GOD WERE PLEADING. As believers present the gospel, God speaks (lit. "calls," or "begs") through them and urges unbelieving sinners to come in an attitude of faith and accept the gospel, which means to repent of their sins and believe on Jesus (cf. Acts 16:31; James 4:8).

[c] WHO KNEW NO SIN. Jesus Christ, the sinless Son of God (cf. Luke 23:4, 14, 22, 47; John 8:46; Gal. 4:4–5; Heb. 4:15; 7:26; 1 Peter 1:19; 2:22–24; 3:18; Rev. 5:2–10).

[d] SIN FOR US. God the Father, using the principle of imputation, treated Christ as if He were a sinner though He was not and had Him die as a substitute to pay the penalty for the sins of those who believe in Him (cf. Isa. 53:4–6; Gal. 3:10–13; 1 Peter 2:24). On the cross He did not become a sinner (as some suggest), but remained as holy as ever. He was treated as if He were guilty of all the sins ever committed by all who would ever believe, though He committed none. The wrath of God was exhausted on Him and the just requirement of God's law met for those for whom He died.

[e] THE RIGHTEOUSNESS OF GOD. Another reference to justification and imputation. The righteousness that is credited to the believer's account is the righteousness of Jesus Christ, God's Son (cf. Rom. 1:17; 3:21–24; Phil. 3:9). As Christ was not a sinner, but was treated as if He were, so believers who have not yet been made righteous (until glorification) are treated as if they were righteous. He bore their sins so that they could bear His righteousness. God treated Him as if He committed believers' sins and treats believers as if they did only the righteous deeds of the sinless Son of God.

Behold, now *is* the accepted time; behold, [f]now *is* the day of salvation.

1TIM For this *is* good and acceptable in the sight of God our Savior, who [g]desires all men to be saved and to come to the knowledge of the truth. ACTS [For God] now commands all men everywhere to repent, because He has appointed a day on which He will judge the world in righteousness by the Man whom He has ordained. He has given assurance of this to all by raising Him from the dead.

ROM If you [h]confess with your mouth the Lord Jesus and believe in your heart that [i]God has raised Him from the dead, you will be saved. For with the heart one believes unto righteousness, and with the mouth confession is made unto salvation. For the Scripture says, "Whoever believes on Him will not be put to shame." For there is no distinction between Jew and Greek, for the same Lord over all is rich to all who call upon Him. For "whoever calls on the name of the Lord shall be saved."

1JN And we know that the Son of God has come and has given us an understanding, that we may know Him who is true; and we are in Him who is true, in His Son Jesus Christ. This is the true God and eternal life. ACTS To Him all the prophets witness that, through His name, whoever believes in Him will receive remission of sins.

1TIM This *is* a faithful saying and worthy of all acceptance, that Christ Jesus came into the world to save sinners. ACTS Therefore let it be known to you, brethren, that through this Man is preached to you the forgiveness of sins; and by Him everyone who believes is justified from all things from which you could not be justi-

---

[f] Now is the day of salvation. Paul applied Isaiah's words to the present situation. There is a time in God's economy when He listens to sinners and responds to those who are repentant—and it was and is that time (cf. Prov. 1:20–23; Isa. 55:6; Heb. 3:7–8; 4:7). However, there will also be an end to that time (cf. Gen. 6:3; Prov. 1:24–33; John 9:4), which is why Paul's exhortation was so passionate.

[g] Desires all men to be saved. The Greek word for "desires" is not that which normally expresses God's will of decree (His eternal purpose), but God's will of desire. There is a distinction between God's desire and His eternal saving purpose, which must transcend His desires. God does not want men to sin. He hates sin with all His being (Pss. 5:4; 45:7); thus, He hates its consequences—eternal wickedness in hell. God does not want people to remain wicked forever in eternal remorse and hatred of Himself. Yet God, for His own glory, and to manifest that glory in wrath, chose to endure "vessels . . . prepared for destruction" for the supreme fulfillment of His will (Rom. 9:22). In His eternal purpose He chose only the elect out of the world (John 17:6) and passed over the rest, leaving them to the consequences of their sin, unbelief, and rejection of Christ (cf. Rom. 1:18–32). Ultimately, God's choices are determined by His sovereign, eternal purpose, not His desires.

[h] Confess . . . the Lord Jesus. Not a simple acknowledgment that He is God and the Lord of the universe, since even demons acknowledge that to be true (James 2:19). This is the deep personal conviction, without reservation, that Jesus is that person's own Master or Sovereign. This phrase includes repenting from sin, trusting in Jesus for salvation, and submitting to Him as Lord. This is the volitional element of faith (cf. Rom. 1:16).

[i] God has raised Him from the dead. Christ's resurrection was the supreme validation of His ministry (cf. John 2:18–21). Belief in it is necessary for salvation, because it proved that Christ is who He claimed to be and that the Father had accepted His sacrifice in the place of sinners (Rom. 4:24; cf. Acts 13:32–33; 1 Peter 1:3–4). Without the resurrection, there is no salvation (1 Cor. 15:14–17).

fied by the law of Moses. 1JN In this the love of God was manifested toward us, that God has sent His only begotten Son into the world, that we might live through Him. In this is love, not that we loved God, but that He loved us and sent His Son *to be* the [j]propitiation for our sins.

ACTS Believe on the Lord Jesus Christ, and you will be saved. 1JN [For] [k]whoever believes that [l]Jesus is the Christ is [m]born of God. 2COR Therefore, if anyone *is* [n]in Christ, *he is* a [o]new creation; old things have passed away; behold, all things have become new.

1JN And this is the testimony: that God has given us eternal life, and this life is in His Son. He who has the Son has life; he who does not have the Son of God does not have life. These things I have written to you who believe in the name of the Son of God, that you may know that you have eternal life, and that you may *continue to* believe in the name of the Son of God.

---

[j] PROPITIATION. The word means "appeasement" or "satisfaction." The sacrifice of Jesus on the cross satisfied the demands of God's holiness for the punishment of sin (cf. Rom. 1:18; 2 Cor. 5:21; Eph. 2:3). Hebrews 9:5 translates a form of this word as "the mercy seat." Christ lit. became our mercy seat like the one in the Holy of Holies, where the high priest splattered the blood of the sacrifice on the Day of Atonement (Lev. 16:15). Christ did this when His blood, spilled on behalf of others, satisfied the demands of God's holy justice and wrath against sin.

[k] WHOEVER BELIEVES. Saving faith is the first characteristic of an overcomer (cf. 1 John 5:4–5). The term *believes* conveys the idea of continuing faith, making the point that the mark of genuine believers is that they continue in faith throughout their life. Saving belief is not simply intellectual acceptance, but whole-hearted dedication to Jesus Christ that is permanent.

[l] JESUS IS THE CHRIST. The object of the believer's faith is Jesus, particularly that He is the promised Messiah or "Anointed One" whom God sent to be the Savior from sin. Whoever places faith in Jesus Christ as the only Savior has been born again and, as a result, is an overcomer.

[m] BORN OF GOD. This is a reference to the new birth and is the same word that Jesus used in John 3:7. The tense of the Greek verb indicates that ongoing faith is the result of the new birth and, therefore, the evidence of the new birth. The sons of God will manifest the reality that they have been born again by continuing to believe in God's Son, the Savior. The new birth brings us into a permanent faith relationship with God and Christ.

[n] IN CHRIST. These two words comprise a brief but most profound statement of the inexhaustible significance of the believer's redemption, which includes the following: (1) the believer's security in Christ, who bore in His body God's judgment against sin; (2) the believer's acceptance in Him with whom God alone is well pleased; (3) the believer's future assurance in Him who is the resurrection to eternal life and the sole guarantor of the believer's inheritance in heaven; and (4) the believer's participation in the divine nature of Christ, the everlasting Word (cf. 2 Peter 1:4).

[o] NEW CREATION. This describes something that is created at a qualitatively new level of excellence. It refers to regeneration or the new birth (cf. John 3:3; Eph. 2:1–3; Titus 3:5; 1 Peter 1:23; 1 John 2:29; 3:9; 5:4). This expression encompasses the Christian's forgiveness of sins paid for in Christ's substitutionary death (cf. Gal. 6:15; Eph. 4:24).

JUDE Now to Him who is able to keep you from stumbling,
And to [p]present you faultless
Before the presence of His glory with exceeding joy,
To [q]God our Savior,
Who alone is wise,
Be glory and majesty,
Dominion and power,
Both now and forever.
Amen.

---

[p] present you faultless. Cf. 2 Cor. 11:1; Eph. 5:27. Christians possess Christ's imputed righteousness through justification by faith and have been made worthy of eternal life in heaven (cf. Rom. 8:31–39).

[q] God our Savior. God is by nature a saving God, unlike the reluctant and indifferent false deities of human and demon invention (cf. 1 Tim. 2:2; 4:10; 2 Tim. 1:10; Titus 1:3; 2:10; 3:4; 2 Peter 1:1; 1 John 4:14).